MINDFULNESS IN POSITIVE PSYCHOLOGY

Mindfulness in Positive Psychology brings together the latest thinking in these two important disciplines. Positive psychology, the science of wellbeing and strengths, is the fastest growing branch of psychology, offering an optimal home for the research and application of mindfulness. As we contemplate mindfulness in the context of positive psychology, meaningful insights are being revealed in relation to our mental and physical health.

The book features chapters from leading figures from mindfulness and positive psychology, offering an exciting combination of topics. Mindfulness is explored in relation to flow, meaning, parenthood, performance, sports, obesity, depression, pregnancy, spirituality, happiness, mortality and many other ground-breaking topics. This is an invitation to rethink about mindfulness in ways that truly expand our understanding of wellbeing.

Mindfulness in Positive Psychology will appeal to a readership of students and practitioners, as well as those interested in mindfulness, positive psychology or other relevant areas such as education, healthcare, clinical psychology, counselling psychology, occupational psychology and coaching. The book explores cutting-edge theories, research and practical exercises, which will be relevant to all people interested in this area, and particularly those who wish to enhance their wellbeing via mindfulness.

Itai Ivtzan is a positive psychologist, a senior lecturer and the program leader of MAPP (Masters in Applied Positive Psychology) at the University of East London (UEL). His research areas are mindfulness, meditation, spirituality and wellbeing. In addition to many journal papers and book chapters, he is the author of several books and the leading author of *Second Wave Positive Psychology: Embracing the Dark Side of Life*.

Tim Lomas is a lecturer at the University of East London, where he is the associate programme leader for the MSc in Applied Positive Psychology and Coaching Psychology. He has published numerous peer-reviewed papers and books in relation to mindfulness, including a monograph based on his PhD, entitled *Masculinity, Meditation, and Mental Health*.

"The integration of mindfulness and positive psychology could greatly enhance our understanding of these two related fields. This book provides a comprehensive discussion of mindfulness, wellbeing, happiness, flow, meaning and purpose in a wide range of populations and settings. It sheds helpful new light on how the understanding of mindfulness can enhance the study of wellbeing, and how positive psychology can enhance the study of mindfulness."

—**Dr Ruth Baer**, Author of *Mindfulness-based Treatment Approaches*

"This book comes at a time when practitioners and patients alike, are seeking self-management tools that can infiltrate and provide positive interventions into what can appear as an overwhelming sense of despair in our modern world. Ivtzan and Lomas have pulled together contributors from a variety of backgrounds, to trace mindfulness from its historically grounded Buddhist philosophical roots through to its practical application in a wide variety of therapeutic endeavours. The useful instructional elements of the chapters makes the book multifaceted, so it could be used to learn more about the attributes and enabling factors of a mindfulness approach, whether as a manager, educator, practitioner, or as an individual wanting to claim back their life in full technicolour high definition, without any electronic stimulus outside of their own beautiful minds."

—**Professor Sally Hardy**, Head of Mental Health and Learning Disabilities, London South Bank University

"What unique angle does positive psychology offer to mindfulness research? In this book the authors organized varied chapters to address this important question. Some of the world's leading authors, researchers and scholars of mindfulness have been willing to explore mindfulness in relation to different aspects of positive psychology, and have contributed their insights to this inspiring book"

—**Professor Yi-Yuan Tang**, Texas Tech University, USA

MINDFULNESS IN POSITIVE PSYCHOLOGY

The Science of Meditation and Wellbeing

Edited by Itai Ivtzan and Tim Lomas

Routledge
Taylor & Francis Group

LONDON AND NEW YORK

First published 2016
by Routledge
2 Park Square, Milton Park, Abingdon, Oxon OX14 4RN

and by Routledge
711 Third Avenue, New York, NY 10017

Routledge is an imprint of the Taylor & Francis Group, an informa business

British Library Cataloguing in Publication Data
A catalogue record for this book is available from the British Library

Library of Congress Cataloging-in-Publication Data
Names: Ivtzan, Itai, editor. | Lomas, Tim, 1979- editor.
Title: Mindfulness in positive psychology : the science of meditation and
    wellbeing / Itai Ivtzan, Tim Lomas, [editors].
Description: Abingdon, Oxon ; New York, NY : Routledge, 2016.
Identifiers: LCCN 2015039176 | ISBN 9781138808454 (hbk) | ISBN
    9781138808515 (pbk) | ISBN 9781315747217 (ebk)
Subjects: LCSH: Positive psychology. | Mindfulness (Psychology) |
    Meditation

ISBN: 978-1-138-80845-4 (hbk)
ISBN: 978-1-138-80851-5 (pbk)
ISBN: 978-1-315-74721-7 (ebk)

Typeset in Bembo
by Apex CoVantage, LLC
Printed in Great Britain by Ashford Colour Press Ltd

Itai Ivtzan would like to dedicate this book to Netta Uli Ivtzan for her limitless acceptance, zen-like being and deep love. You rock baby.

Tim Lomas would like to dedicate this book to Katie Battle Lomas for her ever-inspiring love, kindness and support.

We would like to thank the authors who contributed chapters to this book — thank you for your exciting and meaningful work.

Finally, we send deep gratitude to Tarli Young, who edited this book with great dedication and sensitivity.

CONTENTS

Mindfulness in positive psychology: An introduction   1
   Itai Ivtzan

PART I
Positive psychology interventions   **13**

1 Mindfulness-based strengths practice (MBSP) for
    enhancing well-being, managing problems, and boosting
    positive relationships   15
    Ryan M. Niemiec and Judith Lissing

2 Self-compassion: Embracing suffering with kindness   37
    Kristin Neff and Oliver Davidson

3 Mindful parenting begins at the beginning: Potential
    benefits of perinatal meditation training for family well-being   51
    Catherine Shaddix and Larissa G. Duncan

4 Mindfulness and performance   64
    Amy L. Baltzell

5 The relevance of mindful eating for addressing youth obesity   80
    Jeanne Dalen

PART II
Positive theory and mechanisms of mindfulness   95

6 Mindfulness: The essence of well-being and happiness   97
   Christelle T. Ngnoumen and Ellen J. Langer

7 Mindfulness, mental health, and positive psychology   108
   Shauna Shapiro, Sarah de Sousa, and Hooria Jazaieri

8 Mortality and mindfulness: How intense encounters with
   death can generate spontaneous mindfulness   126
   Steven Taylor

9 Flowing with mindfulness: Investigating the relationship
   between flow and mindfulness   141
   Sue Jackson

10 Additional mechanisms of mindfulness: How does
   mindfulness increase wellbeing?   156
   Tarli Young

PART III
Mindfulness for health practitioners and carers   173

11 Contemplative pedagogy and nursing education   175
   Anne Bruce and Betty Poag

12 Mindfulness-Based Medical Practice: Eight weeks
   en route to wellness   193
   Patricia Lynn Dobkin

13 Mindfulness-based positive behavior support in intellectual
   and developmental disabilities   212
   *Nirbhay N. Singh, Giulio E. Lancioni, Ramasamy Manikam,
   Larry L. Latham, and Monica M. Jackman*

14 Working it: Making meaning with workplace mindfulness   228
   Michael F. Steger and Eve Ekman

PART IV
Mindfulness in spirituality   243

15 Mindfulness and spirituality in positive youth development   245
    Eleanor F. Cobb, Clayton H. McClintock, and Lisa J. Miller

16 Nourishment from the roots: Engaging with the Buddhist
    foundations of mindfulness   265
    Tim Lomas

17 Mindfulness and wellbeing: Towards a unified operational
    approach   280
    Edo Shonin, William Van Gordon, and Mark D. Griffiths

PART V
Mindful therapy   293

18 Mindfulness and person-centred therapy   295
    Stephen Joseph, David Murphy and Tom G. Patterson

19 Beyond mindfulness: The power of self-compassion,
    purpose, play, and confidence in the clinical treatment of
    the depressed client   308
    Elisha Goldstein

20 Mindfulness yoga in pregnancy: A promising positive
    treatment augmentation for women experiencing
    depression or anxiety   321
    Maria M. Muzik and Susan E. Hamilton

Index   341

MINDFULNESS IN POSITIVE PSYCHOLOGY

An introduction

Itai Ivtzan

Mindfulness has emerged as a prominent research topic in psychology (Brown, Ryan, & Creswell, 2007) and now seems to attract much interest in the specific context of positive psychology (Malinowski, 2013). The never-ending stream of studies that show the broad variety of wellbeing benefits offered by mindfulness has triggered our fascination and curiosity. If the quest for an ultimate tool that would consistently increase individual wellbeing is the holy grail of positive psychology, could mindfulness be the answer? Every year, more and more MAPP (Masters in Applied Positive Psychology) students tell me they are looking forward to researching mindfulness as part of positive psychology. Their growing interest has sparked in me the inevitable question: What is actually the relationship between mindfulness and positive psychology? Mindfulness, a meditative practice, has been around for thousands of years, and has been researched extensively in mainstream psychology since the 1970s (Williams & Kabat-Zinn, 2013). I therefore believe that we should explore the added value that positive psychology brings into our understanding of mindfulness. What unique angle does positive psychology offer to mindfulness research? To answer this question we must first define and discuss the ways in which positive psychology is able to enrich and deepen the discussion and investigation of mindfulness. Needless to say, such exploration would also enrich our understanding of positive psychology and its benefits. The varied chapters we offer in this book attempt to address and meet these needs. Some of the world's leading authors, researchers and scholars of mindfulness have been willing to explore mindfulness in relation to different aspects of positive psychology, and have contributed their insights to this book.

This introduction begins with an overview of the book and the chapters it contains. It then introduces mindfulness and positive psychology while offering a new context for the relationship between these two areas. As part of this context a flourishing-based approach is offered where intention, a prominent dimension of mindfulness, is focused on the increase of positive variables and outcomes. The chapter also describes the positive mindfulness program (PMP) as an example of this flourishing-based approach to mindfulness.

Structure of the book

The book is divided into parts, each covering a different area of positive psychology, and each part is divided into chapters. These parts present cutting-edge research chosen for its relevance, and intended to extend the boundaries of positive psychology in relation to mindfulness. The title of the first part is *Positive Psychology Interventions*. It encapsulates a number of mindfulness intervention programs that are highly relevant to positive psychology. This part begins with the chapter "Mindfulness-Based Strengths Practice (MBSP) for Enhancing Well-Being, Managing Problems, and Boosting Positive Relationships", written by Ryan Niemiec and Judith Lissing. The chapter explores the relationship between character strengths and mindfulness, focusing on the mindfulness-based strengths practice (MBSP) program. The chapter indicates that existing mindfulness programs target strengths indirectly, and shows the great importance that the link between mindfulness and strengths has for positive psychology. The next chapter is titled "Self-Compassion: Embracing Suffering with Kindness". This chapter, by Kristin Neff and Oliver Davidson, describes the shift positive psychology has made towards the ideal of eudaimonia, and the greater emphasis consequently placed on concepts such as compassion and self-compassion. The chapter identifies mindfulness as a component of compassion and illustrates the benefits of self-compassion. The authors also discuss interventions which specifically target self-compassion, including the mindful self-compassion (MSC) program. The third chapter in this section is "Mindful Parenting Begins at the Beginning: Potential Benefits of Perinatal Meditation Training for Family Well-Being", authored by Catherine Shaddix and Larissa Duncan. The chapter discusses the effects of mindfulness on parenting. It raises fascinating questions concerning the effects of mindfulness on the mother during pregnancy, and discusses the influence of parental mindfulness practice on the parents' relationship with their children. The Mindfulness-Based Childbirth and Parenting intervention program (MBCP) is discussed as an applied dimension of the above. The following chapter is "Mindfulness and Performance", written by Amy Baltzell. It describes mindfulness interventions applied to performance, focusing on sports. Mindfulness and positive psychology are utilised here to address performance optimisation, and offer an understanding of the connection between mindfulness, flow and performance. The final chapter in this section is "The Relevance of Mindful Eating for Addressing Youth Obesity", authored by Jeanne Dalen. The chapter discusses meditation-based mindful eating programs and the way they could assist in expanding treatment for youth obesity. Three key therapeutic components of mindful eating interventions are emphasised: (1) Experiential acceptance, (2) Self-regulation and (3) Compassion.

The second part of the book, *Positive Theory and Mechanisms of Mindfulness*, raises questions related to the theory, components and mechanisms of mindfulness, linking them to positive psychology concepts and findings. The first chapter in this part, titled "Mindfulness: the Essence of Well-being and Happiness", was written by Christelle Ngnoumen and Ellen Langer. It contemplates various definitions of mindfulness, also addressing mindlessness. The authors decode attitudes and emotions in relation to mindfulness, leading to fascinating insights about our happiness and wellbeing. The following chapter in this part is "Mindfulness, Mental Health, and Positive Psychology" written by Shauna Shapiro, Sarah de Sousa, and Hooria Jazaieri. Outlining the core elements of mindfulness, attention, intention and attitude, this chapter discusses various mindfulness-based interventions for both clinical and non-clinical populations. Integrated in the chapter are insights regarding positive psychology concepts such as optimism, happiness in treatment and psychological flexibility. The following chapter is "Mortality and mindfulness: How Intense Encounters with Death Can Generate Spontaneous Mindfulness", written by Steve Taylor. The chapter describes how intense encounters with mortality can have positive transformational effects, leading to a heightened sense of appreciation for life, and an increased ability to be mindful. Reasons for this positively transformative process include an enhanced sense of appreciation, a wider sense of perspective and the dissolution of psychological attachments. The fourth chapter of this part is titled "Flowing with Mindfulness: Investigating the Relationship Between Flow and Mindfulness" and was written by Sue Jackson. This chapter brings flow and mindfulness together while investigating definitions, models and outcomes relating to both. Future directions for flow and mindfulness research are covered as well. The final chapter in this part is titled "Additional Mechanisms of Mindfulness: How Does Mindfulness Increase Wellbeing?" and was written by Tarli Young. This chapter investigates how mindfulness increases both hedonic and eudaimonic wellbeing. It summarises previously established mechanisms and then makes additional suggestions using past research and positive psychology concepts. Suggested mechanisms include hope, meaning, savouring, gratitude, self-acceptance, autonomy, positive reappraisal and body awareness.

The third part of the book, *Mindfulness for Health Practitioners and Carers*, investigates the role of mindfulness and positive psychology in relation to health professionals and individuals supporting others, such as medical practitioners, nurses and parents. The first chapter in this part, "Contemplative Pedagogy and Nursing Education", written by Anne Bruce and Betty Poag, addresses the field of nursing. The chapter discusses mindfulness in the theoretical and practical studies of nursing, and brings important insights concerning ways in which mindfulness is able to combat burnout at work. It also evaluates ways in which mindfulness could help students strengthen positive emotions and mind states (e.g. empathy, self-compassion) that contribute to their ability to help others. The second chapter in this part is titled "Mindfulness-Based Medical Practice: Eight Weeks En Route to Wellness" and was written by Patricia Dobkin. The chapter outlines in detail the Mindfulness-Based Medical Practice (MBMP), and describes the implications of mindfulness for medical practitioners. The next chapter, "Mindfulness-Based Positive Behaviour Support in Intellectual and Developmental Disabilities", was written by Nirbhay

Singh and colleagues, and helps us understand the contribution mindfulness has for individuals with intellectual and developmental disabilities (IDDs). The chapter also outlines mindfulness-based positive behavior support (MBPBS), which provides a mindful approach for caregivers of individuals with a diverse range of behavioural challenges. The final chapter of this part is "Working It: Making Meaning with Workplace Mindfulness", written by Michael Steger and Eve Ekman. The chapter connects meaning and mindfulness as mutually supportive components in reduction of stress in health service workers. It also summarises meaning research and the benefits of meaning in work while providing a model on how mindfulness and meaning could work together.

In the fourth part of the book, *Mindfulness in Spirituality*, mindfulness and positive psychology are contextualised with spirituality, mainly relating to Buddhism. The first chapter, "Mindfulness and Spirituality in Positive Youth Development", written by Eleanor Cobb, Clayton McClintock and Lisa Miller, describes the effects of mindfulness in schools for both clinical and non-clinical populations. The chapter also links mindfulness and positive psychology with spirituality, and describes their benefits to our wellbeing. The second chapter, "Nourishment from the Roots: Engaging with the Buddhist Foundations of Mindfulness", was written by Tim Lomas. This chapter illustrates how the comprehension of mindfulness has been somewhat limited in the West by its removal from its original Buddhist context. The chapter aims to re-contextualise mindfulness by exploring the deeper spiritual and Buddhist roots of the concept. In the third and final chapter of this part, "Mindfulness and Wellbeing: Towards a Unified Operational Approach", Edo Shonin, William Van Gordon and Mark Griffiths offer a new model of mindfulness, which aims to encompass both Buddhist and Western perspectives. In their chapter they emphasise that by adapting to Western values, mindfulness had lost some of its original spiritual meaning. The chapter places mindfulness within the greater context of Buddhist teachings, where components such as other meditative and spiritual-practice agents also take part in any progress one makes in one's spiritual journey.

The book's final part, *Mindful Therapy*, addresses the relationship between mindfulness, positive psychology and therapeutic or clinical disciplines. This part begins with the chapter "Mindfulness and Person-Centred Therapy", written by Stephen Joseph, David Murphy and Tom Patterson. They address the relationship between person-centred therapy (P-CT), positive psychology and mindfulness, and assess the influence of mindfulness on the therapeutic experience. The chapter argues that P-CT is a kind of mindfulness therapy, and that mindfulness practice could assist therapists. The second chapter in this part is titled "Beyond Mindfulness: The Power of Self-Compassion, Purpose, Play and Confidence in the Clinical Treatment of the Depressed Client", written by Elisha Goldstein. The chapter discusses the benefits of mindfulness meditation and recognises the difficulty depressed individuals have in sustaining their meditation practice. The chapter deals with important areas that are based upon positive psychology and mindfulness, including self-compassion, purpose, play and growth mindsets. The final part ends with the chapter "Mindful

Yoga in Pregnancy: A Promising Positive Treatment Augmentation for Women Experiencing Depression or anxiety", written by Maria Muzik and Susan Hamilton. The chapter explains the importance of alternative treatments for pregnant women at risk for depression. It goes on to describe "mindful yoga" as a possible solution, and offers evidence to support its benefits, including promotion of the mother's mindful stance towards pregnancy, enhanced connection with her child and long-term gains of child wellbeing.

Mindfulness in positive psychology

Before beginning exploration of the wealth of material contained within these chapters it is worthwhile to first consider the unique contribution positive psychology makes to mindfulness. Mindfulness is perceived as a form of awareness that arises from attending to the present moment in a non-judgemental and accepting manner (Bishop et al., 2004). This invites the practitioner to attend to the full range of internal and external experiences in this non-judgemental attitude (Hart, Ivtzan, & Hart, 2013). Research has indicated that mindfulness enhances both hedonic (Brown & Cordon, 2009) and eudaimonic wellbeing (Brown, Ryan, & Creswell, 2007), which are both at the heart of positive psychology research and application. Hedonic wellbeing is linked with pain relief and intensified pleasure (Deci & Ryan, 2008), and eudaimonic wellbeing involves living a meaningful, self-realised and fully functional life (Ryff & Keyes, 1995). The concept of mindfulness originates in traditional Buddhist contemplative practices, where the development of psychological wellbeing is regarded as a primary goal (Shapiro, 2009). Buddhist mindfulness practitioners aspire to improve positive psychological experiences including joy, awareness and compassion.

Within its original religious context, mindfulness is a fundamental part of a broad program of psycho-spiritual development, aiming to help people reach 'enlightenment'. Although terms such as 'enlightenment' are difficult to rationalise within the ontological and epistemological contexts of Western psychology, it may be conceived of as the superlative state of happiness, equanimity and freedom that a human being is capable of experiencing. However, with the transference to Western psychology, the term mindfulness has been interpreted in a way that made it lose some of its initial potential as a means of psycho-spiritual transformation. And although it has been investigated for over 40 years in the West, some of its beneficial objectives have been disregarded. It has been applied along the lines of the deficit model of Western psychology, whose primary concern remains treating or weakening dysfunction or illness, and has been adapted for implementation in clinical populations (Malinowski, 2013). Even though this altered practice has yielded successful mindfulness programs and studies in the West, it has failed to fully actualise the capacity of mindfulness to enhance flourishing because it has overlooked some of the original key positive principles and intentions. The fourth part of this book, *Mindfulness in Spirituality*, offers a number of chapters that investigate in depth the original intentions of mindfulness within the Buddhist context and practice.

Several programs targeting clinical populations have been created in the West, of which the most prominent are mindfulness-based stress reduction (MBSR; Kabat-Zinn, 1982); mindfulness-based cognitive therapy (MBCT; Teasdale et al., 2000) and dialectical behaviour therapy (DBT; Linehan, 1993). As its name suggests, MBSR, originally designed to manage chronic pain, aimed to ease stress, anxiety and depression. MBCT was specifically designed to prevent depression relapses, and DBT was developed to treat borderline personality disorder. All of these programs have been empirically tested (Grossman et al., 2004) and have been shown to be effective in reducing disorder symptoms, including psychosis (Bach & Hayes, 2002), depression (Teasdale et al., 2000) and chronic pain (Kabat-Zinn, 1982). They all focus on reducing negative variables, in keeping with the emphasis Western psychology places on reducing deficits (Seligman & Csikszentmihalyi, 2000). Yet although they concentrate on deficit reduction, Western mindfulness programs have actually brought about improvements in certain positive variables such as positive affect (Geschwind, Peeters, Drukker, Van Os, & Wichers, 2011), cognitive functioning (Hölzel et al., 2011), self-regulation (Ryan & Deci, 2000), positive reappraisal of thoughts (Hanley & Garland, 2014) and improved interpersonal interaction (Goleman, 2006). This is liable to lead to the erroneous conclusion that because existing deficit-focused mindfulness programs increase positive variables, there is no need for a different approach to mindfulness which specifically targets positive variables. A standpoint such as this would overlook the crucial impact of the intentions and goals of an intervention program, the influence of which will be discussed next. Once these are taken into consideration, the important role of wellbeing objectives in the context of mindfulness practice becomes very clear.

Applying positive psychology in mindfulness: mechanisms

Shapiro, Carlson, Astin, and Freedman (2006) propose that mindfulness is made up of three principal components: intention, attention and attitude (IAA). Attention and attitude cover the actual practice of mindfulness and the way we approach it. Attention is concerned with becoming fully aware of our moment-to-moment internal experience; attitude describes the quality of the practitioner's attention, which is filled with acceptance, kindness and curiosity. The first component, intention, is the one that allows the integration of positive psychology in mindfulness practice. First, we must understand the full meaning of the intention component. Intention is defined as the aims and motivations that underlie a practitioner's mindfulness practice. Shapiro et al. (2006) argue that intention has been often overlooked in relevant discussions because Western psychology sought to "extract the essence of mindfulness practice from its original religious/cultural roots" (2006, p. 375). However, they state that the intention embedded in the practice of mindfulness has an important role in the very experience of mindfulness exercises, and naturally affects their consequences. Kabat-Zinn (1990) regards intention as essential in generating positive change through mindfulness: "Your intentions set the stage for what is possible. They remind you from moment to moment of why

you are practicing in the first place" (p. 32). Shapiro (1992) underlines the significance of intention, showing that most mediators in his study have achieved the
effects they had originally aimed for: if they intended to focus on self-regulation
(control over self), they tended to attain it; if their intention was self-exploration
(knowledge of self), their self-exploration increased. In other words, the intention
behind our practice has a significant impact on the actual benefits we draw from
it. Now that we understand the importance of intention in mindfulness practice,
we can investigate further its relevance to positive psychology and to mindfulness
programs in general.

The question of intention is fully addressed in positive psychology, particularly
with regards to the criteria that define a positive psychology intervention (PPI). Sin
and Lyubomirsky (2009, p. 469) describe this as follows: "The study must empirically test an intervention, therapy, or activity, primarily aimed at increasing positive feelings, positive behaviors, or positive cognitions, as opposed to ameliorating
pathology or fixing negative thoughts or maladaptive behavior patterns". More
recently, a number of rigorous parameters have been put forward by Parks and
Biswas-Diener (2013) for the classification of PPIs, beginning with a flourishing-
based method according to which PPIs have a clear aim and intention – to boost
positive variables.

In reality, the paramount purpose of all major mindfulness programs, including
MBSR and MBCT, is to reduce negative variables. This is a deficit-based approach,
where the disease model is the point of departure as well as the implied motivation
and intention (Green, Carrillo, & Betancourt, 2002). According to this approach we
are broken, we must be fixed and we harness mindfulness to that purpose. Most of
the contemporary mindfulness-based interventions focus on remedying or reducing a deficit such as depression, anxiety, insomnia, aggression, pain and substance
abuse (Craigie et al., 2008; Heidenreich et al., 2006; Teasdale et al., 2000). As such,
these programs are not aligned with the spirit of PPIs, whose intentions look at
mental health from a different angle. In PPIs, the absence of mental illness does not
constitute mental health. PPI programs do not regard eliminating illness as a guarantee that an individual is healthy, thriving and competent (Ryff & Singer, 1998).
This state of flourishing exceeds the removal of psychological anguish, and can only
be attained by involving the positive variables and outcomes.

The Western approach to mindfulness has generated much research on the ability of mindfulness to reduce negative variables (e.g. Hölzel et al., 2011), and yet few
studies have been dedicated to interventions based on mindfulness, whose purpose
is increasing positive outcomes (Garland, Gaylord, & Fredrickson, 2011). This does
not aim to critique in any way current mindfulness programs such as MBSR and
MBCT, which have proven highly beneficial and have brought relief to thousands
of psychologically distressed individuals worldwide. Essentially, my point is that it
is possible to approach mindfulness, and more specifically the component of intention, in a different way – one that is aligned with positive psychology. This would
allow individuals to choose between mindfulness programs that intend to alleviate
mental illness and those that seek to improve mental health.

Positive psychology and mindfulness

Positive psychology explores methods that enhance flourishing in an individual's life. Shapiro, Schwartz, and Santerre (2002) propose that this flourishing-oriented approach may introduce perspectives that are more in line with the original aims of mindfulness. Their recommendation to integrate positive outcome variables into mindfulness research stands at the heart of our book. The different chapters of this book offer the integration of positive outcomes with mindfulness, and extend the traditional boundaries of mindfulness application in research and practice by pressing forward towards further positive outcomes, mechanisms and intentions.

Several mindfulness programs that focus on positive variables have already been launched in the West. One of them is the mindfulness-based strengths practice (Niemiec, Rashid, & Spinella, 2012), where strengths (a central theme in positive psychology) and mindfulness are married to create a fascinating program. Another is the MSC program, designed to heighten self-compassion and kindness (Neff & Germer, 2013) by emphasising the compassion dimension of mindfulness. The creators of both of these programs have each contributed a chapter to this book, and their work is highly relevant to positive psychology and mindfulness research. We have also included other programs in this book, which display a similar spirit and intention. These programs offer inspiring models that effectively incorporate mindfulness and positive variables. Because of the insight we feel positive psychology offers for mindfulness research and application, we have combined the two fields into the PMP (Ivtzan et al., in press), which incorporates a variety of prominent positive psychology variables, bringing them together in mindfulness practice. It is introduced here as an example of the process and value of combining positive psychology (PP) and mindfulness.

Positive mindfulness program

The PMP is an 8-week online program that combines mindfulness practice with several positive psychology interventions and theories, in order to improve wellbeing (Ivtzan et al., in press). Each of the 8 PMP weeks focuses on a different topic: (1) self-awareness, (2) positive emotions, (3) self-compassion, (4) self-efficacy (strengths), (5) autonomy, (6) meaning, (7) positive relations with others and (8) engagement (savouring).

At the beginning of each week, the participants are shown an 8–10 minute video, summarising the theoretical basis of that week's topic. They are also provided with a 12–15 minute audio file, which contains a daily guided meditation and an additional daily activity related to the week's topic. The PMP is fully protocoled, including all video materials, daily meditations and daily activities.

The PMP has been tested by Ivtzan et al. (in press), showing excellent increases in participants' levels of wellbeing measures. It is currently being tested with various populations including educators, athletes, CEOs, older persons (60+) and patients suffering from chronic pain.

Outline of PMP eight weekly topics and activities

Week	Variable	Theory Video	Meditation	Daily Practice
1	Self-awareness	Introduction to mindfulness, self-awareness, positive psychology and meditation	Introductory meditation focusing on awareness of breath, body and emotions	Keeping aware of thoughts and reactions throughout the day
2	Positive emotions	Discussion of the benefits of positive emotions and gratitude	Gratitude meditation focusing on who or what one appreciates	Expressing gratitude for positive situations
3	Self-compassion	Explanation of the self-compassion concept, research review, and methods to increase self-compassion	Adapted version of loving kindness meditation focusing on self-compassion (Neff & Germer, 2013)	Replacing internal criticism with statements of kindness
4	Self-efficacy	Introduction to character strengths and self-efficacy including enhancement methods	Meditation focusing on a time when participant was at his/her best and using character strengths	Completing the VIA character strengths questionnaire (Park, Peterson, & Seligman, 2006) and using strengths
5	Autonomy	Introduction to autonomy and its connection with wellbeing	Meditation on authentic self and action	Taking action in line with one's values and noticing external pressure on choices
6	Meaning	Discussion of meaning and wellbeing. Completion of writing exercise, "Best Possible Legacy," adapted from the Obituary Exercise (Seligman, Rashid, & Parks, 2006).	Meditation on future vision of self, living one's best possible legacy	Acting according to best possible legacy. Choosing meaningful activities.
7	Positive relations with others	Discussion of benefits of positive relationships and methods for relationship enhancement	Loving kindness meditation (Scheffel, 2003)	Bringing feelings of loving kindness into interactions
8	Engagement	Introduction to engagement and savouring and their connection with positive emotions	Savouring meditation focusing on food	Using savouring to engage with experiences
	Conclusion	Summary of the program. Discussion of personal growth and invitation to keep meditating.		

The PMP reflects this book's perspective and offering. It exemplifies the IAA components of mindfulness (Shapiro et al., 2006) – intention, attention and attitude – and their relevance to the integration of mindfulness and positive psychology. Each of the daily meditations begins with a short positive psychology intervention followed by mindfulness practice. The positive psychology interventions provide a clear foundation for the intention component, focusing the participants' intention on positive outcomes such as a feeling of autonomy, increased experience of personal meaning in life, greater connection with one's strengths and a deep feeling of self-compassion. Once the intention has been established, the practice shifts to the application of the other two components of mindfulness practice, attention and attitude. As the practitioners' approach the practice, their aims and vision engage with their strengths and virtues. The PMP has positive outcomes because its participants apply mindful, deep attention to their internal experiences with an accepting and kind attitude, while experiencing the intention of strengths and virtues.

Summary

The present chapter has introduced the concept of mindfulness in positive psychology, offering another possible approach to mindfulness within the context of positive psychology. This approach incorporates mindfulness practice with the intention of achieving positive outcomes, which are at the heart of positive psychology. Intention, a central mindfulness component, thus becomes the mechanism through which positive psychology can be applied in mindfulness practice. This introduction has also summarised the other chapters included in this book which I believe the reader will find highly illuminating regarding the connection between mindfulness and positive psychology. Finally, the chapter illustrates the Positive Mindfulness Program (PMP) as an example of a mindfulness program rooted within the intentions of positive psychology outcomes.

Bibliography

Bach, P., & Hayes, S. C. (2002). The use of acceptance and commitment therapy to prevent the rehospitalization of psychotic patients: A randomized controlled trial. *Journal of Consulting and Clinical Psychology, 70*(5), 1129.

Bishop, S. R., Lau, M., Shapiro, S., Carlson, L., Anderson, N. D., Carmody, J., . . . Devins, G. (2004). Mindfulness: A proposed operational definition. *Clinical Psychology: Science and Practice, 11*(3), 230–241.

Brown, K. W., & Cordon, S. (2009). Toward a phenomenology of mindfulness: Subjective experience and emotional correlates. In F. Didonna (Ed.), *Clinical handbook of mindfulness* (pp. 59–81). New York, NY: Springer.

Brown, K. W., Creswell, J. D., & Ryan, R. M. (2015). *Handbook of mindfulness: Theory, research, and practice.* New York, NY: Guilford Publications.

Brown, K. W., Ryan, R. M., & Creswell, J. D. (2007). Mindfulness: Theoretical foundations and evidence for its salutary effects. *Psychological Inquiry, 18*(4), 211–237.

Craigie, M. A., Rees, C. S., Marsh, A., & Nathan, P. (2008). Mindfulness-based cognitive therapy for generalized anxiety disorder: A preliminary evaluation. *Behavioural and Cognitive Psychotherapy, 36*, 553–568.

Deci, E. L., & Ryan, R. M. (2008). Hedonia, eudaimonia, and well-being: An introduction. *Journal of Happiness Studies, 9*(1), 1–11.

Garland, E. L., Gaylord, S., & Fredrickson, B. L. (2011). Positive reappraisal mediates the stress-reductive effects of mindfulness: An upward spiral process. *Mindfulness, 2*(1), 59–67.

Geschwind, N., Peeters, F., Drukker, M., Van Os, J., & Wichers, M. (2011). Mindfulness training increases momentary positive emotions and reward experience in adults vulnerable to depression: A randomized controlled trial. *Journal of Consulting and Clinical Psychology, 79*, 618–628.

Goleman, D. (2006). *Social intelligence: The new science of human relationships*. New York, NY: Bantam.

Green, A. R., Carrillo, J. E., & Betancourt, J. R. (2002). Why the disease-based model of medicine fails our patients. *Western Journal of Medicine, 176*(2), 141–143.

Grossman, P., Niemann, L., Schmidt, S., & Walach, H. (2004). Mindfulness-based stress reduction and health benefits. A meta-analysis. *Journal of Psychosomatic Research, 57*(1), 35–43.

Hanley, A. W., & Garland, E. L. (2014). Dispositional mindfulness co-varies with self-reported positive reappraisal. *Personality and Individual Differences, 66*, 146–152.

Hart, R., Ivtzan, I., & Hart, D. (2013). Mind the gap in mindfulness research: A comparative account of the leading schools of thought. *Review of General Psychology, 17*(4), 453–466.

Heidenreich, T., Tuin, I., Pflug, B., Michal, M., & Michalak, J. (2006). Mindfulness-based cognitive therapy for persistent insomnia: A pilot study. *Psychotherapy and Psychosomatics, 75*(3), 188–189.

Hölzel, B. K., Lazar, S. W., Gard, T., Schuman-Olivier, Z., Vago, D. R., & Ott, U. (2011). How does mindfulness meditation work? Proposing mechanisms of action from a conceptual and neural perspective. *Perspectives on Psychological Science, 6*(6), 537–559.

Ivtzan, I., Young, T. K., Jeffrey, A. D., Martman, J. L., Hart, R., & Eiroa-Orosa, F. J. (in press). Integrating mindfulness in positive psychology: A randomised controlled trial of an 8-week Positive Mindfulness Programme (PMP). Manuscript submitted for publication.

Kabat-Zinn, J. (1982). An outpatient program in behavioral medicine for chronic pain patients based on the practice of mindfulness meditation: Theoretical considerations and preliminary results. *General Hospital Psychiatry, 4*(1), 33–47.

Kabat-Zinn, J. (1990). *Full catastrophe living: The program of the stress reduction clinic at the University of Massachusetts medical center*. New York, NY: Delta.

Krishnamurti, J. (1975). *Freedom from the known*. London: HarperOne.

Linehan, M. (1993). *Cognitive behavioral treatment of borderline personality disorder*. New York, NY: Guilford Press.

Malinowski, P. (2013). Flourishing through meditation and mindfulness. In S. A. David, I. Boniwell & A. Conley Ayers (Eds.), *The Oxford handbook of happiness* (pp. 384–396). Oxford: Oxford University Press.

Neff, K. D., & Germer, C. K. (2013). A pilot study and randomized controlled trial of the mindful self-compassion program. *Journal of Clinical Psychology, 69*(1), 28–44.

Niemiec, R. M., Rashid, T., & Spinella, M. (2012). Strong mindfulness: Integrating mindfulness and character strengths. *Journal of Mental Health Counseling, 34*(3), 240.

Park, N., Peterson, C., & Seligman, M. E. P. (2006). Character strengths in fifty-four nations and the fifty US states. *The Journal of Positive Psychology, 1*(3), 118–129.

Parks, A. C., & Biswas-Diener, R. (2013). Positive interventions: Past, present and future. In T. Kashdan & J. Ciarrocchi (Eds.), *Mindfulness, acceptance and positive psychology: The seven foundations of well-being*. Oakland, CA: Context Press.

Ryan, R. M., & Deci, E. L. (2000). Self-determination theory and the facilitation of intrinsic motivation, social development, and well-being. *American Psychologist, 55*(1), 68.

Ryff, C. D., & Keyes, C. L. M. (1995). The structure of psychological well-being revisited. *Journal of Personality and Social Psychology, 69*(4), 719.

Ryff, C. D., & Singer, B. (1998). The contours of positive human health. *Psychological Inquiry*, *9*(1), 1–28.

Scheffel, B. (2003). *Loving-kindness meditation: Meditations to help you love yourself, love others and create more love and peace in the world*. Gloucester, MA: Fair Winds Press.

Seligman, M. E. P., & Csikszentmihalyi, M. (2000). Positive psychology: An introduction. *American Psychologist*, *55*, 5–14.

Seligman, M.E.P., Rashid,T., & Parks,A.C. (2006). *Positive psychotherapy*. *American Psychologist*, *61*, 774–788.

Shapiro, D. H. (1992). A preliminary study of long term meditators: Goals, effects, religious orientation, cognitions. *Journal of Transpersonal Psychology*, *24*(1), 23–39.

Shapiro, S. L. (2009). The integration of mindfulness and psychology. *Journal of Clinical Psychology*, *65*(6), 555–560.

Shapiro, S. L., Carlson, L. E., Astin, J. A., & Freedman, B. (2006). Mechanisms of mindfulness. *Journal of Clinical Psychology*, *62*(3), 373–386.

Shapiro, S. L., Schwartz, G. E., & Santerre, C. (2002). Meditation and positive psychology. *Handbook of Positive Psychology*, *2*, 632–645.

Sin, N. L., & Lyubomirsky, S. (2009). Enhancing well-being and alleviating depressive symptoms with positive psychology interventions: A practice-friendly meta-analysis. *Journal of Clinical Psychology*, *65*(5), 467–487.

Teasdale, J. D., Segal, Z. V., Williams, J. M. G., Ridgeway, V. A., Soulsby, J. M., & Lau, M. A. (2000). Prevention of relapse/recurrence in major depression by mindfulness-based cognitive therapy. *Journal of Consulting and Clinical Psychology*, *68*(4), 615.

Williams, J. M. G., & Kabat-Zinn, J. (2013). *Mindfulness: Diverse perspectives on its meaning, origins and applications*. New York, NY: Routledge.

PART I

Positive psychology interventions

1

MINDFULNESS-BASED STRENGTHS PRACTICE (MBSP) FOR ENHANCING WELL-BEING, MANAGING PROBLEMS, AND BOOSTING POSITIVE RELATIONSHIPS

Ryan M. Niemiec and Judith Lissing

> We can't understand what is happening to 'something' if we aren't looking. But nothing is going to happen to that 'something' if we don't look *deeply*. That's why so many things with incredible potential go unnoticed because nobody bothers to look.
>
> Alejandro Gonzalez Inarritu, director of *21 Grams* (2003), *Babel* (2006), *Biutiful* (2010), and *Birdman* (2014)

The science of mindfulness and character

Positive psychology has two natural bedfellows that, despite some overlapping routes and similar benefits when practiced, have grown up separately over the centuries. These are mindfulness meditation and strengths of character. Each has a number of misconceptions associated with it so we begin by clarifying terms and offering some brief research findings before delving into their integration.

There are many ways to define mindfulness. Each author, researcher, practitioner, and thought leader has their own take on it. The lack of a common, consensual definition poses problems for researchers and practitioners in terms of understanding what is being discussed, studied, and practiced. It is for this reason that a large group of mindfulness scientists gathered at the turn of the century to derive a consensual, operational definition. What emerged was a two-part definition for mindfulness (Bishop et al., 2004): Mindfulness involves the self-regulation of attention with an approach of curiosity, openness, and acceptance.

Ultimately, mindfulness is not about getting relaxed or achieving a particular state; rather, mindfulness refers to being present to what is happening in the unfolding moment to moment experience, without pre-conceptions or judgments. Mindfulness meditation practices and mindfulness-based programs have been associated with many positive outcomes. Meta-analyses have found clear evidence for the positive effects of meditation on well-being (Sedlmeier et al., 2012) and that meditation is beneficial for both clinical and non-clinical populations (Grossman et al., 2004).

Character is another term that has traditionally lacked a consensual definition. Character has typically been viewed over the decades in a narrow and myopic way – conceived of as a solitary construct such as honesty or integrity or characterized by a random selection of four or five qualities such as responsibility, respect, loyalty, and kindness. Studies of such groupings of character frequently found in character education programs have typically lacked scientific rigor (Berkowitz & Bier, 2007). A new science of character emerged at the turn of the century. In 2004, a common language emerged for understanding these positive aspects of our personality. This was catalyzed by a 3-year project involving 55 scientists, significant cross-cultural work, and extensive research finding 24 character strengths to be universal in human beings (Biswas-Diener, 2006; Park, Peterson, & Seligman, 2006; Peterson & Seligman, 2004). This groundbreaking system of character strengths and virtues is known as the VIA Classification (Peterson & Seligman, 2004), which can be seen in detail in Table 1.1. The accompanying scientific measurement tool to assess these 24 strengths is widely known as the VIA Survey. (The word "VIA" in these instances was formerly an acronym for "values in action.") The VIA Survey, a free online tool (accessible at www.viacharacter.org) has been taken by over three million people reaching every country around the globe. There are over 200 peer-reviewed publications on character strengths, the majority emerging in the last several years.

TABLE 1.1 VIA classification of character strengths and virtues

The Virtue of Wisdom – cognitive strengths that entail the acquisition and use of knowledge

- *Creativity* [originality, ingenuity]: Thinking of novel and productive ways to conceptualize and do things; includes artistic achievement but is not limited to it
- *Curiosity* [interest, novelty-seeking, openness to experience]: Taking an interest in ongoing experience for its own sake; finding subjects and topics fascinating; exploring and discovering
- *Judgment* [open-mindedness; critical thinking]: Thinking things through and examining them from all sides; not jumping to conclusions; being able to change one's mind in light of evidence; weighing all evidence fairly
- *Love of Learning*: Mastering new skills, topics, and bodies of knowledge, whether on one's own or formally; related to the strength of curiosity but goes beyond it to describe the tendency to add systematically to what one knows
- *Perspective* [wisdom]: Being able to provide wise counsel to others; having ways of looking at the world that make sense to oneself/others

The Virtue of Courage – emotional strengths that involve the exercise of will to accomplish goals in the face of opposition, external or internal

- *Bravery* [valor]: Not shrinking from threat, challenge, difficulty, or pain; speaking up for what's right even if there's opposition; acting on convictions even if unpopular; includes physical bravery but is not limited to it

- *Perseverance* [persistence, industriousness]: Finishing what one starts; persevering in a course of action in spite of obstacles; "getting it out the door"; taking pleasure in completing tasks
- *Honesty* [authenticity, integrity]: Speaking the truth but more broadly presenting oneself in a genuine way and acting in a sincere way; being without pretense; taking responsibility for one's feelings and actions
- *Zest* [vitality, enthusiasm, vigor, energy]: Approaching life with excitement and energy; not doing things halfway or halfheartedly; living life as an adventure; feeling alive and activated

The Virtue of Humanity – interpersonal strengths that involve tending and befriending others

- *Love* (capacity to love and be loved): Valuing close relations with others, in particular those in which sharing & caring are reciprocated; being close to people
- *Kindness* [generosity, nurturance, care, compassion, altruistic love, "niceness"]: Doing favors and good deeds for others; helping them; taking care of them
- *Social Intelligence* [emotional intelligence, personal intelligence]: Being aware of the motives/feelings of others and oneself; knowing what to do to fit into different social situations; knowing what makes other people tick

The Virtue of Justice – civic strengths that underlie healthy community life

- *Teamwork* [citizenship, social responsibility, loyalty]: Working well as a member of a group or team; being loyal to the group; doing one's share
- *Fairness:* Treating all people the same according to notions of fairness & justice; not letting feelings bias decisions about others; giving everyone a fair chance
- *Leadership:* Encouraging a group of which one is a member to get things done and at the same time maintain good relations within the group; organizing group activities and seeing that they happen

The Virtue of Temperance – strengths that protect against excess

- *Forgiveness* [mercy]: Forgiving those who have done wrong; accepting others' shortcomings; giving people a second chance; not being vengeful
- *Humility* [modesty]: Letting one's accomplishments speak for themselves; not regarding oneself as more special than one is
- *Prudence:* Being careful about one's choices; not taking undue risks; not saying or doing things that might later be regretted
- *Self-Regulation* [self-control]: Regulating what one feels and does; being disciplined; controlling one's appetites and emotions

The Virtue of Transcendence – strengths that forge connections to the universe & provide meaning

- *Appreciation of Beauty and Excellence* [awe, wonder, elevation]: Noticing and appreciating beauty, excellence, and/or skilled performance in various domains of life, from nature to art to mathematics to science to everyday experience
- *Gratitude*: Being aware of and thankful for the good things that happen; taking time to express thanks

- *Hope* [optimism, future-mindedness, future orientation]: Expecting the best in the future and working to achieve it; believing that a good future is something that can be brought about
- *Humor* [playfulness]: Liking to laugh and tease; bringing smiles to other people; seeing the light side; making (not necessarily telling) jokes
- *Spirituality* [religiousness, faith, purpose]: Having coherent beliefs about the higher purpose & meaning of the universe; knowing where one fits within the larger scheme; having beliefs about the meaning of life that shape conduct and provide comfort

---

Character strengths are core, positive, trait-like capacities for thinking, feeling, and behaving in ways that help us achieve our best potential and bring out the best in others. These character strengths have been found to correlate with many of the valued outcomes that humans pursue. Reviews and examples have been published elsewhere (Niemiec, 2013; Peterson, 2006; Peterson & Seligman, 2004) and include the link between creativity and posttraumatic growth (Forgeard, 2013), the connection between curiosity and intimacy (Kashdan et al., 2011), the alignment of humility with generosity (Exline & Hill, 2012), and the connection between the strength of appreciation of beauty and well-being and self-transcendence (Martinez-Marti et al., 2014), to name a recent few.

There is good reason to explore and deepen the synergy of these exciting positive psychology domains. Mindfulness has been found to provide greater exposure to our internal environment (Brown, Ryan, & Creswell, 2007), to help overcome our blind spots in self-knowledge (Carlson, 2013), and to align our actual self (who we think we are) and our ideal self (who we would like to be; Ivtzan, Gardner, & Smailova, 2011). In practical terms, mindfulness helps people to look within, sift through the judgments, comparisons, distortions, etc., and clearly see who we really are (i.e., our authentic self; our core strengths).

Positive psychology – and its countless researchers and practitioners – strives to not only bring a more careful examination of what is best in people (e.g., positive traits, positive emotions, resilience) but also to use what is best to confront, manage, and/or transcend what is disordered, afflictive, or discomforting (e.g., human suffering, disease, conflict, problems). Mindfulness and character strengths each address these two points and it is suspected that the synergy between the two provides an additive benefit for helping humans to not only champion what is best in them but also to face and manage suffering.

Mindfulness and character strengths integration: past and present

Until recently, minimal attention has been given to synergies of the universal character strengths of the VIA Classification (Peterson & Seligman, 2004) and mindfulness-based practices. Previous synergies had been piecemeal (e.g., focusing on one strength), indirect, or non-inclusive. We outline previous and current approaches.

Indirect focus: The most popular mindfulness-based programs to date, mindfulness-based stress reduction (MBSR; Kabat-Zinn, 1990) and mindfulness-based cognitive therapy (MBCT; Segal, Williams, & Teasdale, 2013), do not directly target character strengths. That said, one is not hard-pressed to discover character strengths being addressed throughout these programs. For example, MBSR places emphasis on cultivating attitudes such as patience, openness, and letting go; the character strengths of self-regulation, curiosity, judgment/open-mindedness, and forgiveness are closely linked with these MBSR attitudes. The newest edition to the MBCT manual (Segal et al., 2013) places an explicitly stronger emphasis on targeting love/kindness/compassion. In addition, projected benefits and focus areas in MBCT are as follows (our observation of the matched character strengths are in parentheses):

- Observe negative thoughts with curiosity and kindness (curiosity, kindness, judgment/critical thinking, self-regulation).
- To accept themselves and stop wishing things were different (forgiveness, perspective).
- To let go of old habits and choose a different way of being (forgiveness, bravery, perseverance).
- To be present in the moment and notice small beauties and pleasures in the world (curiosity, appreciation of beauty and excellence).

Single strength integration: To be sure, many scientists and practitioners have studied, aligned, and taught about the connection between meditation and mindfulness and particular character strengths. Kindness and the recent surge of loving-kindness meditation and compassion practices is one of the more prominent examples. Indeed, entire programs have been created around mindfulness practices and this strength (e.g., Germer, 2009; Gilbert, 2010). Other examples that have merged mindfulness/meditation with a specific strength include creativity (Langer, 2006), spirituality (Ivtzan et al., 2011), hope (Hanson, 2013), forgiveness (Kornfield, 2008), and gratitude (Brach, 2003). Related to this type of integration, researchers have frequently found correlations between individual character strengths and mindfulness practices. For example, nonreactive and nonjudging elements of mindfulness predicted perseverance (Evans, Baer, & Segerstrom, 2009), authenticity/honesty correlates positively with mindfulness (Lakey et al., 2008), and vitality/zest is not infrequently found to be an outcome of mindfulness (Reibel et al., 2001).

Buddhist philosophy and religious approaches: Buddhism, specifically Tibetan Buddhism, has a rich history of meditation teachings, approaches, and metta (loving-kindness) practices. Substantial emphasis is placed on meditation avenues aligned with compassion and wisdom, i.e., the character strengths of kindness and perspective (e.g., Chödrön, 1994; Dalai Lama, 2006). Meditative practices in Christianity date back at least to the early desert fathers centuries ago (Carrigan, 2001) to centering prayer advocates (Keating, 2006) and to contemporary theologians (Rehg, 2002) who have linked mindfulness with Christian 'spirituality, where it is easy to see additional links with open-mindedness/judgment, love, perseverance, and humility.

Total strength integration: Prior to the publication of *Mindfulness and Character Strengths* and the launching of mindfulness-based strengths practice (MBSP), there were three publications that discussed an integration of mindfulness and the universal VIA Classification of character strengths (see Baer & Lykins, 2011; Niemiec, 2013; Niemiec, Rashid, & Spinella, 2012). MBSP, like other mindfulness-based programs, provides a "scaffolding" or "launching pad" to invite cultivation (Kabat-Zinn, 2003) of core positive qualities and attention in participants. MBSP enhances the inclusiveness and depth of previous approaches to virtue, strength, and character by encompassing the following:

- The plurality of our character (e.g., Peterson, 2006): Each individual has a unique constellation of character strengths that are uniquely expressed in different combinations, to different degrees, dependent on the context. Mindfulness practices support the complexity and idiosyncratic nature of these individual differences and contextual issues.
- Exploring over prescribing: A descriptive and exploratory approach to character strengths discovery and application is prioritized over a prescriptive approach that focuses on a handful of strengths that all people must develop (see Linkins et al., 2014, for a full explanation of this difference).
- Targeting strengths: Indeed, single strength integration approaches have been fruitful in boosting up specific strengths, thus this was viewed as an important approach to integrate into MBSP. A mindful targeting of specific strengths, chosen by participants themselves, creates the opportunity for the enhancement of any of the 24 character strengths. Participants sometimes attempt to boost a character strength because it is low in their profile and they wish to build it up; they may be confused by it, disagree with its placement in the rank-order, or simply wish to expand and deepen their understanding and application of the given strength.
- The new science of character: Since the publication of the VIA Classification, peer-reviewed science on character has ballooned to over 200 publications in a short period of time. These contemporary strengths areas are therefore addressed in MBSP, for example, applying mindfulness to signature strengths, overuse and underuse of strengths, the golden mean of strengths, strengths appreciation, strengths constellations, using strengths with problems, and setting goals with strengths.

The mindfulness-based strengths practice program

MBSP is the first of its kind in many respects. It represents the first manualized program to help individuals understand and build their character strengths and is the first program to integrate these two popular areas of positive psychology. It is one of the first mindfulness programs to explicitly target something positive – those characteristics which are strongest in human beings.

MBSP integrates the latest science and best practices involving mindfulness-based approaches and character strengths knowledge. The 8-week, manualized MBSP program underwent numerous iterations based on expert feedback, scientific findings, and early cross-cultural, pilot research of eight groups involving advanced practitioners applying the MBSP program in six countries. These culminated in the version of MBSP outlined in Niemiec (2014). Sessions 1 and 2 offer primers on mindfulness and character strengths, respectively, while the remaining six sessions explore the integration and application of mindfulness and strengths. Table 1.2 provides the core themes covered in each of the eight sessions.

TABLE 1.2 Core topic areas of MBSP (Niemiec, 2014)

Session	Core Topic	Description
1	Mindfulness and autopilot	The autopilot mind is pervasive; insights and change opportunities start with mindful attention.
2	Your signature strengths	Identify what is best in you; this can unlock potential to engage more in work and relationships and reach higher personal potential.
3	Obstacles are opportunities	The practice of mindfulness and of strengths exploration leads immediately to two things – obstacles/barriers to the practice and a wider appreciation for the little things in life.
4	Strengthening mindfulness in everyday life	Mindfulness helps us attend to and nourish the best, innermost qualities in ourselves and others, while reducing negative judgments of self and others; conscious use of strengths can help us deepen and maintain a mindfulness practice.
5	Valuing your relationships	Mindful attending can nourish two types of relationships: relationships with others and our relationship with ourselves. Our relationship with ourselves contributes to self-growth and can have an immediate impact on our connection with others.
6	Mindfulness of the golden mean	Mindfulness helps to focus on problems directly, and character strengths help to reframe and offer different perspectives not immediately apparent.
Optional Retreat	MBSP ½-day retreat	Mindful living and character strengths apply not only to good meditation practice but also to daily conversation, eating, walking, sitting, reflecting, and the nuances therein (e.g., opening the refrigerator door, turning a doorknob, creating a smile). This day is therefore, a *practice* day.
7	Authenticity and goodness	It takes character (e.g., courage) to be a more authentic "you" and it takes character (e.g., hope) to create a strong future that benefits both oneself and others. Set mindfulness and character strengths goals with authenticity and goodness in the forefront of the mind.
8	Your engagement with life	Stick with those practices that have been working well and watch for the mind's tendency to revert back to automatic habits that are deficit-based, unproductive, or that prioritize what's wrong in you and others. Engage in an approach that fosters awareness and celebration of what is strongest in you and others.

The underlying, basic assumptions of MBSP reflect many of the core themes that are practiced. These include that individuals can improve upon their mindful awareness and character strengths; that these lead to valued outcomes such as developing or enhancing mindfulness in relationships; that mindfulness in particular can enhance character strengths awareness, deployment, and balanced use; and that character strengths can support individuals' practice of meditation and mindful living and assist in maintenance of mindfulness in the long-run.

To help participants understand and experience these tenets, there is an optimal structure within each MBSP session that incorporates meditation experiences, mindfulness/strengths integration exercises, group and dyadic discussion, and lecture input. Table 1.3 provides the breakdown of a typical MBSP session.

As viewed in Table 1.3, there are a number of activities participants engage in each week. In an attempt to provide the reader with a sense of some of the priority focus areas each week, Table 1.4 offers an example of the centerpiece activity (main exercise) for each of the MBSP sessions. The table offers a rationale for each activity.

There are two overarching ways in which mindfulness and character strengths can be integrated. One approach is to focus on strengthening one's mindfulness practice, mindful living, and consistency and maintenance of meditation. This can be achieved by deliberately bringing in one's naturally occurring character strengths, referred to as "strong mindfulness." The other approach is to bring mindful awareness to the understanding, exploration, spotting, appreciating, balancing, and deployment of one's character strengths. The bringing of mindfulness to one's character strengths is referred to as "mindful strengths use."

There are many activities that participants engage in within group experiences and in home practice that involve integrating these practices. To review all of them is beyond the scope of this chapter. Therefore, a sampling of activities is covered in Table 1.5, along with their research base and/or source.

TABLE 1.3 Standard structure of MBSP sessions (2014)

Part	Focus Area	Description
I	Opening meditation	Start group with "practice," allows for letting go of preceding tension and ushers in a different focus.
II	Discussion: whole group or multiple small groups	Review participants' practice from last week with the following catalyst: What went well?
III	Lecture/input	Offering new material aligned with core themes.
IV	Experiential	Core practice with mindfulness and character strengths is experienced.
V	Virtue circle	Structured, respectful approach for mindful listening/speaking practice and strengths-spotting/appreciating practice.
VI	Suggested homework	Review of focus areas in between sessions.
VII	Closing meditation	Letting go of session to come fully into present moment; mindful transitioning to the next part of the day.

TABLE 1.4 Novel practices across the eight MBSP sessions (2014)

Session	Core Practice	Explanation	Rationale
1	Raisin exercise/mindful eating	Eating one raisin as if "for the first time"; eating with all 5 senses.	Poignant practice in beginner's mind; offers a microcosm by which mindfulness can be applied into daily life.
2	Strengths-spotting	In pairs or triads, participants share recent positive experiences and practice steps involving the spotting of strengths.	Offers a shift in how we perceive stories and how we typically approach conversations; combats strength blindness.
3	Statue meditation	Participants engage in a challenge involving holding up their arms and facing the mental and physical obstacles and discomforts that ensue.	Facing meditation obstacles and reframing difficulties and stressors that arise as "obstacles" that can be targeted with *any* of the 24 character strengths and mindful breathing.
4	Mindful walking/ movement	Practicing standing and walking meditation, and spotting strengths that arise and that are used during walking.	Strengthening mindfulness in daily life; bringing strengths to a task often taken for granted; deepening the experience of mindfulness through strengths.
5	Loving-kindness meditation (targeting strengths)	Practice of traditional meditation focused on cultivating warmth and compassion; followed by an open meditation on a strength of the participants' choosing.	Experiencing the potential to target any of the 24 strengths; distinction of 2 different types of meditation in doing so.
6	Character Strengths 360	Review of feedback of a 2–5 minute survey in which participants receive feedback from several people on his or her character strengths.	Offers numerous mindfulness opportunities involving strengths awareness, blindness, potential opportunities, appreciation, and handling feedback; implications for positive relationships.
7	Best possible self and defining moments exercise	Structured exercises involving a choice of envisioning a future best self or reflecting on a defining moment.	Mindful reflection or mindful envisioning with strengths; linking goals, identity, and strengths.
8	Golden nuggets	Sharing key insights and long-term practices.	Linking current experiences with next steps; use of positive cueing.

TABLE 1.5 A sampling of 10 integration activities in MBSP (2014)

Name of Practice	Description	Type of Integration	Research Base or Source
Signature strengths use	Bring attention to the use of one of your highest strengths in a new way each day.	Mindful strengths use	Gander et al. (2012); Seligman et al. (2005)
Strengths-spotting	Spot strengths in another person's sharing; spot strengths in your daily routines; spot strengths in the media (e.g., movies, books).	Mindful strengths use	Linley (2008); Niemiec (2013); Niemiec and Wedding (2014)
Strengths appreciation (also called the "Speak Up!" exercise)	Share the value and impact that someone else's strengths expression had upon you.	Mindful strengths use	Adler and Fagley (2005);Algoe, Gable, and Maisel (2010); Bao and Lyubomirsky (2013)
Facing meditation obstacles	Name one barrier to your meditation practice (e.g., mind wandering, noises, scheduling, discomfort), and describe how each of your top strengths could help you face or overcome it.	Strong mindfulness	Brahm (2006); Kornfield (1993); Lomas et al (2014); Niemiec (2014); Niemiec, Rashid, and Spinella (2012)
Bring strengths to mindful living	Identify one area of routine that you could bring mindfulness to (e.g., driving, eating, listening, walking). Notice the strengths that are already present in the experience. How might the experience be invigorated with additional strengths?	Strong mindfulness	Nhat Hanh (1979); Nhat Hanh (1993); Niemiec (2013)
Body mindfulness meditation	Pure present moment mindfulness while using strengths to explore, maintain attention, and be gentle to oneself.	Strong mindfulness	Call, Miron, and Orcutt (2013); Kabat-Zinn (1990); Kabat-Zinn (2005); Mirams et al. (2012); Ussher et al. (2012)
Find balance by attending to strengths overuse and underuse	Examine life situations for strengths overuse and underuse and consider how other strengths can bring balance.	Mindful strengths use	Biswas-Diener, Kashdan, and Minhas (2011); Grant and Schwartz (2011); Niemiec (2014)
Targeting specific strengths	Use meditation to explore and boost any of the 24 strengths.	Mindful strengths use	Amaro (2010); Brach (2003); Fredrickson et al. (2008); Salzberg (1995)
Positive reappraisal with strengths	Skillful use of mindful listening and speaking to reframe challenges with character strengths language.	Both	Garland, Gaylord, and Fredrickson (2011); Garland, Gaylord, and Park (2009)
Character strengths breathing space	Mindfulness practice involving the use of curiosity, self-regulation, and perspective.	Both	Bishop et al. (2004); Niemiec (2014); Segal, Williams, and Teasdale (2013)

At its best, the practice of mindfulness *is* strengths and the practice of strengths *is* mindfulness. They cannot be separated. To practice mindful walking or mindful eating is to exercise self-regulation as well as many other strengths. To express a curious and kindly openness to the unfolding present moment experience is to practice mindfulness. When we deploy character strengths in a mindful way we are strengthening our mindfulness, and when we strengthen our mindfulness we are nurturing the conditions for virtuous behavior and balanced character strengths use (Niemiec, 2014).

As this chapter's opening quote suggests, so much potential in human beings goes unnoticed because people either don't know to look, don't know how to look, or don't look deeply. Mindfulness and character strengths provide a mechanism for looking and a common language for what to look for. When merged synergistically, the result is deep looking – both inwardly and outwardly – and the potential for constructive, authentic, and altruistic action unfolds.

MBSP pilot research and reports from the field

Pilot research

Niemiec (2014) conducted some initial studies of MBSP to determine the efficacy of the intervention program, to attain cross-cultural feedback, and to assist in making improvements to the program. One small non-randomized, controlled study found substantial improvements for the experimental group and when compared with controls. Improvements for flourishing, engagement, and signature strengths use were the strongest effects. In addition to the United States, the program was piloted in five countries by practitioners who met strict criteria in terms of mindfulness knowledge, personal practice, and application and character strengths knowledge and practice. Feedback from these practitioners and their MBSP group participants was unanimously positive and assisted in improving the program. Feedback forms were distributed among all groups with reported improvements in overall well-being, sense of identity, meaning in life, sense of purpose, engagement with life tasks, stress management, quality of relationships, sense of accomplishment, and management of problems. This trend toward a host of positive outcomes has continued with the implementation of online MBSP programs offered by the first author and by additional MBSP leaders across several countries (including the second author).

Core areas participants report they are able to do as a result of the MBSP program include the following:

- Greater awareness of signature strengths (an element of "mindful strengths use") and using strengths more often.
- Deepening of a previously existing mindfulness practice (the element of "strong mindfulness").

    For experienced meditators, this benefit appears to be related to another reported outcome – the overcoming of obstacles in the practice of mindfulness. For new meditators, this outcome is particularly important because in many instances mindfulness barriers are what prevent new meditators from maintaining their practice.

- Using both mindfulness and character strengths to deal with problems and difficulties.
- Both spotting and appreciating strengths more frequently in others.
- When piloted in the workplace, MBSP helped staff develop a common language with one another, and was useful in resolving tension and disputes.

Another study (Briscoe, in press) involved a non-randomized controlled model with participants in the experimental condition ($N = 19$) completing the MBSP program and a waitlist control condition ($N = 20$) that did not receive an intervention. The intervention group was delivered online, which is becoming a popular, successful trend for delivering mindfulness programs as many studies are revealing positive effects with online delivery (e.g., Aikens et al., 2014; Boggs et al., 2014; Cavanagh et al., 2013; Gluck & Maercker, 2011; Krusche et al., 2012; Morledge et al., 2013). This study, with groups equivocal in age and gender, used a number of measures including the Satisfaction with Life Scale (Diener, Emmons, Larsen, & Griffin, 1985), Flourishing Scale (Diener, Lucas, Schimmack, & Helliwell, 2009), engagement questions (a subscale of the Positive Psychotherapy Inventory [Rashid, 2008]), and questions on signature strengths use and its link with flourishing, work, relationships, and community (Niemiec, 2014). Questions from the latter include: "My greatest fulfillments in life occur when I express those parts of myself that are core to who I am," "My work is an expression of who I am at my core, not just something I do well," "My personal relationships give me the opportunity to express the best parts of myself," and "My activities in my community are vehicles by which I express my best self." Even though the experimental group had initially higher baseline levels of all measures compared to the control group, all well-being variables (life satisfaction, flourishing, engagement, and signature strengths use) in the experimental group showed significant increases. The control group demonstrated a significant increase only in life satisfaction. This study offers support for the theoretical and conceptual foundations of MBSP and the initial MBSP pilot study.

These studies are also consistent with preliminary findings from other researchers who found that more time spent using strengths correlates significantly with mindfulness (Jarden et al., 2012), and early results from a Dutch study (Alberts, 2014) of MBSP elements using a correlational and experimental design that found positive correlations between strengths use and life satisfaction, strengths use and authenticity, strengths use and mindfulness, and strengths use and acceptance.

Positive relationships: a standout finding in MBSP groups

One meta-analysis of meditation discovered that the strongest meditation effects were found for emotionality and relationship issues (Sedlmeier et al., 2012). Positive relationships are critical to well-being and are one of the most important pathways to greater happiness (Diener & Seligman, 2002a; 2002b). There are countless factors that may contribute to the creation, rekindling, bolstering, and/or maintenance of positive, healthy relationships; it goes beyond the scope of this chapter to explore the various dynamics and activities therein. Nevertheless, it is interesting to note that one of the more striking, overarching findings we have observed in leading MBSP is the benefits participants experience in the domain of positive relationships. Following MBSP, participants are asked anonymously if MBSP had a direct positive effect on one of their relationships and if so, to describe the impact. Nearly every participant who has completed MBSP to date is able to draw a direct connection between MBSP and positive changes in one of their relationships. There are a number of activities in MBSP that may account for this salient impact on participants' relationships, such as the strengths interview, the Character Strengths 360, weekly strengths-spotting and strengths-appreciating practice, weekly mindful listening and mindful speaking practice, and character strengths meditations that are "other-focused," to name a few examples.

A sampling of cross-cultural examples across several MBSP group experiences reveals participants experiencing both incremental changes that are meaningful over time as well as transformative changes. Here are several examples relating to the domain of positive relationships:

- I decided to renew contact with my estranged son of 15 years. I deliberately used mindful listening and speaking and strengths-based dialogue in the conversations.
- A couple who had been married for 35 years reported the following: MBSP has enhanced our communication, pulled us out of automaton responding to one another, and helped us renew and appreciate the joys and strengths of our marriage.
- I appreciate other people's strengths more and tell them that. I have written a forgiveness letter to my brother with whom I have a difficult relationship and I asked him to forgive me for always wanting to try and rescue him.
- During the program, I started making mindful visits to my 75-year-old dad who lives in a nursing home. His condition is difficult and very sad. Character strengths reflections and mindful walking to his residence cultivated joy and peace within me so I was able to approach him fresh and with mindfulness. The first days he looked at me in the same way; then over time, he became more affectionate with me. He took my hand and kissed it for the first time. My mindfulness visits had touched his soul.
- I am friendlier with myself. And therefore am now expressing more love toward my wife and daughters.
- I have slowed down my thought processes, learned to recognize my strengths and strengths in others. I am a calmer, happier, more joyous person with my friends, family, and colleagues. I am not afraid to face interpersonal challenges or life's obstacles. In fact, I welcome them!
- A new channel of communication has opened with my husband. The Character Strengths 360 deepened our connection as well as my relationships with

friends and family. I feel more appreciated by my kids and friends because of the feedback they gave me and in turn I am easily reciprocating.

- A worker at a nonprofit reported: During these weeks I've had the opportunity to practice mindfulness and strengths-spotting in my co-workers. The results have been very positive because communication flows easily now. The huge problems of the past have now become manageable situations. The tools we have now as a team help us to not be defensive, and I'm aware that we are now showing results at every level. Day by day, our actions are slowly improving our workplace.

- One MBSP practitioner, working with young, impoverished teen mothers, gathered feedback at the end of the program from each participant on three areas – "new discoveries about myself," "my use of strengths," and "my use of mindfulness." Each teen clearly articulated benefits in all three domains, without exception. One teen's example follows:

  - "I overuse my bravery. I need to use the golden mean of character strengths in order to not harm myself" (new discovery);
  - "I can use my bravery with love and these two strengths together can help me serve others" (strengths use);
  - "Through mindfulness practice, I realize now that I can feel OK with myself and who I am and that this use of perspective can help me make decisions" (mindfulness use).

Case discussions of MBSP

[Authors' note: For confidentiality purposes, the identifying information and other elements discussed in the following cases have been edited while maintaining core themes/outcomes of the MBSP experience.]

"Supporting teams in the workplace"

Background: A small marketing firm located in a suburb of Melbourne, Australia, and co-owned by two middle-aged male executives, invited one of the authors [JL] to meet and discuss possible solutions to perceived problems within the organization. One executive, the CEO, was interested in exploring and implementing mindfulness as a tool for enhancing awareness within the organization. Initially, the other executive, the CFO, did not want to participate, saying that the staff would benefit, but he didn't need it. Following discussions around the importance of pursuing greater transparency and unity among all the members of the organization, and the potential of MBSP to be a catalyst for this change, the CFO changed his mind, and both openly participated.

Description of the problem: This small business consisted of two teams, each with its own manager who then reported to one of the owners. Each team addressed different functions but the intention was that they work alongside each other, supporting mutual goals for the organization. Political differences between the two teams had previously led to competition between the teams rather than collaboration. This was, in turn, leading to increased levels of staff stress and claims of workplace bullying. Tension was often high in the workplace environment. Prior to the implementation of MBSP, one of the owners described concerns that the levels of stress, anger, and frequent employee disengagement within the organization seemed to be unusually high when compared with other companies in the same sector. The owners had previously attempted to address disengagement and presenteeism with outside consultants, webinars, incentives, and other methods without success. The goals in bringing MBSP to their firm were twofold:

1   Help staff manage personal and work-related stresses.
2   Build greater team cohesion within the organization.

Implementation: 87% of staff (including the two owners and two managers) commenced MBSP, which was conducted over 10 weeks because of travel/work commitments of senior management. Homework was completed by half of the participants with all participants doing at least a minimal amount. Participation was generally guarded, but 80% of commencing staff completed the 8-week course. The owners were interviewed after 4 weeks and all staff completed pre- and post-questionnaires.

Results: The owners perceived significant changes in staff interactions between the first and last weeks of the program. A common and positive language encouraged teams to focus on individual and group strengths, instead of focusing on competition and flaws (building their strength of perspective). One of the owners observed: "The VIA Survey and character strengths work was used to effectively solve disputes and successfully resolve tension on four occasions. We all spoke the same language and took an objective perspective." A participant commented that what struck her most about the course was the "positive, here and now focus; looking for the good; and appreciating others' strengths." Another said, "MBSP provided us with a shared experience that was honest and open, and it allowed us to better understand and value each other's strengths."

There were two key departures from the organization within 6 months of completing the course and both of these were individuals who had embraced the program and the ongoing practice of mindfulness. It is possible that the insight afforded to these individuals through the program and ongoing mindfulness practice gave them the clarity to see they were the wrong fit for the organization (or the organization was the wrong fit for them). One person who also embraced the program sought additional coaching support following completion of MBSP. Her resilience continued to improve and after mindful deliberation, she decided to stay with the organization and build her strength of leadership.

One-hundred percent of staff who attended every session (80% of commencing staff) gave feedback that the program had helped them better manage stressful situations, both within and outside of work. The MBSP program helped them recognize, appreciate, and prioritize the character strengths of their colleagues, rather than ruminate and fault-find. These improvements proved to be critical factors in improving team cohesion and boosting the strength of teamwork.

Conclusion: The owners were very satisfied with the engagement and positive outcomes of the program. In particular, they stated that, as a multi-week program with ongoing support over 2 full months, MBSP was more valuable to them than other courses they've provided to their staff. Discussions are currently underway for a monthly maintenance program.

"Prevention is better than cure"

Background: A busy restaurant business located near the central business district in Sydney, Australia, was looking to support its staff with a stress management program. Staff mentioned they were interested in learning to meditate, so to enhance commitment and attendance to MBSP, the middle-aged business owner requested that each of his staff participants contribute a weekly co-payment to attend the program.

Description of the problem: The owner became aware that his staff were having difficulties in managing their stress levels. Although there were no serious issues at present, recent legislation regarding duty of care for the health of staff (including mental health) meant that he was driven to teach them skills that would prevent any major problems arising due to the stressful nature of the work. All staff were under 30 years of age and single, often switched on to phone and social media and experiencing the everyday stressors of 21st-century living in a fast-paced city. In addition, nearly every employee worked long hours, usually standing or walking for most of their shift, without structured meal breaks, and experienced the implicit demands that come with working with the public such as having to maintain an upbeat façade even when feeling tired, unwell, or unhappy. The owner felt that staff were distracted and not present enough with the clients.

Implementation: Weekly, 2-hour sessions were conducted before the restaurant opened for business. All 17 staff members (including the owner) commenced and completed the MBSP program. They were committed to the program and always on time, and the majority completed the recommended homework activities, including journaling and meditating.

Results: The owner was impressed with the group participation and engagement and with the application of concepts from MBSP into the workplace setting (e.g., using the character strengths verbiage; displaying mindful listening to one another). The feedback from staff was that the group experience "got better each week" and that it "exceeded expectations." The program theme that helped them most was "Mindfulness of the Golden Mean," which emphasizes using mindfulness for balanced character strengths expression, including context sensitivity, the use of character strength constellations, and managing strengths overuse and underuse. Staff were especially engaged in learning and practicing the loving-kindness meditation and building their strength of perspective when meditating on a problem. During discussion they expressed their strength of gratitude, saying they "felt proud" that they were participating in the course. The owner, a protective and nurturing man who readily displayed his signature strengths of kindness and love, enjoyed seeing the personal growth that took place each week among his staff. He felt that he had provided an opportunity for staff to learn important life skills (e.g., a new way to practice leadership), and observed that even the quieter staff had gained greater confidence (e.g., realizing they could turn mindful attention to their signature strengths during the busy restaurant hours). One participant in particular who was struggling with a difficult personal situation was able to step back with his perspective strength to view his stressors in a different way, use his bravery strength to face his problems directly, and manage his suffering through self-kindness.

At the conclusion of the program, the staff requested MBSP booster sessions on a bimonthly basis. The booster sessions, arranged as an interactive and informative experience, were particularly valued and gathered a full attendance at each session. These have supported the staff in maintaining their MBSP practices.

"Encouraging self-care for enhanced clinical care"

Background: A grant was received by a large city children's hospital in the United States to provide well-being training for a multidisciplinary team, including case workers, nurses, therapists, and administrative staff. The MBSP program was capped at 20 participants and a co-payment was made by each participant to ensure their commitment for the full 8 weeks.

The program coordinator who managed logistics each week explained that the staff needed to learn better self-care to help avoid burnout. Offering wellness programs for staff (e.g., physical fitness programs) had been used in the past with only modest success. On this occasion, the coordinator and team believed that an optimal match might be found in a staff "mental fitness" program.

Description of the problem: Staff working with medically ill children may experience more than the usual amount of workplace stress as they manage the expectations and fears of the parents, handle a variety of administrative requirements, and attend to the emotional and physical needs of the children. This particular staff explained how these stressors are compounded when their own professional and personal stress loads are factored in.

Implementation: The program was open to both clinical and non-clinical staff. The staff who engaged in the opportunity were either working in direct care or administrative roles. No physicians enrolled in the program and while this was not investigated it was suspected that scheduling was the main barrier. Although the program was funded by a grant, a nominal co-payment was requested to encourage full participation and attendance.

Results: Sixteen of the 20 staff (80%) who originally enrolled in the program attended 100% of the sessions. Verbal participation in class was initially guarded as there were concerns about confidentiality between co-workers. Once this was addressed with open discussion, participation improved. For home practice, several participants kept journals and engaged in a routine mindfulness meditation practice, finding that it helped them feel happier, less stressed, and more in control both at work and at home.

One man attending the course had a terminally ill child that the team was caring for, and when the child passed away he explained that her chronic and terminal illness was the reason he had decided to attend the course and that it helped him enormously in terms of acceptance, coping, letting go, and strengths expression (e.g., love, forgiveness, hope, bravery). He also described a positive carryover effect to family members who had not attended the course.

Another participant had a chronic skin condition that visibly and profoundly improved over the 8 weeks. Such effects have previously been documented by Kabat-Zinn et al. (1998), who concluded that mindfulness meditation delivered by audiotape during ultraviolet light therapy increased the healing rate of lesions in patients with psoriasis.

The group expressed interest in two types of MBSP booster sessions: monthly follow-up that reviewed and reinforced core concepts from MBSP, integrated in additional ideas (e.g., positivity), and continued engaging in practices; second, the group decided to meet between themselves as an open group for 15–30 minutes once per week to practice meditation with one another prior to work.

Conclusion: The majority of participants stated that MBSP gave them the skills they were seeking when they enrolled in the course. Some of these skills were put to the test of life in a significant way (e.g., with the death of a child). Those that attend the booster sessions benefit from the regular connection, support, and knowledge they gain.

Future research

MBSP, while based in the science of mindfulness-based practice and the emerging science of character, is a new program and therefore the opportunities for further research are significant. We, and other MBSP leaders, have observed boosts to well-being, engagement, meaning, strengths use, mindfulness practice, purpose in life, problem management, emotional resilience, and positive relationships, but we encourage more rigorous studies of MBSP that would involve randomization and follow-up analyses over longer time periods examining these outcomes. We suggest researchers study the effects of MBSP with other populations (e.g., disabilities, psychological disorders, chronic illness, youth, geriatric) and settings (e.g., medical, business, psychiatric, education, defense, corrective services). Also, what are the mediating variables in the MBSP program? Are the benefits and mediators consistent with what is found in other mindfulness-based programs? Are there unique benefits of MBSP in particular?

Delivering MBSP in the business context raises additional research questions relating to productivity. For example, research conducted by the iOpener Institute in the UK (Pryce-Jones, 2010) found that employees who are happy at work stay up to four times longer in their job, remain at least twice as focused on task, and take one-tenth of the sick leave compared to their less happy colleagues. Studies have shown that both mindfulness and character strength expression can increase a person's well-being. It would therefore be of interest to measure whether MBSP, which combines both of these, could be as, or more, effective in increasing productivity at work than other work-based employee engagement programs.

The integration of mindfulness and character strengths programmatically in lecture points, discussion themes, meditations, and homework practices is a novel contribution. But what is the additive effect of integrating these areas of positive psychology? Does the integration lead to greater maintenance of meditation practices (i.e., termed "strong mindfulness")? What is the role of signature strengths in overcoming meditation barriers? Does the integration lead directly to more balanced and sustained character strengths expressions (i.e., termed "mindful strengths use")?

We are also interested in different delivery mechanisms for MBSP. In addition to the initial successes of face-to-face and online delivery to groups and to individuals, what additional modalities might be utilized? One of the authors (RN) is beginning the adaptation of a self-guided MBSP process by use of a workbook and CD. Would this lead to additional or distinct benefits for participants? Might other web-based and smartphone app mechanisms be routes of delivery that would also reveal positive benefits?

As noted in the case discussions, we find that the integration of mindfulness and character strengths is strikingly empowering in helping participants to manage problems effectively and improve relationships. Further analysis of the underlying factors and mechanisms for each is warranted.

Bibliography

Adler, M. G., & Fagley, N. S. (2005). Appreciation: Individual differences in finding value and meaning as a unique predictor of subjective well-being. *Journal of Personality, 73*(1), 79–114.

Aikens, K. A., Astin, J., Pelletier, K. R., Levanovich, K., Baase, C. M., Park, Y.Y., & Bodnar, C. M. (2014). Mindfulness goes to work: Impact of an online workplace intervention. *Journal of Occupational & Environmental Medicine, 56*(7), 721–731.

Alberts, H. (2014). Personal communication. June 2014.

Algoe, S. B., Gable, S. L., & Maisel, N. C. (2010). It's the little things: Everyday gratitude as a booster shot for romantic relationships. *Personal Relationships, 17,* 217–233.

Amaro, A. (2010). Thinking II: Investigation, the use of reflective thought. *Mindfulness, 1*(4), 65–268.

Baer, R. A., & Lykins, E. L. M. (2011). Mindfulness and positive psychological functioning. In K. M. Sheldon, T. B. Kashdan & M. F. Steger (Eds.), *Designing positive psychology: Taking stock and moving forward* (pp. 335–348). New York, NY: Oxford University Press.

Bao, K. J., & Lyubomirsky, S. (2013). Making it last: Combating hedonic adaptation in romantic relationships. *Journal of Positive Psychology, 8*(3), 196–206.

Berkowitz, M.W., & Bier, M. C. (2007). What works in character education. *Journal of Research in Character Education, 5*(1), 29–48.

Bishop, S. R., Lau, M., Shapiro, S. L., Carlson, L., Anderson, N. D., Carmody, J., . . . Devins, G. (2004). Mindfulness: A proposed operational definition. *Clinical Psychology: Science and Practice, 11,* 230–241.

Biswas-Diener, R. (2006). From the equator to the North Pole: A study of character strengths. *Journal of Happiness Studies, 7,* 293–310.

Biswas-Diener, R., Kashdan, T. B., & Minhas, G. (2011). A dynamic approach to psychological strength development and intervention. *Journal of Positive Psychology, 6*(2), 106–118.

Boggs, J. M., Beck, A., Felder, J. N., Dimidjian, S., Metcalf, C. A., & Segal, Z. V. (2014). Web-based intervention in mindfulness meditation for reducing residual depressive symptoms and relapse prophylaxis: A qualitative study. *Journal of Medical Internet Research, 16*(3), 87.

Brach, T. (2003). *Radical acceptance: Embracing your life with the heart of a Buddha.* New York, NY: Bantam.

Brahm, A. (2006). *Mindfulness, bliss, and beyond: A meditator's handbook.* Boston, MA: Wisdom Publications.

Briscoe, C. (in press). A study investigating the effectiveness of mindfulness-based strengths practice (MBSP). Thesis submitted to University of East London.

Brown, K. W., Ryan, R. M., & Creswell, J. D. (2007). Mindfulness: Theoretical foundations and evidence for its salutary effects. *Psychological Inquiry, 18*(4), 211–237.

Call, D., Miron, L., & Orcutt, H. (2013). Effectiveness of brief mindfulness techniques in reducing symptoms of anxiety and stress. *Mindfulness, 5*(6), 658–668.

Carlson, E. N. (2013). Overcoming the barriers to self-knowledge: Mindfulness as a path to seeing yourself as you really are. *Perspectives on Psychological Science, 8*(2), 173–186.

Carrigan, H. L. (Ed.) (2001). *Eternal wisdom from the desert: Writings from the desert fathers.* Brewster, MA: Paraclete Press.

Cavanagh, K., Strauss, C., Cicconi, F., Griffiths, N., Wyper, A., & Jones, F. (2013). A randomised controlled trial of a brief online mindfulness-based intervention. *Behavior Research Therapy, 51*(9), 573–578.

Chödrön, P. (1994). *Start where you are: A guide to compassionate living.* Boston, MA: Shambhala.

Dalai Lama, His Holiness. (2006). *How to see yourself as you really are.* New York, NY: Atria Books.

Diener, E., Emmons, R. A., Larsen, R. J., & Griffin, S. (1985). The satisfaction with life scale. *Journal of Personality Assessment, 49*, 71–75.

Diener, E., Lucas, R., Schimmack, U., & Helliwell, J. (2009). *Well-being for public policy.* Oxford: Oxford University Press.

Diener, E., & Seligman, M. E. P. (2002a). Very happy people. *Psychological Science, 13*, 80–83.

Diener, E., & Seligman, M. E. P. (2002b). Beyond money: Toward an economy of well-being. *Psychological Science in the Public Interest, 5*(1), 1–31.

Diener, E., Wirtz, D., Tov, W., Kim-Prieto, C., Choi, D., Oishi, S., & Biswas-Diener, R. (2009). New measures of well-being: Flourishing and positive and negative feelings. *Social Indicators Research, 39*, 247–266.

Dunning, D. (2005). *Self-insight: Roadblocks and detours on the path to knowing thyself.* New York, NY: Psychology Press.

Evans, D. R., Baer, R. A., & Segerstrom, S. C. (2009). The effects of mindfulness and self-consciousness on persistence. *Personality and Individual Differences, 47*(4), 379–382.

Exline, J. J., & & Hill, P. (2012). Humility: A consistent and robust predictor of generosity. *Journal of Positive Psychology, 7*(3), 45–56.

Forgeard, M. J. C. (2013). Perceiving benefits after adversity: The relationship between self-reported posttraumatic growth and creativity. *Psychology of Aesthetics, Creativity, and the Arts, 7*(3), 245–264.

Fredrickson, B. L., Cohn, M. A., Coffey, K. A., Pek, J., & Finkel, S. M. (2008). Open hearts build lives: Positive emotions, induced through loving-kindness meditation, build consequential personal resources. *Journal of Personality and Social Psychology, 95*(5), 1045–1062.

Gander, F., Proyer, R. T., Ruch, W., & Wyss, T. (2012). Strength-based positive interventions: Further evidence for their potential in enhancing well-being. *Journal of Happiness Studies, 14*(4), 1241–1259. Advance online publication.

Garland, E., Gaylord, S. A., & Park, J. (2009). The role of mindfulness in positive reappraisal. *Explore: The Journal of Science and Healing, 5*(1), 37–44.

Garland, E. L., Gaylord, S. A., & Fredrickson, B. L. (2011). Positive reappraisal mediates the stress-reductive effects of mindfulness: An upward spiral process. *Mindfulness, 2*(1), 59–67.

Germer, C. (2009). *The mindful path to self-compassion.* New York, NY: Guildford Press.

Gilbert, P. (2010). *Compassion focused therapy: Distinctive features.* London: Routledge.

Gluck, T., & Maercker, A. (2011). A randomised controlled pilot study of a brief, web-based mindfulness training. *BMC Psychiatry, 11,* 175.

Grant, A. M., & Schwartz, B. (2011). Too much of a good thing: The challenge and opportunity of the inverted U. *Perspectives on Psychological Science, 6*(1), 61–76.

Grossman, P., Niemann, L., Schmidt, S., & Walach, H. (2004). Mindfulness-based stress reduction and health benefits: A meta-analysis. *Journal of Psychosomatic Research, 57*(1), 35–43.

Hanson, R. (2013). *Hardwiring happiness: The new brain science of contentment, calm, and confidence.* New York, NY: Harmony.

Ivtzan, I. (2015). *Awareness is freedom: The adventure of psychology and spirituality.* London: John Hunt Publishing.

Ivtzan, I., Gardner, H. E., & Smailova, Z. (2011). Mindfulness meditation and curiosity: The contributing factors to wellbeing and the process of closing the self-discrepancy gap. *International Journal of Wellbeing, 1*(3), 316–326.

Jarden, A., Jose, P., Kashdan, T., Simpson, O., McLachlan, K., & Mackenzie, A. (2012). International well-being study. Unpublished raw data.

Kabat-Zinn, J. (1990). *Full catastrophe living: Using the wisdom of your body and mind to face stress, pain, and illness.* New York, NY: Dell.

Kabat-Zinn, J. (2003). Mindfulness-based interventions in context: Past, present, and future. *Clinical Psychology: Science and Practice, 10*(2), 144–156.

Kabat-Zinn, J. (2005). *Coming to our senses.* New York, NY: Hyperion.

Kabat-Zinn, J., Wheeler, E., Light, T., Skillings, A., Scharf, M. J., Cropley, T. G., . . . & Bernhard, J. D. (1998). Influence of a mindfulness meditation-based stress reduction intervention on rates of skin clearing in patients with moderate to severe psoriasis undergoing phototherapy (UVB) and photochemotherapy (PUVA). *Psychosomatic Medicine, 60*(5), 625–632.

Kashdan, T. B., McKnight, P. E., Fincham, F. D., & Rose, P. (2011). When curiosity breeds intimacy: Taking advantage of intimacy opportunities and transforming boring conversations. *Journal of Personality, 79,* 1369–1401.

Keating, T. (2006). *Open mind, open heart* (20th anniversary edition). New York, NY: Continuum.

Kornfield, J. (1993). *A path with heart: A guide through the perils and promises of spiritual life.* New York, NY: Bantam.

Kornfield, J. (2008). *The art of forgiveness, lovingkindness, and peace.* New York, NY: Bantam.

Krusche, A., Cyhlarova, E., King, S., & Williams, M. G. (2012). Mindfulness online: A preliminary evaluation of the feasibility of a web-based mindfulness course and the impact on stress. *BMJ Open, 2*(3), e000803.

Lakey, C. E., Kernis, M. H., Heppner, W. L., & Lance, C. E. (2008). Individual differences in authenticity and mindfulness as predictors of verbal defensiveness. *Journal of Research in Personality, 42*(1), 230–238.

Langer, E. (2006). *On becoming an artist.* New York, NY: Ballantine Books.

Linkins, M., Niemiec, R. M., & Gillham, J., Mayerson, D. (2014). Through the strengths lens: A framework for educating the heart. *Journal of Positive Psychology, 10*(1), 64–68.

Linley, A. (2008). *Average to A+: Realising strengths in yourself and others.* Coventry, UK: CAPP Press.

Lomas, T., Cartwright, T., Edginton, T., & Ridge, D. (2014). A qualitative analysis of experiential challenges associated with meditation practice. *Mindfulness, 6*(4), 848–860. doi:10.1007/s12671-014-0329-8

Martinez-Marti, M. L., Avia, M. D., & Hernandez-Lloreda, J. (2014). Appreciation of beauty training: A web-based intervention. *Journal of Positive Psychology, 9*(6), 477–481. doi: 10.1080/17439760.2014.920512

Mirams, L., Poliakoff, E., Brown, R. J., & Lloyd, D. M. (2012). Brief body-scan meditation practice improves somatosensory perceptual decision making. *Consciousness and Cognition, 22*(1), 348–359.

Morledge, T. J., Allexandre, D., Fox, E., Fu, A. Z., Higashi, M. K., Kruzikas, D. T., Pham, S. V., & Reese, P. R. (2013). Feasibility of an online mindfulness program for stress management: A randomized, controlled trial. *Annals of Behavioral Medicine, 46*(2), 137–148. Epub.

Nhat Hanh, T. (1979). *The miracle of mindfulness: An introduction to the practice of meditation.* Boston, MA: Beacon.

Nhat Hanh, T. (1993). *For a future to be possible: Commentaries on the five mindfulness trainings.* Berkeley, CA: Parallax Press.

Niemiec, R. M. (2012). Mindful living: Character strengths interventions as pathways for the five mindfulness trainings. *International Journal of Wellbeing, 2*(1), 22–33.

Niemiec, R. M. (2013). VIA character strengths: Research and practice (the first 10 years). In H. H. Knoop & A. Delle Fave (Eds.), *Well-being and cultures: Perspectives on positive psychology* (pp. 11–30). New York, NY: Springer.

Niemiec, R. M. (2014). *Mindfulness and character strengths: A practical guide to flourishing.* Cambridge, MA: Hogrefe.

Niemiec, R. M., Rashid, T., & Spinella, M. (2012). Strong mindfulness: Integrating mindfulness and character strengths. *Journal of Mental Health Counseling, 34*(3), 240–253.

Niemiec, R. M., & Wedding, D. (2014). *Positive psychology at the movies: Using films to build character strengths and well-being.* Cambridge, MA: Hogrefe.

Park, N., Peterson, C., & Seligman, M. E. P. (2006). Character strengths in fifty-four nations and the fifty US states. *Journal of Positive Psychology, 1*(3), 118–129.

Peterson, C. (2006). *A primer in positive psychology.* New York, NY: Oxford University Press.

Peterson, C., & Seligman, M. E. P. (2004). *Character strengths and virtues: A handbook and classification.* New York, NY: Oxford University Press.

Pryce-Jones, J. (2010). *Happiness at work: Maximizing your psychological capital for success.* Oxford, UK: Wiley-Blackwell.

Rashid, T. (2008). Positive psychotherapy. In S. J. Lopez (Ed.), *Positive psychology: Exploring the best in people, vol. 4* (pp. 187–217). Westport, CT: Praeger.

Rehg, W. (2002). Christian mindfulness: A path to finding God in all things. *Studies in the Spirituality of Jesuits, 34*(3), 1–32.

Reibel, D. K., Greeson, J. M., Brainard, G. C., & Rosenzweig, S. (2001). Mindfulness-based stress reduction and health-related quality of life in a heterogeneous patient population. *General Hospital Psychiatry, 23*(4), 183–192.

Salzberg, S. (1995). *Lovingkindness: The revolutionary art of happiness.* Boston, MA: Shambhala.

Sedlmeier, P., Eberth, J., Schwarz, M., Zimmermann, D., Haarig, F., Jaeger, S., & Kunze, S. (2012). The psychological effects of meditation: A meta-analysis. *Psychological Bulletin, 138*(6), 1139–1171.

Segal, Z. V., Williams, J. M. G., & Teasdale, J. D. (2013). *Mindfulness-based cognitive therapy for depression: A new approach to preventing relapse* (2nd edition). New York, NY: Guilford Press.

Seligman, M. E. P., Steen, T. A., Park, N., & Peterson, C. (2005). Positive psychology progress: Empirical validation of interventions. *American Psychologist, 60*, 410–421.

Ussher, M., Spatz, A., Copland, C., Nicolaou, A., Cargill, A., Amini-Tabrizi, N., & McCracken, L. M. (2012). Immediate effects of a brief mindfulness-based body scan on patients with chronic pain. *Journal of Behavioral Medicine, 37*(1), 127–134. Epub.

2

SELF-COMPASSION

Embracing suffering with kindness

Kristin Neff and Oliver Davidson

> As human beings, we all want to be happy and free from misery.
>
> Dalai Lama

This sentiment pervades Eastern and Western philosophical traditions; however, this sentiment has been interpreted in slightly different ways, which has impacted the ways we think about happiness and wellbeing. In the West, this idea has typically been expressed in terms of hedonism, the belief that humans are motivated to seek pleasure and avoid pain. From this perspective, happiness represents a positive ratio of pleasant to unpleasant experiences. In contrast, the Buddhist perspective on happiness recognizes that painful and unpleasant experiences are a natural part of the human condition, which should be embraced rather than avoided. Buddhists see happiness and suffering as cyclically influencing each other.

This difference has also strongly influenced the way we research happiness in the West. Since the beginning of the century, psychology has refocused its emphasis on learning what makes humans thrive and flourish. Consistent with the hedonic perspective, the emerging positive psychology movement initially dichotomized the relationship between positive and negative experiences with the assumption that positive experiences utilized distinct processes that were not contingent upon their negative counterparts (Fredrickson, 2001). Based on this assumption, many have concluded that the alleviation of suffering does not produce happiness and wellbeing but, instead, only the absence of suffering (Duckworth, Steen, & Seligman, 2005). As a result, positive psychology has tended to focus on positive states and traits, such as joy, gratitude, optimism, hope, curiosity, and awe, as well as the conditions that enrich or impoverish these states and traits. More recently, however, there has been a greater emphasis on eudaimonic happiness in positive psychology, which entails finding purpose and meaning in one's life rather than merely pursuing pleasure and avoiding pain. This perspective is in line with the Buddhist construct of self-compassion (Ryan & Deci, 2001).

Self-compassion entails turning directly toward one's suffering – whether that suffering stems from personal failures and mistakes or general life difficulties – and embracing it with feelings of kind, connected presence. As such, it transforms suffering in a way that enhances wellbeing, resilience, and coping with difficult thoughts and emotions. The current chapter will discuss self-compassion and its link to positive psychological health, as well as areas of overlap and difference between self-compassion and mindfulness – another Buddhist construct that is currently receiving attention within the field of positive psychology.

Self-compassion

To better understand what is intended by the term *self-compassion,* it is helpful to first consider what it means to feel compassion for others, a concept many of us have more familiarity with. Compassion involves sensitivity to the experience of suffering. This means opening one's awareness to the pain of others, without avoiding or disconnecting from it, and allowing feelings of kindness towards others and a desire to ameliorate their suffering to emerge (Wispe, 1991). Compassion also involves an understanding of the shared human condition, fragile and imperfect as it is, as well as a willingness to extend that understanding to others when they fail or make mistakes. Instead of looking away or rolling up your window when you pull up next to a homeless man at a stoplight, for example, you pause and take a moment to reflect on how difficult things are for him. By stepping out of your usual frame of reference and placing yourself in his position, you start to see him as an actual human being who is in pain. Once this happens, your heart can't help but resonate with his; compassion literally means "to suffer with" (Lewis & Short, 1879). Rather than trying to tune him out, you might discover that his situation has emotionally moved you, compelling you to help ease his pain in some way.

Just as we can feel compassion for the suffering of others, we can extend compassion towards the self when we experience suffering, regardless of whether the suffering resulted from external circumstances or our own mistakes, failures, and personal inadequacies. Self-compassion, therefore, involves being touched by and open to one's own suffering, not avoiding or disconnecting from it, and generating the desire to alleviate one's suffering and to heal oneself with kindness. Self-compassion also involves offering nonjudgmental understanding to one's pain, inadequacies, and failures, so that one's experience is seen as part of the larger human experience.

The three facets of self-compassion

Although self-compassion originates from the insight tradition of Buddhism, Neff (2003b) has conceptualized the construct in secular terms within the scientific literature. According to Neff's definition, self-compassion involves three main components: self-kindness, a sense of common humanity, and mindfulness.

Self-kindness

In Western culture, we generally value being kind to others; however, we rarely place as much value on being king to ourselves. When we fail or make mistakes, we often relate to ourselves in a harsh, self-critical manner and routinely say things to ourselves that we would not say to a stranger or, in some cases, even someone we disliked. Self-compassion recognizes that inadequacies and difficulties are a natural part of life that should not be resisted (e.g. self-criticism) or denied (e.g. avoidance) but, instead, embraced with warmth, kindness, and acceptance. When noticing a behavioral tendency that has been a source of frustration or embarrassment in the past, for example, the imperfection is approached in kind, understanding manner, and the emotional tone of the language is gentle and supportive. Similarly, when difficult life circumstances arise, the self-compassionate person takes some time to reflect on the emotional toll of the situation and offer the self some soothing and comfort, instead of stoically soldiering through the situation.

Common humanity

One of the biggest problems with harsh self-judgment is that it tends to make us feel isolated. When considering our personal failures and shortcomings, we have a propensity to feel isolated and separated from others, irrationally believing that our struggles are abnormal compared to others who appear to be having an easier time of it. The common humanity component of self-compassion recognizes that all people fail, make mistakes, and feel inadequate in some way. Self-compassion connects one's imperfections to the shared human experience, so that features of the self are considered from a broad, inclusive perspective. By locating our pain within the broader human experience, we tend to feel less isolated and cut off in difficult moments. In this way, self-compassion distinguishes itself from self-pity, which involves feeling sorry for one's own difficulties and, often, immerses people in their own problems to the point that they forget others experience similar problems.

Mindfulness

Mindfulness involves being aware of present moment experience in a clear and balanced manner (Brown & Ryan, 2003), so that one neither ignores nor ruminates on disliked aspects of oneself or one's life. Before one can extend compassion toward the self, one must first recognize that self is suffering. While one's own pain might seem blindingly obvious, we often fail to acknowledge the full extent of our pain, especially emotional pain that stems from self-criticism. Similarly, during difficult times in our lives, we have a tendency to jump immediately into problem solving mode, without recognizing the need to provide ourselves comfort for the struggles we're experiencing. Mindfulness also helps people avoid getting swept up and carried away by the narrative of one's pain, a process Neff (2003b) labeled as "over-identification." When in the throes of over-identification, people tend to exaggerate and obsessively fixate on negative self-relevant thoughts and emotions, meaning that they can't see themselves or their predicament clearly. Eventually, these negative self-referential thoughts become embedded into our self-concept, thus, confounding our unfavorable beliefs about the self with our actual selves. By recognizing that our thoughts and feelings are just that – thoughts and feelings, mindfulness helps us to drop the dramatic storylines about our inadequacies and past failures and gain a more balanced perspective on the self.

Self-compassion and wellbeing

Whereas the traditional, hedonistic psychologist views wellbeing as equivalent to happiness, which is conceptualized as a ratio of positive to negative experiences, researchers in the field of positive psychology increasingly acknowledge the need to more fully address negative experiences in conceptualizations of wellbeing. Because it is often not possible or beneficial to avoid all painful experiences, Wong (2011) proposes that psychology should seek to help individuals achieve an optimal level of functioning in spite of difficult life circumstances, transforming and transcending negative experiences into sources of strength and wellbeing. In many respects, this perspective on wellbeing closely resembles self-compassion. Self-compassion accepts suffering as a natural part of the human condition and holds it in the warm embrace of compassion, generating positive feelings of love, kindness, and connectedness in the process. By providing warmth and support in difficult times, self-compassion gives people the emotional resources necessary to endure painful or challenging experiences. It also softens and soothes negative emotions, allowing them to dissipate more easily, so that people can bounce back quicker. Finally, the knowledge that one possesses an inner strength capable of carrying them through the most difficult times makes them stronger and more willing to face adverse situations in the future. In this way, self-compassion allows people to thrive and grow in the face of adversity.

A burgeoning literature on the mental health benefits of self-compassion supports this point of view (Neff, 2011). During stressful life events, self-compassion has been shown to promote psychological resiliency. For instance, Sbarra, Smith, and Mehl (2012) found that self-compassion was key in helping people adjust after divorce. Researchers asked divorcing adults to discuss their thoughts and feelings about the separation in a 4-minute stream of consciousness recording. Afterwards, independent judges rated the degree to which the dialogs expressed self-compassion. People who exhibited greater self-compassion when talking about their break-up evidenced better psychological adjustment both at the time of the study and at a 9-month follow up. Self-compassion has also been found to aid adjustment to university life. Undergraduates with higher levels of self-compassion have been shown to experience fewer feelings of homesickness in the first semester (Terry, Leary, & Mehta, 2012), and less psychological distress when faced with academic pressure and social difficulties throughout their academic careers (Kyeong, 2013). Research also indicates that self-compassion helps women deal with their breast cancer treatment, resulting in less psychological distress and greater adjustment to cancer-related body changes (Przezdziecki et al., 2013). Finally, self-compassion appears to help veterans adjust after returning from war. Hiraoka et al. (2015)

examined the mental health functioning of combat veterans returning from their tours in Iraq or Afghanistan, and found that more self-compassionate veterans had lower levels of psychopathology, and better functioning in daily life, including fewer symptoms of post-traumatic stress as a result of combat exposure. In fact, regression analysis revealed self-compassion to be a stronger predictor of whether or not vets developed PTSD than level of combat exposure itself.

As mentioned earlier, the adaptive benefits of self-compassion are not merely a result of looking on the bright side. Self-compassionate people recognize when they are suffering, but are kind toward themselves in these moments, acknowledging their connectedness with the rest of humanity. For example, in a study examining self-compassionate individuals' responses to difficult life events, Leary, Tate, Adams, Allen, and Hancock (2007) found that individuals scoring higher in self-compassion were more likely to take a global perspective on their problems and experienced fewer feelings of isolation, anxiety, and self-consciousness when reflecting on their problems. Similarly, a study conducted by Neff, Kirkpatrick, and Rude (2007) asked participants to "describe their greatest weakness" in the context of a fake job interview. Even though self-compassionate people used as many negative self-descriptors as those low in self-compassion when describing their weaknesses, they were less likely to experience anxiety as a result of the task. They also found that self-compassionate individuals tended to use more connected language (e.g. third person pronouns and social references) when writing about their personal weakness. Neff, Hsieh, and Dejitterat (2005) found that self-compassionate college students were more apt to cope with a failure by reinterpreting the event in a more positive light and emphasizing the potential for growth. Furthermore, the ability of self-compassionate individuals to relate in a warm, inclusive manner to difficult emotions and circumstances may partly explain the study's other finding that self-compassionate students had less fear of academic failure and showed greater resiliency in maintaining their intrinsic motivation and sense of competency after a failure experience.

Responding to suffering in this way not only helps people endure painful life events, but, ultimately, allows them to thrive and prosper. Self-compassion has been linked to less depression, anxiety, and stress (for a review, see Barnard & Curry, 2011). In fact, a recent meta-analysis by MacBeth and Gumley (2012) found a large effect size when examining the link between self-compassion and psychopathology across 20 studies. Of course, a key feature of self-compassion is the lack of self-criticism, and self-criticism is known to be an important predictor of anxiety and depression (Blatt, 1995). However, self-compassion still offers protection against anxiety and depression when controlling for self-criticism (Neff, 2003a). Self-compassionate people have also been found to ruminate much less than those who lack self-compassion (Neff, 2003a), presumably because they can break the cycle of negativity by accepting their human imperfection with kindness. A study by Raes (2010) found that rumination mediated the association between self-compassion and depression and anxiety, suggesting that reduced rumination is one of the key benefits of self-compassion.

In addition to reducing negative mind states, the feelings of love, kindness, and caring engendered by self-compassion appear to also bolster positive states and traits. For instance, in a study examining the relationship between self-compassion and other psychological strengths Neff, Rude, and Kirkpatrick (2007) found that self-compassion was related to greater happiness, optimism, positive affect, wisdom, curiosity and exploration, and personal initiative. Similarly, a study by Breen, Kashdan, Lenser, and Fincham (2010) found that self-compassion was positively related to gratitude and satisfaction with life. Self-compassion is also associated with greater emotional intelligence (Neff, 2003a; Neff, Rude, & Kirkpatrick, 2007). Finally, self-compassion is also linked to intrinsic motivation, mindfulness, autonomy, competence, and relatedness (Neff, 2003a; Neff, Hseih, & Dejitterat, 2005), which Ryan, Huta, and Deci (2013) argue are fundamental aspects of eudaimonic wellbeing.

Self-compassion versus self-esteem

Research suggests that while self-compassion yields similar mental health benefits as self-esteem, it doesn't have the same pitfalls (Neff, 2011). In a survey involving a large community sample in the Netherlands (Neff & Vonk, 2009) for instance, self-compassion was associated with more stability in state feelings of self-worth than the trait self-esteem over an 8-month period (assessed 12 different times). This may be related to the fact that self-compassion was also found to be less contingent than self-esteem on things like physical attractiveness or successful performances. Results indicated that self-compassion was associated with lower levels of social comparison, public self-consciousness, self-rumination, anger, and close-mindedness than self-esteem. Also, self-esteem had a robust association with narcissism while self-compassion had no association with narcissism. These findings suggest that in contrast to those with high self-esteem, self-compassionate people are less focused on evaluating themselves, feeling superior to others, worrying about whether or not others are evaluating them, defending their viewpoints, or angrily reacting against those who disagree with them.

Leary et al. (2007) compared self-compassion and self-esteem using mood induction. Participants were instructed to recall a previous failure, rejection, or loss that made them feel badly about themselves, and were then asked a series of questions that assessed their feelings about the event. Half of the participants responded in writing to prompts designed to encourage thinking about the event with self-compassion, while the other half responded to prompts designed to bolster their self-esteem. Participants who received the self-compassion instructions reported reduced levels of negative emotions when thinking about the past event than those in the self-esteem condition. They also took more personal responsibility for the event than those in the self-esteem condition, suggesting that self-compassion does not lead to "letting oneself off the hook" but rather provides the ego-resilience needed to admit one's mistakes.

Self-compassion, motivation, and health

One of the biggest obstacles to self-compassion is the belief that it undermines motivation and encourages overindulgence (Gilbert, McEwan, Matos, & Rivis, 2011).

Upon learning about self-compassion, people express reluctance to let go of their self-critical tendencies because they believe that these tendencies hold them accountable for their behavior and motivate them to achieve their goals. They also fear that becoming too self-compassionate will cause them to sit around all day surfing the Internet and eating junk food. To the extent that self-criticism does work to direct and motivate behavior, it's because we're driven by the desire to avoid self-judgment when we fall short of expectations and standards; however, when we know that failure will be met with a barrage of self-criticism, sometimes it can be too frightening to even try (Petersen, 2014). With self-compassion, we strive to achieve for a very different reason – because we care. If we truly want to be kind to ourselves and do not want to suffer, we'll do what is necessary in the short term to ensure our overall health and happiness, such as taking on a challenging project or starting a new exercise routine. Moreover, because self-compassion gives us the safety needed to acknowledge our weaknesses, we're in a better position to change them for the better.

Research largely supports the idea that self-compassion enhances motivation. In a series of four experimental studies, Breines and Chen (2012) assigned participants to one of three mood induction conditions: self-compassion condition ("express kindness and understanding"), a self-esteem control condition ("describe your positive qualities"), and a positive mood control condition ("describe a hobby you like"). Compared to the control groups, they found that participants who had been induced to feel self-compassion for personal weaknesses and failures exhibited greater motivation to change for the better, try harder to learn, repair past harms, and avoid repeating past mistakes. In other correlational studies, self-compassion has been associated with increased personal initiative: the desire to reach one's full potential (Neff, Rude, & Kirkpatrick, 2007). Self-compassionate people are also more likely to adopt mastery goals, which focus on improving understanding and competence, and less likely to adopt performance goals, which are more concerned with demonstrating ability and avoiding negative judgments (Neff, Hseih, & Dejitterat, 2005). Additionally, students high in self-compassion are less likely to engage in self-handicapping strategies like procrastination (Sirois, 2014). This finding may in part be related to the fact that self-compassionate people tend to have less fear of failure and more willingness to try again after a failure (Neely, Schallert, Mohammed, Roberts, & Chen, 2009).

Research also suggests that self-compassion promotes health-related behaviors as opposed to overindulgent behaviors. For instance, a study by Adams and Leary (2007) demonstrated that self-compassion can help people stick to their diets. Research finds that self-compassionate women tend to be more intrinsically motivated to exercise – and their exercise goals are less likely to involve ego concerns – than women low in self-compassion (Magnus, Kowalski, & McHugh, 2010). Self-compassion also appears to help people overcome addiction issues. For example, a study of self-compassion and smoking cessations conducted by Kelly, Zuroff, Foa, and Gilbert (2009) found that individuals trained to feel compassionate about the difficulties of giving up smoking reduced their smoking to a greater extent than those trained to reflect upon and monitor their smoking. This self-compassion intervention was especially effective among those who were highly self-critical or resistant to change. Similarly, Brooks, Kay-Lambkin, Bowman, and Childs (2012) found that increasing self-compassion helps alcohol-dependent individuals reduce their alcohol use.

Self-compassion, disordered eating, and body image

Research suggests self-compassionate people tend to be less critical of body image and have fewer body image concerns. For example, a recent study examining the relationship between self-compassion and body image in a sample of female under-graduates found a negative association between self-compassion and body dissat-isfaction, body preoccupation, and weight worries. Moreover, they also found that self-compassion continues to predict body image after controlling for self-esteem (Wasylkiw, MacKinnon, & MacLellan, 2012). Albertson, Neff, and Dill-Shackleford (2014) conducted a study among women with body image concerns that involved them listening to guided self-compassion meditations on the Internet for 3 weeks. They found that the intervention produced significant decreases in body dissat-isfaction, body shame, and contingent self-worth based on appearance, as well as increases in body appreciation. Self-compassion appears to buffer against eating pathology as well as body dissatisfaction. It has been linked to less severe binge eat-ing (Webb & Forman, 2013), as well as lower levels of disordered eating in women with clinical eating disorders (Ferreira, Pinto-Gouveia, & Duarte, 2013).

Self-compassion and interpersonal relationships

Beyond the intrapersonal personal benefits of self-compassion already described, self-compassion appears to promote better interpersonal functioning as well. Although people may believe that offering themselves kindness for personal difficulties is tantamount to selfishness, taking care of the self's needs appears to help people respond to others' needs. In a study of romantic couples, Neff and Beretvas (2013) found that self-compassionate individuals were described by their partners as being more emotionally connected, accepting, and autonomy-supporting while being less detached, controlling, and verbally or physically aggressive than those lacking self-compassion. Self-compassion was also linked to greater relationship satisfaction and attachment security. Other research suggests that self-compassionate people tend to have more compassionate goals in relationships, such as providing social support and engendering trust (Crocker & Canevello, 2008). Finally, self-compassion has been associated with the tendencies to compromise in conflict situations (Yarnell & Neff, 2013) and make amends for past relationship harms (Breines & Chen, 2012). Taken together, these findings suggest that self-compassion helps people better meet their own needs, which, in turn, allows them to dedicate more emotional resources to meeting the needs of friends, family, and relationship partners.

Developing self-compassion

Fortunately, self-compassion appears to be a modifiable trait that can be enhanced with training. Mindfulness-based interventions are an important way to increase self-compassion (Keng, Smoski, Robins, Ekblad, & Brantley, 2012). Given that mindfulness is a pre-requisite to self-compassion and is one of its constituent components, it makes sense that learning to be mindful of negative thoughts and emotions also increases one's ability to be self-compassionate; however, beyond simply increasing one's ability to hold painful experiences in balanced awareness, many programs designed to teach mindfulness also include components that develop the capacity to relate to the self in a kind, understanding way. Mindfulness-based stress reduction (MBSR) is the most widespread mindfulness-based intervention (Kabat-Zinn, 1982). Although teaching self-compassion is not an explicit component of the MBSR curriculum, program leaders attempt to convey implicit messages about the benefits of being kind and gentle with oneself, both in their response to participants' questions and by embodying a general quality of emotional warmth (Kabat-Zinn, 2003). In addition MBSR typically teaches loving-kindness meditation (LKM), a meditation designed to generate feelings of positivity and goodwill toward the self and others (Santorelli & Kabat-Zinn, 2003).

In fact, some researchers have proposed that self-compassion may be a key mechanism by which mindfulness-based interventions improve wellbeing (Baer, Lykins, & Peters, 2012; Hölzel et al., 2011). Supporting this contention, Shapiro, Astin, Bishop, and Cordova (2005) examined the impact of the MBSR program on a group of healthcare professionals, and found that the MBSR program significantly increased self-compassion and reduced stress for the treatment group compared to a wait-list control group. Further analysis revealed that self-compassion mediated the stress reductions associated with the program.

Although mindfulness-based interventions have been shown to increase self-compassion, these programs do not directly teach skills of self-compassion, focusing primarily on teaching techniques to enhance mindfulness. This is one of the reasons why Germer and Neff (2013) developed a self-compassion training program called mindful self-compassion (MSC). The term "mindful" is included in the name of the program because it also teaches basic mindfulness skills, which – as discussed above – are crucial to the ability to give oneself compassion. In the MSC program participants meet for 2 hours once a week over the course of 8 weeks, and also meet for a half-day "mini retreat." The program uses discussion, experiential exercises, and contemplative meditations designed to increase awareness of self-compassion and how to practice it in daily life.

Neff and Germer (2013) conducted a randomized controlled trial of the MSC program, comparing outcomes for participants in MSC condition to outcomes for participants in a wait-list control condition. Results suggested that participation in the workshop significantly increased self-compassion, mindfulness, compassion for others, and life satisfaction, while significantly decreasing depression, anxiety, stress, and emotional avoidance. Results from the randomized control trial indicate that the MSC program raised participants' self-compassion levels by 43%, and that gains in all outcomes were maintained at least 1 year later. This suggests that explicit self-compassion training is an effective way to teach self-compassion.

In addition to the MSC program, there are also several new and promising short interventions for teaching self-compassion. Smeets and colleagues (2014) developed a 3-week self-compassion intervention for college students. The intervention involved a combination of discussion, self-compassion activities, and loving-kindness meditation, focusing on identifying the inner critic and finding compassionate ways to motivate the self. At the end of the intervention, students in the self-compassion training condition showed significantly greater increases in mindfulness, optimism, and self-efficacy, as well as significantly greater decreases in rumination in comparison to a time management control group. Shapira and Mongrain (2010) examined the impact of a self-compassionate letter writing intervention, which involved writing a paragraph about a recent difficulty in a kind, understanding way, as a good friend would do. After 7 days of letter writing, they found that this activity not only decreased depression levels for 3 months, but it also increased happiness levels for 6 months. These results indicate that even brief self-compassion interventions can be effective in enhancing wellbeing.

The relationship between mindfulness and self-compassion

Given that they're both Buddhist constructs related to psychological wellbeing, readers may wonder what distinguishes self-compassion from mindfulness. In general, mindfulness refers to the ability to nonjudgmentally bring awareness to any experience, positive, negative, or neutral, whereas self-compassion focuses on holding negative thoughts and emotions with kindness (Germer, 2009). Although the mindfulness component of self-compassion is narrower in scope than general mindfulness, the overall construct of self-compassion is broader in scope than mindfulness, given that it also involves components of common humanity and self-kindness.

Beyond the scope of the constructs, self-compassion and mindfulness also differ in terms of their respective targets. Whereas mindfulness is concerned with the nature and quality of our relationship to the present moment experience, self-compassion is concerned with the nature and quality of our relationship with the *experiencer* who is suffering (Germer, 2009). When a person relates mindfully to a difficult experience, they gently bring their attention to the thoughts, emotions, and sensations that arise without judgment or resistance, letting the experience be as it is – no more, no less (Kabat-Zinn, 1994). However, when self-compassion accompanies mindful awareness of a difficult experience, feelings of care and concern emerge for oneself in the midst of experiencing pain, as well as a desire for the self to be free from suffering in the future. In this sense, self-compassion involves a bit of a paradox; it both completely accepts an experience as it is and also wishes it could be different. In the MSC program, this apparent contradiction is resolved by explaining that "we give ourselves compassion not to feel better but because we feel bad" (Germer & Neff, 2013, p. 386). Put differently, we learn to fully accept our present moment situation while still holding our pain in the tender embrace of compassion, thus, preventing self-compassion from becoming a way of resisting negative thoughts and emotions and providing the emotional safety to fully experience one's pain. In this way, self-compassion and mindfulness work together to mutually enhance each other.

Conclusion

The idea that our response to negative events influences wellbeing is not new within the field of positive psychology. In his 1998 presidential address, Martin Seligman, then acting president of American Psychological Association, referred to this potential for positive psychology when he wrote, "... psychology's focus on the negative has left us knowing too little about the many instances of growth, mastery, drive, and character building that can develop out of painful life events" (p. 561). Still, positive psychologists have tended to focus on the buffering effects of positive emotions, ignoring the transformative aspects of negative emotions. If positive psychology is indeed finally heading toward a more balanced model, which both focuses on enhancing the positive and transforming the negative, it may be time to bring self-compassion under the broad umbrella of positive psychology.

Bibliography

Adams, C. E., & Leary, M. R. (2007). Promoting self-compassionate attitudes toward eating among restrictive and guilty eaters. *Journal of Social and Clinical Psychology, 26*(1), 1120–1144.

Albertson, E. R., Neff, K. D., & Dill-Shackleford, K. E. (2014). Self-compassion and body dissatisfaction in women: A randomized controlled trial of a brief meditation intervention. *Mindfulness, 6*(3), 444–454.

Baer, R. A., Lykins, E. L. B., & Peters, J. R. (2012). Mindfulness and self-compassion as predictors of psychological wellbeing in long-term meditators and match nonmeditators. *Journal of Positive Psychology, 7*, 230–238.

Barnard, L. K., & Curry, J. F. (2011). Self-compassion: Conceptualizations, correlates, & interventions. *Review of General Psychology, 15*(4), 289–303.

Blatt, S. J. (1995). Representational structures in psychopathology. In D. Cicchetti & S. Toth (Eds.), *Rochester symposium on developmental psychopathology: Emotion, cognition, and representation* (Vol. 6., pp. 1–34). Rochester, NY: University of Rochester Press.

Breen, W. E., Kashdan, T. B., Lenser, M. L., & Fincham, F. D. (2010). Gratitude and forgiveness: Convergence and divergence on self-report and informant ratings. *Personality and Individual Differences, 49*, 932–937.

Breines, J. G., & Chen, S. (2012). Self-compassion increases self-improvement motivation. *Personality and Social Psychology Bulletin, 38*, 1133–1143.

Brooks, M., Kay-Lambkin, F., Bowman, J., & Childs, S. (2012). Self-compassion amongst clients with problematic alcohol use. *Mindfulness, 3*, 308–317.

Brown, K. W., & Ryan, R. M. (2003). The benefits of being present: Mindfulness and its role in psychological well-being. *Journal of Personality and Social Psychology, 84*, 822–848.

Crocker, J., & Canevello, A. (2008). Creating and undermining social support in communal relationships: The role of compassionate and self-image goals. *Journal of Personality and Social Psychology, 95*, 555–575.

Duckworth, A. L., Steen, T. A., & Seligman, M. E. (2005). Positive psychology in clinical practice. *Annual Review of Clinical Psychology, 1*, 629–651.

Ferreira, C., Pinto-Gouveia, J., & Duarte, C. (2013). Self-compassion in the face of shame and body image dissatisfaction: Implications for eating disorders. *Eating Behaviors, 14*(2), 207–210.

Fredrickson, B. L. (2001). The role of positive emotions in positive psychology: The broaden-and-build theory of positive emotions. *American Psychologist, 56*(3), 218.

Germer, C. K. (2009). *The mindful path to self-compassion.* New York, NY: Guilford Press.

Germer, C., & Neff, K. (2013). The mindful self-compassion training program. In T. Singer & M. Bolz (Eds.), *Compassion: Bridging theory and practice: A multimedia book* (pp. 365–396). Leipzig, Germany: Max-Planck Institute.

Gilbert, P. (2009). *The compassionate mind.* London: Constable.

Gilbert, P., McEwan, K., Matos, M., & Rivis, A. (2011). Fears of compassion: Development of three self-report measures. *Psychology and Psychotherapy: Theory, Research and Practice, 84*, 239–255.

Gilbert, P., & Procter, S. (2006). Compassionate mind training for people with high shame and self-criticism: Overview and pilot study of a group therapy approach. *Clinical Psychology & Psychotherapy, 13*, 353–379.

Goetz, J. L., Keltner, D., & Simon-Thomas, E. (2010). Compassion: An evolutionary analysis and empirical review. *Psychological Bulletin, 136*, 351–374.

Hiraoka, R., Meyer, E. C., Kimbrel, N. A., B. DeBeer, B. B., Gulliver, S. B., & Morissette, S. B. (2015). Self-compassion as a prospective predictor of PTSD symptom severity among trauma-exposed U.S. Iraq and Afghanistan war veterans. *Journal of Traumatic Stress, 28*, 1–7.

Hollis-Walker, L., & Colosimo, K. (2011). Mindfulness, self-compassion, and happiness in non-meditators: A theoretical and empirical examination. *Personality and Individual Differences, 50*, 222–227.

Hölzel, B. K., Lazar, S. W., Gard, T., Schuman-Olivier, Z., Vago, D. R., & Ott, U. (2011). How does mindfulness meditation work? Proposing mechanisms of action from a conceptual and neural perspective. *Perspectives on Psychological Science, 6*, 537–559.

Kabat-Zinn, J. (1982). An outpatient program in behavioral medicine for chronic pain patients based on the practice of mindfulness meditation: Theoretical considerations and preliminary results. *General Hospital Psychiatry, 4*(1), 33–47.

Kabat-Zinn, J. (1994). *Wherever you go, there you are: Mindfulness meditation in everyday life.* New York, NY: Hyperion.

Kabat-Zinn, J. (2003). Mindfulness-based interventions in context: Past, present, and future. *Clinical Psychology: Science and Practice, 10*, 144–156. http://doi.org/10.1093/clipsy.bpg016

Kelly, A. C., Zuroff, D. C., Foa, C. L., & Gilbert, P. (2009). Who benefits from training in self-compassionate self-regulation? A study of smoking reduction. *Journal of Social and Clinical Psychology, 29*, 727–755.

Keng, S., Smoski, M. J., Robins, C. J., Ekblad, A. G., & Brantley, J. G. (2012). Mechanisms of change in mindfulness-based stress reduction: Self-compassion and mindfulness as mediators of intervention outcomes. *Journal of Cognitive Psychotherapy, 26*(3), 270–280.

Klimecki, O. M., Leiberg, S., Lamm, C., & Singer, T. (2013). Functional neural plasticity and associated changes in positive affect after compassion training. *Cerebral Cortex, 7*, 1552–1561.

Kyeong, L. W. (2013). Self-compassion as a moderator of the relationship between academic burn-out and psychological health in Korean cyber university students. *Personality and Individual Differences, 54*(8), 899–902.

Leary, M. R., Tate, E. B., Adams, C. E., Allen, A. B., & Hancock, J. (2007). Self-compassion and reactions to unpleasant self-relevant events: The implications of treating oneself kindly. *Journal of Personality and Social Psychology, 92*, 887–904.

Lewis, C. T., & Short, C. (1879). *A Latin dictionary.* New York, NY: Harper & Brothers

Lutz, A., Brefczynski-Lewis, J., Johnstone, T., & Davidson, R. J. (2008). Regulation of the neural circuitry of emotion by compassion meditation: Effects of meditative expertise. *Public Library of Science, 3*, 1–5.

MacBeth, A., & Gumley, A. (2012). Exploring compassion: A meta-analysis of the association between self-compassion and psychopathology. *Clinical Psychology Review, 32*, 545–552.

Magnus, C. M. R., Kowalski, K. C., & McHugh, T. L. F. (2010). The role of self-compassion in women's self-determined motives to exercise and exercise-related outcomes. *Self & Identity, 9*, 363–382.

Neely, M. E., Schallert, D. L., Mohammed, S. S., Roberts, R. M., Chen, Y. (2009). Self-kindness when facing stress: The role of self-compassion, goal regulation, and support in college students well-being. *Motivation and Emotion, 33*, 88–97.

Neff, K. D. (2003a). Development and validation of a scale to measure self- compassion. *Self and Identity, 2*, 223–250.

Neff, K. D. (2003b). Self-compassion: An alternative conceptualization of a healthy attitude toward oneself. *Self and Identity, 2*, 85–102.

Neff, K. D. (2004). Self-compassion and psychological well-being. *Constructivism in the Human Sciences, 9,* 27–37.

Neff, K. D. (2011). Self-compassion, self-esteem, and well-being. *Social and Personality Compass, 5,* 1–12.

Neff, K. D., & Beretvas, S. N. (2013). The role of self-compassion in romantic relationships. *Self and Identity, 12*, 78–98.

Neff, K. D., & Germer, C. K. (2013). A pilot study and randomized controlled trial of the mindful self-compassion program. *Journal of Clinical Psychology, 69*, 28–44.

Neff, K. D., Hseih, Y., & Dejitterat, K. (2005). Self-compassion, achievement goals, and coping with academic failure. *Self and Identity, 4*, 263–287.

Neff, K. D., Kirkpatrick, K., & Rude, S. S. (2007). Self-compassion and its link to adaptive psychological functioning. *Journal of Research in Personality, 41*, 139–154.

Neff, K. D., Rude, S. S., & Kirkpatrick, K. (2007). An examination of self-compassion in relation to positive psychological functioning and personality traits. *Journal of Research in Personality, 41*, 908–916.

Neff, K. D., & Vonk, R. (2009). Self-compassion versus global self-esteem: Two different ways of relating to oneself. *Journal of Personality, 77,* 23–50.

Petersen, L. E. (2014). Self-compassion and self-protection strategies: The impact of self-compassion on the use of self-handicapping and sandbagging. *Personality and Individual Differences, 56*, 133–138.

Przezdziecki A., Sherman K. A., Baillie A., Taylor, A., Foley, E., & Stalgis-Bilinsky, A. (2013). My changed body: Breast cancer, body image, distress and self-compassion. *Psycho-Oncology, 22*(1), 1872–1879.

Raes, F. (2010). Rumination and worry as mediators of the relationship between self-compassion and depression and anxiety. *Personality and Individual Differences, 48,* 757–761.

Ryan, R. M., & Deci, E. L. (2001). On happiness and human potentials: A review of research on hedonic and eudaimonic well-being. *Annual Review of Psychology, 52*, 141–166.

Ryan, R. M., Huta, V., & Deci, E. L. (2013). Living well: A self-determination theory perspective on eudaimonia. *Journal of Happiness Studies, 9,* 139–170.

Santorelli, S., & Kabat-Zinn, J. (2003). *MBSR curriculum guide and supporting materials: Guidelines for presenting this work.* Worcester, MA: Center for Mindfulness in Medicine, Health Care & Society.

Sbarra, D. A., Smith, H. L., & Mehl, M. R. (2012). When leaving your ex, love yourself: Observational ratings of self-compassion predict the course of emotional recovery following marital separation. *Psychological Science, 23*, 261–269.

Seligman, Martin E. P. (1999). The President's Address (Annual Report). *American Psychologist,* *54,* 559–62.

Shapira, L. B., & Mongrain, M. (2010). The benefits of self-compassion and optimism exercises for individuals vulnerable to depression. *The Journal of Positive Psychology, 5,* 377–389.

Shapiro, S. L., Astin, J., Bishop, S., & Cordova, M. (2005). Mindfulness-based stress reduction and health care professionals. *International Journal of Stress Management, 12,* 164–176.

Sirois, F. M. (2014). Procrastination and stress: Exploring the role of self-compassion. *Self and Identity, 13,* 128–145. doi:10.1080/15298868.2013.763404

Smeets, E., Neff, K., Alberts, H., & Peters, M. (2014). Meeting suffering with kindness: Effects of a brief self-compassion intervention for female college students. *Journal of Clinical Psychology, 70*(9), 794–807.

Terry, M. L., Leary, M. R., & Mehta, S. (2012). Self-compassion as a buffer against homesickness, depression, and dissatisfaction in the transition to college. *Self and Identity, 12*(3), 1–13. doi:10.1080/15298868.2012.667913

Van Dam, N. T., Sheppard, S. C., Forsyth, J. P., & Earleywine, M. (2011). Self-compassion is a better predictor than mindfulness of symptom severity and quality of life in mixed anxiety and depression. *Journal of Anxiety Disorders, 25,* 123–130.

Wasylkiw, L., MacKinnon, A. L., & MacLellan, A. M. (2012). Exploring the link between self-compassion and body image in university women. *Body Image, 9*(2), 236–245.

Webb, J. B., & Forman, M. J. (2013). Evaluating the indirect effect of self-compassion on binge eating severity through cognitive–affective self-regulatory pathways. *Eating Behaviors, 14*(2), 224–228.

Wispe, L. (1991). *The psychology of sympathy.* New York, NY: Plenum.

Wong, P. T. P. (2011). Positive psychology 2.0: Towards a balanced interactive model of the good life. *Canadian Psychology, 52,* 69–81.

Yarnell, L. M., Neff, K. D. (2013). Self-compassion, interpersonal conflict resolutions, and well-being. *Self and Identity, 2,* 146–159.

3

MINDFUL PARENTING BEGINS AT THE BEGINNING

Potential benefits of perinatal meditation training for family well-being

Catherine Shaddix and Larissa G. Duncan

Mindfulness training in the perinatal period: preliminary research

Interest in bringing mindfulness training into childbirth and early parenting programs has grown in recent years because of the positive outcomes that have been shown in the application of mindfulness for parenting (Bögels, Lehtonen, & Restifo, 2010; Coatsworth, Duncan, Greenberg, & Nix, 2010). Programs integrating mindfulness training into childbirth and parenting education have shown promise for helping to reduce perinatal stress and anxiety, as well as for providing psychological support to women during pregnancy (Vieten & Astin, 2008), mothers and fathers/partners jointly during childbirth and early parenting (Duncan & Bardacke, 2010), and breastfeeding mothers (Perez-Blasco, Viguer, & Rodrigo, 2013). Reducing maternal stress in the prenatal period may have enduring effects on the physical health of the child due to changes in the intrauterine environment that impact prenatal programming (e.g., Fowden et al., 2006). The emotional aspects of early parent-child relationships can also have long-term health consequences (Miller, Lachman, Chen, Karlamangla, & Seeman, 2011). Thus an intervention such as mindfulness training for childbirth and parenting, which may both buffer antenatal stress effects on the fetus and enhance infant-parent emotional relatedness, could have lasting effects on the health and well-being of the child.

Building internal psychological resources for mothers in the form of self-awareness and emotion regulation has emerged as an increasingly important factor in promoting healthy caregiver-infant relationships (Snyder, Shapiro, & Treleaven, 2011), and fits within the growing field of positive psychology, which is concerned with realizing the human potential for well-being. Acknowledgement that mindfulness training could provide a means of maternal psychological support, as well as provide enhanced coping in the perinatal period (Duncan & Bardacke, 2010), has supported the growing interest in the integration of mindfulness with childbirth and parenting programs. As well, two aspects of mindfulness training for parents with older children may be especially relevant for application to early parenting: (1) becoming more in tune with their child's emotions (Coatsworth et al., 2010), and (2) mindful appraisal (Williams & Wahler, 2010), wherein the mother may make connections between her parenting style and the child's behavior, potentially leading to positively reinforcing patterns of mutual interaction. The findings from mindful parenting programs with older children suggest that mindfulness training may contribute to reduced parental stress and reactivity, improved parental self-regulation, and reduced child behavior problems, all of which could be beneficial in the phase of early parenting (Coatsworth et al., 2010; Dawe & Harnett, 2007; Singh et al., 2006; Singh et al., 2007; Singh et al., 2010).

Recent applications of mindfulness-based interventions have shown promise in reducing the impact of stress and increasing positive affect during pregnancy. In a small RCT ($N = 31$) with mothers in the second half of their pregnancy, using an 8-week mindfulness-based intervention aimed at reducing stress and improving mood in pregnancy and early postpartum, results showed that mothers who received the intervention had a 20–25% reduction in anxiety, negative affect, and stress, and a similar percentage of improvement in positive affect (Vieten & Astin, 2008). The intervention, called Mindful Motherhood, incorporated three methods of working with mindfulness: mindfulness of thoughts and feelings, primarily using the breath as the focus of attention; mindfulness of the body through hatha yoga and body awareness meditations; and instruction in accepting the whole of one's experience through the cultivation of an observing self. Training sessions included education, discussion, and experiential exercises, some of which were tailored to the specific issues of pregnancy such as anxiety about labor. Participants in the program were given home practice in the form of 20-minute guided meditations that they were encouraged to use daily. Limitations of the study were its small sample size, its limited generalizability because of the ethnic and socioeconomic representation in the sample, reliance on self-report measures, and lack of structured interviews.

Results of a pilot study of an adaptation of MBCT for pregnant women with anxiety, Coping with Anxiety through Living Mindfully, found that participants ($N = 24$) with generalized anxiety disorder (GAD) showed statistically and clinically significant decreases in anxiety, worry, and depression, and significant increases in self-compassion and mindfulness (Goodman et al., 2014). The study included pre- and post-intervention self-report measures, a structured diagnostic interview, and qualitative feedback as means of assessment. Of the 17 participants who met criteria for GAD at the start of the study, only one continued to meet criteria post-intervention. Strengths of the study included its sample, which was drawn from a community-based obstetric population and consisted of women who were suffering significant psychiatric distress and who were not currently receiving mental health care at the time of the study. In addition to the salubrious effects of diminished anxiety for the pregnant mothers participating in the study, the study findings are also significant in that they support the possibility that a mindfulness-based intervention could be used during the perinatal period to address generalized anxiety, when pharmacological interventions are not advised.

In a mixed-methods pilot study, $n = 27$ pregnant women and their birthing partners participated in the Mindfulness-Based Childbirth and Parenting (MBCP) program during their third trimester of pregnancy (Duncan & Bardacke, 2010). MBCP was developed by Nancy Bardacke, CNM, in 1998 (Bardacke, 2012), and it is a formal adaptation of the mindfulness-based stress reduction (MBSR) program, designed by Jon Kabat-Zinn (1990). MBCP is oriented towards reducing the perception of pregnancy, childbirth, and parenting-related stressors as overwhelming or frightening, and promoting mindfulness skills in the service of more adaptive functioning and family well-being.

Two central themes of the program, which are interwoven throughout the training, are that the capacity to be fully present for labor and delivery can support the normal course of childbirth, and that parenting that is present-centered and attentive can greatly enhance the development of a healthy, empathic parent-child relationship (Duncan & Bardacke, 2010). A core tenet of the MBCP program is that through the cultivation of mindful awareness, with which one can more willingly and receptively encounter one's emotional, physical, or cognitive experience, one can gain the freedom to be with life's moment-to-moment unfolding without the need to withdraw from, alter, or deny any of its particular manifestations, thus allowing for spaciousness, creativity, and psychological balance to arise spontaneously (Bardacke, 2012).

MBCP consists of nine weekly sessions of 3 hours' duration, during which the participants are taught the secular mindfulness meditation practices from MBSR specifically adapted for pregnant women and their birthing partners. These strategies include sitting meditation, mindful yoga, a body awareness practice called the body scan, and walking meditation. For the specific childbirth and parenting practices, participants are given psychoeducation in regards to the processes of pregnancy, labor, childbirth, breastfeeding, postpartum adjustment, and the psychological needs of the infant. Information about the physiological effects of perceived stress and its detrimental effects on pregnancy and labor are offered, and the beneficial effects of coping with stress through mindful awareness to all of the dimensions of one's experience are emphasized (Bardacke, 2012).

Participants are encouraged throughout the course to simply be present for the unfolding process of pregnancy, which eventually includes labor, without overlaying their experience with thoughts about anticipated or feared outcomes (Bardacke, 2012). Participants are given a wide variety of mind-body pain coping skills for childbirth, awareness skills for coping with stress in daily life, and techniques for cultivating loving communication between partners through touch and mindful speaking and listening. Exercises which direct the mother and partner to identify and share emotions around birth and parenting, including those related to family of origin issues and the participant's feelings about becoming a parent themselves, are presented as guided meditations to be done in the group as well as part of the program homework. The role of the partner's own cultivation of mindfulness is held to be equally as important as that of the mother's in the exercises.

In the pilot study, quantitative measures were used to assess changes in perceived stress, pregnancy anxiety, depression, mindfulness, and the frequency and intensity of positive and negative affect pre- and post-course. Results revealed statistically significant decreases in pregnancy anxiety, negative affect, and depression symptoms; increases in the frequency and intensity of positive affect; and an improvement in the nonreactivity dimension of mindfulness on the Five Factor Mindfulness Questionnaire (FFMQ; Baer, Smith, Hopkins, Krietemeyer, & Toney, 2006) at the conclusion of the MBCP training. In addition, 85% of the pregnant women reported using mindfulness to cope with a salient stressful aspect of pregnancy at post-intervention, more than double the frequency at pre-test (37%) (Duncan & Bardacke, 2010).

Qualitative results from post-course interviews supported the quantitative findings. Participants stated they used the formal and informal practices of mindfulness in coping with the stress of pregnancy, labor, delivery, and postpartum. Reported benefits of the practices included being able to stay in the present moment during the birth experience in the midst of pain and fear, to stay present with infants and partners with more mindful presence and less emotional reactivity, and to accept internal experiences and external situations with a non-judgmental attitude. These findings suggest that the participants gained an expanded set of coping skills from having received the mindfulness training. Participants also described the importance of having birthing partners be a part of the training, and being able to receive the mindful support of their partners during birth and postpartum. Both quantitative and qualitative results showed that the majority of participants continued to experience the perceived benefits of mindfulness training during the perinatal period and into the period of early parenthood (Duncan & Bardacke, 2010).

Limitations of the study were its small sample size, lack of a control group, selection effects, reliance solely on self-report measures, and the relatively high educational level and socioeconomic status of the participants. However, even with the study design limitations and small sample size, numerous statistically significant effects were found for the central hypothesized mechanism of action of more adaptive stress appraisal and enhanced coping processes.

A unique strength of the MBCP program is the emphasis on how mindfulness skills may be beneficial in parenting a newborn, and in nurturing the partner relationship after the birth of the child (Duncan & Bardacke, 2010). The transition to parenthood impacts both parents, in that both will need to be able to attend to their inevitable anxieties and uncertainties, which may carry them back to the struggles and ambivalences of earlier relationships (Brazelton & Cramer, 1990). As well, the risk for pregnant women of depression during pregnancy and postpartum may be ameliorated by the support of their partners (Feeny, Alexander, Noller, & Hohaus, 2003; Lancaster et al., 2010). Partners who can use mindfulness skills as self-regulation strategies for dealing with their own internal processes around becoming a parent may have more capacity in regulating their own emotional ups and downs, as well as having attentional resources to devote to the needs of the mother and infant when inevitable needs arise.

Mindfulness in the perinatal period and its potential impact on the parent-child relationship

Increasing resources in parent-child interactions through increased parental awareness

The current research on mindfulness training in the perinatal period has supported the hypothesis that such training could lessen maternal stress, anxiety, and negative affect, as well as increase partner support. While it has not yet been thoroughly investigated, it is also possible that mindfulness training during this transitional time could have long-lasting effects on the relationship between the parent and child by increasing the parent's capacity for awareness of their own cognitive, emotional, and behavioral patterns. Increased parental self-awareness would be beneficial for the parent-child dyad at any point in the developing relationship, whether just after birth or in parenting a toddler. Through increased self-awareness, the parent could gain more access to their internal experience, especially when distressed, and thus have the potential for greater self-regulation when with their child. Through greater self-regulation, the parent may also have access to more psychological resources with which to attend to their child, even in distressing circumstances.

This increased capacity for self-awareness would be cultivated initially through formal mindfulness practices such as sitting meditation, walking meditation, yoga, and the body scan, and could then potentially be integrated into the parent's moment-to-moment experience through an ongoing practice of informal mindfulness. Research on mindfulness training programs for the perinatal period suggests that the participants do continue to practice informally while in the activity of parenting (Duncan & Bardacke, 2010; Shaddix, Duncan, Cook, & Bardacke, 2014). It is also possible that the most efficacious time to train parents to parent mindfully is during the perinatal period, where the parent-to-be has heightened motivation to engage in the practices because of the knowledge of the challenges that lie ahead, and also because during the perinatal period the parent-to-be has the attentional resources needed to undertake this kind of formal training, which may be limited once the demands of parenthood begin.

Research on mindfulness training in other contexts suggests that enhanced awareness may be an outcome of such training. For example, in a small study of MBSR using daily diaries of home practice ($N = 8$), a grounded theory analysis of the diaries revealed that all of the study participants were experiencing moments of distress related to practice during the training. However, those participants who completed the training displayed increased detail and clarity in their descriptions over the course of the training, improved affect, and the emergence of an observing self. A second analysis of the data, specifically undertaken to explore this development of an observing self, revealed that the observing self emerged regardless of whether the reported experience of the subject had a negative valence or not. By the end of the 8-week trial, even those subjects whose diary entries had been predominantly negative were able to display an observing, witnessing attitude towards their own distress (Kerr, Josyula, & Littenberg, 2011).

The first implication of such an increased ability to observe one's distress is that one could adopt an internal stance of fluidity in regards to changing internal and external phenomena. One could then reduce the need to fixate or alter these phenomenal experiences, thereby gaining more ability to tolerate and accept a wider range of psychologically challenging thoughts, feelings, and mind-states. For a parent, this may lead to greater equanimity, especially in stressful conditions with their infant or child.

Secondly, the parent with enhanced self-awareness would have more cognitive and emotional resources available to attend to the emotional experience of the child. For parents, this could translate into being able to remain in contact with their own as well as their child's emotions, cognitions, and behaviors. This may lead to the parent having greater empathy for their child's emotional experiences. In addition, the parent, through having greater equanimity in moments of distress, may be able to make more balanced attributions about their child's distress-inducing behavior, which may keep open the possibility that the parent will be able to access positive emotions even when angry or frustrated with their child. Experiencing positive emotion towards their child when the child is distressed could play an important role in the parent remaining attuned to their child by buffering the challenging experience of contacting a child's negative affect. It may also enable a parent to avoid negative affect reciprocity. Negative affect reciprocity, wherein one responds to another's negative affect with one's own negative affect, has been noted in the analysis of marital interactions to be a primary contributor to dissatisfaction (Gottman, 1999), and may function in a similar way in parent-child relationships.

Access to positive emotion during stressful interactions has been shown to be an outcome of mindful relating in committed relationships (Wachs & Cordova, 2007). It is possible that mindfulness training during the perinatal period could augment the ability of the participant to access positive emotions when engaging in stressful situations with their child. Mothers who attended MBCP in their third trimester of pregnancy ($N = 10$) reported that the skills acquired during their mindfulness training enabled them to consider possible underlying reasons for their child's distressing behaviors, and to access positive emotions for and while with their child, despite those behaviors (Shaddix et al., 2014).

This finding supports the view that mindfulness training may facilitate the caregiver having more internal resources to draw upon in times of distress with their child. Mindfulness may promote spaciousness in the midst of complex, emotionally triggering experiences and provide a caregiver the platform for responding to their child, rather than reacting. Parental use of mindfulness while parenting may also have an impact on the child's ability to form a secure attachment with the caregiver, as described below.

Attachment theory and parent-child attunement

According to early research on attachment (Bowlby, 1980), the internal representational map that the child forms in relation to their primary caregiver, also called the internal working model of attachment (Bowlby, 1982), develops during the middle months of the first year of the child's life. This internal working model both reflects and forms the basis of the child's attachment relationship to their caregiver. In addition, the internal working model underlies a global relational pattern that is referred to as an attachment style, which can be reliably classified as "secure," or "insecure," which is further categorized as "avoidant," "anxious/ambivalent," or "unresolved/disorganized" by the end of the first year of a child's life (Slade, 2000). Based on the emergence of these representational patterns at this stage of development, there is a strong suggestion that the establishment of flexibility, balance, and attunement in the domain of affect is tied to the dynamics of the early caregiver-child relationship, inclining those representational patterns towards more or less security of attachment (Slade, 2000). However, it should be noted that changes in attachment security can occur during the first 5 years of life due to the interaction between the developing child and its changing environment (Bowlby, 1982).

In the matrix of the interdependent caregiver-child dyad, the quality of attunement is predicated on the caregiver's ability to assess his or her own internal experience, as well as the body-based emotions and needs of the infant. An ongoing experience of mutual attunement in the dyad depends upon the caregiver's ability to attune to and communicate the mental states of the child, which provides the foundation for the co-regulation of emotion and can aid in establishing the base for the child's later psychological resilience (Siegel, 2007). Such an attuned process is also referred to as "collaborative communication" (Siegel, 1999). This construct of collaborative communication works in conjunction with another construct, that of the "Theory of Mind," in which the ability to attribute mental states such as thoughts, beliefs, emotions, and desires to oneself and others allows for everyday predictions and explanations of human actions (Sodian & Kristen, 2010). Collaborative communication requires close observation of the child's preverbal initiatives, through which the child communicates their needs and motives and the associated meanings the child makes in regards to these needs and motives (Lyons-Ruth, 1999). An attuned parent will provide mirroring, structuring, and emotion coaching for their child, thereby helping the child to articulate their preverbal experience, including their difficulties. The child's ability to notice and communicate their vulnerabilities can create the foundation wherein the child will ultimately be able to deal with those vulnerabilities more effectively (Mikulincer & Shaver, 2007).

Enhancing attachment security through mindfulness training in the perinatal period

Mindfulness training in the perinatal period may influence and enhance attachment security in the relationship between the caregiver and the child in a number of ways. Perhaps the most important way it may do this is by increasing the capacity of the caregiver to reflect on their own internal states, a process known in the field of attachment research as "mentalizing" (Fonagy, Gergely, Jurist, & Target, 2002). This has been defined as simply noticing one's own as well as another's thoughts, feelings, needs, and motivations (Shaver, Lavy, Saron, & Mikulincer, 2007). In the *Satipatthana Sutta* (Nanamoli & Bodhi, 1995), an early Buddhist text in which mindfulness training was detailed, mindfulness was considered to be both "internal," through directing it towards one's own subjective experience, as well as "external," through directing it to the subjective experience of others by observing another person's posture, facial expression, and tone of voice as indicators of their feelings or state of mind (Analayo, 2006). In this way, mindfulness may be an analogue of mentalizing.

Because of the proposed increase in self-awareness, it has been speculated that mindfulness training may impact a practitioner's own level of attachment security (Shaver et al., 2007). This impact on adult attachment security may be the second way that mindfulness training in the perinatal period could have an impact on parent-child attachment. One means by which this may occur is known in attachment theory as "earned security" (Hesse, 1999; Hesse, 2008). Earned security refers to the capacity of certain individuals to regard their early life experiences in a way that is balanced and objective, even if they are negative, especially when the nature of their early experiences would normally have created a pathway to an insecurely attached state of mind (Siegel & Hartzell, 2003). Mindfulness training may cultivate an essential aspect of earned security, metacognitive processing, which is the ability to reflect on one's own cognitive processes as they are arising (Brown & Ryan, 2003). Through mindfully investigating one's cognitive patterns, the resultant metacognitive processing may allow previously unconscious contents and patterns of mind to become available for reflection (Brown, Ryan, & Creswell, 2007), and through repeated contemplation, for repair and healing.

A third way that mindfulness training in the perinatal period could be important for parent-child attachment is through what is considered to be the intergenerational transmission of attachment, wherein the caregiver's attachment pattern, whether secure or insecure, is passed to the child. Although influenced by a number of factors, attachment patterns are thought to be transmitted intergenerationally to a significant degree (Bowlby, 1988; Siegel & Hartzell, 2003). Lieberman (1997) suggested that maternal attributions and their subsequent internalization in the child as mind and body states are a possible vehicle for the transmission of intergenerational attachment. She defined attributions as "the inferences mothers make about the developmentally-determined motives and age-specific limitations of their children" (p. 283), which become internalized by an infant to become part of its internal working model.

The mother's own internal working model provides the rules by which the mother selects and organizes information relevant to the activity of relating to her child, and is used as a filter that guides her responses to her child's affect and behavior. When the mother is unconscious of this process, attributions can reflect the mother's fears, anger, or other suppressed or unacknowledged parts of herself, and can be pervasively rigid, constricting, and negative. Early mis-attunement experiences based on these attributions can be encoded at the most visceral, nonverbal levels of the child's sense of self, even before the infant can form a stable mental representation of the mother. Unless negative maternal attributions can be trans-formed through the mother's own conscious internal development, these experi-ences become integrated with similar ongoing experiences that are semantically encoded by the child, giving rise to symbolic representations of self and mother that are embedded in a matrix of mind and body states in the child (Lieberman, 1997).

Through what means could mindfulness training influence the psychological processes that contribute to the transmission of attachment security from parent to child?

Mindfulness training could possibly help in the coherent organization of experi-ence on the most basic somatic, emotional, and cognitive levels through the repeated turning of attention to very simple phenomenal components such as sensation, feeling, thought, and mental states (Nanamoli & Bodhi, 1995). This may allow one to contact and eventually re-organize with more clarity what may have been origi-nally experienced as a jumble of thoughts, feelings, and intentions. Mindful atten-tion to how the self is being structured, moment by moment, from the constantly shifting array of sensations, thoughts, feelings, and mental states could reduce the tendency towards rigid identification with negative, one-dimensional, or disor-ganized internal representations, thereby creating more freedom in the mindful observer to hold an internal representation of greater complexity. An understanding of the ultimately impermanent nature of any internal representation may also allow for a lighter grasp of all self-representations. Through this process, more flexibility in cognitive, emotional, and behavioral patterns may be gained (Brown et al., 2007).

Along those lines, mindfulness may offer more psychological space in which to review actions, situations, and thinking processes. In such expanded psychological space, thinking is not compartmentalized because of defensive processes, which may distort, disorganize, or limit access to memories, feelings, intentions, and recogni-tion of options (Emavardhana & Tori, 1997; Main, Kaplan, & Cassidy, 1985). With more psychological space a parent may be able to acknowledge their own affective and cognitive patterns, and to reflect on those patterns prior to enacting them with their child. Attributions that the parent is making about their child's behavior could come to awareness and be considered rather than unconsciously incorporated into the parent's understanding of their child. Mindfulness training may also enhance one's awareness of intention (Wallace & Shapiro, 2006), which could help to ori-ent parents towards their intentions while parenting, thus steering the behavioral course of the parent in challenging interactions with their child towards behaviors that embody patience, clarity, and responsiveness.

As previously discussed, mindfulness may facilitate more thoughtful regulation of subjective emotional states in parents and more capacity to recognize subjec-tive emotional states in their infant or child. Mindfulness training in the perinatal period may also confer other emotional benefits to the parent through the increas-ing of compassion and empathy (Lutz, Brefczynski-Lewis, Johnstone, & Davidson, 2008). This becomes crucial during times when attachment security is especially at risk, such as after a difficult labor when the mother may be exhausted or the newborn may initially be unresponsive, underweight, or stressed; when an infant is consistently difficult to soothe; or if the temperamental fit between mother and infant is less than ideal.

The capacity of the mother to observe her own difficult experiences and soothe her own frustration, confusion, or disappointment may mean the difference between her navigating the challenging times or distancing herself from her child unconsciously (Brazelton & Cramer, 1990). Self-compassion, which is seen to be the capacity to regard oneself with kindness and understanding rather than with harshness when feelings of pain or failure arise (Neff, 2009), has been hypothesized to be a fundamental component of mindfulness (Hölzel et al., 2011). Self-compassion may contribute to the ability to hold painful thoughts and feelings in mindful awareness when anxious or psychologically threatened without identifying with them (Neff, Kirkpatrick, & Rude, 2007). Self-compassion may play a large role in the formation of well-functioning mother-infant dyads by helping the mother to weather her own emotional challenges as well as disturbances in the relationship.

All of these aspects of mindfulness could be helpful for caregivers who are encountering the complex challenges that must be met for attachment security to be formed in the early period of the caregiver-infant relationship, and to be sustained in the later stages of parenting.

Conclusions and future directions

Mindfulness training in the perinatal period may have beneficial outcomes in the parent-child relationship that reach far beyond the timeframe of the intervention delivery. There are several means by which mindfulness training may have long-term impacts, such as through increasing parental resources during parent-child interactions, and by enhancing attachment security between parent and child. By teaching contemplative practices that provide a means for participating in the activity of parenting in a more attuned way, mindfulness training during this period may provide tools that can be used in childbirth as well as throughout the whole of parenting. Further research, including longitudinal studies of parent-child dyadic functioning and child development outcomes following mindfulness training in the perinatal period, is essential to provide a more thorough understanding of the potential outcomes of such training.

Bibliography

Analayo, B. (2006). Mindfulness in the āali *Nikayas*. In D. K. Nauriyal, M. S. Drummond & Y. B. Lal (Eds.), *Buddhist thought and applied psychological research* (pp. 229–249). New York, NY: Taylor & Francis Routledge.

Baer, R. A., Smith, G. T., Hopkins, J., Krietemeyer, J., & Toney, L. (2006). Using self-report assessment methods to explore facets of mindfulness. *Assessment, 13*(1), 27–45.

Bardacke, N. (2012). *Mindful birthing: Training the mind, body and heart for childbirth and beyond.* New York, NY: HarperCollins.

Benoit, D., & Parker, K. (1994). Stability and transmission of attachment across three generations. *Child Development, 65*(5), 1444–1456.

Bögels, S. M., Lehtonen, A., Restifo, K. (2010). Mindful parenting in mental health care. *Mindfulness, 1*(2), 107–120.

Bowlby, J. (1980). *Attachment and loss:* Vol. 3. *Loss, sadness and depression.* New York, NY: Basic Books.

Bowlby, J. (1982). *Attachment and loss:* Vol. 1. *Attachment* (2nd edition). New York, NY: Basic Books.

Bowlby, J. (1988). *A secure base: Parent-child attachment and healthy human development.* New York, NY: Basic Books.

Brazelton, T. B., & Cramer, B. G. (1990). *The earliest relationship: Parents, infants, and the drama of early attachment.* Boston, MA: DaCapo Press.

Brown, K. W., & Ryan, R. M. (2003). The benefits of being present: Mindfulness and its role in psychological well-being. *Journal of Personality and Social Psychology, 84*(4), 822–848.

Brown, K. W., Ryan, R. M., & Creswell, J. D. (2007). Mindfulness: Theoretical foundations and evidence for its salutory effects. *Psychological Inquiry, 18*(4), 211–237.

Coatsworth, J. D., Duncan, L. G., Greenberg, M. T., & Nix, R. L. (2010). Changing parent's mindfulness, child management skills and relationship quality with their youth: Results from a randomized pilot intervention trial. *Journal of Child and Family Studies, 19*(2), 203–217.

Dawe, S., & Harnett, P. (2007). Reducing potential for child abuse among methadone-maintained parents: Results from a randomized controlled trial. *Journal of Substance Abuse Treatment, 32*(4), 381–390.

Duncan, L. G., & Bardacke, N. (2010). Mindfulness-based childbirth and parenting education: Promoting family mindfulness during the perinatal period. *Journal of Child and Family Studies, 19*(2), 190–202.

Emavardhana, T., & Tori, C. D. (1997). Changes in self-concept, ego defense mechanisms, and religiosity following seven-day Vipassana meditation retreats. *Journal for the Scientific Study of Religion, 36*(2), 194–206.

Feeny, J., Alexander, R., Noller, P., & Hohaus, L. (2003). Attachment insecurity, depression, and the transition to parenthood. *Personal Relationships, 10*(4), 475–493.

Fonagy, P., Gergely, G., Jurist, E., & Target, M. (2002). *Affect regulation, mentalization, and the development of the self.* New York, NY: Other Press.

Fowden, A. L., Giussani, D. A., & Forhead, A. J. (2006). Intrauterine programming of physiological systems: Causes and consequences. *Physiology, 21*(1), 29–37.

Goodman, J. H., Guarino, A., Chenausky, K., Klein, L., Prager, J., Petersen, R., Forqet, A., & Freeman, M. (2014). CALM Pregnancy: Results of a pilot study of mindfulness-based cognitive therapy for perinatal anxiety. *Archives of Women's Mental Health, 17*(5), 373–387.

Gottman, J. M. (1999). *The marriage clinic: A scientifically based marital therapy.* New York, NY: Norton.

Hesse, E. (1999). The adult attachment interview: Historical and current perspectives. In J. Cassidy & P. R. Shaver (Eds.), *Handbook of attachment: Theory, research, and clinical applications* (pp. 395–433). New York, NY: Guilford Press.

Hesse, E. (2008). The adult attachment interview: Protocol, method of analysis, and empirical studies. In J. Cassidy & P. R. Shaver (Eds.), *Handbook of attachment: Theory, research, and clinical applications* (2nd edition, pp. 552–598). New York, NY: Guilford Press.

Hölzel, B. K., Lazar, S. W., Gard, T., Schuman-Olivier, Z., Vago, D. R., & Ott, U. (2011). How does mindfulness meditation work? Proposing mechanisms of action from a conceptual and neural perspective. *Perspectives on Psychological Science, 6*(6), 537–559.

Kabat-Zinn, J. (1990). *Full catastrophe living: Using the wisdom of your body and mind to face stress, pain, and illness.* New York, NY: Delacourt.

Kerr, C. E., Josyula, K., & Littenberg, R. (2011). Developing an observing attitude: An analysis of meditation diaries in an MBSR clinical trial. *Clinical Psychology and Psychotherapy, 18*(1), 80–93.

Lancaster, C. A., Gold, K. J., Flynn, H. A., Yoo, H., Marcus, S. M., & Davis, M. M. (2010). Risk factors for depressive symptoms during pregnancy: A systematic review. *American Journal of Obstetrics and Gynecology, 202*(1), 5–14.

Lieberman, A. F. (1997). Toddler's internalizations of maternal attributions as a factor in quality of attachment. In K. Zucker & L. Atkinson (Eds.), *Attachment and psychopathology* (pp. 277–291). New York, NY: Guilford Press.

Lutz, A., Brefczynski-Lewis, J., Johnstone, T., & Davidson, R. J. (2008). Regulation of the neural circuitry of emotion by compassion meditation: Effects of meditative expertise. *PloS ONE, 3*(3), e1897.

Lyons-Ruth, K. (1999). The two-person unconscious: Intersubjective dialogue, enactive relational representation, and the emergence of new forms of relational organization. *Psychoanalytic Inquiry, 19*(4), 576–617.

Main, M. (1991). Metacognitive knowledge, metacognitive monitoring, and singular (coherent) versus multiple (incoherent) models of attachment: Finding directions for future research. In C. Parkes, J. Stevenson-Hinde & P. Marris (Eds.), *Attachment across the life cycle* (pp. 127–159). New York, NY: Guilford Press.

Main, M., Kaplan, N., & Cassidy, J. (1985). Security in infancy, childhood, and adulthood: A move to the level of representation. In J. Bretherton & E. Waters (Eds.), *Growing Points of Attachment Theory and Research, Monographs of the Society for Research in Child Development, 50*(1–2), 66–104.

Mikulincer, M., & Shaver, P. R. (2007). Reflections on security dynamics: Core constructs, psychological mechanisms, relational contexts, and the need for an integrative theory. *Psychological Inquiry, 18*(3), 139–156.

Miller, G., Lachman, M., Chen, E., Karlamangla, A., & Seeman, T. (2011). Pathways to resilience: Maternal nurturance as a buffer against the effects of childhood poverty on metabolic syndrome at midlife. *Psychological Science, 22*(12), 1591–1599.

Nanamoli, B., & Bodhi, B. (Trans.) (1995). *The middle-length discourses of the Buddha: A new translation of the Majjhima Nikaya.* Boston, MA: Wisdom Publications.

Neff, K. D. (2009). The role of self-compassion in development: A healthier way to relate to oneself. *Human Development, 52*(4), 211–214.

Neff, K. D., Kirkpatrick, K. L., & Rude, S. S. (2007). Self-compassion and adaptive psychological functioning. *Journal of Research in Personality, 41*(1), 139–154.

Perez-Blasco, J., Viguer, P., & Rodrigo, M. F. (2013). Effects of a mindfulness-based intervention on psychological distress, well-being, and maternal self-efficacy I breast- feeding mothers: Results of a pilot study. *Archives of Women's Mental Health, 16*(3), 227–236.

Shaddix, C., Duncan, L. G., Cook, J. G., & Bardacke, N. (2014). *Mindfulness training in the prenatal period increases parental awareness, self-regulation, and flexibility in the process of parent-child attunement.* Poster presented at the 2nd biennial International Symposium for Contemplative Studies. Boston, MA.

Shaver, P. R., Lavy, S., Saron, C. D., & Mikulincer, M. (2007). Social foundations of the capacity for mindfulness: An attachment perspective. *Psychological Inquiry, 18*(4), 264–271.

Siegel, D. (1999). *The developing mind.* New York, NY: Guilford Press.

Siegel, D. (2007). *The mindful brain: Reflection and attunement in the cultivation of well-being.* New York, NY: Norton.

Siegel, D., & Hartzell, M. (2003). *Parenting from the inside out: How a deeper self-understanding can help you raise children who thrive.* New York, NY: Penguin.

Singh, N. N., Lancioni, G. E., Winton, A. S., Fisher, B. C., Wahler, R. G., McAleavey, K., Singh, J., & Sabaawi, M. (2006). Mindful parenting decreases aggression, noncompliance, and self-injury in children with autism. *Journal of Emotional and Behavioral Disorders, 14*(3), 169–177.

Singh, N. N., Lancioni, G. E., Winton, A. S., Singh, J., Curtis, W. J., Wahler, R. G., & McAleavey, K. M. (2007). Mindful parenting decreases aggression and increases social behavior in children with developmental disabilities. *Behavior Modification, 31*(6), 749–771.

Singh, N. N., Singh, A. N., Lancioni, G. I., Singh, J. W., Winton, A. S., & Adkins, A. D. (2010). Mindfulness training for parents and their children with ADHD increases the children's compliance. *Journal of Child and Family Studies, 19*(2), 157–166.

Slade, A. (2000). The development and organization of attachment: Implications for psychoanalysis. *Journal of the American Psychoanalytic Association, 48*(4), 1147–1174.

Snyder, R., Shapiro, S., & Treleaven, T. (2011). Attachment theory and mindfulness. *Journal of Child and Family Studies, 21*(5), 709–717.

Sodian, B., & Kristen, S. (2010). Theory of mind. In B. Glatzeder, V. Goel, & A. Müller (Eds.), *Towards a theory of thinking* (pp. 189–201). Berlin: Springer.

Vieten, C., & Astin, J. (2008). Effects of a mindfulness-based intervention during pregnancy on prenatal stress and mood: Results of a pilot study. *Archives of Women's Mental Health, 11*(1), 67–74.

Wachs, K., & Cordova, J. V. (2007). Mindful relating: Exploring mindfulness and emotion repertoires in intimate relationships. *Journal of Marital and Family Therapy, 33*(4), 464–481.

Wallace, B. A., & Shapiro, S. L. (2006). Mental balance and well-being. *American Psychologist, 61*(7), 690–701.

Williams, K. L., & Wahler, R. G. (2010). Are mindful parents more authoritative and less authoritarian? An analysis of clinic-referred mothers. *Journal of Child and Family Studies, 19*(2), 230–235.

4

MINDFULNESS AND PERFORMANCE

Amy L. Baltzell

Introduction

This chapter provides an overview of the study of mindfulness within the realm of performance. Performance can be conceptualized as competing against others or executing skills to the best of one's abilities (e.g. athlete, dancer or musician) in a public event in which individuals or groups aspire to win and/or optimally execute their skills and abilities. There has been a growing interest in exploring the benefits of a mindfulness approach to enhance psychological preparation for optimizing performance.

The burgeoning interest in mindfulness, in general, aligns with the field of positive psychology, which is concerned with happiness, positive human development and flourishing. Though the majority of empirical research in mindfulness has been focused on clinical issues (Baer, 2003; Keng, Smoski, & Robin, 2011), whether psychological issues or physical ailments, there also has been a focus on the benefits of mindfulness for healthy people. For example in a meta-analysis, Chiesa and Serretti (2009) explored the efficacy of mindfulness-based stress reduction (MBSR) with healthy participants. For non-clinical participants (absence of psychological or medical issues) MBSR participation resulted in reduced stress, enhanced spiritual values, reduced ruminative thinking and trait anxiety, and enhanced empathy and self-compassion.

Mindfulness interventions designed to help athletes and other performers optimize performance are a relatively new application. Applying mindfulness approaches within the performance realm has helped performers cope with competitive pressure (e.g. Gardner & Moore, 2012), experience increased flow, and become more engaged in their moment-to-moment experience (e.g. Kaufman, Glass, & Arnkoff, 2009); it has also enhanced the quality of their performance, ranging from the athletic field (e.g. John, Verma, & Khanna, 2011) to the musician's stage (e.g. Langer, Russel, & Eisenkraft, 2009). An overview of mindfulness research across performance realms, which typically relies on an Eastern/Buddhist approach to mindfulness, along with consideration of future applications of Langerian mindfulness will be provided.

Sport and athletics have been the focus of most published accounts of mindfulness interventions within the performance realm. The focus on sport versus other performance realms may be due less to sportspeople's inherent interest in mindfulness, and more that sport psychology is the most formalized pathway of studying mindfulness-based interventions and approaches within the performance realm (e.g. Gardner & Moore, 2012; Pineau, Glass & Kaufman, 2014). Thus the review of empirical support is heavily weighted on research that intentionally used athlete participants.

Most interventions within the performance realm are based on an aspect of Eastern/Buddhist mindfulness, with an emphasis on intentional acceptance of present moment experience. Much of this current work was drawn directly from the work of Jon Kabat-Zinn, with such sport interventions inspired by either formal mindfulness meditation practice or Kabat-Zinn's MBSR. MBSR has served as the intervention for a majority of non-performance mindfulness studies, with a focus on improving medical or psychological disorders (see Keng et al., 2011). Specifically in sport, researchers implement formal mindfulness meditation training (e.g. Aherne, Moran, & Lonsdale, 2011; Kabat-Zinn, Beall, & Rippe, 1985; Stankovic & Baltzell, 2015), programs modeled after Kabat-Zinn's MBSR program (e.g. Kaufman's Mindful Sport Performance Enhancement [MSPE]) or they have implemented the MAC approach to sport (e.g. Gardner & Moore, 2007), modeled after Hayes's (2004) acceptance commitment therapy (ACT). A more detailed description of these interventions will be presented later in the chapter.

Kabat-Zinn (2005) defines mindfulness as "an open-hearted, moment-to-moment non-judgmental awareness" (p. 24). Such awareness requires an acceptance of what is occurring, which can be conceptualized as, ". . . taking a stance of non-judgmental awareness and actively embracing the experience of thoughts, feelings and bodily sensations as they occur" (Hayes, Strohsahl, Bunting, Twohig, & Wilson, 2004, p. 7). With the practice of *allowing,* and not resisting internal and external experience, the individual can learn to experience a changed relationship to emotions, thoughts, patterns of thoughts and habitual reactions.

Kabat-Zinn, Beall and Rippe (1985) were the first on record to use mindfulness meditation training within the modern performance realm. Rowers preparing for the Olympics were given group introduction to the meditation practice, provided guided mindfulness meditation for daily use, and had access to guided daily practice at the Olympic Games. The U.S. Olympic team rowers, some of whom were medalists, reported the usefulness of mindfulness meditation in preparing them for Olympic level racing (Kabat-Zinn et al., 1985).

Why mindfulness training in sport? Anxiety

It took about 20 years for other sport psychology researchers to take an interest and, subsequently, conduct empirical studies focused on athlete participants. The most studied intervention in sport is based on Hayes's (2004) ACT: Clinical sport psychologists Frank Gardner and Zella Moore (2004, 2007, 2012) created the MAC approach – a seven module protocol developed to help athletes learn to effectively cope with aversive feelings and thoughts to enable optimized performance.

Anxiety is an essential issue addressed by the MAC approach in sport. Trying to help performers cope more effectively is not a new concern within applied sport psychology research and practice. Anxiety-based symptom reduction is of great interest to sport and performance consultants and psychologists. Typically, performance anxiety is the sole emotion addressed in sport psychology textbooks (e.g. Weinburg & Gould, 2015), with such textbooks consistently replete with theoretical models that explain the "arousal and performance" relationship. And of particular interest in these models is the mediating factor of performance anxiety, in the performance-arousal relationship, including emotions, thoughts, and patterns of thought that threaten to thwart athletic performance. When athletes focus on negative thoughts and emotions, the ability to focus on task-relevant and/or performance-relevant cues greatly diminishes (Gardner & Moore, 2007). Distraction from sport-relevant cues due to aversive emotion is also supported by the concept of choking in sport (Hill, Hanton, Fleming, & Matthews, 2009). Choking in sport occurs when the athlete *perceives* the given athletic demand to exceed their resources and their attention becomes inflexibly focused on internal, narrow concerns – which can result in the athlete getting caught up in fears and unable to focus effectively on task-relevant cues (Williams, Nideffer, Wilson, & Sagal, 2014). An interest in mindfulness interventions in sport is born out of a practical need to find alternate solutions to help athletes cope effectively with such debilitating outcomes of performance anxiety.

In the past 10 years some researchers and practitioners have created mindfulness interventions (e.g. Gardner & Moore, 2007) to address such cognitive-emotional disruption in sport – a distinctly different approach from traditional cognitive behavioral interventions in performance psychology. Goal setting, imagery/mental rehearsal, arousal control, self-talk and pre-contemplative routines (e.g. Anderson, 2005; Orlick & Partington, 1988) are typically used as "control-based" interventions, used to control or change thoughts with the goal of addressing performance related issues (Gardner & Moore, 2012; Wegner, 1994). The efficacy of this cognitive behavioral approach may be less effective with aversive emotions given such an approach leads performers to suppress or control unwanted negative thoughts and/or emotions to improve performance (Craft, Magyar, Becker, & Feltz, 2003). Though there remains a great interest in implementing control-based cognitive behavioral interventions to address performance anxiety, mindfulness interventions to enhance performance are gaining international attention (see Baltzell, 2016).

With clear evidence of the reduction in anxiety symptoms from mindfulness meditation interventions in clinical populations (Baer, 2003; Keng et al., 2011), it is logical that there would be an interest in the performance community to look to mindfulness interventions as an alternate intervention to address the challenges associated with performance anxiety. Clinical and medical issues are quite different from high-pressure demands in performance realms and the reduction in anxiety that results from the practice of a formal, sedentary mindfulness practice. How does mindfulness practice contribute to the dynamic needs of performers while they are engaged in their performance realm – from the dancer on stage to the golfer preparing to take a put?

Optimizing performance and anxiety

Enhanced mental efficiency is the ultimate performance benefit of mindfulness practices (Gardner & Moore, 2012). With less attention on aversive emotions such as fears, anxiety and self-doubt (resulting from a mindful practice and approach) the athlete's attention is gradually freed up to place more attention on the task at hand. By cultivating acceptance of external events and internal information, mindfulness training can help the performer reduce distraction and thus focus more effectively on relevant moment-to-moment information for best performance (Bernier, Thienot, Codron, & Fournier, 2009). Experiencing less frequent and intense negative thoughts, a complementary benefit of mindfulness practice, may also support enhanced mental efficiency (Frewen, Evans, Maraj, Dozois, & Partridge, 2008).

The one place that may most benefit from a mindfulness approach, instead of a control-based strategy, is in high-pressure performance events that elicit anxiety or similar cognitive-emotional, aversive internal experiences for some performers. When athletes or performers must be able to give full attention to the task at hand and are temporarily distracted by elaborate processing (Bishop et al., 2004), such as unintentionally bringing to mind fears of failure or self-doubt, they need a pathway to re-focus on performance demands. Being able to simply accept such unintentional thinking and bring one's focus back to the task at hand may be the key contribution that a mindfulness approach brings to helping the individual optimize performance.

Elizabeth Stanley (2014), whose research has primarily focused on helping soldiers cope with life threatening encounters, brings to light the essential element of courage when faced with challenges in high stress environments. Focused on the challenge of military service – from threats of personal safety to inflicting harm, and sometimes death, on others – she emphasizes the myriad detriments of military stress and the curative benefits of mindfulness practices. Stanley points to two key benefits of a mindfulness approach: "attentional control and tolerance for challenging experience" (p. 970).

Similarly, the call to not suppress, but instead re-focus on the task at hand in sport, was also called for over 30 years ago by social psychologist Albert Bandura (1986). He stated, "The cognitive control task is to stop rumination over a mistake or failure, which is likely to breed only further mistakes . . . efforts to control unwanted thoughts by suppressing them can backfire because such attempts only draw attention to them or create reminders of them. People can better rid themselves of disruptive thinking by concentrating their attention on the task at hand and generating helpful thinking" (p. 391). Bandura wisely advises the athlete to develop the ability to intentionally focus on the task at hand. Mindfulness training offers an avenue for athletes, and performers, to do just that – particularly when facing performance anxiety.

Mindfulness training in sport has been born out of the commitment to offer interventions that are effective when helping athletes cope with intense, aversive and distracting emotions and thoughts. Mindfulness interventions in sport are focused on helping the performer change or modify their relationship with moment-to-moment experience (e.g. Baltzell, Caraballo, Chipman, & Hayden, 2014; Gardner & Moore, 2007). Specifically, mindfulness training in performance enhancement involves strengthening non-judgmental awareness and acceptance of in-the-moment cognitive, affective and sensory experiences, and this awareness is expected, ultimately, to be useful to aid performance during competitive situations by freeing up the athlete's attention to focus on task-relevant cues, moment to moment (Gardner & Moore, 2004, 2007).

Mindfulness and performance: empirical support

Mindfulness-based research in sport offers a wide range of mindfulness meditation interventions (e.g. Aherne, Moran, & Lonsdale, 2011; Baltzell, Caraballo et al., 2014; Gardner & Moore, 2007; John et al., 2011; Kabat-Zinn et al., 1985; Kaufman et al., 2009). The main interventions include formal (traditional) mindfulness meditation (MM). In such practices participants sit or lie down for a specified period of time and are guided by an instructor, guided by an audio-tape or self-guided to observe physical sensations, sounds, emotions and thoughts with an interested, open-hearted, accepting-present-moment focus.

Audio-tapes and formal mindfulness meditation practice

Though enhancing performance is of utmost interest, only a few studies to date have directly demonstrated enhanced performance resulting from a mindfulness-based intervention. These same studies also have used traditional, formal MM as the sole intervention. In John, Verma and Khanna's (2011) experimental study, elite Indian pistol shooters increased shooting performance and decreased pre-competitive stress after completing 20-minute daily group sessions of MM training over a 4-week period. The MM training was formal with all members of the experimental group, together, meditating each morning in a climate controlled room. With a total of 96 athletes participating in the study, performance in mean score of pistol shooting improved for the MM group ($p < .001$), compared to the control group, and similarly, salivary cortisol levels significantly decreased (John et al., 2011).

In another formal MM intervention in sport, using guided audio-files, Stankovic and Baltzell (2015) conducted a mindfulness meditation study with masters-level, adult female tennis players. The experimental group ($n = 43$) listened to a pre-recorded 10-minute MM audio-tape daily over an 8-week period while the control group ($n = 39$) listened daily to a pre-recorded 10-minute audio-tape focused on tennis coaching tips. The experimental group won significantly more games and matches ($p < .001$) compared to the controls. Total wins and losses were tallied from the end of the intervention over a subsequent 7-week period (see Table 4.1).

TABLE 4.1 Games and matches won and lost, 7-weeks post-intervention

	Intervention	Control
Games won	449	242
Matches won	211	99
Games lost	188	428
Matches lost	120	205

In addition the experimental group significantly increased ($p < .001$) in mindfulness, measured by the Mindful Attention and Awareness Scale (Brown & Ryan, 2003), and significantly decreased in frequency of negative thoughts as measured by the University of British Columbia Cognitive Inventory – 'Letting Go' Revised Version (Woody, Taylor, McLean, & Koch, 1998). And finally, based on regression analysis, athletes with higher levels of mindfulness also won more games and matches (Stankovic & Baltzell, 2015).

Two other studies, using only MM, indicated other performance related benefits. Aherne et al. (2011) conducted a quasi-experimental mindfulness-based intervention with elite athletes. Participants completed a 10-minute daily MM and a 30-minute weekly MM exercise for 6 weeks. The athletes used a CD-guided MM created by Kabat-Zinn and colleagues (Williams, Teasdale, Segal, & Kabat-Zinn, 2007), thus the intervention also was a formal, MM intervention practiced individually. The meditation group experienced significantly more flow post-intervention, with flow assessed using Flow State Scale-2 (FSS-2; Jackson & Eklund, 2004). And Baltzell and LoVerme-Ahktar (2014) studied the impact of an MM intervention with collegiate soccer players: The program ran for 6 weeks, with two 30-minute sessions per week. The athletes showed increased mindfulness scores, with the Mindful Attention Awareness Scale (MAAS) used to assess mindfulness. Mindfulness Meditation Training in Sport (MMTS) includes both formal MM practice and focused compassion exercises based on Paul Gilbert's work (e.g. Gilbert, 2010), founder of compassion focused therapy.

Mindful sport performance enhancement (MSPE)

Mindful Sport Performance Enhancement (MSPE) is a mindfulness meditation training program designed for athletes (Kaufman et al., 2009), which was initially a 2.5-hour session per week, 4-week program, and has been revised to a 6-week, 90-minutes per week program (Kaufman, Glass, & Pineau, 2016) in which part of the time is spent in formal MM practices. MSPE is modeled closely after Kabat-Zinn's MBSR program (e.g. formal sitting meditation, walking mediation, and body scans) with an addition of directed discussions within sessions about application to sport.

Research conducted on MPSE has resulted in performance related benefits, including enhanced dispositional mindfulness and state flow for archers, while golfers experienced a reduction in somatic anxiety and thought disruption and increases in sport confidence, dispositional optimism and mindfulness (Kaufman et al., 2009), In addition, mindfulness increased and sport related worries decreased for runners (De Petrillo, Kaufman, Glass, & Arnkoff, 2009). Thompson, Kaufman, De Petrillo, Glass and Arnkoff (2011) conducted a follow up study with the runners and 50% of the athletes had significantly higher mindfulness scores and the runners' mile times were significantly faster than at pre-test assessment, at the 1-year follow up.

The mindfulness acceptance commitment (MAC) in sport

Based theoretically on Hayes's acceptance commitment therapy (ACT) (Hayes, 2004), Gardner and Moore (2004, 2007) adopted ACT for the sport realm and entitled their approach, the Mindful Acceptance Commitment (MAC) approach in sport. The MAC approach is currently the most heavily researched mindfulness-based intervention in sport (see Gardner & Moore, 2012). With the goal of helping athletes optimize performance, the MAC approach was designed to help athletes self-regulate attention during sport performance. This mindfulness-based approach facilitates athletes' acceptance of potentially aversive internal experiences (i.e. thoughts, feelings, and sensations) and, instead of trying to suppress and change them, committing to personally valued actions that support performance (see Gardner & Moore, 2007). The MAC approach includes educational, self-reflective and mindfulness practices that are delivered one-on-one over seven modules.

Both ACT and MAC stand on the shoulders of relational frame theory: Humans relate to their environment through language and derive relational meaning between and among external experiences (Hayes, 2004). Hayes (2004) summarizes, "When we think, reason, speak with meaning, or listen with understanding, we do so by deriving relations among events – among words and events, words and words, events and events" (p. 649). Thus, when applied to sport, athletes can create generalized meanings in performance contexts that cause great internal unease and discomfort, which can manifest in performance anxiety.

The MAC approach, following ACT, uses a mindfulness approach to address such internal angst, which can become evident as either *cognitive fusion*, "the strangle hold of literal verbal meaning of thoughts", or *experiential avoidance*, "the attempt to escape or avoid private events" (Hayes, 2004, p. 650). The performer's relationship to thoughts becomes the problem, not the thoughts themselves. Hayes (2004) notes, "It is the tendency to take these experiences literally and then to fight against them that is viewed as harmful" (p. 651).

Thoughts such as "I'll never be able to win this one" or "I hate this, all I want to do is quit", thus, are not the problem. The problem in performance occurs when an athlete has such a thought and then gets tangled up in the belief that such thoughts are the unequivocal truth. Uninvited, unintentional, harsh, destructive thoughts are quite common for performers, based on my experience as a sport psychologist. When destructive, critical thoughts emerge they can often result in 'performance dukkha'. I conceptualize *performance dukkha* as the psychic pain and performance distraction that athletes experience as a function of over-engaging with or trying to avoid such aversive, internal sport experiences. And, in concert with ACT, the MAC approach emphasizes the importance of allowing such thoughts to occur – thus minimizing such performance dukkha – and, at once, committing to value-driven behaviors instead of getting lost (and distracted) by difficult internal psychological experiences.

Single case studies comprise the majority of MAC-based studies with many reported positive results including a springboard diver's enhanced performance (Schwanhausser, 2009); a male swimmer's reported decrease in worry and increased enjoyment of sport experience and a female power lifter's personal best lift (Gardner & Moore, 2004); and improved coach rated performance (Lutkenhouse, 2007). Bigger sample studies ($n = 11$) have also resulted in improved coach rated performance for women's field hockey and volleyball players (for more in-depth consideration of the MAC approach, please refer to Gardner & Moore, 2007, 2012; Moore & Gardner, 2014).

Mindfulness and acceptance combined with psychological skills training (PST)

Bernier and colleagues (2009) implemented a time intensive traditional PST program with mindfulness and acceptance concepts with seven national golfers. Season 1 focused on PST (i.e. goal setting, imagery) and season 2 focused on mindfulness and acceptance post-intervention; all seven golfers increased their national ranking. Improved performance may be a result of participants' heightened attention to relevant internal and external sport context information. Bernier and colleagues' (2009) study points to the possibility that combining a traditional PST and mindfulness approach may offer great, practical benefits to the performer.

Mindfulness interventions: design and dosage in sport

Mindfulness training within sport is greatly varied, with interventions ranging from exclusively traditional sitting mindfulness meditation (e.g. Aherne et al., 2011; Kabat-Zinn et al., 1985) to a clinical approaches focused on mindfulness and acceptance (e.g. Gardner & Moore, 2007). It may be that a range of mindfulness approaches are beneficial for particular performance challenges facing the performer, though to date we do not know which mindfulness approach or how much practice is most efficacious regarding performance factors such as cultivating flow, reducing performance anxiety and/or, ultimately, enhancing performance itself.

One current concern is the dosage of mindfulness practice and duration of the program. Most of the sport interventions to date, in terms of dosage, are quite time intensive. For example, MSPE began with four 2.5-hour training sessions, including 45 to 90 minutes of mindfulness-based practices. More recently the MSPE, designed for group or team interventions, has been redesigned to six, 90-minute sessions (Kaufman et al., 2016). The MAC approach includes seven modules, requiring up to 12 sessions conducted one-on-one, with an emphasis on an educational, prompted self-reflective intervention with the integration of brief, traditional MM practices. The MM session in Kabat-Zinn and colleagues' (1985) intervention included 30-minute sessions, with one or two recommended daily independent practice sessions of 15 minutes. Such time intensive demands may make such approaches untenable for some athletes or performers.

In sport, only a few studies have implemented a relatively low dose of MM (20 minutes or less), including a 20-minute daily group session of MM training over a 4-week period (John et al., 2011), a 10-minute mindfulness exercise most days per week and a 30-minute mindfulness exercise once per week over a 6-week period (Aherne et al., 2011), and 10 minutes of formal practice within a 30-minute session twice a week (Baltzell & LoVerme-Ahktar, 2014).

These lower MM dose studies in sport indicate benefits. However, we don't yet know the best dosage per session of MM paired with the optimal number of sessions for offering clear performance benefits. The non-sport, general literature offers initial support for brief MM interventions concerning both duration and number of sessions (10 to 20 minutes over 3 to 4 days), resulting in benefits such as anxiety reduction (e.g. Zeidan, Johnson, Diamond, David, & Goolkasian, 2010) and reduction in psychological stress (e.g. Creswell, Pacilio, Lindsay, & Brown, 2014). Next steps in sport and other performance realms will be to explore brief MM interventions geared toward performance related benefits for athletes and performers to make such an intervention more feasible.

Participant experience of MMTS

How does the competitive athlete respond to being introduced to sitting MM? What aspects of such a program are compelling or difficult for the athlete? Baltzell, Caraballo et al. (2014) conducted a qualitative study of Division I female soccer players who participated in a 6-week MM program for sport entitled Mindfulness Meditation Training in Sport (MMTS), for 30 minutes two times per week. Athletes' receptiveness and perception of the impact of the mindfulness practice in sport emerged from thematic analysis of interview data.

Frustration was a typical complaint of the athletes when asked about their initial participation in MMTS: They had a difficult time understanding how to meditate and the connection between formal meditation practice and sport performance. The frustration makes sense, given the athletes were mandated to participate in the program by their head coach. Yet, they reported benefits: Enhanced ability to accept and experience a different relationship with negative emotions, both on and off the field, was a common experience. One athlete noted, "I think that [meditation] helped me, just because I wasn't always focusing on all the bad stuff and I was able to kind of let it go" (Baltzell, Caraballo et al., 2014, p. 231). Sub-themes of benefits from the female collegiate soccer players participating in MMTS included being "able to accept (negative feelings), calm down" and "decide how to react" and being more "able to move past negative occurrences on the field". Following prompts regarding future program recommendations, the athletes offered specific suggestions including not offering the program after practice and before dinner, extending the numbers of sessions for group MM practices, and making a clear connection between formal sitting practice and on-field performance early in the training.

Mindfulness and flow

A paucity of studies have offered a clear connection between mindfulness and performance, with only a few exceptions reported to date (e.g. John et al., 2011; Stankovic & Baltzell, manuscript submitted), perhaps because experimental studies with a traditional mindfulness-based (MM or clinical) intervention in competitive sport are difficult to secure because of time constraints, understanding and/or interest.

The state of flow, however, correlates strongly with optimal performance (e.g. Bakker, Oerlemans, Demerouti, Slot, Ali, & Ali, 2011) and mindfulness (Kee & Wang, 2008), and research in flow in sport has already been established (e.g. Jackson, 1992, 1995). Being mindful shares many core features with flow, namely being fully present and interested in moment-to-moment experience. Mihaly Csikszentmihalyi (1975, 1999), who coined the term flow, describes flow as "a particular kind of experience that is so engrossing and enjoyable that it becomes autotelic, that is, worth doing for its own sake even though it may have no consequence outside itself"(1999, p. 824).

Thus, the study of the relationship between mindfulness and flow has recently garnered strong attention in the research of sport (e.g. Kaufman et al., 2009; Kee & Wang, 2008; Langer et al., 2009) because of the aligned relationship between optimal performance and flow experiences. Why study flow and mindfulness in sport? Understanding factors that contribute to performance is essential in performance psychology. Given we know that flow aligns with optimal performance and that mindfulness is aligned with flow, then it is logical to want to understand if mindfulness cultivates flow (which in turn would, subsequently, be hypothesized to enhance performance).

Thus, there is strong interest in the relationship between mindfulness and flow, the state of full engagement, often associated with best or peak sport performance (Jackson & Csikszentmihalyi, 1999). A positive relationship between mindfulness and flow in sport has emerged in more recent mindfulness and sport research (Kaufman et al., 2009; Kee & Wang, 2008). Some authors suggest that the mindfulness–flow relationship may be mediated by self-efficacy and sport confidence (Pineau, Glass, Kaufman, & Bernal, 2014). Regardless, in Aherne, Moran and Lonsdale's (2011) experimental study, the MM group of high performance athletes reported significantly greater flow states after using mindfulness training, a Kabat-Zinn MM audiotape for 6 weeks.

Bernier and colleagues (2009) conducted interviews with 10 French national training center swimmers regarding their optimal swimming experience. In addition to the eight dimensions of flow (Jackson & Csikszentmihalyi, 1999), mindfulness emerged as a ninth dimension, an awareness and acceptance of somatic experience prior to performing. Bernier and colleagues' (2009) study suggests that the experience of flow and being mindful (on a focused performance) may almost be synonymous within the optimal performance experience itself.

How then is flow cultivated? Susan Jackson (1992, 1995) conducted landmark studies on flow in sport, which offered an initial understanding of flow antecedents. Some of the factors that prime the flow experience offered by Jackson (2012) include *being well prepared, the right level of intensity, high motivation, a clear performance plan, staying focused on the task at hand, and managing distractions* (Flow and Performance section, para. 4). There is initial evidence that mindfulness approaches that cultivate an open acceptance of moment-to-moment experience may help performers cultivate being more mindful which, in turn, would facilitate both pre-performance and performance relationships to thoughts, feelings and somatic cues for prompting flow, and at once enhance performance in sport (e.g. Baltzell, Caraballo, Chipman, & Hayden, 2014; Kaufman et al., 2009).

Langerian and Eastern/Buddhist mindfulness in 21st-century performance

Ellen Langer offers a very different understanding of mindfulness, which has not yet been embraced by researchers in performance psychology (Pineau, Glass, & Kaufman, 2014). She defines mindfulness as "a process of actively making novel distinctions about objects in one's awareness" (Langer, Cohen, & Djikic, 2012, p. 1114). According to this, a Langerian conceptualization of mindfulness – improved focus, presence and openness to novelty – would be expected to enhance performance of all kinds because of the fresh engagement with one's experience (Langer et al., 2009). How would noticing novel stimuli help cultivate mindfulness?

In 2009, Langer and colleagues found strong support for the value of a Langerian mindful approach for highly skilled performers, in the realm of orchestral musicians performing in front of an audience. Langer purposefully chose a group of performers who were expected to be both reliably highly skilled and who performed low-challenge tasks, performing the same score of music literally hundreds of times per year. In their study, the 60 orchestra players played Brahms's Symphony No. 1 twice. In the intervention condition the musicians were prompted to play in the "finest manner [they could], offering subtle new nuances to [their] performance" and in the control condition the musicians were prompted to "think about the finest performance of this piece that [they could] remember, and try to play it" (p. 127).

The subtle nuances in performance were preferred by the orchestral musicians and the audience compared to the more uninspired, robotic, pre-programmed approach. Langer and colleagues (2009) offer convincing preliminary evidence that noticing new stimuli can also contribute to performance for unpressured, well-learned goal-oriented tasks. Helping performers re-engage in well-learned tasks from a wide range of disciplines is ripe with possibility for offering an approach to improve performance.

Csikszentmihalyi's (1975) flow model offers a framework for understanding the benefits of both Eastern/Buddhist mindfulness and Langerian mindfulness for performance (e.g. Moore & Gardner, 2014 and Langer et al., 2009, respectively). When considered in the framework of the flow model, an understanding of the relationship between challenge and skill is essential. When perceived challenge is greater than perceived skill, anxiety results. When perceived skill is greater than perceived challenge, boredom results. When there is a balance of challenge and skill, flow is hypothesized to emerge (see Jackson & Csikszentmihalyi, 1999). The Eastern/ Buddhist mindfulness approach, applied to sport, helps with focus and concentration on the task at hand by helping athletes tolerate unpleasant thoughts, feelings and physical sensations and thereby helps them move from feeling over-challenged (and anxious) towards a more engaged (flow) state.

However, there has been minimal consideration of interventions for those athletes who are under-challenged – when perceived skill far exceeds perceived challenges. In Csikszentmihalyi's (1975) flow model, being under-challenged results in boredom and under-performance. This is just the issue that Langer and colleagues sought out (highly skilled and under-challenged musicians) and found a solution for: having orchestra musicians intentionally paying attention to what is novel. Such a focus, within the framework of performing a musical piece, resulted in better performance (compared to trying to re-create best past performance). Langerian mindfulness and the Eastern/Buddhist approach to mindfulness may offer different pathways to fully engage, moment to moment, within the performance realm.

Conclusion

There is great variation in the types of mindfulness-based interventions offered that could contribute to performers' wellbeing and performance. These range from the clinical approach adopted in sport (i.e. the MAC approach), to traditional mindfulness meditation practices (e.g. Kabat-Zinn, 2005), and to the intentional attendance to novel stimuli as championed by Langer (e.g. Langer et al., 2009).

There is much to be learned about the efficacy of mindfulness practices in performance and matching mindfulness intervention type to the needs of the performer within the performance context. We need to consider factors such as matching the mindfulness practice for the challenge of the performer, quantifying the best dose of practice and duration of program (for MM interventions), and expanding the research beyond sport to areas of performance such as dance, music, acting and teaching. Regardless of the mindfulness approach, helping performers be open, accepting and interested in performance experiences offers them enhanced opportunities to better engage in routine, mundane tasks (e.g. Langer et al., 2009), tolerate aversive internal stimuli and still perform well (e.g. Gardner & Moore, 2007) and increase the likelihood of experiencing flow (Aherns, Moran, & Lonsdale, 2011).

Though presented in the literature as opposing approaches (Gardner & Moore, 2012), it is most likely that mindfulness approaches paired with mental skills can be efficacious (Baltzell, McCarthy, & Greenbaum, 2014). This hypothesis is warranted when considering one of the main findings from Kee and Wang's (2008) study showing that athletes with higher levels of mindfulness were also more likely to value traditional mental skills training (e.g. self-talk; imagery). In addition, Bernier and colleagues' (2009) study, which implemented an integration of both a PST program (e.g. self-talk; visualization) along with mindfulness and acceptance, resulted in better performance (compared to PST only). Instead of having to choose between cognitive behavioral interventions and mindfulness, we need to continue to develop a better understanding of how to integrate mindfulness approaches into performance interventions. Current research suggests that addressing issues of cognitive-emotional distress in performance with Eastern/Buddhist-based mindfulness interventions may be most helpful. And, though only supported by preliminary research, a Langerian approach may be most efficacious for helping elite performers better engage and optimize performance in well-learned, low-challenge tasks. In essence, as noted by Stanley (2014), mindfulness practices can cultivate two essential abilities that can enhance performance: attentional control and tolerance for challenging experiences.

Bibliography

Aherne, C., Moran, A., & Lonsdale, C. (2011). The effect of mindfulness training on athletes' flow: An initial investigation. *The Sport Psychologist, 25*, 177–189.

Anderson, M. (Ed.) (2005). *Sport psychology in practice*. Champaign, IL: Human Kinetics.

Baer, R. A. (2003). Mindfulness training as a clinical intervention: A conceptual and empirical review. *Clinical Psychology: Science and Practice, 10*, 125–143.

Bakker, A. B., Oerlemans, W., Demerouti, E., Slot, B. B., Ali, D. D., & Ali, D. K. (2011). Flow and performance: A study among talented Dutch soccer players. *Psychology of Sport and Exercise, 12*, 442–450.

Baltzell, A. L. (2016). *The Cambridge companion to mindfulness and performance*. New York, NY: Cambridge University Press.

Baltzell, A. L., Caraballo, N., Chipman, K., & Hayden, L. (2014). A qualitative study of the Mindfulness Meditation Training for Sport (MMTS): Division I female soccer players' experience. *Journal of Clinical Sport Psychology, 8*(3), 221–244.

Baltzell, A. L., & LoVerme-Ahktar, V. (2014). Mindfulness Meditation Training for Sport (MMTS) intervention: Impact of MMTS with division I female athletes has been successfully submitted online and is presently being given full consideration for publication. *Journal of Happiness and Well-being, 2*(2), 160–173.

Baltzell, A. B., McCarthy, J. M., & Greenbaum, T. (2014). Mindfulness strategies: Consulting with coaches and athletes: Background and presentation of the 2013 AASP annual convention workshop. *Journal of Sport Psychology in Action, 5*(3), 147–155.

Bandura, A. (1986). *Social foundations of thought and action: A social cognitive theory*. Englewood Cliffs, NJ: Prentice-Hall.

Bandura, A. (1997). *Self-efficacy: The exercise of control*. New York, NY: Freeman.

Bernier, M., Thienot, E., Codron, R., & Fournier, J. (2009). Mindfulness and acceptance approaches in sport performance. *Journal of Clinical Sport Psychology, 4*, 320–333.

Bishop, S. R., Lau, M., Shapiro, S., Carlson, L., Anderson, N. D., Carmody, J., Segal, S. V., Abbey, S., Speca, M., Velting, D., Devins, G. (2004). Mindfulness: A proposed operational definition. *Clinical Psychology: Science and Practice, 11*, 230–241.

Brown, K. W. & Ryan, R. M. (2003). The benefits of being present: Mindfulness and its role in psychological well-being. *Journal of Personality and Social Psychology, 84*(4), 822–848.

Chiesa, A., & Serretti, A. (2009). Mindfulness-based stress reduction for stress management in healthy people: A review and meta-analysis. *The Journal of Alternative and Complementary Medicine, 15*(5), 593–600. doi:10.1089/acm.2008.0495

Craft, L. L., Magyar, T. M., Becker, B. J., & Feltz, D. L. (2003). The relationship between the Competitive State Anxiety Inventory-2 and sport performance: A meta-analysis. *Journal of Sport and Exercise Psychology, 25*, 44–65.

Creswell, D., Pacilio, L., Lindsay, E., & Brown, K. W. (2014). Brief mindfulness meditation training alters psychological and neuroendocrine responses to social evaluative stress. *Psychoneuroendocrinology, 44*, 1–12. doi:10.1016/j.psyneuen.2014.02.007

Csikszentmihalyi, M. (1975). *Beyond boredom and anxiety.* Washington, DC: Jossey-Bass.

Csikszentmihalyi, M. (1999). If we are so rich, why aren't we happy? *American Psychologist, 54*(10), 821–827.

De Petrillo, L., Kaufman, K., Glass, C., & Arnkoff, D. (2009). Mindfulness for long-distance runners: An open trial using Mindful Sport Performance Enhancement (MSPE). *Journal of Clinical Sport Psychology, 4*, 357–376.

Frewen, P. A., Evans, E. M., Maraj, M., Dozois, D. J. A., & Partridge, K. (2008). Letting go: Mindfulness and negative automatic thinking. *Cognitive Therapy Research, 32*, 758–774.

Gardner, F. L., & Moore, Z. E. (2004). A Mindfulness-Acceptance-Commitment (MAC) based approach to performance enhancement: Theoretical considerations. *Behavior Therapy, 35*, 707–723.

Gardner, F., & Moore, Z. (2007). *The psychology of enhancing human performance: The Mindfulness-Acceptance-Commitment (MAC) approach.* New York, NY: Springer.

Gardner, F. L., & Moore, Z. E. (2012). Mindfulness and acceptance models in sport psychology: A decade of basic and applied scientific advancements. *Canadian Psychology, 53*(4) 309–318.

Gilbert, P. (2010). *Compassion focused therapy: The distinctive features series.* New York, NY: Routledge.

Gilbert, P. (2011). Shame in psychotherapy and the role of compassion focused therapy. In R. Dearing & J. Tangney (Eds.), *Shame in therapy hour* (pp. 325–354). Washington, DC: American Psychological Association.

Gooding, A., & Gardner, F. L. (2009). An investigation of the relationship between mindfulness, preshot routine, and basketball free throw percentage. *Journal of Clinical Sport Psychology, 3*(4), 303–319.

Hayes, S. C. (2004). Acceptance and commitment therapy, relational frame theory, and the third wave of behavioral and cognitive therapies. *Behavior Therapies, 35*, 639–665.

Hayes, S. C., Strohsahl, K. D., Bunting, K., Twohig, M., & Wilson, K. G. (2004). What is acceptance and commitment therapy? In S. C. Hayes & K. D. Strohsahl (Eds.), *A practical guide to acceptance and commitment therapy* (pp. 1–30). New York, NY: Springer.

Hill, D. M., Hanton, S., Fleming, S., & Matthews, N. (2009). A re-examination of choking under pressure. *European Journal of Sport Science, 9,* 203–212.

Jackson, S. A. (1992). Athletes in flow: A qualitative investigation of flow states in elite figure skating. *The Journal of Applied Sport Psychology, 4*, 161–180.

Jackson, S. A. (1995). Factors influencing the occurrence of flow state in elite athletes. *Journal of Applied Sport Psychology, 7*, 138–166.

Jackson, S. A. (2012). Flow: The mindful edge in sport and performing arts. *InPsych: The Bulletin of the Australian Psychological Society Limited* (December 2012), 14–15.

Jackson, S., & Csikszentmihalyi, M. (1999). *Flow in sports: The keys to optimal experiences and performances.* Champaign, IL: Human Kinetics.

Jackson, S. A., & Eklund, R. C. (2004). *The flow scale manual.* Morgantown, WV: Fitness Information Technology

John, S., Verma, S., & Khanna, G. (2011). The effect of mindfulness meditation on HPA-Axis in pre-competition stress in sports performance of elite shooters. *National Journal of Integrated Research in Medicine, 2*(3), 15–21.

Kabat-Zinn, J. (2005). *Coming to our senses: Healing ourselves and the world through mindfulness.* New York, NY: Hyperion.

Kabat-Zinn, J., Beall, B., & Rippe, J. (1985). A systematic mental training program based on mindfulness meditation to optimize performance in collegiate and Olympic rowers. Poster presented at the World Congress in Sport Psychology, Copenhagen, Denmark.

Kaufman, K., Glass, C., & Arnkoff, D. (2009). Evaluation of Mindful Sport Performance Enhancement (MSPE): A new approach to promote flow in athletes. *Journal of Clinical Sport Psychology, 4,* 334–356.

Kaufman, K. A., Glass, C. R., & Pineau, T. R. (2016). Mindful Sport Performance Enhancement (MSPE): Development and applications. In A. L. Baltzell (Ed.), *The Cambridge companion to mindfulness and performance* (153–85). Cambridge, UK: Cambridge University Press.

Kee, Y. H., & Wang, C. K. J. (2008). Relationships between mindfulness, flow dispositions and mental skills adoption: A cluster analytic approach. *Psychology of Sport and Exercise, 9*(4), 393–411. doi:10.1016/j.psychsport.2007.07.001

Keng, S. L., Smoski, M. J., & Robin, C. J. (2011). Effects of mindfulness on psychological health: A review of empirical studies. *Clinical Psychology Review, 31,* 1041–1056. doi:10.1016/j.cpr.2011.04.006

Langer, E., Cohen, M., & Djikic, M. (2012). Mindfulness as a psychological attractor: The effect on children. *Journal of Applied Social Psychology, 42*(5), 1114–1122. doi:10.1111/j.1559-1816.2011.00879.x

Langer, E., Russell, T., & Eisenkraft, N. (2009). Orchestral performance and the footprint of mindfulness. *Psychology of Music, 37*(2), 125–136.

Lutkenhouse, J. M. (2007). The case of Jenny: A freshman collegiate athlete experiencing performance dysfunction. *Journal of Clinical Sport Psychology, 1,* 166–180.

Moore, Z. E., & Gardner, F. L. (2014). *Mindfulness and performance. The Wiley Blackwell handbook of mindfulness,* Vol. II. Chichester, UK: John Wiley & Sons.

Orlick, T., & Partington, J. (1988). Mental links to excellence. *The Sport Psychologist, 2,* 105–130.

Pineau, T. R., Glass, C. R., & Kaufman, K. A. (2014). Mindfulness in sport performance. In A. Le, C. T. Ngnoumen & E. J. Langer (Eds.), *The Wiley Blackwell handbook of mindfulness* (Vol. II, pp. 1004–1033). Chichester, UK: John Wiley & Sons.

Pineau, T. R., Glass, C. R., Kaufman, K. A., & Bernal, D. R. (2014). Self- and team-efficacy beliefs of rowers and their relation to mindfulness and flow. *Journal of Clinical Sport Psychology, 8,* 142–158.

Schwanhausser, L. (2009). Application of the Mindfulness-Acceptance-Commitment (MAC) protocol with an adolescent springboard diver. *Journal of Clinical Sport Psychology, 4,* 377–395.

Stankovic, D., & Baltzell, A. L. (2015). *Mindfulness Meditation in Sport: Improved Sport Performance of Masters Tennis Players.* Manuscript submitted for publication.

Stanley, E. A. (2014). Mindfulness-based mind fitness training: An approach for enhancing performance and building resilience in high-stress contexts. *The Wiley Blackwell handbook of mindfulness* (Vol. II, pp. 964–985). Chichester, UK: John Wiley & Sons.

Thompson, R., Kaufman, K., De Petrillo, L., Glass, C., & Arnkoff, D. (2011). One year follow-up of Mindful Sport Performance Enhancement (MSPE) with archers, golfers, and runners. *Journal of Clinical Sport Psychology, 5,* 99–116.

Wegner, D. M. (1994). Ironic processes of mental control. *Psychological Review, 101*(1), 34–52.

Weinburg, R. & Gould, D. (2015). *Foundations of sport and exercise psychology* (6th edition). Champaign, IL: Human Kinetics.

Williams, J. M., Nideffer, R. M., Wilson, V. E., & Sagal, M.-S. (2014). Concentration and strategies for controlling it. In J. M. Williams (Ed.), *Applied sport psychology: Personal growth to peak performance* (6th edition, pp. 304–325). Mountain View, CA: Mayfield Publishing.

Williams, M., Teasdale, J., Segal, Z., & Kabat-Zinn, J. (2007). *Guided meditation practices for the mindful way through depression*. CD Narrated by Jon Kabat-Zinn. New York, NY: Guilford.

Woody, S. R., Taylor, S., McLean, P. D., & Koch, W. J. (1998). Cognitive specificity in panic and depression: Implications for comorbidity. *Cognitive Therapy & Research, 22*, 427–443.

Zeidan, F., Johnson, S. K., Diamond, B. J., David, Z., & Goolkasian, P. (2010). Mindfulness meditation improves cognition: Evidence of brief mental training. *Conscious and Cognition, 597*–605. doi:10.1016/j.concog.2009.03.014

5

THE RELEVANCE OF MINDFUL EATING FOR ADDRESSING YOUTH OBESITY

Jeanne Dalen

Introduction

The continued exploration of the benefits of mindfulness has led to a natural extension of bringing mindfulness training to ever younger populations. Over the last decade the literature has begun to flourish with data that suggests that teaching mindfulness skills to our younger counterparts can incur great benefits (Black, 2015). A broad range of issues have been targeted to date, with data suggesting that increased mindfulness in youth is associated with improvement across a host of domains including anxiety (Sibinga et al., 2013), attention deficit hyperactivity disorder (van der Oord, Bogels, & Peijnenburg, 2012), blood pressure (Barnes, Davis, Murzynowski, & Treiber, 2004; Gregoski, Barnes, Tingen, Harshfield, & Treiber, 2011), chronic health conditions (Cotton et al., 2010; Jastrowski Mano et al., 2013), autism (de Bruin, Blom, Smit, van Steensel, & Bogels, 2014), sleep quality (Bei et al., 2013), and mental health disorders (Tan & Martin, 2013). In addition, these interventions have shown high acceptability and feasibility and speak to the interest apparent within this demographic in learning positive mind-body techniques (Black, Milam, & Sussman, 2009).

One area that could have particular saliency is the role of mindfulness in addressing the current youth obesity epidemic, as researchers and clinicians have begun to advocate for a positive psychology approach as an adjunct to traditional behavioral weight management programs (Lillis, Hayes, Bunting, & Masuda, 2009). Positive psychology is a branch of psychology that, unlike other branches, turns away from the focus on abnormal behavior and dysfunctional symptomatology, and instead shifts attention on how to increase well-being and happiness so that individuals may thrive and flourish (Seligman & Csikszentmihalyi, 2000). Mindfulness-based approaches have begun to be specifically adapted for addressing eating behavior change in adults and seek to provide a balanced and integrated approach to the prevention of weight-related problems (Dalen et al., 2010; Katterman, Kleinman,

Hood, Nackers, & Corsica, 2014; O'Reilly, Cook, Spruijt-Metz, & Black, 2014). Though still emerging, the early success of these programs demonstrates an opportunity to expand these programs for use in children and adolescent populations, as currently, no formal research has been published on adapting and assessing mindful eating interventions for youth obesity. Therefore, the purpose of this chapter is to offer a perspective on how mindful eating interventions could advance treatment development efforts by directly addressing key psychological risk factors that prior to now have been missing from traditional weight loss programs in youth. Specifically, the discussion will focus on how mindful eating corresponds directly to two intervention targets implicated in both the development and maintenance of youth obesity. These include (1) reduced psychosocial functioning including depression and body dissatisfaction; and (2) disordered eating behaviors including unhealthy weight control behaviors (UWCB), frequent dieting, and emotional binge eating. A review of the research in this area will be highlighted followed by an overview of how three central therapeutic components of mindful eating can specifically target these risk factors. Conclusions will present considerations for future research.

Associations between obesity and reduced psychological functioning

The high prevalence of youth overweight (Body Mass Index [BMI] > 85th percentile) and obesity (BMI > 95th percentile) has become a significant public health concern worldwide given the detrimental health, psychological, and social consequences associated (Falkner et al., 2001; Ogden, Carroll, Kit, & Flegal, 2014). The determinants of youth obesity are thought to be complex, with factors ranging from environment and policy, to family dynamics all playing a role (Fulkerson, Strauss, Neumark-Sztainer, Story, & Boutelle, 2007; Wyatt, Winters, & Dubbert, 2006). However, individual psychosocial functioning in particular stands out as being highly correlated with eating behaviors and overall quality of life in youth (Butryn et al., 2010; Cossrow & Falkner, 2004; Crow, Eisenberg, Story, & Neumark-Sztainer, 2006; Falkner et al., 2001; Wilson & Sato, 2014). For example, symptoms of depression, anxiety, body dissatisfaction, and physiological stress have been reported to be significantly higher in overweight adolescents compared with average weight peers (Melnyk et al., 2006; Young-Hyman et al., 2006), and reported health-related quality of life in some studies has been equivalent to adolescents diagnosed with cancer (Schwimmer, Burwinkle, & Varni, 2003). Depression in particular seems to be a significant mental health correlate of youth obesity present in both clinical and community samples (de Wit et al., 2010; Goldfield et al., 2010; Luppino et al., 2010; Nemiary, Shim, Mattox, & Holden, 2012; Sjoberg, Nilsson, & Leppert, 2005). Researchers contend that the effects of psychological distress in youth may be even more pronounced than in adult populations given that these formative years are a sensitive and vulnerable developmental period (Butryn et al., 2010; Neumark-Sztainer et al., 2002).

Weight-based teasing and discrimination, social pressure to be thin, and negative messages regarding weight may mediate the relationship between obesity and psychosocial functioning (Eisenberg, Neumark-Sztainer, Haines, & Wall, 2006; Puhl & Latner, 2007; Storch et al., 2007; Tang-Peronard & Heitmann, 2008). The adverse effects of social stigmatization on psychosocial functioning, and body dissatisfaction in particular, have been well documented in the literature (Israel & Ivanova, 2002; Krukowski et al., 2009; Morgan, Tanofsky-Kraff, Wilfley, & Yanovski, 2002; Strauss, 2000). Higher BMI is associated with more frequent and intense stigmatization in youth of both sexes (Eisenberg, Neumark-Sztainer, & Story, 2003) and findings seem to hold true even when messages come from seemingly benign sources such as family members and health professionals (Keery, Boutelle, van den Berg, & Thompson, 2005; Mellin et al., 2002; Wertheim, Martin, Prior, Sanson, & Smart, 2002).

Psychological functioning as a risk factor for disordered eating behaviors

Decreased psychosocial functioning (i.e., depression, low self-esteem, low body satisfaction) can exact a heavy toll by, not only affecting overall quality of life, but in increasing youths' vulnerability to engage in disordered eating behaviors (Decaluwe, Braet, & Fairburn, 2003; Neumark-Sztainer et al., 2002). Body dissatisfaction in particular seems to be a key psychosocial outcome and strong predictor for disordered eating behaviors including the use of unhealthy weight control practices (Latzer & Stein, 2013; Neumark-Sztainer, 2012; Pesa, Syre, & Jones, 2000; Shaw, Ramirez, Trost, Randall, & Stice, 2004), dietary restraint (Goldfield et al., 2010; Hawks, Madanat, & Christley, 2008), and binge eating (Danielsen et al., 2012; Herbozo, Schaefer, & Thompson, 2015; Puhl, Moss-Racusin, & Schwartz, 2007).

Unhealthy weight control behaviors

UWCB include skipping meals, using laxatives, diet pills, food substitutes (i.e., cigarettes), and/or engaging in self-induced vomiting. A consistent body of research reveals significantly higher levels of UWCB among overweight youth (Mellin et al., 2002; Neumark-Sztainer, 2012) and has been particularly noted among adolescent girls (Eisenberg et al., 2006), with studies reporting prevalence rates of up to 76% (Neumark-Sztainer et al., 2002). However, it is clear that even young males struggle with UWCB, as research has also found behaviors such as skipping meals to be significantly higher in overweight males when compared to those of normal weight (Mellin & et al., 2002; Neumark-Sztainer, Flattum, Story, Feldman, & Petrich, 2008).

Dietary restraint

Overweight youth also report more frequent dieting attempts or the use of dietary restraint, which is the conscious restriction of calories to control body weight (Goldfield et al., 2010). Research paradoxically suggests that dieting attempts, along with the use of UWCB, are not only ineffective for weight loss, but can actually increase weight gain over time (Field, Haines, Rosner, & Willett, 2010; Neumark-Sztainer, Wall, Haines, Story, & Eisenberg, 2007; Stice, Presnell, Groesz, & Shaw, 2005). Robust evidence for this association comes from the longitudinal study, Project EAT, which examined the socio-environmental, personal, and behavioral determinants of nutritional intake and weight status in a diverse adolescent population with a large sample size (Haines, Neumark-Sztainer, Eisenberg, & Hannan, 2006). One of the strongest findings from this study was that frequent dieting was a significant predictor of large weight gains at both 5-year and 10-year follow-ups (Neumark-Sztainer, Wall, Larson, Eisenberg, & Loth, 2011). Furthermore, higher levels of dieting and UWCB have been associated with higher levels of emotional distress (Gillen, Markey, & Markey, 2012; Hawks et al., 2008), and put overweight youth at risk for binge eating (Neumark-Sztainer et al., 2008; Stice, 1998).

Binge eating

In the Project EAT study, binge eating behavior mediated the relationship between frequent dieting and weight gain over time (Neumark-Sztainer et al., 2007). This finding seems to be consistent with the body of research demonstrating dietary restraint as a risk factor in the development and maintenance of binge eating and eating disorders (Cachelin & Regan, 2006; Morgan, Yanovski, et al., 2002; Stice, Presnell, Groesz, et al., 2005; Tanofsky-Kraff et al., 2004). Binge eating behavior, characterized by the consumption of large amounts of food and loss of control over eating, is relatively frequent among overweight youth (Birch & Davison, 2001; Goossens, Soenens, & Braet, 2009). Though typically not reaching full clinical significance in the majority of population-based studies, the prevalence of sub-threshold binge eating behavior in overweight youth has been reported upward of 30% (Decaluwe & Braet, 2003).

Not only is binge eating associated with increased risk of developing a clinical eating disorder, it is significantly correlated with greater eating-related distress, depression, anxiety, and lower self- and body-esteem (Marcus & Kalarchian, 2003; Morgan, Yanovski, et al., 2002; Tanofsky-Kraff et al., 2004). Indeed, research shows that emotional distress increases in relation to severity of binge eating behavior in overweight youth (Goossens, Braet, Van Vlierberghe, & Mels, 2009). It has also been correlated with poorer response to weight loss interventions (Tanofsky-Kraff et al., 2007), and weight gain (Stice, Presnell, Shaw, & Rohde, 2005).

The potential role of mindful eating for overweight youth

Overall, there appears to be a consistent association between reduced psychosocial functioning and disordered eating behaviors in overweight youth, in that they appear to interact and sustain each other in a cyclical pattern. Based on these findings, it is important to begin to identify protective factors that can assist overweight youth with feeling good in their bodies, in developing positive coping skills for stress, and in finding healthier balanced ways of addressing eating and weight loss (Neumark-Sztainer, 2012). The high prevalence of both psychosocial distress and disordered eating behaviors in overweight youth illustrates the need to expand treatment efforts beyond traditional weight loss programs (Haines & Neumark-Sztainer, 2006), which tend to focus primarily on teaching dietary restraint and exercise education (Kong et al., 2012).

Mindfulness is broadly defined in the literature as paying attention in a particular way: "on purpose, in the present moment and non-judgementally" (Kabat-Zinn, 1990, p. 4). Though considered an inherent quality, mindfulness can be strengthened through the practice of meditation, in which participants learn to regulate their attention through various exercises, and this can include both formal and informal training components (Baer, 2003). Jean Kristeller, one of the pioneers of mindful eating research, and developer of the MB-EAT program, states that within the framework of mindful eating interventions, "mindfulness meditation is conceptualized as a way of training attention to increase nonjudgmental awareness of internal experience and automatic patterns related to eating, emotional regulation, and self-acceptance" (Kristeller & Wolever, 2011, p. 51).

There are many reasons why mindful eating skills could be considered an effective adjunct to obesity treatment programs for youth. In the following section, an overview of three key therapeutic components that form the foundation of mindful eating interventions are presented including (1) Experiential acceptance as a positive coping skill for controlling responses to psychological distress; (2) Self-regulation through developed awareness of the emotional and physical cues to eat; and (3) Compassion as a way to cultivate self-acceptance and body satisfaction. Overall, these skills seek to reduce risk factors associated with psychological distress, promote healthy eating behaviors, and enhance protective factors such as body acceptance, self-compassion, and overall quality of life.

Experiential acceptance

One relevant aspect of binge eating is emotional eating, defined as overeating in response to psychological distress (Alberts, Thewissen, & Raes, 2012; Goossens, Braet, et al., 2009). Several mechanisms have been proposed to explain this association, including escape theory (Heatherton & Baumeister, 1991) and affect regulation models (Polivy & Herman, 1993). In essence, these theories propose that emotional binge eating is a maladaptive coping mechanism based on an inability to tolerate negative emotional arousal (Gianini, White, & Masheb, 2013; Leehr et al., 2015; Spoor, Bekker, Van Strien, & van Heck, 2007). An important element is the concept of experiential avoidance, defined as the unwillingness to experience negative feelings, sensations, or thoughts (Whiteside et al., 2007). Individuals high in experiential avoidance take immediate steps to avoid or distract themselves when distressed, even when doing so is maladaptive (Bennett, Greene, & Schwartz-Barcott, 2013). Seen from this position, overeating becomes a method of escape or distraction that is reinforced by temporary reductions in psychological distress (Gianini et al., 2013; Ricca et al., 2009).

Thus, psychological methods for youth that promote experiential acceptance could be particularly useful in reducing avoidance-based coping, such as emotional binge eating (Alberts, Schneider, & Martijn, 2012; Farb, Anderson, & Segal, 2012). Indeed, a core tenet of mindfulness is the notion that the more we try avoid negative thoughts and feelings, the more likely we are to paradoxically experience them (Gross & John, 2003; Lillis et al., 2009). Mindfulness could assist youth in not over-identifying with strong emotional states and thus, instead of distress serving as a trigger for overeating, mindfulness can provide a space for youth to recognize that an emotional trigger has presented itself and allow for alternative stress management strategies to be considered and potentially employed (Alberts, Thewissen, et al., 2012). Second, mindfulness provides the ability to experience emotions as short-lived events that eventually lose their strength over time. This may reduce the need for impulsive responses as one begins to recognize through mindfulness that over time intense emotions dissipate of their own accord (Baer, Fischer, & Huss, 2006).

Self-regulation

The second therapeutic component of mindful eating relevant to youth obesity is promoting intuitive eating, an eating style that relies on physiologic hunger and satiety cues to guide eating rather than externally driven emotional factors or dieting behaviors (Daubenmier et al., 2011; Kristeller & Wolever, 2011). According to self-regulation theory, regulation of internal physical processes, such as hunger, depends on one's ability to detect and act on internal cues (Schwartz, 1975). However, research shows that emotional eaters may not be able to differentiate between automatic, emotional eating and physical hunger (Smith, Shelley, Leahigh, & Vanleit, 2006).

Another aspect of mindful eating that allows for self-regulation is giving oneself permission to eat with no restrictions being placed on calorie or nutrition content (Avalos & Tylka, 2006). Instead of foods being labeled as 'good' or 'bad,' the focus becomes more on balanced food choice selections while finding enjoyment with smaller quantities of food (Kristeller & Wolever, 2011). Research suggests that when pre-specified dietary restrictions are taken away, and foods are no longer labeled as 'good' or 'bad,' not only is weight loss obtainable, but vast improvements in psychosocial health outcomes are found (Augustus-Horvath & Tylka, 2011; Avalos & Tylka, 2006; Godsey, 2013). For example, in a study conducted by Denny and colleagues (2013), teens and young adults who reported trusting their bodies to tell them how to eat were less likely to engage in disordered eating and frequent dieting (Denny, Loth, Eisenberg, & Neumark-Sztainer, 2013). In particular, eating for physical rather than emotional reasons and relying on internal hunger and satiety cues uniquely contribute to psychological well-being (Avalos & Tylka, 2006).

Self-acceptance, self-care, and compassion

The third therapeutic component central to mindful eating is promotion of self-acceptance, self-care, and compassion, all of which are highly pertinent for addressing the widely prevalent body dissatisfaction and body image issues found in over-weight youth (Crow et al., 2006; Menzel et al., 2010; Tylka, Russell, & Neal, 2015). Fundamental to this idea is developing an improved self-relationship by promoting lower self-criticism and higher self-compassion through non-judgmental aware-ness of thoughts, feelings, and experiences (Neff & Germer, 2013; Shapiro, Carlson, Astin, & Freedman, 2006). When seen within a mindful framework, self-acceptance allows mistakes to be a natural part of the learning process, rather than reasons for failure and giving up (Mantzios & Wilson, 2014). Self-care is also reinforced by increasing the enjoyment to be found in eating (Kristeller & Wolever, 2011) and reinforced in the physical body through cultivating body acceptance and body appreciation (Schaefer & Magnuson, 2014).

The ability for mindfulness to target these internal behaviors related to body issues is through fostering an acceptance for the present moment. Instead of being dissatisfied with one's current body shape and size, mindfulness promotes acceptance of the body in its present state, rather than accepting artificial soci-etal notions of what is deemed acceptable. By accepting the body as is, strong judgments and self-critical evaluations can be reduced (Alberts, Thewissen, et al., 2012) and feeling good about one's body can help promote the need for self-care (Mantzios & Wilson, 2014; Neff & Germer, 2013; Neumark-Sztainer, 2012).

Conclusions

The purpose of this chapter was to offer a perspective on how meditation-based mindful eating programs could assist in expanding treatment development efforts for youth overweight and obesity. Obesity in youth has increased substantially over the past decades worldwide (Ogden et al., 2014), and it has been well documented that these youth face incredible risk for reduced psychosocial functioning including depression, anxiety, body dissatisfaction, and physiological stress (Butryn et al., 2010; Cossrow & Falkner, 2004; Crow et al., 2006; Faith et al., 2011; Falkner et al., 2001; Wilson & Sato, 2014). Not only does reduced psychosocial functioning affect over-all quality of life, it puts overweight youth at high risk of engaging in disordered eating behaviors (Goldfield et al., 2010; Stice, 1998).

Mindful eating interventions represent a promising approach to youth obesity by addressing key psychological variables related to quality of life and eating behav-iors. Mindful eating seeks to provide a balanced and integrated approach to the prevention of weight-related problems in youth through decreasing emotional dis-tress, teaching positive coping skills, promoting healthier sustainable eating habits, and increasing self-compassion and body acceptance (Kristeller & Wolever, 2011). Though the research in this field is still in the early stages, the success of other meditation-based programs used in youth populations (Black et al., 2009; Sibinga et al., 2011) speaks to an untapped opportunity to expand mindful eating interven-tions to overweight youth.

It is hoped that this chapter spurs movement towards a new line of treatment development research aimed at adapting mindful eating programs for younger overweight populations. Future research efforts should (1) consider how best to adapt, modify, or tailor program content in order to enhance effectiveness, (2) include examination of primary outcomes as well as key mechanisms of change, (3) isolate the effects associated with specific components of these interventions, and (4) conduct comparative efficacy studies between mindfulness-based interventions and traditional behavioral weight loss programs for youth.

Bibliography

Alberts, H. J., Schneider, F., & Martijn, C. (2012). Dealing efficiently with emotions: Acceptance-based coping with negative emotions requires fewer resources than suppression. *Cogn Emot, 26*(5), 863–870. doi:10.1080/02699931.2011.625402

Alberts, H. J., Thewissen, R., & Raes, L. (2012). Dealing with problematic eating behaviour. The effects of a mindfulness-based intervention on eating behaviour, food cravings, dichotomous thinking and body image concern. *Appetite, 58*(3), 847–851. doi:10.1016/j.appet.2012.01.009

Augustus-Horvath, C. L., & Tylka, T. L. (2011). The acceptance model of intuitive eating: A comparison of women in emerging adulthood, early adulthood, and middle adulthood. *J Couns Psychol, 58*(1), 110–125. doi:10.1037/a0022129

Avalos, L., & Tylka, T. (2006). Exploring a model of intuitive eating with college women. *J Couns Psychol, 53*(4), 486–497.

Baer, R. A. (2003). Mindfulness training as a clinical intervention: A conceptual and empirical review. *Clin Psychol-Sci Pr, 10*(2), 125–143.

Baer, R. A., Fischer, S., & Huss, D. B. (2006). Mindfulness and acceptance in the treatment of disordered eating. *J Ration Emot Cogn Behav Ther, 23*(4), 281–300.

Barnes, V. A., Davis, H. C., Murzynowski, J. B., & Treiber, F. A. (2004). Impact of meditation on resting and ambulatory blood pressure and heart rate in youth. *Psychosom Med, 66*(6), 909–914.

Bei, B., Byrne, M. L., Ivens, C., Waloszek, J., Woods, M. J., Dudgeon, P., …Allen, N. B. (2013). Pilot study of a mindfulness-based, multi-component, in-school group sleep intervention in adolescent girls. *Early Interv Psychiatry, 7*(2), 213–220. doi:10.1111/j.1751-7893.2012.00382.x

Bennett, J., Greene, G., & Schwartz-Barcott, D. (2013). Perceptions of emotional eating behavior. A qualitative study of college students. *Appetite, 60*(1), 187–192.

Birch, L. L., & Davison, K. K. (2001). Family environmental factors influencing the developing behavioral controls of food intake and childhood overweight. *Pediatr Clin North Am, 48*(4), 893–907.

Black, D. S. (2015). Mindfulness training for children and adolescents: A state-of-the-science review. In K. C. Brown, J. D. Creswell, & R. M. Ryan, (Eds.), *Handbook of mindfulness theory, research, and practice* (pp.283–311). New York, NY: Guilford Press.

Black, D. S., Milam, J., & Sussman, S. (2009). Sitting-meditation interventions among youth: A review of treatment efficacy. *Pediatrics, 124*(3), e532–e541.

Butryn, M. L., Wadden, T. A., Rukstalis, M. R., Bishop-Gilyard, C., Xanthopoulos, M. S., Louden, D., & Berkowitz, R. I. (2010). Maintenance of weight loss in adolescents: Current status and future directions. *J Obes, 2010*, 789280.

Cachelin, F. M., & Regan, P. C. (2006). Prevalence and correlates of chronic dieting in a multi-ethnic U.S. community sample. *Eat Weight Disord, 11*(2), 91–99.

Cossrow, N., & Falkner, B. (2004). Race/ethnic issues in obesity and obesity-related comorbidities. *J Clin Endocrinol Metab, 89*(6), 2590–2594.

Cotton, S., Humenay Roberts, Y., Tsevat, J., Britto, M. T., Succop, P., McGrady, M. E., & Yi, M. S. (2010). Mind-body complementary alternative medicine use and quality of life in adolescents with inflammatory bowel disease. *Inflamm Bowel Dis, 16*(3), 501–506.

Crow, S., Eisenberg, M. E., Story, M., & Neumark-Sztainer, D. (2006). Psychosocial and behavioral correlates of dieting among overweight and non-overweight adolescents. *J Adolesc Health, 38*(5), 569–574. doi:10.1016/j.jadohealth.2005.05.019

Dalen, J., Smith, B. W., Shelley, B. M., Sloan, A. L., Leahigh, L., & Begay, D. (2010). Pilot study: Mindful Eating and Living (MEAL): Weight, eating behavior, and psychological outcomes associated with a mindfulness-based intervention for people with obesity. *Complement Ther Med, 18*(6), 260–264.

Danielsen, Y. S., Stormark, K. M., Nordhus, I. H., Maehle, M., Sand, L., Ekornas, B., & Pallesen, S. (2012). Factors associated with low self-esteem in children with overweight. *Obes Facts, 5*(5), 722–733. doi:10.1159/000338333

Daubenmier, J., Kristeller, J., Hecht, F. M., Maninger, N., Kuwata, M., Jhaveri, K., . . . Epel, E. (2011). Mindfulness intervention for stress eating to reduce cortisol and abdominal fat among overweight and obese women: An exploratory randomized controlled study. *J Obes, 2011*, 651936. doi:10.1155/2011/651936

de Bruin, E. I., Blom, R., Smit, F. M., van Steensel, F. J., & Bogels, S. M. (2014). My mind: Mindfulness training for youngsters with autism spectrum disorders and their parents. *Autism, 19*(8), 906–911. doi:10.1177/1362361314553279

de Wit, L., Luppino, F., van Straten, A., Penninx, B., Zitman, F., & Cuijpers, P. (2010). Depression and obesity: A meta-analysis of community-based studies. *Psychiatr Res, 178*(2), 230–235. doi:10.1016/j.psychres.2009.04.015

Decaluwe, V., & Braet, C. (2003). Prevalence of binge-eating disorder in obese children and adolescents seeking weight-loss treatment. *Int J Obes Relat Metab Disord, 27*(3), 404–409. doi:10.1038/sj.ijo.0802233

Decaluwe, V., Braet, C., & Fairburn, C. G. (2003). Binge eating in obese children and adolescents. *Int J Eat Disord, 33*(1), 78–84. doi:10.1002/eat.10110

Denny, K. N., Loth, K., Eisenberg, M. E., & Neumark-Sztainer, D. (2013). Intuitive eating in young adults. Who is doing it, and how is it related to disordered eating behaviors? *Appetite, 60*(1), 13–19. doi:10.1016/j.appet.2012.09.029

Eisenberg, M. E., Neumark-Sztainer, D., Haines, J., & Wall, M. (2006). Weight-teasing and emotional well-being in adolescents: Longitudinal findings from project EAT. *J Adolesc Health, 38*(6), 675–683. doi:10.1016/j.jadohealth.2005.07.002

Eisenberg, M. E., Neumark-Sztainer, D., & Story, M. (2003). Associations of weight-based teasing and emotional well-being among adolescents. *Arch Pediatr Adolesc Med, 157*(8), 733–738. doi:10.1001/archpedi.157.8.733

Faith, M. S., Butryn, M., Wadden, T. A., Fabricatore, A., Nguyen, A. M., & Heymsfield, S. B. (2011). Evidence for prospective associations among depression and obesity in population-based studies. *Obes Rev, 12*(5), e438–e453. doi:10.1111/j.1467-789X.2010.00843.x

Falkner, N. H., Neumark-Sztainer, D., Story, M., Jeffery, R. W., Beuhring, T., & Resnick, M. D. (2001). Social, educational, and psychological correlates of weight status in adolescents. *Obes Res, 9*(1), 32–42. doi:10.1038/oby.2001.5

Farb, N. A., Anderson, A. K., & Segal, Z. V. (2012). The mindful brain and emotion regulation in mood disorders. *Can J Psychiatr, 57*(2), 70–77.

Field, A. E., Haines, J., Rosner, B., & Willett, W. C. (2010). Weight-control behaviors and subsequent weight change among adolescents and young adult females. *Am J Clin Nutr, 91*(1), 147–153. doi:10.3945/ajcn.2009.28321

Fulkerson, J. A., Strauss, J., Neumark-Sztainer, D., Story, M., & Boutelle, K. (2007). Correlates of psychosocial well-being among overweight adolescents: The role of the family. *J Consult Clin Psychol, 75*(1), 181–186. doi:10.1037/0022-006X.75.1.181

Gianini, L. M., White, M. A., & Masheb, R. M. (2013). Eating pathology, emotion regulation, and emotional overeating in obese adults with binge eating disorder. *Eat Behav, 14*(3), 309–313. doi:10.1016/j.eatbeh.2013.05.008

Gillen, M. M., Markey, C. N., & Markey, P. M. (2012). An examination of dieting behaviors among adults: Links with depression. *Eat Behav, 13*(2), 88–93. doi:10.1016/j.eatbeh.2011.11.014

Godsey, J. (2013). The role of mindfulness based interventions in the treatment of obesity and eating disorders: An integrative review. *Complement Ther Med, 21*(4), 430–439. doi:10.1016/j.ctim.2013.06.003

Goldfield, G. S., Moore, C., Henderson, K., Buchholz, A., Obeid, N., & Flament, M. F. (2010). Body dissatisfaction, dietary restraint, depression, and weight status in adolescents. *J Sch Health, 80*(4), 186–192. doi:10.1111/j.1746-1561.2009.00485.x

Goossens, L., Braet, C., Van Vlierberghe, L., & Mels, S. (2009). Loss of control over eating in overweight youngsters: The role of anxiety, depression and emotional eating. *Eur Eat Disord Rev, 17*(1), 68–78. doi:10.1002/erv.892

Goossens, L., Soenens, B., & Braet, C. (2009). Prevalence and characteristics of binge eating in an adolescent community sample. *J Clin Child Adolesc Psychol, 38*(3), 342–353. doi:10.1080/15374410902851697

Gregoski, M. J., Barnes, V. A., Tingen, M. S., Harshfield, G. A., & Treiber, F. A. (2011). Breathing awareness meditation and life skills training programs influence upon ambulatory blood pressure and sodium excretion among African American adolescents. *J Adolesc Health, 48*(1), 59–64. doi:10.1016/j.jadohealth.2010.05.019

Gross, J. J., & John, O. P. (2003). Individual differences in two emotion regulation processes: Implications for affect, relationships, and well-being. *J Pers Soc Psychol, 85*(2), 348–362.

Haines, J., & Neumark-Sztainer, D. (2006). Prevention of obesity and eating disorders: A consideration of shared risk factors. *Health Educ Res, 21*(6), 770–782. doi:10.1093/her/cyl094

Haines, J., Neumark-Sztainer, D., Eisenberg, M. E., & Hannan, P. J. (2006). Weight teasing and disordered eating behaviors in adolescents: Longitudinal findings from project EAT (Eating Among Teens). *Pediatrics, 117*(2), e209–e215. doi:10.1542/peds.2005-1242

Hawks, S., Madanat, H., & Christley, H. (2008). Psychosocial associations of dietary restraint: Implications for healthy weight promotion. *Ecol Food Nutri, 47*(5), 450–483.

Heatherton, T. F., & Baumeister, R. F. (1991). Binge eating as escape from self-awareness. *Psychol Bull, 110*(1), 86–108.

Herbozo, S., Schaefer, L. M., & Thompson, J. K. (2015). A comparison of eating disorder psychopathology, appearance satisfaction, and self-esteem in overweight and obese women with and without binge eating. *Eat Behav, 17*, 86–89. doi:10.1016/j.eatbeh.2015.01.007

Israel, A. C., & Ivanova, M. Y. (2002). Global and dimensional self-esteem in preadolescent and early adolescent children who are overweight: Age and gender differences. *Int J Eat Disord, 31*(4), 424–429. doi:10.1002/eat.10048

Jastrowski Mano, K. E., Salamon, K. S., Hainsworth, K. R., Anderson Khan, K. J., Ladwig, R. J., Davies, W. H., & Weisman, S. J. (2013). A randomized, controlled pilot study of mindfulness-based stress reduction for pediatric chronic pain. *Altern Ther Health Med, 19*(6), 8–14.

Kabat-Zinn, J. (1990). *Full catastrophe living: Using the wisdom of your body and mind to face stress, pain, and illness.* New York, NY: Delacourt.

Katterman, S. N., Kleinman, B. M., Hood, M. M., Nackers, L. M., & Corsica, J. A. (2014). Mindfulness meditation as an intervention for binge eating, emotional eating, and weight loss: A systematic review. *Eat Behav, 15*(2), 197–204. doi:10.1016/j.eatbeh.2014.01.005

Keery, H., Boutelle, K., van den Berg, P., & Thompson, J. K. (2005). The impact of appearance-related teasing by family members. *J Adolesc Health, 37*(2), 120–127. doi:10.1016/j.jadohealth.2004.08.015

Kong, A. S., Dalen, J., Negrete, S., Sanders, S. G., Keane, P. C., & Davis, S. M. (2012). Interventions for treating overweight and obesity in adolescents. *Adolesc Med State Art Rev, 23*(3), 544–570.

Kristeller, J. L., & Wolever, R. Q. (2011). Mindfulness-based eating awareness training for treating binge eating disorder: The conceptual foundation. *Eat Disord, 19*(1), 49–61. doi: 10.1080/10640266.2011.533605

Krukowski, R. A., West, D. S., Philyaw Perez, A., Bursac, Z., Phillips, M. M., & Raczynski, J. M. (2009). Overweight children, weight-based teasing and academic performance. *Int J Pediatr Obes, 4*(4), 274–280. doi:10.3109/17477160902846203

Latzer, Y., & Stein, D. (2013). A review of the psychological and familial perspectives of childhood obesity. *J Eat Disord, 1*, 7. doi:10.1186/2050-2974-1-7

Leehr, E. J., Krohmer, K., Schag, K., Dresler, T., Zipfel, S., & Giel, K. E. (2015). Emotion regulation model in binge eating disorder and obesity: A systematic review. *Neurosci Biobehav Rev, 49*, 125–134. doi:10.1016/j.neubiorev.2014.12.008

Lillis, J., Hayes, S. C., Bunting, K., & Masuda, A. (2009). Teaching acceptance and mindfulness to improve the lives of the obese: A preliminary test of a theoretical model. *Ann Behav Med, 37*(1), 58–69. doi:10.1007/s12160-009-9083-x

Luppino, F. S., de Wit, L. M., Bouvy, P. F., Stijnen, T., Cuijpers, P., Penninx, B. W., & Zitman, F. G. (2010). Overweight, obesity, and depression: A systematic review and meta-analysis of longitudinal studies. *Arch Gen Psychiatr, 67*(3), 220–229. doi:10.1001/archgenpsychiatry.2010.2

Mantzios, M., & Wilson, J. C. (2014). Making concrete construals mindful: A novel approach for developing mindfulness and self-compassion to assist weight loss. *Psychol Health, 29*(4), 422–441. doi:10.1080/08870446.2013.863883

Marcus, M. D., & Kalarchian, M. A. (2003). Binge eating in children and adolescents. *Int J Eat Disord, 34*(Suppl), S47–S57. doi:10.1002/eat.10205

Mellin, A. E., Neumark-Sztainer, D., Story, M., Ireland, M., &, & Resnick, M. D. (2002). Unhealthy behaviors and psychosocial difficulties among overweight adolescents: The potential impact of familial factors. *J Adolesc Health, 31*(2), 145–153.

Melnyk, B. M., Small, L., Morrison-Beedy, D., Strasser, A., Spath, L., Kreipe, R., . . . Van Blankenstein, S. (2006). Mental health correlates of healthy lifestyle attitudes, beliefs, choices, and behaviors in overweight adolescents. *J Pediatr Health Care, 20*(6), 401–406. doi:10.1016/j.pedhc.2006.03.004

Menzel, J. E., Schaefer, L. M., Burke, N. L., Mayhew, L. L., Brannick, M. T., & Thompson, J. K. (2010). Appearance-related teasing, body dissatisfaction, and disordered eating: A meta-analysis. *Body Image, 7*(4), 261–270. doi:10.1016/j.bodyim.2010.05.004

Morgan, C. M., Tanofsky-Kraff, M., Wilfley, D. E., & Yanovski, J. A. (2002). Childhood obesity. *Child Adolesc Psychiatr Clin North Am, 11*(2), 257–278.

Morgan, C. M., Yanovski, S. Z., Nguyen, T. T., McDuffie, J., Sebring, N. G., Jorge, M. R., . . . Yanovski, J. A. (2002). Loss of control over eating, adiposity, and psychopathology in overweight children. *Int J Eat Disord, 31*(4), 430–441. doi:10.1002/eat.10038

Neff, K. D., & Germer, C. K. (2013). A pilot study and randomized controlled trial of the mindful self-compassion program. *J Clin Psychol, 69*(1), 28–44. doi:10.1002/jclp.21923

Nemiary, D., Shim, R., Mattox, G., & Holden, K. (2012). The relationship between obesity and depression among adolescents. *Psychiatr Ann, 42*(8), 305–308. doi:10.3928/0048 5713-20120806-09

Neumark-Sztainer, D. (2012). Integrating messages from the eating disorders field into obesity prevention. *Adolesc Med State Art Rev, 23*(3), 529–543.

Neumark-Sztainer, D., Falkner, N., Story, M., Perry, C., Hannan, P. J., & Mulert, S. (2002). Weight-teasing among adolescents: Correlations with weight status and disordered eating behaviors. *Int J Obes Relat Metab Disord, 26*(1), 123–131. doi:10.1038/sj.ijo.0801853

Neumark-Sztainer, D., Flattum, C., Story, M., Feldman, S., & Petrich, C. (2008). Dietary approaches to healthy weight management for adolescents: The New Moves model. *Adolesc Med State Art Rev, 19*(3), 421–430, viii.

Neumark-Sztainer, D., Wall, M., Haines, J., Story, M., & Eisenberg, M. E. (2007). Why does dieting predict weight gain in adolescents? Findings from project EAT-II: A 5-year longitudinal study. *J Am Diet Assoc, 107*(3), 448–455. doi:10.1016/j.jada.2006.12.013

Neumark-Sztainer, D. R., Wall, M. M., Haines, J. I., Story, M. T., Sherwood, N. E., & van den Berg, P. A. (2007). Shared risk and protective factors for overweight and disordered eating in adolescents. *Am J Prev Med, 33*(5), 359–369. doi:10.1016/j.amepre.2007.07.031

Neumark-Sztainer, D., Wall, M., Larson, N. I., Eisenberg, M. E., & Loth, K. (2011). Dieting and disordered eating behaviors from adolescence to young adulthood: Findings from a 10-year longitudinal study. *J Am Diet Assoc, 111*(7), 1004–1011. doi:10.1016/j.jada.2011.04.012

Ogden, C. L., Carroll, M. D., Kit, B. K., & Flegal, K. M. (2014). Prevalence of childhood and adult obesity in the United States, 2011–2012. *JAMA, 311*(8), 806–814. doi:10.1001/jama.2014.732

O'Reilly, G. A., Cook, L., Spruijt-Metz, D., & Black, D. S. (2014). Mindfulness-based interventions for obesity-related eating behaviours: A literature review. *Obes Rev, 15*(6), 453–461. doi:10.1111/obr.12156

Pesa, J. A., Syre, T. R., & Jones, E. (2000). Psychosocial differences associated with body weight among female adolescents: The importance of body image. *J Adolesc Health, 26*(5), 330–337.

Polivy, J., Herman, C. P. (1993). Etiology of binge eating: Psychological mechanisms. In R. Palmer (Ed.), *Binge eating – nature, assessment, and treatment* (pp. 173–205). New York, NY: Guilford Press.

Puhl, R. M., & Latner, J. D. (2007). Stigma, obesity, and the health of the nation's children. *Psychol Bull, 133*(4), 557–580. doi:10.1037/0033-2909.133.4.557

Puhl, R. M., Moss-Racusin, C. A., & Schwartz, M. B. (2007). Internalization of weight bias: Implications for binge eating and emotional well-being. *Obesity (Silver Spring), 15*(1), 19–23. doi:10.1038/oby.2007.521

Ricca, V., Castellini, G., Lo Sauro, C., Ravaldi, C., Lapi, F., Mannucci, E., . . . Faravelli, C. (2009). Correlations between binge eating and emotional eating in a sample of overweight subjects. *Appetite, 53*(3), 418–421. doi:10.1016/j.appet.2009.07.008

Schaefer, J. T., & Magnuson, A. B. (2014). A review of interventions that promote eating by internal cues. *J Acad Nutr Diet, 114*(5), 734–760. doi:10.1016/j.jand.2013.12.024

Schwartz, G. E. (1975). Biofeedback, self-regulation, and the patterning of physiological processes. *Am Sci, 63*(3), 314–324.

Schwimmer, J. B., Burwinkle, T. M., & Varni, J. W. (2003). Health-related quality of life of severely obese children and adolescents. *JAMA, 289*(14), 1813–1819.

Seligman, M. E., & Csikszentmihalyi, M. (2000). Positive psychology. An introduction. *Am Psychol, 55*(1), 5–14.

Shapiro, S. L., Carlson, L. E., Astin, J. A., & Freedman, B. (2006). Mechanisms of mindfulness. *J Clin Psychol, 62*(3), 373–386. doi:10.1002/jclp.20237

Shaw, H., Ramirez, L., Trost, A., Randall, P., & Stice, E. (2004). Body image and eating disturbances across ethnic groups: More similarities than differences. *Psychol Addict Behav, 18*(1), 12–18. doi:10.1037/0893-164X.18.1.12

Sibinga, E. M., Kerrigan, D., Stewart, M., Johnson, K., Magyari, T., & Ellen, J. M. (2011). Mindfulness-based stress reduction for urban youth. *J Altern Complement Med, 17*(3), 213–218. doi:10.1089/acm.2009.0605

Sibinga, E. M., Perry-Parrish, C., Chung, S. E., Johnson, S. B., Smith, M., & Ellen, J. M. (2013). School-based mindfulness instruction for urban male youth: A small randomized controlled trial. *Prev Med, 57*(6), 799–801. doi:10.1016/j.ypmed.2013.08.027

Sjoberg, R. L., Nilsson, K. W., & Leppert, J. (2005). Obesity, shame, and depression in school-aged children: A population-based study. *Pediatrics, 116*(3), e389–e392. doi:10.1542/peds.2005-0170

Smith, B. W., Shelley, B. M., Leahigh, L., & Vanleit, B. (2006). A preliminary study of the effects of a modified mindfulness intervention on binge eating. *Complement Health Prac Rev, 11*(3), 133–143.

Spoor, S. T., Bekker, M. H., Van Strien, T., & van Heck, G. L. (2007). Relations between negative affect, coping, and emotional eating. *Appetite, 48*(3), 368–376. doi:10.1016/j.appet.2006.10.005

Stice, E. (1998). Relations of restraint and negative affect to bulimic pathology: A longitudinal test of three competing models. *Int J Eat Disord, 23*(3), 243–260.

Stice, E., Presnell, K., Groesz, L., & Shaw, H. (2005). Effects of a weight maintenance diet on bulimic symptoms in adolescent girls: An experimental test of the dietary restraint theory. *Health Psychol, 24*(4), 402–412. doi:10.1037/0278-6133.24.4.402

Stice, E., Presnell, K., Shaw, H., & Rohde, P. (2005). Psychological and behavioral risk factors for obesity onset in adolescent girls: A prospective study. *J Consult Clin Psychol, 73*(2), 195–202. doi:10.1037/0022-006X.73.2.195

Storch, E. A., Milsom, V. A., Debraganza, N., Lewin, A. B., Geffken, G. R., & Silverstein, J. H. (2007). Peer victimization, psychosocial adjustment, and physical activity in overweight and at-risk-for-overweight youth. *J Pediatr Psychol, 32*(1), 80–89. doi:10.1093/jpepsy/jsj113

Strauss, R. S. (2000). Childhood obesity and self-esteem. *Pediatrics, 105*(1), e15.

Tan, L., & Martin, G. (2013). Taming the adolescent mind: Preliminary report of a mindfulness-based psychological intervention for adolescents with clinical heterogeneous mental health diagnoses. *Clin Child Psychol Psychiatr, 18*(2), 300–312. doi:10.1177/1359104512455182

Tang-Peronard, J. L., & Heitmann, B. L. (2008). Stigmatization of obese children and adolescents, the importance of gender. *Obes Rev, 9*(6), 522–534. doi:10.1111/j.1467-789X.2008.00509.x

Tanofsky-Kraff, M., Wilfley, D. E., Young, J. F., Mufson, L., Yanovski, S. Z., Glasofer, D. R., & Salaita, C. G. (2007). Preventing excessive weight gain in adolescents: Interpersonal psychotherapy for binge eating. *Obesity (Silver Spring), 15*(6), 1345–1355. doi:10.1038/oby.2007.162

Tanofsky-Kraff, M., Yanovski, S. Z., Wilfley, D. E., Marmarosh, C., Morgan, C. M., & Yanovski, J. A. (2004). Eating-disordered behaviors, body fat, and psychopathology in overweight and normal-weight children. *J Consult Clin Psychol, 72*(1), 53–61. doi:10.1037/0022-006X.72.1.53

Tylka, T. L., Russell, H. L., & Neal, A. A. (2015). Self-compassion as a moderator of thinness-related pressures' associations with thin-ideal internalization and disordered eating. *Eat Behav, 17*, 23–26. doi:10.1016/j.eatbeh.2014.12.009

van der Oord, S., Bogels, S. M., & Peijnenburg, D. (2012). The effectiveness of mindfulness training for children with ADHD and mindful parenting for their parents. *J Child Fam Stud, 21*(1), 139–147. doi:10.1007/s10826-011-9457-0

Wertheim, E. H., Martin, G., Prior, M., Sanson, A., & Smart, D. (2002). Parent influences in the transmission of eating and weight related values and behaviors. *Eat Disord, 10*(4), 321–334. doi:10.1080/10640260214507

Whiteside, U., Chen, E., Neighbors, C., Hunter, D., Lo, T., & Larimer, M. (2007). Difficulties regulating emotions: Do binge eaters have fewer strategies to modulate and tolerate negative affect? *Eat Behav, 8*(2), 162–169. doi:10.1016/j.eatbeh.2006.04.001

Wilson, S. M., & Sato, A. F. (2014). Stress and paediatric obesity: What we know and where to go. *Stress Health, 30*(2), 91–102. doi:10.1002/smi.2501

Wyatt, S. B., Winters, K. P., & Dubbert, P. M. (2006). Overweight and obesity: Prevalence, consequences, and causes of a growing public health problem. *Am J Med Sci, 331*(4), 166–174.

Young-Hyman, D., Tanofsky-Kraff, M., Yanovski, S. Z., Keil, M., Cohen, M. L., Peyrot, M., & Yanovski, J. A. (2006). Psychological status and weight-related distress in overweight or at-risk-for-overweight children. *Obesity (Silver Spring), 14*(12), 2249–2258. doi:10.1038/oby.2006.264

Positive theory and mechanisms of mindfulness

PART II

Positive theory and mechanisms of mindfulness

6

MINDFULNESS

The essence of well-being and happiness

Christelle T. Ngnoumen and Ellen J. Langer

Laughter becomes happiness

The American philosopher and psychologist William James once wrote, "We don't laugh because we're happy, we're happy because we laugh" (James, 1902). According to James, a preexisting state of happiness is not necessary for laughter. Rather, laughter itself can create happiness. Happiness is a choice and emerges from an active taking of joy from life through laughter. James's observation suggests that happiness is readily available to any individual and can be attained by simply reorienting the mind and body in a different way. Laughter becomes happiness. Since James, pain and emotion researchers have confirmed that mere, decontextualized laughter sends positive feedback to the body that can reduce stress and pain and boost positive emotion (Smith-Lee, 1990). Moreover, embodiment research, such as Langer's Counter Clockwise experiment, has demonstrated that positive thinking and environmental mirroring can affect physiological functioning and performance. In their experiment, elderly men taken to a retreat retrofitted to 20 years earlier were instructed to mentally embody their younger selves. Participants in the experimental group demonstrated more psychological and physiological improvements compared to matched controls. Altogether, emotion and embodiment research show that, contrary to expectations, well-being and happiness can be embodied.

Findings from emotion and embodiment research also reinforce a unitary view of mind and body. Human beings have always been characterized as having both a mind (e.g., a nonphysical entity) and a body (e.g., a physical entity). Early dualist models of the mind and body, such as those proposed by Plato and other classical Greek philosophers, viewed the mind and body as fundamentally distinct entities with limited interaction. Increasing research from psychology, however, particularly following the advent of behaviorism and neuroscience, supports a unitary perspective of the mind and body. According to mind-body unity theory, the mind and body comprise a single system, and every change in the human being is simultaneously a change at the level of the mind (e.g., cognitive changes) as well as the body (e.g., hormonal; neural; behavioral changes).

Mind-body dualism's early influence on Western philosophy and science, however, continues to significantly inform current common sense intuition regarding the nature of mental and physical experiences as distinct. This is apparent in the biomedical model of health that is still widely applied today (Langer, 2009). A critical assumption of the biomedical model of health is that social, emotional, and cognitive factors play little role in health. As such, the biomedical model subscribes to the reductionistic view of mind-body dualism. Moreover, perhaps because of its relatively younger historical presence, the wealth of evidence showing how good health can be directly embodied or produced through positive evaluation is obscured as researchers devote their efforts to finding mediating links between psychological (e.g., the mind) and physical experiences (e.g., the body). This bias of focusing on mediating—as opposed to direct—links reflects how common sense expectations are still grounded in early dualist notions, and assumes a necessary split between the mind and body whereby choice (e.g., a mental event) cannot affect behavior and biology (e.g., the body).

Controlling choice ≠ choosing control

Most positive experiences and their consequences are a function of choice and of the evaluations one chooses to make. The idea that positive experiences and good health are choices does not align with the information given to us at an earlier age that we've now come to adopt and apply generally. Common sense expectations borrowed from early sociocultural experiences depict the world as unpredictable, and depict well-being and happiness as products of external factors rooted in chance and luck as opposed to choice. More often than not, people in good physical or psychological health are viewed as merely having low genetic predispositions for chronic illness. Rarely do we consider the choices they actively make to allow themselves to be healthy such as smiling more, adding humor into their personal narratives, seeking out positive social supports, engaging in work that has personal meaning, and learning to differentiate the thoughts that are helpful to them from those that are not.

In the rare instance that common sense expectations borrowed from early sociocultural experiences do allow for a role of choice in well-being, well-being and happiness are nevertheless depicted as attainable only through extreme control in the form of structure, order, and overly applied discipline (Langer, 1989). Control and choice are not synonymous, however. While choice promotes control (e.g., exercising choice provides greater engagement in one's environment and life outcomes), extreme control hinders choice (e.g., rigid fixation on one outcome closes off access to alternative, and possibly more appropriate, outcomes). The rigid adherence to routine and notions that characterize control restricts access to more creative ways of thinking and of choosing to behave.

From a young age, humans are taught to value control; control holds things still and creates a sense of stability (Langer, 2009). Over time, however, unmoderated illusions of control become seemingly still images that close off access to more flexible and creative ways of thinking and viewing, and of responding to the world. Locked within a self-imposed view of the world as static, the individual quickly forgets that nothing is still in reality, and that experiences in the real world are marked by great variability. As the individual develops, rigid adherence to early sociocultural preferences for control can limit his ability to access novel information in the environment that could inform positive emotions and cultivate well-being. Control limits his ability to make choices. Furthermore, strong preferences for control generate an equally strong avoidance of the loss of that control. An individual with enough fear of losing control may grow to avoid displays of positive emotion such as laughter, out of a concern that these overt, physical displays represent an internal loss of control. By removing laughter from his behavioral repertoire, the individual also seals off a natural process of emotional release and a potential avenue for reducing stress and for inducing positive emotion (Miller et al., 2006).

Insistence of control is therefore a mindless process that lends itself to more negative experiences whereas choice is a mindful one that lends itself to more positive experiences. A mindful attitude involves identifying the positives in a situation, regardless of whether the situation itself initially seems positive or negative. A mindful attitude allows a person to recognize that positive and negative represent two alternative interpretations for the same event, each accompanied by very different outcomes that involve gains and losses (respectively) (Langer, 2008). Often, the path toward well-being and happiness is as direct as choosing to gain via positive evaluations.

Our emotions are choices

We take for granted that our evaluations of the world exist independently of it. We assume that our feelings and thoughts are facts that accurately capture objective truths in the world. However, a closer look at the things that we think are supposed to provide happiness, as compared to the things that actually provide it, reveals that happiness resides in our thoughts about objects and situations rather than in the objects and situations themselves. There is no such thing as an objective reality in which particular situations or objects guarantee a positive experience. Experience, which includes our emotions, is a product of evaluation. Evaluation is a choice.

Social psychology research shows that well-being and happiness depend more on the freedom to make choices rather than on having money (Fischer & Boer, 2011). We are often mistaken in our assumptions regarding the kinds of things that will afford happiness and promote well-being. Common sense expectations lead us to believe that factors such as wealth, high social and professional standing, and beauty supply happiness. While having money can certainly buy us things that make us happy, relative deprivation theory research (Vanneman & Pettigrew, 1972) has shown that nothing dejects the winner of a $500 bonus like learning of his coworker's $550 bonus. The perception of an unfair disparity between his situation and that of his coworker reflects a choice to negatively evaluate the scenario. There exists a positive, alternative evaluation for the same scenario that he has chosen to overlook. Overlooking the positive introduces a new theme of deprivation in his narrative that further fuels negative emotions and stress, ultimately reducing his capacity for happiness and increasing his vulnerabilities to poorer health.

Unbeknownst to him, the winner chooses to lose. While the difference between the two bonuses could, in fact, reflect an objective difference in the world, the winner's interpretation of that difference as an unfairness leads to feelings of inadequacy and lowers him to a subjective position of losing. The greatest unfairness met by the winner is therefore the theft of his own happiness caused by not considering alternative factors that may have played into these differences in bonuses, and by overlooking the fact that he is no more or less a winner compared to his coworker. A more mindful evaluation of the situation might have allowed him to consider the definition of a winner and consider all the forms in which winning takes shape. Overcoming an adversary is but one form of winning. Gaining a bonus is another form of winning.

Poor health as a product of mindlessness and outdated expectations

Whereas mindful evaluations promote positive experiences and well-being, mindless evaluations stemming from rigid adherence to common sense expectations impede health and happiness. Mindlessness is an inactive state of mind that relies on distinctions and categories drawn in the past and over-applies them to the present. Mindlessness is rooted in automaticity and undermines personal control, trapping the individual within a single perspective without awareness of contextual information (Langer, 1989; Langer et al., 1978). Deeply rooted and automatic sentiments about the nature of the world prevent us from accessing alternative information in the world around us that could inform our happiness and promote well-being.

Mindlessness has pervasive negative effects on health and well-being. Langer et al. (1988) found that uncritical acceptance of new health-related information locks individuals into premature cognitive commitments that resist change. Premature cognitive commitments are perspectives that are adapted at a particular time to make sense of the world; however, they are held onto mindlessly and never updated against present realities (Chanowitz & Langer, 1981). In one study, a sample of alcoholics were divided according to their childhood exposure to alcoholism. Their degree of premature cognitive commitments to information mindlessly learned about alcoholism during childhood predicted their treatment success. In another study, the authors found that participants' mindless attachment to views about old age learned during childhood was inversely related to their assessed alertness, activity levels, and independence in adulthood. Together, both studies demonstrate how mindless clinging to outdated expectations about health and aging can impede recovery and functioning. Langer's research also revealed how the language of illness and aging primes expectations and dictates attention and behavior (Langer et al., 2010.

A narrow understanding of illness and of happiness promotes a limited under-standing of well-being, which consequently closes us off to the benefits of alterna-tive therapeutic interventions and to positive experiences. The language commonly used to describe illness, such as "chronic" and "in remission," constrains individuals' experiences by priming expectations of long-term poor health. This language cre-ates the illusion that symptoms are stable and unmanageable. Individuals' identities tend to crystallize around the labels they are given, leading to an adoption of ste-reotypical behaviors that are in line with particular illnesses. It is in this manner that labels corresponding to chronic conditions rob individuals of personal control and potentially prevent the achievement of optimal health (Langer, 2009).

Research rooted in labeling theory has demonstrated that people who are labeled ill experience a decline in their general functioning and self-esteem that is more pronounced compared to individuals suffering from the same symptoms who are not labeled (Lai, Hong, & Chee, 2000). Carson and Langer (2006) com-pared the general health and well-being of breast cancer survivors who understood their cancer as in remission and as cured. Whereas the label cured primes the idea of health, the label in remission primes the idea of illness. Results revealed higher scores on measures of general health and emotional well-being among cancer sur-vivors who considered themselves cured compared to participants who considered themselves in remission. Participants in the cured group also had relatively fewer intrusive thoughts and lower depression scores. These results suggest a direct link between how participants view their relationships to illness and health outcomes. These results also suggest that mindset manipulations such as priming may serve as effective alternative therapeutic interventions for chronic illness.

The label chronic also primes the idea of illness (Langer, 2009). Most chronic conditions like depression and anxiety are subject to attention and interpretation, however. According to the *DSM-5,* a manual used to diagnose mental disorders, common symptoms people with depression experience include low mood and/or loss of interest in activities once enjoyed on a daily basis (or nearly daily) for at least 2 weeks (American Psychiatric Association, 2013). Symptoms of depression are all too often mindlessly perceived as definitive markers of chronic illness rather than as conditional occurrences, however. This is particularly problematic in cases where 2 weeks of intense sadness following the loss of a loved one is defined according to a diagnosis that does not specify when a person no longer meets its require-ments for eligibility. The lack of defining markers for when a person no longer has a chronic condition such as depression or anxiety makes its diagnosis, alone, more psychologically devastating than the condition itself. Not only is the end state of the condition not defined, but neither is the course of the condition, which is marked by high individual variation.

People experiencing depressive symptoms tend to believe that they are always depressed. The chronic label of their condition renders depression and its symp-toms a constant in their lives, and any temporary positive states that may emerge intermittently are overlooked. In a similar vein, people who experience chronic pain are not likely to track down the various contextual triggers of their pain for the unconditional view of their condition suggests little variation. Overtime, individuals with symptoms of depression and pain might cling to the expectations of their symptoms in a manner that makes the symptoms appear more familiar and frequent. Furthermore, the prescribing and use of pharmaceutical interventions to treat the depression and pain further fuels the beliefs people already have about their conditions being permanent. Thus begins a vicious cycle wherein the stability of their expectations gets interpreted as representing a stability in their objective realities (Langer, 2009).

Well-being as a product of mindfulness and choice

The essence of well-being is a mindful attitude, which involves noticing new things, active orientation in the present, openness to new information, continuous creation of new categories and distinctions, sensitivity to different contexts, and awareness of multiple perspectives (Langer et al., 1978). A mindful state of mind is guided—rather than governed—by rules, routines, and categories drawn in the past. A substantial body of research rooted in mindfulness theory demonstrates that people achieve better health through shifting their mindsets and by reorienting their attitudes toward themselves and their environments (e.g., Cohen, Doyle, Turner, Alper, & Skoner, 2003; Kamen-Siegel, Rodin, Seligman, Dwyer, 1991; Langer, Beck, Janoff-Bulman, & Timko, 1984; Langer, Janis, & Wolfer, 1975; Langer, Perlmuter, Chanowitz, & Rubin, 1988; Langer & Rodin, 1976; Langer, Rodin, Beck, Weinman, & Spitzer, 1979; Levy, Hausdorff, Hencke, & Wei, 2000; Levy & Langer, 1994; Levy & Leifheit-Limson, 2009; Levy, Slade, & Gill, 2006; Levy, Slade, Kunkel, & Kasl, 2002; Levy, Zonderman, Slade, & Ferrucci, 2009; Maier & Smith, 1999; Miller & Seligman, 1975; Peterson, Seligman, & Vaillant, 1988). Studies consistently show that mindful traits reduce negative affect and stress, cultivate creativity, and improve psychological well-being and quality of life (Creswell et al., 2007; Idler & Kasl, 1991; Kaplan & Camacho, 1983; Levy et al., 2002).

In the aforementioned Langer et al. (1990) Counter Clockwise experiment, elderly men taken to a retreat retrofitted to 20 years earlier were instructed to live for a week as if it were 20 years earlier. More specifically, participants in the experimental group were instructed to be psychologically where they were 20 years ago, but also to hold all discussions about the past in the present tense. By comparison, participants in the control group merely reminisced about the past 20 years without actively reliving the past in the present. The control group was instructed to hold all discussions about the past in the past tense. The experimental group demonstrated greater dexterity, grip strength, flexibility, hearing, vision, and memory and cognition compared to matched controls. This experiment showed that humans have the capacity to shift discontinuously to an "earlier" context and that such a mindset shift, when performed mindfully, is followed by a reverse temporal shift in physical and cognitive functioning.

In another experiment, Langer and Rodin (1976) found that institutionalized elderly adults who were encouraged to assume a more engaged role in their lives by making more decisions about their living space became more alert, more active, happier, healthier, and they lived longer. In this study, nursing home residents were encouraged to make more decisions for themselves such as where to receive visitors, what movies to watch at the home and when, which houseplants they could care for, where to place the houseplants in their rooms, and how frequently to water the houseplants. Compared to control participants, participants who exercised more choices demonstrated higher mood, greater activity, greater alertness, and greater longevity. This study showed that letting people make choices about their immediate environment engages them more fully in their own lives (e.g., increases personal responsibility), and affords them with a greater sense of personal control. Both of these factors promote health and well-being.

Crum and Langer (2007) primed female room attendants to view their work as a form of exercise and found that reorienting their attention toward the health benefits of their work resulted in decreases in BMI, waist-to-hip ratio, and weight. This study showed that – especially for individuals unaware that they are getting required amounts of physical exercise – priming the idea of exercise can result in benefits without actually changing daily habits.

Other studies have demonstrated that cognitive reappraisals provide relief from the pains of major surgery. Langer, Janis, and Wolfer (1975) instructed a group of patients undergoing surgery to replace their worries about surgery with thoughts about the positive aspects of the hospital experience and to rehearse these positive thoughts. Patients in the experimental group involving the cognitive reappraisal intervention demonstrated better post-surgery adjustment, less post-operative anxiety, less pain, and less pain medication usage compared to matched placebo control and information groups.

Studies by Levy and colleagues have also found that perceived health was a better predictor of mortality than actual health (Levy et al., 2006; Levy et al., 2009). Hsu, Ching, and Langer et al. (2010) discovered that cues that directly and indirectly signal aging primed diminished capacity. Moreover, the removal of these age cues primed health and longevity. Across five experiments, they found that cut or colored hairstyles cued youth and were associated with decreased blood pressure; clothing served as an age-related cue that influenced longevity; baldness cued old age and sped aging; the presence of children around women who gave birth later in life served as an age-related cue associated with positive outcomes; and large spousal age difference served as an age-related cue that shortened and expanded the longevity of younger and older spouses, respectively.

Mindfulness promotes well-being. Mindfulness challenges assumptions and prior beliefs by generating positive potential outcomes of meaning in a manner that may be more advantageous. Mindful cognitive reappraisals such as those adopted in the aforementioned studies all serve to test outdated assumptions against novel circumstances. Ideally, these forms of reality-testing afford individuals the chance to refine their expectations in a manner that resonates with their current contexts.

Mindful cognitive reappraisals hence reintroduce a firm grip on choice without the loss of control.

Engagement: a new look at happiness

The simple act of noticing new things, which defines mindfulness, generates engagement and leads to happiness. The process of looking at something familiar in new ways allows us to realize that we didn't know what we thought we did as well as we did. The world constantly changes and all of its components look different from different perspectives. The act of noticing new things allows the familiar to become interesting again and fosters engagement. Exercising choice—as demonstrated in Langer and colleagues' 1978 study wherein nursing home residents who exercised more choices showed improved mood and greater longevity—also fosters engagement. Engagement with both familiar and unfamiliar things causes a person to live in the present moment, is energizing, and bolsters creativity by opening up new ways of thinking and of choosing to behave (Brown & Langer, 1990; Langer, 1997). Research shows that high engagement promotes mindfulness and feelings of serenity, and it is intrinsically rewarding (Csikszentmihalyi, 1999).

Little attention is paid to the daily variability of positive emotions. Similar to depression and pain, happiness is perceived as an ongoing personal quality (e.g., a trait) as opposed to discontinuous positive experiences (e.g., states). There is an expectation that happiness must occur continually in order for its experience to be valid. Just as depressed people are expected to be depressed all the time, happy people are expected to be happy all the time. This expectation of happiness mindlessly excludes and isolates an individual as incapable of experiencing real happiness if he is not continuously happy. This can invalidate and dampen his isolated instances of joy. Over time, the systematic discounting of isolated instances of joy lends itself to ongoing unhappiness.

By paying attention to ourselves and to our bodies, we may also come to find that we're happier than we thought! This is to say, most clinical diagnoses consist of lists of negative symptoms that have been found to appear across a majority of individuals. Rarely does an individual experience all the symptoms from that general list. It is therefore important for the individual to recognize the extent to which s/he diverges from – as opposed to converges with – that general list of diagnostic criteria. It is also equally crucial to pay attention to those instances of positive emotion. Consider that the 'luck' of discovering a four-leaf clover exponentially increases when one starts actively looking for it. The process of finding happiness is similar: by paying attention to when we are happy, to how frequently we are happy, and to how long we remain happy, we allow ourselves to be happy. Attending to our happiness allows the happiness that is already readily available to us to be experienced. Contrary to expectations, finding a four-leaf clover and finding happiness therefore do not require luck. Rather, both are attainable through active looking and by noticing new things.

Establishing health and joy through mindfulness

A mindful attitude involves identifying the positive aspects of a negative situation, defining negatives in terms of positives, looking for variation within stability, and creating novel ways of distinguishing preexisting categories. All of these forms of cognitive reappraisal run counter to the human tendency of attending to negative stimuli and of organizing information into unified wholes based on old principles. Mindfulness therefore involves accepting and actively applying a new and different orientation to one's prior way of understanding the world.

Contrary to popular belief, illness, happiness, and aging are highly varying processes, susceptible to human choice and cultivation. In fact, the only stable things about our physical and mental health are our mindsets about them (Langer, 2009). Mindfulness-based research shows that stress is often the byproduct of outdated or untested assumptions about the negative outcomes of illness and aging. Stress also results from choosing to believe in our own negative evaluations of events. Mindfulness attacks these outdated assumptions and negative evaluations by generating positive alternative evaluations. This process of validating outdated assumptions against novel circumstances allows for exercising choice in the present, and the engagement that accompanies making choices also allows for happiness to be experienced. Exercising choice in the present yields greater control over health and happiness. Mindful and active engagement with our surroundings, such as paying closer attention to variations in our symptoms of illness, allows us to create labels that fit those experiences more appropriately. Furthermore, closer attention to the variations in our emotional experiences also allows us to notice and fully experience happiness when it emerges in a manner that common sense expectations would not predict.

Bibliography

American Psychiatric Association. (2013). *Diagnostic and statistical manual of mental disorders* (5th edition). Washington, DC.

Brown, J., & Langer, E. (1990). Mindfulness and intelligence: A comparison. *Educational Psychologists, 25*(3–4), 305–336.

Carson, S. H., & Langer, E. J. (2006). Mindfulness and self-acceptance. *Journal of Rational-Emotive and Cognitive Behavior Therapy, 24*(1), 29–4.

Cohen, S., Doyle, W. J., Turner, R. B., Alper, C. M., & Skoner, D. P. (2003). Emotional style and susceptibility to the common cold. *Psycho-somatic Medicine, 65*(1), 652–657.

Chanowitz, B., & Langer, E. (1981). Premature cognitive commitment. *Journal of Personality and Social Psychology, 41*, 1051–1063.

Creswell, J. D., Way, B. M., Eisenberger, N. I., & Lieberman, M. D. (2007). Neural correlates of dispositional mindfulness during affect labeling. *Psychosomatic Medicine, 69*(6), 560–565.

Crum, A., & Langer, E. (2007). Mind-set matters: Exercise and the placebo effect. *Psychological Science, 18*(2), 165–171.

Csikszentmihalyi, M. (1999). If we are so rich, why aren't we happy? *American Psychologist, 54*, 821–82.

Fischer, R., & Boer, D. (2011). What is more important for national well-being: Money or autonomy? A meta-analysis of well-being, burnout and anxiety across 63 societies. *Journal of Psychology and Social Psychology, 101*, 164–184.

Hsu, L. M., Chung, J., & Langer, E. J. (2010). The influence of age-related cues on health and longevity. *Perspectives in Psychological Science, 5*, 632–48.

Idler, E. L., & Kasl, S. (1991). Health perceptions and survival: Do global evaluations of health status really predict mortality? *Journal of Gerontology, 46*, S55–S65.

James, W. (1902). *The varieties of religious experience*. Edenborough: Longmans, Green, and Co.

Kamen-Siegel, L., Rodin, J., Seligman, M. E., Dwyer, J. (1991) Explanatory style and cell-mediated immunity in elderly men and women. *Health Psychology, 10*(1), 229–235.

Kaplan, G. A., & Camacho, T. (1983). Perceived health and mortality: A nine-year follow-up of the human population laboratory cohort. *American Journal of Epidemiology, 117*, 292–304.

Lai, Y. M., Hong, C. P., & Chee, C. Y. (2000). Stigma of mental illness. *Singapore Medical Journal, 42*(3), 111–114.

Langer, E. (1989). *Mindfulness*. Reading, MA: Addison-Wesley.

Langer, E. (2006). *On becoming an artist: Reinventing yourself through mindful creativity*. New York, NY: Ballentine.

Langer, E. (2008). Mindfulness/ mindlessness. In S. Lopez (Ed.), *Encyclopedia of positive psychology* (pp. 311–312). London, England: Blackwell Publishing.

Langer, E., Beck, P., Janoff-Bulman, R., & Timko, C. (1984). The relationship between cognitive deprivation and longevity in senile and non-senile elderly populations. *Academic Psychology Bulletin, 6*, 211–226.

Langer, E., Chanowitz, B., Palmerino, M., Jacobs, S., Rhodes, M., & Thayer, P. (1990). Non-sequential development and aging. In C. Alexander & E. Langer (Eds.), *Higher stages of human development: Perspectives on adult growth* (pp. 114–138). New York, NY: Oxford University Press.

Langer, E., Djikic, M., Pirson, M., Madenci, A., & Donohue, R. (2010). Believing is seeing: Using mindlessness (mindfully) to improve visual acuity. *Psychological Science, 21*(5), 661–666.

Langer, E., Perlmuter, L., Chanowitz, B., & Rubin, R. (1988). Two new applications of mindlessness theory: Aging and alcoholism. *Journal of Aging Studies, 2*, 289–299.

Langer, E., Pirson, M., & Delizonna, L. (2010). The mindlessness of social comparisons. *Psychology Aesthetics, Creativity, and the Arts, 4*(2), 68–74.

Langer, E., & Rodin, J. (1976). Effects of choice and enhanced personal responsibility for the aged: A field experiment in an institutional setting. *Journal of Personality and Social Psychology, 34*(2), 191–199.

Langer, E. J. (1997). *The power of mindful learning*. Reading, MA: Addison-Wesley.

Langer, E. J. (2009). *Counter clockwise: Mindful health and the power of possibility*. New York, NY: Ballantine Books.

Langer, E. J., & Abelson, R. F. (1974). A patient by any other name . . .: Clinician group difference in labeling bias. *Journal of Consulting and Clinical Psychology, 42*, 4–9.

Langer, E. J., Blank, A., & Chanowitz, B. (1978). The mindlessness of ostensibly thoughtful action: The role of "placebic" information in interpersonal interaction. *Journal of Personality and Social Psychology, 36*(6), 635–642.

Langer, E. J., Janis, I. L., & Wolfer, J. A. (1975). Reduction of psychological stress in surgical patients. *Journal of Experimental Social Psychology, 11*, 155–165.

Langer, E., J. Rodin, P. Beck, C. Weinman, & L. Spitzer. (1979). Environmental determinants of memory improvement in late adulthood. *Journal of Personality and Social Psychology, 37*(11), 2003–2013.

Lee, J. R. (1990). Osteoporosis reversal: The role of progesterone. *International Journal of Clinical Nutrition, 10,* 384–91.

Levy, B., Hausdorff, J., Hencke, R., & Wei, J. (2000). Reducing cardiovascular stress with positive self-stereotypes of aging. *Journal of Gerontology: Psychological Sciences, 55,* 1–9.

Levy, B., & Langer, E. (1994). Aging free from negative stereotypes: Successful memory in China and among the American deaf. *Journal of Personality and Social Psychology, 66,* 989–997.

Levy, B. R., & Leifheit-Limson, E. (2009). The stereotype-matching effect: Greater influence on functioning when age stereotypes correspond to outcomes. *Psychology and Aging, 24,* 230–233.

Levy, B. R., Slade, M. D., & Gill, T. (2006). Hearing decline predicted by elders' age stereotypes. *Journal of Gerontology: Psychological Sciences, 61,* 82–87.

Levy, B. R., Slade, M., Kunkel, S., & Kasl, S. (2002). Longevity increased by positive self-perceptions of aging. *Journal of Personality and Social Psychology, 83,* 261–270.

Levy, B. R., Zonderman, A., Slade, M. D., & Ferrucci, L. (2009). Negative age stereotypes held earlier in life predict cardiovascular events in later life. *Psychological Science, 20,* 296–298.

Maier, H., & Smith, J. (1999). Psychological predictors of mortality in old age. *Journals of Gerontology: Psychological Sciences, 54B,* 44–54.

Miller, M., Mangano, C., Park, Y., Goel, R., Plotnick, G., & Vogel, R. (2006). Impact of cinematic viewing on endothelial function. *Heart, 92*(2), 261–262.

Miller, W. R. and Seligman, M.E.P. (1975). Depression and learned helplessness in man. *Journal of Abnormal Psychology, 84*(1), 228–238.

Peterson, C. Seligman, M. E. P. & Vaillant, G. E. (1988). Pessimistic explanatory style is a risk factor for physical illness: A thirty-five year longitudinal study. *Journal of Personality and Social Psychology, 55*(1), 23–27.

Smith-Lee, B. (1990). Humor relations for nurse managers. *Nursing Management, 21,* 86.

Vanneman, R. D., & Pettigrew, T. F. (1972). Race and relative deprivation in the urban United States. *Race, 13,* 461–486.

7

MINDFULNESS, MENTAL HEALTH, AND POSITIVE PSYCHOLOGY

Shauna Shapiro, Sarah de Sousa,
and Hooria Jazaieri

Introduction

Clinical psychology has long been focused on the alleviation of human suffering through the assessment and treatment of psychological disorders. Correspondingly, mental health has long been defined as the absence of disorder rather than as the presence of positive characteristics and traits. Positive psychology expands this definition to include a fuller sense of human potential and flourishing through the recognition that positive characteristics are not only salient markers of mental health, but indeed form the heart of what it means to live a full and rewarding human life. As Wood and Tarrier (2010) suggest, the future of clinical psychology lies in integrating the contributions of positive psychology into the daily research and practice of clinical work. Central to the development and practice of positive clinical psychology is the call for clinicians to embrace a concept of wellbeing that honors the interdependence of negative and positive emotions, thoughts, and experience (Wood & Tarrier, 2010). The study of mindfulness as a clinical intervention, as well as a theoretical framework, offers much to this emerging focus in clinical work (Shapiro, de Sousa, & Hauck, in press).

We begin our exploration of mindfulness, mental health, and positive psychology by offering an operational definition of mindfulness. We review the clinical applications of mindfulness, dividing this into four categories: (1) Diagnostic disorders, (2) Prevention and healthy stressed populations, (3) Positive physiological findings, and (4) Positive psychological findings. We explore future directions in research and clinical applications and lastly, we posit that mindfulness offers something unique and deeply healing to the mental health professions, through its acceptance of negative and positive experiences as equally important and valid.

What is mindfulness?

Mindfulness is much more than paying attention. It is a way of training the mind, heart, and body to be fully present with life. It is both a practice (e.g., meditation) and a way of being. Fundamentally, it is a way of relating to all experience – positive, negative, and neutral – with kindness, openness, and receptivity.

Shapiro and Carlson (2009) offer a model that integrates three core elements of mindfulness, *intention, attention,* and *attitude* (IAA) into an operational definition, at once practical in the clinical environment, and nuanced in its rendering of the complex, multifaceted and paradoxically irreducible nature of what is essentially an experiential process. Here, we present the IAA model of mindfulness as a framework for understanding the applications of mindfulness to clinical work, and the potential it holds for expanding the paradigm of human wellbeing.

Three core elements of mindfulness

The IAA model of mindfulness comprises three core elements: intention, attention, and attitude (Shapiro & Carlson, 2009). Intention creates the context and motivation that fuel our practice of mindfulness because intention connects us to what is of greatest value: our ultimate aim, our vision, and our aspiration. Attention involves bringing our awareness into focus and observing our moment-to-moment internal and external experience in the here and now. Attitude describes the quality of our attention – harsh and exacting or kind, curious, and gentle. These three elements are inextricably bound in the moment-to-moment process that is mindful practice. According to the IAA model, mindfulness is the ongoing cyclical interplay of these core elements as they unfold in the present moment.

Intention

The first core component of mindfulness is intention. According to Jon Kabat-Zinn (1990), "Your intentions set the stage for what is possible. They remind you from moment to moment of why you are practicing in the first place" (p. 32). Discerning our intentions involves inquiring into our deepest hopes, desires, and aspirations. Explicitly reflecting on our intentions helps us bring unconscious values to awareness and decide whether they are really the values we want to pursue (Shapiro & Carlson, 2009). And yet, it is important to note that intention is not about becoming goal oriented or attached to a specific outcome. At the deepest level, intention is simply a reflection upon why we are practicing, what we value, and what is most important to us. Intention involves setting the compass of the heart in the direction we want to head. As Jack Kornfield guides us, "Intention is not a destination, it is a direction" (personal communication, 2012).

Attention

The second fundamental component of mindfulness is attention. It has been suggested in the field of psychology that attention is critical to the healing process that occurs in therapy (Shapiro & Carlson, 2009). Paying attention involves a clear seeing of what is here, now, in this present moment. In the context of mindfulness, we learn to attend not only to the world around us but to the contents of our own consciousness. And yet, this can be challenging. Recent research demonstrates that our mind wanders approximately 47% of the time (Killingsworth & Gilbert, 2010). The human mind is often referred to as a "monkey mind," swinging from thought to thought as a monkey swings from limb to limb. Mindfulness helps us cultivate attention that is sustained and concentrated, despite our mind's inclination to wander. Therefore, attention is the component of mindfulness that facilitates greater focus, discernment, and the capacity to note what arises in our field of experience without engaging in reflexive reactivity.

Often, as we try to pay attention, our attention becomes tense and contracted. This is because we mistakenly think we have to be stressed or vigilant to focus our attention in a rigorous way. However, the meditation traditions teach us of a different kind of attention, a "relaxed alertness" that involves clarity and precision without stress or vigilance (Wallace, 2006; Shapiro, Jazaieri, & de Sousa, in press). This relaxed alertness is the kind of attention that is essential to mindfulness. Mindful attention is also deep and penetrating; as Bhikkhu Bodhi notes ". . . whereas a mind without mindfulness 'floats' on the surface of its object the way a gourd floats on water, mindfulness sinks into its object the way a stone placed on the surface of water sinks to the bottom" (Wallace, 2006, p. 7).

Attitude

As we learn to attend with clarity and discernment to our own experience, we may also begin to notice that the mind is constantly judging. How we pay attention, our attitude, is therefore essential to mindfulness. As Khalil Gibran (n.d.) says, "Your living is determined not so much by what life brings to you as by the attitude you bring to life." Attention can be cold and critical or curious, kind, and compassionate. The latter is what brings out the best of our humanity and enhances our clinical work, and it is what we are talking about when we speak in terms of mindfulness (Shapiro, de Sousa, & Hauck, in press). Attending without bringing the attitudinal qualities of curiosity, openness, acceptance, and love (COAL; Siegel 2007) into the practice may result in an attention that is condemning or shaming of inner (or outer) experience – our own or our client's. This may well have consequences contrary to the intentions of mindful practice; what we practice becomes stronger. When we practice judgment and criticism, we strengthen neuropathways of negativity. Conversely, when we practice equanimity, openness, and acceptance, we strengthen our capacity to be with whatever arises in our field of experience, negative or positive.

Thus, the attitudes of mindfulness do not alter our experience, but simply contain it. When a negative thought or emotion arises during our practice, we simply note what is without attempting to suppress or replace it. When our minds wander, as they inevitably will, we do not berate ourselves for the failure; we gently invite our attention to return with graciousness, as though greeting a dear one returning home. When we practice mindfulness, we cultivate new habits of relating to our inner and outer worlds, and gradually learn to transcend our ingrained reactivity. This way of being begins to shift our brain circuits toward empathy, understanding, and acceptance. As this shift occurs, we find ourselves clinging less to our positive experiences and meeting our negative experiences with less resistance. Learning to attend within a context of curiosity, openness, acceptance, and love not only makes it much easier to stay present, it can also transform our ability to foster wellbeing in those who seek our clinical care.

Formal and informal practice

Cultivating mindfulness requires practice. As with any skill, developing our capacity to intentionally pay attention with a kind, open, curious attitude involves making time to train ourselves in this mode of being. What we refer to as *formal* practice is the time we allocate to structured practices such as sitting meditation, body scan meditation, or other forms of systematic training. *Informal* practice describes our efforts to transfer the skills acquired through formal practice to the moments and events of our everyday lives. For example, we can apply the mindfulness skills of intention, attention, and attitude to washing the dishes, reading a book, or meeting with a client.

Fundamentally, all clinical work can be considered informal mindfulness practice. In the clinical art of being with another human, the ability to sustain focused attention, respond with a nonreactive and empathic presence to what arises in each moment, and stay connected to our wholesome intention as helping professionals are essential skills that both constitute and enhance informal practice (Shapiro, Thakur, & de Sousa, 2014). As Bien (2006) says, "The most important thing we offer [in therapy] is our true presence and our deep listening. . . . To offer true presence and deep listening, we need ways to become more clear and centered. If we are not clear and centered, how will we offer these qualities to those who seek our help?" (p. xv).

Clinical applications

Research investigating the efficacy of mindfulness-based interventions for the treatment of psychological symptoms and disorders is continuing to grow at a fast pace. As it stands, there is solid evidence that mindfulness-based treatments can be successfully applied to the treatment of symptoms of anxiety and depression. Research investigating psychological outcomes in healthy community populations, however, is currently quite minimal, as is research that addresses the possibilities for personal growth and transcendence (Shapiro & Carlson, 2009). Below we review the current and most relevant literature in each of these domains of clinical research and offer suggestions regarding those areas of research that merit significant future attention.

Diagnostic disorders

We begin our review by examining the effects of mindfulness-based interventions across diverse clinical populations. Research spanning the past 30 years has evaluated the effectiveness of mindfulness-based interventions. In a recent meta-analysis evaluating 209 studies of mindfulness-based therapies (MBTs) with participants of diverse clinical profiles, Khoury, Lecomte, Fortin, et al. (2013) found MBTs to show clinically significant effects, particularly in the treatment of anxiety and depression.

One study compared mindfulness-based stress reduction (MBSR) with the gold-standard treatment of 12 weekly sessions of cognitive-behavioral therapy (CBT) in 53 patients with social anxiety disorder (Koszycki, Benger, Shlik, & Bradwejn, 2007). Both interventions resulted in improved mood, functionality, and quality of life, but CBT proved superior in terms of improving specific measures of the severity of social anxiety. Wiess, Nordlie, and Siegel (2005) added MBSR training to psychotherapy for a group of outpatients with primarily anxiety and depressive symptoms. When compared with a group that received psychotherapy only, both groups improved similarly on psychological distress, but those in MBSR showed greater gains on a measure of goal achievement and were able to terminate therapy sooner.

MB-EAT is an adapted form of MBSR specifically designed for persons with binge eating disorder. In a recent study, Kristeller, Wolever, and Sheets (2014) reported decreased bingeing frequency and related symptoms at a clinically meaningful level post-intervention when comparing MB-EAT to both a psychoeducational/cognitive-behavioral intervention and a wait-list control across 150 randomly assigned participants, 66% of whom met full DSM-IV-R criteria for binge eating disorder. Furthermore, improvement in the degree of symptom reduction was related to the degree of mindfulness practice.

Further clinical research has been conducted on adapted applications of MBSR for psychological and behavioral disorders including insomnia, addiction, and ADHD. However, the research base supporting MBSR's efficacy as a psychological intervention is significantly less robust than the research base addressing efficacy in medical populations. There continues to be a need to investigate the efficacy of MBSR compared with other gold-standard treatments for mental health issues, utilizing stringently designed clinical trials.

Mindfulness-based cognitive therapy (MBCT) is a mindfulness-based intervention that has received considerable attention for its efficacy in treating patients with major depressive disorder (MDD) and in preventing relapse. MBCT studies originate from experienced psychotherapy researchers; therefore, MBCT research tends to be quite strong methodologically. Much of this research has been conducted by Teasdale, Williams, and colleagues in the United Kingdom. Multiple studies conducted by this group have documented significantly fewer relapses in depression when comparing MBCT to treatment as usual (TAU) in at-risk populations (Ma & Teasdale, 2004; Williams, Teasdale, Segal, & Soulsby, 2000). These findings are consistent with a recent meta-analysis by Piet and Hougaard (2011), which found that MBCT showed clinically significant effects in reducing the risk of relapse/recurrence for patients diagnosed with recurrent MDD.

Mindfulness-based relapse prevention (MBRP; Witkiewitz, Marlatt, & Walker, 2005) is an innovative therapy designed as an aftercare treatment to prevent relapse in patients diagnosed with substance abuse disorders. In an RCT comparing MBRP to TAU, Bowen and colleagues (2006) found that MBRP reduced rates of substance use and that results were maintained at the 4-month follow-up. These findings were extended by Witkiewitz, Bowen, Douglas, and Hsu (2013), who proposed that a latent factor representing the interdependent processes of acceptance, awareness, and nonjudgment would significantly mediate the reduction in self-reported levels of craving immediately following treatment with MBRP. Interestingly, the mindfulness subscales of acceptance, awareness, and nonjudgment were not found to independently mediate the association between MBRP and the level of craving. As in the IAA model of mindfulness, these findings suggest that only in concert can the awareness and attitudinal qualities instilled by mindful practice predict healthier outcomes.

Acceptance and commitment therapy (ACT), another form of mindfulness-based intervention, has produced a number of RCTs evaluating the effect of ACT on a range of psychological disorders, including borderline personality disorder (BPD; Gratz & Gunderson, 2006), opiate dependence (Hayes et al., 2004), smoking cessation (Gifford et al., 2004), math anxiety (Zettle, 2003), and trichotillomania (Woods, Wetterneck, & Flessner, 2006). A 2008 review of RCTs of ACT described 13 RCTs in which ACT, singly or in combination with another treatment, was compared with a control group or another active treatment (Ost, 2008). The overall effect size on a variety of psychosocial and symptom-related outcome measures when combined with a meta-analysis was 0.68. As with other mindfulness-based treatment modalities, this research suggests that mindfulness-based treatments may be applicable across a wide range of clinical populations, though further research is necessary to determine the details of what is effective for whom.

Dialectical behavior therapy (DBT) was developed as a therapy to be applied to people with BPD (Linehan, 1987, 1993), so it is not surprising that the bulk of the evidence supporting its efficacy is from that treatment population. A 2008 review by Ost identified 13 RCTs of DBT, nine of which were for patients with BPD. The review by Ost (2008) found that the average effect size of the DBT interventions was 0.58, which is considered to be a medium-sized effect and likely clinically significant. A meta-analysis of five RCTs by Panos, Jackson, Hasan, and Panos (2014) found that DBT was most effective at stabilizing and controlling self-destructive behaviors and improving compliance in patients diagnosed with BPD. DBT has also been adapted and applied to other groups, primarily people with symptoms of depression (Harley, Sprich, Safren, Jacobo, & Fava, 2008; Lynch, Chapman, Rosenthal, Kuo, & Linehan, 2006). In the case of mixed-modality intensive treatments such as DBT, the underlying mechanisms of action have only begun to be explored, and applicability to diverse populations, as well as the efficacy of such interventions in treating specific symptoms, offers rich opportunities for clinical research.

Prevention and healthy stressed populations

Though limited in scope, research on healthy stressed populations suggests that mindfulness training offers a wide range of physical, emotional, and psychological benefits (Shapiro & Jazaieri, 2015). In a group of healthy university students, six individual sessions of mindfulness training were compared with two guided-imagery sessions (Kingston, Chadwick, Meron, & Skinner, 2007). Students who had the mindfulness training showed significant increases pre- to post-treatment in their pain tolerance compared with those in the other condition, although there were no differences on mood or blood pressure.

Carson, Carson, Gil, and Baucom (2004) evaluated the preliminary efficacy of mindfulness-based relationship enhancement using a randomized wait-list trial in a group of relatively happy, nondistressed couples. Couples participating in the intervention reported improvements in their relationship's satisfaction, autonomy, relatedness, and closeness, as well as improvements in their acceptance of each other and a lessening in distress about their relationship. As individuals, they were also more optimistic and relaxed and reported less distress than did those in the wait-list group. Benefits were maintained at a 3-month follow-up, and the amount of meditation practice was related to the magnitude of the benefits reported.

Although most mindfulness research has focused on patient benefits, recent research has found that mindfulness training may be particularly useful for clinical professionals as a means of managing stress and promoting self-care (Irving, Dobkin, & Park, 2009; Shapiro & Carlson, 2009). Studies evaluating the effectiveness of mindfulness-based stress reduction (MBSR) have found decreased anxiety, depression, rumination, and stress, as well as increased empathy, self-compassion, spirituality, and positive mood states among premedical students, nursing students, and therapists in training after completion of the MBSR program (Beddoe & Murphy, 2004). Similar findings have been obtained with studies on nurses and doctors.

In a controlled trial of premedical students, Jain et al. (2007) determined that students receiving an MBSR intervention experienced increases in positive mood states and significant decreases in rumination and stress, compared with a control group. Notably, effect sizes for mood state increases were moderate to large in the MBSR group, whereas the control group showed no effect. Practicing nurses have reported significant improvements in aspects of burnout (personal accomplishment and emotional exhaustion) after MBSR training (Cohen-Katz, Wiley, Capuano, Baker, & Shapiro, 2005), and primary care doctors showed improvements in burnout, depersonalization, empathy, total mood disturbance, consciousness, and emotional stability after an 8-week mindfulness course and a 10-month maintenance phase (2.5 hours per month) (Krasner et al., 2009).

Though research investigating psychological outcomes in healthy community populations as well as healthy stressed populations is growing, future research in these areas would be most welcome.

Positive physiological findings

An emerging field of research that holds valuable implications for mental health professionals seeks to better understand the physiological underpinnings of psychological wellbeing. A growing body of research suggests that positive traits and attributes can be assessed and cultivated, leading to improved psychological resilience, and buffering against psychological disorder (Kobau et al., 2011). Furthermore, "positive emotions and positive evaluations of life are associated with decreased risk of disease, illness and injury; healthier behaviors; better immune functioning; speedier recovery; and increased longevity" (Kobau et al., 2011, p. 2). As Ryff and Singer (1998) aptly point out, "human wellness is at once about the mind and the body and their interconnections" (p. 2). Although the implications of the physiological correlates of mindfulness meditation are as yet unclear, it seems likely that some of the changes represent "physiological substrates of flourishing" (Ryff & Singer, 1998, p. 2; Shapiro, Jazaieri, & de Sousa, in press).

Immune function

Improvements in immune system functioning or reversal of immune suppression may be an important marker of such physiological substrates of health and wellbeing (Shapiro, Jazaieri, & de Sousa, in press). A significant body of work has evaluated the effects of mindfulness-based interventions on psychological and biological outcomes for cancer patients. In one such study, Carlson et al. (2004) found that MBSR had a number of effects on immune parameters that are consistent with a shift to a more normal profile. This study also looked at salivary cortisol, because daily salivary cortisol levels have been related to stress and health and are often dysregulated in cancer survivors. Dysregulated cortisol secretion patterns are associated with poorer clinical outcomes (Shapiro & Carlson, 2009). Carlson et al. (2004) found fewer evening cortisol elevations and some normalization of abnormal diurnal salivary cortisol profiles post-MBSR.

Recent research in the field of psychoendocrinology sheds additional light on a possible mechanism of action linking physical health to psychological functioning in clinical populations (Schutte & Malouff, 2014). Telomere length (TL) has been established as an important "psychobiomarker" linking psychological stress and disease because of the role TL plays in cellular longevity (Epel et al., 2009; Willeit, Willeit, Kloss-Brandstätter, Kronenberg, & Kiechl, 2011; Lin, Epel, & Blackburn, 2012). Lengacher and colleagues (2014) conducted an RTC to assess the effects of MBSR on TL in 142 women with breast cancer and found that MBSR was associated with significant increases in telomerase activity (TA) compared to the wait-list control. Although the clinical benefits of increased TA remain as yet unclear, emerging evidence suggests that TA and TL may be important outcome variables to consider in future studies evaluating the salutary effects of mindfulness-based interventions.

Neuroplasticity

Converging data indicate that mindfulness practice contributes to the development of neurophysiological structures undergirding key markers of psychological health, including cognitive flexibility, affective plasticity, emotion regulation, and attentional deployment (Goldin & Gross, 2010; Hölzel, Carmody, Vangel, et al., 2011;

Lazar et al., 2005). A recent study evaluating the effects of MBSR on emotion regulation in patients diagnosed with social anxiety disorder (SAD) found significant MBSR-related changes in regions of the brain associated with visual attention, attentional deployment, and emotional reactivity (Goldin & Gross, 2010). Research on healthy stressed populations also provides evidence that meditation experience influences changes in the brain's physical structure.

In a longitudinal MRI study with 26 participants, Hölzel, Carmody, Evans, et al. (2010) investigated the relationship between changes in perceived stress with changes in amygdala gray matter density following an 8-week MBSR intervention. Participants in the study were screened using the perceived stress scale (PSS) and eligibility was defined as a PSS score at least one standard deviation above the population mean. Reductions in perceived stress correlated positively with decreased amygdala gray matter density post-treatment. Though a growing body of research is beginning to elaborate the linkages between meditation experience and neuroplasticity, ongoing research is needed that investigates the relationship between neuroplastic changes and the effects of mindfulness-based interventions for clinical and healthy populations.

Several meta-analyses have shown that mindfulness meditation programs such as MBSR reliably decreases symptoms of stress, anxiety, and depression, and increases wellbeing across clinical and non-clinical samples (Baer, 2003; Bishop, 2002; Grossman, Niemann, Schmidt, & Walach, 2004) and is associated with increased positive-affective and decreased negative-affective states (Baer, Carmody, & Hunsinger, 2012; Brown & Ryan, 2003; Hofmann, Sawyer, Witt, & Oh, 2010). These programs, as we'll briefly review, have also been shown to improve a number of other important areas related to positive psychology for those experiencing a variety of mental health issues.

Memory, attention, and concentration

Preliminary research indicates that mindfulness training influences a number of measures associated with cognitive performance. In a study evaluating the impact of mindfulness training on working memory capacity (WMC) and affective experience, Jha and colleagues (2010) measured the effects of mindfulness training (MT) on a military cohort during the high-stress predeployment interval preceding a deployment to Iraq. Results from the MT group on the OSPAN (Operation Span), as well as the PANAS (Positive and Negative Affect Schedule), a 10-item self-report mood scale, were compared to results from a military control (MC) sample drawn from the same parent unit as the MT group (Jha et al., 2010). Results in this study supported the hypothesis that mindfulness training enhances WMC, demonstrating statistically significant improvements on the OSPAN in the MT group (Jha et al., 2010). Results also suggest that improvements in WMC may increase positive affect and mitigate negative affect, buffering against the psychological and cognitive deterioration associated with prolonged exposure to high-stress conditions (Jha et al., 2010).

When considering persons who experience depression, MBCT has been shown to improve autobiographical memory specificity and reduce categorical overgeneral memories (Williams et al., 2000). The study by Williams and colleagues (2000) was replicated and extended by Heeren, Van Broeck, and Philippot (2009). In a quasi-experimental mixed design, Heeren et al. (2009) found that MBCT increased specific and decreased general autobiographical memory retrieval, improved the capacity to inhibit secondary elaborative processing of responses that arise in one's stream of consciousness, and improved the ability to switch between cognitive tasks.

Mindfulness meditation can be considered a form of an attention training practice. Increasing evidence suggests that for clinical populations and those experiencing mental health issues mindfulness training may be beneficial for improving attention and concentration. In a randomized controlled treatment trial comprised of individuals who have experienced a traumatic brain injury or who have suffered a stroke, Johansson and colleagues (2012) found that a standard 8-week MBSR program demonstrated statistically significant improvement in self-reported mental fatigue as well as improvements on neuropsychological tests quantifying information processing speed.

Happiness and positive affect

It has been well documented in the empirical literature that mindfulness and meditation programs are associated with a reduction in negative affect such as stress and depression in patients with a variety of mental and physical health conditions (e.g., Baer, 2003). Recently, researchers have examined whether these programs also have the ability to increase positive affect within clinical populations. For example, having a sense of coherence or experiencing life as meaningful and manageable has been suggested to be a protective factor for psychological health in stressful circumstances. One study examined the effects of an MBSR program in women with fibromyalgia and found that when compared to the control condition, women in the MBSR group reported a significant increase in their sense of coherence following the program (Weissbecker et al., 2002). Another study examined a mindfulness intervention in cancer patients who were undergoing hematopoietic stem cell transplant (Bauer-Wu et al., 2008). The intervention consisted of one-on-one sessions with a mindfulness meditation instructor prior to hospitalization and twice weekly one-on-one sessions during hospitalization. Patients also listened to guided mindfulness meditation CDs at least three times per week immediately prior to and during hospitalization. Findings demonstrated increases in happiness over the course of the mindfulness program.

Optimism

Empirical literature has documented the link between optimism and greater well-being (e.g., Carver, Scheier, & Segerstrom, 2010). For example, a recent study evaluated the effectiveness of a 10-day silent Vipassana (mindfulness) meditation course on substance use and positive psychosocial outcomes in an incarcerated population

(Bowen et al., 2006). Participants in the course completed baseline assessments 1 week before the start of the course, 1 week after completion of the course, and at 3 months following release from jail. Results indicated that compared to those in a TAU control condition, participants in the meditation course showed significant increases in optimism as measured by the Life Orientation Test (LOT; Scheier & Carver, 1985) 3 months after release. Also when compared to the control condition, the participants in the meditation condition demonstrated reductions in alcohol, marijuana, and crack cocaine use, as well as decreases in alcohol-related problems and psychiatric symptoms 3 months after release from jail.

Psychological flexibility

Psychological flexibility is considered to be fundamental to health and yet is absent in many mental health disorders (Kashdan & Rottenberg, 2010). When examining the effects of ACT on psychological flexibility for adults with chronic pain, there were significant improvements in four aspects of psychological flexibility – acceptance of pain, values-based action, psychological acceptance, and mindfulness (McCracken & Gutiérrez-Martínez, 2011). In another study an 8-week ACT plus mindfulness intervention was utilized within a sample of adults with mild to moderate psychological distress (Fledderus, Bohlmeijer, Smit, & Westerhof, 2010). When compared to the control condition, the ACT plus mindfulness intervention improved psychological flexibility immediately following the intervention. Furthermore, the improvement in psychological flexibility during the intervention mediated the effects of the intervention on positive mental health both immediately following the treatment and at the 3-month follow-up.

Self-esteem

Low self-esteem has been linked to numerous mental health issues (Mann, Hosman, Schaalma, & de Vries, 2004). Meditation and mindfulness-based interventions have sought to examine the effects of these programs on self-esteem. For example, in an MBSR program for adolescents between the ages of 14–18 years old in an outpatient psychiatric facility, when compared to the TAU control participants, those receiving MBSR reported reductions in clinical symptoms (anxiety, depression) and improved self-esteem and sleep quality (Biegel, Brown, Shapiro, & Schubert, 2009). MBSR has also been shown to improve self-esteem in adults diagnosed with social anxiety disorder (Goldin & Gross, 2010; Goldin, Ramel, & Gross, 2009). MBCT has been associated with improvements in self-esteem in psychiatric outpatients with mood and/or anxiety disorders (Ree & Craigie, 2007).

Quality of life and satisfaction with life

It has become increasingly common for clinical studies to examine not only the absence of clinical features following an intervention but also the improvement of an overall reported quality of – or satisfaction with – life. A small pilot study examined the effects of a 12-week mindfulness-based intervention on improving quality of life in individuals with mild to moderate brain injuries (1 year or longer following their injury) (Bédard et al., 2003). The preliminary results from this study suggest that mindfulness-based interventions may improve the quality of life of those who have experienced a traumatic brain injury.

Within the context of a randomized controlled trial, 150 patients with mild to moderate multiple sclerosis (MS) were randomized to either an 8-week mindfulness training program or TAU (Grossman et al., 2010). In addition to improving depression, fatigue, and anxiety, participants in the mindfulness group reported a higher quality of life following the program. MBSR for patients with social anxiety disorder was also found to improve quality of life following the 8-week program (Koszycki et al., 2007).

One study examined the effects of MBSR on health-related quality of life, which includes both physical and mental functioning and wellbeing, within a patient population with heterogeneous medical diagnoses (Reibel, Greeson, Brainard, & Rosenzweig, 2001). The results from this prospective, observational study suggested that in addition to reducing physical symptoms and psychological distress, MBSR can improve health-related quality of life immediately following the intervention and these benefits are also maintained at the 1-year follow-up.

Several other studies have examined quality of life and life satisfaction improvements following mindfulness programs in a variety of clinical populations including chronic pain and fibromyalgia patients (for a review, see Veehof, Oskam, Schreurs, & Bohlmeijer, 2011). Another study examining a standard-week MBSR intervention in patients with social anxiety disorder found an increase in patients' self-reported life satisfaction following the MBSR program (Jazaieri, Goldin, Werner, Ziv, & Gross, 2012). These benefits were also sustained at the 3-month follow-up period.

Future directions

The shifting focus in clinical psychology toward an integration of the negative and positive in research and clinical work invites those interested in the effects of mindfulness on mental health to consider broadly the treatment, prevention, and positive applications of mindfulness-based interventions. Continued research in the effects of mindfulness-based programs on positive physiological and psychological outcomes within clinical populations is needed. For example, examining the effects of mindfulness-based programs on compassion, empathy, moral reasoning, and spirituality (e.g., Labelle, Lawlor-Savage, Campbell, Faris, & Carlson, 2014) are all areas ripe for examination within clinical research. Further research investigating the relationship between mindfulness and neural correlates of positive affect, emotion regulation, and attentional deployment may support clinical professionals in developing improved interventions, and in understanding the mechanisms of action in interventions that are highly effective across diverse populations.

Mindfulness extends the invitation to expand our paradigm of wellbeing beyond the presence or absence from our lives of illness, distress, anger, sadness, joy, optimism, or health. It is an invitation to welcome all of our experience and explore it with equanimity, discernment, and kindness. As psychotherapist and mindfulness teacher Jack Kornfield (1993) says, it is "in accepting all the songs of our life that we can begin to create for ourselves a much deeper and greater identity in which our heart holds all within a space of boundless compassion" (p. 48). By facilitating this examination of the full range of one's own experience as well as the experience of others, mindfulness supports those dealing with mental health issues in living more meaningful and fulfilling lives.

Bibliography

Astin, J. A. (1997). Stress reduction through mindfulness meditation. Effects on psychological symptomatology, sense of control, and spiritual experiences. *Psychotherapy & Psychosomatics, 66*, 97–106.

Baer, R. A. (2003). Mindfulness training as a clinical intervention: A conceptual and empirical review. *Clinical Psychology: Science and Practice, 10*, 125–143.

Baer, R. A., Carmody, J., & Hunsinger, M. (2012). Weekly change in mindfulness and perceived stress in a mindfulness-based stress reduction program. *Journal of Clinical Psychology, 68*(7), 755–765. doi:10.1002/jclp.21865

Bauer-Wu, S., Sullivan, A. M., Rosenbaum, E., Ott, M. J., Powell, M., McLoughlin, M., & Healey, M. W. (2008). Facing the challenges of hematopoietic stem cell transplantation with mindfulness meditation: A pilot study. *Integrative Cancer Therapies, 7*, 62–69.

Bédard, M., Felteau, M., Mazmanian, D., Fedyk, K., Klein, R., Richardson, J., . . . Minthorn-Biggs, M. B. (2003). Pilot evaluation of a mindfulness-based intervention to improve quality of life among individuals who sustained traumatic brain injuries. *Disability & Rehabilitation, 25*, 722–731.

Beddoe, A. E., & Murphy, S. O. (2004). Does mindfulness decreases stress and foster empathy among nursing students? *Journal of Nursing Education, 43*, 305–312.

Biegel, G. M., Brown, K. W., Shapiro, S. L., & Schubert, C. M. (2009). Mindfulness-based stress reduction for the treatment of adolescent psychiatric outpatients: A randomized clinical trial. *Journal of Consulting and Clinical Psychology, 77*, 855.

Bien, T. (2006). *Mindful therapy: A guide for therapists and helping professionals.* Boston, MA: Wisdom Publications.

Bishop, S. R. (2002). What do we really know abut mindfulness-based stress reduction? *Psychosomatic Medicine, 64*, 71–83.

Bowen, S., Witkiewitz, K., Dillworth, T. M., Chawla, N., Simpson, T. L., Ostafin, B. D., Larimer, M. E., Blume, A. W., Parks, G. A., & Marlatt, G. A. (2006). Mindfulness meditation and substance use in an incarcerated population. *Psychology of Addictive Behaviors, 20*, 343–347.

Brown, K. W., & Ryan, R. M. (2003). The benefits of being present: Mindfulness and its roles in psychological well-being. *Journal of Personality and Social Psychology, 84*, 822–848.

Carlson, L. E., Angen, M., Cullum, J., Goodey, E., Koopmans, J., Lamont, L., et al. (2004). High levels of untreated distress and fatigue in cancer patients. *British Journal of Cancer, 90*(4), 2297–2304.

Carson, J. W., Carson, K. M., Gil, K. M., & Baucom, D. H. (2004). Mindfulness-based relationship enhancement. *Behavior Therapy, 35*(3), 471–494.

Carver, C. S., Scheier, M. F., & Segerstrom, S. C. (2010). Optimism. *Clinical Psychology Review, 30*, 879–889.

Cohen-Katz, J., Wiley, S., Capuano, T., Baker, D. M., & Shapiro, S. (2005). The effects of mindfulness-based stress reduction on nurse stress and burnout: A qualitative and quantitative study, part III. *Holistic Nursing Practice, 19*(2), 78–86.

Creswell, J. D., Way, B. M., Eisenberger, N. I., & Lieberman, M. D. (2007). Neural correlates of dispositional mindfulness during affect labeling. *Psychosomatic Medicine, 69*, 560–565.

DeYoung, C. G., Peterson, J. B., & Higgins, D. M. (2005). Sources of openness/intellect: Cognitive and neuropsychological correlates of the fifth factor of personality. *Journal of Personality, 73*, 825–858.

Epel, E. S., Merkin, S. S., Cawthon, R., Blackburn, E. H., Adler, N. E., Pletcher, M. J., & Seeman, T. E. (2009). The rate of leukocyte telomere shortening predicts mortality from cardiovascular disease in elderly men. *Aging, 1*(1), 81.

Fledderus, M., Bohlmeijer, E. T., Smit, F., & Westerhof, G. J. (2010). Mental health promotion as a new goal in public mental health care: A randomized controlled trial of an intervention enhancing psychological flexibility. *American Journal of Public Health, 100*, 2372.

Gibran, K. (n.d.). *A poet's voice XV by Khalil.* www.poetry.net/poem/25185 Pearls of Wisdom.

Gifford, E.V., Kohlenberg, B. S., Hayes, S. C., Antonuccio, D. O., Piasecki, M. M., Rasmussen-Hall, M. L., & Palm, K. A. (2004). Acceptance based treatment for smoking cessation. *Behavior Therapy, 35*, 689–705.

Goldin, P., Ramel, W., & Gross, J. (2009). Mindfulness meditation training and self-referential processing in social anxiety disorder: Behavioral and neural effects. *Journal of Cognitive Psychotherapy, 23*, 242–257.

Goldin, P. R., & Gross, J. J. (2010). Effects of mindfulness-based stress reduction (MBSR) on emotion regulation in social anxiety disorder. *Emotion, 10*, 83–91.

Gratz, K. L., & Gunderson, J. G. (2006). Preliminary data on an acceptance-based emotion regulation group intervention for deliberate self-harm among women with borderline personality disorder. *Behavior Therapy, 37*, 25–35.

Grossman, P., Kappos, L., Gensicke, H., D'souza, M., Mohr, D. C., Penner, I. K., & Steiner, C. (2010). MS quality of life, depression, and fatigue improve after mindfulness training a randomized trial. *Neurology, 75*, 1141–1149.

Grossman, P., Niemann, L., Schmidt, S., & Walach, H. (2004). Mindfulness-based stress reduction and health benefits: A meta-analysis. *Journal of Psychosomatic Research, 57*, 35–43.

Harley, R., Sprich, S., Safren, S., Jacobo, M., & Fava, M. (2008). Adaptation of dialectical behavior therapy skills training group for treatment resistant depression. *Journal of Nervous and Mental Disease, 196*, 136–143.

Hayes, S. C., Wilson, K. G., Gifford, E. V., Bissett, R., Piasecki, M., Batten, S.V., Byrd, M., & Gregg, J. (2004). A preliminary trial of twelve-step facilitation and acceptance and commitment therapy with polysubstance-abusing methadone-maintained opiate addicts. *Behavior Therapy, 35*, 667–688.

Hayes, S. C., Wilson, K. G., Gifford, E.V., Follette, V. M., & Strohsahl, K. (1996). Experiential avoidance and behavioral disorders: A functional dimensional approach to diagnosis and treatment. *Journal of Consulting and Clinical Psychology, 64*, 1152–1168.

Heeren, A., Van Broeck, N., Philippot, P. (2009). The effects of mindfulness on executive processes and autobiographical memory specificity. *Behaviour Research and Therapy, 47*(1), 403–409.

Hofmann, S. G., Sawyer, A. T., Witt, A. A., & Oh, D. (2010). The effect of mindfulness-based therapy on anxiety and depression: A meta-analytic review. *Journal of Consulting and Clinical Psychology, 78*, 169–183.

Hölzel, B., Carmody, J., Evans, K., Hoge, E., Dusek, J., Morgan, L., . . . Lazar, S. (2010). Stress reduction correlates with structural changes in the amygdala. *Social Cognitive and Affective Neuroscience, 5*(1), 11–17.

Hölzel, B., Carmody, J., Vangel, M., Congleton, C., Yerramsetti, S., Gard, T., & Lazar, S. (2011). Mindfulness practice leads to increases in regional brain gray matter density. *Psychiatry Research: Neuroimaging, 191*(1), 36–43.

Hölzel, B. K., Lazar, S. W., Gard, T., Schuman-Olivier, Z., Vago, D. R., Ott, U. (2011). How does mindfulness meditation work? Proposing mechanisms of action from a conceptual and neural perspective. *Perspectives in Psychological Science, 6*, 537–559.

Irving, J. A., Dobkin, P. L., & Park, J. (2009). Cultivating mindfulness in health care professionals: A review of empirical studies of mindfulness-based stress reduction. *Complementary Therapies in Clinical Practice, 15*, 61–66.

Jain, S., Shapiro, S. L., Swanick, S., Roesch, S. C., Mills, P. J., Bell, I., & Schwartz, G. (2007). A randomized control trial of mindfulness meditation versus relaxation training: Effects on distress, positive states of mind, rumination, and distraction. *Annals of Behavioral Medicine, 33*, 11–21.

Jazaieri, H., Goldin, P. R., Werner, K., Ziv, M., & Gross, J. J. (2012). A randomized trial of MBSR versus aerobic exercise for social anxiety disorder. *Journal of Clinical Psychology, 68*, 715–731.

Jha, A. P., Krompinger, J., & Baime, M. J. (2007). Mindfulness training modifies subsystems of attention. *Cognitive, Affective and Behavioral Neuroscience, 7*, 109–119.

Jha, A. P., Stanley, E. A., Kiyonaga, A., Wong, L., & Gelfand, L. (2010). Examining the protective effects of mindfulness training on working memory capacity and affective experience. *Emotion, 10*, 54–64.

Johansson, B., Bjuhr, H., & Rönnbäck, L. (2012). Mindfulness-based stress reduction (MBSR) improves long-term mental fatigue after stroke or traumatic brain injury. *Brain Injury, 26*, 1621–1628.

Johnson, D., Penn, D., Fredrickson, B., Kring, A., Meyer, P., Catalino, L., & Brantley, M. (2011). A pilot study of loving-kindness meditation for the negative symptoms of schizophrenia. *Schizophrenia Research, 129*, 137–140.

Kabat-Zinn, J. (1990). *Full catastrophe living: Using the wisdom of your body and mind to face stress, pain and illness.* New York, NY: Delacourt.

Kabat-Zinn, J. (2005). Coming to our senses: *Healing ourselves and the world through mindfulness.* New York, NY: Hyperion.

Kashdan, T. B. (2009). *Curious? Discover the missing ingredient to a fulfilling life.* New York, NY: William Morrow.

Kashdan, T. B., & Rottenberg, J. (2010). Psychological flexibility as a fundamental aspect of health. *Clinical Psychology Review, 30*, 865–878.

Khoury, B., Lecomte, T., Fortin, G., Masse, M., Therien, P., Bouchard, V., Chapleau, M. A., Paquin, K., & Hofman, S. G. (2013). Mindfulness-based therapy: A comprehensive meta-analysis. *Clinical Psychology Review, 33*(6), 763–771.

Killingsworth, M. A., & Gilbert, D. T. (2010). A wandering mind is an unhappy mind. *Science, 330*, 932.

Kingston, J., Chadwick, P., Meron, D., & Skinner, T. C. (2007). A pilot randomized control trial investigating the effect of mindfulness practice on pain tolerance, psychological well-being, and physiological activity. *Journal of Psychosomatic Research, 62*, 297–300.

Kornfield, J. (1993). *A path with heart: A guide through the perils and promises of spiritual life.* New York, NY: Bantam Books.

Kobau, R., Seligman, M. E. P., Peterson, C., Diener, E., Zack, M. M., Chapman, D., & Thompson, W. (2011) Mental health promotion in public health: Perspectives and strategies from positive psychology. *American Journal of Public Health, 101*(8), 1–9.

Koszycki, D., Benger, M., Shlik, J., & Bradwejn, J. (2007). Randomized trial of a meditation-based stress reduction program and cognitive behavior therapy in generalized social anxiety disorder. *Behaviour Research and Therapy, 45*, 2518–2526.

Krasner, M. S., Epstein, R. M., Beckman, H., Suchman, A. L., Chapman, B., Mooney, C. J., & Quill, T. E. (2009). Association of an educational program in mindful communication with burnout, empathy, and attitudes among primary care physicians. *The Journal of the American Medical Association, 302,* 1284–1293.

Kristeller, J., Wolever, R., & Sheets, V. (2014). Mindfulness-Based Eating Awareness Training (MB-EAT) for binge eating: A randomized clinical trial. *Mindfulness,* 5, 282–297.

Labelle, L. E., Lawlor-Savage, L., Campbell, T. S., Faris, P., & Carlson, L. E. (2014). Does self-report mindfulness mediate the effect of Mindfulness-Based Stress Reduction (MBSR) on spirituality and posttraumatic growth in cancer patients? *The Journal of Positive Psychology, 10*(2), 1–14.

Lazar, S. W., Kerr, C. E., Wasserman, R. H., Gray, J. R., Greve, D. N., Treadway, M. T., McGarvey, M., Quinn, B. T., Dusek, J. A., Benson, H., Rauch, S. L., Moore, C. I., & Fischl, B. (2005). Meditation experience is associated with increased cortical thickness. *Neuroreport, 16,* 1893–1897.

Lengacher, C. A., Shelton, M., Reich, R., Barta, M., Johnson-Mallard, V., & Moscoso, M. S. (2014). Mindfulness based stress reduction (MBSR) in breast cancer: Evaluating fear of recurrence (FOR) as a mediator of psychological and physical symptoms in a randomized control trial (RCT). *Journal of Behavioral Medicine, 37*(1), 185–195.

Lin, J., Epel, E., Blackburn, E. (2012). Telomeres and lifestyle factors: Roles in cellular aging. *Mutation Research/Fundamental Molecular Mechanism Mutagenesis, 730*(1) 85–89.

Linehan, M. M. (1987). Dialectical behavior therapy for borderline personality disorder. Theory and method. *Bulletin of the Menninger Clinic, 51,* 261–276.

Linehan, M. M. (1993). *Cognitive-behavioral treatment of borderline personality disorder.* New York, NY: Guilford Press.

Lynch, T. R., Chapman, A. L., Rosenthal, M. Z., Kuo, J. R., & Linehan, M. M. (2006). Mechanisms of change in dialectical behavior therapy: Theoretical and empirical observations. *Journal of Clinical Psychology, 62,* 459–480.

Ma, S. H., & Teasdale, J. D. (2004). Mindfulness-based cognitive therapy for depression: Replication and exploration of differential relapse prevention effects. *Journal of Consulting and Clinical Psychology, 72,* 31–40.

Mann, M. M., Hosman, C. M., Schaalma, H. P., & de Vries, N. K. (2004). Self-esteem in a broad-spectrum approach for mental health promotion. *Health Education Research, 19,* 357–372.

McCracken, L. M., & Gutiérrez-Martínez, O. (2011). Processes of change in psychological flexibility in an interdisciplinary group-based treatment for chronic pain based on acceptance and commitment therapy. *Behaviour Research and Therapy, 49,* 267–274.

Oschner, K. N., & Gross, J. J. (2008). Cognitive emotion regulation: Insights from social cognitive and affective neuroscience. *Current Directions in Psychological Science, 17,* 153–158.

Ost, L. G. (2008). Efficacy of the third wave of behavioral therapies: A systematic review and meta-analysis. *Behaviour Research and Therapy, 46,* 296–321.

Panos, P. T., Jackson, J. W., Hasan, O., Panos, A. (2014). Meta-analysis and systematic review assessing the efficacy of Dialectical Behavior Therapy (DBT). *Research on Social Work Practice, 24*(2), 213–223.

Piet, J., & Hougaard, E. (2011). The effect of mindfulness-based cognitive therapy for prevention of relapse in recurrent major depressive disorder: A systematic review and meta-analysis. *Clinical Psychology Review, 31,* 1032–1040.

Ree, M. J., & Craigie, M. A. (2007). Outcomes following mindfulness-based cognitive therapy in a heterogeneous sample of adult outpatients. *Behaviour Change, 24,* 70–86.

Reibel, D. K., Greeson, J. M., Brainard, G. C., & Rosenzweig, S. (2001). Mindfulness-based stress reduction and health-related quality of life in a heterogeneous patient population. *General Hospital Psychiatry, 23,* 183–192.

Ryan, R. M., & Deci, E. L. (2000). Self-determination theory and the facilitation of intrinsic motivation, social development, and well-being. *American Psychologist, 55,* 68–78.

Ryff, C. D., & Singer, B. H. (1998). The contours of positive human health. *Psychological Inquiry, 9*(1), 1–28.

Salzberg, S. (1995). *Lovingkindness: The revolutionary art of happiness.* Boston, MA: Shambhala.

Scheier, M. F., & Carver, C. S. (1985). Optimism, coping, and health: Assessment and implications of generalized outcomes expectancies. *Health Psychology, 4,* 219–247.

Schutte, N., & Malouff, J. (2014). A meta-analytic review of the effects of mindfulness meditation on telomerase activity. *Psychoneuroendocrinology, 42,* 45–48.

Segal, Z. V., Williams, M. G., & Teasdale, J. D. (2002). *Mindfulness-based cognitive therapy for depression: A new approach to preventing relapse.* New York, NY: Guilford Press.

Shapiro, S., & Carlson, L. (2009). *The art and science of mindfulness: Integrating mindfulness into psychology and the helping professions.* Washington, DC: American Psychological Association.

Shapiro, S. L., Carlson, L. E., Astin, J. A., & Freedman, B. (2006). Mechanisms of mindfulness. *Journal of Clinical Psychology, 62,* 373–386.

Shapiro, S., de Sousa, S., & Hauck, C. (in press). Mindfulness in positive clinical psychology. In *Positive clinical psychology: An integrative approach to improving well-being.* Wiley.

Shapiro, S. L., & Jazaieri, H. (2015). Mindfulness-based stress reduction for healthy stressed adults. In K. W. Brown, D. Creswell & R. Ryan (Eds.), *Handbook of mindfulness: Theory and research* (pp. 269–306). New York, NY: Guilford Press.

Shapiro, S., Jazaieri, H., & de Sousa, S. (in press). Mindfulness and positive psychology. In *Oxford handbook of positive psychology* (3rd edition). Oxford University Press.

Shapiro, S., Thakur, S., & de Sousa, S. (2014). Mindfulness for health care professionals and therapists in training. In R. A. Baer (Ed.), *Mindfulness-based treatment approaches: Clinician's guide to evidence base and applications* (pp. 319–345). San Diego, CA: Academic Press.

Siegel, D. J. (2007) *The mindful brain: Reflection and attunement in the cultivation of well-being.* New York: W. W. Norton & Company

Veehof, M. M., Oskam, M. J., Schreurs, K. M., & Bohlmeijer, E. T. (2011). Acceptance-based interventions for the treatment of chronic pain: A systematic review and meta-analysis. *Pain, 152,* 533–542.

Wallace, B. A. (2006). *The attention revolution.* Sommerville, MA: Wisdom Publications, Inc.

Wallace, B. A., & Bodhi, B. (2006). *The nature of mindfulness and its role in Buddhist meditation: A correspondence between B. Alan Wallace and the venerable Bhikkhu Bodhi.* Unpublished manuscript. Santa Barbara, CA: Santa Barbara Institute for Consciousness Studies.

Weiss, M., Nordlie, J., & Siegel, E. P. (2005). Mindfulness-based stress reduction as an adjunct to outpatient psychotherapy. *Psychotherapy and Psychosomatics, 74,* 108–112.

Weissbecker, I., Salmon, P., Studts, J. L., Floyd, A. R., Dedert, E. A., & Sephton, S. E. (2002). Mindfulness-based stress reduction and sense of coherence among women with fibromyalgia. *Journal of Clinical Psychology in Medical Settings, 9,* 297–307.

Willeit, P., Willeit, J., Kloss-Brandstätter, A., Kronenberg, F., Kiechl, S. (2011). Fifteen-year follow-up of association between telomere length and incident cancer and cancer mortality. *JAMA, 306*(1), 42.

Williams, J. M. G., Teasdale, J. D., Segal, Z. V., & Soulsby, J. (2000). Mindfulness-based cognitive therapy reduces overgeneral autobiographical memory in formerly depressed patients. *Journal of Abnormal Psychology, 109,* 150.

Wilson, K. G., & Murrell, A. R. (2004). Values work in acceptance and commitment therapy: Setting a course for behavioral treatment. In S. C. Hayes, V. M. Follette & M. Linehan (Eds.), *Mindfulness and acceptance: Expanding the cognitive–behavioral tradition* (pp. 120–151). New York, NY: Guilford Press.

Witkiewitz, K., Bowen, S., Douglas, H., & Hsu, S. (2013). Mindfulness-based relapse prevention for substance craving. *Addictive Behaviors, 38*(2), 1563–1571.

Witkiewitz, K., Marlatt, G. A., & Walker, D. (2005). Mindfulness-based relapse prevention for alcohol and substance use disorders. *Journal of Cognitive Psychotherapy, 19*(3), 211–228.

Wood, A., & Tarrier, N. (2010). Positive clinical psychology: A new vision and strategy for integrated research and practice. *Clinical Psychology Review, 30*(7), 819–829.

Woods, D. W., Wetterneck, C. T., & Flessner, C. A. (2006). A controlled evaluation of acceptance and commitment therapy plus habit reversal for trichotillomania. *Behaviour Research and Therapy, 44*, 639–656.

Zettle, R. D. (2003). Acceptance and commitment therapy (ACT) vs. systematic desensitization in treatment of mathematics anxiety. *The Psychological Record, 53*, 197–215.

8

MORTALITY AND MINDFULNESS

How intense encounters with death can generate spontaneous mindfulness

Steven Taylor

Introduction

In 1994, the British author Dennis Potter – well known for plays like *The Singing Detective* – gave a television interview, just a few weeks before his death from prostate cancer, at the age of 59. The interview became famous, because of the serenity and acceptance which Potter displayed in the face of his own mortality. He admitted that, for most of his life, he had been an angry and bitter person, but suggested that had really only been a mask he had used to hide his natural timidity. During the interview, he remarked that he didn't feel sad or sorry for himself, only for the close friends and family who were going to be losing somebody they loved. He said that he was, in fact, happier and more at peace with the world than he had ever been before. He described a new intensity of perception, an increased appreciation of the beauty and vividness of his surroundings, and an increased awareness of the importance of the present. As he remarked during the interview:

> We forget that life can only be defined in the present tense. It is is is. And it is now only . . . That nowness becomes so vivid to me that in a perverse sort of way, I'm serene. I can celebrate life . . . The nowness of everything is absolutely wonderful . . . The fact is that if you see, in the present tense – boy, can you see it; boy, can you celebrate it.
>
> *(in Fenwick & Fenwick, 1995, p.201)*

Potter described how phenomena he had rarely paid attention to before now seemed beautiful and full of significance; as if it were the first time he had really seen them. Looking through the window at an apple blossom in his garden, it seemed to him "the whitest, frothiest, blossomiest blossom that there ever could be" (in Fenwick & Fenwick, 1995, p. 201).

Research suggests that such a positive psychological shift is not an uncommon response to a direct and intense encounter with mortality. Kastner (1998) studied a group of breast cancer patients and used the term "thriving" to describe their experience. She found that they reported living more authentically, felt a stronger relationship to the 'divine', took more responsibility for their own lives and had a more accepting attitude to death. Other studies have highlighted improved relationships, increased self-confidence and higher levels of spirituality and appreciation for life in cancer patients (Stanton, Bower, & Low, 2006; Tedeschi & Calhoun, 1996, 2004; Tomich & Helgeson, 2004). In positive psychology, the potentially transformative effects of encountering mortality have been examined by Wong (e.g. 2007, 2009), whose "existential positive psychology" emphasises the importance of facing up to and embracing death. This enables the individual to live more authentically and to move towards self-actualisation.

The transformational effects of encountering mortality have also been investigated within the wider context of post-traumatic growth. Post-traumatic growth has been identified across a wide range of traumatic experiences, such as bereavement, rape, stroke, heart events, and in parents of hospitalised children (Sheikh and Marotta, 2005). PTG typically features positive changes such as a new sense of appreciation, enhanced and more authentic relationships, enriched spiritual/philosophical attitudes and a new sense of self-confidence and possibility (Cryder, Kilmer, Tedeschi, & Calhoun, 2006; Fosse, 2005; Lindstrom, Cann, Calhoun, & Tedeschi, 2013). In terms of encounters with mortality, PTG has been identified following life-threatening experiences such as combat (Maguen, Vogt, King, & Litz, 2006); natural disasters (Cryder et al., 2006); accidents (Snape, 1997) and other chronic illness besides cancer (Abraído-Lanza, Guier, & Colón, 1998). Bereavement – encountering mortality through the death of significant others – has also been shown to generate PTG (Bray, 2011; Calhoun, Tedeschi, Cann, & Hanks, 2010).

Studies of the after-effects of 'near-death experiences' (NDEs) show similar findings. In NDEs, an individual undergoes a series of unusual conscious experiences during a medical emergency (often a cardiac arrest) featuring an apparent cessation of physiological and neurological functioning. According to researchers (Fenwick, 1995; Greyson, 1999), there are a number of "core characteristics" of NDEs which appear in most cases. Typically, the person experiences a sense of separation from their body, a sense that they are moving or gliding through darkness, with an intense sense well-being, or even euphoria. They may experience a 'life review' of significant experiences of their lives. Leaving aside the debate about the validity of these experiences (concerning whether they can be explained in physicalist terms, or offer evidence of a more controversial non-materialistic conception of reality), from a psychological point of view, the most significant aspect of them is their after-effects. Van Lommel (2004) conducted a follow up study of 62 NDE patients and found that almost all had experienced a major shift in perspective and in values. They reported a decreased interest in material wealth and personal success, and an increased sense of connection to nature, together with an increased sense of love and compassion, both for themselves and others. In van Lommel's words, "The long lasting transformational effects of an experience that lasts only a few minutes was a surprising and unexpected finding" (2004, p. 118). Similarly, on a life changes questionnaire given by the researcher Michael Sabom (1998), individuals who had NDEs several years previously showed an increase in sense of meaning, capacity for love and involvement with family.

To some extent, these transformational effects may be due to the *content* of the near-death experience, but it is very likely that they are also due to the encounter with mortality itself.

Given modern Western culture's general attitude of denial and negativity towards death, these positive effects might seem surprising. If sex was the great taboo of the 19th century, then death is perhaps the great taboo of the late 20th and early 21st centuries (Niemiec et al., 2010). At earlier times, *mementos mori* (literally, 'remember you must die') were widely used to remind individuals of their own mortality. In the 16th century, it was common for scholars to keep skulls on their desks to remind them that they were always close to death, while in the Victorian era it was common for people to wear lockets containing the hair of their deceased loved ones, and mourning veils. But perhaps because of the materialism and youth-orientation of modern Western culture – and perhaps because many people no longer believe in an afterlife – mortality awareness tends to be suppressed. Ivtzan et al. (2015) suggest three further reasons for the death-denying tendencies of Western cultures: the habit of shielding children and family members from the deaths of others; the fact that we have become removed from the process of death and burial now that most deaths occur in hospital settings, with hospital staff taking over roles which once belonged to family members; and finally, that death is seen as a 'failure' of the medical profession rather than a natural and inevitable process.

However, this attitude of denial means that the potentially transformative aspects of mortality awareness have become less accessible to us, which is unfortunate. As Elizabeth Kubler-Ross wrote, ". . . the promise of death and the experience of dying, more than any other force in life, can move a human being to grow" (Kubler-Ross, 1975, p. 117).

Spontaneous mindfulness

One potentially transformative aspect of intense encounters with death (or mortality awareness in general) may be the development of spontaneous mindfulness, an effortless ongoing form of attentiveness.

Mindfulness has been described as conscious attention to one's present moment experience with an attitude of non-judgemental acceptance (Kabat-Zinn, 1994). One further perspective of mindfulness I would like to suggest here is that it has two orientations: an internal and external. The internal aspect is the practice or ability to observe and experience one's own mental processes, emotional reactions and physical experiences. It implies an ability to 'stand back' from the processes, to observe neutrally without being immersed in them. The external orientation of mindfulness involves experience of the phenomenal world. It involves focusing one's attention on one's surroundings, on the natural and man-made phenomena unfolding around us as we move through our lives – on the sky, trees and plants, buildings and streets, animals and other species, other human beings and so forth.

This does not imply a distinction between these two aspects of mindfulness, or that they should be seen as two different 'types' of mindfulness. In a sense awareness of the phenomenal world is also an 'internal' phenomenon, since externally oriented attention produce 'qualia' (in the terminology of consciousness studies) of internal conscious experience. This is simply a matter of attention. 'Internally oriented mindfulness' means attending to internal psychological, emotional or physiological processes, while 'externally oriented mindfulness' means attending to one's surroundings or environment.

This terminology is useful because the development of enhanced 'externally oriented mindfulness' has been found to be a common after-effect of an intense encounter with mortality (or IEM) (Taylor, 2011, 2012b). At the same time, it is not so clear whether 'internally oriented mindfulness' is enhanced by an IEM. This did not emerge as a clear theme from the research which will be described below, although it is perhaps implied by characteristics such as an increased appreciation of health and the body, and awareness of a sense of well-being.

Spontaneous mindfulness has been identified as a result of the ongoing regular practice of mindfulness. In other words, once mindfulness has been consciously practised for a certain amount of time, it should become established as a trait (at least to some degree), so that one becomes naturally more mindful, without conscious effort. As Siegel notes, for example, "What was once an effortful activity to intentionally create a state (regular mindful practice) becomes an effortless intentionally automatic aspect of our personality. We call this a trait" (2010, p. 181). Fralich states that just as, for an advanced musician, music becomes ". . . a spontaneous part of who she is, so too can our mindfulness become a spontaneous aspect of our personality that flows effortlessly into our lives" (2013, p. 37). This spontaneous aspect of mindfulness is also noted in the Mahamudra Buddhist tradition (mostly associated with Tibetan Buddhism), where the practice of mindfulness is seen as leading to an 'all-round mindfulness' which is maintained without mental effort or activity.

The development of spontaneous mindfulness makes sense in terms of the evidence that the ongoing practice of mindfulness increases attentiveness, bringing a de-automatisation of cognitive processes (Tang et al., 2007; Valentine & Sweet, 1999). Studies have found that mindfulness practice brings increased attentional control and heightened awareness, which can override automatic processing and behaviour (Moore & Malinowski, 2009; Sauer, Walach, Offenbächer, Lynch, & Kohls, 2011). In one of the earliest studies of the effects of meditation, Deikman (1963) concluded that meditation created a "deautomatization of perception", which led to an increased sense of the vividness and beauty of everyday objects.

However, following an IEM, mindfulness – in an 'externally oriented' form – may become established as a trait without a history of practice. That is, individuals may develop a stable, ongoing attitude of attentiveness and receptiveness to the phenomenal world, and to their experience in it, because of a re-orienting of attention away from the future and the past – and from associational mental chatter – and into their experience in the present. In other words, mindfulness emerges as a trait. This leads to a new sense of appreciation of the vividness and beauty of seemingly 'ordinary' phenomena which were rarely attended to before. (Significantly, studies of post-traumatic growth have identified characteristics of a shift in attention towards 'small things' which were previously considered unimportant, and a greater appreciation of life in general [Lindstrom et al., 2013; Tedeschi & Calhoun, 2004]).

We'll now examine some examples of this.

Transformation through turmoil

In a qualitative phenomenological study, 32 individuals who reported positive psychological transformation following periods of intense turmoil and trauma were interviewed (Taylor, 2011, 2012b). The types of turmoil and trauma included serious illness (most commonly cancer), intense stress, disability, bereavement, depression and alcoholism. Eight of the experiences were reported as being temporary – that is, the turmoil and trauma the participants underwent triggered intense or expanded states of consciousness lasting for periods of between a few seconds to a few days. The prevalent characteristics of these experiences were an intense sense of well-being, a sense of meaning and relief, intensified perception and a sense of connection (to nature, to other people, or to the world in general). However, after a certain amount of time these participants reported that the positive characteristics faded. There was a return to a more 'normal' state of consciousness.

However, most of the participants – 24 out of 32 – felt that they had undergone permanent change. Their transformational experience led to what they felt was a permanently transformed state. They reported feeling that they had taken on a different identity, with a different perception of and relationship to the world, a different attitude to life, new values and perspectives and more authentic and intimate relationships. Some initially expected this transformation to fade, but it had not done so. Some reported an extremely intense initial phase which had diminished slightly, settling into a more stable, ongoing state, but with the same basic characteristics. In some cases, it had been decades since their shift, but the state had remained stable and ongoing. For example, one person's traumatic experience happened 25 years ago, another 30 years ago, and longest of all – in the case of an 89-year-old man – 60 years ago. One participant described the shift as follows: "It's like there are two people – there's a before and after" (in Taylor, 2012b, p. 36). Another remarked, "There's no going back. I'm a different person now, for the rest of my life" (in Taylor, 2012b, p. 36).

A woman who experienced positive transformation after a long period of turmoil following the death of her daughter described the transformation beautifully:

> The way it feels is that I've permanently broken through to another state. I've moved up to another level of awareness which I know is going to stay with

me. One day, a shift occurs, and a different picture suddenly emerges . . . there's no going back. It's like the transformation a caterpillar goes through during the chrysalis stage before emerging as a butterfly.

(in Taylor, 2011, p. 55)

In some cases, these experiences were clearly examples of 'post-traumatic growth', taking place gradually over a long period of time. However, the majority of the cases of permanent transformation were described as occurring suddenly and dramatically. These participants could pinpoint a specific moment when a sudden shift occurred, or when a transformational process began. In these cases, the alternate term 'post-traumatic *transformation*' would be more accurate (Taylor, 2013).

An analysis of the types of turmoil and trauma which triggered these 24 experiences of reported permanent transformation – both gradual and sudden – found that 13 of them involved intense encounters with mortality. Nine of these were direct individual encounters with death – for example, being diagnosed with cancer, or returning from a close brush with death due to a medical emergency or an accident (such as a heart attack or near-drowning). Three others were the result of bereavement – that is, an intense encounter with mortality via the death of a person close to them. One further case involved both bereavement and an encounter with one's own mortality.

Following a thematic analysis of interviews with the participants, a number of primary themes emerged. One of them was an enhanced sense of well-being. Many participants described this in terms of an intense sense of appreciation and gratitude. They felt grateful just to be alive, and they could appreciate aspects of life that they used to take for granted, such as their health, their friends, nature and simple pleasures such as eating and walking. As one participant noted, "I'm just so fortunate to be alive on this planet . . . I just feel so privileged to be on this earth and to have been given this awareness" (in Taylor, 2011, p. 145).

An equally strongly featured theme – reported by all participants – was 'intensified perception'. The participants described a heightened sense of beauty, a sense that the world around them had become real and vivid, and an enjoyment of simply sitting or standing still to observe their surroundings. One person who had survived a close encounter with death through a fall (which left him paralysed) reported, "Everything I look at has this beautiful and uncanny clarity" (in Taylor, 2011, p. 76), while another person who was diagnosed with breast cancer described how "the air is clean and fresh and everything is just so vibrant and vivid" (in Taylor, 2011, p. 145).

Another participant was diagnosed with cancer and recovered, but still reported an intensified perception 4 years later. She described this very succinctly and clearly:

It's completely different. I definitely take in things a lot more. When other people see a bird flying they just think it's a normal thing, but I feel like I see it in perspective, as if it's more real. When I'm out in the countryside and I see animals I feel like I really see them. It's difficult to describe, but it's like there's an extra dimension. Water looks different – it's more see through. When you look at a stream you just see the stream moving but I see the layers of the stream and the flotsam and the tones in between.

(in Taylor, 2011, p. 30)

A related theme was a heightened sense of connection. The woman quoted above who underwent 'post-traumatic transformation' following the death of her daughter described this as a "knowing that you are a part of something far more wonderful, far more mysterious" (in Taylor, 2011, p. 183). Sometimes this was described more specifically as a sense of connection with nature. One participant – a successful television writer – experienced turmoil following the death of her baby nephew, and was shortly afterwards diagnosed with breast cancer. Following her diagnosis, and during the course of her treatment, she underwent a major shift of perspective and values. She became less ambitious in her career, less interested in material things and much more connected to nature:

I have a completely different attitude to nature. I walk every day with my dog, but before I would think of it as a chore, and now it's the best part of my day. After my diagnosis I went to Cornwall for six months, and I just spent the whole time by the sea. I felt a really strong connection with nature, feeling a part of it for the first time ever. It felt joyous to be outside.

(in Taylor, 2011, p. 35)

Others spoke in terms of a strong sense of connection specifically with other people. Another participant who was diagnosed with cancer described an "inner connectedness with other people, with the whole universe, this sense of how we're all related" (in Taylor, 2011, p. 146). The man quoted above who came close to death through a fall described feeling a sense of unity between himself and other people, which he felt other people could sense too.

Another strong theme was an increased 'present-ness'. Participants were less interested in the future or the past. They focused less on future plans or hopes, spent less time ruminating over past events and gave correspondingly more attention to the present. One participant recovered from Hodgkin's disease over 40 years ago – he was diagnosed in his mid-20s – but was still aware of the disease as a powerful positive influence in his life. He described, "[It] continues to bring me back to the present, makes me feel that I have to live in the now, to focus on what's really important" (in Taylor, 2011, p. 158).

Similarly, the television writer quoted above reported, "Now I live very much in the present" (in Taylor, 2011, p.187), and she remarked on how this had improved her relationships. She was more present with her friends, rather than getting lost in her own thoughts: "Before I'd just follow my thoughts. And because I'm more present with other people, I'm connecting with them more. They've responded to the change in me and become more present as well. So my relationships have definitely improved" (in Taylor, 2011, p. 187).

In fact, 'improved relationships' emerged as another strong theme from this study. Participants described how their relationships had become deeper, more fulfilling and more authentic. They reported greater empathy and compassion, a heightened sensitivity towards the feelings of others and an enhanced ability to respond to them. One person who came close to death by drowning described how he no longer took his parents for granted, and felt an increased affection for them, so that when he saw them he no longer asked superficial questions but was genuinely interested in them.

All of these characteristics – an increased sense of appreciation, heightened perception, increased connection and increased 'present-ness' – can be seen as related to, or resulting from, an increased attentiveness to one's experience. They can be seen as examples of ongoing, spontaneous mindfulness, manifesting itself particularly as 'externally oriented mindfulness'.

Why do IEMs generate spontaneous mindfulness?

Why do intense encounters with mortality have this transformational effect – and in particular, why do they generate an ongoing state of mindfulness? The reasons for this have already been indicated in the discussion above, but I'll highlight them more specifically here. I will suggest three possible reasons: increased sense of value of life and experience; an increased focus on the present; and a decreased tendency to be immersed in associational mental chatter.

First, intense encounters with mortality may dramatically increase our sense of the value of our experience in the world, which prompts us to pay more attention to it. Life becomes intensely valuable simply because we realise that it is fragile and temporary. The world around us becomes intensely valuable to us because we realise that we are only here for a finite amount of time, and could potentially leave it at any moment. The people in our lives become more valuable to us for the same reason. The same applies to the everyday activities and pleasures of our lives. As Wong and Tomer (2011) suggest, increased awareness of death can alter individuals' time perspective, giving them a view of their lifetime as limited and precious. This sense of the value of life brings about a 're-orienting' of attention. This may be equivalent to what Deikman (1963) referred to as a "deautomatization of perception". Ordinarily, it may be that subconsciously we don't deem our experience valuable enough to pay real attention to it. But following an IEM, this changes drastically.

Another effect of this increased sense of the value of life – although not directly related to mindfulness – may be a 'life re-evaluation'. People may question the course their life has been taking, and feel dissatisfied with their previous careers, hobbies, character traits and goals. They may feel a strong impulse to follow a more meaningful and productive path, and an increased willingness take risks, knowing that they only have a limited amount of time in this life. This can lead to a new sense of purpose, a desire to put their limited time to good use, to help others or to further their own personal development. Many of the participants of the study (Taylor, 2011, 2012b) described here exemplified this. After a near fatal heart attack, one person decided to wind down his business, so that he had more time to himself and with his family. After recovering from cancer, a woman sold her business, and trained to be a counsellor, at the same time as giving herself the opportunity to fulfil ambitions that she had always put off before. (For example, she did a parachute jump, went white-water rafting, and went away for the weekend on her own for the first time.) Another participant described herself as a workaholic – she was an IT manager for a medical company, constantly travelling around the country, with no real interests or ambitions outside her job. But after her IEM, she realised that she had been neglecting herself for years, and shifted her focus to her own well-being and development. She learned meditation and yoga, studied Buddhism, trained to be a life coach and ran a lifestyle club at the local hospital for breast cancer patients. These findings accord with Wong's suggestion that increased awareness of mortality leads to a more intentional search of meaning in life and more intrinsically motivated goals (Wong, 2007).

The second reason why an IEM may lead to ongoing mindfulness is an increased focus on the present. This is partly related to the increased sense of value described above. A heightened sense of the value of life, and an enhanced sense of appreciation of different aspects of our lives, inevitability leads to increased present-orientation, since the present is the place where the experience which we appreciate takes place. (There is probably a reverse causation here too, in that an increased present-orientation brings enhanced appreciation. Both modes may work together in a feedback process, intensifying each other.)

An increased focus on the present is also a result of the fact that an encounter with death places the whole of a person's projected future into doubt. The whole edifice of one's ambitions and plans may be revealed as a meaningless fiction. The fragility and temporariness of life may make it seem absurd to invest so much attention in such constructs, and to depend on them for our identity or well-being. As a result, psychological attachments to future hopes and ambitions may dissolve away, and the individual may become disinterested in the whole concept of the future (Taylor, 2013). There may be a similar reaction to a person's past. The edifice of one's past achievements, failures and successes – or failures or conflicts – may also become meaningless, after coming so close to losing everything through death. As a result, psychological attachments to the past may dissolve away too. And this orientation away from the future and the past brings an increased orientation towards the present, with a realisation that, in the words of Dennis Potter above, "life can only be defined in the present tense" (in Fenwick, 1995, p. 201).

The third reason IEMs may lead to ongoing spontaneous mindfulness is that they may have the effect of reducing the amount of time a person spends immersed in associational mental chatter. A great deal of associational chatter is based on the future and the past – thoughts about what we have to do at work next week, daydreaming about achieving our ambitions; or, in the past, thoughts about what we did last week, or reliving pleasant or painful memories. So as the future and the past become less significant, we spend less time ruminating over them.

This may also be connected to the expanded sense of perspective which an IEM often brings. A great deal of associational chatter is centred on worries and anxieties.

For example, we may ruminate over whether people respect or dislike us or whether our careers are going well enough; we may feel guilty that we're not working hard enough or not doing enough exercise, or that we haven't contacted friends for some time or haven't achieved our ambitions. But in the shadow of death, such 'problems' no longer seem so significant. It may no longer seem justifiable to spend time mulling over such concerns. As Wong and Tomer note, "Death exposes the fragility of life and the futility of everyday busyness and strivings. Death focuses and clarifies" (2011, p. 103). And being less immersed in associational mental chatter means that we are much more likely to attend to other forms of experience – in particular, our experience of the phenomenal world. In Taylor (2012a) it is suggested that there are three basic attentional modes which human beings can experience: absorption (when attention is immersed in an activity or entertainment); abstraction (when attention is immersed in associational mental chatter); and awareness (when attention is focussed on present moment experience). These are referred to as the 'Three As' in shorthand. Often more than one of the three modes are in operation simultaneously – e.g. we are often partly absorbed in an activity at the same time as partly attentive to our experience, just as we are often partly in a state of abstraction at the same time as being partly attentive to our experience. At the same time, the three modes can be seen as mutually exclusive. In other words, the more of one's attention is given to abstraction, the less is given to absorption or awareness; and the more is given to absorption, the less is given to abstraction or awareness. Following an intense encounter with death, therefore, a decreased tendency to be immersed in associational mental chatter may mean that attention is more likely to be devoted to moment to moment awareness.

Terror management theory

A potentially problematic area of these findings relates to terror management theory (TMT). TMT suggests that death awareness generates a sense of insecurity and anxiety which encourages individuals to engage in protective or defensive behaviour. As Goldenberg et al. write, for example, "When one is indirectly confronted with their own mortality, the individual engages in defences to enhance their personal value and so to enhance their symbolic mortality" (2006, p. 155). In TMT, the creation of 'mortality salient' environments – where people are subtly made aware of their own mortality – has been shown to make individuals more prone to status-seeking, materialism, greed, prejudice and aggression. They are more likely to conform to culturally accepted attitudes, and to identify with their national or ethnic groups (Vail et al., 2012). According to TMT, the motivation of these behaviours is to enhance one's sense of significance or value in the face of death, or to gain a sense of security or belonging, as a way of protecting oneself against the threat of mortality. (In fact, some TMT research has indicated positive outcomes, although these have been much less prevalent than the negative [Vail et al., 2012].)

How does TMT fit with the findings of this chapter? How is it possible that mortality awareness can bring positive transformation in some cases, and insecurity and anxiety in others?

Part of the answer may lie in Goldenberg et al.'s comment that TMT involves being "*indirectly* confronted" [my italics] with mortality. TMT tasks offer a brief, manipulated and subtle form of "mortality salience" (Ivtzan et al., 2015). As such, they are only likely to generate a very superficial – and artificial – awareness of mortality, completely different to a life-threatening situation, or even to the serious contemplation of one's own mortality.

In contrast, it may be that intense encounters with mortality often have a positive transformational effect precisely *because* they are intense. They illustrate the importance of facing up to mortality directly, with an attitude of acceptance. Kubler-Ross (2005) suggested that individuals who are aware that they are going to die go through five stages of grief: anger, denial, bargaining, depression and finally acceptance. According to this model, the positive transformational aspects of dying are only accessible once one has progressed through the first four stages, and reached the point of acceptance. Before then, one is likely to experience anxiety and depression. And since TMT only involves superficial and indirect encounters with mortality, it is highly unlikely that – in terms of Kubler-Ross's model – a person would have the opportunity to move beyond the initial stages of this process, to the point where positive transformation is possible.

In other words, it may be that mortality awareness only has positive transformational effects when the individual faces up to death directly, with an attitude of acceptance (that is, with a *mindful* perspective). The 'mortality salient' environments of TMT are unlikely to generate this mindful perspective and so are much less likely to have positive effects. Cozzolino (2006) suggests that awareness of death can involve "dual-existential" systems: *mortality-induced defensiveness* (as identified in TMT) or *mortality-induced growth*. Similarly, Wong and Tomer (2011) suggest the two existential systems of "defensive management" or "meaning management" in relation to mortality.

The intensity of a person's encounter with death, together with the degree to which they face up and accept the reality of their mortality, may be the main factor that determines which of these systems (in both formulations) they experience most prominently.

Facing death without the danger of dying

Is it possible for us to gain access to the transformational power of death without actually encountering it directly? That is, do we actually have to come close to death – through an illness or accident – in order to become conscious enough of our mortality to experience the positive effects described above?

The serious contemplation of one's own mortality can certainly be very powerful. In Buddhism, 'cemetery meditations' are recommended as a way of making oneself conscious of the reality and inevitability of death. In the *Satipatthana Sutta,* the Buddha tells his monks that if they see a dead body – one that is newly dead, one being eaten by animals or one that is nothing more than a skeleton or a pile of bones – they should tell themselves: "Verily, also my own body is of the same nature;

such it will become and will not escape it" (*Satipatthana Sutta,* 2005). In this way, the monk becomes aware of the impermanence of life, and, in the Buddha's words, "lives detached, and clings to nothing in the world" (*Satipatthana Sutta,* 2015).

One method of contemplating death I have personally found very effective is the 'Year to Live' therapy developed by the poet and author Stephen Levine (1997). According to this, we should imagine that we're going to die exactly 1 year from now, and treat the next 365 days as if they genuinely are the last days of our life. During the first part of the year, Levine suggests, we should discuss our attitude to death, including our fear of it. Then we should start to review our lives, developing an attitude of gratitude and forgiveness towards people we've known. Later, we should begin to contemplate what will happen to our body after death, and then write a will and an epitaph, together with letters and poems for the loved ones we are leaving behind. In the tenth month of the programme, we imagine how our possessions are going to be distributed when we die, and consciously 'let go' of them. In the eleventh month, we spend more time with relatives and friends, and contemplate their mortality too. And finally, in the twelfth month, we say goodbye to our loved ones, thank our body for its perseverance, and prepare for death.

I have used an abbreviated form of this exercise with many groups of students and workshop participants over several years, and consistently found it to be very effective. In my adaptation, students are simply given today's date next year and told that this is the date of their death. They are given a worksheet and asked to think about – and write down – what changes they are going to make over the last year of their lives, under different categories such as 'changes to relationships', 'changes to lifestyle' and 'changes in attitude'. They are then told to stand up, and walk around the room, sharing their ideas with other students. I have consistently found that this exercise has a powerfully positive effect, generating a sense of the value of life itself and an expanded sense of perspective. Similarly, when King et al. (2009) induced "death reflection" conditions in students they found that it generated an intensified sense of gratitude. Cozzolino et al. (2004) found similar results from a "death reflection scenario" (although because of its graphic and specific nature, this exercise was also linked to distress and anxiety). In contrast to the subtle exposure to mortality of TMT, these exercises involve serious and sustained contemplation of one's mortality – that is, confronting death directly rather than indirectly – which helps to explain their positive transformational potential.

Outside of specific exercises, it is important for us to make a conscious effort to remind ourselves of our own mortality, simply by regularly contemplating the reality of death. Ultimately, we are all in the same position as a person who has cancer and has been told that they may only have a certain amount of time left to live – it's just that we don't know *how much* time we have left, and it's probable that most of us will have more time than the cancer patient.

In terms of positive psychology, this highlights the importance of avoiding a simplistic dichotomy between the 'negative' and the 'positive'. As both post-traumatic growth and post-traumatic transformation illustrate, negative experiences may possess an underlying transformational potential, which can lead to intense flourishing across all aspects of a person's life. This is particularly true of intense encounters with mortality. What may appear to be the most intensely negative aspect of our lives – our own mortality – is potentially the most powerfully transformational aspect of our lives. And this interdependence is reflected in terms of mindfulness: being mindful of the reality of death helps us to become mindful of the reality of life.

Bibliography

Abraído-Lanza, A. F., Guier, C., & Colón, R. M. (1998). Psychological thriving among Latinas with chronic illness. *Journal of Social Issues*, *54*(2), 405–424.

Bray, P. (2011). Bereavement and transformation: A psycho-spiritual and post-traumatic growth perspective. *Journal of Religion and Health, 52*(3), 890–903.

Calhoun, L. G., Tedeschi, R. G., Cann, A., & Hanks, E. A. (2010). Positive outcomes following bereavement: Paths to posttraumatic growth. *Psychologica Belgica*, *50*(1), 125–143.

Cozzolino, P. J. (2006). Death contemplation, growth, and defense: Converging evidence of dual-existential systems? *Psychological Inquiry*, *17*(4), 278–287.

Cozzolino, P. J., Staples, A. D., Meyers, L. S., & Samboceti, J. (2004). Greed, death, and values: From terror management to transcendence management theory. *Personality and Social Psychology Bulletin*, *30*(3), 278–292.

Cryder, C. H., Kilmer, R. P., Tedeschi, R.G., & Calhoun, L. G. (2006). An exploratory study of posttraumatic growth in children following a natural disaster. *The American Journal of Orthopsychiatry*, *76*(1), 65–9.

Deikman, A. J. (1963). Experimental meditation. *The Journal of Nervous and Mental Disease*, *136*(4), 329–343.

Fenwick, P., & E. (1995). *The truth in the light*. London: Headline.

Fosse, M. J. (2005). Posttraumatic growth: The transformative potential of cancer. *Dissertation Abstracts International: Section B: The Sciences and Engineering, 66*(3-B).

Fralich, T. (2013). *Five core skills of mindfulness: A direct path to more confidence, joy and love*. Wisconsin: PESI.

Frias, A., Watkins, P. C., Webber, A. C., & Froh, J. J. (2011). Death and gratitude: Death reflection enhances gratitude. *The Journal of Positive Psychology*, *6*, 154–162.

Goldenberg, J. L., Hart, J., Pyszczynski, T., Warnica, G. M., Landau, M. J., & Thomas, L. (2006). Terror of the body: Death, neuroticism, and the flight from physical sensation. *Personality and Social Psychology Bulletin*, *32*, 1264–1277.

Greyson, B. (1999). Defining near-death experiences. *Mortality*, *4*(1), 7–19.

Ivtzan, I., Lomas, T., Hefferon, K., & Worth, P. (2015). *Second wave positive psychology: Embracing the dark side of life*. London: Routledge.

Kabat-Zinn, J. (1994). *Wherever you go, there you are: Mindfulness meditation for everyday life*. New York: Hyperion.

Kastner, R. S. (1998). Beyond breast cancer survival: The meaning of thriving. *Dissertation Abstracts International: Section B: The Sciences and Engineering, 59*(5-B).

King, L. A., Hicks, J. A., & Abdelkhalik, J. (2009). Death, life, scarcity and value: An alternative perspective on the meaning of death. *Psychological Science*, *20*, 1459–1462.

Kubler-Ross, E. (1975). *Death: The final stage of growth*. New York, NY: Simon & Schuster.

Kubler-Ross, E. (2005). *On grief and grieving: Finding the meaning of grief through the five stages of loss*. New York, NY: Simon & Schuster.

Levine, S. (1997). *A year to live*. New York, NY: Three Rivers Press.

Lindstrom, C. M., Cann, A., Calhoun, L. G., & Tedeschi, R. G. (2013). The relationship of core belief challenge, rumination, disclosure, and sociocultural elements to posttraumatic growth. *Psychological Trauma: Theory, Research, Practice, and Policy, 5*(1), 50–55. doi:10.1037/a0022030

Lommel, P., & van Lommel, P. (2004). About the continuity of our consciousness. *Advances in Experimental Medicine and Biology, 550*(1), 115–132.

Maguen, S., Vogt, D. S., King, L. A., King, D. W., & Litz, B. T. (2006). Posttraumatic growth among Gulf War I veterans: The predictive role of deployment-related experiences and background characteristics. *Journal of Loss and Trauma, 11*, 373–388.

Moore, A., & Malinowski, P. (2009). Meditation, mindfulness and cognitive flexibility. *Consciousness and Cognition, 18*(1), 176–186.

Niemiec, C. P., Brown, K. W., Kashdan, T. B., Cozzolino, P. J., Breen, W. E., Levesque-Bristol, C., & Ryan, R. M. (2010). Being present in the face of existential threat: The role of trait mindfulness in reducing defensive responses to mortality salience. *Journal of Personality and Social Psychology, 99*(2), 344–365. doi:10.1037/a0019388

Niemiec, C. P., Brown, K. W., Kashdan, T. B., Cozzolino, P. J., Breen, W. E., Rosenblatt, A., . . . Lyon, D. (1989). Evidence for terror management theory I: The effects of mortality salience on reactions to those who violate or uphold cultural values. *Journal of Personality and Social Psychology, 57*, 681–690.

Sabom, M. B. (1998). *Light and death: One doctor's fascinating account of near-death experiences.* Grand Rapids, MI: Zondervan.

Satipatthana Sutta. (2005). www.accesstoinsight.org/tipitaka/mn/mn.010.than.html

Sattipatthana Sutta. Majjhima Nikāya 10.

Sauer, S., Walach, H., Offenbächer, M., Lynch, S., & Kohls, N. (2011). Measuring mindfulness: A Rasch analysis of the Freiburg mindfulness inventory. *Religions, 2*(4), 693–706.

Sheikh, A. I., & Marotta, S. A. (2005). A cross-validation study of the posttraumatic growth inventory. *Measurement and Evaluation in Counseling and Development, 38*(2), 66–77.

Siegel, D. J. (2010). *The mindful therapist: A clinician's guide to mindsight and neural integration* (1st edition). New York, NY: W.W. Norton & Company.

Snape, M. C. (1997). Reactions to a traumatic event: The good, the bad and the ugly? *Psychology, Health & Medicine, 2*(3), 237–242.

Stanton, A. L., Bower, J. E., & Low, C. A. (2006). Posttraumatic growth after cancer. In L. G. Calhoun & R. G. Tedeschi (Eds.). *Handbook of posttraumatic growth: Research and practice* (pp. 138–175). Mahwah, NJ: Erlbaum.

Tang, Y. Y., Ma Y., Wang, J., Fan, Y., Feng, S., Lu, Q., . . . Posner, M. I. (2007). Short-term meditation training improves attention and self-regulation. *Proceedings of the National Academy of Sciences, 104*, 17152–17156.

Taylor, S. (2011). *Out of the darkness: From turmoil to transformation.* London: Hay House.

Taylor, S. (2012a). *Back to sanity: Healing the madness of our minds.* London: Hay House.

Taylor, S. (2012b). Transformation through suffering: A study of individuals who have experienced positive psychological transformation following periods of intense turmoil and trauma. *The Journal of Humanistic Psychology, 52*, 30–52.

Taylor, S. (2013). The peak at the nadir: Psychological turmoil as the trigger for awakening experiences. *The International Journal of Transpersonal Studies, 32*(2), 1–12.

Tedeschi, R. G., & Calhoun, L. G. (1996). The posttraumatic growth inventory: Measuring the positive legacy of trauma. *Journal of Traumatic Stress, 9*(3), 455–471.

Tedeschi, R., & Calhoun, L. (1998). *Posttraumatic growth: Positive changes in the aftermath of crisis.* Mahwah, NJ: Lawrence Erlbaum Associates.

Tedeschi, R., & Calhoun, L. (2004). Posttraumatic growth: Conceptual foundation and empirical evidence. *Psychological Inquiry, 15*(1), 1–18.

Tomich, P. L., & Helgeson, V. S. (2004). Is finding something good in the bad always good? Benefit finding among women with breast cancer. *Health Psychology, 23*, 16–23.

Vail, K. E., Juhl, J., Arndt, J., Vess, M., Routledge, C., & Rutjens, B. T. (2012). When death is good for life considering the positive trajectories of terror management. *Personality and Social Psychology Review, 16*(4), 303–329.

Valentine, E. R., & Sweet, P. L. G. (1999). Meditation and attention: A comparison of the effects of concentrative and mindfulness meditation on sustained attention. *Mental Health, Religion & Culture, 2*(1), 59–70.

van Lommel, P. (2004). About the continuity of our consciousness. In C. Machado & D. A. Shewmon (Eds.), *Brain death and disorders of consciousness* (Vol. 550, pp. 115–132). New York: Springer.

Wong, P. (2009). Existential psychology. In S. Lopez (Ed.), *The Encyclopaedia of positive psychology* (pp. 361–368). Chichester: Blackwell Publishing Ltd.

Wong, P. T., & Tomer, A. (2011). Beyond terror and denial: The positive psychology of death acceptance. *Death Studies, 35*(2), 99–106.

Wong, P. T. P. (2007). Meaning management theory and death acceptance. In A. Tomer, E. Grafton & P. T. P. Wong (Eds.), *Death attitudes: Existential & spiritual issues* (pp. 65–87). Mahwah, NJ: Lawrence Erlbaum Associates.

Wong, P. T. P., & Tomer, A. (2011). Beyond terror and denial: The positive psychology of death acceptance. *Death Studies, 35*(2), 99–106. doi:10.1080/07481187.2011.535377

9

FLOWING WITH MINDFULNESS

Investigating the relationship between flow and mindfulness

Sue Jackson

Introduction

Flow is a central construct in the science of positive psychology. Seligman and Csikszentmihalyi (2000) placed flow as a key positive individual experience in their outlining of three areas central to the science of positive psychology: positive subjective experience, positive individual traits, and positive institutions. Thus, flow has a home in the science of positive psychology.

Flow is an optimal mindset. When in flow, there is a total focus on the task at hand, and performance unfolds as one clear action after another. Flow is intrinsically rewarding, drawing those who experience it back to this optimal psychological state. In this chapter, an overview of flow, and some of the research that has been conducted on this state, will be provided. How flow is relevant to an understanding of mindfulness, and mindfulness to flow, will be explored.

The experience of flow

Flow is the name given by Csikszentmihalyi (1975) to the experience of total involvement in what one is doing, following his research in the 1970s of people in diverse types of activities describing a consistent psychological state that co-occurred with everything coming together during performance of their activity. Csikszentmihalyi operationally defined flow as occurring when the challenges of a situation and an individual's skills are balanced, both above an individual's average levels of challenges and skills. So flow is predicted to occur when an individual is being extended by virtue of performing in a challenging situation, and has a skill level that matches the challenge being faced. Flow experiences lead to optimal functioning, and are often linked with peak levels of performance and experience.

Perceptions of challenges and skills, in the flow model, describe a variety of psychological experiences. In what have become known as the four and eight quadrant flow models (Csikszentmihalyi & Csikszentmihalyi, 1988), a range of psychological experiences is predicted to result from different mixes of perceived challenges and skills in a situation. Anxiety, for example, is predicted to occur when perceived challenges are high, but perception of skills low. Boredom is predicted to occur when skills are perceived to be high, but the challenges in a situation are perceived to be low. Flow occurs between the boundaries of anxiety and of boredom, where challenges are high, and extending the individual, but not creating a situation where confidence is called into question.

The relative mix of challenges and skills is an important starting point for understanding flow. It is the first and a necessary component of the flow experience. It is liberating to be engaged in a situation where we sense that the balance between challenges and skills is just right, enabling us to climb the mountain in front of us without fear. During flow, there are many wonderful aspects to our experience: we know exactly what it is we want to do; we receive clear feedback about how well we are doing; we become totally immersed in what we are doing, to the point of action and awareness merging; we are totally focused on the task at hand; we experience a sense of control and a loss of self-consciousness; we may have a sense of change in the normal passage of time; and what we experience provides such a high level of intrinsic reward that we are motivated to return to this state. These experiences collectively are known as the (nine) dimensions of flow, and are described in more depth elsewhere (e.g., Csikszentmihalyi, 1990; Jackson & Csikszentmihalyi, 1999).

Flow has received considerable research attention since the early studies of the late 1970s, and in settings ranging from daily living, to reflections on states of mind during major scientific advances (e.g., see Csikszentmihalyi, 1996, 1997). There has been remarkable consistency in how flow has been described by individuals across diverse settings. Flow can occur at different levels of complexity, but, by definition, flow is intrinsically rewarding, regardless of whether it involves a simple task, or a complicated and dangerous gymnastics routine. During his initial studies of people being absorbed in what they were doing, Csikszentmihalyi (1975) used the term, autotelic experience, to describe what he later called flow. The word, autotelic, is derived from the Greek, 'auto' (self) and 'telic' (goal) and signifies an activity one does for the reward inherent in that activity. Hearing his interviewees describe the state of total absorption with descriptors like 'flow' and 'flowing', Csikszentmihalyi (1975) decided that what he initially referred to as autotelic experiences would be better understood through calling them flow experiences.

Csikszentmihalyi (1975) categorised the different levels of flow into micro and macro flow experiences. Micro flow experiences were proposed to fit the patterns of everyday life, whereas macro flow was reserved for experiences associated with higher levels of complexity and demand on the participant. These latter experiences are often associated with peak performance, and peak experience (Jackson, 1996; Jackson & Csikszentmihalyi, 1999). While flow has great potential to help with extending possible levels of performance and achievement, the opportunity it creates for individuals to experience full engagement in the present moment is what makes flow matter most from a wellbeing perspective.

Exploring relationships between flow and mindfulness

Flow represents those moments when everything comes together to create a special state of absorption and enjoyment in what one is doing (Csikszentmihalyi, 1975, 1990). Complete involvement in a task at hand defines flow. Having a present-focused awareness is key to experiencing flow. Focus and awareness can be developed through the practice of mindfulness. There have been many commendable definitions of mindfulness (e.g., Bishop et al., 2004; Black, 2011; Brown & Ryan, 2004); the one being used as a point of reference in this chapter is that provided by the founder of Western mindfulness programs, Jon Kabat-Zinn (1994): "Paying attention in a particular way: on purpose, in the present moment, non-judgmentally" (Kabat-Zinn, 1994, p. 4). Mindfulness-based approaches to psychology and health have experienced a rapid increase in recent years, demonstrating a pervasive recognition of the value of present-moment awareness.

The purposeful, present-moment awareness that defines mindfulness also defines the experience of flow, creating an immediate synergy between the two constructs. Bringing present-moment awareness to what one does enhances experience, and tasks are performed better when fully focused on the task. It is this concentrated focus that may help with the finding of flow in performance. Present-moment awareness is cultivated through mindfulness training, and there are a number of approaches that develop the skill of mindfulness, some of which are described in this book.

When in flow, nothing disturbs or detracts one from this concentrated state. Neither external nor internal distractions take up mental space, which is fully focused in the present. This present-moment focus is congruent with the aims of increasing mindfulness, and thus by helping individuals to be more mindful, psychologists may also be helping create the conditions for flow. Empirical support has been demonstrated for the premise that mindfulness enhances propensity to experience flow. For example Kee and Wang (2008) found an association between being mindful and self-reported flow in college athletes. Using a cluster analytic approach, Kee and Wang found that the high mindfulness cluster of athletes scored significantly higher in the flow dimensions of challenge-skill balance, clear goals, concentration on the task at hand, sense of control, and loss of self-consciousness. Aherne, Moran, and Lonsdale (2011) found a mindfulness training program for college athletes increased flow scores on the flow dimensions of clear goals and sense of control, as assessed by the Flow State Scale-2 (Jackson & Eklund, 2002). Cathcart, McGregor, and Groundwater (2014) similarly found associations between self-reported mindfulness and flow as assessed by the Dispositional Flow Scale-2 (Jackson & Eklund, 2002), in a sample of elite athletes. Cathcart and colleagues (2014) found no differences in global measures of flow or mindfulness across gender, sport types, or years of practice in sport. Another interesting finding of Cathcart et al. (2014) was that global mindfulness and flow scores were negatively correlated with number of illnesses and injuries. Positive associations between mindfulness and flow were also found in Kaufman, Glass, and Arnkoff (2009) with a community sample of athletes, and in Moore (2013) with college students. Moore found support for cognitive flexibility and mindfulness predicting disposition to experience flow, using Jackson and Eklund's (2002) dispositional flow scale.

Through using multidimensional measures of both flow (Jackson & Eklund, 2002) and mindfulness (Five Factor Mindfulness Questionnaire [FFMQ]; Baer, Smith, Hopkins, Krietemeyer, & Toney, 2006), the Cathcart et al. (2014) study was able to examine the association between mindfulness and flow at a more detailed level. Consistent with other research (e.g., Aherne et al., 2011; Swann, Keegan, Piggott, & Crust, 2012), the flow dimension of total focus on the task at hand was demonstrated to be key to the association between mindfulness and flow. Correlations were found between this flow dimension and several of the FFMQ mindfulness dimensions, and in particular, describing, acting with awareness, and nonjudging of inner experience.

To further examine the relationship between flow and mindfulness, Kee and Wang (2008) and Cathcart et al. (2014) created high and low flow groups, based on responses to the flow scales (Jackson & Eklund, 2002). High flow groups had higher mindfulness scores, leading to conclusions that "elite athletes with the highest flow propensity also have the highest disposition to mindfulness" and "propensity to achieve flow states may be enhanced by increasing mindfulness" (Cathcart et al., 2014, p. 137). Directionality of any relationship between flow and mindfulness is an area awaiting further research, but it does seem likely at a conceptual level that the relationship between flow and mindfulness is symbiotic (Kee & Wang, 2008). As Kee and Wang rightly point out, flow can be an elusive state, and therefore developing mindfulness skills as a pathway to flow experiences makes sense from an applied perspective. While flow cannot be deliberately increased, mindfulness can. Therefore, one of the benefits of developing mindfulness is an enhanced opportunity for flow experiences.

Approaching challenge with an attitude of openness, or moving towards challenging tasks, and letting go of fear of judgements, or evaluations of performance, helps develop skills of mindfulness, and the mindset of flow. Both states involve a letting go of worrying about the self, as attention is focused fully on a present-moment experience. Brown and Cordin (2009) refer to the distinction between what has been termed the 'narrative self' (a coherent group of cognitions around an individual's place in the world), and an 'experiential self' (an individual's immediate experience of reality, also described as 'bare attention'). Mindfulness, in its simplest form, is described as bare attention, or attention fully in the present, and encourages movement away from the narrative self. Experiencing times of flow, when attention is fully immersed in the task at hand, can help to build the capacity for 'bare attention'. Similarly, by developing mindfulness skills, the capacity for flow experiences increases.

While it seems to make sense that a state of mindfulness can facilitate an experience of flow, a study by Sheldon, Prentice, and Halusic (2015) concluded that mindfulness can disrupt a person's ability for flow absorption, though it is conducive to flow control. Sheldon et al. based their argument regarding the experiential incompatibility of flow absorption and mindfulness on the role of self-awareness in both states. The authors argued that self-awareness is antithetical to flow, but that mindfulness involves maintaining self-awareness throughout an activity. The studies conducted by Sheldon et al. (2015) were innovative and yielded interesting findings on a subject that is intriguing and holds promise for further understanding of both states of mindfulness and states of flow. However, the premise that mindfulness practice involves, ". . . striving for sustained self-awareness" (Sheldon et al., 2015, p. 277) is one requiring further clarification. While mindfulness involves developing awareness, there is no 'striving' in a mindful state, and the intent of mindfulness is not so much on sustaining a focus on self, but rather an openness to experience, and without the judgement that typically accompanies self-awareness. Mindfulness is certainly about awareness, defined by Brown and Ryan (2004) as the "subjective experience of internal and external phenomena" (p. 242). The freedom of mindfulness is that it is awareness without the evaluation of self and others that inhabits our minds for a considerable amount of our waking hours. Further, the argument by Sheldon et al. that absorption is ". . . plausibly limited by mindfulness" may be true for some, but not all, mindfulness practices. Becoming absorbed in the present moment, while being able to let the past and future thoughts come and go, is central to a mindful awareness, and the level of absorption resulting from some mindfulness-meditation practices is deep. The operational definition of mindfulness provided by Brown and Ryan (2004, p. 245), "open or receptive attention to and awareness of ongoing events and experiences", reinforces this notion of becoming absorbed in the present when in a mindful state. Nonetheless, the extent of absorption likely to be experienced in mindfulness and in flow does offer a point of difference between these two constructs, as argued by Sheldon et al. While both involve attention being invested in the present moment, flow is a total absorption, with concomitant lack of awareness of thoughts. The awareness and receptiveness to all of one's experience that defines mindfulness leave space for thoughts to be experienced (although they are unlikely to be experienced in deeply meditative states). This meta-cognitive aspect of mindfulness thus can be seen to provide a point of distinction from flow.

In summary, while mindfulness and flow are different mind states, they are closely related. Both are positive, present-centred states of mind. Both are associated with enhanced performance and positive emotional states. Some of the research that has examined the relationships between flow and performance or psychological wellbeing outcomes will be briefly overviewed next. Relationships between mindfulness and performance enhancement (e.g., Bernier, Thienot, Codron, & Fournier, 2009; Gardner & Moore, 2007), as well as mindfulness and wellbeing are reviewed elsewhere (e.g., Brown & Ryan, 2003).

The study of flow and its antecedents across performance domains

Research in flow has encompassed a great diversity of domains, from daily living (Csikszentmihalyi, 1997) to major scientific and creative discoveries, and everything in between (e.g., Csikszentmihalyi & Csikszentmihalyi, 1988). One area that has

received considerable research attention has been that of sport. In Csikszentmihalyi's landmark 1975 book, *Beyond Boredom and Anxiety,* wherein the flow construct
was initially conceptualized, sport was one of the areas investigated. Sport has been
recognised as an excellent setting in which to examine flow (Csikszentmihalyi,
1990; Jackson & Csikszentmihalyi, 1999). Sport offers the opportunity to do something better than it has been done before, and so, once a commitment to achievement in the sport domain takes place, a focused mindset often follows. Further, the
experience of sport is generally one of enjoyment – people engage in sport for the
quality of experience it provides; as explained by Jackson and Csikszentmihalyi
(1999, p. 4), "Contrary to what happens in most of life, sport can offer a state of
being that is so rewarding one does it for no other reason than to be a part of it".
Thus, sport can be considered an autotelic activity, and this also makes it an environment conducive to flow.

Research in sport and other performance domains (e.g., Jackson 1996) has demonstrated strong support for Csikszentmihalyi's nine-dimensional flow model. Further, across various quantitative studies, illustrative examples of which are briefly
reviewed below, positive associations between flow and several important constructs
in sport/performance psychology have been reported, including mastery-focused
motivation, perceptions of ability, positive engagement, self-determined forms of
motivation, and use of psychological skills. As well, there have been consistent negative relationships between flow and anxiety.

In one of the early studies of flow in sport, Jackson and Roberts (1992) examined associations between peak performance and flow with 200 elite athletes across
a wide range of sports. Flow was related to athletes' peak performances. Further,
athletes high in orientation toward mastery of the task reported experiencing flow
more frequently than athletes low in mastery orientation. As an example of research
in a broader physical activity context, Karageorghis, Vlachopoulos, and Terry (2000)
investigated relationships between subjective feelings of enjoyment and flow in
exercise. Using Jackson's original Flow State Scale (Jackson & Marsh, 1996), they
found in their sample of over 1,200 aerobic dance exercise participants, a positive
and significant association between levels of flow and the post-exercise feelings of
revitalization, tranquility, and positive engagement.

Research on flow has continued to unfold in a number of contexts, including various domains of sport, work, and the performing arts (e.g., Csikszentmihalyi, 1996, 2003; Jackson & Eklund, 2004; Koehn, Morris, & Watt, 2006; Martin &
Cutler, 2002; Moyle, Jackson, & McCloughan, 2014; Perry, 1999; Wrigley, 2005).
Understanding factors that facilitate flow has been one focus of Jackson's research
(e.g., 1992, 1995; Jackson et al., 1998, 2001), and the findings of this research consistently demonstrate the importance of focus and mental attitude while performing to experiencing flow. In a qualitative study with US national champion figure
skaters, Jackson (1992) found that skaters were more likely to achieve flow when
they held a positive mental attitude, experienced positive pre-competitive and
competitive affect, maintained appropriate focus, felt physically ready, and experienced a unity with their dance partner. Skaters' experiences of flow were more

likely to be prevented or disrupted if they experienced physical problems and made mistakes, had an inability to maintain focus, held a negative attitude, or experienced a lack of audience response.

In a larger and more diverse sample of elite athletes, Jackson (1995) found considerable consistency with results from the earlier study with figure skaters (Jackson, 1992). A set of 10 factors were synthesised from the elite athletes' descriptions of what helped or hindered flow from occurring. This set of 10 factors included physical, psychological, nutritional, and situational variables. These included being well prepared for the challenge, having high levels of motivation, having the right level of energy for the performance, having a clear plan for their performance, having a sense that performance was progressing to this plan, staying focused on the task, remaining confident, experiencing good team work, and managing distractions. These are examples of the types of factors that performers can focus on to help them be prepared for the challenges they face, and to face those challenges with a mindset that can lead to flow.

Jackson and colleagues (Jackson, 1995; Jackson & Roberts, 1992; Jackson et al., 1998, 2001) have found that a high perception of ability is an important factor to facilitating flow. This led Jackson (Jackson et al., 2001) to suggest that the perceived skills component of the challenge-skill balance that defines flow is a critical aspect in the acquisition of the flow state in sport or other performance-based domains. Perceptions of skill and challenge in a situation, as described in the flow model, also help to explain when the experience of anxiety, rather than flow, is likely to occur. When the challenges are greater than perceived skills, anxiety is the predicted outcome, according to the flow model. Research has consistently demonstrated that anxiety is a factor preventing flow (Jackson, 1995; Jackson & Roberts, 1992; Jackson et al., 1998; Stein, Kimiecik, Daniels, & Jackson, 1995; Taylor, 2001). Developing skill, and confidence in one's skill, facilitates flow. One implication for the link between flow and mindfulness is that by cultivating a mindful attitude toward challenging tasks, the experience of flow may be cultivated. Through approaching challenge with openness and interest, and suspending judgement, opportunity for the full engagement of flow is created.

The concept of flow can assist with understanding what educational tasks and environments keeps students engaged and productive in in their studies (Shernoff, Csikszentmihalyi, Schneider, & Shernoff, 2003). A longitudinal study of high school students ($n = 526$) measured student engagement, attention, and quality of experience; also measured were level of challenge, skill, relevance, and control associated with tasks. Student level of engagement was highest when participating in individual or group work, and lowest during lectures, watching videos, or undertaking an exam. Participants experienced increased engagement in individually challenging environments, where there was relevant instruction, and the learning environment was under their control. Shernoff et al. (2003) argued that optimal engagement is facilitated through the relationship between the challenge level of a task and the skill level of the individual, with the ideal challenge level just beyond current level of skill (i.e., the flow model). Suggestions by these authors for how to encourage student engagement focused on provision of activities that are challenging and relevant, and where the student feels a sense of autonomy and confidence in his ability.

While it is not possible to engineer a flow experience, it is possible to increase its occurrence, as Jackson and Csikszentmihalyi (1999, p. 138) argued: "It is not possible to make flow happen at will . . . and attempting to do so will only make the state more elusive. However, removing obstacles and providing facilitating conditions will increase its occurrence. . ." (Jackson & Csikszentmihalyi, 1999, p. 138). Learning the skills of mindfulness provides one way to facilitate the occurrence of flow. Future research examining flow and mindfulness holds promise for helping individuals to move from fragmented states of mind to focused and calm awareness.

Assessing flow

Interest in flow as a research concept has continued to grow and flourish across a number of domains. Concurrent with this growing interest has been an interest in development and application of research tools to investigate what is by nature a somewhat elusive concept. A brief review of some of the tools used to assess flow will be provided, to illustrate the ways in which flow can be assessed empirically. Concurrent use of flow assessment instruments with the diversity of mindfulness assessment instruments available will help to further understanding of the relationship between these constructs.

Csikszentmihalyi (1975) developed his model of flow through the use of experience sampling (Csikszentmihalyi & Larson, 1987). The experience sampling method (ESM) involves multiple sampling of experience as it occurs, through having respondents complete experience sampling forms when paged randomly throughout the day. The ESM approach has yielded fascinating insights into the quality of subjective experience across a diversity of life experiences (see, e.g., Csikszentmihalyi, 1996, 2003; Csikszentmihalyi & Csikszentmihalyi, 1988; Csikszentmihalyi, Rathunde, & Whalen, 1993, 1997), and has also been used as a tool in mindfulness research (e.g., Brown & Ryan, 2003). The ESM offers one method of examining differences in propensity for mindfulness and flow experiences across individuals and settings.

Jackson and colleagues (e.g., Jackson & Eklund, 2002; Jackson, Eklund, & Martin, 2010; Jackson & Marsh, 1996; Jackson, Martin, & Eklund, 2008; Marsh & Jackson, 1999; Martin & Jackson, 2008) developed and validated a suite of self-report scales to suit a diversity of research and applied purposes. In the *Flow Manual,* Jackson, Eklund, and Martin (2010) describe these scales, which they categorized into three subsets: Long, Short, and Core Flow Scales. Central to the approach of Jackson and colleagues to assessing flow has been to do so at two levels: (a) the *dispositional level,* or frequency of flow experience across time in particular domains (e.g., sport, work, school), and (b) the *state level,* or extent of flow experienced in a particular event or activity (e.g., a race, a work project, or a test). A similar distinction has been made between trait and state mindfulness (e.g., Brown & Ryan, 2003), and with measurement instruments available to assess both constructs at state and trait levels, the opportunities for fruitful research combining flow and mindfulness are considerable.

The dispositional and state flow scales are parallel forms, with wording differences reflecting whether the disposition to experience flow, or a specific flow experience, is being assessed. By designing dispositional and state versions of the scales, it is possible to assess both a general tendency to experience flow, as well as particular incidence (or non-incidence) of flow characteristics during a particular event. The Long Flow Scales were developed first (Jackson & Eklund, 2002; Jackson & Marsh, 1996) and thus to date have the most empirical support, and are probably the most widely known of the flow scales. They are 36-item instruments, designed to assess the nine dimensions of flow (Csikszentmihalyi, 1990), and are called Flow State Scale-2 (FSS-2), and the Dispositional Flow Scale-2 (DFS-2). The Short Flow Scales are 9-item (dispositional and state) scales, which are abbreviated versions of Long Flow. These flow scales provide a brief assessment, which is useful when research or practical constraints prevent use of a longer scale. The Core Flow Scales are 10-item (dispositional and state) scales, designed to assess the central subjective experience of flow. They complement the dimensional flow assessments provided by the Long and Short Flow Scales. All versions of the scales have been validated through confirmatory factor analyses, and the scales have demonstrated good psychometric properties (e.g., Jackson & Eklund, 2002; Jackson & Marsh, 1996; Jackson, Martin, & Eklund, 2008; Marsh & Jackson, 1999; Martin & Jackson, 2008).

Understanding the flow experience, including what have been termed the pre-conditions for flow (the dimensions of challenge-skill balance, clear goals, and unambiguous feedback; Nakamura & Csikszentmihalyi, 2002) has been facilitated through the ability to assess the nine-dimensional flow model via the Long Flow Scales. Intercorrelations between the flow dimensions have been assessed in several studies (e.g., Jackson et al., 1998, 2001; Stavrou, Jackson, Zervas, & Karteroliotis, 2007) and help to provide a more fine-tuned description of what it is like to enter into flow, and what the process of flow is like.

Understanding this process of being in flow has also been facilitated through qualitative research approaches. Csikszentmihalyi's (1975) initial investigations of the flow experience were based on qualitative data from interviews with participants when they were deeply absorbed in an activity. Jackson (1992, 1995, 1996) analysed the in-depth interview-based responses of elite athletes to questions of what being in flow was like, as well as what hindered or helped them get to this state. Qualitative research, through allowing for the voice of the experiencer to be the focus of enquiry, holds promise for helping to understand what are by definition, subjective experiences – flow and mindfulness. Qualitative research approaches may facilitate knowledge about the quality of the experience, pathways to both flow and mindfulness experiences, as well as how these two pathways may intersect. Taking a multi-method approach to the study of mindfulness and flow, incorporating both quantitative and qualitative methods of enquiry, will allow for the greatest gains in knowledge about these important states of human experience.

Future directions for flow and mindfulness research

The wealth of training programs available to develop mindfulness offer opportunities to examine the potential of mindfulness to impact a number of subjective experiences, including the experience of flow. Training programs to enhance potential for flow experiences could benefit from the inclusion of mindfulness skills, and there is some initial research support for such undertakings (e.g., Aherne, Moran, & Lonsdale, 2011). Intervention studies across a variety of settings could examine the impact of mindfulness training on the experience of flow. Conversely, the impact of flow experiences on developing the capacity to be mindful, and the relationship between the autotelic (flow) personality and propensity for mindfulness could also be examined empirically. The opportunities and potential for concurrent research of flow and mindfulness are plentiful, and could provide much-needed insights into cultivating a present-focused attention in an age where living in the present is challenged on many fronts.

While mindfulness and flow are different mind states, they are closely related. Both are positive, present-centred states of mind. Both are associated with enhanced performance and emotional wellness, and it seems to make sense that a state of mindfulness can facilitate an experience of flow. Future research could examine both points of similarity and points of difference between mindfulness and flow. For example, the study by Sheldon et al. (2015) highlighted points of difference between mindfulness and flow, concluding that mindfulness can disrupt a person's ability for flow absorption, and argued that self-awareness is antithetical to flow, but part of being mindful. As discussed earlier, part of what makes both mindfulness and flow such enjoyable states of consciousness is the freedom from self-evaluations and judgements that arise through deliberate focusing of attention, and this is an interesting area for future research. The flow dimensions of action-awareness merging and loss of self-consciousness may be able to help shed light on relationships between awareness and absorption in flow, as well as help clarify what is happening in relation to these aspects of the self during mindful states. The inhibition of the thinking mind in mindfulness may facilitate a loss of self-consciousness and absorption in the task, which in turn can lead to flow experiences (e.g., Cathcart et al., 2014; Kee & Wang, 2008; Salmon, Hanneman, & Harwood, 2010; Swann et al., 2012). The multidimensional structure of the Long Flow Scales (Jackson & Eklund, 2002; Jackson et al., 2010) provides a tool to empirically examine the associations between action-awareness merging, loss of self-consciousness, as well as other flow dimensions, and various aspects of attention and experience.

Csikszentmihalyi (e.g., 1982, 1990, 2014; Csikszentmihalyi & Figurski, 1982) has written extensively about the tenuous relationship between the self and flow, as illustrated in this quote: "The relationship between optimal experiences and the self is fraught with apparent paradox. On the one hand, the self is hidden during a flow experience; it cannot be found in consciousness. On the other hand, the self appears to thrive and grow as a result of such experiences" (1982, p. 29). Distinguishing between the loss of self focus *during* a flow state, and the growth in complexity of the self *through* flow experiences, Csikszentmihalyi has also highlighted one of the points of similarity between flow and mindfulness. Letting go of worrying about the self occurs in mindfulness and flow states, with attention fully focused on a present-moment experience. The result of spending time in both states has similarly positive outcomes for the growth of the self, and longitudinal research on outcomes of experiencing mindfulness and flow would be useful in understanding the benefits of spending time in these states of consciousness.

The development of research approaches that can examine what is happening at a physiological level during different states of subjective experience will provide a way forward with understanding what is happening in the brain-body interactions during states of mindfulness and flow. The neurophysiology of flow is starting to be understood (e.g., de Manzano, Theorell, Harmat, & Ullen, 2010; Dietrich, 2004), and there is considerable research support for neurophysiological changes associated with mindfulness (e.g., Holzel et al., 2011; Ivanovski & Malhi, 2007; Lazar et al., 2005). Concurrent neurophysiological examination of states of mindfulness and flow could open up new understandings of both experiences.

Future research opportunities abound for the challenge-seeking researcher interested in furthering understanding of positive experiential states. The synergy between the concepts of flow and mindfulness mean that research endeavours that include concurrent study of both experiences offer the greatest potential gains in knowledge going forward.

Conclusion

Flow is an optimal psychological state that has been defined as occurring when challenges and skills are balanced and extending an individual. The total focus of flow, and the associated positive experiential characteristics of this state, provides an opportunity for individuals to move their experience from average to optimal. One outcome of this heightened level of experience is that peak performance is often achieved. In this chapter, the idea that the flow state associated with high-level performance in any endeavour can be one outcome of being mindful in a challenging situation has been discussed. However, also discussed has been the premise that flow is important not so much for any performance outcomes that may ensue, but (and primarily) for the opportunity it provides to experience full engagement in the present moment. This, too, is one reason that makes mindfulness an important state to experience as one travels through life.

Flow can be experienced in any human endeavour, from the tasks of daily living, to demonstrations of outstanding levels of performance in sport, and in the world of work. Having interviewed many athletes at the very top of their sport, this author has found a consistent theme of performers valuing their experience of flow, appreciating the opportunity to speak about their *experiences* (rather than just their results), and being motivated to have more flow in their performances.

Flow is an internal, conscious process that lifts experience from the ordinary to the optimal. It is the simultaneous experiencing of several positive aspects that makes the flow experience so special (Jackson & Csikszentmihalyi, 1999). Some of these aspects, or dimensions of flow as they have come to be known, include total focus, involvement, and absorption in what one is doing. Mind and body work together effortlessly, so that there is an intrinsic experience of harmonious enjoyment (Jackson & Csikszentmihalyi, 1999). This leads to a feeling of being so involved in the activity that nothing else seems to matter and we continue in it ". . . even at great cost, for the sheer sake of doing it" (Csikszentmihalyi, 1990, p. 4). This experience of flow, from a mindfulness perspective, could be viewed as mindfulness in action, with similarity between one's mental state when one is mindfully engaged in a task, and when one is experiencing flow in a task.

Flow is the embodiment of positive subjective experience. Flow matters, because the quality of our experience matters; as Csikszentmihalyi (1982) so eloquently expressed, "It is useful to remember occasionally that life unfolds as a chain of subjective experiences . . . . The quality of these experiences determine whether, and to what extent, life was worth living" (p. 13). Flow provides researchers and practitioners with a key to understanding those moments in time that help to make life worth living. Mindfulness, through cultivating present-moment and non-judgmental awareness, provides one pathway for developing a state of mind that can help unlock the door to flow.

Bibliography

Aherne, C., Moran, A., & Lonsdale, C. (2011). The effect of mindfulness training on athletes' flow: An initial investigation. *The Sport Psychologist, 25*(2), 177–189.

Baer, R., Smith, G., Hopkins, J., Krietemeyer, J., & Toney, L. (2006). Using self-report assessment methods to explore facets of mindfulness. *Assessment, 13*(1), 27–45.

Bernier, M., Thienot, E., Codron, R., & Fournier, J. F. (2009). Mindfulness and acceptance approaches in sport performance. *Journal of Clinical Sports Psychology, 4*, 320–333.

Bishop, S., Lau, M., Shapiro, S., Carlson, L., Anderson, N., Carmody, J., . . . Devins, G. (2004). Mindfulness: A proposed operational definition. *Clinical Psychology: Science and Practice, 11*, 230–241.

Black, D. S. (2011). A brief definition of mindfulness. *Mindfulness research guide.* www.mindful experience.org

Brown, K. W., & Cordin, S. L. (2009). Toward a phenomenology of mindfulness: Subjective experience and emotional correlates. In F. Didonna (Ed.), *Clinical handbook of mindfulness* (pp. 59–81). New York, NY: Springer.

Brown, K., & Ryan, R. (2003). The benefits of being present: Mindfulness and its role in psychological well-being. *Journal of Personality and Social Psychology, 84*, 822–848.

Brown, K., & Ryan, R. (2004). Perils and promise in defining and measuring mindfulness: Observations from experience. *Clinical Psychology: Science and Practice, 11*, 242–248.

Cathcart, S., McGregor, M., & Groundwater, E. (2014). Mindfulness and flow in elite athletes. *Journal of Clinical Sport Psychology JCSP, 8*, 119–141.

Csikszentmihalyi, M. (1975). *Beyond boredom and anxiety.* San Francisco, CA: Jossey-Bass.

Csikszentmihalyi, M. (1982). Towards a psychology of optimal experience. In L. Wheeler (Ed.), *Review of personality and social psychology* (Vol. 2, pp. 13–35). Beverly Hills, CA: Sage.

Csikszentmihalyi, M. (1990). *Flow: The psychology of optimal experience.* New York, NY: Harper & Row.

Csikszentmihalyi, M. (1996). *Creativity: Flow and the psychology of discovery and invention.* New York, NY: Harper Collins.

Csikszentmihalyi, M. (1997). *Finding flow: The psychology of engagement with everyday life.* New York, NY: Harper Collins.

Csikszentmihalyi, M. (2003). *Good business: Leadership, flow, and the making of meaning.* London: Hodder & Stoughton.

Csikszentmihalyi, M. (2014). *Flow and the foundations of positive psychology: The collected works of Mihaly Csikszentmihalyi.* Dordrecht, Netherlands: Springer.

Csikszentmihalyi, M., & Csikszentmihalyi, I. (Eds.) (1988). *Optimal experience: Psychological studies of flow in consciousness.* New York, NY: Cambridge University Press.

Csikszentmihalyi, M., & Figurski, T. J. (1982). Self-awareness and aversive experience in everyday life. *Journal of Personality, 50,* 15–28.

Csikszentmihalyi, M., & Larson, R. (1987). Validity and reliability of the experience-sampling method. *The Journal of Nervous and Mental Disease, 175,* 526–536.

Csikszentmihalyi, M., Rathunde, K., & Whalen, S. (1993). *Talented teenagers: The roots of success and failure.* New York, NY: Cambridge University Press.

Csikszentmihalyi, M., Rathunde, K., & Whalen, S. (1997). *Talented teachers: The roots of success and failure.* New York, NY: Cambridge University Press.

De Manzano, O., Theorell, T., Harmat, L., & Ullen, F. (2010). The psychophysiology of flow during piano playing. *Emotion, 10,* 301–311. doi:http://dx.doi.org/10.1037/a0018432

Dietrich, A. (2004). Neurocognitive mechanisms underlying the experience of flow. *Consciousness and Cognition, 13,* 746–761. doi:10.1016/j.concog.2004.07.002

Gardner, F. L., & Moore, Z. E. (2007). *The psychology of enhancing human performance: The Mindfulness-Acceptance-Commitment (MAC) approach.* New York, NY: Springer.

Holzel, B. K., Carmody, J., Vangel, M., Congleton, C., Yerramsetti, S. M., Gard, T., & Lazar, S. (2011). Mindfulness practice leads to increases in regional brain gray matter density. *Psychiatry Research, 191,* 36–43. doi:10.1016/j.pscychresns.2010.08.006

Ivanovski, B., & Malhi, G. S. (2007). The psychological and neurophysiological concomitants of mindfulness forms of meditation. *Acta Neuropsychiatrica, 19,* 76–91. doi:10.1111/j.1601-5215.2007.00175.x

Jackson, S. A. (1992). Athletes in flow: A qualitative investigation of flow states in elite figure skaters. *Journal of Applied Sport Psychology, 4,* 161–180.

Jackson, S. A. (1995). Factors influencing the occurrence of flow states in elite athletes. *Journal of Applied Sport Psychology, 7,* 135–163.

Jackson, S. A. (1996). Toward a conceptual understanding of the flow experience in elite athletes. *Research Quarterly for Exercise and Sport, 67,* 76–90.

Jackson, S. A., & Csikszentmihalyi, M. (1999). *Flow in sports: The keys to optimal experiences and performances.* Champaign, IL: Human Kinetics.

Jackson, S. A., & Eklund, R. C. (2002). Assessing flow in physical activity: The FSS-2 and DFS-2. *Journal of Sport and Exercise Psychology, 24,* 133–150.

Jackson, S. A., & Eklund, R. C. (2004). *The flow scales manual.* New York: Fitness Information Technology.

Jackson, S. A., Eklund, R. C., & Martin, A. J. (2010). *The flow manual.* Menlo Park, CA: Mind Garden Inc.

Jackson, S. A., Kimiecik, J., Ford, S., & Marsh, H. W. (1998). Psychological correlates of flow in sport. *Journal of Sport and Exercise Psychology, 20,* 358–378.

Jackson, S. A., & Marsh, H. W. (1996). Development and validation of a scale to measure optimal experience: The flow state scale. *Journal of Sport and Exercise Psychology, 18,* 17–35.

Jackson, S.A., Martin, A. J., & Eklund, R. C. (2008). Long and short measures of flow: Examining construct validity of the FSS-2, DFS-2, and new brief counterparts. *Journal of Sport and Exercise Psychology, 30,* 561–587.

Jackson, S.A., & Roberts, G. C. (1992). Positive performance states of athletes: Toward a conceptual understanding of peak performance. *The Sport Psychologist, 6,* 156–171.

Jackson, S.A., Thomas, P. R., Marsh, H.W., & Smethurst, C. J. (2001). Relationships between flow, self-concept, psychological skills, and performance. *Journal of Applied Sport Psychology, 13,* 154–178.

Kabat-Zinn, J. (1994). *Wherever you go, there you are: Mindfulness meditation in everyday life.* New York, NY: Hyperion.

Karageorghis, C. I., Vlachopoulos, S. P., & Terry, P. C. (2000). Latent variable modelling of the relationship between flow and exercise-induced feelings: An intuitive appraisal perspective. *European Physical Education, 6*(3), 230–248.

Kaufman, K., Glass, C., & Arnkoff, D. (2009). Evaluation of Mindful Sport Performance Enhancement (MSPE): A new approach to promote flow in athletes. *Journal of Clinical Sports Psychology, 4,* 334–356.

Kee, Y., & Wang, C. (2008). Relationships between mindfulness, flow dispositions and mental skills adoption: A cluster analytic approach. *Psychology of Sport and Exercise, 9,* 393–411.

Koehn, S., Morris, T., & Watt, A. P. (2006). Efficacy of an imagery intervention on flow and performance in tennis competitions *Society for Tennis Medicine and Science, 11,* 12–14.

Lazar, S. W., Kerr, C. E., Wasserman, R. H., Gray, J. R., Greve, D. N., Treadway, M. T., & Fischl, B. (2005). Meditation experience is associated with increased cortical thickness. *Neuroreport, 16,* 1893–1897.

Marsh, H.W., & Jackson, S.A. (1999). Flow experience in sport: Construct validation of multidimensional, hierarchical state and trait responses. *Structural Equation Modelling, 6,* 343–371.

Martin, A. J., & Jackson, S. A. (2008). Brief approaches to assessing task absorption and enhanced subjective experience: Examining 'short' and 'core' flow in diverse performance domains. *Motivation and Emotion, 32,* 141–157.

Martin, J. J., & Cutler, K. (2002). An exploratory study of flow and motivation in theater actors. *Journal of Applied Sport Psychology, 14,* 344–352.

Moore, W. (2013). Propensity for experiencing flow: The roles of cognitive flexibility and mindfulness. *The Humanistic Psychologist, 41,* 319–332. doi:10.1080/08873267.2013.820954

Moyle, G., Jackson, S. A., & McCloughan, L. J. (2014). *Mindfulness on the move: The impact of mindfulness training within a university dance program.* Manuscript in preparation.

Nakamura, J., & Csikszentmihalyi, M. (2002). The concept of flow. In C. R. Snyder & S. J. Lopez (Eds.), *Handbook of positive psychology* (pp. 89–105). New York, NY: Oxford University Press.

Perry, S. K. (1999). *Writing in flow.* Cincinnati, OH: Writer's Digest.

Salmon, P., Hanneman, S., & Harwood, B. (2010). Associative/dissociative cognitive strategies in sustained physical activity: Literature review and proposal for a mindfulness-based conceptual model. *The Sport Psychologist, 24,* 127–156.

Seligman, M. E., & Csikszentmihalyi, M. (2000). Positive psychology: An introduction. *American Psychologist, 55*(1), 5–14.

Sheldon, K. M., Prentice, M., & Halusic, M. (2015). The experiential incompatibility of mindfulness and flow absorption. *Social Psychological and Personality Science, 6,* 276–283.

Shernoff, D., Csikszentmihalyi, M., Schneider, B., & Shernoff, E. (2003). Student engagement in high school classrooms from the perspective of flow theory. *School Psychology Quarterly, 18,* 158–176.

Stavrou, N., Jackson, S. A., Zervas, Y., & Karteroliotis, K. (2007). Flow experience and athletes' performance with reference to the orthogonal model of flow. *The Sport Psychologist, 21,* 438–457.

Stein, G., Kimiecik, J., Daniels, J., & Jackson, S. A. (1995). Psychological antecedents of flow in recreational sport. *Personality and Social Psychology Bulletin, 21,* 125–135.

Swann, C., Keegan, R., Piggott, D., & Crust, L. (2012). A systematic review of the experience, occurrence, and controllability of flow states in elite sport. *Psychology of Sport and Exercise, 13,* 807–819.

Taylor, M. K. (2001). *The relationships of anxiety intensity and direction of flow in collegiate athletes.* Unpublished master's thesis, University of North Carolina at Greensboro, North Carolina.

Wrigley, W. J. (2005). *An examination of ecological factors in music performance assessment.* Unpublished doctoral thesis, Griffith University, Brisbane.

10

ADDITIONAL MECHANISMS OF MINDFULNESS

How does mindfulness increase wellbeing?

Tarli Young

Introduction

Bishop and colleagues (2004) define mindfulness as a 'mode of awareness' that results from paying attention to current experiences, while adopting an approach of acceptance, openness and curiosity. This includes awareness of both external and internal experiences (Grossman, Niemann, Schmidt, & Walach, 2004). Mindfulness originated in Buddhist contemplative practices where the development of psychological wellbeing was seen as a central aim (Shapiro, 2009). Western psychology has adapted mindfulness into new interventions, and mindfulness practices have been the focus of extensive research and widespread popularity (Brown, Ryan, & Creswell, 2007).

Within mindfulness research, there have been numerous studies on mindfulness-based interventions, developed to alleviate physical or mental health issues such as chronic pain (Kabat-Zinn, 1982), psychosis (Bach & Hayes, 2002) and depression (Teasdale et al., 2000). There have also been many studies on the outcomes of mindfulness which include decreases in depression, stress and anxiety (Bishop et al., 2004), and improvements in wellbeing (Brown et al., 2007), self-compassion, empathy (Neff, 2003), positive affect (Geschwind, Peeters, Drukker, Van Os, & Wichers, 2011), joy and contentment (Davidson et al., 2003).

While research has grown around the outcomes of mindfulness, there has been less research on the mechanisms that produce these effects (Baer, 2009). This is slightly problematic, as identifying distinct mechanisms of mindfulness is an important endeavour, not only to enhance our understanding of mindfulness, but also to amplify the treatment benefits of mindfulness interventions (Kabat-Zinn, 2003) and assist in tailoring interventions for different outcomes or populations (Hölzel et al., 2011).

Within the Western research that does exist on mechanisms, there has been a strong focus on how mindfulness reduces negative variables such as depression, pain and stress, and relatively little research on how mindfulness brings about positive outcomes such as positive affect and wellbeing (Garland, Gaylord, & Fredrickson, 2011). This focus on mindfulness mechanisms which reduce negative variables reflects the prevalent use of mindfulness-based interventions with clinical populations to alleviate negative variables (Malinowski, 2013). This does not mean that the mechanisms established by Western researchers do not also increase positive variables such as wellbeing; it is likely they do; but this has not been the focus of the investigations into mechanisms thus far.

This chapter seeks to further understand the mechanisms of mindfulness which lead to positive outcomes. Specifically it explores the question: 'How does mindfulness lead to increased wellbeing?' This refers to both hedonic and eudaimonic wellbeing which research shows are both enhanced through mindfulness (Brown & Cordon, 2009; Brown et al., 2007). Hedonic wellbeing encompasses short-term pleasure attainment and pain avoidance and includes the presence of high positive affect (Huta & Ryan, 2009). On the other hand, eudaimonic wellbeing is focused on living in a meaningful and deeply satisfying manner in the long term (Deci & Ryan, 2008). Huta and Ryan (2009) describe eudaimonia and hedonia as complementary types of wellbeing, and suggest that embracing both can bring about the greatest and most diverse wellbeing. It is important to note that both hedonic and eudaimonic wellbeing are more than the absence of mental illness or negative states; they include positive states and are characterised by positive functioning in life (Keyes, 2002). Garland et al. (2011) relate this to mindfulness in a study showing the positive effects of a mindfulness programme were partially mediated by increases in positive emotional and cognitive processes, as opposed to just a decrease of negative processes.

To investigate how mindfulness leads to increased wellbeing, the chapter will first summarise the key mechanisms of mindfulness that have been established across multiple Western psychology studies including decentring, exposure, acceptance, self-compassion, self-regulation, values clarification, changes in modes of mental processing, shifts in perception of the self, and flexibility in cognitive, emotional and behavioural responses. These established mechanisms are included to lay the groundwork for the main body of the chapter which proposes additional mechanisms of mindfulness that may explain increases in wellbeing. In order to do this, it incorporates previous research suggestions and also makes new suggestions using theories from the field of positive psychology, which has made significant progress in identifying mechanisms that increase wellbeing (Parks & Biswas-Diener, 2013). Suggested mechanisms include hope, meaning, savouring, gratitude, self-acceptance, autonomy, positive reappraisal and body awareness. Following these suggested mechanisms is a section on upward spirals which proposes that the identified mechanisms may be mutually supportive. The final section discusses possible future directions for mindfulness research.

By taking a positive psychology perspective, this chapter builds on mindfulness research within Western psychology, while acknowledging Buddhist psychology has extensive writings on mindfulness (e.g. see Grabovac, Lau, & Willett, 2011). Likewise this chapter does not seek to cover the neurological mechanisms of mindfulness (e.g. see Chiesa, Calati, & Serretti, 2011; Tang & Posner, 2013) and instead focuses on psychological processes.

Established mechanisms

Research into how mindfulness works has led to a number of proposed mechanisms. This section summarises mechanisms that have been established across a number of studies. They are included to lay the groundwork for the additional mechanisms suggested in the following section, as many of the mechanisms discussed are interdependent. As mentioned previously, several of these mechanisms may play a role in increasing wellbeing, but most have been identified in prior research for their role in decreasing negative variables. This focus is represented in the summaries below.

A key mechanism of mindfulness studied in the West relates to practitioners' mindful observation of their own internal experience. As practitioners begin to hold their experiences and reactions in broader awareness they are better able to see their internal experiences as transient events rather than permanent realities (Kabat-Zinn, 1982, 1990). This is a skill known as **decentring** and similar concepts include deautomisation (Safran & Segal, 1990), reperceiving (Shapiro, Carlson, Astin, & Freedman, 2006), and cognitive diffusion (Hayes, Strohsahl, & Wilson, 1999). Decentring involves non-judgemental observation of internal experiences, 'labelling' them as opposed to engaging with their content (Baer, 2009). This introduces a mental gap between one's awareness and the contents of consciousness (Brown et al., 2007) and helps decrease habitual cognitive and behavioural reactions. Decentring is identified by Shapiro et al. (2006) as a meta-mechanism which allows subsequent mechanisms to take place. It also helps avert repetitive, analytical processing seen in forms of rumination (Baer, 2009) thus reducing psychological distress.

As mindfulness practitioners decentre from their internal stimuli this enables a process known as **exposure**, whereby individuals observe internal stimuli (particularly negative stimuli) without attempts to avoid them (Linehan, 1993). Exposure is a central mechanism of mindfulness and can lead to desensitisation as it enables practitioners to encounter very intense internal experiences with less reactivity and more objectivity (Shapiro et al., 2006). Through exposure, practitioners discover that their emotions, thoughts and sensations are not as overpowering or frightening as they may have believed. This reduces fear responses, emotional reactivity, and avoidance behaviours (Linehan, 1993).

In addition to exposing practitioners to their internal experiences, mindfulness training encourages **acceptance** of whatever arises within one's experience, abandoning attempts to judge or change the current internal and external experiences (Hayes et al., 1999). An attitude of non-judgemental acceptance helps practitioners manage negative experiences without avoidance behaviours and cognitions (Hayes et al., 1999). Acceptance is a mechanism of mindfulness associated with decreased depressive symptoms and rumination (Hayes & Feldman, 2004).

While mindfulness encourages acceptance, it also encourages practitioners to be compassionate and kind with themselves, which leads to enhanced **self-compassion** (Neff, Rude, & Kirkpatrick, 2007). Neff et al. (2007) define self-compassion as being understanding and kind to oneself in times of suffering. Self-compassion encourages positive states such as equanimity, empathy, kindness, inter-connectedness and psychological wellbeing (Neff & Germer, 2013). As such it is identified as a mechanism of mindfulness that increases wellbeing (Hölzel et al., 2011).

As mindfulness practitioners learn to decentre from and accept their internal experiences, this reduces automatic reactions to these experiences and greater freedom to respond effectively, thus enhancing **self-regulation** (Shapiro et al., 2006). Self-regulation in turn acts as a mechanism of mindfulness as it reduces avoidance behaviours and cognitions, enhances efficacy in mood repair and helps practitioners self-regulate in a manner which increases wellbeing (Hayes, Luoma, Bond, Masuda, & Lillis, 2006).

The increased objectivity that comes through decentring and acceptance also enables greater **cognitive, emotional and behavioural flexibility**, which Shapiro et al. (2006) identify as another mechanism of mindfulness. By encouraging direct contact with the present moment, mindfulness helps practitioners to see the current situation and their reactions more clearly, with less distortion from past conditioning and beliefs (Brown & Cordon, 2009). This leads to reductions in experiential avoidance and pathology and increased ability to regulate emotions effectively, cope with challenging experiences and undertake actions which are appropriate to the situation and in line with one's values (Hayes et al., 2006).

Freedom from past conditioning also helps in **values clarification** (Ryan, Kuhl, & Deci, 1997). Decentring allows mindfulness practitioners to step back from their current values, reappraise them and possibly choose different values (Brown & Ryan, 2003). In this way mindfulness helps people recognise what they truly value as opposed to what society values (Brown & Ryan, 2003). This is an important aspect of psychological health, and as such Shapiro et al. (2006) identify values clarification as a mechanism of mindfulness.

By bringing attention to the present moment, mindfulness also brings about **changes in the mode of mental processing**. There are two broad modes of mental processing: conceptual (language-based) processing and sensory-perceptual processing (Williams, 2010). In a conceptual mode of processing, judgements are made on each stimuli based on past experience. Each new judgement can be easily assimilated into existing cognitive schema, thus strengthening the tendency to make future automatic judgements (Brown & Cordon, 2009). Mindfulness encourages the individual to maintain attention on the current reality, rather than processing it through habitual conceptual filters (Brown & Cordon, 2009), thus encouraging more frequent use of sensory-perceptual processing. This reduces reflexive reactions and further enables the aforementioned mechanism of cognitive, emotional and behavioural flexibility, which promotes psychological health and reduces pathology (Hayes et al., 2006).

Shifts in the mode of mental processing and decentring also lead to **changes in perceptions of the self**. Some philosophical traditions delineate two conceptions of the self: the 'narrative self', which involves a coherent set of cognitions about an individual's place in the world; and an 'experiential self', which is an individual's direct experience of reality, also known as 'bare attention' (Brown & Cordon, 2009). Mindfulness promotes a shift from the narrative to the experiential self, as practitioners decentre from the mental processes which provide an impression of a static self (Treadway & Lazar, 2009). De-identification from the perception of a constant self has been identified as a mechanism of mindfulness which leads to reduced psychological distress; and those who have felt this shift describe feelings of freedom and spaciousness (Hölzel et al., 2011).

Additional mechanisms of mindfulness that promote wellbeing

While the aforementioned mechanisms explain many of the outcomes of mindfulness, they do not fully explain the outcomes of wellbeing and enhanced positive emotions such as joy and bliss which are reported by some mindfulness practitioners (Kornfield, 2006). Where studies of statistical mediation have been undertaken, the mechanisms outlined above do not fully account for the positive outcomes of mindfulness practice (e.g. Carmody, Baer, Lykins, & Olendzki, 2009; Coffey, Hartman, & Fredrickson, 2010; Jimenez, Niles, & Park, 2010). This section seeks to suggest additional mechanisms of mindfulness that may further promote hedonic and eudaimonic wellbeing. It is important to note that some of the mechanisms suggested below can be viewed as positive outcomes in themselves (e.g. gratitude, self-acceptance, etc.), and these are included because they may help explain how mindfulness increases wellbeing and therefore act as a mechanism between the two.

The mechanisms are discussed under the three components of mindfulness proposed by Shapiro et al. (2006): (1) intention, (2) attention and (3) attitude. Within this model, 'intention' relates to the identification of intentions or purpose by individuals undertaking mindfulness practice. The component of 'attention' relates to the activity of observing one's current internal and external experiences (Shapiro et al., 2006). The component of 'attitude' relates to the attitude practitioners bring to their attention, including acceptance, non-judgement, non-reactivity, curiosity and kindness (Bishop et al., 2004). The three components and also the mechanisms suggested within them are not separate stages, but interwoven, concurrent parts of a cyclical process (Shapiro et al., 2006). As such, the mechanisms depend on all three components, but in this section they are included under the most relevant.

Intention

Mindfulness practitioners are encouraged to mentally identify the personal intentions they bring to their practice and these intentions will often evolve over time

(Shapiro et al., 2006). Shapiro (1992) found the majority of meditators attained positive effects which aligned with their original intentions, and Kabat-Zinn (1990) suggests that setting an intention is essential to facilitate positive change through mindfulness. This section outlines two mechanisms that may be associated with intention: hope and meaning.

Hope

Positive psychology offers an additional perspective regarding intention in the form of hope theory, which also focuses on progress towards goals (Rand & Cheavens, 2009). Snyders's cognitive hope theory (1989) includes three components: desired goals, perceived capacity to generate pathways to achieve these goals, and agency or perceived ability to sustain movement along pathways (Rand & Cheavens, 2009). These three components are a learned set of cognitive abilities and higher levels of hope correspond with greater physical and psychological wellbeing (Rand & Cheavens, 2009). According to hope theory, positive emotions are the result of perceived progress towards goals (Snyder et al., 1996).

Mindfulness practice can be viewed in terms of hope theory's components. When mindfulness practitioners affirm their intentions, this can be seen as setting goals. As they plan different activities to achieve mindfulness (e.g. meditation, mindful eating, etc.), this can be seen as generating pathways to their goal. And finally, when mindfulness practitioners undertake their practice, this can be seen as building agency and increasing their perceived ability to continue. According to hope theory, as mindfulness practitioners perceive progress towards their intentions, this would produce positive affect (Rand & Cheavens, 2009), a key component of hedonic wellbeing. Thus hope theory may explain one source of hedonic wellbeing within mindfulness.

Meaning

Meaning is another area studied extensively within positive psychology which relates well to intentions. Meaning emerged as a clinical construct through the work of Victor Frankl (1963), who saw meaning as personally (rather than universally) defined, evolving over time, and bigger than the individual self. The relationship between mindfulness and meaning has not been studied to date but it is possible that they promote each other.

A meaningful life involves developing awareness of one's personal meaning, and undertaking behaviour in line with the identified meaning (McGregor & Little, 1998). Mindfulness would encourage both these aspects. Awareness of meaning would be enhanced through the increased self-awareness and reduced automatic conditioning afforded by mindfulness. Mindfulness reduces the influence of conditioning (by society, family, etc.), which would help practitioners better identify their own personal meaning, in a similar manner seen in the mechanisms of values clarification. In terms of behaviour in line with one's meaning, mindfulness enables the cognitive and behavioural flexibility to allow such reflective action.

This connection is somewhat supported by a study which found that when individuals act mindfully, they also act in ways that are more aligned with their values (Brown & Ryan, 2003), and increased clarity of values is also associated with greater life meaning (McGregor & Little, 1998).

This increase in meaning through mindfulness acts as a link to enhanced wellbeing. Greater meaning in life has been associated with hope, optimism (Steger, 2012) and positive affect (Hicks & King, 2009). Meaning is also a key element of the psychological wellbeing model which was developed by Ryff (1989) in an effort to define key aspects of eudaimonic wellbeing. Thus, meaning may be a mechanism of mindfulness that leads to increases in both hedonic and eudaimonic wellbeing.

While mindfulness supports enhanced meaning, the relationship could be reciprocal, as a practitioner's personal meaning could provide their intention for mindfulness practice. Similarly to meaning as defined by Frankl (1963), mindfulness intentions are also personal and dynamic visions. Linking mindfulness intention to one's personal meaning would create a powerful motivator for mindfulness practice, as undertaking personally meaningful activities enhances intrinsic motivation and promotes rapid development towards goals (Sheldon, Kasser, Smith, & Share, 2002). This could be particularly important in mindfulness throughout the day, as meaning could provide a guide for mindful action – linking practitioners' daily action to a greater purpose such as kindness to others. The relationship between meaning and mindfulness needs further exploration, but it is a promising area of study.

Attention

Attention regulation is a key component of mindfulness as it allows people to self-regulate to choose more positive stimuli (Hamilton, Kitzman, & Guyotte, 2006) and enables adaptive outcomes such as enhanced emotional regulation, self-knowledge and self-regulation (Baer, 2009). It is proposed here that attention also enables subsequent mechanisms including gratitude and savouring.

Gratitude

Gratitude is enabled by mindfulness and in turn produces a variety of positive outcomes. Emmons and Mishra (2012) describe gratitude as mindful awareness of the benefits in one's life while Wood, Joseph and Maltby (2009) see trait gratitude as a tendency to notice and appreciate the positive in life. Mindfulness increases awareness of experiences, and this allows practitioners more opportunities for gratitude, as one can only experience a positive event if the event enters one's awareness (Watkins, 2014).

This connection was supported in a study of 130 adults with depression, 64 of whom undertook a mindfulness-based cognitive therapy (MBCT) programme (Geschwind et al., 2011). Experimental participants showed significantly greater appreciation of pleasant daily-life activities. The authors suggest this may have occurred because mindfulness facilitates broadened attention, which in turn enables greater awareness of pleasant situations (which are overlooked more easily than unpleasant situations) (Geschwind et al., 2011). Thus mindfulness may counteract the 'negativity bias' whereby people tend to notice negative information more than positive information (Vaish, Grossmann, & Woodward, 2008). Mindfulness increases awareness of all stimuli and reduces prior conditioning, so individuals are better able to notice, and be grateful for, the large amount of positive stimuli they may otherwise take for granted.

As mindfulness enables gratitude, gratitude in turn leads to increased satisfaction with one's current reality. Gratitude correlates with positive affect and satisfaction with life (McCullough, 2002), which are key aspects of hedonic wellbeing. McCullough (2002) also suggests that mindful attentiveness facilitates gratitude, which in turn allows individuals to extract meaning from experiences – an important element of eudaimonic wellbeing (Ryff & Keyes, 1995). As such gratitude may be a mechanism of mindfulness that increases both hedonic and eudaimonic wellbeing.

Savouring

Savouring entails the self-regulation of positive affect, typically in order to create or enhance positive feelings (Bryant & Veroff, 2007). It is an area that has received significant attention from positive psychology. Bryant, Chadwick and Kluwe (2011) distinguish between four aspects of savouring: experiences, processes, strategies and beliefs. Mindfulness is most related to savouring experiences which are one's internal experiences (such as sensations, emotions and thoughts) when mindfully focusing on a positive stimulus (Bryant et al., 2011). Mindfulness practice could allow increased access to savouring experiences by enhancing the ability to mindfully focus on positive stimuli. For example, mindfulness enhances awareness of internal experiences, including positive experiences such as contentment or joy; and thus mindfulness would enable practitioners the opportunity to savour and maintain such feelings. As savouring leads to the production and maintenance of positive affect, it is possible it acts as a mechanism of mindfulness that increases hedonic wellbeing.

Savouring could also be an important process to prevent erosion of hedonic wellbeing gained through mindfulness. Hedonic adaption suggests people quickly adjust to changes, making it difficult to sustain gains in wellbeing (Frederick & Loewenstein, 1999). Sheldon, Boehm and Lyubomirsky (2013) suggest that appreciation and variety are important in preventing hedonic adaption as they hinder increased aspirations and sustain positive affect. Savouring promotes appreciation (Bryant & Veroff, 2007) while increased attention would produce a greater variety in perceptions; as such savouring could be a mechanism which prevents erosion of hedonic wellbeing gained through mindfulness practice.

While mindfulness and savouring are similar there are also differences. For example savouring can include focus on the past, present or future (Bryant, 2003), while mindfulness is associated with the current moment (Shapiro et al., 2006).

Additionally savouring is related to positive experiences alone (Jose, Lim, & Bryant, 2012) whereas mindfulness encompasses all experiences (Brown et al., 2007). This second difference could be explained if we viewed savouring as a form of mindfulness in the presence of positive experiences.

Attitude

Practitioners are encouraged to approach mindfulness practice with an attitude of acceptance, non-judgement, non-reactivity, curiosity and kindness (Bishop et al., 2004). This attitude is a key component of mindfulness (Kabat-Zinn, 1990) and allows many subsequent mechanisms to occur. Additional mechanisms suggested under this component include self-acceptance, autonomy, positive reappraisal and body awareness.

Self-acceptance

Acceptance of internal experiences has been highlighted as an established mechanism of mindfulness, but this could be extended further to acceptance of the self. Markus and Wurf (1987) suggest that self-concept – the changeable representations of what an individual thinks or feels about himself – is a key regulator of affect and behaviour. Threats to the self-concept can be detrimental; for example, narratives of past-imperfect selves have been linked with depression (Jimenez et al., 2010). Mindfulness training can counteract such threats as it encourages practitioners to accept whatever arises within their experience, including non-judgemental regard for past, present and future aspects of the self (Jimenez et al., 2010).

Mindfulness interventions have been shown to increase levels of self-acceptance (Cohen-Katz et al., 2005). In addition to counteracting threats, self-acceptance facilitated through mindfulness can enhance positive variables such as positive emotions. For example, in a study of 514 college students, Jimenez et al. (2010) found self-acceptance partly mediated the relationship between mindfulness and positive emotions; this was the strongest effect found in the study. Self-acceptance is also a component of the psychological wellbeing model which represents eudaimonic wellbeing (Ryff & Keyes, 1995). As such self-acceptance may be a mechanism of mindfulness that enhances both hedonic and eudaimonic wellbeing.

Autonomy

As mindfulness promotes psychological flexibility and insight into one's own values and meaning, this could enhance autonomy. According to Ryan and Deci's (2000) self-determination theory, autonomous people demonstrate enhanced awareness of their emotions and motives, and the ability to freely choose how they regulate their behaviour. Mindfulness promotes this process by enhancing self-awareness and the ability to choose what has formerly been reflexively adopted or habituated (Baer, 2009). This can facilitate autonomy as practitioners choose behaviours consistent

with their own values, interests and needs. Mindful attention also enhances awareness of prompts (such as emotions) originating from an individual's motivations
and needs, allowing practitioners to more skilfully respond to these prompts in how
they regulate their behaviour (Brown & Ryan, 2003).

Increased autonomy could act as a link between mindfulness and wellbeing
since autonomy is a key component of eudaimonic wellbeing (Ryan & Deci, 2000)
and is associated with increased positive affect and life satisfaction (Ryff & Keyes,
1995). This relationship is supported by a study of 717 high-risk students which
found that autonomy partially mediated the relationship of mindfulness with both
reduced psychological distress and increased psychological wellbeing (Parto &
Besharat, 2011). Self-regulation and autonomy together explained 11% of the variance in decreased psychological distress and 19% of the variance in increased psychological wellbeing. This study has limitations, however, as it used newly adapted
scales which would need further validation, but it offers an interesting avenue for
future research.

Positive reappraisal

Garland, Gaylord and Park (2009) introduce positive reappraisal as a possible mechanism of mindfulness. They define positive reappraisal as the adaptive process of
reappraising distressing events to be either benign, meaningful or beneficial. Garland et al. (2011) describe positive reappraisal as an active coping strategy, which
allows the individual to step back and shift to new cognitive appraisals of experiences, rather than endeavouring to suppress or manipulate negative cognitive
appraisals. They suggest that decentring through mindfulness allows practitioners
the cognitive flexibility to disengage from initial reflexive appraisals and select more
adaptive appraisals, which can help give new meaning to previously stressful events.
Such reappraisals can enhance hope and resilience and result in positive emotions,
even in adverse circumstances (Garland et al. 2009). Hence, positive reappraisal can
be seen as a mechanism of mindfulness which increases wellbeing in the presence
of distressing events.

To investigate these suggestions, Garland et al. (2011) studied 339 participants
who undertook a programme in mindfulness-based stress and pain management.
Results demonstrated that mindfulness practice increased positive reappraisals and
that these increases mediated decreases in stress levels. This relationship needs further research however as the study was missing substantial amounts of data and
could not cite causality because of lack of a control group. There is also a slight
paradox in the relationship between mindfulness and positive reappraisals, as the
former is a mode of non-judgemental, accepting awareness, while the latter actively
attributes positive valence to experiences (Garland et al., 2009). Garland et al.
(2009) counter this point by suggesting mindfulness facilitates positive reappraisals
but they are separate components. However, Garland et al. (2011) acknowledge the
need for further research to firmly ascertain the relationship between mindfulness
and positive reappraisals.

Body awareness

As mindfulness training encourages a shift to sensory-perceptual (as opposed to conceptual) processing, this encourages increased awareness of the sensations within the body, and enhanced body awareness (Mehling et al., 2009). Body awareness involves attention on and awareness of internal body sensations, including physical sensations (e.g. breathing, heat, etc.) and complex syndromes (e.g. pain or 'somatic markers' of emotions) (Mehling et al., 2009).

Research implies body awareness can be both adaptive and maladaptive, and Mehling et al. (2009) suggest the differentiating factor is whether the mode of mind is ruminative and self-focused (which leads to maladaptive body awareness), or focused directly on the current experience (leading to adaptive body awareness). Mindfulness is signified by current-moment, experiential focus and thus could encourage adaptive body awareness. Adaptive body awareness includes the ability to recognise subtle body sensations, which was found to be useful in managing chronic diseases and pain (Baas, Beery, Allen, Wizer, & Wagoner, 2004). As such body awareness may be a mechanism which helps explain the success of mindfulness programmes with chronic pain (e.g. Kabat-Zinn, 1982).

While mindfulness increases adaptive body awareness, the relationship may be reciprocal, as body awareness is frequently used to develop mindfulness by providing an anchor to the current moment. This process is seen in mindfulness meditations which actively encourage increased perception of body sensations, such as body scans and breathing mediations (Kabat-Zinn & Hanh, 2009). There have been few studies which measure changes in body awareness following mindfulness practice, but Lazar et al. (2005) found meditation is associated with enlarged cortical thickness in a subset of brain areas linked with bodily attention and sensory processing, although they could not cite causality for this effect.

Frank (1997) suggests people often do not notice their bodies until something goes wrong, in the form of trauma or pain. Adaptive body awareness developed through mindfulness may address this tendency as it leads to greater sensitivity to neutral or positive sensations (Mehling et al., 2009). This is important as people experience pleasure and positive emotions through the body (Hefferon & Boniwell, 2011). Increased body awareness can lead to greater sensitivity of positive emotions and sensations. As Greeson (2009) suggests, mindfulness may lead to positive physical effects in part by allowing practitioners to notice there is usually more right with the body than wrong. This links to the previously discussed mechanisms of savouring and gratitude in that, through enhancing awareness of positive physical sensations, mindfulness could allow savouring and appreciation of such sensations. Mehling et al. (2009) also notes that awareness of the somatic markers of emotions is important for emotional regulation and the sense of self, which both affect overall wellbeing. It is therefore suggested that mindfulness increases adaptive body awareness, which in turn acts as mechanism to build further mindfulness, enhance experiences of positive emotions, increase gratitude for neutral and positive sensations, and enhance self-regulation. As such body awareness could be an important mechanism that links mindfulness and wellbeing.

Upward spirals

The suggested mechanisms above are positive psychological processes, and research suggests such processes are frequently energised through the reciprocal processes of upward spirals whereby the positive effects accumulate and compound (Fredrickson & Joiner, 2002). These spirals can be self-sustaining as the positive outputs simultaneously input back into the upward spiral (Garland et al., 2011).

Garland et al. (2011) link upward spirals with mindfulness in their work on positive reappraisals. They suggest mindfulness enhances positive reappraisals of stressful events, which enhances positive affect, decreases stress and encourages further development of mindfulness. Upward spirals could be encouraged through many mechanisms of mindfulness including gratitude, self-compassion, meaning, autonomy and body awareness. For example, as mindfulness increases body awareness, this enhances awareness of pleasant sensations within the body (Mehling et al., 2009). This could lead to an upward spiral as greater sensitivity to positive sensations produces greater appreciation and savouring of such sensations, which in turn prolongs or increases positive sensations and positive affect, and supports further mindfulness practice. This mutually supportive upward spiral (between mindfulness, body awareness, positive sensations, savouring and positive affect) may explain experiences of joy and bliss, which are reported by some mindfulness practitioners (Kornfield, 2006) but have not been sufficiently explained in Western mindfulness research. The above process could be likened to the reverse of panic attacks, which are typified by a downward spiral of negative physical sensations and negative affect, both of which increase maladaptive body awareness in a mutually reinforcing manner (Mehling et al., 2009).

Upward spirals are important to wellbeing, as more frequent experiences of positive affect can shift the hedonic balance of negative to positive affect, enhancing life satisfaction (Wood, Froh, & Geraghty, 2010). Positive emotions can also have longer lasting effects as explained within the 'broaden and build' theory (Fredrickson, 2001). This is a key theory within positive psychology and posits that positive emotions broaden the range of thoughts and behaviours individuals use, which in turn assists individuals in building durable psychological, physical and social resources. The result is that positive emotions support the production of more positive emotions in an upward spiral (Fredrickson, 2001). Mindfulness is associated with both increased positive affect, and broadened and more flexible thoughts (Garland et al., 2011). As such Garland et al. (2011) have linked the broaden and build theory to mindfulness, suggesting that enhanced positive emotions facilitate enhanced mindfulness and vice versa.

It is possible that mindfulness could greatly enhance upward spirals, as it increases practitioners' awareness of positive processes. While there has been some preliminary research on mindfulness and upward spirals (e.g. Garland et al., 2011), this area would benefit from more research and may help explain the full effects of mindfulness.

Future research

This chapter has made some brief, preliminary suggestions for mechanisms of mindfulness which may lead to increased wellbeing. These proposed mechanisms are supported by past research but remain theoretical suggestions. As such, additional research is needed to test the validity of the proposed mechanisms. For example, while it may be intuitive, it is not logical to say (1) mindfulness increases gratitude and (2) gratitude increases wellbeing; (3) therefore mindfulness increases wellbeing via increased gratitude. Future research using statistical models of mediation would be needed to assess whether the proposed mechanisms account for significant variance in the changes brought about through mindfulness.

The mechanisms of mindfulness overlap and mutually support each other (Hölzel et al., 2011), but it is important to identify how this occurs. Tests of mediating effects should be used to ascertain whether certain mechanisms are pre-requisites to others, in order to combine identified mechanisms into an integrated model. Many existing studies of mindfulness identify mechanisms but do not explain the full effects of mindfulness, especially outcomes such as wellbeing. It is possible a model of mechanisms may be developed by identifying a few meta-mechanisms that facilitate many other direct-mechanisms. For example Shapiro et al. (2006) suggest reperceiving (or decentring) is a meta-mechanism of mindfulness which enables exposure, emotional regulation, values clarification and flexibility in cognitive, emotional and behavioural responses. Attention could also be a viable meta-mechanism which allows exposure, savouring and gratitude. These outcomes could in turn act as secondary mechanisms which lead to further outcomes. For example, decentring enhances emotional regulation and values clarification, which leads to increased autonomy, which results in increased eudaimonic wellbeing. A successful model would fit together meta-mechanisms and secondary and tertiary mechanisms in a multi-levelled model, which could account for a significant amount of the variance in the changes brought about through mindfulness. Such a model could be tested using longitudinal studies of mindfulness interventions to identify the paths of causality between the intervention and outcomes. Studies with large sample sizes would allow concurrent investigations of different potential pathways and mechanisms.

While research on the links between mindfulness and wellbeing continues, it would also be logical to apply this through the development of mindfulness programmes which specifically aim to increase positive variables. Some such programmes have already been developed such as the mindful self-compassion programme (Neff & Germer, 2013). Similar programmes could be developed focusing on processes that overlap with mindfulness, such as meaning, gratitude, self-acceptance, autonomy or adaptive body awareness.

Conclusions

This chapter has outlined established mechanisms of mindfulness and suggested additional mechanisms which may help explain how mindfulness increases wellbeing, including both hedonic and eudaimonic wellbeing. These suggestions have built on positive psychology theory but further studies are needed to move beyond theoretical discussions. Additional research could focus on incorporating new and existing mechanisms into a coherent model to provide a full picture around how mindfulness works. Where the mechanisms suggested within this chapter can be further established, it is hoped these findings will enhance future mindfulness research and aid in amplifying the benefits of mindfulness interventions.

Bibliography

Baas, L. S., Beery, T. A., Allen, G., Wizer, M., & Wagoner, L. E. (2004). An exploratory study of body awareness in persons with heart failure treated medically or with transplantation. *Journal of Cardiovascular Nursing, 19*(1), 32–40.

Bach, P., & Hayes, S. C. (2002). The use of acceptance and commitment therapy to prevent the rehospitalization of psychotic patients: A randomized controlled trial. *Journal of Consulting and Clinical Psychology, 70*(5), 1129.

Baer, R. A. (2009). Self-focused attention and mechanisms of change in mindfulness-based treatment. *Cognitive Behaviour Therapy, 38*(S1), 15–20.

Bishop, S. R., Lau, M., Shapiro, S., Carlson, L., Anderson, N. D., Carmody, J., . . . Devins, G. (2004). Mindfulness : A proposed operational definition. *Clinical Psychology: Science and Practice, 11*(3), 230–241.

Brown, K. W., & Cordon, S. (2009). Toward a phenomenology of mindfulness: Subjective experience and emotional correlates. In D. Fabrizio (Ed.), *Clinical handbook of mindfulness* (pp. 59–81). New York, NY: Springer.

Brown, K. W., & Ryan, R. M. (2003). The benefits of being present: Mindfulness and its role in psychological well-being. *Journal of Personality and Social Psychology, 84*(4), 822–848.

Brown, K. W., Ryan, R. M., & Creswell, J. D. (2007). Mindfulness: Theoretical foundations and evidence for its salutary effects. *Psychological Inquiry, 18*(4), 211–237.

Bryant, F. (2003). Savoring Beliefs Inventory (SBI): A scale for measuring beliefs about savouring. *Journal of Mental Health, 12*(2), 175–196.

Bryant, F. B., Chadwick, E. D., & Kluwe, K. (2011). Understanding the processes that regulate positive emotional experience: Unsolved problems and future directions for theory and research on savoring. *International Journal of Wellbeing, 1*(1), 107–126.

Bryant, F. B., & Veroff, J. (2007). *Savoring: A new model of positive experience.* Mahwah, NJ: Lawrence Erlbaum Associates.

Carmody, J., Baer, R. A., Lykins, E. L. B., & Olendzki, N. (2009). An empirical study of the mechanisms of mindfulness in a mindfulness-based stress reduction program. *Journal of Clinical Psychology, 65*(6), 613–626.

Chiesa, A., Calati, R., & Serretti, A. (2011). Does mindfulness training improve cognitive abilities? A systematic review of neuropsychological findings. *Clinical Psychology Review, 31*(3), 449–64.

Coffey, K. A., Hartman, M., & Fredrickson, B. L. (2010). Deconstructing mindfulness and constructing mental health: Understanding mindfulness and its mechanisms of action. *Mindfulness, 1*(4), 235–253.

Cohen-Katz, J., Wiley, S., Capuano, T., Baker, D. M., Deitrick, L., & Shapiro, S. (2005). The effects of mindfulness-based stress reduction on nurse stress and burnout: A qualitative and quantitative study, part III. *Holistic Nursing Practice, 19*(2), 78–86.

Davidson, R. J., Kabat-Zinn, J., Schumacher, J., Rosenkranz, M., Muller, D., Santorelli, S. F., . . . Sheridan, J. F. (2003). Alterations in brain and immune function produced by mindfulness meditation. *Psychosomatic Medicine, 65*(4), 564–570.

Deci, E. L., & Ryan, R. M. (2008). Hedonia, eudaimonia, and well-being: An introduction. *Journal of Happiness Studies, 9*(1), 1–11.

Emmons, R. A., & Mishra, A. (2012). Why gratitude enhances well-being: What we know, what we need to know. In K. Sheldon, T. Kashdan, & M. F. Steger (Eds.), *Designing the future of positive psychology: Taking stock and moving forward* (pp. 248–262). New York: Oxford University Press.

Frank, A. W. (1997). *The wounded storyteller: Body, illness and ethics.* Chicago: University of Chicago Press.

Frank, A. W. (1998). Stories of illness as care of the self: A Foucauldian dialogue. *Health, 2*(3), 329–348.

Frankl, V. E. (1963). *Man's search for meaning: An introduction to logotherapy: A newly rev. and enl. ed. of from death-camp to existentalism.* Translated by Ilse Lasch. Boston: Beacon Press.

Frederick, S., & Loewenstein, G. (1999). Hedonic adaptation. In D. Kahneman, E. Diener & N. Schwartz (Eds.), *Scientific perspectives on enjoyment, suffering, and well-being.* New York, NY: Russell Sage Foundation.

Fredrickson, B. L. (2001). The role of positive emotions in positive psychology: The broaden-and-build theory of positive emotions. *American Psychologist, 56*(3), 218.

Fredrickson, B. L., & Joiner, T. (2002). Positive emotions trigger upward spirals toward emotional well-being. *Psychological Science, 13*(2), 172–175.

Garland, E., Gaylord, S., & Park, J. (2009). The role of mindfulness in positive reappraisal. *Explore: The Journal of Science and Healing, 5*(1), 37–44.

Garland, E. L., Gaylord, S., & Fredrickson, B. L. (2011). Positive reappraisal mediates the stress-reductive effects of mindfulness: An upward spiral process. *Mindfulness, 2*(1), 59–67.

Geschwind, N., Peeters, F., Drukker, M., Van Os, J., & Wichers, M. (2011). Mindfulness training increases momentary positive emotions and reward experience in adults vulnerable to depression: A randomized controlled trial. *Journal of Consulting and Clinical Psychology, 79*, 618–628.

Grabovac, A. D., Lau, M. a., & Willett, B. R. (2011). Mechanisms of mindfulness: A Buddhist psychological model. *Mindfulness, 2*(3), 154–166.

Greeson, J. M. (2009). Mindfulness research update: 2008. *Complementary Health Practice Review, 14*(1), 10–18.

Grossman, P., Niemann, L., Schmidt, S., & Walach, H. (2004). Mindfulness-based stress reduction and health benefits. A meta-analysis. *Journal of Psychosomatic Research, 57*(1), 35–43.

Hamilton, N. A., Kitzman, H., & Guyotte, S. (2006). Enhancing health and emotion: Mindfulness as a missing link between cognitive therapy and positive psychology. *Journal of Cognitive Psychotherapy, 20*(2), 123–134.

Hayes, A. M., & Feldman, G. (2004). Clarifying the construct of mindfulness in the context of emotion regulation and the process of change in therapy. *Clinical Psychology: Science and Practice, 11*(3), 255–262.

Hayes, S. C., Luoma, J. B., Bond, F. W., Masuda, A., & Lillis, J. (2006). Acceptance and commitment therapy: Model, processes and outcomes. *Behaviour Research and Therapy, 44*(1), 1–25.

Hayes, S. C., Strohsahl, K. D., & Wilson, K. G. (1999). *Acceptance and commitment therapy: An experiential approach to behaviour change.* New York, NY: Guilford Press.

Hefferon, K., & Boniwell, I. (2011). *Positive psychology: Theory, research and applications.* London: McGraw-Hill Education.

Hicks, J. A., & King, L. A. (2009). Positive mood and social relatedness as information about meaning in life. *The Journal of Positive Psychology, 4*(6), 471–482.

Hölzel, B. K., Lazar, S. W., Gard, T., Schuman-Olivier, Z., Vago, D. R., & Ott, U. (2011). How does mindfulness meditation work? Proposing mechanisms of action from a conceptual and neural perspective. *Perspectives on Psychological Science, 6*(6), 537–559.

Huta, V., & Ryan, R. M. (2010). Pursuing pleasure or virtue: The differential and overlapping well-being benefits of hedonic and eudaimonic motives. *Journal of Happiness Studies, 11*(6), 735–762.

Jimenez, S. S., Niles, B. L., & Park, C. L. (2010). A mindfulness model of affect regulation and depressive symptoms: Positive emotions, mood regulation expectancies, and self-acceptance as regulatory mechanisms. *Personality and Individual Differences, 49*(6), 645–650.

Jose, P. E., Lim, B. T., & Bryant, F. B. (2012). Does savoring increase happiness? A daily diary study. *The Journal of Positive Psychology, 7*(3), 176–187.

Kabat-Zinn, J. (1982). An outpatient program in behavioral medicine for chronic pain patients based on the practice of mindfulness meditation: Theoretical considerations and preliminary results. *General Hospital Psychiatry, 4*(1), 33–47.

Kabat-Zinn, J. (1990). *Full catastrophe living: The program of the stress reduction clinic at the University of Massachusetts medical center.* New York, NY: Delta.

Kabat-Zinn, J. (2003). Mindfulness-based interventions in context: Past, present, and future. *Clinical Psychology: Science and Practice, 10*(2), 144–156.

Kabat-Zinn, J., & Hanh, T. N. (2009). *Full catastrophe living: Using the wisdom of your body and mind to face stress, pain, and illness.* London: Delta.

Keyes, C. L. (2002). The mental health continuum: From languishing to flourishing in life. *Journal of Health and Social Behavior,* 207–222.

Kornfield, J. (2006). *Mindfulness, bliss, and beyond: A meditator's handbook.* Somerville, MA: Wisdom Publications Inc.

Lazar, S. W., Kerr, C. E., Wasserman, R. H., Gray, J. R., Greve, D. N., Treadway, M. T., . . . Fischl, B. (2005). Meditation experience is associated with increased cortical thickness. *Neuroreport, 16*(17), 1893.

Linehan, M. (1993). *Cognitive behavioral treatment of borderline personality disorder.* New York, NY: Guilford Press.

Malinowski, P. (2013). Flourishing through meditation and mindfulness. In S. A. David, I. Boniwell & A. Conley Ayers (Eds.), *The Oxford handbook of happiness* (pp. 384–396). Oxford: Oxford University Press.

Markus, H., & Wurf, E. (1987). The dynamic self-concept: A social psychological perspective. *Annual Review of Psychology, 38*(1), 299–337.

McCullough, M. E. (2002). Savoring life, past and present: Explaining what hope and gratitude share in common. *Psychological Inquiry, 13*(4), 302–304.

McGregor, I., & Little, B. R. (1998). Personal projects, happiness, and meaning: On doing well and being yourself. *Journal of Personality and Social Psychology, 74*(2), 494.

Mehling, W. E., Gopisetty, V., Daubenmier, J., Price, C. J., Hecht, F. M., & Stewart, A. (2009). Body awareness: Construct and self-report measures. *PloS One, 4*(5), e5614.

Neff, K. (2003). Self-compassion: An alternative conceptualization of a healthy attitude toward oneself. *Self and Identity, 2*(2), 85–101.

Neff, K. D., & Germer, C. K. (2013). A pilot study and randomized controlled trial of the mindful self-compassion program. *Journal of Clinical Psychology, 69*(1), 28–44.

Neff, K. D., Rude, S. S., & Kirkpatrick, K. L. (2007). An examination of self-compassion in relation to positive psychological functioning and personality traits. *Journal of Research in Personality, 41*(4), 908–916.

Parks, A. C., & Biswas-Diener, R. (2013). Positive interventions: Past, present, and future. In T. B. Kashdan & J. Ciarrocchi (Eds.), *Mindfulness, acceptance, and positive psychology: The seven foundations of well-being* (pp. 140–165). Oakland, CA: Context Press/New Harbinger Publications.

Parto, M., & Besharat, M. A. (2011). Mindfulness, psychological well-being and psychological distress in adolescents: Assessing the mediating variables and mechanisms of autonomy and self-regulation. *Procedia-Social and Behavioral Sciences, 30*, 578–582.

Rand, K. L., & Cheavens, S. (2009). Hope theory. In S. J. Lopez & C. R. Snyder (Eds.), *Oxford handbook of positive psychology* (pp. 323–334). Oxford: Oxford University Press.

Ryan, R. M., & Deci, E. L. (2000). Self-determination theory and the facilitation of intrinsic motivation, social development, and well-being. *American Psychologist, 55*(1), 68.

Ryan, R. M., Kuhl, J., & Deci, E. L. (1997). Nature and autonomy: An organizational view of social and neurobiological aspects of self-regulation in behavior and development. *Development and Psychopathology, 9*(4), 701–728.

Ryff, C. D. (1989). Happiness is everything, or is it? Explorations on the meaning of psychological well-being. *Journal of Personality and Social Psychology, 57*(6), 1069.

Ryff, C. D., & Keyes, C. L. M. (1995). The structure of psychological well-being revisited. *Journal of Personality and Social Psychology, 69*(4), 719.

Safran, J. D., & Segal, Z. V. (1990). *Interpersonal process in cognitive therapy.* New York, NY: Basic Books.

Seligman, M. E. (2011). *Learned optimism: How to change your mind and your life.* New York, NY: Random House Digital, Inc.

Shapiro, D. H. (1992). A preliminary study of long term meditators: Goals, effects, religious orientation, cognitions. *Journal of Transpersonal Psychology, 24*(1), 23–39.

Shapiro, S. L. (2009). The integration of mindfulness and psychology. *Journal of Clinical Psychology, 65*(6), 555–560.

Shapiro, S. L., Carlson, L. E., Astin, J. A., & Freedman, B. (2006). Mechanisms of mindfulness. *Journal of Clinical Psychology, 62*(3), 373–386.

Sheldon, K. M., Boehm, J., & Lyubomirsky, S. (2013). Variety is the spice of happiness: The hedonic adaptation prevention model. In S. A. David, I. Boniwell & A. Conley Ayers (Eds.), *The Oxford handbook of happiness* (pp. 901–914). New York, NY: Oxford University Press.

Sheldon, K. M., Kasser, T., Smith, K., & Share, T. (2002). Personal goals and psychological growth: Testing an intervention to enhance goal attainment and personality integration. *Journal of Personality, 70*(1), 5–31.

Snyder, C. R. (1989). Reality negotiation: From excuses to hope and beyond. *Journal of Social and Clinical Psychology, 8*(2), 130–157.

Snyder, C. R., Sympson, S. C., Ybasco, F. C., Borders, T. F., Babyak, M. A., & Higgins, R. L. (1996). Development and validation of the state hope scale. *Journal of Personality and Social Psychology, 70*(2), 321.

Steger, M. F. (2012). Experiencing meaning in life: Optimal functioning at the nexus of spirituality, psychopathology, and well-being. In P. T. P. Wong (Ed.), *The human quest for meaning* (2nd edition, pp. 165–184). New York, NY: Routledge.

Tang, Y.-Y., & Posner, M. I. (2013). Special issue on mindfulness neuroscience. *Social Cognitive and Affective Neuroscience, 8*(1), 1–3.

Teasdale, J. D., Segal, Z. V., Williams, J. M. G., Ridgeway, V. A., Soulsby, J. M., & Lau, M. A. (2000). Prevention of relapse/recurrence in major depression by mindfulness-based cognitive therapy. *Journal of Consulting and Clinical Psychology, 68*(4), 615.

Treadway, M. T., & Lazar, S. W. (2009). The neurobiology of mindfulness. In F. Didonna (Ed.), *Clinical handbook of mindfulness.* (pp. 45–57). New York, NY: Springer Science and Business Media.

Vaish, A., Grossmann, T., & Woodward, A. (2008). Not all emotions are created equal: The negativity bias in social-emotional development. *Psychological Bulletin, 134*(3), 383.

Watkins, P. C. (2014). *Gratitude and the good life, toward a psychology of appreciation.* Dordrecht: Springer Science & Business Media.

Wood, A. M., Froh, J. J., & Geraghty, A. W. (2010). Gratitude and well-being: A review and theoretical integration. *Clinical Psychology Review, 30*(7), 890–905.

Wood, A. M., Joseph, S., & Maltby, J. (2009). Gratitude predicts psychological well-being above the big five facets. *Personality and Individual Differences, 46*(4), 443–447.

Williams, J. M. G. (2010). Mindfulness and psychological process. *Emotion, 10*(1), 1.

PART III

Mindfulness for health practitioners and carers

11

CONTEMPLATIVE PEDAGOGY AND NURSING EDUCATION

Anne Bruce and Betty Poag

> Around the world a quiet revolution is unfolding in teaching and learning through the introduction of contemplative practices in higher education.
>
> (Zajonc, 2013, p. 91)

In the summer of 2009 I (AB) attended a weeklong summer program at Smith College, Massachusetts, called, 'Contemplative Practices in Higher Education'. During that summer I met educators from disciplines as diverse as English literature, chemistry, psychology, anthropology, physics, law, women's studies and my own profession of nursing. As educators working in colleges and universities across the United States and Canada, we came together seeking ways to integrate practices such as meditation into our courses. As teachers we longed to return to the roots of liberal education by *drawing forth* (Latin *educare*) the brilliance of our students, to awaken their inherent curiosity so they could be transformed through education. We wanted to introduce direct experiences of the subject matter we were teaching in order to help students find meaningful connection with the topics they were studying. We believed that by incorporating contemplative practices such as meditation we could foster such flourishing in our classrooms. Even back in 2009, we knew we were part of a growing movement of educators who were interested in preparing students to be attentive, emotionally balanced and compassionate members of their communities; we left that summer in an embrace of appreciation knowing that we'd found what we were looking for.

Today, these summer programs continue to be offered and are part of a rapidly growing movement in this quiet revolution of contemplative pedagogy (Zajonc, 2013). Leading the way is the Center for Contemplative Mind in Society (www. contemplativemind.org) and its sister organization for professional educators, the Association for Contemplative Mind in Higher Education (ACMHE) (www. acmhe.edu) that was founded in 2009. These organizations host the summer program mentioned above, along with academic conferences, supportive webinar sessions, blog sites and practice fellowships that fund professors to integrate contemplative practices into academic courses. A recent text, *Contemplative Practices in Higher Education: Powerful Methods to Transform Teaching and Learning* (2014) was co-authored by past director of ACMHE, Daniel Barbezat, and senior fellow and co-founder of the Center for Contemplative Mind in Society (CCMS), Mirabai Bush. The revolution is gaining momentum.

In this chapter we will explore the aligned goals of contemplative pedagogy and those of positive psychology. Educators employing contemplative pedagogy and clinicians rooted in positive psychology share a common focus on human wholeness. The goals of both disciplines are to foster optimal health and wellness through strengthening positive emotions and mind states such as empathy, authenticity, courage, flow, attentiveness, forgiveness, self-compassion and mindfulness (Schmidt, Ziemer, Piontkowski, & Raque-Bogdan, 2013; Zajonc, 2006). We begin by describing contemplative practices and contemplative pedagogy with a brief discussion of their link with the aims of positive psychology. Next, we draw from our experiences as a university professor (AB) working with students to incorporate contemplative approaches, and as a master's student in nursing (BP) exploring contemplative pedagogy within a web-based graduate-level course that prepares nurse educators. And finally we explore potential challenges to consider when using contemplative practices in educational contexts.

Contemplative practice aligns with positive psychology

There is a close fit between the quiet revolution of contemplative practices in higher education and what Seligman and Csikszentmihalyi (2000) called the new science of positive psychology. A comparison of the similarities and differences between these emerging fields is beyond the scope of this chapter; however, readers will recognize a complementarity in our focus on contemplative pedagogy and beginning links with positive psychology.

Positive psychology as broadly described by the International Positive Psychology Association (www.ippannetwork.org) is the scientific examination of what facilitates individuals and communities to thrive. In the context of education there are synergies (Donaldson, Csikszentmihalyi, & Nakamura, 2011; Seligman, Ernst, Gillham, Reivich, & Linkins, 2009) between the studies in positive psychology that generate new understandings of happiness (Buss, 2000; Jose, Kemp, & Grimm, 2015), creativity, (Ryan, James, & Hogan, 2013; Simonton, 2000) giftedness (Winner, 2000) and the scholarship of contemplative pedagogy using contemplative practices to foster these same emotions, traits and learning environments. In its broadest sense contemplative practice is understood as a process of quieting the mind in order to cultivate a capacity for calm, concentration and insight. Miller (1994a; 1994b) describes contemplation as a way of knowing that interrupts habitual thinking patterns and opens us into a deeper awareness. Similarly, Hart (2004) defines contemplation as "the natural human capacity for knowing through silence, looking inward, pondering deeply, beholding, [and] witnessing the contents of our consciousness" (p. 30). On the CCMS website (www.contemplativemind.org/practices) contemplative practices are defined as methods incorporated into daily life that remind us to slow down, focus and feel more connected to what we find most meaningful. Contemplative practices are "practical, radical, and transformative" and foster deep concentration and quieting that can be sustained in the midst of activities and the distractions of everyday life. These practices include a wide range of approaches including mindfulness, meditation, yoga, quiet pondering, poetry, mindful walking and reflective journaling (Beddoe & Murphy, 2004; Hart, 2004; McGarrigle & Walsh, 2011; Zajonc, 2013).

Duerr and Bergam created a useful image of a Tree of Contemplative Practices. The tree provides an overview of the practices available. The roots of the tree represent the intentions of these practices to foster awareness, connection and communion and the branches organize practices into clusters. Of the seven main branches the following three are making their way into nursing education classrooms: the *stillness practices* (e.g. meditation, centring and silence to quiet the mind and body and foster calm and focus), the branch of *relational practices* (that foster connection with self and other through deep listening, storytelling, dialogue) and the branch of *creative practices* (reflective journal writing, music, poetics). Despite the diversity, all of these practices evoke present experience – and foster introspection and relational awareness of self-and-other. Engaging with these activities consistently is said to strengthen attunement with what is happening in our body and mind in the present moment.

There has been an explosion of empirical evidence that is examining outcomes of contemplative practices, especially a growth in rigorous intervention studies of mindfulness meditation. A brief search of publications using the search engine Summon 2.0 emphasises this point. Using the search terms 'mindfulness' and 'research' resulted in a sharp increase in publications: from 2000 to 2005 only 4,417 articles were published; from 2006 to 2010 this number doubled to 10,446 and from 2010 to 2015 the number doubled again with 22,167 published articles cited. Mindfulness is often defined as awareness that comes from paying attention to present moment experience in a purposeful and non-judgemental manner (Kabat-Zinn, 1994). The most widely used contemplative practice in classrooms seems to be mindfulness or mindfulness-based activities. Perhaps this is to be expected, given the strength and growing body of evidence that reports positive health outcomes along with enhanced concentration and attention from mindfulness practice. Much of this evidence overlaps with – or indeed is generated by researchers linked to – positive psychology (Donaldson, Dollwet, & Rao, 2015).

Recent meta-analyses have found that mindfulness practice is associated with less anxiety and depression in both non-clinical and clinical populations (Goyal et al., 2014), improved focus and attention, reduced stress and burnout (Brainstrom, Duncan, & Moskowitz, 2011; Hassed, de Lisle, Sullivan, & Pier 2009; Krasner et al., 2009) and enhanced empathy (Birnie, Speca, & Carlson, 2010). Of particular interest is the mounting evidence that mindfulness interventions may improve well-being in health care professionals and nurses in particular (Chen, Yang, Wang, & Zhang, 2013; Cohen-Katz, 2005). For example, Westphal, Bingisser, Feng and Kleim (2014) examined whether practicing mindfulness, even for a short time, would protect against the negative impact of work-related stressors on burnout and mental health indices in emergency room (ER) nurses. In their descriptive study, nurses (with a response rate of 49%) completed questionnaires of work-related questions as well as measures of anxiety, depressive symptoms, burnout and mindfulness. The researchers found mindfulness was associated with lower symptoms of anxiety, depression and burnout in these ER nurses. In addition, mindfulness was found to moderate the effect of interpersonal stress on anxiety arising from conflict.

In a recent concept analysis, White (2014) identified mindfulness as an important and emerging concept for nursing. White reviewed a sample of 59 English theoretical and research-based articles from the Cumulative Index to Nursing and Allied Health Literature database from 1981 to 2012. She identified five interconnected attributes of mindfulness as a transformative process where practitioners experience "an increasing ability to 'experience being present', with 'acceptance', 'attention' and 'awareness'" (p. 282). Given the increasingly fast-paced and complex heath care settings in which nurses work, mindfulness offers significant potential for fostering and sustaining the qualities of presence, attention and acceptance that are essential to therapeutic nursing care. With such growing evidence that associates contemplative practices with enhanced health and wellness, educational settings are well poised to introduce them and continue to investigate their impact and limitations.

Contemplative knowing

According to Arthur Zajonc, director of the CCMS and professor of physics at Amherst College, students are generally unaware of the habits and ruts their thinking follows because this is usually automatic and associative (Zajonc, 2009). Self-knowledge and awareness are hallmarks of education, and contemplative practices in pedagogical contexts are said to foster students' skills of introspection, and attention/attunement to relationships and their environment (Dufon & Christian, 2013; Kang, Gruber, & Gray, 2013). Zajonc (2009) also describes contemplative knowing as a new way of thinking that complements the more privileged epistemologies encouraged in the academy, that is, materialistic thinking (e.g. rational-logical reasoning, inductive and deductive reasoning) and mechanistic thinking (identifying patterns and systematic analysis). While these are important mental capacities and skills required for professionals in health care, they are not enough. Contemplative cognition as a way of knowing and being augments these more conventional cognitive skills. Rather than seeing illness as an object of investigation, or patients as enacting behaviours that in turn are the objects of investigation (i.e. a science of objects and behaviours), contemplative cognition explores relationships of being-and-knowing vis-à-vis illness experience, of metamorphosis instead of stasis, and of agency rather than mechanisms (see Zajonc, 2009, p. 156).

Zajonc (2009, 2013) refers to a kind of contemplative knowing that includes a sense of the world as alive, with phenomena expressing their own form of agency

and connection. And although Zajonc (2009) does not use the language of rela-
tionality, it is perhaps implied in his illustration of how contemplative knowing
manifests through an example of composing music. A composer creates and writes
down notation for a melody and associated harmonies. The notes convey a set of
relationships that when played on the piano evoke morphing tonal relationships
that change and move as the music unfolds. As the creator and enactor of the melody, the pianist is an agent of the music, but in turn the music has a life of its own
that shapes the musician – "agency is the activity that creates and maintains the life
of the musical piece" (p. 157).

This view of agency within the universe is a way of thinking that is emerging in
the 21st century. It is a way of relating to the phenomenal world that goes beyond
humans as the centre (or top of a hierarchy), with all non-human and inanimate
life forms as less important. With current global and environmental challenges, it
seems we need to rethink relationships as interdependent and inherently complex
where there is agency within the environment (exerting influence and activity) in a
fluid and unfolding interplay. This way of thinking decentres the self and decentres
human beings while acknowledging an inter-dependence of all phenomena within
a web of relations.

This view is emerging in variety of domains. In nursing, the theories of *Health as
Expanding Consciousness* (Newman, 1994), *Human Becoming Theory* (Parse & National
League for Nursing, 1999) and Roger's *Science of Unitary Beings* (Wright, 2006) are
only a few examples. In the context of narrative inquiry, sociologist Arthur Frank
(2010) also moves in this direction, encouraging researchers to engage with narratives as living phenomena that breathe (*Letting Stories Breathe,* 2010), rather than as
inanimate, dead objects to be analysed under a methodological microscope. Similarly, contemplative thinking offers new epistemologies to emerge.

Contemplative pedagogy

Contemplative pedagogies are considered to be philosophies of education that promote the use of contemplative practices in teaching, learning and generating new
knowledge (Repetti, 2010). Contemplative pedagogy makes conscious use of a
wide range of practices "to cultivate student attention and emotional balance, compassion, empathic connection, and altruistic behaviour" and develop "pedagogical
approaches that support student creativity, insight and learning course content"
(Zajonc, 2013, p. 83).

In general, a distinguishing feature of contemplative pedagogies is the valuing
and use of subjective, 'first-person' epistemological approaches to knowing. This is
contrasted with conventional reliance on didactic, 'third-person' approaches (Britton et al., 2013; Roth, 2006; Shapiro, Brown, & Astin, 2011; Zajonc, 2006). The
distinction between first-, second- and third-person knowing is a useful conceptualization used by scholars in this field and is summarized here, beginning with the
most well-known in conventional, secular colleges and universities.

Third-person knowing and experience is found predominantly in the sciences, medicine, psychology and nursing and is oriented to external knowledge,

rational, logic and analytic approaches to inquiry. Current evidence-based movements in nursing reflect the importance of third-person approaches that foreground objectivity while minimizing or excluding subjective dimensions of the learner's experience. In nursing education, tensions exist in trying to balance the increasing content-laden curriculum that requires pathophysiology, pharmacology and all that constitutes the science of nursing without overshadowing the phenomenological, narrative, person-centred processes integral for the art of nursing care.

Second-person approaches are more process oriented and bring the learner into the realm of the creative (Sarath, 2006). Nursing students can learn theories of care and what it means to be cared for in health care settings (third-person knowledge), but this understanding is enriched and deepened by reflecting on their own experiences of being cared for (second-person knowledge) and the impact this has on students as people and hence their approach to providing care for others. Reflective practices and the importance of critical reflection have been incorporated into many nursing curricula (Johns & Freshwater, 2005) but are often under threat of being squeezed out by demands for additional science-based content.

And finally, first-person knowing and experience overlaps with second-person knowing. At its core, first-person knowing is an experience of self-awareness and includes mind-training technologies drawn from wisdom traditions including Buddhism, Hinduism and Taoism alongside modern sciences of psychology and neuroscience (Britton et al., 2013). It is suggested that the cultivation of first-person knowing enhances second- and third-person knowing. Consider the following description of a meditation experience from a master's nursing student who practiced a loving kindness meditation as part of a course that will be described later; her description exemplifies first-person epistemology.

> I chose to try one of the loving kindness meditations, because I had a difficult relational experience at work that left me feeling tense. Though I regularly practice breathing and relaxation techniques and meditation, I thought this was the perfect opportunity to try a new type of contemplative practice. I recognized that part of why I was feeling upset was because I wanted to be my authentic self and bring kindness and love to the situation. As I began the meditation, my breathing became more regular and I could feel my chest muscles relax, then shoulders, arms, hands, until my whole body was relaxed. As this happened, I tried to "breathe into my heart spot" and send out loving messages. I honestly felt a softening in my centre and an increased feeling of openness. I finished the meditation feeling less tense and more positive in my outlook.

First-person pedagogies heighten awareness of inner feelings, sensations and thoughts and are said to support important educational goals including self-knowledge. Recent research shows that contemplative practices such as meditations as cited above improve attention (Tang, et al. 2007), cognitive flexibility (Zeidan, Johnson, Diamond, David, & Goolkasian, 2010) and emotional balance (Britton et al., 2013; Kroll, 2010; Repetti, 2010; Shapiro, et al., 2011).

Integrating contemplative practices and first-person inquiry into nursing education

Nursing is a profession that demands emotional, cognitive and physical labor. The following case illustrates how emotional balance, the ability to be present and aware of inner and outer feelings, is integral to providing holistic care to patients and families.

> Mrs. Mary Wood was a lovely, delicate, white-haired lady of 78 years, with her right jaw and cheek carefully wrapped in gauze. She had a large tumor that was invading her face, and she had reached the terminal stage of her illness. Although she could still speak, the tumor had pushed her mouth over so that she could only drink from a straw and could no longer eat . . . the tumor was bleeding and smelled. It was emotionally difficult for the nurses to clean her tumor because it was so advanced that her jawbone was exposed. Indeed, the gauze on her face had evidence of dried blood from her weeping tumor, and there was a distinct odor that pervaded the room. The nurse practitioner reassured her that her tumor was not what her professional team and her family and friends saw – that the beautiful person inside was the person they saw.
>
> *(Taylor & McCann, 2005, p. 144)*

In the face of overpowering smells and sights, nursing students can sometimes feel overwhelmed and experience feelings of fear, revulsion or even disgust. Such feelings are often accompanied by guilt and doubt about their ability to practice nursing. In the face of patients' suffering and distress students must learn to connect deeply with who they are, with their own suffering, when facing another's sickness and ultimately with the human condition. In this context, nurse educators have the moral obligation to ensure students develop resources and supports for processing these experiences. Over time, students must learn to competently facilitate helping, caring relationships which are patient and family centred, where they can genuinely see the person – Mrs. Mary Wood – rather than her illness or tumour.

First-person contemplative practices of meditation, reflective journaling and loving kindness practices offer potential approaches to help develop these capacities in students. As noted earlier, growing empirical evidence suggests that meditation fosters non-judgemental awareness without needing to react, judge or suppress. Becoming aware of their own fears and reactions increases students' capacity to compassionately care for others (Baugher, 2008). However, more research is needed within educational and clinical contexts; nevertheless, our experience with students has been encouraging.

This next section is not rooted in empirical research but is a reflection drawing on the authors' experiences integrating contemplative pedagogy with nursing students in an on-line course. What follows are two learning activities as examples illustrating how contemplative practices have been incorporated into a master's-level course for nurse educators. Although it may seem incongruous to use contemplative practices with on-line formats, our experience has been reassuring. The asynchronous nature of on-line courses allows students to engage on their own time and in their own way; they have greater control and privacy. Also, the easily accessible guided meditations and instructions by qualified and experienced practitioners available on-line provides choice and diversity for leading guided meditations.

Background

For the last 2 years I (AB) have included opportunities for students to explore, practice and critique contemplative pedagogy in an on-line course entitled "Critical Pedagogies in Nursing Education". In one assignment, students select a topic from a list of current educational discourses that includes contemplative pedagogy. Even though most students are not familiar with the term, many have experienced either meditation or yoga in their personal lives and have been receptive to this topic. For the assignment students are asked to design a 'Peer Lead Session' for a small group to which they have been assigned. They are encouraged to draw on aesthetic knowing and experiential approaches as the assignment is an opportunity to practice teaching/facilitation skills. Therefore, they are interested in understanding the assumptions and discourses embedded in the pedagogical topic and also what learning occurred as a result of their peer lead session. The following two learning activities were developed (BP) and illustrate the kinds of approaches and responses students share when contemplative approaches are critically introduced and practiced on-line.

LEARNING ACTIVITY 1

Introducing the activity: Contemplative pedagogy may be described as a teaching approach which "cultivates inner awareness through first-person investigation" (Grace, 2011, p. 99). Kahane (2009) suggests that major pedagogical approaches in education directed at understanding power and privilege in a globalized and interconnected world "remain within a paradigm of education and scholarship as third person knowing" (p. 53). Contemplative practices offer an opportunity to shift from the third-person distant, empathic knowing to a connected awareness and knowledge of our personal habits of mind, judgements and beliefs, developing deepened self-knowledge (Kahane, 2009). Self-knowledge is a first step in transformative experience and new ways of knowing and "radically enhances the constructive development of critical thinking" (Grace, 2011, p. 114).

Step one

To give you an opportunity to evaluate contemplative pedagogical practices, I invite you to experience one of two forms of daily contemplative practice over the course of this Peer Lead Session.

These include a:

• 5-minute daily guided meditation practice

OR

• 10-minute daily free writing practice

Meditation

Meditation practice may be used to develop *mindfulness*. Mindfulness practice "means paying attention in a particular way: on purpose, in the present moment, and nonjudgmentally" (Kabat-Zinn, 1994, p. 4).

Focussing on the present moment fosters increased awareness of the minute details of each moment, our experiences and the thinking that determines our responses. As Kabat-Zinn (1994) states, "If we are not fully present for many of those moments, we may not only miss what is most valuable in our lives but also fail to realize the richness and depth of our possibilities for growth and transformation" (p. 4).

Free writing

The process of free writing serves as a contemplative practice by inviting one to relax and let thoughts flow freely and without inhibition or judgement (Elbow, 1981).

Free writing is writing without stopping for a fixed period of time. The writing is done with pen or pencil on paper and not on a computer, tablet or smartphone. The pen and the thoughts that flow from the writer's mind during the activity flow onto the page. Conscious and unconscious thoughts are given voice in the form and one "writes things that one didn't know one had to say" (Kahane, 2009, p. 55).

Step two

5-minute daily guided meditation practice

I invite you to take 5 minutes in each day in the contemplative practice of mindfulness meditation, focussing on your breathing and watching your thoughts float through your mind like twigs gently drifting down a stream.

Please find a quiet space where you will be comfortable and undisturbed. The following link will take you to a 5-minute guided meditation which ends with the sound of a bell.

http://marc.ucla.edu/mpeg/01_Breathing_Meditation.mp3

Alternatively, you may choose to download this mediation as a voice file app on your mobile phone.

> *Please take the time to note your thoughts and how you are feeling prior to beginning your chosen practice activity and following your chosen contemplative practice each day.*

Free writing activity

Please find a quiet space where you will be comfortable and undisturbed. You will need a watch, clock or timer to time your writing. You will also need a pen or pencil and paper or a notebook for writing.

Begin to write. Do not stop; keep the pen moving across the page. Write without hurrying or focussing on the end of the activity. Do not lift the pen from the page; do not edit; do not worry about spelling or grammar. Do not judge your efforts; simply write; write whatever comes into your mind. If you can't think of what to write, write "I can't think of what to write" over and over again until something does come into your mind. Just continue to write anything for 10 minutes.

To assist you in your free writing activity, you may wish to choose one of the writing prompts below, and write whatever comes to mind after you have read one of them.

- "To speak a true world is to transform the world" – Paulo Friere
- "Muddy water, let stand, becomes clear" – Laozi
- "I am large; I contain multitudes" – Walt Whitman, *Leaves of Grass.*
- "The oppressed, want at any cost, to resemble the oppressors" – Paulo Friere

> *Please take the time to note your thoughts and how you are feeling prior to beginning your chosen practice activity and following your chosen contemplative practice each day.*

Step three

At the end of the week, in 250–300 words, describe what, if any, impact the contemplative practice you chose had on your learning this week. If you are comfortable doing so, please include in your posting any reflections or thoughts that came to the fore as a result in undertaking the contemplative practice of your choice.

References

Elbow, P. (1981). *Writing with power: Techniques for mastering the writing process.* New York, NY: Oxford University Press.

Friere, P. (2000). *Pedagogy of the oppressed.* New York, NY: Bloomsbury Publishing Inc.

Grace, F. (2011). Learning as a path, not a goal: Contemplative pedagogy – Its principles and practices. *Teaching Theology and Religion, 14*(2), 99–124.

Kabat-Zinn, J. (1994). *Wherever you go, there you are.* New York, NY: Hyperion.

Kahane, D. (2009). Learning about obligation, compassion, and global justice: The place of contemplative pedagogy. *New Directions in Teaching and Learning, 118,* 49–60.

Whitman, W. (2007). *Leaves of grass.* Radford, VA: Wilder Publications

LEARNING ACTIVITY 2

Introducing the activity: Grace (2011) describes three forms of teaching and learning which form the journey of her own educator experience. The first is described as *"content-based, third-person, analytical teaching"* (p. 106). With this form of teaching, the teacher provides the content to the learner. This form of teaching is akin to Friere's (2000) description of teaching as the "banking" (p. 72) method wherein the teacher narrates the information to be learned and the student accepts the information. Knowledge delivered in such a way "becomes lifeless and petrified" (Friere, 2000, p. 71).

The next form of teaching on Grace's (2011) pedagogical journey is described as *"context-based, second-person, interactive teaching"* (p. 106). Recognizing students' lack of engagement, Grace (2011) began to invite individuals currently working in the field of study to speak to the class about their work. Students responded with lively discussion and engagement, viewing one another as "living texts" (p. 106) and experts in many aspects of content under discussion. Although the author felt her role was to encourage students to explore their personal perspectives and beliefs and encourage action against oppression and inequity, such "second-person interactions" (p. 106) frequently resulted in conflict, preventing productive dialogue. Grace contends the reason lies in students' lack of insight and awareness of their deeply held judgements and biases, resulting in an inability to explore and interpret other perspectives and their contribution to knowledge construction.

The final form of teaching that Grace (2011) describes is the form that is the focus of this Peer Lead Session: *"contemplative-based, first-person, interior teaching"* (p. 106).

Grace (2011) describes the use of contemplative practices as offering teachers the opportunity to explore inner or self-knowledge. The exploration of one's "interior (contemplative) dimension" (p. 106) of teaching, blended with the two other dimensions, mentioned previously, provides a balanced and integrated approach to teaching and learning. Grace (2011) notes students have reported that the use of meditation has "substantially improved their academic success and overall flourishing" (p. 106).

As you read the following articles and explore the tenets of contemplative pedagogy, I invite you to consider Grace's (2011) view of contemplative teaching as first-person knowledge.

Step one

Please watch the following videos about contemplative pedagogy:

> "Fostering Attention: Contemplative Pedagogy at Vanderbilt" www.youtube.com/watch?v=wqRGJhW5wZE (9 minutes)
> "What Is Mindfulness? Dr. Jon Kabat-Zinn" www.youtube.com/watch?v=HmEo6RI4Wvs (5 minutes)

Read the following articles:

> Hart, T. (2004). Opening the contemplative mind in the classroom. *Journal of Transformative Education, 2*(1), 28–46.
> Sharts-Hopko, N. C. (2007). Personal and professional impact of a course on contemplative practices in health and illness. *Holistic Nurse Practitioner, 21*(1), 3–9.

1 Please choose one of the questions below and in 300–500 words, provide a response.
2 Respond to *one* other member of the group by asking a thought-provoking question or commenting on their posting.

  a. Based on the readings, what do you see as the strengths and limitations of using contemplative pedagogical approaches in your teaching practice?
  b. How do contemplative pedagogy, and the practices associated with it, support critical pedagogy in nursing?
  c. What are the epistemological underpinnings of contemplative practice? Please explain your reasoning.

Step two

1 Describe how you might use contemplative pedagogy and its practices in your own teaching setting.

Student experiences and feedback of learning activities

Learning Activity #1 offered learners an opportunity to regularly practice a contemplative activity for 1 week. Most students chose the guided meditation practice and all reported noticing increased relaxation and an ability to clear their minds or take a mental break, to centre oneself. Several students noted that the practices afforded them an opportunity to stop in the midst of a stressful day, to take a deep breath and to focus on the current moment. One learner shared how she is already using similar practices in her nursing work.

> When I first started working on a mixed palliative-and-medical floor . . . I wondered how I would be able to come across as peaceful and calm with my palliative clients / family members when I was busily running around like a chicken with its head cut off for my acutely ill clients. But one day, one of my colleagues approached me and discussed a strategy to help ground me and get me out of the crazy busy frame of mind before I went into my palliative clients' rooms. She told me that just before entering a palliative client's room, I was to touch the door knob and hold it for 10 seconds while I focused on slowing my breathing down with the goal of trying to quiet my mind. I tell you, that I still use this technique even today. We can incorporate small contemplative practices into our workplaces which help to center and ground us, and these will enable us to better assist our clients in the end because we are totally ready to be present with them in the moment.

Another student added how using a bell sound meditation during the week helped her during the stressful work week.

> The meditation session I chose was a 4-part Bell Sound Practice by Arthur Zajonc, from the website of the Center for Contemplative Mind in Society — sounds like a most interesting place! I picked this practice because, as an ICU nurse [intensive care unit], my working life is dominated by bells and whistles sounding throughout my shifts. I would love for someone to count the number of alarms ringing throughout a 12-hour period in any given location within my Unit — I'm sure it would be a spectacular number! I chose this practice because it constitutes a kind of redemption-by-non-work-bells for me — also I love meditative bells in general, and I thought that this practice could contribute to my current goal of changing my stress level in relation to my work bells. In other words, if I had at least the memory of meditative bells and where they took me at a deeper level of my being, I think it would lower my overall stress level and increase my overall relaxation level. This was my hope going into the meditation. I got it downloaded into my iPod so I could listen to it and go through the meditation at various locations including my workplace during my breaks this week.
> During the meditation sessions, I found that I was able to enter into them quite quickly and I found the themes very meaningful, eg., the theme of focused attention, open awareness, memory of the bell sound and release of it to go beyond it, and gratitude. Afterwards — I used this practice several times during this past week and I found

> *that it met my expectations of lowering my overall stress level and increasing my*
> *relaxation level. It also allowed several images to emerge that I will continue to ponder*
> *for their personal meaning to me over time.*

In Learning Activity #2, students critically examined contemplative pedagogy from several perspectives. Contemplative pedagogy was described as arising from a constructivist epistemology using experiential learning theories. One learner described contemplative pedagogy as "knowledge being obtained from inside ourselves". She also described a shifting from knowledge inquiring *what we know* to that of inquiring *how we know*. Contemplative pedagogy seemed to foster awareness and knowledge of their personal habits of mind, judgements and beliefs, developing deepened self-knowledge. There were also some reservations about using these kinds of practices in the educators' teaching.

> *In order to do anything more advanced I feel that I'd have to take a course or get com-*
> *fortable and confident with leading an activity that was more than personal reflection.*
> *I have been in learning situations where the instructor had made us do an activity –*
> *one that stands out for me was a guided relaxation exercise that was performed for a*
> *staff retreat on vicarious trauma. Quite a few nurses in the group broke down in tears*
> *during the exercise and I felt rather uncomfortable as it seemed to precipitate some*
> *issues in public that we were not equipped to deal with. So I think that if you use*
> *these techniques they can be powerful but one needs to be able to support learners if the*
> *exercise brings out the unexpected.*

The group identified additional challenges to using contemplative pedagogy. Foremost was that the educator must first believe in the value of a practice or pedagogical approach before taking it up and introducing it to students. Other limitations fell under institutional barriers and individual barriers. For example, barriers include questioning whether academic or clinical agencies would support the implementation of such approaches. With value placed firmly on 'science' and the 'gold standard' of random-clinical trials, students question if there is enough convincing evidence for administrators and policy makers to support the integration of 'soft' skills. In terms of individual barriers, challenges included the lack of instruction about how to incorporate or carry out contemplative pedagogy and how to attend to unexpected emotional responses in students.

Finally, the group identified the many practices they currently use which fall into the contemplative pedagogical approach: critical questioning; providing time for self-reflection; creating a classroom environment which is relaxed, supportive and safe for discussion. A student suggested trying some of the practices throughout the semester and inviting students to identify what practice they found helpful.

While the benefits of contemplative pedagogy in teaching were also noted, there remain many questions about how and whether it can be implemented and what further knowledge will assist with integrating contemplative pedagogy into the educators' teaching practice. Concrete examples in publications illustrating how contemplative pedagogical teaching in nursing has been used were seen to be helpful.

Factors to consider when using contemplative practices in educational contexts

Barbezat and Bush (2014) outline four broad objectives for educators to consider when integrating first-person contemplative practices into coursework. First, they recommend beginning with focusing and attention-building exercises using meditation exercises to strengthen mental stability. Attention and focusing exercises are easy to explain and help familiarize students with their mental activity and the settling of mind. Useful exercises include awareness of sense perceptions: attending to sounds, sensations of breathing, sitting, walking or mindfully eating (a well-known activity of mindfully observing, feeling and eating a raisin).

Second, help students deepen their understanding of course material using contemplation and introspection activities to support their discovery of the material in themselves. Awareness practices should be linked explicitly and clearly to course content. For example, Daniel Barbezat is an economist who uses meditation exercises where students imagine the impact of different forms of distribution of goods and income; students attend to images and feelings when goods are distributed primarily to those who are loved ones and those who are strangers. Students become aware of their own reactions "without having to adopt any ideology or specific belief" (Barbezat & Bush, 2014, p. 6).

Third, explore connections to compassion and a deepening sense of the moral and spiritual aspect of education. The separation of church and state has long been an important hallmark of education in democratic societies. Incorporating contemplative practices that do not advocate a particular spiritual or ideological tradition but recognize the diversity of religious and ideological perspectives seems important.

And finally, foster inquiry into the nature of their minds, what is personally meaningful, creative and insightful. Including not only a rationale for why and how contemplative practices support the course material, but leaving room for critique and opting out are also important considerations.

Conclusion

A growing body of empirical evidence (mostly in relation to mindfulness practice) suggests that first-person experience fostered through enhanced attention and self-awareness yields increased empathy, self-compassion and connection with the world (Birnie, Speca, & Carlson, 2010). As educators of health professionals, we have the moral obligation to equip students with the knowledge, skills and capacity to be able to care for patients and families competently and compassionately and to sustain their well-being in the process. Contemplative epistemologies and practices offer new directions for teaching and learning in the 21st century that are catching hold of educators' imaginations in higher education. This tide of change aims to prepare future nurses, doctors, therapists, psychologists, lawyers and citizens to engage in life with more awareness, gentleness and dynamism. While contemplative practices are not a panacea, current evidence and anecdotal experience from our own educational contexts offer compelling cases for incorporating contemplative pedagogy. It is our belief and aspiration that these practices can help students strengthen positive emotions and mind states that contribute to the greater good.

Bibliography

Barbezat, D., & Bush, M. (2014). *Contemplative practices in higher education: Powerful methods to transform teaching and learning.* San Francisco, CA: Jossey-Bass

Baugher, J. E. (2008). Facing death: Buddhist and Western hospice approaches. *Symbolic Interaction, 31*(3), 259–284. doi:10.1525/si.2008.31.3.259

Beddoe, A. E., & Murphy, S. O. (2004). Does mindfulness decrease stress and foster empathy among nursing students? *Journal of Nursing Education, 43*(7), 305–312.

Birnie, K., Speca, M., & Carlson, L. E. (2010). Exploring self-compassion and empathy in the context of mindfulness-based stress reduction (MBSR). *Stress and Health, 26*(5), 359–371.

Brainstrom, R., Duncan, L. G., & Moskowitz, J. T. (2011). The association between dispositional mindfulness, psychological well-being and perceived health in a Swedish population-based sample. *British Journal of Health Psychology, 16*(2), 300–316. doi. org/10.1348/135910710x501683.

Britton, W., Brown, A.-C., Kaplan, C. T., Goldman, R. E., DeLuca, M., Rojiani, R., . . . Frank, T. (2013). Contemplative science: An insider prospectus. *New Directions for Teaching & Learning, 134,* 13–29.

Bruce, A., & Davies, B. (2005). Mindfulness in hospice care: Practicing meditation-in-action. *Qualitative Health Research, 15*(10), 1329–1344.

Buss, D. M. (2000). The evolution of happiness. *American Psychologist, 55,* 15–23.

Chen, Y., Yang, X., Wang, L., & Zhang, X. (2013). A randomized controlled trial of the effects of brief mindfulness meditation on anxiety symptoms and systolic blood pressure in Chinese nursing students. *Nurse Education Today, 33*(10), 1166–1172 doi.org/10.1016/j. nedt.2012.11.014

Cohen-Katz, J. (2005). The effects of mindfulness-based reduction on nurse stress and burnout, Part II: a quantitative and qualitative study. *Holistic Nursing Practice, 19*(1), 26–35.

Donaldson, S., Dollwet, M., & Rao, M. (2015). Happiness, excellence, and optimal human functioning revisited: Examining the peer-reviewed literature linked to positive psychology. *The Journal of Positive Psychology, 10*(3), 185–195, doi.org/10.1080/17439760.2014 .943801

Donaldson, S. I, Csikszentmihalyi, M., & Nakamura, J. (Eds.) (2011). *Applied positive psychology: Improving everyday life, health, schools, work, and society.* London: Routledge Academic.

Doty, J. (2012). *The place for compassion in a modern age.* Center for Compassion and Altruism Research and Education webcast. www.ccare.stanford.edu/videos/the-place-for-compass ion-in-a-modern-age-james-doty

Dufon, M. A., & Christian, J. (2013). The formation and development of the mindful campus. *New Directions for Teaching & Learning: Contemplative Studies in Higher Education, 134,* 65–72.

Frank, A. W. (2010). *Letting stories breathe: A socio-narratology.* Chicago: University of Chicago Press.

Friere, P. (2000). *Pedagogy of the oppressed.* New York: Continuum.

Goyal, M., Singh, E. S., Sibinga, E., Gould, N., Rowland-Seymour, A., Sharma, R., . . . Haythornthwaite, J. (2014). Meditation programs for psychological stress and well-being: A systematic review and meta-analysis. *JAMA Internal Medicine, 174*(3), 357–368,. doi. org/10.1001/jamainternmed.2013.13018

Hart, T. (2004). Opening the contemplative mind in the classroom. *Journal of Transformative Education, 2*(1), 28–46.

Hassed, C., de Lisle, S., Sullivan, G., Pier, C. (2009). Enhancing the health of medical students: Outcomes of an integrated mindfulness and lifestyle program. *Advances in Health Sciences Education: Theory and Practice, 14,* 387–398.

Johns, C., & Freshwater, D. (2005). *Transforming nursing through reflective practice.* Malden, MA; Oxford: Blackwell Pub.

Jose, P. E., Kemp, S., & Grimm, C. (2015). Orientations to happiness and the experience of everyday activities. *The Journal of Positive Psychology, 10*(3), 207–218. doi:10.1080/17439 760.2014.941382

Kabat-Zinn, J. (1994). *Wherever you go, there you are.* New York, NY: Hyperion.

Kang, Y., Gruber, J., & Gray, J. R. (2013). Mindfulness and de-automatization. *Emotion Review, 5*(2), 192–201. doi:10.1177/1754073912451629

Krasner, M. S., Epstein, R. M., Beckman, H., Suchman, A. L., Chapman, B., Mooney, C. J., & Quill, T. E. (2009). Association of an educational program in mindful communication with burnout, empathy and attitudes among primary care physicians. *JAMA, 302*(12), 1284–1293. doi:10.1001/jama.2009.1384

Kroll, K. (2010). Contemplative practice in the classroom. In K. Kroll (Ed.), *Contemplative teaching and learning, new directions for community colleges, no 151* (pp. 111–113). San Francisco, CA: Jossey-Bass.

McGarrigle, T., & Walsh, C. A. (2011). Mindfulness, self-care, and wellness in social work: Effects of contemplative training. *Journal of Religion & Spirituality in Social Work: Social Thought, 30*(3), 212–233.

Miller, J. (1994a). *The contemplative practitioner: Meditation in education and the professions.* Westport, CT: Bergin & Garvey.

Miller, J. (1994b). Contemplative practice in higher education: Experiment in teacher development. *Journal of Humanistic Psychology, 34*(4), 53–69.

Newman, M. A. (1994). *Health as expanding consciousness.* New York, NY: National League for Nursing Press.

Parse, R. R., & National League for Nursing. (1999). *Illuminations: The human becoming theory in practice and research.* Sudbury, MA: Jones and Barlett Publishers.

Repetti, R. (2010). The case for a contemplative philosophy of education. In K. Kroll (Ed.), *Contemplative teaching and learning: New directions for community colleges, no 151* (pp. 5–15). San Francisco, CA: Jossey-Bass.

Roth, H. (2006). Contemplative studies: Prospects for the new field of contemplative studies. *Teachers College Record, 108*(9), 1787–1815.

Ryan, C., James, M., & Hogan, M. (2013). Nurturing creativity in the classroom. *The Journal of Positive Psychology, 8*(1), 81–83. doi:10.1080/17439760.2012.733725

Sarath, E. (2006). Meditation, creativity, and consciousness: Charting future terrain within higher education. *Teachers College Record, 108*(9), 1816–1841.

Schmidt, C., Ziemer, K. Z, Piontkowski, S., & Raque-Bogdan, T. L (2013). The history and future directions of positive health psychology. In J. Sinnott (Ed.), *Positive psychology and adult motivation* (pp. 207–228). London: Springer.

Seligman, M. E., & Csikszentmihalyi, M. (2000). Positive psychology: An introduction. *American Psychologist, 55,* 4–14. doi:10.1037/0003-066X.55.1.5

Seligman, M. E., Ernst, R. M., Gillham, J., Reivich, K., & Linkins, M. (2009). Positive education: Positive psychology and classroom interventions. *Oxford Review of Education, 35*(3), 293–311. doi:10.1080/03054980902934563

Shapiro, S., Brown, K., & Astin, J. (2011). Toward the integration of meditation into higher education: A review of research. *Teachers College Record, 113*(3), 493–598.

Simonton, D. K. (2000). Creativity: Cognitive, personal, developmental, and social aspects. *American Psychologist, 55,* 151–158.

Tang, Y. Y., Ma, J., Wang, J., Fan, Y. Feng, S., Lu, Q., Yu, Q. (2007). Short-term meditation training improves attention and self-regulation. *Proceedings of the National Academy of Sciences, 104,* 17152–17156.

Taylor, B. R., & McCann, R. M. (2005). Controlled sedation for physical and existential suffering? *Journal of Palliative Medicine, 8*(1), 144–147.

The Center for Contemplative Mind in Society. (n.d.). *Meditation and mindfulness.* www.contemplativemind.org

Westphal, M., Bingisser, M. B., Feng, T., & Kleim, B. (2014). Protective benefits of mindfulness in emergency room personnel. *Journal of Affective Disorders, 175,* 79–85. doi:10.1016/j.jad.2014.12.038

White, L. (2014). Mindfulness in nursing: An evolutionary concept analysis. *Journal of Advanced Nursing, 70*(2), 282–294. doi:10.1111/jan.12182

Winner, E. (2000). The origins and ends of giftedness. *American Psychologist, 55,* 159–169.

Wright, B. W. (2006). Rogers' science of unitary human beings. *Nursing Science Quarterly, 19*(3), 229–230. doi:10.1177/0894318406289888

Zajonc, A. (2006). Love and knowledge: Recovering the heart of learning through contemplation. *Teachers College Record, 108*(9), 1742–1759.

Zajonc, A. (2009). *Meditation as contemplative inquiry: When knowing becomes love.* Great Barrington, MA: Lindisfarne Books.

Zajonc, A. (2013). Contemplative pedagogy: A quiet revolution in higher education. *New Directions for Teaching & Learning: Contemplative Studies in Higher Education, 134,* 83–94.

Zajonc, A. (n.d.). *The 4-part bell sound practice.* The Center for Contemplative Mind in Society. Audio recording. www.contemplativemind.org/audio/AZ-Four_Part_Bell_Sound.mp3

Zeidan, F., Johnson, S. K., Diamond, B. J., David, Z., & Goolkasian, P. (2010). Mindfulness meditation improves cognition: Evidence of brief mental training. *Consciousness and Cognition, 19*(2), 597–605.

12

MINDFULNESS-BASED MEDICAL PRACTICE

Eight weeks en route to wellness

Patricia Lynn Dobkin

Introduction

While early research on mindfulness for health care professionals (HCPs) was conducted with trainees (e.g., Rosenzweig, Reibel, Greeson, Brainard, & Hojat, 2003), a number of studies have highlighted the potential for mindfulness to support the wellness of practicing HCPs through mechanisms such as attention and self-compassion (Irving, Dobkin, & Park, 2009). In a randomized trial with a mixed-group of HCPs enrolled in the mindfulness-based stress reduction (MBSR) program, Shapiro and colleagues (Shapiro, Astin, Bishop, & Cordova, 2005) found that self-compassion predicted changes in perceived stress. Krasner and colleagues (Krasner et al., 2009) conducted an open trial of a modified version of MBSR with primary care physicians; results showed increases in mindfulness and empathy, improved emotional stability, and decreases in physician burnout. Moreover, increases in mindfulness were correlated with improved mood, perspective taking, and decreased burnout. Two studies explored the impact of mindfulness upon clinical encounters. Connelly (2005) used case studies to illustrate how being present and aware during medical visits improved patient care. Grepmair and colleagues (Grepmair et al., 2007) conducted a randomized controlled study of psychotherapy trainees, which revealed that the patients of meditating trainees demonstrated greater reductions in psychological distress.

In a more recent, pragmatic controlled trial, conducted in Spain by Asuero and colleagues (Asuero et al., 2014) with 68 professionals, it was found that those who took the mindfulness education program showed improvements in mood, empathy, mindfulness, and burnout. In the first study to examine if practitioners' mindfulness influenced the medical encounter, Beach and colleagues (Beach et al., 2013) conducted an observational study of 45 clinicians caring for patients infected with HIV. Medical visits were audio recorded and coded by raters blinded to mindfulness scores; patients independently rated their perceptions following the visit. Clinicians who scored high on mindfulness were more likely to engage in patient-centered communication (e.g., discussed psychosocial issues, built rapport) and they displayed a more positive emotional tone with patients. Patients reported better communication with the more mindful physicians and they were more satisfied with their care.

It is apparent that the practice of mindfulness is a promising approach towards improving the wellness of practicing clinicians and patient care. Given the inherently demanding nature of the work carried out by HCPs, our program, Mindfulness-Based Medical Practice (MBMP), recognizes the relationship between perceived stress and wellness as well as the moderating effects of mindfulness and self-compassion. Our courses have been taught by the same two instructors: a PhD level psychologist (PLD) and a palliative care physician (Dr. Thomas Hutchinson) with certification in family therapy and 8 years of experience. Instructors had completed training through the University of Massachusetts Center for Mindfulness, and one instructor (PLD) has completed the third level of training, is certified, and teaches MBSR to patients with chronic illness as well. Course participants receive a home practice manual and four CDs created by the instructor (PLD) to guide the following meditation practices: body scan, sitting meditation, hatha yoga, and meditation involving visual imagery. At the end of each class, participants are asked to complete specific home practice exercises including informal practice (awareness of breath; being mindful while engaging in various daily tasks). Group discussions throughout the course focus on the various practices and how they are being integrated into the participants' daily lives and work. In Irving's dissertation work (Irving, 2011) results from 90 HCPs (half of whom were physicians) who took the course over a 4-year period were similar to existing research. Significant decreases were observed in participants' perceived stress and burnout, as well as significant increases in mindfulness, self-compassion, and wellness following the program. Hierarchical regression analyses indicated that while stress negatively predicted wellness, mindfulness and self-compassion predicted greater wellness (Irving et al., 2014). Attendance and self-reported satisfaction were high.

Rather than present a review of the literature in this chapter, I have written a narrative (Charon, 2006) to showcase HCPs' experiences in one of my MBMP courses. Participants' identities have been masked; they were mix of physicians and other HCPs. What transpired was similar to what occurs typically in this course and thus my intention was to provide the reader with insight into how MBMP is taught and how participation in the course over 8 weeks leads to wellness. This aim is consistent with positive psychology.

Beginning

The Zendo, with its mahogany floors and bamboo plants basking in the sunshine, was silent upon my arrival. Twenty HCPs – physicians, a nurse, a few psychologists, an osteopath, a social worker, and two hospital-based spiritual counselors – had been interviewed individually and pre-tested online prior to beginning the MBMP.

I arrived early to set up and practice a walking meditation. A bronze statue of the Buddha graced the room; it reminded me of my intentions for leading this group. Joy filled my heart. While I have provided 21 MBSR courses for patients with chronic illness, with about 20 people per group, I realized years ago that teaching MBMP would serve more patients than I could ever work with directly. The standard MBSR program was modified to suit HCPs; emphasis was placed on building resilience and enhancing communication skills in recognition of the needs of this population, where they work, and the nature of the stressors in their lives (Dobkin, Hickman, & Monshat, 2013).

Week #1

We sat in a circle until everyone arrived and began by reviewing guidelines regarding how to work together. I invited them to remove their watches, a symbolic gesture bowing to the present moment. With the ring of Tibetan bells we sat for a brief awareness of breath meditation. This set the stage for the next 8 weeks. We noticed what we noticed: mind clutter, a stiff neck, shallow breath, calmness. In voicing what they experienced, the universal nature of the human experience was revealed. We are more similar than different.

The second meditation was contemplative in nature: I asked, "What brings you here now?" Throughout the years, some physicians have been referred by the Quebec Physician Assistance Program, a government-funded agency – four staff doctors have taken the course so they know what it offers. Some psychologists wanted to ride the third wave of mindfulness-based interventions; a few hoped to teach MBSR and this was their first step towards that goal. When they said why they had come, a few mentioned feeling overwhelmed by the suffering they witness daily; a few sought the company of like-minded HCPs. Several had tried to meditate alone but felt the need for structure to maintain a regular practice. A few mentioned the desire to extend compassion to themselves and be more present with patients. One woman was honest enough, with herself and us, when she said, "I don't know why I am here." Not knowing and the acceptance of not knowing are important aspects of mindfulness.

A mixed array of emotions permeated the room: hope, happiness, relief. Their thoughts reflected openness to experience and curiosity. Most spoke in French, while I and a few others spoke in English or switched back and forth – a common phenomenon in Montreal. This is a unique aspect of this course: its bilingual nature extends the invitation to "come as you are/be who you are"; it is welcoming.

One physician who noticed her busy mind during the first meditation smiled when I asked, "Who else experienced this?" Most hands went up. This gave me the opportunity to state clearly, "We are here to train the mind. When we go to the gym we train the body. Is it not curious that so little attention is paid to this, especially for those of us who have studied for decades in educational institutions? During this program we will be scientists exploring our own minds." A gynecologist appreciated the analogy. Clearly she was in the right place at the right time in her life.

Week #2

I arrived a half hour early in order to set up and set my intention for teaching the class. When I began a walking meditation I read, "Une fleur s'ouvre à chaque pas," i.e., "A flower opens with each step," written in calligraphy style posted on the wall. Just minutes beforehand I had stopped to admire an entire front yard colored with tulips while coming to class, so I smiled. Then I sat on my cushion with the Buddha behind me – literally and figuratively. My intentions were right effort, right mindfulness, right view, right thought, right speech, and right action – knowing that these signposts on the eight-fold path would guide me during the class.

The nurse arrived early. When she saw me walking she fell into step. Since she has been wounded deeply she casts a victim shadow. In my mind I pictured her being bullied as a child, harassed as an adult. I imagined her aggressors gnawing on her vulnerabilities with delight. My heart opened. Her suffering is welcome here in this sanctuary. The group will offer her acceptance. I will ensure that the space is safe for her and the other HCPs who signed in, sat down, and waited in silence for the second class to begin.

The body scan meditation was purposefully long and slow. We were explorers noting sensations as they came and went in the various parts of the body. We were learning not to rush. We were training our minds to aim and sustain attention. We were observing the breath as it entered each cell in the body. It is our best friend. Forty minutes later we described our observations, like scientists debriefing. One class member, the one who was surprised last week by how slow the body scan was, noted that this time and during her home practice she simply observed differences when practicing slowly and then more quickly. Another class member declared that she could not stay awake, ever, here or at home. I recalled a chapter I had just read by Goldstein on sloth and torpor (Goldstein, 2013) and suggested that she open her eyes, sit up, or even stand up to fall awake. I added that yoga or walking meditation may be easier for her. Her energy and concentration seemed to be out of balance. She was not alone to struggle with this hindrance. A more experienced meditator noticed "denseness" in parts of her body. I recalled my 10-day Goenka (Vipassana) retreat years ago when we were instructed to sweep awareness through the body and notice if there were areas that were blocked. . . . I made no comment since none was needed.

Home practice of the body scan varied across class members. Some were able to carve out 30 minutes to practice daily; others were not. A student felt guilty for missing 1 day so she doubled up the next. I commented that unlike forgetting a pill there was no need to double up. While discipline is important, HCPs tend to criticize themselves when they fail to complete required tasks so I encouraged them to examine what got in the way of their intention to practice (Irving et al., 2014). Harshness is habitual among them; it's a mind habit that the course aims to soften through kindness.

As for eating mindfully during the week this was a challenge for most who commented on it taking too long. Time pressure is a stressor for them. One person mentioned that she started to eat this way but then forgot, as did the person next to me who got halfway through the exercise and then was distracted. I commented on how our attention is constantly pulled in multiple directions such that we miss the moment most of the time. We bypass the joy of eating, of the sun on our face, the laughter of children, and so much more. I revisited this notion later when giving the "Pleasant Events" home practice assignment. It is important to emphasize the joy that mindfulness can bring to our lives to give people hope that they can live full, happy lives.

The 9-dot exercise calls up self-judgment in those who fail to solve the puzzle. Feelings of inadequacy, competition, frustration . . . this is one point of the exercise. In contrast to their conditioning, it does not matter if they succeed in solving the problem. We examine process: What went through your minds? Can we notice when our inner voice is unkind? This is how the course helps them be aware of harmful thoughts.

The class ended with a 15-minute awareness of breath meditation with little guidance on my part. They sat on chairs, cushions, benches, and lifted their chests to allow the breath to fill their lungs completely. Silence permeated the room.

Week #3

Rain and congested roads prevented me from arriving early for the third class. Most were waiting near the locked door when I arrived. Years ago I would have felt bad about having made people wait for me. This time, even though I was "almost late," I coped by moving quickly without rushing, without criticizing myself, setting up things and beginning at precisely 3 p.m. Whew . . . I knew that the yoga practice would help us all to stay grounded in the present moment. I used my arriving "just in time" as an opportunity to examine informal practice. I related how I drove slowly in the pouring rain, seeing the trucks and cars, taking care to release projections about being late. A spiritual counselor who travels 2 to 3 hours from a smaller city in Quebec related how he noticed the heavy rain, the smell of it, the sound it made. He was calm.

Once settled in corpse pose I asked everyone to note the body's energy level. We followed the standard sequences from the MBSR program. I emphasized that this practice is an extension of the body scan in that we meditate in movement. I asked them to notice sensations as we stretched and held postures. A social worker was concerned she could not move in certain ways. This gave me the opportunity to remind everyone to listen to their bodies, respect their limits, and accept things just as they are. The exercise adage "No pain, no gain" has no place in this practice. I underscored the importance of not comparing or judging as if this were a performance. In this way, I integrated the attitudes that are central to being mindful. Afterwards I surveyed the group with regard to their energy levels; many found that theirs had increased.

In reviewing the home practice a psychologist who works long hours indicated that she did the body scan at 11 p.m., before bed, and that her sleep deepened because of it. She related feeling joyful and light during the day. When she asked if this was similar to relaxation training I explained the difference between the two. Because they are trained to provide rationale-based, evidence-based treatments I recognized the need for an answer to this question. Nonetheless, it is important not to fall into a professor role to be consistent with the way MBSR is taught. A student noted that she stopped projecting into the future, even though she is young and preparing for her career.

With regard to informal home practice, one person related how she stopped multitasking at work, focusing on one thing at a time, and consequently was much less tired when she arrived at home. Another told of not reacting when another driver did a U-turn to dart into her parking space. By being aware she was able to see another spot. She said that in the past she may have been too upset to notice it.

Not all the people were practicing daily. I encouraged them to do as much as they could. When someone said, "This takes discipline!" I simply agreed. Over the years I have heard of this struggle over and over again. Week by week, especially after the retreat, their practice develops. I maintained confidence in this process.

They formed groups of three to exchange their experiences with "Pleasant Events." This gave them an opportunity to move into the group process phase. Sharing and helping each other allowed the isolation of clinical practice to diminish. I moved between groups and allowed them the time needed for this to occur. When the room became quieter I knew it was time to move to on.

To end the class we sat in silence for 20 minutes. Enough words had been spoken for the day. David Whyte's (2004) poem came to mind:

ENOUGH

> Enough. These few words are enough.
> If not these words, this breath.
> If not this breath, this sitting here.
> This opening to the life
> we have refused
> again and again
> until now.
> Until now.

Week #4

The theme of Week 4 is stress management. This class was co-led with the director of McGill Programs in Whole Person Care, a palliative care physician trained in family therapy. He brings to this class Satir's communication stances (Satir, 1988) as part of our communication training. It is good for the physicians in the room to have a member of their profession teach them; this validates the application of mindfulness in medicine.

Tom and I have taught together for 8 years. We wondered what effect his dropping in on the group at this point in time (rather than co-lead the entire program with me as we have in the past) would have. In fact, another physician – a psychiatrist from South America who could not come earlier because of a strike at his university – also just arrived. The group was open, accepting these two newcomers without any resistance. I had informed the group beforehand about these two men coming that day. The South American physician aims to infuse mindfulness into his work in addiction in his country – a noble intention. He arrived after 30 hours of travel that day and was grateful to be with us. I was thankful that he made it safely to Canada.

Tom began the class with a guided sitting meditation, gently mentioning that they need not work now.

Next, we examined the stressors in our lives. In popcorn style participants named what they found stressful: multitasking at work, angry people, bureaucracy, time. Then they checked off in the home practice manual their stress reactions. The completion of the "Unpleasant Events" form helped one person realize that her stressors were not external; she ruminated about unresolved issues. We referred to the two figures in the manual that contrast stress reactivity and responding. This is a key message of the course: while stress will always be part of our lives, how we choose to respond is what matters.

I used two teaching tools: the Triangle of Awareness and STOP to give them the means to deal with stress more effectively. STOP is an acronym for S = slow down/stop; T = take a breath; O = observe; P = proceed. With the Triangle of Awareness (see Figure 12.1), we examined the links between thoughts, emotions, and body sensations. I made the connection with the body scan: it helps you to discern when you are stressed. "Where in your body do you feel this?" I asked. One class member replied that she gets headaches. When one is at the O stage of STOP one can observe the three parts of the triangle, the Satir stance one is in, and then choose an appropriate response.

A physician related that during an especially charged week she was abruptly asked to solve a problem between co-workers. She was not happy with how she handled it. A psychologist described waking up feeling sad for "no reason." This event led to an exploration of how we deal with emotions. She wanted to know if "staying with" the mood state was a form of indulgence. I replied that it could be "feeding it" but it also offers an opportunity to gain insight into the nature of the experience. Goldstein (2013) guided my elaboration: "You can investigate a feeling state (negative, positive, or neutral). Notice what triggers it; examine what co-occurs with an open, curious attitude." This exchange was followed by the student who described when she wakes up "feeling down" she seeks a way to change it by doing something more pleasant – "Is this OK? Does this mean I am not accepting it?" she queried. I was aware of the importance of not being in my role of professor so I asked her, "What do you think?" She had been schooled in cognitive behavior therapy so I wanted her to understand the difference. We were not here to

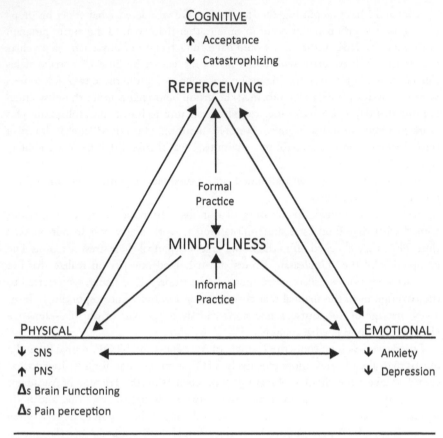

SNS = Sympathetic Nervous System; PNS = Parasympathetic Nervous System

FIGURE 12.1 Triangle of awareness

restructure thoughts or use logic to dismantle them. I recalled the exercise RAIN used by Buddhist teachers (R = recognize; A = accept; I = investigate; N = non-identification; Kornfield, 2008), so I pointed out the importance of befriending and accepting what arises before letting it go. Referring back to STOP, I said, what you choose to do (for example, go for a walk with your dog) should follow the step of acceptance.

Following a brief break, Tom taught the Satir communication stances: placating, blaming, super-reasonable, irrelevant, and congruent. He used body language/sculpting and role plays to do so. He had one group member play the role of a diabetic patient refusing an amputation, and five others to play the other roles. Focus was placed on the patient: how she felt with a blaming doctor versus a congruent one. This exercise helps the HCPs be more compassionate with the whole person of the patient. Tom linked it to stress in that often what we consider to be stressful is interpersonal in nature.

When I reviewed the home practice with them they tended to describe it at the logistic level: "Oh, it's not good right before bed, or I can't get up early to practice because I have too much to do." The scientist among us said he realized that he was approaching yoga as exercise rather than meditation, so he tried to do it differently. "What are you discovering?" I inquired. The South American doctor (who had the CDs while still in his country) said he found the practice relaxing and his sleep had improved. The social worker noticed that when she came home tired from a long day of work she would eat unhealthy foods. She felt guilty afterwards. "This is awareness," I noted.

We ended the class with a 3-minute breathing space exercise. I asked them to recall a recent stressful event at work, to breathe with and through it.

Week #5

We began with a soundscape meditation; I chose Deva Primal's perfect pitch mantras in Sanskrit with the intention of engaging the right brains and hearts of the listeners. HCPs' left brains are over-trained and overactive. I suggested that they use the Triangle of Awareness to guide them in being aware of the music's impact on their thoughts, emotions, and body sensations. This music is ancient and healing in nature; Westerners are not versed in Sanskrit so it invites them to go beyond words and feel the vibrations. Before we started I noticed the nurse with a strained look on her face; it relaxed as she opened to this experience. The social worker, when I asked the group to describe their experiences, said, "I did not like it at all" (judgment: not good). She added, "I was uncomfortable and could not find a position to sit still in" (reactivity in the body). I pointed out the link between thoughts and body sensations – both negative in valance for her. In general, this person appeared to be having difficulty, in part because she did not always understand my English, but I sensed there was more behind her struggle. A spiritual counselor mentioned that it transported him close to God and his heart opened as he recognized the music, having attended Kirtans (group mantra singing celebration) in the past. The woman next to me described how she felt like she was being led by a snake to dance.

In class five I ask those who always sit in the same spot to move. I invited them to view things from another perspective. Was that really "your seat"? I asked, helping them to let go of attachment to "my place."

They named the four seasons in a round-robin manner to form four groups. They were instructed to write out a response to the "Mid-way" form to indicate what they were learning or what challenges they were facing. These small group exercises are intended to help them learn from each other and get to know their fellow classmates.

At the end of the fourth class as part of their home practice, they were instructed to notice where or how they were stuck in their lives, be it at work, in a relationship, with a health problem, etc. One student took the risk to say she felt like she was "in prison" with regard to romantic relationships. A spiritual counselor who has been at the same hospital for years saw no way out of what has become routine and uninspiring for him. I asked the group, "How about ruminations? Anyone stuck in repeated thought patterns?" Most nodded. MBSR research shows that one positive outcome of taking the course is a reduction in ruminations (e.g., Jain, Shapiro, Swanick, Bell, & Schwartz, 2004).

Next I taught the group walking meditation as another way of being in the body, in the moment: "We are going nowhere." I pointed out that we are typically rushed and driven to get "there," wherever that is. With this practice we can undo years of the habit to rush through life. I recalled overhearing Kabat-Zinn say, "If I were to rewrite the title of my book, rather than *Wherever You Go There You Are* (1994), it would be *Wherever You Go Here You Are*." I shared with the group that this practice has taught me patience. Moreover, it is helpful when obsessions fill the mind; one can drop down to the feet or stand in yoga mountain position to find stability.

Following a 10-minute pause, we engaged in a communication exercise that focused on being stuck in unhealthy relationship patterns – a source of stress for many. I reviewed Satir's stances from the previous week and suggested that they may be stuck in one of the four patterns. Colored pencils and paper were distributed and I asked them to engage their right brains by drawing the pattern – it could be with one person, in particular, or something more general (such as blaming people at work). The next step of the exercise is done in dyads. Given we were not an even number of class members I paired up with the South American physician. While it is a challenge to lead and participate at the same time, when I do I get a good idea of how the exercise is being approached. Plus, it is important that even though I am the instructor, they see that I am one of them. What I observed was that this man took the exercise to another level. His body was relaxed, his voice tone was soft, and he made eye contact readily. Rather than drawing a picture depicting a negative pattern, he drew one of light and harmony. I wondered if he was reluctant to reveal conflict or if he had misunderstood the instructions. No, when he thought about an angry encounter he was able to accept and not judge or blame the other, so there were no dark clouds or jagged lines depicting thunder. This reminded me not to assume another's mindset, what Epstein calls "premature closure" (Epstein, 2003). When it was my turn, I let my guard down. He noted that my emotions and body language were congruent and "rewarded" me with the flower of friendship that grew in the sunny landscape of his drawing.

We ended the class with a choiceless awareness meditation. Rather than focus on an object (e.g., sound or breath) this practice encourages "being with" what arises. No need to look for thoughts, or focus on an emotion; one simply notices what emerges in awareness. This is "practice" for mindfulness in our daily lives. Can we be with, accept, and allow what life has to offer, be it a joy or sorrow? It takes practice to do so. When the meditation was over I pointed out the calligraphy on the meditation hall walls that said, "Vous êtes vraiment à la maison," i.e., "You are really home" and "Je suis bien arrivé," i.e., "I have already arrived."

Week #6

While the main theme for the class was mindfulness in interpersonal relationships, the second notion transmitted was acceptance. This enables us to maintain equanimity. The S-T-O-P tool would be better with an 'A' following the 'O,' for accept what you observe before you proceed, but that would not fit with the mnemonic. Thus, when we practiced the choiceless awareness meditation for a longer period the instruction was to simply be with what emerged (e.g., a thought, a sound, a body sensation). This is practice for life. Last week this meditation was 10 minutes long; in this class it was 20 minutes yet they were more able to sit still. I let go of words (i.e., gave sparse instructions and listened to the silence).

My colleague Tom co-led the class with me. He followed up on the Satir stances by asking the class to relate the kind of stressors they experience at work. Here is what came up:

- Having to juggle too many tasks simultaneously
- Giving bad news
- Dying patients
- Being afraid of making an error that would harm the patient
- Having an aggressive co-worker
- Hospital closures/forced changes
- Heavy patient loads
- 'Difficult' patients
- Not enough time in the day to do all that was required
- Feeling inadequate

While they listed what stresses them, Tom was considering which one to use for a role play. The gynecologist was chosen as she mentioned several of the listed stressors. She was led around the room to select a classmate to 'play' her, and another to 'play' her former boss. She quit her post several months ago, feeling unable to cope with the pressures and her own distress. She related what had happened prior to her decision to leave and instructed the players as to how the situation unfolded. She had been placating for 2 years but then became so angry that she confronted her boss, her former mentor who was respected for his medical skills but not his interpersonal style. Tom guided them and the others in the class in seeing how both were blaming each other and that led them to an impasse. He asked the person playing the gynecologist to use another stance. As it happened, the person substituting for her was a psychiatrist and she did an excellent job of being more congruent (i.e., taking herself, the other, and the context into account; using I statements). The 'boss' felt less defensive and responded differently. Tom had her articulate what had changed. Once the dyad had almost come to a resolution, Tom asked the gynecologist to step back in and be herself now that she could see the situation from another viewpoint. She was able to do so, albeit not perfectly, as she has yet to come to terms with its outcome. Throughout the role play Tom asked, "How does mindfulness fit in here?" Tom pointed out how difficult it is to change patterns but that mindfulness helps us see what is occurring within ourselves (e.g., anger, thoughts such as, 'He does not appreciate my work.') as well as in the encounter. He stated that mindfulness allows us to be authentic and it opens 'space' to choose another response.

During the pause the person who had mentioned how multitasking was stressful for her spoke with Tom as she had another issue she wanted to work out with the group. This involved a 2-year struggle with a verbally aggressive colleague. She, being a psychologist, had listened and tried to understand and empathize with the person in question to a breaking point when she was too upset to feel any empathy anymore. Moreover, it drained her energy. Similar to the previous example, long-term placating led to anger. She stopped trying so hard when she understood she could not fix her. Since she still sees this person daily her solution was to avoid her and withdraw from the relationship. But, of course, this was not a resolution and she continued to harbor some uncomfortable thoughts and feelings. Tom noted that she was not 'free' from the situation, as it continues to trouble her through rumination, an internal stressor.

When Tom asked the group, "How has what you have learned thus far influenced your relationships?," the scientist related two events. Before the course he had a conflict with a competitive co-worker; he felt righteous and stuck to his perception that the other was wrong. In the previous week when he was having lunch with the same person, he was aware of his thoughts and feelings and was able to let go rather than react to him. He had ruminated for some time about the first, but not the second, encounter. Tom noted that we are freer when we are congruent.

The next exercise was aimed at the notion acceptance. Rumi's poem, "The Guest House" (Barks, 1995) was handed out with the instructions to write a narrative about an event that was unexpected or unwanted that recently occurred. They were to write what stance they were in and what were their reactions in terms of the Triangle of Awareness. Then they chose a partner, taking turns relating their respective stories, with the instructions for the listener to not add to the exchange. There was a buzz in the room and I knew they were learning . . . when the exchanges were over I asked the group to speak about the process: What was it like to relate the story? To listen to the story? As usual there was discomfort with the instruction not to intervene. Yet another person indicated that it was 'liberating.' I brought up two issues: HCPs' inclination and training to 'fix' others and our desire to be 'in control.' These approaches to events can block being with, allowing, trusting emergence. I said this keeping in mind Irving et al.'s (2014) findings about HCPs in our earlier groups indicating that it was difficult to change this in ourselves.

As the time was almost up, rather than do a walking meditation we stood in yoga mountain pose to be present to ourselves and what we just learned. As the next day was our retreat day, I gave instructions and took questions because for some people anxiety arises about the projection of what it will be like to remain in silence with no eye contact or distractions for most of the day.

Retreat day

The guidelines for the day, provided at the end of Class 6 were to arrive in silence, not make eye contact, stay in silence, not to read or write throughout the retreat, keep cell phones off, and bring a lunch for a mindful meal.

I woke up with referred pain down my right leg (stemming from osteoarthritis and stenosis at L4–L5 in my spine) that made it difficult to use stairs or walk normally. "Ah," I said to myself, "an uninvited guest . . . one who visited me four months ago and decided to return." When my mind added with a touch of anxiety, "How will you be able to lead the retreat today?" I thought, "You will embody the practice: be with what is, with curiosity and acceptance."

We sat in silence waiting for the group members to arrive; one was late and another did not come.

I led the yoga practice with the instruction to approach the mat as if it were the first time, exploring boundaries, accepting limits. This message was for me as well, of course. In fact, my body surprised me as it loosened up and began to move with more fluidity. Yet, I noticed one class member who sat the practice out and was holding his knee clearly in pain. He could not walk and another class member helped him into a chair outside the room.

Later, when I was able to speak with him (while the others were doing a walking meditation), he told me that the same thing happened 4 months ago and he needed to see an osteopath as soon as possible. I lent him my phone to make the arrangements. He added, "I am so frustrated! I was looking forward to today." I replied that ". . . this *was* his retreat practice – to be with and accept this uninvited guest." I reminded him that when he feels frustrated the pain gets worse and suggested that he experiment with exploring the changing nature of the sensations. He commented when I delivered his sweater and lunch, "Thank you for taking pity upon me." I told him that I did not pity him, that I understood his experience (especially since I was living it with him) and was responding to it. His face lit up when he understood and said simply with a smile, "Compassion." I returned his smile.

The rest of the day was a seamless series of practices – sitting, walking, eating – and I introduced the loving kindness meditation for the first time towards the end of the day. They were deep in the practice, respecting themselves and each other.

When we debriefed at the end, I asked: "What surprised you? What was challenging? What did you learn?" The South American doctor was surprised at how relaxing the day felt to him – he had wondered what a day of silence would be like with a bit of apprehension. The social worker who had been reading during the lunch hour said when we sat with the instruction not to move it reminded her of her youth when she was told, "Don't move!" She moved, but was aware of what compelled her to do so. One woman felt overwhelming body heat during the same meditation. She wanted relief but did not give in to the impulse to take off a layer of clothing. The nurse had spoken to the man with the knee pain at lunchtime, not being able to resist breaking silence to advise him to ice it. Habits die hard. I suggested that they ease back into "normal" life gently and observe how they feel over the next few days as sometimes what is learned surfaces later.

Week #7

The theme of the sitting meditation was letting go. Letting go of thoughts, body sensations, emotions, sounds, anything that presented to their consciousness. At this point in the course they need much less guidance. I was preparing them for when I, along with the other members of the group, would be gone.

We seamlessly moved into a yoga practice right after the sitting meditation, much like the retreat day when one practice flowed into the next. The man with the injured knee was not present; I made a mental note to contact him to check in.

Six days following the retreat is enough time to explore the effects of the experience. The social worker who seemed to distract herself by reading began by saying all week she ate mindfully. She realized that when she eats with awareness she can tackle her weight problem from a different angle. Rather than try to control what and how much she eats, she savors foods that she chooses for their nurturing qualities. It's paradoxical, she said twice. Yes, I agreed, it's paradoxical. I was pleasantly surprised by her progress and insight.

Another class member said she had fleeting moments of being totally in the moment, but they were ephemeral. Nonetheless, she was encouraged. A doctor who traveled 2 hours to take the course noted how much she likes and needs silence in her life. The student wondered how to deal with people who think she is somewhat odd when she related to them with open hearted honesty. I added that we work in a group so that we can be supported by others who value this way of being.

A palliative care physician said that she was startled by my statement that this practice is preparation for dying. All week she reflected on that. I reiterated that this practice is a radical way of living. While she confronts others' deaths daily, I asked her if has she come to terms with the fact that she will be one of them someday. I noted that Tom has told me many times how working in palliative medicine makes him feel totally alive and reminds him to live fully every day as his are finite.

The scientist's mother was gravely ill and the practice was helping him cope with the multitude of medical and psychological challenges. He saw clearly how his stance of being super-reasonable is a defense – blocking his feelings of despair, frustration, anxiety. When he spoke about this I asked him if he was aware of his pressured speech. This is a sign that can help him know how he is feeling. "Take a deep breath and be with the feeling," I suggested. Moreover, I said, "Emotions are part of the human experience, not to be rejected but allowed to come and go like clouds in the sky."

Following the break I taught the group the steps in insight dialogue (Kramer, 2007): pause, relax, open, trust emergence, speak your truth, listen deeply. Once they were in dyads I asked them to contemplate: "Who am I in the face of suffering?" Then I slowly guided them through the exercise. They took turns with regard to who the speaker and listener was. They were able to "hold the space" for one another. I could feel the energy of their exchanges as I allowed time for this work to deepen. When they had finished, I queried, "How does this relate to clinical practice?" A psychologist replied, "Totally!" Of course, this exercise is practice for presence.

Finally, I addressed home practice. The palliative care physician said she could not do it . . . but she practices yoga often; this *is* formal practice I reminded her. She said the group helped her to sit still. Yes, I added, that is why we offer the course in groups and why meditation societies offer retreats and group meditation time. Nonetheless, she has noticed that this has helped her work better in teams. She is open and listens deeply to her patients and their families.

We need to be OK with our own suffering to be OK with the suffering of others. The usual way of handling this in medical practice is to disconnect the mind and heart. Yet, this fails because when we lose touch with ourselves we cannot relate authentically with others. As I concluded in the final chapter of *Mindful Medical Practice: Clinical Narratives and Therapeutic Insights,* mindful attitudes open hearts in clinical practice (Dobkin, 2015). The spiritual counselor was clear in his view when he said that patients know the difference when you are acting with professionalism and when you are congruent. Indeed.

Week #8

We started the class with the first meditation practice: the body scan. Full circle. Afterwards when we debriefed about *this* body scan a few people mentioned that they were able to stay with their sensations and not be carried off by thoughts or fall into slumber.

I distributed a follow-up questionnaire that prompts them to reflect on what was learned, lifestyle changes made, practices they engaged in, and which ones they found most beneficial.

Next, the class members were asked to sit with the contemplation: "What do I want to remember when this course is over? What have I learned about myself?" Then I asked them to write themselves a letter (a love letter) based on what emerged, "Dear Me . . . ," and then seal it in an envelope addressed to themselves. Their letters will be mailed out 6 months later. While they wrote I asked myself the same questions as I too learn while teaching and each group brings new insights into the processes underlying the transformative power of living in the present moment.

We explored what their hopes were at the beginning of the course, what they learned, and how they felt about the course ending. Several mentioned that they initially wanted to consolidate their meditation practice. In line with this aim was to integrate mindfulness in their work and personal lives. The scientist said that in the beginning he did not understand the distinction between a goal and an intention. He registered for the course to learn about mindfulness thinking and how it may be useful in his research. Now his intention was to infuse his life with kindness. He was able to let go of the struggle to change his super-reasonable stance and allow self-compassion to do this for him. In line with positive psychology, several others noticed that they were less self-critical. The social worker elaborated upon how her entire practice has become eating mindfully. She learned that when she truly cares about herself she has less desire to eat foods that are not nourishing. She no longer judges herself when she eats a cookie. Moreover, she sees that in each moment she can make a choice. I reiterated that this is a forgiving practice. A psychologist described a similar experience with coffee. She switched to drinking herbal teas and water, which has had a dramatic impact on her health. By exploring in depth the consequences of her actions and asking herself, "Why am I choosing something that is harmful for me?," she was able to act in her best interest. The student mentioned that even though she had been attending meditation groups before this course that this one was special because of its continuity (typical of a closed group where people do not drop in and out). She realized that she was only now beginning to see with clarity. Yes, I agreed, this is a lifelong practice.

A genetic counselor said for her, enlightenment was not found in formal practice but in informal practice, e.g., when she notices the beauty surrounding her as she walks. A psychiatrist mentioned that when he did the body scan, pain from a former injury disappeared. The palliative care doctor found that 'fierce compassion' invigorated her while tending to dying patients. Another class member spoke of how her life had many unsettling events during the past 2 months, which interfered with her formal practice – but she was able to be flexible and not judge herself for not 'sticking with the program.' Being flexible is very important to wellness. I told them that a few years ago I would have not allowed the South American doctor to join us so late in the course but I too have become more flexible. This is a gift of the yoga practice. Finally, there was a consensus that the course helped them to manage stress better.

When asked what was most helpful in the course, they stated: the retreat, the group, the weekly format, and the silence. The injured class member said that having to sit out the retreat and be with his knee pain for the past 2 weeks made him more conscious of how his thoughts and feelings impact his pain. I reflected that this is exactly how their patients feel: those confined to hospital beds and those disabled by chronic illnesses. Hmm . . . we all thought about our patients for a few moments. I wanted them to see the link to their patient care.

It is important for maintenance of lifestyle changes to examine how to keep practicing once they no longer have the group support and structure of the class to guide them. I referred them to Saki Santorelli's "Integrating Mindfulness into Daily Living" in their manuals. I handed out "Hints and Reminders" that overviews the course and suggests that this is the beginning of the rest of their lives. We discussed what helped them thus far to practice. Having it be part of their routine is one way. Another is to know themselves and life circumstances to best fit it in. One spiritual counselor said he meditates in his office for 10 minutes before seeing patients. This reminded me of Dr. Ron Epstein relating in a presentation that when he turns the doorknob to enter a patient's room he lets go of the experience with the previous patient so that he can be fully present for the next one. We can link mindfulness in this way to ordinary tasks in order to remember to be awake.

As the last hour of the class approached I queried them how they felt about the course ending. While one person said anxious, most stayed silent. The social worker announced that she belongs to a group of HCPs who meditate together and invited them to join.

The way I ended the course was by having them form a circle; then we each rang the Tibetan bells in turn and stated with one word what each person felt summarized their experience: words such as serenity, calm, silence, joy, peace, and community filled the space.

Conclusions

When I teach MBSR or MBMP, the eight-fold path guides me during the 8 weeks of our work together. We engage in right effort, right concentration, right mindfulness, right view, right speech, and right action – right meaning wise. In His Holiness the Dalai Lama's book *The Art of Happiness at Work* (2003) he underscores that when one is happy there is no separation between the person and the worker because they are integrated, leading one to being authentic (or congruent in Satir's terminology). He explains that being able to focus attention (learned in meditation) is not enough; while it brings stability to the mind it cannot be sustained nor is it reliable. Thus, it's more important to shape one's attitudes (e.g., non-judgment, non-striving, acceptance, loving kindness). He emphasizes that satisfaction results from being challenged, using your talents, and being creative, and this all provides a sense of accomplishment for a job well done. Happiness at work results when it is a 'calling' – you work at something worthwhile, e.g., help others/relieve suffering, have a higher purpose/contribute to society. Importantly he says, "Change the work environment if you can; change yourself if you cannot."

The people in this class became more attuned to themselves and consequently became more compassionate. They learned much more than how to manage stress. They gained insight into patterns that were not healthy, as well as the link between the mind-heart-body and how this influenced their interpersonal encounters. They saw how this translates into working in the manner described by His Holiness the Dalai Lama. In the follow-up questionnaire two-thirds endorsed the item 'improved capacity to work.' I observed that they improved their capacity to live fully in the present moment.

Bibliography

Asuero, A. M., Queraltò, J. M., Pujol-Ribera, E., Berenguera, A., Rodriguez-Balnco, T., & Epstein, R. (2014). Effectiveness of a mindfulness education program in primary HCPs: A pragmatic controlled trial. *Journal of Continuing Education in the Health Professions, 34*, 4–12.

Barks, C. (1995). *The essential Rumi*. San Francisco, CA: Harper Press.

Beach, M. C., Roter, D., Korthuis, P.T., Epstein, R. M., Sharp, V., Ratanawongsa, N., . . . Saha, S. (2013). A multicenter study of physician mindfulness and health care quality. *Annals of Family Medicine, 11*, 421–428.

Charon, R. (2006). *Narrative medicine: Honoring the stories of illness*. New York, NY: Oxford University Press.

Connelly, J. E. (2005). Narrative possibilities: Using mindfulness in clinical practice. *Perspectives in Biology and Medicine, 48,* 84–94.

Dalai Lama, & Cutler, H. (2003). *The art of happiness at work: The conversation continues about job, career, and calling.* New York, NY: Riverside Books.

Dobkin, P. L. (2009). Fostering healing through mindfulness in the context of medical practice [Guest Editorial]. *Current Oncology, 16,* 4–6.

Dobkin, P. L. (2015). Mindful attitudes open hearts in clinical practice. In P. L. Dobkin (Ed.), *Mindful medical practice: Clinical narratives and therapeutic insights* (pp. 155–160). New York, NY: Springer Press.

Dobkin, P. L., Hickman, S., & Monshat, K. (May 2013). Holding the heart of MBSR: Balancing fidelity and imagination when adapting MBSR. *Mindfulness, 5*(6), 710–718. doi:10.1007/s12671–013–0225–7

Dobkin, P. L, Irving, J., & Amar, S. (2012). For whom may participation in a mindfulness-based stress reduction program be contraindicated? *Mindfulness, 3,* 44–50.

Epstein, R. M. (2003). Mindful practice in action (II): Cultivating habits of mind. *Family, Systems & Health, 21,* 1–17.

Epstein, R. M., & Krasner, M. S. (2013). Physician resilience: What it means, why it matters, and how to promote it. *Academic Medicine, 88,* 382–389.

Goldstein, J. (2013). *Mindfulness: A practical guide to awakening.* Boulder, CO: Sounds True.

Grepmair, L., Mitterlehner, F., Loew, T., Bachler, E., Rother, W., & Nickel, M. (2007). Promoting mindfulness in psychotherapists in training influences the treatment results of their patients: A randomized, double-blind, controlled study. *Psychotherapy and Psychosomatics, 76,* 332–338. doi:10.1159/000107560

Irving, J. A. (2011). *Mindfulness-based medical practice: A mixed-methods investigation of an adapted mindfulness-based stress reduction program for HCPs.* Unpublished doctoral dissertation, McGill University, Montreal, Canada.

Irving, J. A., Dobkin, P. L., & Park, J. (2009). Cultivating mindfulness in HCPs: A review of empirical studies of mindfulness-based stress reduction (MBSR). *Complimentary Therapies in Clinical Practice, 15,* 61–66.

Irving, J. A., Park, J., Fitzpatrick, M., Dobkin, P. L., Chen, A., & Hutchinson, T. (2014). Experiences of HCPs enrolled in mindfulness-based medical practice: A grounded theory model. *Mindfulness, 5,* 60–71.

Jain, S., Shapiro, S., Swanick, S., Bell, I., & Schwartz, G. (2004). Mindfulness meditation versus relaxation training for medical, premedical, nursing, and prehealth students: Differential effects on response style and psychological distress. Poster presented at the Second Annual Mindfulness in Medicine and Health Care Conference, Worcester, MA.

Jain, S., Shapiro, S. L., Swanick, S., Roesch, S. C., Mills, P. J., Bell, I., & Schwartz, G. E. (2007). A randomized controlled trial of mindfulness meditation versus relaxation training: Effects on distress, positive states of mind, rumination, and distraction. *Annals of Behavioral Medicine, 33,* 11–21.

Kabat-Zinn, J. (1994). *Wherever you go, there you are: Mindfulness meditation in everyday life.* New York, NY: Hyperion.

Kornfield, J. (2008). *The wise heart: A guide to the universal teachings of Buddhist psychology.* New York, NY: Bantam Books.

Kramer, G. (2007). *Insight dialogue: The interpersonal path to freedom.* Boston, MA: Shambhala.

Krasner, M. S, Epstein, R. M., Beckman, H., Suchman, A. L., Chapman, B., Mooney, C. J., & Quill, T. E. (2009). Association of an educational program in mindful communication with burnout, empathy, and attitudes among primary care physicians. *Journal of the American Medical Association, 302,* 1284–1293.

Rosenzweig, S., Reibel, D. K., Greeson, J. M., Brainard, G. C., & Hojat, M. (2003). Mindfulness-based stress reduction lowers psychological distress in medical students. *Teaching and Learning in Medicine, 15,* 88–92.

Satir, V. (1988). *The new peoplemaking.* Palo Alto, CA: Science and Behavior Books.

Shapiro, S. L., Astin, J. A., Bishop, S. R., & Cordova, M. (2005). Mindfulness-based stress reduction for health care professionals: Results from a randomized trial. *International Journal of Stress Management, 12*(2), 164–176. doi:10.1037/1072-5245.12.2.164

Styron, C. W. (2005). Positive psychology: Awakening to the fullness of life. In C. K. Germer, R. D. Siegel & P. R. Fulton (Eds.), *Mindfulness and psychotherapy* (pp. 262–282). New York, NY: Guilford Press.

Whyte, D. (2004). *Where many rivers meet.* Langley, WA: Many Rivers Press.

13

MINDFULNESS-BASED POSITIVE BEHAVIOR SUPPORT IN INTELLECTUAL AND DEVELOPMENTAL DISABILITIES

Nirbhay N. Singh, Giulio E. Lancioni, Ramasamy Manikam, Larry L. Latham, and Monica M. Jackman

Introduction

Some individuals with intellectual and developmental disabilities (IDDs) engage in challenging behaviors, with physical aggression being the most difficult to treat. Various prevalence surveys indicate levels of aggression in individuals with IDDs to be about 35% in institutions and between 9.7% and 17% in community settings (Novaco & Taylor, 2004; Taylor, 2002). While substantial progress has been made in integrating individuals with IDDs in community settings in the last several decades, those who exhibit aggression still face restricted opportunities for physical and social community involvement (Kampert & Goreczny, 2007; Verdonschot, De Witte, Reichrath, Buntinx, & Curfs, 2009). Furthermore, high levels of anger and aggression put individuals at risk for negative health outcomes that may affect their long-term wellness (Suinn, 2001).

Psychopharmacological and psychosocial interventions are currently the mainstay of anger and aggression management in individuals with IDDs (Brosnan & Healy, 2011; Singh, Lancioni, Winton, & Singh, 2011a). In terms of psychopharmacological interventions, the new generation antipsychotics (e.g., risperidone, aripiprazole, and olanzapine) are used fairly frequently, but the evidence for their effectiveness in reducing aggression in this population is limited (Singh et al., 2011a). In addition, while there is a hint in the research literature that some antidepressants (e.g., fluvoxamine, fluoxetine, and sertraline) might have beneficial effects in controlling aggression, the data are too limited for drawing any general conclusions about their effectiveness for controlling aggression in individuals with IDDs (Singh et al., 2011a). In general, caution is needed when using psychopharmacological agents to treat aggression in individuals with IDDs because the evidence base for their effectiveness is limited and the risks associated with the drugs may outweigh their effectiveness (Matson & Wilkins, 2008; Tyrer et al., 2008). In terms of psychosocial approaches, behavioral interventions have the strongest evidence base for their effectiveness in treating challenging behaviors in general and aggression in particular (Brosnan & Healy, 2011; Singh et al., 2011a). These interventions are based on assessed functions of the aggressive behavior exhibited by an individual with an IDD in specific contexts (Hastings et al., 2013). Behavioral interventions focus not only on reducing or eliminating the aggressive behavior, but also on teaching the individual alternative means of achieving the same ends as those produced by the aggressive behavior.

Both psychopharmacological and behavioral interventions are delivered by the carers of individuals with IDDs, most often with little input from the individuals themselves. Even when effective, psychopharmacological interventions carry multiple risks for the individuals in terms of unintended effects of the drugs, suggesting that it is not a very positive approach to helping them manage their challenging behaviors. While behavioral interventions are typically effective when adequately programmed by skilled behavior analysts and implemented by trained direct support professionals, these too have associated problems. Research suggests that in practice, in both institutional and community settings, planned behavioral interventions often give way to the use of reactive and restrictive strategies in real life conditions (Allen, 2001; Emerson, 2002; Feldman, Atkinson, Foti-Gervais, & Condillac, 2004). These strategies often include the use of medication for sedation and behavior control, physical and mechanical restraints, seclusion, and other aversive interventions, such as confinement timeout. While effective behavioral approaches are available, direct support professionals sometimes resort to aversive strategies when dealing with individuals with aggressive and other challenging behaviors.

Carers have found behavioral programs to be time consuming and stressful to implement in the context of daily life. Indeed, parents often report that their stress level escalates when they are required to implement intensive behavioral programs with their children (Singh et al., 2014). Even when parents are well versed in implementing behavioral strategies, they do so fairly inconsistently and with decreased fidelity when they are stressed, resulting in their child's behavior becoming more challenging, which in turn raises the parents' stress level even further (Hastings, 2002a). This bidirectional relationship between the child's challenging behaviors and parental stress escalates into generally negative on-going transactions that lead to negative outcomes for both (Lecavalier, Leone, & Wiltz, 2006; McGrath, 2013; Neece, Green, & Baker, 2012). Furthermore, research suggests that similar processes occur with direct care professionals and individuals with IDDs who engage in challenging behaviors (Hastings, 2002b).

A new approach has emerged over the last decade that suggests an entirely positive approach may be possible when providing services to individuals with IDDs in general and treating their challenging behaviors in particular. Mindfulness-based approaches have proven to be effective not only in helping individuals with IDDs learn how to control their own challenging behaviors, but also in assisting carers to better manage their stress when providing services to individuals with IDDs (Myers, Winton, & Lancioni, 2014). Furthermore, carers appear to be most effective when their behavioral training is paired with mindfulness-based procedures

(Myers et al., 2014). In this chapter, we present the rudiments of this approach and discuss how this positive approach needs to be developed further.

Mindfulness-based positive behavior support

Mindfulness-based positive behavior support (MBPBS) is a hybrid approach to providing services to individuals with challenging behaviors, regardless of the disorder or disability, gender, age, race, and other related variables of the individuals. MBPBS is also intended for caregivers of individuals with a diverse range of behavioral challenges, such as those with IDDs, early stage Alzheimer's disease or dementia, multiple sclerosis, psychiatric disorders, and medical conditions that may give rise to challenging behaviors. While MBPBS is not intended to treat the primary diagnosis or disorder, or medical condition, it is intended to provide a mindful approach for caregivers when faced with aggressive, destructive, or disruptive behaviors that may be secondary to these conditions. Of course, not all individuals with these diagnoses, disorders, or medical conditions exhibit challenging behaviors, but this approach is intended to be used with those that do. Caregivers include family members, clinicians, direct care professionals, and teachers who provide services to individuals with challenging behaviors. By overlaying a mindfulness-based approach on the scientific foundations of behavioral technology, we can achieve a totally positive approach to the care of a broad range of individuals with challenging behaviors.

Mindfulness-based approaches

At the core of mindfulness-based approaches is the simple notion that we cannot control what happens – what people say or do, what events take place in the world – but we can certainly control how we respond to events that take place in our lives. To be human (or, more generally, a sentient being) is to have suffering, because that is an integral part of our existence. While we cannot avoid suffering, how we respond to it determines the quality of our lives. Mindfulness provides a way of making a dramatic change, a transformation, in how we view and respond to what happens in and around us on a moment-to-moment basis.

Mindfulness has been defined in numerous ways (Van Gordon, Shonin, Griffiths, & Singh, 2015) and there does not appear to be much consensus on how it can be defined in a unitary manner (Singh, Lancioni, Wahler, Winton, & Singh, 2008). For example, it has been defined as "the awareness that emerges through paying attention on purpose, in the present moment, and non-judgmentally to the unfolding of experience moment to moment" (Kabat-Zinn, 2003, p. 145). A more descriptive understanding of mindfulness in the context of daily life has been presented as, "It is not thinking, but experiencing from moment to moment, living from moment to moment, without clinging, without condemning, without judging, without criticizing – choiceless awareness . . . . It should be integrated into our whole life. It is actually an education in how to see, how to hear, how to smell, how to eat, how to drink, how to walk with full awareness" (Knaster, 2010, p. 1). We have noted previously that mindfulness requires remembrance or recalling of memories from the past while being fully aware of what is happening in the present moment (Singh & Jackman, in press). This means that mindfulness entails bringing "memories from the past to bear on a clear alertness of events and actions in the present with the purpose of abandoning unskillful qualities and developing skillful ones both in the present and on into the future" (Thānissaro Bhikkhu, 2012, p. 15).

Origins of MBPBS

In our work with individuals with IDDs, we noticed that direct care professionals rely more on contingency management techniques to treat the challenging behaviors of individuals than on using contextual strategies to maintain their wellness. Implementing contingency management programs generally produces one or more of these three outcomes: changes in the rate of challenging behaviors of the individuals; increasingly negative social interactions between the staff and the individuals with challenging behaviors; and increased staff stress and burnout (Lucyshyn et al., 2015). It is totally understandable that well-designed behavior plans, implemented with some degree of fidelity, would produce changes in the rate of the challenging behaviors of the individuals. Given the primary focus of staff is on managing challenging behaviors, their attention to and reinforcement of socially acceptable behaviors is reduced (Carr, Taylor, & Robinson, 1991). From a transactional analysis viewpoint, a heavy emphasis on contingency management, in the absence of attention to enhancing wellness, gives rise to a negative trajectory in the interactions between staff and the individuals with challenging behaviors (Sameroff, 1995). Taking care of individuals with seriously challenging behaviors, implementing labor-intensive behavior plans, overlaid by increasingly negative social transactions, almost inevitably results in staff stress and burnout (Hastings, 2002b; Noone, 2013).

In an early study, we found that teaching mindfulness practices to direct care professionals increased wellness in individuals with IDDs in the absence of explicit programming for wellness (Singh, Lancioni, Winton, Wahler, Singh, & Sage, 2004). At the same time, other research showed that stress in various populations could be reduced by engaging in mindfulness practices (see Didonna, 2009). In addition, there was a substantial evidence base attesting to the effectiveness of behavioral interventions for treating challenging behaviors. Thus, we wondered if we could develop a model of care for individuals with challenging behaviors based on these two approaches that would not only effectively manage the individuals' challenging behaviors, but also enhance the wellness of the staff by reducing their stress and burnout. Furthermore, by focusing solely on changing the behavior of the staff through training in these two approaches, we wondered if positive changes would arise in the individuals without explicit programming to treat their maladaptive behaviors.

We answered this question in a study with group home staff (Singh et al., 2006a). We provided the group home staff with behavioral training and later with mindfulness training, and assessed the effects of behavioral training alone and combined with mindfulness on aggressive behavior and the number of learning objectives mastered by individuals in the group homes. The results showed that, when compared to baseline, the number of staff interventions for aggression was reduced following behavioral training, but aggression decreased substantially only following mindfulness training. In addition, the number of learning objectives mastered by the individuals increased following behavioral training, but greater and more consistent increases were obtained only after mindfulness training. Improvements also occurred on other measures assessed after behavioral training, but these were always greater and more consistent following mindfulness training. In this study, the addition of mindfulness practices to behavioral training considerably enhanced the ability of the group home staff to effectively manage the aggressive behavior and learning of individuals with IDDs.

In another study with group home staff, we wondered if adding mindfulness practices to the behavioral training of group home staff would obviate the need for using physical restraints to manage the aggressive and destructive behavior of individuals with IDDs (Singh et al., 2009). Staff who had previously received formal behavioral training participated in a 12-week mindfulness-based training program. Data were collected on the number of incidents, staff observations of incidents, staff verbal redirections, restraints used, emergency medications administered, staff injuries, and peer injuries. Results showed that following mindfulness training the use of restraints decreased, with almost none being recorded by the end of the study. In addition, use of emergency medications administered to control aggressive behavior also substantially decreased, together with staff and peer injuries. This study reinforced our belief that adding mindfulness practices to the repertoire of direct care professionals greatly reduces their use of aversive procedures.

To assess the generality of these findings, we undertook similar studies with parents of children with autism and developmental disabilities. Research shows that parent-child transactions provide an important social context for the development of adaptive as well as maladaptive behaviors in young children with autism (Singh et al., 2006b). We hypothesized that adding mindfulness-based training to their existing knowledge of behavioral principles would help develop alternative transactional pathways that might lead to more positive behavioral patterns in their children. We taught mothers a 12-week mindfulness-based course and assessed the outcome of the training on their children's behavior (Singh et al., 2006b). In addition, the mothers rated their satisfaction with their parenting skills and interactions with their children. We found that the mothers' mindful parenting decreased aggression, noncompliance, and self-injury in their children and increased the mothers' satisfaction with their parenting skills and interactions with their children. These results were obtained in the absence of specific, programmed contingencies for their children's challenging behaviors. We replicated and extended these findings with parents of children with IDDs (Singh et al., 2007). The parents reported that their children exhibited aggressive behavior and had limited social skills. When we provided mindfulness-based training to parents of children with IDDs, who already had acquired behavior management skills, there was a clinically significant decrease in aggressive behavior and an increase in the social skills of their children. The parents also reported a greater practice of mindfulness, increased satisfaction with their parenting, more social interactions with their children, and lower parenting stress. Furthermore, the children with IDDs showed increased positive and decreased negative social interactions with their siblings. In a related study, we found that compliance to parental requests increased in children with Attention Deficit/Hyperactivity Disorder when their behaviorally trained parents were provided training in mindfulness-based practices (Singh et al., 2010).

We further assessed the generality of these findings with preschool teachers of children with mild IDDs who exhibited challenging behaviors (Singh, Lancioni, Winton, Karazsia, & Singh, 2013). To the teachers' existing behavior management skills, we added mindfulness practices based on an 8-week mindfulness training program. Results showed decreases in the children's challenging behaviors and increases in their compliance with teacher requests commensurate with the mindfulness training for the teachers. Furthermore, the children showed a decrease in negative social interactions and an increase in independent play. These results indicated that mindfulness-based training provided to the teachers was effective in changing teacher-children interactions in desirable ways.

According to Buddhist ontology, the arising of parent-child interactions, staff-client interactions, and teacher-student interactions are interdependent, and changes in the behavior of one affects the behavior of the other (Dalai Lama, 2002). Thus, when individuals with IDDs engage in challenging behaviors, it negatively affects the behavior of their carers and manifests as stress and burnout. Furthermore, when parents, staff, and teachers are stressed they tend to behave in ways that increase the likelihood of maintaining the individuals' challenging behaviors (Hastings & Remington, 1994) and may lead to further decline in their own well-being (Mitchell & Hastings, 2001). The findings in our studies suggested to us that adding mindfulness-based training to the repertoire of behaviorally trained carers – parents, staff, teachers – changes the bidirectional parent-child, staff-client, and teacher-student interactions in a positive direction. For example, adding mindfulness-based training to the parents' existing behavioral knowledge produces not only clear and measurable positive changes in the individuals' challenging behaviors, but also a decrease in parental stress (see Myers et al., 2014 for a review). These findings led us to develop the MBPBS training model for the care of individuals with challenging behaviors.

Positive behavior support

Positive behavior support (PBS) is based on the foundational concepts of applied behavior analysis, particularly assessment and intervention strategies, but it also incorporates concepts from person-centered planning and normalization (Carr, 2007; Carr et al., 2002; Dunlap & Carr, 2009). While the concepts and applications of PBS are still evolving and being refined, it has always focused on broader goals than just eliminating challenging behaviors, i.e., it "uses educational and systems change methods to enhance quality of life" (Carr et al., 2002, p. 4). The core features of PBS include a philosophy of respect for the individual with an IDD, a desire to enhance the person's lifestyle, a focus on function-based interventions, and teaching of adaptive skills to replace challenging behaviors. PBS approaches incorporate social, curricular, and ecological contexts in the PBS plans, and include antecedent, consequence, and contextual changes aligned with the assessed needs of each individual. In practice, well-designed PBS programs tend to focus on lifestyle changes by enhancing the individual's social and physical ecology, providing multi-element supports, and utilizing proactive and reactive behavioral change interventions. Generally, PBS interventions have been found to be effective for severe and high-rate challenging behaviors in both institutional and community settings (LaVigna & Willis, 2012) and are viewed favorably by families of individuals with IDDs as an approach to behavioral interventions for challenging behaviors (Lucyshyn, Dunlap, & Albin, 2002; Lucyshyn et al., 2015).

A systematic review of training studies in PBS with direct care professionals indicated increased knowledge, decreased emotional responding, and changes in the staff's attributions of the challenging behaviors, as well as decreased challenging behaviors in the individuals in their care (MacDonald & McGill, 2013). Training in PBS has typically been diverse, with researchers including different components of the model and assessing different outcomes. In the MBPBS model, we have adhered to the seven essential elements of PBS training as advocated by Dunlap, Hieneman, Knoster, Fox, Anderson, and Albin (2000, p. 23):

1   Establishing a collective vision and goals for intervention,
2   Collaborating and building teams among families and professionals,
3   Conducting functional assessments,
4   Designing hypothesis-driven, multicomponent support plans,
5   Implementing intervention strategies that include environmental adjustments, replacement skills, appropriate consequences, and lifestyle enhancement,
6   Monitoring and evaluating intervention outcomes, and
7   Infusing positive behavior support into broader systems.

These components are taught as principles and within the context of specific prototypic "cases," with demonstration of the use of these principles with individuals the staff are currently providing services to. In addition, there is an emphasis on how to undertake these procedures and processes in a mindful way.

MBPBS Training and Curriculum

MBPBS is a hybrid training program that integrates mindfulness-based meditations and PBS behavioral technology. There are two training formats for MBPBS: (1) a regular course that begins with a 2-hour pretraining session followed by 1-day a week training for 8 weeks and (2) an intensive 7-day course.

The 8-week course

The format for the regular 8-week course (i.e., 1 day a week for 8 days) is presented in Table 13.1. This program begins with a 2-hour Samatha meditation pretraining session a month prior to the 8-week training session. Participants receive instructions on the fundamentals of meditation posture: sit comfortably with a straight spine, without slouching or stretching the shoulders; head tilted slightly forward; eyes slightly open; tip of the tongue lightly touching the upper palate; right hand resting over the left hand on the lap, with thumbs just touching; and breathing evenly (Buksbazen, 2002). They are taught to focus on their breathing, without deliberately changing the length of each breath. They learn to count an inhalation and exhalation as one breath until they reach 10 breaths, before restarting the counting cycle. They are taught to simply observe their discursive thoughts and emotions, without paying attention to them or trying to suppress them. That is, they are required to focus their awareness on whatever takes place in their mind without judgment or engagement. In addition, the participants are taught Kinhin and Vipassana (insight) meditations (Buksbazen, 2002; McDonald, 2005). Following the pretraining, they are instructed to develop a personal meditation practice, beginning with a few minutes each day and slowly increasing it until they reach between 20 and 30 minutes of disciplined daily practice.

TABLE 13.1 Outline of the 8-week MBPBS program

Training Sessions	Topics Covered
Pretraining: Basic meditations (1 month prior to baseline)	What is mindfulness?
	Everyday mindfulness
	Samatha meditation
	Kinhin meditation
	Insight meditation
	Practice: Samatha, Kinhin, and insight meditations
Week 1	Review of pretraining practices
	Samatha, Kinhin, and insight meditations
	The five hindrances to meditation
	The four foundations of insight
	The Four Immeasurables
	Beginner's mind, premature cognitive commitment, confirmation bias
	Applications of mindfulness training to PBS
	Practice: Journaling and meditation practices
Week 2	Review of Week 1 and meditation practices
	Samatha, Kinhin, and insight meditations
	Equanimity visualization
	Being in the present moment
	Applications of mindfulness training to PBS
	Practice: Journaling and meditation practices

(Continued)

TABLE 13.1 (Continued)

Training Sessions	Topics Covered
Week 3	Review of Week 2 and meditation practices
	Samatha, Kinhin, and insight meditations
	Equanimity visualization
	Lovingkindness visualization
	The three poisons: attachment, anger, and ignorance
	Applications of mindfulness training to PBS
	Practice: Journaling and meditation practices
Week 4	Review of Week 3 and meditation practices
	Samatha, Kinhin, and insight meditations
	Equanimity and lovingkindness visualizations
	Compassion visualization
	Discussion of anger
	Applications of mindfulness training to PBS
	Practice: Journaling and meditation practices
Week 5	Review of Week 4 and meditation practices
	Samatha, Kinhin, and insight meditations
	Equanimity, lovingkindness, and compassion visualizations
	Joy visualization
	Applications of mindfulness training to PBS
	Practice: Journaling and meditation practices
Week 6	Review of Week 5 and meditation practices
	Samatha, Kinhin, and insight meditations
	Equanimity, lovingkindness, compassion, and joy visualizations
	Shenpa
	Shenpa meditation and compassionate abiding
	Applications of mindfulness training to PBS
	Practice: Journaling and meditation practices
Week 7	Review of Week 6 and meditation practices
	Samatha, Kinhin, and insight meditations
	Equanimity, lovingkindness, compassion, and joy visualizations
	Compassionate abiding
	Compassionate abiding meditation
	Applications of mindfulness training to PBS
	Practice: Journaling and meditation practices
Week 8	Review of Week 7 and meditation practices
	Equanimity, lovingkindness, compassion, and joy visualizations
	Shenpa and compassionate abiding
	Anger: Meditation on the soles of the feet
	Mindfulness and PBS: Putting it all together
	Review of the MBPBS course and arrangements for individual follow-up interviews
	Post-course interviews

The MBPBS training phase consists of 1 day of training, once a week, for 8 weeks. The training includes instruction on the Four Immeasurables (lovingkindness, compassion, joy, and equanimity), the three poisons (attachment, anger, and ignorance), shenpa and compassionate abiding, and meditation on the soles of the feet (Chödrön, 2007, 2010; Kongtrül, 2008; Kyabgon, 2003; Singh et al., 2011b). Although most participants have some knowledge of behavior management, they are given training in PBS as indicated above. Throughout the MBPBS training, they are taught how to use PBS within the context of mindfulness practices. They are required to practice what they learned in the pretraining and previous week(s), thus making their practice of MBPBS cumulative as the training progresses through the MBPBS program. In addition, they are taught to apply their newly learned MBPBS skills in their interactions with individuals with IDDs, clients, or students.

The MBPBS practice phase immediately follows the MBPBS training phase and lasts 48 weeks. The participants are required to continue with all meditation practices they learned in the MBPBS training phase and to mindfully utilize the PBS techniques in their interactions with individuals with IDDs, clients, or students. During the practice phase, any questions that arise about the mindfulness-based practices and the PBS techniques are fully answered.

The 7-day intensive course

The format for the intensive 7-day course is presented in Table 13.2. The program begins with a 1-day meditation pretraining session a month prior to the 5 consecutive days of mindfulness and PBS training. The participants learn the three basic meditations (Samatha, Kinhin, and Vipassana), as well as the five hindrances. They also begin their daily practice logs and journaling. The intensive training on days 2 to 6 covers all the materials as presented in the 8-week mindfulness program, with a final 1-day follow-up 1 month following the termination of the intensive training. The MBPBS practice phase follows the MBPBS intensive training, under the same conditions as in the 8-week MBPBS training, and lasts 48 weeks.

Training Adherence

Attendance of the participants at the training sessions is recorded by the trainer and each participant is required to complete daily logs of meditation practices from pretraining to the end of the MBPBS practice phase.

Trainer

The trainer is required to have a long-standing personal meditation practice, clinical expertise in the subject population, and experience in mindful delivery of services in behavioral health.

TABLE 13.2 Outline of the 7-day MBPBS program

Day 1 Pretraining (1 month before Day 2)	Samatha meditation
	Kinhin meditation
	Insight meditation
	Five hindrances
	Daily logs and journaling
Day 2	Review of meditation practice
	Introduction to the Four Immeasurables (Brahmavihara)
	Equanimity meditation
	Beginner's mind
	Applications to PBS practice
Day 3	Review of Day 2 instructions and practices
	Further instructions on the Four Immeasurables
	Equanimity meditation
	Lovingkindness meditation
	Being in the present moment
	Applications to PBS practice
Day 4	Review of Days 2 and 3 instructions and practices
	Further instructions on the Four Immeasurables
	Equanimity meditation
	Lovingkindness meditation
	Compassion meditation
	The three poisons
	Applications to PBS practice
Day 5	Review of Days 2 to 4 instructions and practices
	Further instructions on the Four Immeasurables
	Equanimity meditation
	Lovingkindness meditation
	Compassion meditation
	Joy meditation
	Attachment and anger – shenpa and compassionate abiding meditations
	Applications to PBS practice
Day 6	Review of Days 2 to 5 instructions and practices
	Review and practice Samatha, Kinhin, and insight meditations
	Review of the Four Immeasurables
	Practice equanimity, lovingkindness, compassion, and joy meditations
	Attachment and anger – meditation on the soles of the feet
	Review of applications to PBS practice
	Review of the MBPBS training program
Day 7 (1 month after Day 6)	Review of the meditation instructions and practices (daily logs)
	Review and practice Samatha, Kinhin, and insight meditations
	Review of the Four Immeasurables
	Practice equanimity, lovingkindness, compassion, and joy meditations
	Emotion regulation and anger – meditation on the soles of the feet
	Applications to PBS practice
	Review of the 7-day MBPBS training program

Fidelity of Training

Teaching sessions are video recorded and a (pre-specified) randomly chosen sample of sessions, which can be stratified by key variables, is assessed for fidelity of training by another qualified mindfulness trainer. The fidelity of mindfulness training is acceptable if it reaches at least an average of 95% agreement between two independent trainers.

Measuring Outcomes

Most research utilizing mindfulness-based interventions include self-reported changes in mindfulness of the participant (as measured by rating scales), as well as outcomes such as levels of stress, pain, and other variables, depending on the context of the study. In most of our research, we have not provided data on self-reported changes in the participants' mindfulness, because we have been uncertain as to what is actually measured by these rating scales (see Grossman & Van Dam, 2011). Our view has been that we engage in mindfulness practice to alleviate the suffering of others and thus our best indicator of success should be observational measures of change in those around us. This approach is particularly applicable when working with individuals with severe levels of cognitive disabilities such that they may not be able to engage in mindfulness practice themselves, but might rely on the benefits of mindfulness practices of their carers. Thus, outcome measures can include any target behaviors of the individuals with IDDs.

Research on MBPBS

In addition to the studies reviewed above, one study has evaluated the effects of the standard 8-week MBPBS program with mothers of adolescents with autism spectrum disorder (Singh et al., 2014), and one with the 7-day intensive MBPBS training with staff in group homes (Singh et al., 2015). Obviously, much more research is needed to establish an evidence base for the MBPBS model of caregiver training in managing challenging behaviors in diverse populations.

Future directions

The MBPBS model is in the most rudimentary stage of development, but it offers a new way of conceptualizing how effective interventions can be delivered in a positive manner to people with challenging behaviors. Instead of focusing on changing the behavior of individuals with IDDs and challenging behaviors, the model suggests that changing the behavior of the carers – parents, staff, and teachers – through mindfulness training will result in greater and more positive outcomes for the individuals. In this respect, it is a paradigm shift because it suggests that greater therapeutic gains can be obtained not by focusing on the individual's challenging behaviors, but by focusing on transformational change within the carer through enhanced mindfulness.

The model is, at present, a vision of possibility and in the chrysalis stage of development. To fully actualize it in practice will require several developments by several research teams beyond the current developers. This will include explicating the core elements of the MBPBS model in greater detail and providing instructions that translate these core elements into daily practice by carers in natural settings. In addition, it will require explicating the core competencies of the trainers because the interfacing of two distinct approaches – mindfulness and PBS – will require operationalizing the skills that practitioners will need to use MBPBS with some degree of precision.

The current evidence supporting the effectiveness of the model is sparse and will need to be buttressed not only with much more research, but also replications and extensions by independent researchers. While there is an inkling that this process has started (e.g., Brooker et al. [2014] conceptually replicated the Singh et al. [2009] findings), this will require the coming together of researchers and clinicians well versed in mindfulness and PBS, as well as openness to this approach. Such research will need to determine not only the comparative effectiveness of the MBPBS model against existing evidence-based approaches, but also its acceptability, durability, and sustainability over time in enhancing the quality of life of individuals with challenging behaviors.

Bibliography

Allen, D. (2001). *Training carers in physical interventions: Research towards evidence-based practice.* Kidderminster, UK: British Institute of Learning Disabilities.

Brooker, J. E., Webber, L., Julian, J., Shawyer, F., Graham, A. L., Chan, J., & Meadows, G. (2014). Mindfulness-based training shows promise in assisting staff to reduce their use of restrictive interventions in residential services. *Mindfulness.* In advance of print. doi:10.1007/s12671–014–0306–2.

Brosnan, J., & Healy, O. (2011). A review of behavioral interventions for the treatment of aggression in individuals with developmental disabilities. *Research in Developmental Disabilities, 32*, 437–446.

Buksbazen, J. D. (2002). *Zen meditation in plain English.* Boston, MA: Wisdom Publications.

Carr, E. G. (2007). The expanding vision of positive behavior support: Research perspectives on happiness, helpfulness, and hopefulness. *Journal of Positive Behavior Interventions, 9,* 3–14.

Carr, E. G., Dunlap, G., Horner, R. H., Koegel, R. L., Turnbull, A. P., Sailor, W., Andereson, J. L., Albin, R. W., Koegel, L. K. & Fox, L. (2002). Positive behavior support: Evolution of an applied science. *Journal of Positive Behavior Interventions, 4,* 4–16.

Carr, E. G., Taylor, J. C., & Robinson, S. (1991). The effects of severe behavior problems in children on the teaching behavior of adults. *Journal of Applied Behavior Analysis, 24,* 523–535.

Chödrön, P. (2007). *Don't bite the hook: Finding freedom from anger, resentment, and other destructive emotions.* Boston, MA: Shambhala Audio.

Chödrön, P. (2010). *Taking the leap: Freeing ourselves from old habits and fears.* Boston, MA: Shambhala.

Dalai Lama. (2002). *How to practice: The way to a meaningful life.* New York, NY: Atria Books.

Didonna, F. (2009). *Clinical handbook of mindfulness.* New York, NY: Springer.

Dunlap, G., & Carr, E. G. (2009). Positive behavior support and developmental disabilities: A summary and analysis of research. In S. L. Odom, R. H. Horner, M. E. Snell, & J. Blacher (Eds.), *Handbook of developmental disabilities* (pp. 469–482). New York, NY: Guilford Press.

Dunlap, G., Hieneman, M., Knoster, T., Fox, L., Anderson, J., & Albin, R. W. (2000). Essential elements of inservice training in positive behavior support. *Journal of Positive Behavior Interventions, 2,* 22–32.

Emerson, E. (2002). The prevalence of use of reactive management strategies in community-based services in the UK. In D. Allen (Ed.), *Ethical approaches to physical interventions. Responding to challenging behaviour in people with intellectual disabilities* (pp. 15–30). Plymstock, UK: British Institute of Learning Disabilities.

Feldman, M. A., Atkinson, L., Foti-Gervais, L., & Condillac, R. (2004). Formal versus informal interventions for challenging behavior in persons with intellectual disabilities. *Journal of Intellectual Disabilities Research, 48,* 60–68.

Grossman, P., & Van Dam, N. T. (2011). Mindfulness, by any other name . . . : trials and tribulations of *sati* in Western psychology and science. *Contemporary Buddhism, 12,* 219–239.

Hastings, R. P. (2002a). Parental stress and behavior problems of children with developmental disability. *Journal of Intellectual and Developmental Disability, 27,* 149–160.

Hastings, R. P. (2002b). Do challenging behaviors affect staff psychological well-being? Issues of causality and mechanism. *American Journal on Mental Retardation, 107,* 455–467.

Hastings, R. P., Allen, D., Baker, P., Gore, N. J., Hughes, J. C., McGill, P., Noone, S. J., & Toogood, S. (2013). A conceptual framework for understanding why challenging behaviours occur in people with developmental disabilities. *International Journal of Positive Behavioural Support, 3,* 5–13.

Hastings, R. P., & Remington, B. (1994). Staff behaviour and its implications for people with learning disabilities and challenging behaviors. *British Journal of Clinical Psychology, 33,* 423–438.

Kabat-Zinn, J. (2003). Mindfulness-based interventions in context: Past, present, and future. *Clinical Psychology: Science & Practice, 10,* 144–156.

Kampert, A. L., & Goreczny, A. J. (2007). Community involvement and socialization among individuals with mental retardation. *Research in Developmental Disabilities, 28,* 278–286.

Knaster, M. (2010). *Living this life fully: Stories and teachings of Munindra.* Boston, MA: Shambhala.

Kongtrül, D. (2008). *Light comes through: Buddhist teaching on awakening to our natural intelligence.* Boston, MA: Shambhala.

Kyabgon, T. (2003). *Mind at ease: Self-liberation through Mahamudra meditation.* Boston, MA: Shambhala.

LaVigna, G. W., & Willis, T. J. (2012). The efficacy of positive behavioural support with the most challenging behavior: The evidence and its implications. *Journal of Intellectual and Developmental Disability, 37,* 185–195.

Lecavalier, L., Leone, S., & Wiltz, J. (2006). The impact of behavior problems on caregiver stress in young people with autism spectrum disorders. *Journal of Intellectual Disability Research, 50,* 173–183.

Lucyshyn, J. M., Dunlap, G., & Albin, R. W. (2002). *Families and positive behavior support: Addressing problem behavior in family contexts* (pp. 3–43). Baltimore, MD: Paul H. Brookes.

Lucyshyn, J. M., Fossett, B., Bakeman, R., Cheremshynski, C., Miller, L., Lohrmann, S., Binnendyk, L., Kahn, S., Chinn, S., Kwon, S., & Irvin, L. K. (2015). Transforming parent-child interaction in family routine: Longitudinal analysis with families of children with developmental disabilities. *Journal of Child and Family Studies.* In advance of print. doi:10.1007/s10826-015-0154-2

MacDonald, A., & McGill, P. (2013). Outcomes of staff training in positive behavior support: A systematic review. *Journal of Developmental and Physical Disabilities, 25*, 17–23.

Matson, J. L., & Wilkins, J. (2008). Antipsychotic drugs for aggression in intellectual disability. *Lancet, 371*, 9–10.

McDonald, K. (2005). *How to meditate: A practical guide*. Boston, MA: Wisdom Publications.

McGrath, A. (2013). Links between the conduct of carers and clients' challenging behaviour. *Learning Disability Practice, 16*, 30–32.

Mitchell, G., & Hastings, R. P. (2001). Coping, burnout, and emotion in staff working in community services for people with challenging behaviors. *American Journal on Mental Retardation, 106*, 448–459.

Myers, R. E., Winton, A. S. W., Lancioni, G. E., & Singh, N. N. (2014). Mindfulness in developmental disabilities. In N. N. Singh (Ed.), *Psychology of meditation* (pp. 209–240). New York, NY: Nova Science.

Neece, C. L., Green, S. A., & Baker, B. L. (2012). Parenting stress and child behavior problems: A transactional relationship across time. *American Journal on Intellectual and Developmental Disabilities, 117*, 48–66.

Noone, S. J. (2013). Supporting care staff using mindfulness- and acceptance-based approaches. In J. L. Taylor, W. R. Lindsay, R. Hastings & C. Hatton (Eds.), *Psychological therapies for adults with intellectual disabilities* (pp. 207–221). Chichester, UK: John Wiley.

Novaco, R. W., & Taylor, J. L. (2004). Assessment of anger and aggression in male offenders with developmental disabilities. *Psychological Assessment, 16*, 42–50.

Sameroff, A. J. (1995). General systems theories and developmental psychopathology. In D. Cicchetti & D. J. Cohen (Eds.), *Developmental psychopathology. Vol. 1: Theory and methods* (pp. 659–695). New York, NY: John Wiley.

Singh, N. N., & Jackman, M. M. (in press). Teaching mindfulness to individuals with intellectual and developmental disabilities and their caregivers. In D. McCown, D. K. Reibel & M. S. Micozzi (Eds.), *Resources for teaching mindfulness: A cross-cultural and international handbook*. New York, NY: Springer.

Singh, N. N., Lancioni, G. E., Karazsia, B. T., Myers, R. E., Winton, A. S. W., Latham, L. L., & Nugent, K. (2015). Effects of training staff in MBPBS on the use of physical restraints, staff stress and turnover, staff and peer injuries, and cost effectiveness in developmental disabilities. *Mindfulness*. ePub ahead of Print.

Singh, N. N., Lancioni, G. E., Wahler, R. G., Winton, A. S. W., & Singh, J. (2008). Mindfulness approaches in cognitive behavior therapy. *Behavioural and Cognitive Psychotherapy, 36*, 659–666.

Singh, N. N., Lancioni, G. E., Winton, A. S. W., Curtis, W. J., Wahler, R. G., Sabaawi, M., Singh, J., & McAleavey, K. (2006a). Mindful staff increase learning and reduce aggression by adults with developmental disabilities. *Research in Developmental Disabilities, 27*, 545–558.

Singh, N. N., Lancioni, G. E., Winton, A. S. W., Fisher, B. C., Wahler, R. G., McAleavey, K., Singh, J., & Sabaawi, M. (2006b). Mindful parenting decreases aggression, noncompliance and self-injury in children with autism. *Journal of Emotional and Behavioral Disorders, 14*, 169–177.

Singh, N. N., Lancioni, G. E., Winton, A. S. W., Karazsia, B. T., Myers, R. E., Latham, L. L., & Singh, J. (2014). Mindfulness-based positive behavior support (MBPBS) for mothers of adolescents with Autism Spectrum Disorder: Effects on adolescents' behavior and parental stress. *Mindfulness, 5*, 646–657.

Singh, N. N., Lancioni, G. E., Winton, A. S. W., Karazsia, B. T., & Singh, J. (2013). Mindfulness training for teachers changes the behavior of their preschool students. *Research in Human Development, 10*, 211–233.

Singh, N. N., Lancioni, G. E., Winton, A. S. W., Singh, A. N., Adkins, A. D., & Singh, J. (2009). Mindful staff can reduce the use of physical restraints when providing care to individuals with intellectual disabilities. *Journal of Applied Research in Intellectual Disabilities*, *22*, 194–202.

Singh, N. N., Lancioni, G. E., Winton, A. S. W., Singh, J., Curtis, W. J., Wahler, R. G., & McAleavey, K. M. (2007). Mindful parenting decreases aggression and increases social behavior in children with developmental disabilities. *Behavior Modification*, *31*, 749–771.

Singh, N. N., Lancioni, G. E., Winton, A. S. W., Wahler, R. G., Singh, J., & Sage, M. (2004). Mindful caregiving increases happiness among individuals with profound multiple disabilities. *Research in Developmental Disabilities*, *25*, 207–218.

Singh, N. N., Singh, A. N., Lancioni, G. E., Singh, J., Winton, A. S. W., & Adkins, A. D. (2010). Mindfulness training for parents and their children with ADHD increases the children's compliance. *Journal of Child and Family Studies*, *19*, 167–174.

Singh, N. N., Lancioni, G. E., Winton, A. S. W., & Singh, J. (2011a). Aggression, tantrums, and other externally driven challenging behaviors. In J. L. Matson & P. Sturmey (Eds.), *International handbook of autism and pervasive developmental disorders* (pp. 413–435). New York, NY: Springer.

Singh, N. N., Singh, J., Singh, A. D. A., Singh, A. N. A., & Winton, A. S. W. (2011b). *Meditation on the Soles of the Feet for anger management: A trainer's manual.* Raleigh, NC: Fernleaf. (www.fernleafpub.com).

Suinn, R. M. (2001). The terrible twos – anger and anxiety: Hazardous to your health. *American Psychologist*, *56*, 27–36.

Taylor, J. L. (2002). A review of the assessment and treatment of anger and aggression in offenders with intellectual disability. *Journal of Intellectual Disability Research*, *46*, 57–73.

Thānissaro Bhikkhu. (2012). *Right mindfulness: Memory and ardency on the Buddhist path.* www.accesstoinsight.org/lib/authors/thanissaro/rightmindfulness.pdf

Tyrer, P., Oliver-Africano, P. C., Ahmed, Z., Bouras, N., Cooray, S., Deb, S., . . . Crawford, M. (2008). Risperidone, haloperidol, and placebo in the treatment of aggressive challenging behavior in patients with intellectual disability: A randomized controlled trial. *Lancet*, *371*, 57–63.

Van Gordon, W., Shonin, E., Griffiths, M. D., & Singh, N. N. (2015). There is only one mindfulness: Why science and Buddhism need to work together. *Mindfulness*, *6*. doi:10.1007/s12671-014-0379-y

Verdonschot, M. M. L., De Witte, L. P., Reichrath, E., Buntinx, W. H. E., & Curfs, L. M. G. (2009). Community participation of people with an intellectual disability: A review of empirical findings. *Journal of Intellectual Disability Research*, *53*, 303–318.

14

WORKING IT

Making meaning with workplace mindfulness

Michael F. Steger and Eve Ekman

Man was made for Joy and Woe;
And when this we rightly know
Thro' the World we safely go.
William Blake

> Life is never made unbearable by circumstances, but only by lack of meaning and purpose.
>
> Viktor E. Frankl

What is the goal of life? What do people pursue? What do people live for? How can we make sense of our direct experiences of life both good and bad? What keeps people moving when joy is replaced by woe, inspiration by hopelessness?

There are as many answers to these questions as there are ways of being distracted from asking them in the first place. Contemporary life thrusts an unprecedented arsenal of beguiling, empty distractions our way, many honed by computer algorithms that harvest information about us to sharpen their barbs, others refined by behavioral research and persuasion science. Every website we consult on our computers, phones, and wearable devices tantalizes us with aptly named hyperlinks, and offers us innocuous-sounding cookies to make our future visits more enjoyable (and create a crumb trail to track us through cyberspace). Like the sailors who succumbed to the narcotic feasts of the lotus-eaters during the voyages of Odysseus, our beleaguered minds often long for mundane and pleasurable sinkholes that offer effortlessly attainable cravings and comforts, along with escape from the complex existential demands and stressful dilemmas of our lives. And certainly since at least the time of Odysseus, curmudgeons have complained about people getting distracted by from the core of life's meaning by unimportant rubbish. We share with our ancestors the proclivity to fall under the dual scepters of wanton idleness and of the stress and 'busyness' that further distracts us from the pursuit of meaning. "Beware the bareness of a busy life," said Socrates, an admonishment that could easily be applied to our current day.

Some of the appeal of the topic of this book – mindfulness – must be as an ancient antidote for this affliction: *In a mindless world, we need to be mindful.* In this chapter, we agree with the importance of mindfulness and suggest that there may be a useful corollary: *In a busy, trivial world, we need meaning.* Here, meaning is understood to refer to the most important elements of life, those that provide a purpose, a sense of significance, and appreciation of the incredible good fortune of living. If you put these notions together you get something like our thesis: *In a mindless, busy world, we need to be mindful to live a meaningful life.* For the majority of us our work is a primary part of our everyday life; work is the arena we choose to focus this enormous topic of meaning in life. It is our hope that this chapter shares a vision of how mindfulness and meaningfulness together can help us live a deep, enjoyable, and authentic life.

This chapter is framed by a contemplation of how meaning and mindfulness may provide benefits specifically to those who engage in challenging work, explicitly through cultivating empathy and compassion. People can prosper through cultivating empathy and compassion in all working life, but we focus on those jobs that are especially reliant on interpersonal interactions. Many empathy-reliant jobs, including the human service jobs we use as an example in this chapter, carry both enormous stress and enormous opportunity for connection and meaning making through serving others. We argue that there are two compelling and complementary ways to try to manage the stress of this work: meaning and mindfulness. Meaning in this work can be achieved through interpersonal interactions, empathy, and connecting with people who are struggling, among other ways. Mindfulness practices can provide the tools for recognizing and alleviating the sympathetic distress of working with people who we may not be able to cure or truly help. Together they work to help maintain a sincere and vital sense of purpose, dedication, and resilience that encourages awareness of one's limits and one's achievements. Both are needed to manage the hyper-stressful situations that require our vigilance and discernment and the hyper-meaningful situations that carry the opportunity for deep connection and resilience.

This chapter will move from definitions and background of meaning, mindfulness, and work and then to the threat stress poses in the human service environment, and across various job and life domains. We then explore how mindfulness practices may reduce the stress that is the obstacle of maintaining empathy and compassion in a human service setting. Finally, we seek to integrate mindfulness practices and meaning and consider how they might work together to not only withstand stress but also locate and nurture new avenues for personal expansion and optimal living.

Meaning in life: significance and purpose

At its heart, the study of meaning in life is one way of trying to understand and articulate how people can make the most of their lives. The underlying assumption long has been that if one lives a meaningful life, one will experience true fulfill-ment and be empowered to stave off stresses and setbacks met along the way. In psychology, this understanding of meaning is traced primarily to the life and work of Viktor Frankl (e.g., 1984). Around the time that the Nazi movement was coming to power in Austria, Frankl developed the theory that humans have a core need for meaning and purpose, and that satisfying this need and finding one's purpose would give people a reason to live. Frankl's theory was tested in excruciating fashion in Nazi concentration camps with his own incarceration and the killing of his family. Frankl's experiences in the camps are detailed in his most influential book, *Man's Search for Meaning*. Roughly divided between a gripping and tragic account of the camps and a formal description of his theory, the book makes the case that those who were lucky enough to survive the physical brutalities of the camps were then able to withstand succumbing to the mental misery because they had a reason to live, and a purpose that enabled them to surpass the deprivation, violence, and abuse of their imprisonment. Frankl's view of meaning focuses on a highly active sense of purpose. That is, meaning and purpose are what people *do with* their lives. Each individual is the sole match for a unique purpose awaiting them in the world, in Frankl's view. It is incumbent upon each of us to identify, find, and embrace that purpose, whether it leads us along a difficult or easy path.

Modern theories of meaning have expanded upon many of Frankl's ideas and left others alone. For example, research from cognitive and social psychology has persuaded many scholars that humans are highly flexible in ascribing meaning to all manner of stimuli (e.g., Heine, Proulx, & Vohs, 2006). This knowledge has sup-ported a more constructivistic view of meaning that assumes people have the ability to find meaning in many things and to have the ability to pursue any number of purposes rather than idiosyncratically predestined ones (e.g., Battista & Almond, 1973; Reker, Peacock, & Wong, 1987; Ryff, 1989). The most common definitions of meaning in life now focus on two primary dimensions: significance and purpose (Steger, Frazier, Oishi, & Kaler, 2006). The first dimension refers to people's ability to make sense of and understand their lives, including having a clear vision of who they are, what the world around them is like, and how they are best able to interact with the world. The second dimension refers to people's possession and embrace of one or more highly valued, expansive life goals, aims, or missions. Others have argued that meaning should include a dimension capturing how worthwhile or valued living is to people (George & Park, 2013). The definition we generally use states that meaning in life is "the extent to which people comprehend, make sense of, or see significance in their lives, accompanied by the degree to which they perceive themselves to have a purpose, mission, or overarching aim in life" (Steger, 2009, p. 682).

As Frankl originally argued, meaning in life appears to provide people with fortitude and resilience during times of strife and struggle. Research and more contemporary theory largely support Frankl's contention, as survivors of all sorts of traumas, illnesses, losses, and adverse events who report finding meaning fol-lowing their suffering have better outcomes than those who do not find meaning

(e.g., Davis, Wortman, Lehman, & Silver, 2000; Park & Folkman, 1997). This part-
nership with meaning is not confined to the interpreted meaning (or appraisal) of
difficult events; it also includes people's broader meaning in life (e.g., Park, 2010;
Steger, Owens, & Park, 2015; Steger & Park, 2012). The literature on meaning's
potential capacity to bestow resilience in the face of adversity is firmly in line
with our idea that meaning plays a critical role in helping those in challenging
professions, such as human service providers, retain their empathy under difficult
circumstances at work.

Meaning and motivation in work

Frankl first proposed that people could find meaning and purpose through their
work over 50 years ago; however, research on the subject is just picking up steam
(Frankl, 1984; Morrison, Burke, & Greene, 2007). Frankl described meaning as the
principal human need, and wrote that meaning allows self-transcendence – an ability to develop a purpose beyond the self. He stated that meaning could be found
in three ways: through work and creative efforts, through relationships, and through
the attitude we take (or reappraisals we make) toward unavoidable suffering (Frankl,
1984). Frankl was not writing with human service care providers in mind, but
each of these three avenues to meaning are available through human service work.
Human service work directly involves encounters with other humans as well as
an exposure to their unavoidable suffering in the form of illness, mental health
struggles, incarceration, and myriad other circumstances, especially among under-
resourced populations.

The idea that a workplace can fulfill a variety of needs beyond financial com-
pensation has been recognized for decades (Warr, 1987). Organizational psychology
literature that addresses the role of meaning in work has highlighted the role of
interpersonal interactions and relationships, such as working with clients in human
service settings, in finding meaning in work (Baron & Pfeffer, 1994; Wrzesniewski,
Dutton, & Debebe, 2003). A workplace can foster intrinsic motivation by increasing
the potential and reward of quality interpersonal interactions (Morrison, Burke, &
Green, 2007).

As meaningful work has become more popular in the working world and in
academia, new perspectives and approaches have emerged. Meaningful work is seen
to consist of a strong sense of purpose and motivation toward one's work, to draw
on the motivation for one's work to serve a greater good or to benefit others,
and to take root most readily when one is able to express valued characteristics
in an autonomous fashion (Rosso, Dekas, & Wrzesniewski, 2010; Steger & Dik,
2009; Steger, Dik, & Duffy, 2012). Other research has focused more tightly on how
meaningful work arises from the match between individual skills and values – how
one's abilities can be used in alignment with personal, intrinsic motivations (Cartwright & Holmes 2006; Chalofsky, 2003). When work cultivates meaning, it can
change the experience of spent effort, allowing hard work to feel significant instead
of merely exhausting (Brickman, 1987). Meaningful work is linked to a host of

other psychological benefits as well, such as greater well-being and reduced anxiety and hostility (Steger et al., 2012). In the next section we examine human service work, which, through its emphasis on both relationships and service, allows for many potential opportunities to find meaning.

Human service work, appraisal, stress, and meaning

There is an implicit and largely untested assumption that human service care providers self-select into their profession because of an altruistic motivation: They seek the rewards associated with empathic connection, and its sense of meaning (Batson, Lishner, Cook, & Sawyer, 2005; Keltner, 2009; Morrison, Burke, & Greene, 2007). Despite the organizational stressors, client-based demands, and inability to fully help that arise in human service work, there is also a great opportunity to cultivate feelings of meaning from the empathic connection to clients (Halifax, 2012). For example, doctors working in palliative care settings, in which there are high volumes of human suffering and death, often still report high levels of satisfaction and personal accomplishment (Graham, Ramirez, Cull, Finlay, Hoy, & Richards, 1996; Halifax, 2012).

Personal accomplishment is often derived from the provider's ability to sustain emotionally meaningful relationships and support clients and coworkers (Graham et al., 1996; Morrison, Burke, & Greene, 2007). This can make the human service setting an ideal location to connect with helping others (Brickman, 1987; Porter, Steers, & Boulian, 1973). Unfortunately, in human service settings where authentic empathy and emotional connections could create meaning for workers, the burdens of workplace stress can eclipse the altruistic motivation and desire for connection. Supporting the personal efficacy of providers so that they can manage their stress is a critical component to finding and maintaining meaning and well-being (Poulin, Brown, Dillard, & Smith 2013). It is important to note that despite the well-researched prevalence of workplace stress across a variety of human service settings, there is minimal research on the ancillary opportunities for mindfulness and meaning (Edwards, Burnard, Coyle, Fothergill, & Hannigan, 2000).

Stress, empathy, and the role of appraisal

Individuals differ in the degree to which they experience sympathetic distress for the suffering of others. For some, emotional resonance with another person's suffering feels overwhelming; for others, it is simply a call to react. The variation in stress triggers has to do with individual assessment or appraisal of the situation, instead of merely the situation or environment itself (Lazarus & Folkman, 1984). In the famous words of early stress researcher Hans Selye (1936), it is not stress that harms us, it is our (over)reaction to that stress. Developing awareness of our appraisals and the subsequent thoughts that accompany our emotional responses has been found to be a successful coping strategy by both the fields of stress research and thousands of years of contemplative practice. In fact mindfulness's emergence in the West has been the result of its application to help us manage stress by becoming aware of our emotions and thoughts as they arise.

Prior research indicates that appraisals predict how the individual sees the demands of the world around them (stressors) in relation to their perceived resources to manage the situation (Lazarus & Folkman, 1984). Some of our stress appraisals help us by rallying our physiological responses to the demands of a situation appropriately, whereas other stress appraisals are more a rapid, rigid survival-based response, which helps briefly but taxes our physiological system. The same situation can elicit threat-based (taxing) or challenge-based (rallying) stress responses corresponding to the individual's unique appraisal of their resources in relation to the stressors (Akinola & Mendes, 2012; Blascovich, Mendes, Hunter, & Salomon, 1999; Lazarus & Folkman, 1984). Many people suffer from chronic stressors at work, feel their resources depleted, and reach a state of chronic threat-based stress. This is untenable, and a common strategy to manage this experience is to withdraw emotionally. Critically, emotional withdrawal also prevents empathic engagement, derailing the rewards of connection with others and the meaning of one's work. Simply stated: The strategy of avoiding feelings in work to avoid stress makes work less meaningful.

Empathy and appraisal

Within human service work, as is the case within many professions, the opportunity to use empathy to forge and enjoy strong emotional bonds with clients is a valued part of the work. Empathy is defined as two distinct processes occurring in concert: (1) the emotional resonance with another's plight, and (2) the cognitive appraisal of what is occurring (Davis, 1983; Decety, 2011; Ekman & Halpern, 2015). Experiencing emotional resonance occurs faster than cognitive appraisal, but that resonance can devolve to self-related anxiety and sympathetic distress when the experiencer of empathy appraises the situation as overwhelming emotionally (Decety, 2011; Hein & Singer, 2008). The appraisal process can incorporate perspective-taking to allow a more targeted or accurate empathy, helping to distinguish another's personal distress situation from one's own; thus, appraisals can actually serve to manage and decrease sympathetic distress (Decety, 2011; Halpern, 2001; Ickes, Funder, & West, 1993). Unencumbered by distress, a provider can feel more resources to approach their work with compassion (Ekman & Halpern, 2015). See Figure 14.1 below.

Conversely, sympathetic distress also can be avoided by refusing to feel empathy by suppressing the emotional resonance to another's suffering or automatically appraising every subject of potential empathy as an unrelated 'other,' subsequently detaching from engaged concern and compassion.

It is crucial to understand that there is much to be gained from empathy despite the risk of sympathetic distress. In fact, empathy supplies affective data to inform clinical and treatment decisions, curiosity, and compassion (Halpern, 2001; Krasner et al., 2009; Singer & Klimecki, 2014). Empathy can also make challenging interpersonal work feel more rewarding and increase feelings of efficacy (Halpern, 2001;

FIGURE 14.1 Empathy response

Riess et al., 2012), both of which may help prevent feelings of sympathetic distress and even burnout. As suggested above, many care providers are drawn to emotionally engaging human service work because they are naturally empathic and seek the intrinsic rewards of helping others (Ashforth & Humphrey, 1995; Freudenberger & Richelson, 1980). As Frankl suggested, our work with others and witnessing suffering are the fertile ground from which to grow meaning. The intrinsic rewards of helping others are potentially more sustainable than extrinsic financial sources of success. They have a more powerful and sustainable impact on work well-being and may help workers manage stress and promote positive appraisals of work (Brickman, 1987; Keltner & Haidt, 1999; Wallace & Shapiro, 2006). The intrinsic reward of helping others is directly related to feelings of meaning, purpose, and significance (Baumeister, 1991; Keltner, 2009). Thus, overcoming stress and preserving the ability to generate and experience empathy is a critical challenge for those in human service work. We suggest that using mindfulness practices to manage stress and connect to meaning is an important method to buffer stress and sustain empathy in human service occupations. We hope that an exploration of the interplay between mindfulness, meditation practices, and meaning in one's work might yield insights for their synergy in other occupations and life domains as well.

Mindfulness, meditation, stress, empathy, and compassion

Mindfulness refers to a type of cultivated awareness that emerges through deliberately paying attention to experiences as they occur in the present moment, in real-time, while understanding their temporary nature. Mindfulness-based programs build on the core premise of using the present awareness as an anchor for creating a space of reflection by witnessing thoughts and emotions, yet not becoming carried away by them (Kabat-Zinn, 1990). Mindfulness-based trainings have been at the forefront of wellness and stress reduction interventions in the last decade (Goyal et al., 2014; Keng, Smoski, & Robins, 2011). Specifically, mindfulness practices have been found to reduce stress, depression, and anxiety, and to increase activation in brain regions responsible for regulating attention and positive affective states, including empathy and other pro-social emotions (Davidson et al., 2003; Grossman, Niemann, Schmidt, & Walach, 2004; Hofmann, Sawyer, Witt, & Oh, 2010; Lutz, Slagter, Dunne, & Davidson, 2008).

One of the most basic and widely used techniques is a focus on the present moment through the breath; this builds stable attention and relaxation. In this technique, participants learn to pay attention to the present moment without judgment through a focus on their breathing, on the present activity, or on their body with the intention to relax (Kabat-Zinn, 1990; Wallace & Shapiro, 2006). Simple breath practices are believed to help bring the attention of the mind to the present moment instead of letting the mind ruminate in negative or cynical thoughts. Such a reorientation also helps bring a clearer focus on the present moment. Regular breath practice trains the mind to develop an everyday awareness of habitual patterns of negative self-thoughts and behavior, referred to as meta-cognitive awareness (Davidson & McEwen, 2012; Hayes, Strohsahl, & Wilson, 1999; Keng et al., 2011). Although it is frequently taught in a seated silent posture, mindfulness can be practiced during any moment or any activity by simply drawing attention to the task at hand, the breath, or the body to reorient to the present moment.

Mindfulness practices that focus on relaxation through the breath offer an alternative to being sucked into negative appraisals of threat and being overwhelmed that generate stress. Whereas feeling under siege by unmanageable demands may often elicit strong negative judgments of events, people, or work, mindful awareness ideally allows such judgments to arise and then pass. Circumventing the potentially harmful role of negative appraisals during stress is one of the ways mindfulness may interrupt the mounting damage from stress and consequently help keep the way open for authentic and natural empathy and compassion to arise.

A second way in which mindfulness may both help people cope with stress and relax is by helping people pay better attention to the physiological markers of stress. For example, a worker could be rushing through a hectic day, scrambling to complete paperwork, respond to patient needs, and communicate with coworkers. The first sign that stress might be gaining the upper hand could be a slight, tight feeling in the chest or the beginnings of a headache wrapping around the forehead. Through cultivating the ability to intentionally direct awareness and attention, this worker could recognize her stress level and briefly stop to tune in to her breath and body and give the stress an opportunity to release.

Finally, mindfulness allows people to avoid the impulse to withdraw emotionally because it encourages them to observe that they are facing a significant number of demands without prompting the judgment that therefore they are helpless, under attack, or letting others down. Instead, mindfulness may assist people in seeing demands as what they are, whether that means tasks awaiting completion, patients requesting assistance, coworkers expressing hostility, or a piling up of multiple requests at a time. After all, judging demands to be egregious does not facilitate their completion nor does it really help people feel better. Non-judgmental awareness helps manage stress and elude the snare of negative appraisals concerning environmental stressors.

Additional meditation practices

Mindfulness refers to developing a training to reorient thoughts and ruminations to a more beneficent, present-moment awareness as discussed in the previous paragraph; mindfulness, however, is a practice that emerges from the larger category of meditation skill development. There are many types of meditation practices that can complement mindfulness. One important meditation practice, which has been adapted from the contemplative tradition, has been taught as compassion and/or self-compassion to develop feelings of care towards self and others. Compassion practices are delivered through a guided visualization during a sitting meditation practice that focuses on an aspiration (for self or other) to be free from suffering and the causes of suffering. Self-compassion practices help with self-soothing during difficulties and bolster feelings of efficacy and resilience (Neff, Kirkpatrick, & Rude, 2007). Compassion for others extends these feelings of caring to the suffering and struggles of others, including clients and coworkers. In the latter case, such a stance of compassion helps to provide an avenue of care and concern even when one is not actually able to intervene. Compassion is informed by empathy, recognizing the suffering of others, and without feeling distress compassion can naturally arise. However in the context of human service work, training to sustain that compassion can be critical. Compassion-focused trainings with care providers start by practicing compassion for the self, then move on to practicing compassion for the clients who are suffering (Klimecki, Leiberg, Lamm, & Singer, 2012; Neff et al., 2007; Shapiro, Brown, Thoresen, & Plante, 2011).

Another meditation technique is setting a clear intention with regard for what people want to achieve through meditation, and bringing awareness to it through mindfulness practices. The intention should connect to a person's meaningful life aspirations. Human service workers, for example, can use set an intention to connect (or reconnect) to the intrinsic rewards of altruism and being of service. Practicing the skill of connecting to the core altruistic motivation to be of service could clarify job expectations, mitigate cynicism, and encourage empathy. The intrinsic motivation for seeking a human service job suggests a desire for purpose and meaning. Research with human service providers who are not working in a professional job role, such as family caregivers, has shown the management of stress through 'meaning based coping,' which can be thought of as a way of finding meaning in the difficulty of their work (Folkman & Moskowitz, 2000). Family caregivers have an intrinsic motivation to be of service to their loved ones; however, their care burden can exceed that of professional care providers because of the relationship to their loved one and the continual hours spent in provision of care (Epel et al., 2004). When family care providers find an experience of meaning in their work, they experience less stress (Epel et al., 2004; Folkman, Chesney, & Christopher-Richards, 1994). The pivotal role of meaning as a method for stress reduction for family caregivers is relevant to considering how meaning can promote positive coping in care-providing work.

Meaningful work theoretically includes both the ability to make sense of our work and also the judgment that our work has an identifiable and important purpose (Steger & Dik, 2009). The purpose of our work is thought to continually replenish the core motivation we have to persist through obstacles and roadblocks. Remembering our core motivation can help us reconnect, or strengthen existent experiences of meaning – which is something beyond the trivial and momentary wants of the self (Steger, 2012) and something separate from the finite, extrinsic rewards of money, status, or success (Duerr & Consulting, 2008). Perhaps especially in the case of human service workers, success with high-needs clients who are very sick has inadequate follow-up resources or motivation for care and can be elusive; this can make workers feel hopeless (Schaufeli, Leiter, & Maslach, 2009). Still, interpersonal meaning and compassion for self and others can help workers manage emotional disconnection and cynicism. But only if meaning is *used*.

How meaning and mindfulness can work together

Nothing is more anathematic to meaning than the notion of mindlessly bumbling through life, blindly fidgeting away one's life on hollow, randomly chosen pursuits. The meaningful life is not supposed to be laborious and terrible, but it is supposed to be consciously embraced and lived (Steger, Kashdan, & Oishi, 2008). One must be in close contact with life; one must think, act, choose, engage, and infuse the living of life with one's meaning and purpose.

Unfortunately, this is one of the most important untested assumptions in meaning in life research, that people intentionally discern and hone their sense of significance and valued purposes as they develop, encounter new environments, and discover or accrue new abilities and deficits. Because most meaning research is cross-sectional, and what research there is that is longitudinal only assesses how much meaning people feel they have at various points in time. We do not really know how people are finding meaning, how they are adapting meaning over time, or even whether they are considering meaning when making important decisions in their lives. We would argue that if meaning is to be any kind of important topic of study, then meaning must be used in these ways. If meaning is not able to be found intentionally, modified with ecological flexibility, or perceived and consulted in the living of life, then it is merely some 1 to 7 rating on an opinion scale and not worth bothering with. We think that centuries of human inquiry cannot be *that* far off base, so we are willing to sustain the hypothesis that meaning can be encountered and used to fashion the best life possible for people. Meaning can be used as a source of strength to overcome hardship; meaning can be used to find motivation for self-improvement; meaning can be used to help choose suitable courses of action.

If we peel back one more layer of this argument, we see a natural fusion of meaning and mindfulness. People can shape meaning and use meaning only if they are aware of meaning in the first place, and mindfulness is a natural and robust tool for optimizing awareness. In addition, introspective meditations that remind us of our core aspirations can help us identify our motivations and support us to lead our lives in a meaningful way. In everyday life, this entails making meaning as tangible and observable as breathing, emotional responses, empathy, and compassion.

Life throws many things our way, some of which are deeply impactful whether they bring joy or woe. Much of what life throws our way seems to be completely devoid of importance, despite how strenuously and noisily these things solicit our attention. Like most people, we struggle to evade the notification beeps, flashing lights, gossip, seductive advertisements, blaring umbrage, and flaunted crocodile tears, and like most people we are not always successful. Like potato chips or fun size candy bars, such noise promises savory satisfaction and pleasure that seem hard to deny sometimes. Yet, also like junk food, whatever indulgence they provide is wholly insufficient to nurture life. To truly build a life worth living, we strive to mind our meanings. We see great promise in a fusion of mindfulness and meaning as an antidote for stress, a pathway to our potential, or a bridge to bring us closer to others.

Conclusion

We have begun to develop and deliver interventions and experiences designed to harmonize meaning and mindfulness, particularly in the context of stress, with the intent of cultivating and sustaining empathy and compassion. Figure 14.2 provides a simple schematic of our thesis and a general flow of how sustainable, meaningful work may be achieved. Meaning is introduced as the overarching beliefs, goals, commitments, and values people have. Meaning is the architectural framework on which other important aspects of our development and resilience are built. Motivation is introduced within specific contexts. One of us (EE) has spent many years working with people employed in human service careers, ranging from prison guards to ER nurses. For such people, work is an intensely important context. In other applications of the model, the context might be healing personal relationships, establishing and maintaining a healthier lifestyle, or self-improvement. The motivation for doing difficult work in any of these contexts is built onto each person's personal meaning framework, bolstering that motivation to persist under pressure. Finally, mindfulness and other meditation practices are introduced as a vital way of being in the world, and a powerful set of practices that can be used to lower overall stress loads and lessen the accumulation of stress. We feel that mindfulness – in both perspective and practice – is best applied to an aspiration, a focus, and that meaning can provide a generative focus for mindfulness. For example, as we observe our behavior and the events happening around us, we can better become aware of whether we are aligned with our meaning, whether we are linking our daily motivations with our larger sense of purpose, and whether we are undermining or reinforcing an understanding of our place in the world that gives us the opportunity and incentive to act benevolently. On the flip side, mindfulness gives us powerful

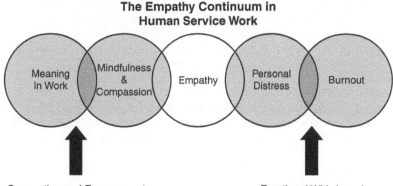

FIGURE 14.2 Our thesis: Meaning and mindfulness may work optimally together to maintain motivation in relationship-intensive occupations, enabling people to experience empathy and compassion while avoiding burnout and exhaustion. Even in challenging jobs, making authentic connections with others helps people find meaning in their work.

tools for accessing and using meaning, helping us transcend the worthless minutia of each day and our own petty, passing concerns, and instead expand ourselves to include the stakes of others, to nurture empathy and compassion, and to build connections that are greater than any one of us. *In a mindless, busy world, we need to be mindful to live a meaningful life.*

Bibliography

Akinola, M., & Mendes, W. B. (2012). Stress-induced cortisol facilitates threat-related decision making among police officers. *Behavioral Neuroscience, 126*(1), 167–174.

Ashforth, B. E., & Humphrey, R. H. (1995). Emotion in the workplace: A reappraisal. *Human Relations, 48*(2), 97–125.

Baron, J. N., & Pfeffer, J. (1994). The social psychology of organizations and inequality. *Social Psychology Quarterly, 57*(3), 190–209.

Batson, C. D., Lishner, D. A., Cook, J., & Sawyer, S. (2005). Similarity and nurturance: Two possible sources of empathy for strangers. *Basic and Applied Social Psychology, 27*(1), 15–25.

Battista, J., & Almond, R. (1973). The development of meaning in life. *Psychiatry, 36,* 409–427.

Baumeister, R. F. (1991). *Meanings of Life.* New York: Guilford Press.

Blascovich, J., Mendes, W. B., Hunter, S. B., & Salomon, K. (1999). Social 'facilitation' as challenge and threat. *Journal of Personality & Social Psychology, 77*(1), 68–77.

Brickman, P. (1987). *Commitment, conflict, and caring.* Englewood Cliffs, NJ: Prentice-Hall.

Cartwright, S., & Holmes, N. (2006). The meaning of work: The challenge of regaining employee engagement and reducing cynicism. *Human Resource Management Review, 16*(2), 199–208.

Chalofsky, N. (2003). An emerging construct for meaningful work. *Human Resource Development International, 6*(1), 69–83.

Davidson, R. J. (2003). Affective neuroscience and psychophysiology: Toward a synthesis. *Psychophysiology, 40*(5), 655–665.

Davidson, R. J., Kabat-Zinn, J., Schumacher, J., Rosenkranz, M., Muller, D., Santorelli, S. F., & Sheridan, J. F. (2003). Alterations in brain and immune function produced by mindfulness meditation. *Psychosomatic Medicine, 65*(4), 564–570.

Davidson, R. J., & McEwen, B. S. (2012). Social influences on neuroplasticity: Stress and interventions to promote well-being. *Nature Neuroscience, 15*(5), 689–695.

Davis, C., Wortman, C. B., Lehman, D. R., & Silver, R. (2000). Searching for meaning in loss: Are clinical assumptions correct? *Death Studies, 24,* 497–540.

Davis, M. H. (1983). Measuring individual differences in empathy: Evidence for a multidimensional approach. *Journal of Personality and Social Psychology, 44*(1), 113–126.

Decety, J. (2011). Dissecting the neural mechanisms mediating empathy. *Emotion Review, 3*(1), 92–108.

Decety, J., & Jackson, P. L. (2004). The functional architecture of human empathy. *Behavioral Cognitive Neuroscience Review, 3,* 71–100.

Duerr, M., & Consulting, F. D. (2008). The use of meditation and mindfulness practices to support military care providers: A Prospectus. *Report Prepared for Center for Contemplative Mind in Society, Northampton, MA,* pp. 1–57.

Edwards, D., Burnard, P., Coyle, D., Fothergill, A., & Hannigan, B. (2000). Stress and burnout in community mental health nursing: A review of the literature. *Journal of Psychiatric and Mental Health Nursing, 7*(1), 7–14.

Ekman & Halpern (2015). Professional distress and meaning in healthcare: Why professional empathy can help. *Social Work in Health Care, 54*(7), 633–650. doi:10.1080/00981389.2015.1046575

Epel, E. S., Blackburn, E. H., Lin, J., Dhabhar, F. S., Adler, N. E., Morrow, J. D., & Cawthorn, R. M. (2004). Accelerated telomere shortening in response to life stress. *Proceedings of the National Academy of Sciences of the United States of America, 101*(49), 17312–17315

Folkman, S., Chesney, M. A., & Christopher-Richards, A. (1994). Stress and coping in caregiving partners of men with AIDS. *Psychiatric Clinics of North America, 17,* 35–55.

Folkman, S., & Moskowitz, J. T. (2000). Stress, positive emotion, and coping. *Current Directions in Psychological Science, 9,* 115–118.

Frankl, V. E. (1984). *Man's search for meaning: An introduction to logotherapy.* New York, NY: Mount Mary College.

Freudenberger, H. J., & Richelson, G. (1980). *Burn-out: The high cost of high achievement.* Garden City, NY: Anchor Press.

George, L. S., & Park, C. L. (2013). Are meaning and purpose distinct? An examination of correlates and predictors. *The Journal of Positive Psychology, 8,* 365–375.

Goyal, M., Singh, S., Sibinga, E. M., Gould, N. F., Rowland-Seymour, A., Sharma, R., . . . Shihab, H. M. (2014). Meditation programs for psychological stress and well-being: A systematic review and meta-analysis. *JAMA internal medicine, 174*(3), 357–368.

Graham, J., Ramirez, A. J., Cull, A., Finlay, I., Hoy, A., & Richards, M. A. (1996). Job stress and satisfaction among palliative physicians. *Palliative Medicine, 10*(3), 185–194.

Grossman, P., Niemann, L., Schmidt, S., & Walach, H. (2004). Mindfulness-based stress reduction and health benefits: A meta-analysis. *Journal of Psychosomatic Research, 57*(1), 35–43.

Halifax, J. (2012). The precious necessity of compassion. *Journal of Pain and Symptom Management, 41*(1), 146–153.

Halpern, J. (2001). *From detached concern to empathy: Humanizing medical practice.* Oxford: Oxford University Press.

Hayes, S. C., Strohsahl, K. D., & Wilson, K. G. (1999). *Acceptance and commitment therapy: An experiential approach to behavior change.* New York, NY: Guilford Press.

Hein, G., & Singer, T. (2008). Cognitive neuroscience. I feel how you feel but not always: The empathic brain and its modulation. *Current Opinion in Neurobiology, 18*(2), 153–158.

Heine, S. J., Proulx, T., & Vohs, K. D. (2006). The meaning maintenance model: On the coherence of social motivations. *Personality and Social Psychology Review, 10*, 88–110.

Hofmann, S. G., Sawyer, A. T., Witt, A. A., & Oh, D. (2010). The effect of mindfulness-based therapy on anxiety and depression: A meta-analytic review. *Journal of Consulting and Clinical Psychology, 78*(2), 169–183.

Ickes, W., Funder, D. C., & West, S. G. (1993). Empathic accuracy. *Journal of Personality, 61*(4), 587–610.

Kabat-Zinn, J. (1990). *Full catastrophe living: Using the wisdom of your body and mind to face stress, pain and illness*. New York, NY: Delta Trade.

Keltner, D. (2009). *Born to be good: The science of a meaningful life*. New York, NY: W.W. Norton & Co.

Keltner, D., & Haidt, J. (1999). Social functions of emotions at four levels of analysis. *Cognition and Emotion, 13*(5), 505–521. doi:10.1080/026999399379168

Keng, S. L., Smoski, M. J., & Robins, C. J. (2011). Effects of mindfulness on psychological health: A review of empirical studies. *Clinical Psychology Review, 31*(6), 1041–1056.

Klimecki, O., Leiberg, S., Lamm, C., & Singer, T. (2012). Neural and behavioral changes related to compassion training. Poster presented at Social & Affective Neuroscience Society Annual Meeting 2012, New York, NY.

Krasner, M. S., Epstein, R. M., Beckman, H., Suchman, A. L., Chapman, B., Mooney, C. J. (2009). Association of an educational program in mindful communication with burnout, empathy, and attitudes among primary care physicians. *JAMA, Journal of American Medical Association, 302*(12), 1284–1293.

Lazarus, R. S., & Folkman, S. (1984). *Stress, coping, and adaptation*. New York, NY: Springer.

Lutz, A., Slagter, H. A., Dunne, J. D., & Davidson, R. J. (2008). Attention regulation and monitoring in meditation. *Trends in Cognitive Sciences, 12*(4), 163–169. doi:10.1016/j.tics.2008.01.005

Morrison, E. E., Burke, G. C., & Greene, L. (2007). Meaning in motivation: Does your organization need an inner life? *Journal of Health and Human Services Administration, 30*(1), 98–115.

Neff, K. D., Kirkpatrick, K. L., & Rude, S. S. (2007). Self-compassion and adaptive psychological functioning. *Journal of Research in Personality, 41*(1), 139–154.

Park, C. L. (2010). Making sense of the meaning literature: An integrative review of meaning making and its effects on adjustment to stressful life events. *Psychological Bulletin, 136*, 257–301.

Park, C. L., & Folkman, S. (1997). The role of meaning in the context of stress and coping. *Review of General Psychology, 1,* 115–144.

Porter, L., Steers, R., & Boulian, P. (1973). *Organizational commitment, job satisfaction, and turnover among psychiatric nurses*. Washington: US Department of Health Education & Welfare National Institute of Education.

Poulin, M. J., Brown, S. L., Dillard, A. J., & Smith, D. M. (2013). Giving to others and the association between stress and mortality. *American Journal of Public Health, 103*(9), 1649–1655.

Reker, G. T., Peacock, E. J., & Wong, P. T. P. (1987). Meaning and purpose in life and wellbeing: A life-span perspective. *Journal of Gerontology, 42,* 44–49.

Riess, H., Kelley, J. M., Bailey, R. W., Dunn, E. J., & Phillips, M. (2012). Empathy training for resident physicians: a randomized controlled trial of a neuroscience-informed curriculum. *Journal of General Internal Medicine, 27*(10), 1280–1286.

Rosso, B. D., Dekas, K. H., & Wrzesniewski, A. (2010). On the meaning of work: A theoretical integration and review. *Research in Organizational Behavior, 30*, 91–127.

Ryff, C. D. (1989). Happiness is everything, or is it? Explorations of the meaning of psychological well-being. *Journal of Personality and Social Psychology, 57*, 1069–1081.

Schaufeli, W. B., Leiter, M. P., & Maslach, C. (2009). Burnout: 35 years of research and practice. *Career Development International, 14*, 204–220.

Selye, H. (1936). A syndrome produced by diverse nocuous agents. *Nature, 138*(3479), 32.

Shapiro, S. L., Brown, K. W., Thoresen, C., & Plante, T. G. (2011). The moderation of mindfulness-based stress reduction effects by trait mindfulness: Results from a randomized controlled trial. *Journal of Clinical Psychology, 67*(3), 267–277.

Singer, T., & Klimecki, O. M. (2014). Empathy and compassion. *Current Biology, 24*(18), R875–R878.

Steger, M. F. (2009). Meaning in life. In S. J. Lopez (Ed.), *Oxford handbook of positive psychology* (2nd edition, pp. 679–687). Oxford: Oxford University Press.

Steger, M. F. (2012). Experiencing meaning in life: Optimal functioning at the nexus of spirituality, psychopathology, and well-being. In P. T. P. Wong (Ed.), *The human quest for meaning* (2nd edition, pp. 165–184). New York, NY: Routledge.

Steger, M. F., & Dik, B. J. (2009). If one is looking for meaning in life, does it help to find meaning in work? *Applied Psychology: Health and Well-Being, 1*(3), 303–320. doi:10.1111/j.1758-0854.2009.01018.x

Steger, M. F., & Dik, B. J. (2010). Work as meaning. In P. A. Linley, S. Harrington & N. Page (Eds.), *Oxford handbook of positive psychology and work* (pp. 131–142). Oxford: Oxford University Press.

Steger, M. F., Dik, B. J., & Duffy, R. D. (2012). Measuring meaningful work: The Work and Meaning Inventory (WAMI). *Journal of Career Assessment, 20,* 322–337.

Steger, M. F., Frazier, P., Oishi, S., & Kaler, M. (2006). The meaning in life questionnaire: Assessing the presence of and search for meaning in life. *Journal of Counseling Psychology, 53*(1), 80–93. doi:10.1037/0022-0167.53.1.80

Steger, M. F., Kashdan, T. B., & Oishi, S. (2008). Being good by doing good: Eudaimonic activity and daily well-being correlates, mediators, and temporal relations. *Journal of Research in Personality, 42,* 22–42.

Steger, M. F., Owens, G. P., & Park, C. L. (2015). Violations of war: Testing the meaning-making model among military veterans. *Journal of Clinical Psychology, 71,* 105–116.

Steger, M. F., & Park, C. L. (2012). The creation of meaning following trauma: Meaning making and trajectories of distress and recovery. In T. Keane, E. Newman & K. Fogler (Eds.), *Toward an integrated approach to trauma focused therapy* (pp. 171–191). Washington, DC: APA.

Wallace, A., & Shapiro, S. L. (2006). Mental balance and well-being: Building bridges between Buddhism and Western psychology. *American Psychologist, 61*(7), 690–701.

Warr, P. (1987). *Work, unemployment and mental health.* Oxford: Clarendon Press.

Wrzesniewski, A., Dutton, J. E., & Debebe, G. (2003). Interpersonal sensemaking and the meaning of work. *Research in organizational behavior, 25,* 93–135.

PART IV

Mindfulness in spirituality

15

MINDFULNESS AND SPIRITUALITY IN POSITIVE YOUTH DEVELOPMENT

Eleanor F. Cobb, Clayton H. McClintock, and Lisa J. Miller

Mindfulness in youth development: an overview

Positive directions

The study of mindfulness as it relates to human development and positive psychological experiences represents a significant area of growth within the larger field of positive psychology (Seligman & Csikszentmihalyi, 2000), and, over the past decade, research and application in this area have extended to youth. School-based mindfulness interventions have become a mainstream option in schools for preparing children to learn through a more comprehensive developmental environment. Many organizations around the United States are currently implementing formalized mindfulness interventions in schools with youth, such as Mindful Schools (2010), Inner Resilience Program (Lantieri & Goleman, 2008), and MindUP (Hawn Foundation, 2011). Extensive research goes to show that "...academic achievement, social and emotional competence, and physical and mental health are fundamentally and multiply interrelated ... [and] the best and most efficient way to foster any of those is to foster all of them" (Diamond, 2010, as cited in Zenner, Herrnleben-Kurz, & Walach, 2014). Given the inextricably intertwined nature of academic performance and emotional health of the child, schools provide the ideal grounds to implement institution-wide interventions to enhance all aspects of performance and well-being.

Referring to the vast array of research highlighting the advantageous effects of mindfulness practices offered in schools, Zenner et al. (2014) asserted that "mindfulness can be understood as the foundation and basic pre-condition for education" (p. 2). Zenner et al. (2014) showed via meta-analysis, outcomes of beneficial academic, psychological, and well-being improvements associated with mindfulness-based training in school settings. A meta-analysis of studies on mindfulness delivered in both clinical and education settings (Zoogman, Goldberg, Hoyt, & Miller, 2014) demonstrated a mild to moderate effect size over a broad range of positive academic and psychological outcomes. In keeping with these findings, a comprehensive review of the literature on school-based mindfulness implementation by Rempel (2012) highlighted the universal effectiveness of teaching mindfulness to children. Hence, the research supports the momentum to implement mindfulness practice into school settings.

Mindfulness and cognitive development in youth

Mindfulness often is selected by schools to improve cognitive and behavioral functioning. Multiple meta-analyses on mindfulness-based interventions in schools with youth have demonstrated promising results in cognitive performance, problem solving skills, and attentional abilities (Zenner et al., 2014; Zoogman et al., 2014). Napoli, Krech, and Holley (2005) demonstrated the classroom benefits of mindfulness with children as young as age 6. Compared to a control group, the mindfulness intervention group of first to third graders demonstrated greater selective attention, less test anxiety, and fewer classroom attention problems overall (Napoli, Krech, & Holley, 2005). Students 7 to 8 years of age who completed a mindfulness meditation intervention program demonstrated decreased anxiety, which can lead to improved academic concentration and performance (Semple, Reid, & Miller, 2005).

While the improvements in performance are consistently linked with mindfulness, we do not know the mechanism by which this functions. One possibility is that positive cognitive outcomes are the result of increased conscious awareness of the self, which is the cornerstone of mindfulness. Increasing the awareness of one's behavior and thoughts, even in young children, could influence the choices and efforts made.

In many of these school-based models, mindfulness practices are being utilized as individual management techniques. Helping children cultivate their capacity to develop techniques they can access whenever they choose can play a crucial role in their growth and development (Semple et al., 2005; Semple, Lee, Rosa, & Miller, 2010; Rempel, 2012). Becoming "present" to the moment and using the breath to decrease sympathetic activity in the nervous system appear to help youth become less anxious and more attentive (Beary, Benson, & Klemchuk, 1974), which consequently enhances both their internal and external worlds and overall psychological well-being.

Mindfulness and emotional development in youth

Beyond improvements in the academically related cognitive domain, mindfulness practice has also shown to improve emotional self-regulation, and increase compassion, empathy, creativity, and ethical sensitivity in youth (Zenner et al., 2014). Mindfulness practices are thought to be able to help improve emotional regulation by the practice of intentionally noticing one's thoughts and feelings in a nonreactive manner (Bishop et al., 2004 and Coffey, Hartman, & Fredrickson, 2010 as cited in Zoogman et al., 2014).

Overall, self-esteem and self-regulation, along with positive externalizing behaviors, have been widely shown to improve in youth with mindfulness practice (Weare, 2013). A study of dispositional mindfulness among students in fourth and fifth grade showed enhancements of the executive control process of inhibition (Oberle, Schonert-Reichl, Lawlor, & Thomson, 2012). Research shows that youth who practice mindfulness have an increased capacity to self-soothe, calm themselves, and consequently become more present and less reactive (Abrams, 2008, as cited in Rempel, 2012). Psychological measures of resilience to stress and coping with challenges have also been linked with mindfulness practice in youth (Zenner et al., 2014).

Social and emotional resiliency also appear to be bolstered by mindfulness practice in youth (Semple et al., 2010). A school-based mindfulness intervention conducted with urban youth showed a positive impact on problematic responses to stress, including rumination, intrusive thoughts, and emotional arousal (Mendelson et al., 2010).

After reviewing the literature on mindfulness in schools, Rempel (2012) asserted that "teaching mindfulness techniques to all students creates the potential for greater self-awareness, improved impulse control, and decreased emotional reactivity to challenging events" (p. 203). Besides mindful meditation practices, mindful movement, such as yoga, has demonstrated advantageous effects for youth. A study of school-age girls who received a mindful yoga intervention were less likely to report stress and more likely to report greater coping than their peers who did not practice mindful yoga (White, 2011).

Overall, research and anecdotal experiences demonstrate the widespread benefits and application of mindfulness for youth.

Beyond the classroom

Beyond classroom interventions, clinical mindfulness interventions hold promise as well. Mindfulness-based practices have been shown to reduce mental health issues, such as depression and anxiety, while also enhancing psychological well-being (Baer, 2003; Beauchemin, Hutchins, & Patterson, 2008; Brown & Ryan, 2003; Lilly & Hedlund, 2010; Rempel, 2012). Joyce, Etty-Leal, Zazryn, and Hamilton (2010) implemented a mindfulness program to target behavioral problems and depression in schools, resulting in a significant reduction in both self-reported behavioral problems and depression, especially for the student with clinically significant levels of behavioral problems and depression before the intervention (as cited in Weare, 2013). A clinical study examining behavioral issues in adolescents diagnosed with attention and behavioral deficits showed that mindfulness practice increased self-reports of happiness, sustained attention, and ability to work on their personal goals (Bogels, Hoogstad, van Dun, de Schutter, & Restifo, 2008). Furthermore, a clinical study of adolescents with Asperger syndrome exhibited the benefits of mindfulness practice with this population, as their mean rates of aggression decreased significantly (Singh, Lancioni, Singh, Winton, Singh, & Singh, 2011b).

A meta-analysis of mindfulness in school-based interventions showed only a mild to moderate statistically significant improvement across a broad range of psychological outcomes, whereas the effects size in clinical samples of youth was nearly three times the magnitude (Zoogman et al., 2014). While this could be attributed to a ceiling effect, in that targeting a clinical sample allows more room for improvement, it also points to the need for the mindfulness research field to more extensively explore the possibilities of mindfulness work with child clinical samples (the meta-analysis only identified three published clinical studies with youth). The well-documented success of mindfulness with adult clinical populations signals great opportunity for future research and further applications among child and adolescent clinical populations.

A larger context for mindfulness

Diverse origins and contexts

It is revealing to trace the recent history of mindfulness, as its origins prior to meeting mainstream psychology can suggest new directions for its application with youth. The construct of mindfulness comes from various sources, Western and Eastern. Within the discipline of social psychology, Ellen Langer's study of mindlessness led to experimental studies on its opposite, mindfulness, described as "a flexible state of mind in which we are actively engaged in the present, noticing new things and sensitive to context," (Langer, 2000, p. 220; Langer, Blank, & Chanowitz, 1978). Langer' s conceptualization when tested within a variety of laboratory and real-life contexts, led to a host of interpersonal, educational, creativity, and health benefits (Alexander et al., 1989; Carson, Shih, & Langer, 2001; Langer & Abelson, 1972; Langer & Piper, 1987; Rodin & Langer, 1977).

Mindfulness in the past 20 years has been studied and applied extensively for the treatment of clinical disorders. Introducing a novel clinical paradigm, Jon Kabat-Zinn translated mindfulness specifically from the millennia-old Buddhist tradition into Western clinical practice through the creation of mindfulness-based stress reduction (MBSR) programs. He defines mindfulness as "paying attention in a particular way: on purpose, in the present moment, and non-judgmentally" (Kabat-Zinn, 1994, p. 4).

The Buddhist-derived practice of Vipassana, or mindfulness meditation, where an individual anchors their attention on the breath without reacting to the stream of thoughts, emotions, and sensations, plays a central role in cultivating the mindful state taught in MBSR. MSBR also features similar practices, like body scans and mindful movement through yoga poses. Other therapies have adapted mindfulness for clinical process, such as acceptance and commitment therapy and dialectical and behavioral therapy. In this context, mindfulness refers not to meditation but to the "domination of the literal and evaluative functions of human language and cognition" (Hayes & Wilson, 2003, p. 161). While differences exist in the origins, contexts, and resulting definitions of the construct of mindfulness, at its essence mindfulness orients individuals to the phenomenological experience of the present moment, resulting in a wide range of positive psychological consequences.

Buddhist origins of mindfulness

It is noteworthy that aspects of mindfulness within MBSR, educational contexts, and other mainstream areas directly descend from Buddhist teachings and practices. With the development of MBSR in the 1970s, a core element of Buddhism was imported into Western mainstream society by using mindfulness meditation to teach individuals "the regular, disciplined practice of moment-to-moment awareness or mindfulness, the complete 'owning' of each moment of your experience, good, bad, or ugly" (Harrington, 2008). Kabat-Zinn and other Buddhist practitioners and scientists deliberately decontextualized the introduction of meditation into the Western world from Buddhist philosophy or religious practice in order to make it non-threatening to the medical establishment and ordinary patients. Kabat-Zinn reasoned that "if you go in talking about the Buddha and inviting masters with shaved heads for lectures, it's going to be perceived right away as some foreign cultural ideology—a belief system" (as cited in Harrington, 2008).

Tracing further the Buddhist origins of mindfulness can illuminate its role in positive human development. In its traditional Buddhist roots, mindfulness is considered one of the components of the Noble Eightfold Path that leads to the cessation of suffering and, ultimately, to liberation. Within this formulation, mindfulness is couched within other elements like right speech, right action, and right livelihood. Other qualities of right view, right intention, right effort, and right concentration complete this list of eight. While mindfulness is intimately connected to all aspects of the Eightfold Path, the components taken together create a mental, emotional, and ethical framework and a "backbone of a spiritual path leading to personal transformation" (Schmidt, 2011).

Thus, the teaching of the Eightfold Path illustrates how mindfulness is a part of a much larger set of injunctions within Buddhism, each of which "exist, operate, and are developed in a mutually dependent and reciprocal relationship" (Gethin, 1998). Without the backdrop of good conduct and livelihood, for example, mindfulness might actually do harm to self and others, and without right effort and intention, mindfulness would likely not endure the pull to revert to mindlessness. So while mindfulness does occupy a central place within the Buddhist spiritual tradition, it is a virtue that is necessarily cultivated in the context of other important elements.

The emerging science of spirituality

Defining spirituality

At the same time that mindfulness has grown to become normative within intervention research and clinical science, so too has burgeoned an enormous body of research on spirituality in mental and physical health (Koenig, King, & Carson,

2012; Miller, 2012). For the purpose of this chapter, it is also important to review the meaning of the word "spirituality."

Research surveys indicate that nearly 90 percent of the world's population is actively involved in some form of spiritual practice (World Christian Database, 2007 as cited in Koenig, 2010). The term "spirituality" often triggers a relation to "religion" or "religiosity." While spirituality undoubtedly can be accessed through religion or include religious expression, spirituality stands as its own construct. Hence, spirituality can experienced within religion, but extends to people who may not be involved in religion and crosses all religious boundaries (Koenig, 2010). Benson, Scales, Syvertsen, and Roehlkepartain (2012) explain that spirituality is a collection of beliefs, practices, and experiences that can be related to religious ritual and doctrine but are definitively distinct from religiosity. In a synthesis of the research across sub-fields over the psychological and psychological correlates of spirituality, Miller (2015) argues that spirituality is an innate human capacity, much like cognition, emotion, or language. "Natural spirituality" is then cultivated by relational and psycho-spiritual developmental opportunities, including a spiritual language, practices, and transcendent experience, which can be found within religious observance but also outside of religion.

Dalton, Eberhardt, Bracken, and Echols (2006) explain: "We use the term 'spirituality' to include all forms of reflection and introspection in which the primary goal is to explore one's relationship to the transcendent in order to deepen and enrich personal meaning, purpose, authenticity, and wholeness" (p. 5). Hay and Nye (1998) emphasize a view of spirituality that exists within or outside of a religious tradition, as "a holistic awareness of reality which is potentially to be found in every human being" (p. 63).

Despite definitions of spirituality that do not rely on religion, the language around spirituality has at times hindered the distinction between religion and spirituality, as the words "religiosity" and "spirituality" are often not distinguished in popular discourse, just as the word "meditation" often holds a connotation more connected with Buddhism. In contrast, the term "mindfulness" has been effectively extricated from Buddhism to make it more accessible to the cultural mainstream. Most definitions of spirituality refer to some aspect of connectedness to a transcendent awareness or larger sense of meaning. Thus, one task of the growing field is to develop an accessible language where no particular religious beliefs are required, and even those who might reject aspects of religion could understand and experience core elements of spirituality.

Speaking in analogy and specifics, mindfulness can encompass meditation but does not rely on meditation, just as spirituality can encompass religion but can also be experienced separately from religion.

Connecting mindfulness and spirituality

Contemplative practices that cultivate greater mindfulness are not unique to the Buddhist tradition, as various kinds of meditations have a place in virtually all the world's spiritual traditions, East and West. From centering prayer in Christianity, to transcendental meditation from Hinduism, to the Sufi dances within Islam, to the qigong of Daoism, spiritual traditions the world over have developed practices to cultivate a more mindful awareness and presence (Keating, 2002; Kelly, 2012; Nisargadatta, 1982; Tzu, 1964; Walsh, 1999).

Mindfulness and spirituality share commonalities in their principal components. In fact, a large cross-cultural study of youth from eight countries found that mindfulness was one of four principle components of spiritual development (Benson et al., 2012). Mindfulness and elements within spiritual traditions provide contemplative experiences that help cultivate conscious awareness, self-awareness, interpersonal awareness, and connectivity. Mindfulness and spirituality both serve as access to interdependence with the universe, including building awareness of one's sense of purpose in the world. Additionally, both of these practices and ways of being in the world are accessible to every child as a possibility to offer a framework for self-growth and purpose. Therefore, our responsibility is to open up these guiding ways in a child's life.

Common elements in most definitions of mindfulness focus on attention and a fostered awareness, which are the fundamental aspects of traditional Buddhist mindfulness practices (Brown & Ryan, 2003; Kabat-Zinn, 2003; Rempel, 2012). Mindfulness interventions shown to directly increase attention (Zoogman et al., 2014). Brown and Ryan (2003) explain mindfulness as form of consciousness that allows for enhanced awareness of the present moment experience. Hence, practicing conscious awareness and cultivating present moment attention remain central to mindfulness.

To return to the conceptualization of spirituality as "a holistic awareness of reality which is potentially to be found in every human being" (Hay & Nye, 1998), it can be seen that mindfulness and spirituality both possess similar underlying processes of attention – to the inner self, to others, and to the greater world (p. 63).

Developmental research shows young children have the capacity to build awareness (Gopnik, Meltzoff, & Kuhl, 1999). From a development perspective that youth possess the ability to cultivate awareness and attention, mindfulness and spirituality have the capacity to play crucial roles in developmental processes. Scott (2003) points out Hay and Nye's (1998) definition of awareness-sensing as one aspect of spirituality. This sense of awareness inherent in spirituality converges with the awareness inherent in mindfulness, clarifying that cultivating one can influence the opening of the other. Furthermore, the early capacity of spiritual development may lay in awareness-building, which can be facilitated by mindfulness practices.

Another common component of mindfulness practice is fostering empathy and compassion for the self and others. A facet of mindfulness practice is adopting many perspectives from a nonjudgmental standpoint, which can further perpetuate the connection to others (Langer, 1993). This practice equips youth with skills they can access in times of distress or conflict throughout their lives. Therefore, mindfulness practice can generate an enhanced sense of trust and closeness with others (Kabat-Zinn, 1994).

Mindfulness can build the social and emotional intelligence that Siegel (2013) conceptualizes as "mindsight," the ability to truly see or know the mind of self and others through insight, empathy, and integration. While mindsight builds awareness that enhances interpersonal interactions, spirituality extends the process to that of an interrelated consciousness, further allowing youth to connect with others and the world around them. Mindfulness can produce an experience of being open and curious in the world, which can allow for spirituality to be fostered to further develop one's sense of being part of the nature of the world. Research on youth has shown that openness to experience is correlated with spiritual awareness and ultimately spiritual development (Kelley, Athan, & Miller, 2007).

Where spirituality and youth development come together

Adolescence is a time of spiritual awakening and questioning, as shown in a recent synthesis of neuroscientific, genetic-epidemiological, and clinical research (Miller, 2015). Adolescent spiritual development is part of a comprehensive understanding of human development that involves the integration of multiple faculties with a spiritual command and control center. This is a model of adolescence that emerges from a review of the biological basis of adolescent development, psychological anthropology, and the science specifically on spirituality and wellness in youth.

In a broader sense, adolescence has long been understood as a time of quest, a hunger for experience and expedition – to know, to feel intensely, and to connect with people. Quest has been conceptualized within developmental psychology primarily as a time of questioning and individuation. One neurophysiological developmental framework shows a burgeoning of gray matter in adolescence, linked to a priming of greater curiosity, emotionality, openness, risk, and exploration (Giedd et al., 1999). At the same time, this is a period of selective pruning and myelination, such that what an adolescent does and practices becomes to some extent how she or he is structurally developed (Dahl, 2004). Developmental psychologist Laurence Steinberg (2014) has found that the adolescent brain is exquisitely sensitive to feeling and perceiving, such that adolescence marks a prime period for perception, memory, and learning. Such finely tuned perception equips the adolescent to individuate, meaning to determine the "me and not me" of self, to include identification of personal interests, values, and goals. Siegel (2013) summarizes the individuation process beautifully in sharing that "adolescence can be seen as a transformative period in which individuals go from being open to everything (in childhood) to becoming expert at a few things (in adulthood)" (p. 74).

As college-age youth go out on their own and gain independence, developmental factors often influence them to go on a quest of inner self-exploration and reflection. This time of exploration can be spiritually foundational as it is a great time of opening. Findings show an increasing number of college students have been seeking out and participating in activities that enhance the process of self-examination, inner reflection, and self-growth (Dalton et al., 2006).

Cross-culturally, the period of pre-adolescence and adolescence has been seen to be a particular time of spiritual emergence, awakening, and growth (Good &

Willoughby, 2008; Scott, 2009). In some cultures, this is an individual and private process, while other cultures have coming of age rituals and ceremonies with spiritual undertones or an overt spiritual focus (Good & Willoughby, 2008; Mahdi, Foster, & Little, 1987;Scott, 2003, 2009).

Benson and colleagues (2012) propose spiritual development as universal and central to positive youth development based on an international survey of over 6,000 youth ages 12–25 years from eight different countries. This study further reveals that in adolescents spirituality emerges regardless of involvement in religious practice (Benson et al., 2012). A study of Israeli middle school students reveals that religious practice and the trait of mindfulness both support adolescent spiritual development, indicating additive and multiple opportunities to provide developmental support (Cobb, Kor, & Miller, 2015).

Multiple explanations could be provided as to why the time during pre-adolescence and adolescence is a burgeoning period of spirituality. For example, the brain development of this time engenders greater awareness and perception (Steinberg, 2014) as well as a peaked curiosity and openness to novel experiences (Siegel, 2013). Scott (2003) argues: "Acknowledging that children are relational, that they can and do have beyond-the-self experiences, that they have perceptions and sensitivities that open them to spiritual experiences can provide an initial framework to inform our understanding of children as spiritual in a variety of cultural settings" (p. 127). Scott proposes that by recognizing that youth have the capacity to be spiritually aware, we can help support their emerging spiritual experiences, and be open to seeing their full potential. While spiritual development is a unique aspect of youth development, it is nonetheless a facet of general positive youth development and, therefore, should be addressed in conjunction with the discussion of other areas of positive youth development. Thus, placing youth spirituality in a developmental context, with the notion that spirituality is a lifelong evolving process, would rightly situate spiritual development with other areas that are so encouraged such as academic, social, and emotional development (Scott, 2003).

Miller (2015) has argued even more strongly, based upon a summation of the research on spirituality in youth, that spirituality is the "central organizing principle" of all other lines of social-moral and emotional development in adolescence. Related research has shown that indeed spirituality is an essential source of thriving, associated with a broad range of inner virtues and outer instrumental character strengths (Barton & Miller, 2015).

The near absence of research on secular, school-based spirituality programs in youth reflects the general shortage of these types of interventions. This is an explorative time for spirituality, and understanding how it relates to mindfulness is an important step in the acceptance of spirituality as a non-threatening process independent of religion.

Spirituality and its positive effects on youth

Spirituality has consistently shown strong benefits to physical and mental well-being (Koenig et al., 2012), yet is nearly absent from the body of research on positive youth interventions. An exiting landscape for intervention research opens with the now empirically justified investigation of spiritually based interventions and spiritual processes, and spiritual growth as an outcome.

We propose that current positive psychology interventions in schools might begin to find ways to integrate important aspects of spirituality, guided by the research to date as well direct experiences of teachers, providers, and other professionals who work with youth.

Spirituality and positive emotion in youth

Spirituality has been linked to a variety of positive emotions like wonder, peace, joy, and compassion (Ciarrocchi, Dy-Liacco, & Deneke, 2008; Koenig et al., 2012; Vaillant, 2008). Peak spiritual experiences almost always induce concomitant feelings of awe, love, and appreciation, and are documented not only among adults but also among children and adolescents (Hart, 2004; James, 1985; Maslow, 1973). In addition, traditional spiritual practices like singing hymns or practicing loving-kindness meditation induce a host of powerful positive emotional states (Fredrickson, Cohn, Coffey, Pek, & Finkel, 2008; Vaillant, 2008). Indeed, these spiritual forms of cultivating positive emotion contribute both to positive development and flourishing for young people as well as to enhanced mental health outcomes (Fredrickson et al., 2008; Seligman, 2012).

Spirituality and mental health in youth

Research has consistently shown a connection between spirituality and enhanced mental health for the general population (Koenig, 2010), and studies among adolescents have demonstrated a similar relationship. In fact, strong evidence shows that relational spirituality is one of the most protective factors against prevalent forms of psychopathology, particularly depression and substance abuse, during this developmental period (Desrosiers & Miller, 2007; Desrosiers & Miller, 2008; Kub & Solari-Twadell, 2013; Miller, Davies, & Greenwald, 2000; Miller & Gur, 2002). In addition, relational spirituality inversely relates to substance use and abuse across a range of substances for adolescents (Miller et al., 2000), and to decreased likelihood of depression among adolescent girls (Miller & Gur, 2002).

Recent neuroscientific research has begun to find biological correlates for the relationship between spirituality and depression (Miller, 2013). Importance placed on spirituality has been shown to directly correlate with cortical thickness in particular regions of the brain, which were also significantly thinner in individuals at high risk for depression (Miller et al., 2014). These regions of the brain have also been shown to be thicker in experienced meditators. These findings suggest that spirituality and meditation, separate and together, may confer resilience by expanding cortical reserve in brain regions where thinning leaves individuals vulnerable to depression. In any case, spirituality provides ample resources to promote mental health during youth development.

Spirituality and moral development in youth

The emphasis upon moral virtues within spiritual traditions can be a tremendous resource for young people. The self-reported importance of spirituality among youth, across traditions, has been shown to directly correlate to the number of prosocial values and behaviors, like kindness, leadership, and gratitude; furthermore, through longitudinal analysis spirituality has accounted for positive character change over time (Ahmed, 2009; James, Fine, & Turner, 2012). Spirituality is also inversely related to risky and delinquent adolescent behaviors like substance use, crime, violence, depression, risk taking, and early sexual behavior (Benson & King, 2005; Wallace & Forman, 1998).

Moral resources have been found to mediate positive outcomes among youth. For example, self-regulation, a character trait positively correlated with spirituality, has been shown to mediate lower prevalence of anti-social behavior as well as depression among adolescents (Black, 2013; Laird, Marks, & Marrero, 2011). Similarly, interpersonal forgiveness among young people has been shown to increase hope and optimism, and positively relate to prosocial behavior and empathy, while negatively relating to aggression and grudge-holding (Al-Mabuk, Enright, & Cardis, 1995; Baskin & Enright, 2004; Pickering & Wilson, 2004).

Spiritual traditions, through their teachings, communities, and practices, have many resources for cultivating moral development among youth. While increased virtue can in turn lead to other positive outcomes, moral development itself is an important and valuable outcome.

Spirituality and supportive relationships in youth

Spiritual traditions across cultures and throughout the ages have emphasized the importance of meeting together in community, and these supportive networks of relationships created within spiritual contexts have an important impact on youth. Spiritual communities have a unique capacity to foster healthy and trustworthy relationships across generations, which for young people promotes identity development, self-worth, and positive engagement with adults outside one's family (Cook, 2000; Jessor, Turbin, & Costa, 1998; King & Roeser, 2009; Scales et al., 2003). These communities also often emphasize essential connection to and social responsibility for others (Scott, 2003). In addition, church attendance and other public forms of religiosity correlate positively with educational progress, especially in economically stressed neighborhoods (Regnerus & Elder, 2003), demonstrating that spiritual community can function as a protective mechanism for youth.

Maternal, paternal, and peer spiritual support have been shown to relate positively to relational spirituality, suggesting that parents and peers have an important role in the spiritual development of adolescents (Desrosiers, Kelley, & Miller, 2011). Similarly, Zenner et al. (2014) found that the beneficial effects of school-based mindfulness programs become magnified when mindfulness practices occur at home with the parents, suggesting the related nature of spiritual and mindful practices.

Spirituality and purpose in youth

A sense of meaning and purpose can be a crucial factor in positive psychological development, and spiritual resources can serve as a primary vehicle for cultivating a sense of meaning and purpose beyond the individual. Among adolescents, research has shown direct correlations between perceived life purpose and various aspects of spirituality, like personal prayer, scripture reading, and organizational participation (Francis, 2000; Francis & Burton, 1994).

In the face of life's challenges and trials, spirituality has the capacity to offer purpose, perspective, and meaning (Koenig, 2010). Levine (1999) suggested that children's ability to "simultaneously practice concrete and fanciful thinking is a spiritual capacity that permits concrete and transcendent sensibility to co-exist for them" (as cited in Scott, 2003). In this way, spirituality has the capacity to expand the thinking of youth that can help them create purpose in their lives.

Research has shown an inverse relationship among high school adolescents between purpose in life and risky behavior, like using alcohol, tobacco, marijuana, and "harder" drugs, as well as driving under the influence of alcohol, a result which was maintained across genders and ethnic groups (Sayles, 1995). In another sample of adolescents, lack of purpose correlated with illicit drug use (Minehan, Newcomb, & Galaif, 2000). Among undergraduate students, purpose in life was strongly and positively related to happiness; furthermore, purpose in life mediated the relationship between religiosity and happiness (French & Joseph, 1999).

The connection between spirituality and purpose for any given person can occur in various ways. Spirituality can influence an intention to contribute, which leads to a sense of purpose. Alternatively, the cultivation of values and a sense of meaning can lead to greater purpose. Service to the community can serve as another pathway to purpose in life. Spiritual traditions have long placed an emphasis upon service and contribution to a larger community outside oneself, and, indeed, research shows that involvement in a spiritual community is consistently related to volunteerism and service (Benson & King, 2005). Youth who view religion as important are more likely to do service than those who do not (Youniss, McLellan, Su, & Yates, 1999). Regardless of the particular pathway, amidst a postmodern culture that often provides little guidance for developing life purpose, spirituality offers important resources to youth for cultivating this character quality.

Putting mindfulness and spirituality back together

This chapter has elucidated how mindfulness has been embedded within a larger set of views and practices in Buddhism and other spiritual traditions, aspects that often complement and even depend upon each other. While the multi-dimensional construct of spirituality includes mindfulness, it also includes other important resources like moral injunctions and character development, supportive relationships and communities, positive emotions, an emphasis on service, and a sense of meaning and purpose.

Mindfulness is uniquely valuable for positive youth development, and it can be increasingly valuable as spirituality is accessed. Mindfulness facilitates attention and perception that can lead to enhanced spiritual awareness. Spiritual development in youth exists; however, because of the lack of spiritual language, we often categorize it as 'mindfulness.' Now the field has progressed to a point where mindfulness and spirituality can both be explored, as separate entities, and as integrated processes that can enhance positive youth development together.

The lack of spiritual support for youth has likely resulted from associating spirituality with religiosity, within the context of separating religion from a secular education system. Recognizing that spirituality relates to the same path of positive youth development as mindfulness allows for the acknowledgement of spirituality as an entity separate from religion. The dearth of accessible language for describing spiritual experiences and explorations compounds the lack of support of spiritual development. Conversely, mindfulness and its open awareness have been effectively integrated into our vocabulary. Hence, the potential exists for mindfulness to offer a platform for spiritual development to be acceptable and accessible within our culture, as the two relate and share commonalities. The understanding of how mindfulness nurtures conscious awareness that influences our brains, and internal and external worlds, can support the unfolding of spirituality as it allows for the discovery of oneself beyond the self.

Mindfulness and spirituality can be individual and stand independently of each other, or they can be theorized as an interactive and additive process. Mindfulness can be conceptualized as a gateway to spirituality, as they are both components of comprehensive positive youth development. Linking mindfulness and spirituality together has the potential to enhance the practice and presence of each in the lives of youth.

Mindfulness, spirituality, and positive youth development

Youth spiritual development in our society has often been disregarded because of the secular and religious split in schools (Blake, 1996; Putnam & Campbell, 2012). Hence, the very places youth spend most of their time are most often intentionally void of spiritual development and learning in order to adhere to the secularity of schools. Furthermore, children are not provided with the language and vocabulary to enable them to express freely and expressively the concepts of spirituality and spiritual experiences (Scott, 2003).

Yet, for many other cultures and eras, spirituality and education have been viewed as natural partners, not antagonists, of developing the whole human being (Palmer, 1983; Thurman, 2006). An examination of the Tibetan monastic system model of education, by way of contrast, might be instructive (Dreyfus, 2003). Devotional chanting, recitation of spiritual and moral teachings, and other rituals characterize the young monk's daily training within these schools. Yet, the training also demands enormous intellectual rigor. Students learn and memorize large amounts of texts and are examined daily. Moreover, formal debates characterized by dramatic flair, in which students quickly and logically analyze complex arguments, feature significantly. In this fashion, the rigorous cultivation of the mind goes hand in hand with the cultivation of heart and spirit. Though many of the specifics may not translate directly into contemporary Western society, skillfully and creatively combining intellectual and spiritual disciplines, and bringing them into educational institutions, is certainly possible (Thurman, 2006).

Our society rewards and celebrates achievement and performance. Consequently, knowing and learning become central to measuring the growth and development of youth. Often the essential component of cultivating a socially, emotionally, and mentally well person are overshadowed by the demands of increasing knowledge and skillsets to further accomplishments. Thus, supporting youth's process of being well becomes a particular pertinent and essential component to youth development. Mindfulness and spirituality both engender that essence of being well, apart from gaining knowledge or learning to perform well.

Mindfulness and spirituality are both access points, and in some circumstances even tools, to enhance social and emotional wellness in youth. Individually, mindfulness and spirituality have been associated with a multitude of positive psychology characteristics, and, therefore, they can be utilized to enhance overall positive youth development. Children have the capacity to be attuned and open at a young age. Hence, our responsibility is to cultivate that innate capacity. Mindfulness and spirituality are two specific avenues to nurture the developmental process of becoming consciously aware of one's own internal life and connections to others and to the world. A spiritual belief or spiritual practice, or a mindful outlook or mindfulness practice, can all be techniques to support youth in their development towards whole and well beings. Children inevitably have responses to their surrounding environments. Mindfulness and spirituality can be fostered as tools to cultivate nonreactivity to life's challenging circumstances, if youth are provided the language to access their potential for inner calm.

Cultivating mindfulness skills and spiritual perspectives can enhance well-being and provide life-long internal capacities that can serve as protective factors against stress and difficulty and promote supportive processes for positive and adaptive growth and development. While spiritual development in youth involves a process of awareness and discovery, mindfulness can support this type of internal development and external awareness by strengthening one's ability to connect internally and outwardly in conscious ways.

Empirical research on mindfulness and youth is a much younger field than adult mindfulness research (Weare, 2013). Hence, great potential exists for future research, particularly with clinical samples, of the benefits of mindfulness among youth. The literature is even more sparse on spirituality in youth, and nearly negligible on how mindfulness and spirituality together affect positive youth development. Thus, much room for further research exists on the pathways and approaches through which mindfulness and spirituality can enhance positive youth development.

While spirituality often emerges in adolescent years, there often lacks a supportive language to provide a framework within which individual spirituality can grow and flourish. Mindfulness provides the opportunity to cultivate a spiritual perception, which can be met with a lens through which youth can organize their experience, eventually to augment and integrate spiritual awareness. Mindfulness might be adduced to spiritually oriented psychotherapy or wellness work for children and adolescents, which adopts a child-centered stance (Miller & Kelly, 2006).

Bibliography

Abrams, H. (2008). Towards an understanding of mindful practices with children and adolescents in residential treatment. *Residential Treatment for Children & Youth, 24*(1–2), 93–109. doi:10.1080/08865710802147497

Ahmed, S. (2009). Religiosity and presence of character strengths in American Muslim youth. *Journal of Muslim Mental Health, 4*(2), 104–123.

Alexander, C. N., Langer, E. J., Newman, R. I., Chandler, H. M., & Davies, J. L. (1989). Transcendental meditation, mindfulness, and longevity: An experimental study with the elderly. *Journal of Personality and Social Psychology, 57*(6), 950.

Al-Mabuk, R. H., Enright, R. D., & Cardis, P. A. (1995). Forgiveness education with parentally love-deprived late adolescents. *Journal of Moral Education, 24*(4), 427–444.

Baer, R. (2003). Mindfulness training as a clinical intervention: A conceptual and empirical review. *Clinical Psychology: Science and Practice, 10*(2), 125–143.

Barton, Y., & Miller, L. (2015). Positive psychology and spirituality go hand in hand. *Journal of Religion and Health, 54*(3), 829–843.

Baskin, T. W., & Enright, R. D. (2004). Intervention studies on forgiveness: A meta-analysis. *Journal of Counseling & Development, 82*(1), 79–90.

Beary, J. F., Benson, H., & Klemchuk, H. P. (1974). A simple psychophysiologic technique which elicits the hypometabolic changes of the relaxation response. *Psychosomatic Medicine, 36*(2), 115–120.

Beauchemin, J., Hutchins, T., Patterson, F. (2008). Mindfulness meditation may lessen anxiety, promote social skills, and improve academic performance among adolescents with learning disabilities. *Complementary Health Practice Review, 13*, 34–45.

Benson, P. L., & King, P. E. (2005). Religion and adolescent development. In H. R. Ebaugh (Ed.), *The handbook of religion and social institutions* (pp. 115–123). New York, NY: Springer.

Benson, P. L., & Scales, P. C. (2009). Positive youth development and the prevention of youth aggression and violence. *European Journal of Developmental Science, 3*, 218–234.

Benson, P., Scales, P., Syvertsen, A., & Roehlkepartain, E. (2012). Is youth spiritual development a universal developmental process? An international exploration. *The Journal of Positive Psychology, 7*(6), 453–470.

Bishop, S. R., Lau, M., Shapiro, S., Carlson, L., Anderson, N. D., Carmody, J., . . . Devins, G. (2004). Mindfulness: A proposed operational definition. *Clinical Psychology: Science and Practice, 11*(3), 230–241. doi:10.1093/clipsy.bph077

Black, B. C. (2013). Intrinsic religiosity and adolescent depression and anxiety: The mediating role of components of self-regulation. *All Theses and Dissertations.* Paper 4155.

Blake, N. (1996). Against spiritual education. *Oxford Review of Education, 22*(4), 443–456.

Bogels, S., Hoogstad, B., van Dun, L., de Schutter, S., & Restifo, K. (2008). Mindfulness training for adolescents with externalizing disorders and their parents. *Behavioural and Cognitive Psychotherapy, 36*(2), 193–209.

Brown, K., & Ryan, R. (2003). The benefits of being present: Mindfulness and its role in psychological well-being. *Journal of Personality and Social Psychology, 84*(4), 822–848.

Carson, S., Shih, M., & Langer, E. (2001). Sit still and pay attention? *Journal of Adult Development, 8*(3), 183–188.

Ciarrocchi, J. W., Dy-Liacco, G. S., & Deneke, E. (2008). Gods or rituals? Relational faith, spiritual discontent, and religious practices as predictors of hope and optimism. *The Journal of Positive Psychology, 3*(2), 120–136.

Cobb, E. F., Kor, A., & Miller, L. (2015). Support for adolescent spirituality: Contributions of religious practice and trait mindfulness. *Journal of Religion and Health, 54*(3), 862–870.

Coffey, K. A., Hartman, M., & Fredrickson, B. L. (2010). Deconstructing mindfulness and constructing mental health: Understanding mindfulness and its mechanisms of action. *Mindfulness, 1*(4), 235–253.

Cook, K. V. (2000). "You have to have somebody watching your back, and if that's God, then that's mighty big": The church's role in resilience of inner city youth. *Adolescence, 35,* 717–730.

Dahl, R. (2004). Adolescent brain development: A period of vulnerabilities and opportunities. *Annals of the New York Academy of Science, 1021,* 1–22.

Dalton, J. C., Eberhardt, D., Bracken, J., & Echols, K. (2006). Inward journeys: Forms and patterns of college student spirituality. *Journal of College and Character, 7*(8), 1–22.

Desrosiers, A., Kelley, B. S., & Miller, L. (2011). Parent and peer relationships and relational spirituality in adolescents and young adults. *Psychology of Religion and Spirituality, 3*(1), 39–54. doi:10.1037/a0020037

Desrosiers, A., & Miller, L. M. (2007). Relational spirituality and depression in adolescent girls. *Journal of Clinical Psychology, 63,* 1021–1037.

Desrosiers, A., & Miller, L. M. (2008). Substance use versus anxiety: Are some disorders more spiritual than others? *Research in the Social Scientific Study of Religion, 19,* 137–154.

Diamond, A. (2010). The evidence base for improving school outcomes by addressing the whole child and by addressing skills and attitudes, not just content. *Early Education and Development, 21*(5), 780–793.

Dreyfus, G. B. (2003). *The sound of two hands clapping: The education of a Tibetan Buddhist monk.* Berkeley, CA: University of California Press.

Francis, L. J. (2000). The relationship between bible reading and purpose in life among 13–15-year-olds. *Mental Health, Religion & Culture, 3*(1), 27–36.

Francis, L. J., & Burton, L. (1994). The influence of personal prayer on purpose in life among Catholic adolescents. *Journal of Beliefs and Values, 15*(2), 6–9.

Freedman, S. R., & Enright, R. D. (1996). Forgiveness as an intervention goal with incest survivors. *Journal of Consulting and Clinical Psychology, 64*(5), 983.

Fredericks, L. (2004, July). A gathering on social and emotional learning, love, and forgiveness. In *Summary of proceedings at the conference of the Fetzer Institute.* Kalamazoo, MI.

Fredrickson, B. L., Cohn, M. A., Coffey, K. A., Pek, J., & Finkel, S. M. (2008). Open hearts build lives: Positive emotions, induced through loving-kindness meditation, build consequential personal resources. *Journal of Personality and Social Psychology, 95*(5), 1045.

French, S., & Joseph, S. (1999). Religiosity and its association with happiness, purpose in life, and self-actualisation. *Mental Health, Religion & Culture, 2*(2), 117–120.

Gethin, R. (1998). *The foundations of Buddhism.* New York, NY: Oxford University Press.

Giedd, J., Blumenthal, J., & Jeffries, N. O., Castellanos, F. X., Liu, H., Zijdenbos, A., . . . Rapoport, J. L. (1999). Brain development during childhood and adolescence: A longitudinal MRI study. *Nature Neuroscience, 2*(10), 861–863.

Good, M., & Willoughby, T. (2008). Adolescence as a sensitive period of spiritual development. *Society for Research in Child Development, 2*(1), 32–37.

Gopnik, A., Meltzoff, A., & Kuhl, P. (1999). *The scientist in the crib: Minds, brains and how children learn.* New York, NY: William Morrow.

Hamer, D. H. (2005). *The God gene: How faith is hardwired into our genes.* New York, NY: Random House.

Harrington, A. (2008). *The cure within: A history of mind-body medicine.* New York, NY: W.W. Norton.

Hart, T. (2004). Opening the contemplative mind in the classroom. *Journal of Transformative Education, 2*(1), 28–46. doi:10.1177/1541344603259311

Hart, T. (2005). Spiritual experiences and capacities of children and youth. In E. C. Roehlkepartain, P. E. E. King, L. M. Wagener & P. L. Benson (Eds.), *The handbook of spiritual development in childhood and adolescence* (pp. 163–177). Newbury Park, CA: Sage Publications.

Hawn Foundation. (2011). *The MindUP curriculum: Brain-focused strategies for learning and living.* Puerto Rico: Scholastic Teaching Resources.

Hay, D., & Nye, R. (1998). *The spirit of the child.* London: Fount.

Hayes, S. C., & Wilson, K. G. (2003). Mindfulness: Method and process. *Clinical Psychology: Science and Practice, 10*(2), 161–165.

Huguelet, P., & Koenig, H. (Eds.) (2009). *Religion and spirituality in psychiatry.* New York, NY: Cambridge University Press.

James, A. J., Fine, M. A., & Turner, L. J. (2012). An empirical examination of spirituality as an internal developmental asset during middle childhood and adolescence. *Applied Developmental Science, 16*(4), 181–194.

James, W. (1985). *The varieties of religious experience: Vol. 13.* Cambridge, MA: Harvard University Press.

Jessor, R. J., Turbin, M. S., & Costa, F. M. (1998). Risk and protection in successful outcomes among disadvantaged adolescents. *Applied Developmental Science, 2,* 194–208.

Joyce, A., Etty-Leal, J., Zazryn, T., & Hamilton, A. (2010). Exploring a mindfulness meditation program on the mental health of upper primary children: A pilot study. *Advances in School Mental Health Promotion, 3*(2), 17–25. doi:10.1080/1754730X.2010.9715677

Kabat-Zinn, J. (1994). *Wherever you go, there you are.* New York, NY: Hyperion.

Kabat-Zinn, J. (2003). Mindfulness-based interventions in context: Past, present, and future. *Clinical Psychology: Science and Practice, 10*(2), 144–156.

Kelly, B. D. (2012). Contemplative traditions and meditation. In L. Miller (Ed.), *The Oxford handbook of psychology and spirituality* (pp. 307–325). Oxford: Oxford University Press.

King, P. E., & Roeser, R. W. (2009). Religion and spirituality in adolescent development. In *Handbook of adolescent psychology.* Newbury Park, CA: Sage Publications.

Keating, T. (2002). *Open mind, open heart: The contemplative dimension of the Gospel.* New York, NY: Continuum International Publishing.

Kelley, B. S., Athan, A. M., & Miller, L. F. (2007). Openness and spiritual development in adolescents. *Research in the Social Scientific Study of Religion, 18,* 3.

King, P. E., & Benson, P. L. (2006). Spiritual development and adolescent well-being and thriving and well-being. In G. C. Roehlkepartain, P. E. King, L. M. Wagener & P. L. Benson (Eds.), *The handbook of spiritual development in childhood and adolescence* (pp. 384–398). Newbury Park, CA: Sage Publications.

Koenig, H. (2010). Spirituality and mental health. *International Journal of Applied Psychoanalytic Studies, 7*(2), 116–122.

Koenig, H., King, D., & Carson, V. B. (2012). *Handbook of religion and health.* New York, NY: Oxford University Press.

Kub, J., & Solari-Twadell, P. A. (2013). Religiosity/spirituality and substance use in adolescence as related to positive development: A literature review. *Journal of Addictions Nursing, 24*(4), 247–262.

Laird, R. D., Marks, L. D., & Marrero, M. D. (2011). Religiosity, self-control, and antisocial behavior: Religiosity as a promotive and protective factor. *Journal of Applied Developmental Psychology, 32*(2), 78–85.

Langer, E. J. (1993). A mindful education. *Educational Psychologist, 28*(1), 43–50.

Langer, E. J. (2000). Mindful learning. *Current Directions in Psychological Science, 9*(6), 220–223.

Langer, E. J., & Abelson, R. P. (1972). The semantics of asking a favor: How to succeed in getting help without really dying. *Journal of Personality and Social Psychology, 24*(1), 26.

Langer, E. J., Blank, A., & Chanowitz, B. (1978). The mindlessness of ostensibly thoughtful action: The role of "placebic" information in interpersonal interaction. *Journal of Personality and Social Psychology, 36*(6), 635.

Langer, E. J., & Piper, A. I. (1987). The prevention of mindlessness. *Journal of Personality and Social Psychology, 53*(2), 280.

Lantieri, L., & Goleman, D. P. (2008). *Building emotional intelligence: Techniques to cultivate inner strength in children.* Boulder, CO: Sounds True.

Levine, S. (1999). Children's cognition as the foundation of spirituality. *International Journal of Children's Spirituality, 4*(2), 121–140

Lilly, M., & Hedlund, J. (2010). Healing childhood sexual abuse with yoga. *International Journal of Yoga Therapy, 1*(1), 120–130.

Mahdi, L. C., Foster, S., & Little, M. (Eds.) (1987). *Betwixt & between: Patterns of masculine and feminine initiation.* La Salle, IL: Open Court.

Maslow, A. H. (1973). *The farther reaches of human nature.* Richmond, CA: Maurice Bassett

Mendelson, T., Greenberg, M., Dariotis, J., Gould, L., Rhoades, B., & Leaf, P. (2010). Feasibility and preliminary outcomes of a school-based mindfulness intervention for urban youth. *Journal of Abnormal Child Psychology, 38*(7), 985–994.

Miller, L. (2013). Spiritual awakening and depression in adolescents: A unified pathway or "two sides of the same coin." *Bulletin of the Menninger Clinic, 77*(4), 332–348.

Miller, L., Bansal, R., Wickramarante, P., Hao, X., Tenke, C., Weissman, M., & Peterson, B. (2014). Neuroanatomical correlates of religiosity and spirituality: A study in adults at high and low familial risk for depression. *JAMA Psychiatry, 71*(2), 128–135.

Miller, L., Davies, M., & Greenwald, S. (2000). Religiosity and substance use and abuse among adolescents in the national comorbidity survey. *Journal of the American Academy of Child and Adolescent Psychiatry, 39,* 1190–1197.

Miller, L., & Gur, M. (2002). Religiosity, depression, and physical maturation in adolescent girls. *Journal of the American Academy of Child & Adolescent Psychiatry, 41,* 206–214.

Miller, L., & Kelley, B. (2006). Spiritually oriented psychotherapy with youth; A child-centered approach. In E. Roehlkepartain (Ed.), *The handbook of spiritual development in childhood and adolescence* (pp. 421–438). New York, NY: Sage.

Miller, L. J. (Ed.) (2012). *The Oxford handbook of psychology and spirituality.* New York, NY: Oxford University Press.

Miller, L. J. (2015). *The spiritual child.* New York, NY: St. Martin's Press.

Minehan, J. A., Newcomb, M. D., & Galaif, E. R. (2000). Predictors of adolescent drug use: Cognitive abilities, coping strategies, and purpose in life. *Journal of Child & Adolescent Substance Abuse, 10*(2), 33–52.

Napoli, M., Krech, P., & Holley, L. (2005). Mindfulness training for elementary school students: The attention academy. *Journal of Applied School Psychology, 21*(1), 99–125.

Newberg, A., & Newberg, S. (2009). A neuropsychological perspective on spiritual development. In G. C. Roehlkepartain, P. E. King, L. M. Wagener & P. L. Benson (Eds.), *The handbook of spiritual development in childhood and adolescence* (pp. 61–68). Newbury Park, CA: Sage Publications.

Nisargadatta, S. (1982). *I am that: Talks with Sri Nisargadatta Maharaj* (M. Frydman, Trans.). Durham, NC: Acorn.

Oberle, E., Schonert-Reichl, K. A., Lawlor, M. S., & Thomson, K. C. (2012). Mindfulness and inhibitory control in early adolescence. *The Journal of Early Adolescence, 32*(4), 565–588. doi:10.1177/0272431611403741

Palmer, P. J. (1983). *To know as we are known: Education as a spiritual journey.* San Francisco, CA: HarperOne.

Park, N., & Peterson, C. (2006). Character strengths and happiness among young children: Content analysis of parental descriptions. *Journal of Happiness Studies, 7*(3), 323–341.

Pickering, S. R., & Wilson, B. J. (2004). Forgiveness in first grade children: Links with social preference, aggression, social problems, and reciprocal friendships. In S. Denham (Chair), *Children's forgiving in behavior, cognition, and affect. Symposium conducted at the biennial meeting of the Conference on Human Development* (pp. 21–42). Washington, DC.

Putnam, R. D., & Campbell, D. E. (2012). *American grace: How religion divides and unites us.* New York, NY: Simon and Schuster.

Regnerus, M. D., & Elder, G. H. (2003). Staying on track in school: Religious influences in high-and low-risk settings. *Journal for the Scientific Study of Religion, 42*(4), 633–649.

Rempel, K. (2012). Mindfulness for children and youth: A review of the literature with an argument for school-based implementation. *Canadian Journal of Counselling and Psychotherapy/Revue canadienne de counseling et de psychothérapie, 46*(3), 1923–6182.

Rodin, J., & Langer, E. J. (1977). Long-term effects of a control-relevant intervention with the institutionalized aged. *Journal of Personality and Social Psychology, 35*(12), 897.

Saroglou, V., Buxant, C., & Tilquin, J. (2008). Positive emotions as leading to religion and spirituality. *The Journal of Positive Psychology, 3*(3), 165–173.

Sayles, M. L. (1995). *Adolescents' purpose in life and engagement in risky behaviors: Differences by gender and ethnicity.* Doctoral dissertation. Cambridge, UK: ProQuest Information & Learning.

Scales, P. C., Benson, P., Mannes, M., Hintz, N., Roehlkepartain, EC., & Sullivan, T. (2003). *Other people's kids: Social expectations and American adults' involvement with children and adolescents.* New York, NY: Springer Science & Business Media.

Schmidt, S. (2011). Mindfulness in east and west–is it the same? In H. Walach, S. Schmidt & W. B. Jonas (Eds.), *Neuroscience, consciousness and spirituality* (Vol. 1, pp. 23–38). Heidelberg: Springer.

Scott, D. (2003). Spirituality in child and youth care: Considering spiritual development and "relational consciousness." *Child and Youth Care Forum, 32*(2), 117–131.

Scott, D. (2009). Coming of age as a spiritual task in adolescence. In M. de Souza, L. Francis, J. O'Higgins-Norman & D. Scott (Eds.), *International handbook of education for spirituality, care, wellbeing* (pp. 453–467). Netherlands: Springer.

Seligman, M. E. (2012). *Flourish: A visionary new understanding of happiness and well-being.* New York, NY: Simon and Schuster.

Seligman, M. E. P., & Csikszentmihalyi, M. (2000). Positive psychology: An introduction. *American Psychologist, 55*(1), 5–14.

Semple, R., Lee, J., Rosa, D., & Miller, L. (2010). A randomized trial of mindfulness-based cognitive therapy for children: Promoting mindful attention to enhance socialemotional resiliency in children. *Journal of Child and Family Studies, 19*(2), 218–229.

Semple, R., Reid, E., & Miller, L. (2005). Treating anxiety with mindfulness: An open trial of mindfulness training for anxious children. *Journal of Cognitive Psychotherapy, 19*(4), 379–392.

Siegel, D. (2013). *Brainstorm: The power and purpose of the teenage brain.* New York, NY: Penguin Group.

Singer, W., & Gray, C. M. (1995). Visual feature integration and the temporal correlation hypothesis. *Annual Review of Neuroscience, 18*(1), 555–586.

Singh, N., Lancioni, G., Singh, A., Winton, A., Singh, A. N., & Singh, J. (2011b). Adolescents with Asperger syndrome can use a mindfulness-based strategy to control their aggressive behavior. *Research in Autism Spectrum Disorders, 5*(3), 1103–1109.

Steinberg, L. (2014). *Age of opportunity: Lessons from the new science of adolescence*. London: Houghton Mifflin Harcourt.

Thurman, R. (2006). Meditation and education: India, Tibet, and modern America. *The Teachers College Record, 108*(9), 1765–1774.

Trends, Barrett and Johnson (William Carey Library 2001). updated February 2007. http://worldchristiandatabase.org/wcd/

Tzu, C. (1964). *Basic writings* (B. Watson, Trans.). New York, NY: Columbia University Press.

Vaillant, G. E. (2008). Positive emotions, spirituality and the practice of psychiatry. *Mens Sana Monographs, 6*(1), 48.

Wallace, A., & Shapiro, S. (2006). Mental balance and well-being: Building bridges between Buddhism and Western psychology. *American Psychologist, 61*(7), 690–701.

Wallace, J. M., & Forman, T. A. (1998). Religion's role in promoting health and reducing risk among American youth. *Health Education & Behavior, 25*(6), 721–741.

Walsh, R. N. (1999). *Essential spirituality: The 7 central practices to awaken heart and mind*. New York, NY: John Wiley.

Warren, A., Lerner, R., & Phelps, E. (Eds.) (2012). *Thriving and spirituality among youth: Research perspective and future possibilities*. New York, NY: John Wiley.

Weare, K. (2013). Developing mindfulness with children and young people: A review of the evidence and policy context. *Journal of Children's Services, 8*(2), 141–153.

White, L. (2011). Reducing stress in school-age girls through mindful yoga. *The Journal of Pediatric Health Care, 26*(1), 45–56.

World Christian Database. (2001). *Atheists/nonreligious by country*. Lancaster, PA: World Christian.

World Christian Database. (2007). Todd M. Johnson and Gina A. Zurlo (Eds.). Leiden/Boston: Brill.

Youniss, J., Mclellan, J. A., Su, Y., & Yates, M. (1999). The role of community service in identity development normative, unconventional, and deviant orientations. *Journal of Adolescent Research, 14*(2), 248–261.

Zenner, C., Herrnleben-Kurz, S., Walach, H. (2014). Mindfulness-based interventions in schools- a systematic review and meta-analysis. *Frontiers in Psychology, 5*, 603.

Zoogman, S., Goldberg, S., Hoyt, W., Miller, L. (2014). Mindfulness interventions with youth: A meta-analysis. *Mindfulness, 6*(2), 1–13.

16

NOURISHMENT FROM THE ROOTS

Engaging with the Buddhist foundations of mindfulness

Tim Lomas

Introduction

Over recent years, the concept of mindfulness has had a dramatic, profound impact on Western society. Not only have mindfulness-based interventions been widely embraced within positive psychology (PP), as attested to by the existence of this book, but by many applied professions, from education (Napoli et al., 2005) to healthcare (Fortney & Taylor, 2010). Given the detailed and wonderful contributions of the other chapters in this book, the value of mindfulness as a means to well-being and psychological development hardly needs to be restated here. However, what this chapter will argue is that our current understanding and appreciation of mindfulness is somewhat *limited,* and that we would have a much greater sense of its profound potential if we were to explore the original Buddhist context in which the notion of mindfulness was first developed. As will be seen here, Western psychology has latched on to one quite specific idea of mindfulness, influenced by the pioneering scholarship of Kabat-Zinn (1982). This particular version of mindfulness, centred around the development of attention and awareness, has often been presented in a de-contextualised way, separated from the wider Buddhist framework of ideas and practices in which mindfulness was originally situated and taught (Shapiro, 1994). This de-contextualisation was not necessarily a bad thing: arguably, this was what enabled mindfulness to take root and be adopted enthusiastically in predominantly secular Western societies (King, 1999). However, as valuable and worthwhile as this particular formulation of mindfulness is, the original Buddhist teachings are replete with profound, nuanced insights and teachings concerning mindfulness. Now that mindfulness *has* been widely accepted within academia, and the West generally, we might benefit from *re*-contextualising it.

This then is what the present chapter aims to do: to re-contextualise mindfulness by considering the deeper Buddhist roots of the concept, thus enabling PP to still further harness the revolutionary power of this practice. This re-contextualisation will necessarily be partial and incomplete: over its 2,500 year history, Buddhism has flowered into numerous traditions, each with their own teachings and interpretations; as such, one can only hope to cover a small portion of this immense wealth of insight. In this light, the approach taken here is to consider three 'types' of mindfulness within Buddhist teachings (as interpreted by the contemporary Buddhist teacher Sangharakshita (1998), who is introduced in an endnote). This idea that there are different 'types' of mindfulness is based on the identification of three Pāli[1] words in the canonical Buddhist teachings that are all conceptually related to awareness: *sati* (awareness of the present moment); *appamada* (awareness infused with a spirit of ethical care); and *sampajañña* (awareness infused with a sense of spiritual progress). As readers may perhaps recognise, most contemporary conceptualisations of mindfulness are generally based on the first type of mindfulness, *sati*. As valuable as 'sati-type' mindfulness is, this chapter will argue that we have much to gain from also embracing and encouraging the other two types. As such, this chapter will be in three sections, exploring the three 'types' in turn. In each case, we will consider how PP could benefit from considering and promoting this 'type' of mindfulness.

Sati: awareness of the present moment

We begin here with *sati,* since the term 'mindfulness' was derived explicitly from this Pāli word. Thus, our first point of exploration here is to consider how *sati* gave rise to the modern notion of 'mindfulness.' Such considerations fit in to an emergent debate in the psychological literature around the term 'mindfulness,' and its adequacy as a translation of concepts in the original Buddhist teachings (McCown et al., 2010). This is a debate about exegesis and hermeneutics (i.e., how we interpret original texts), and about translation and discursive equivalence (i.e., how we capture the nuanced meanings of the original terms in our choice of English words). The rendering of *sati* as 'mindfulness' was first accomplished by the pioneering Buddhist scholar T.W. Rhys Davids, in 1881, who was responsible for many of the initial translations of Buddhist teachings into English. So, in what context is the word *sati* used in these original texts? The term appears frequently throughout. Arguably the most prominent and influential teaching relating to *sati* in the Pāli canon is the *Satipatthana Sutta,* the 'Discourse on the Establishment of Mindfulness' (Bodhi, 2011). Its guidance states: 'Establishing present-moment recollection right where you are, simply breathe in, simply aware, then breathe out, simply aware. Breathing in long, know directly *I am breathing in long* . . . [etc.].' (p. 298). Readers might be familiar with this teaching as the basis for the 'mindfulness of breathing,' a foundational practice within contemporary mindfulness interventions, such as Kabat-Zinn's (1982) mindfulness-based stress reduction (MBSR). Readers may further recognise the phrase 'present-moment recollection' in the *sutta* as the roots for Kabat-Zinn's (2003, p. 145) own influential definition of mindfulness as 'the awareness that arises through paying attention on purpose, in the present moment, and nonjudgmentally to the unfolding of experience moment by moment.' However, the word 'recollection' in the *sutta* is noteworthy. As Peacock (2014, p. 5) explains, in the Brahmanical tradition of India – the cultural context in which the Buddha was born and lived (circa the 5th century BCE; Coningham et al., in press) – the word *sati* had connotations of 'remembrance' and 'recollection.' Within a Buddhist context, this did not mean historical memory per say, but rather 'recollecting' or 'remembering' the activity that one is currently engaged in. As Anālayo (2003, p. 48) puts it, this means bringing to mind 'what is otherwise too easily forgotten: the present moment.'

This type of mindfulness is incredibly important and worth cultivating. The point of this chapter is not to denigrate *sati*-type mindfulness, but just to suggest that PP (and of course people generally) could benefit by augmenting it with the two other forms of mindfulness discussed here too. Before discussing why such augmentation might be useful, let's first remind ourselves why *sati*-mindfulness – which is the basis for all contemporary mindfulness-based interventions – is so valuable. We do not need to go into great detail here; after all, this entire book is dedicated to showcasing the manifold ways in which *sati*-mindfulness, and positive psychology interventions (PPIs) that engender this, is conducive to wellbeing. The early, pioneering, mindfulness-based interventions were developed primarily within medicine and clinical psychology; these showed that *sati*-mindfulness (i.e., attending to the present moment in a non-judgmental way) is helpful in alleviating physical and mental health problems, from chronic pain (Kabat-Zinn, 1982) and fibromyalgia (Kaplan et al., 1993) to depression (Teasdale et al., 2000) and anxiety (Miller et al., 1995). Over recent years, to this growing corpus of interventions have been added others that are more recognisable as PPIs – i.e., rather than alleviating illness or dysfunction, they proactively promote the kind of 'positive' outcomes in which PP specialises. Such mindfulness-based PPIs include interventions focusing specifically on engendering qualities ranging from forgiveness (Recine et al., 2009) and gratitude (McIntosh, 2007) to resilience (Meiklejohn et al., 2012) and spirituality (Goldstein, 2007). The development of such interventions is very much to be welcomed, and many more PPIs based on engendering sati-type mindfulness will hopefully be developed over the years ahead.

However, many people participate in such interventions without engaging with the wider Buddhist teachings in which mindfulness was first developed. This is of course fine! No one should feel any duty to engage with Buddhism, and as emphasised above, many people find great benefits from practising mindfulness on its own terms, without reference to Buddhism. That said, one could argue that people would find even greater benefits if they were to explore these Buddhist teachings. This includes, in the context of this chapter, engaging with the other 'types' of mindfulness, namely *appamada*-mindfulness (with its emphasis on ethical awareness and practice) and *sampajañña*-mindfulness (with its emphasis on spiritual development). This is not to say that people practising *sati*-mindfulness will not necessarily be acting ethically or developing spiritually. However, deliberately cultivating these other two types of mindfulness could help *enhance* their ethical behaviour and *accelerate* their spiritual development, thus engendering greater wellbeing. (The question of *why* ethics and spiritual development are important to wellbeing will be addressed in the two sections below.) As Kabat-Zinn himself acknowledges, by taking mindfulness out of its original Buddhist context, and conceptualising it using cognitive theories of attention, there is the risk that 'Western psychology may wind up denaturing it in fundamental ways,' and that there is 'the potential for something priceless to be lost' (Williams & Kabat-Zinn, 2011, p. 4).

Moreover, without explicitly cultivating ethical and spiritual awareness, there is the possibility of mindfulness being deployed in problematic ways. As Stanley (2012, p. 202) notes, while teachings in the Pāli canon preserved an ethical dimension to *sati,* when taken out of this context and conceptualised purely as an attention training technique, then there is the risk of mindfulness 'becoming de-ethicised.' Some of the ways in which mindfulness interventions have been utilised are arguably reflective of this 'de-ethicised' process. For instance, mindfulness-based mind fitness training has been developed for military personnel as a stress-prevention tool (Stanley et al., 2011). Now, let me emphasise that this intervention has the noble aim of addressing the severe mental health risks that soldiers are liable to, and as such is to be welcomed. However, it is nevertheless also the case that one aim of this intervention is to help military personnel operate more effectively in combat situations, which inevitably includes acts of killing. While this does not necessarily render the use of mindfulness *un*-ethical, it can be recognised at the least that this is a morally tricky area. This is not necessarily just a modern issue: meditative techniques have been harnessed in military contexts previously in history, as reflected by the martial arts and warrior traditions within Buddhism, such as the samurai 'Warrior Zen' of 16th- and 17th-century feudal Japan (Johnson, 2000, p. 9). Nevertheless, even if these cases are exceptions, they show that mindfulness *can* be deployed in a de-contextualised way, for instance just as an attention training technique, without necessarily any reference to ethical or spiritual development.

Moreover, the contention that interventions can be utilised without reference to ethics is a charge that might also be applied to PP more generally, which on the whole has been wary of being prescriptive around ethics (Sundararajan, 2005). For instance, in *Authentic Happiness,* Seligman (2002) characterises the 'good life' as the gratification one obtains from utilising one's 'signature strengths.' However, he suggests that PP cannot be prescriptive over *how* people find such gratification, since PP is a science, and as such should aim for the idea of value-neutrality. He illustrates this with the challenging example of 'a hit man who derives enormous gratification from stalking and slaying' (p. 303). Asking rhetorically whether this person could be deemed to have achieved 'the good life,' Seligman states: 'The answer is yes. I condemn their actions, of course, but on grounds independent of the theory in this book.' (p. 303). That is, while Seligman naturally finds such actions abhorrent, he argues that this condemnation cannot be made *within the context of his theory,* since this theory is 'not a morality or a world-view' but a scientific theory, and as such should be 'morally neutral.' (p. 303). This is a respectable argument, and is certainly in keeping with the objective spirit of scientific enquiry. (Although that said, some theorists suggest that every viewpoint is inextricably made from a 'moral horizon' (Taylor, 1989); for instance, paradoxically, even the scientific ideal of value-neutrality *is itself* a value choice, one which values 'objectivity' over explicit moral commitments.) Nevertheless, the next section will argue that PP would do well to explicitly incorporate reflections on ethics into its theorising. In a sense, this would be a radical departure for a scientific discipline; however, as the next section will explore, from a Buddhist perspective, incorporating ethics into theories of wellbeing is valuable and indeed necessary, because acting ethically (or otherwise) has a strong determining impact on wellbeing.

Appamada: awareness infused with a spirit of ethical care

Having extolled the virtues of *sati*-mindfulness above, this section makes the case that people would further benefit from engaging with the Buddhist teachings in which the concept of mindfulness was first developed. Interestingly, research on converts to Buddhism in Western countries suggests that many people do indeed go on this journey of discovery – from utilising mindfulness in a de-contextualised 'secular' way, to then being intrigued by the broader and potentially more far-reaching possibilities for wellbeing offered by Buddhism. For example, qualitative interviews with meditators in London revealed that although most initially just took up meditation as a stress-management technique (Lomas et al., 2013), nearly all subsequently became interested in the wider Buddhist context of meditation (Lomas et al., 2014b), and many went on to become practising Buddhists to some extent (Lomas et al., 2014a). So, what relevance to such Buddhist teachings holds for PP? This second section focuses on one particular element – a second 'type' of mindfulness found in the Pāli canon, namely *appamada*. (That said, while we are labelling this a 'type' of mindfulness, it is perhaps best not to see *appamada* as distinct from *sati*-mindfulness: rather than a separate state of mind, *appamada* might be best seen as a quality with which one might try to imbue *sati* [Peacock, 2014]. Thus, one would seek to develop one's mindfulness into an enhanced form encompassing both *sati* and *appamada*.) So, what qualities does *appamada* bring to mindfulness? One way of ascertaining these is to consider the diverse range of English words into which the term has been translated. These include 'earnestness' (Müller, 1881), 'vigilant care' (Soeng, 2006), 'unremitting alertness' (Thera, 1941), 'diligence' (Peacock, 2014), and 'carefulness' (Nikaya, 2008). From the perspective of Sangharakshita's interpretation of Buddhism, which underpins this chapter, perhaps the best translation is 'moral watchfulness' (Rao, 2007, p. 69). This translation reflects the commentary on the Dhammapada (the collection of sayings attributed to the Buddha), which describes it as 'awareness . . . with regard to the sphere of qualities of good conduct' (Carter, 2005). As such, we might view *appamada* as 'awareness infused with a spirit of ethical care.' Thus, the overriding significance of *appamada* is that is introduces an *ethical* dimension to mindfulness practice; this takes the concept of mindfulness beyond just being aware of what is happening (i.e., *sati*), and explicitly connects it to Buddhist teachings on ethics and morality.

In this section, we shall consider two questions: what, from a Buddhist perspective, does ethical behaviour consist of; and why, from the perspective of PP, do ethics *matter*? However, before considering these, let us briefly clarify what ethics are, and how they differ from two closely related concepts: values and morals. Values are not necessarily about right/wrong, but are 'conceptions of the desirable' that motivate behaviour and life choices (Schwartz, 1999, p. 24). In contrast, morals *are* explicitly about 'notions of right and wrong' (Hazard Jr., 1994, p. 451). However, there is often a close relationship between values and morals: values held in common in a society often *become* the basis for a commonly held moral framework. As for ethics, while morals may be unarticulated or implicit, the term ethics refers to the explicit codification of such morals in a communally defined and recognised framework. So, firstly, what does Buddhism say about ethics? One central teaching in Buddhism is that one can attain liberation from suffering by following the 'Noble Eightfold path'; this is a prescription for 'right living,' including wisdom (right vision and conception), ethical conduct (right speech, conduct, and livelihood), and meditation (right effort, mindfulness, and concentration) (Thrangu, 1993). Thus, three strands of this path are explicitly about ethics: right speech *(sammā-vācā)*, right action *(sammā-kammanta)*, and right livelihood *(sammā-ājīva)*. Elaborating on these strands, the teachings offer various lists of precepts, specifying in more detail what these consist of. The most widely known set is the 'five precepts' *(pañca-sīla)*, which recommend abstinence from harming living beings; taking the not given (i.e., theft); misconduct concerning sense pleasures (e.g., sexual misconduct); false speech (i.e., lying); and unmindful states related to consumption of alcohol or drugs. For more committed Buddhists, these five are supplemented by additional recommendations in lists of eight and ten precepts (e.g., featuring prescriptions around eating). At a far more detailed level, the Monastic Disciplinary Code *(pāṭimokkha)* features around two hundred rules for monastic life (Keown, 2009). In addition to these prescriptions are various exhortations to virtuous living in the literature. For example, in the Therevadan tradition, there is an emphasis on four *'brahma-viharas'* ('divine' qualities): loving-kindness *(mettā);* compassion *(karuṇā);* sympathetic joy *(muditā);* and equanimity *(upekkha).*

Now, our second question in this section is why, from the perspective of PP, does ethical behaviour matter? Essentially, Buddhist teachings hold that 'skilful' (i.e., ethical) actions should be pursued because they will generate future positive states of mind (i.e., wellbeing), whereas 'unskilful' (i.e., unethical) actions should be avoided because they will lead to future negative states of mind. This reasoning is underpinned by a key Buddhist teaching: *paṭiccasamuppāda,* i.e., the 'law of conditionality.' This teaching is absolutely central: expressed by the Buddha on attaining enlightenment, it may even be described as the fundamental insight of Buddhism, upon which all others rest (Kang, 2009). Essentially, this teaching refers to the causal operation of the universe, i.e., the general principle of ordered relationship between conditions and their effects. As expressed by the Buddha: 'This being, that is; from the arising of this, that arises. . . . This being not, that is not; from the cessation of this, that ceases' (Kang, 2009, p. 72). This is the central insight that underpins all other Buddhist teaching, the 'meta' law that substantiates all other laws. For example, the Noble Eightfold path is a manifestation of this more fundamental notion of *paṭiccasamuppāda* (in this case, that following the path will lead to liberation). Understanding the truth of this teaching is seen as the key to wellbeing and ultimately liberation from suffering. As Sangharakshita and Subhuti (2013, p. 49) put it, 'Once we have understood and are fully convinced about the nature of reality as *paṭiccasamuppāda,* we align ourselves with those regularities or laws that lead us to liberation.'

From this law of *paṭiccasamuppāda* is derived the understanding of the importance of ethical behaviour. This importance is understood through the notion of karma. However, it is important to emphasise that karma is just one aspect of this more general law of conditionality. Although the word *karma* has entered Western discourse, there are many misunderstandings around it, including the notion that it means that *everything* that happens to you is the result of past actions. However, in Buddhism, analysis of the law of conditionality is rather more subtle. One such analysis has been the identification of five different 'orders' of conditionality, referred to as the fivefold *'niyāma.'* In Keown's (2003) *Dictionary of Buddhism, niyāma* are defined as 'laws, conditions or constraints that govern processes or phenomena.' It is worth noting that the Buddha himself is not recorded as presenting these *together* as a fivefold list, rather just mentioning them individually in separate teachings; this model of a collective fivefold *niyāma* only occurred in the 5th century CE in the influential commentaries of Buddhaghosa (Jones, 2012). Essentially, his commentaries recognize five different domains of life that are subject to law-like principles. First, *utu-niyāma* is the 'law of the seasons': this pertains to the observable cyclical regularity of environmental phenomena (e.g., seasonal and diurnal patterns); viewed anachronistically through our contemporary scientific understanding, we could regard this as the domain of physical laws, like the law of gravity. Second, *bīja-niyāma* is the 'law of seeds': this refers to observable patterns in the realm of organic matter, like reproductive continuity; again, anachronistically, this would be the domain of bio-chemistry, featuring principles such as the genetic inheritance of phenotypes. Third, *citta-niyāma* is the 'law of the mind': this refers to psychological processes, such as patterns and causes of mental events; we could see this as the domain of psychology. Fourth, and most crucially in the context of this section, is *kamma-niyāma,* the law of *kamma* (or *karma,* to give it its more commonly used Sanskrit name). This encompasses the general idea that actions in the world tend to have consequences; as expressed by Buddhaghosa, this refers to the desirable and undesirable results following good and bad action. As indicated above, this aspect of conditionality is the domain of ethics and morality. Finally, the *dhamma-niyāma* is the 'law of nature'; while this is a somewhat esoteric notion, one could regard it as referring to the potential of the universe to develop complex qualities such as consciousness, and to produce exemplary beings like the Buddha. From the perspective of a modern scientific understanding, we might associate this law with the theory of evolution, and particularly with emergentist philosophies (e.g., Aurobindo, 2005 [1939–1940]; Wilber, 1995) which view the universe as evolving *towards* complex outcomes such as self-consciousness.

The nuance provided by this list of fivefold *niyāma* is that things happen for all kinds of reasons, some of which are connected to people's actions *(karma niyāma),* and some of which are not (the other four *niyāma).* However, it also states that while not everything is caused by one's past actions, every action will nevertheless cause an outcome in the future. So, to bring the discussion back to the central theme of this chapter, *appamada*-mindfulness means becoming aware and appreciative of the *karma niyāma,* and of the fundamental notion that actions have consequences. It is important to differentiate *karma* from other religious teachings relating to ethics; for instance, Christian notions of sin suggest that we are punished *for* our sins through divine retribution (Swinburne, 1989). However, the Buddhist notion of *karma* does not involve a supernatural agency, but simply proposes that we are rewarded or punished, in a causal sense, *by* our actions. As expressed by Kang (2009, p. 73), 'The law of karma states that any volitional action rooted in non-greed, non-hatred and non-delusion (or in positive terms: generosity, love/compassion, and wisdom) gives rise to virtuous or positive imprints in the mind that would subsequently result in experiences of happiness and pleasure.' Conversely, 'any ethical action rooted in greed, hatred or delusion gives rise to their opposite non-virtuous/negative mental imprints that later result in experiences of suffering and displeasure.' Given this law, Buddhist teachings state that ethical actions are not only beneficial to other people, but have direct benefits for the actor themselves; so, people have a vested interest in acting ethically, and should be motivated to act as such. As Kang (2009, p. 73) puts it, 'A behavioural guideline that emerges from such an ethical view of causality is that one ought to engage mindfully in positive karma rooted in positive volitions.'

Thus, *appamada* introduces a further dimension to mindfulness that is not present in *sati*-mindfulness alone: this goes beyond simply being aware of our thoughts, feelings, and actions, but involves reflecting on whether our actions are 'skilful' (i.e., in tune with the ethical precepts). *Appamada* also involves 'tracing the origins of your mental states [which] helps you to discover more about their background, so that you can make adjustments to the way you live your life' (Sangharakshita, 2003, p. 94). This type of ethical reflection and appreciation is simply not found in contemporary conceptualisations of mindfulness, founded as these are on the concept of *sati,* with its emphasis just on attention. In modern mindfulness-based interventions, if people experience negative cognitions or feelings, they are encouraged to attend to these, and to ideally decentre from them. Of course, this type of mental response is very effective, and is to be encouraged; as emphasised above, interventions involving this kind of attention training can have a potent impact on wellbeing. However, what such interventions do *not* do is make any causal connection between any such negative qualia and people's actions outside of meditation practice. This is an omission, an example of Kabat-Zinn's fear of something 'priceless' being lost (Williams & Kabat-Zinn, 2011, p. 4). That is, although it is useful to learn how to decentre from negative thoughts – the prerogative of many mindfulness interventions – a potentially more powerful solution would be to help people to learn to live skilfully (i.e., ethically), thus lessening the likelihood of negative qualia emerging in the first place. It is this type of ethical appreciation that is developed with the cultivation of *appamada*-mindfulness. As such, the implication of this for PP is that we would do well to develop PPIs that explicitly encourage mindfulness of – and engagement *in* – ethical behaviour. This need not be seen as a radical departure from what is already happening. After all, we already have interventions promoting prosocial qualities such as forgiveness (Lin et al., 2004), compassion (Fredrickson et al., 2008), and kindness (Buchanan & Bardi, 2010). However, there is room for PP to be far more explicit about the value of acting ethically, and to explore the notion of ethical practice through a far more systematic process of empirical and theoretical enquiry.

Sampajañña: awareness infused with a sense of spiritual progress

Finally, we shall touch upon a third 'type' of mindfulness, *sampajañña,* which we might define as awareness infused with a sense of spiritual progress. By including this here, we are suggesting that, as valuable as *sati* and *appamada* are, we can augment mindfulness still further, cultivating an even more powerful approach to wellbeing. As with *appamada,* it is better not to regard this as a distinct 'type' of mindfulness, separate from the others, but a new quality that one can bring to mindfulness, thus creating a compound of *sati-appamada-sampajañña* mindfulness. So, what qualities or abilities are implied by the word *sampajañña*? Some scholars interpret it as the ability to 'effortlessly' sustain *sati*. For example, the influential 8th-century (CE) Indian teacher Śāntideva (2002, p. 22) states that '*Samprajanya* [i.e., *sampajañña*] comes and, once come, does not go again, if *smṛti* [i.e., *sati*] stands guard at the door of the mind.' Maharaj (2013, p. 67) interprets this as meaning that the 'assiduous practice of sati . . . culminates eventually in the achievement of samprajanya, which seems to be a more spontaneous and effortless state of watchfulness of the body and mind.' Beyond this idea of 'effortless' mindfulness, many writers associate the term *sampajañña* specifically with *insight*. For instance, in the seminal teaching on mindfulness, the *Satipatthana Sutta,* there is a refrain of *ātāpi sampajāno satimā,* which Bodhi (2011) translates as 'ardent, clearly comprehending, and mindful.' Thus the refrain encompasses three mental factors: *atapi* (ardent) refers to energy to engage in practice; *sati* is watchful awareness; and *sampajāno* (an adjective relating to the noun *sampajañña*) concerns clear comprehension.

So, what type of insight does *sampajañña* imply? Sangharakshita's (2003) interpretation is that *sampajañña* fundamentally means having an appreciation of the possibility of spiritual development. Thus, Sangharakshita argues that sampajañña might best be translated as 'mindfulness of purpose,' in the sense that 'everything we do should be done with a sense of the direction we want to move in and of whether or not our current action will take us in that direction' (p. 13). This kind of awareness supersedes *appamada*-mindfulness; the latter simply means appreciating the value of living ethically, which one could potentially do in a secular, conventional way (as indeed many people do); however, *sampajañña*-mindfulness involves taking on the profound, revolutionary possibility of spiritual development, and pursuing this goal accordingly. Arguably, this is the overarching 'point' of Buddhism: ultimately, all teachings are about helping people overcome suffering and make progress towards liberation. One way to consider the type of awareness constituted by *sampajañña* is in terms of *paṭiccasamuppādia*, i.e., the law of conditionality introduced above. In particular, Sangharakshita (2003) suggests that *sampajañña* is associated with awareness of the final *niyāma*, the *dhamma niyāma*. This is referred to as the 'law of nature,' which can be interpreted as the potential of the universe to develop complex qualities such as consciousness and exemplary living beings like the Buddha. From this perspective, with the emergence and cultivation of *sampajañña*, one would develop a deep appreciation of the *dhamma-niyāma*, and its implications. One such implication is the idea that all living beings have the potential to become Buddhas, and that the way to progress towards this is by following a spiritual path. So, just as *appamada* would entail an appreciation of the value of living ethically, *sampajañña* would inherently mean being convinced of the value and indeed necessity of diligently following such a path. This awareness would inextricably guide and structure our behaviours, such that we would evaluate and choose all our actions according to whether they facilitated our progress along this path (Sangharakshita, 2003).

There are many ways in which spiritual development is conceptualised in Buddhist teachings, with various nuanced stage-wise depictions of the path. Within the *Tipitaka* (early Buddhist canonical texts), Bucknell (1984) identifies six different lists of stages. The first of these is arguably the most prominent, namely, the Noble Eightfold path, introduced above. A second tenfold stage-wise schema adds two further stages to the end of the eightfold path: right insight *(samma-nana)* and right liberation *(samma-vimutti)*. Other lists identified by Bucknell feature different sequences of stages, which are often greater in number (as many as sixteen in one instance). Further stage-wise models were also developed throughout Buddhism's long history of evolution. For example, the Sarvāstivāda school, which emerged around 240 BCE following a schism within the Therevadan tradition (King, 1995) propounded a Five Path schema, involving five stages (Chong, 2009). First, the foundational path of accumulation *(sambhara-mārga)* involves building up 'merits' (i.e., 'good karma') through three primary practices: giving *(dana)*, moral observance *(sila)*, and the cultivation of meditation *(bhavana)*. Second, the path of preparatory effort *(prayoga-marga)* involves deepening meditative practices, with an initial phase *(mokabhagiya)* of basic practices *(samatha* and *vipassana)*, then more advanced practices *(nirvedhabhagiya)*. The third stage, the path of seeing *(darsana-marga)*, involves 'direct comprehension' *(abhisamaya)* of Buddhist insights into the nature of reality. Fourth comes the path of transformation *(bhavana-marga)*; certain aspects of suffering cannot be extinguished by insight (the third stage), but only by further cultivation of the mind during this more advanced fourth stage. The final stage is the path of the non-trainee/no more learning *(asaika-marga)*, in which the practitioner achieves enlightenment and final liberation from suffering.

This Five Path schema has been reworked by Sangharakshita (1998) into 'four stages of deepening practice: integration; positive emotion; spiritual death; and spiritual rebirth. The stage of integration involves 'recognising oneself as a moral agent and intentionally, cultivating ever-more skilful actions of body, speech and mind, so that progressively more satisfying, subtle, flexible, and open states of consciousness emerge as their fruit' (Sangharakshita & Subhuti, 2013, p. 128). In this sense, one would take one's first steps along the spiritual path with the cultivation of *appamada*. The sense of integration is produced by (a) understanding the connections between one's subjective experiences (e.g., in mindfulness practice) and one's actions; and (b) integrating one's actions with one's values (e.g., Buddhist precepts). This stage is followed by 'positive emotions'; this builds upon the previous stage through the 'systematic cultivation of skilful intentions and actions that bring the karmic fruit of a more finely tuned mind' (Sangharakshita & Subhuti, 2013, p. 133). Subsequently, more advanced practitioners might enter the stage of spiritual death. This involves developing deep insight into the nature of existence; in particular, according to Buddhism, this means appreciating the three *lakshanas* (i.e., 'marks of conditioned existence'): *anicca* (impermanence), *anattā* (insubstantiality), and *dukkha* (suffering). This teaching is central to Buddhism, and describes the fundamental nature of reality: all phenomena are empty of a fixed, enduring, independent nature, but are transitory *(anicca)* and interdependent *(anattā)*; denial or ignorance of these fundamental truths, and the consequent attempt to attach to phenomena that are inherently subject to change, is thus seen as causing suffering *(dukkha)*. Spiritual death occurs when these insights are realised with respect to one's own self, and one understands the impermanence and insubstantiality of one's being. Thus, 'dying' here means giving up our 'self-oriented clinging' (Sangharakshita & Subhuti, 2013, p. 133). However, this is not nihilistic annihilation, but the precursor to the final stage of the path, a liberating spiritual rebirth. This involves re-birth into a deeper sense of self, one that is coterminous with the *dhamma niyāma*, with the spiritual path itself. Here, Sangharakshita and Subhuti suggest that one's own egoic concerns dissipate, and one connects 'more and more deeply with *dhamma niyāma* processes' (p. 134). At the culmination of this fourth stage (which in the Five Path schema is a stage in its own right), there is no longer a 'self' that is making progress, but just the *dhamma niyāma* playing itself out through the medium of the person; this is the omega state of spiritual development, sometimes referred to as enlightenment.

Conclusion

From an orthodox scientific perspective, these ideas – particularly esoteric notions like 'liberation' and 'enlightenment' – might sound challenging. However, it must be emphasised that such Buddhist teachings are not the product of abstract theorising and philosophising, but are the result of empirical observation of the developmental states of mind achieved through meditation, and the systematic structural mapping of these observations (Wilber et al., 1986). Nevertheless, even if we regard these teachings as speculative (which I would strongly argue that we should *not*), at the very least this is territory that is of interest to PP, one which scholars might endeavour to explore and test out according to their preferred methodological protocols. The notion of adaptive psychological and/or spiritual development is central to PP, from Maslow's (1943) pioneering hierarchy of needs, to Ryff's (1989) model of psychological wellbeing. As valuable as such theories are though, PP has much to gain from exploring actual practical activities that can engender such growth. It is the contention here that mindfulness can be one such facilitator of psycho-spiritual development. However, this chapter has also argued that many contemporary mindfulness-based interventions are based on a rather narrow understanding of mindfulness, one derived from the Pāli term *sati,* centred on present-moment awareness. It has been suggested here that people may be able to attain more far-reaching and profound states of wellbeing by engaging with other forms of mindfulness. These include being aware of one's actions and experiences in the light of ethical considerations *(appamada),* and in the context of the pursuit of spiritual development *(sampajañña).* PP has much to gain from exploring these deeper, more radical, forms of mindfulness in the years ahead.

Note

Sangharakshita is one of the foremost contemporary interpreters of Buddhism in the West. Born in London in 1925 as Dennis Lingwood, after serving in India during the Second World War, he stayed on to pursue an interest in Buddhism, studying under revered Buddhist masters (recounted in Sangharakshita, 1997). He was ordained within the Therevadan tradition in 1950, whereupon he received the honorific 'dharma name' Urgyen Sangharakshita, a Pāli term meaning 'Protector of the Sangha.' He returned to England in 1964, and founded the monastic Western Buddhist Order (WBO) in 1967, together with the more inclusive Friends of the Western Buddhist Order (FWBO). In 2010 the movement changed its name to the Triratna Buddhist Order/Community; *'Triratna'* is a Sanskrit term meaning the 'three jewels,' i.e., the triad of Buddha (teacher), *dharma* (teachings), and *sangha* (community) to which members are said to turn for 'refuge' (i.e., commit to) at their ordination. The Triratna is one of the main forms that Buddhism has taken in the West, with around 80 centres/groups in the UK (Bluck, 2006). It is somewhat unorthodox, since it does not exclusively identify with one antecedent Asian Buddhist tradition. Instead, Sangharakshita has chosen practical and doctrinal elements from various traditions, aiming to convey a 'core of common material,' constituting the 'essence' of Buddhism, which may be optimally 'relevant to the West (Subhuti, 1994). For example, the Triratna's two core meditative practices – the mindfulness of breathing and the *metta bhavana* – are derived from the early Therevadan tradition. However, the movement also uses rituals *(pujas)* from the Mayahanan and Vajrayana traditions, such as a 'seven-fold puja' based on the *Bodhicaryāvatāra* by Śāntideva (2002), a teaching on the *Way of the Boddhisattva* from the 8th century CE (Batchelor, 1987).

1   Pāli is an Indo-Aryan language that was indigenous to the Indian subcontinent when Buddhist scriptures were first recorded in writing around the first century BCE, and still serves as the canonical language of Buddhism. All terms here will be written in the text in Pāli, and will generally be defined on first usage.

Bibliography

Anālayo, B. (2003). *Satipaṭṭhāna: The direct path to realization.* Birmingham: Windhorse Publications.
Aurobindo, S. (2005 [1939–1940]). The life divine. Pondicherry, India: Sri Aurobindo Ashram Publication Department.

Batchelor, S. (1987). *Santideva's Bodhicaryāvatāra: A guide to the Bodhisattva's way of life*. Dharamsala: Library of Tibetan Works and Archives.

Bluck, R. (2006). *British Buddhism: Teachings, practice and development*. Oxford: Routledge.

Bodhi, B. (2011). What does mindfulness really mean? A canonical perspective. *Contemporary Buddhism, 12*(01), 19–39.

Buchanan, K. E., & Bardi, A. (2010). Acts of kindness and acts of novelty affect life satisfaction. *The Journal of Social Psychology, 150*(3), 235–237. doi:10.1080/00224540903365554

Bucknell, R. S. (1984). The Buddhist path to liberation: An analysis of the listing of stages. *Journal of the International Association of Buddhist Studies, 7*(2), 7–40.

Carter, J. R. (2005). Buddhist ethics? In W. Schweiker (Ed.), *The blackwell companion to religious ethics* (pp. 278–285). Oxford: Blackwell Publishing.

Chong, L. J. V. D. (2009). *The Sarvāstivāda doctrine of the path of spiritual progress: A study based primarily on the Abhidharma-Mahāvibhāsā-śāstra, the Abhidharmakośa-bhāsya and their Chinese and Sanskrit commentaries*, PhD, University of Hong Kong.

Coningham, R., Acharya, K., Strickland, K., Davis, C., Manuel, M., Simpson, I., . . . Sanderson, D. (in press). The earliest Buddhist shrine: Excavating the birthplace of the Buddha, Lumbini (Nepal). *Antiquity*.

Fortney, L., & Taylor, M. (2010). Meditation in medical practice: A review of the evidence and practice. *Primary Care: Clinics in Office Practice, 37*(1), 81–90.

Fredrickson, B. L., Cohn, M. A., Coffey, K. A., Pek, J., & Finkel, S. M. (2008). Open hearts build lives: Positive emotions, induced through loving-kindness meditation, build consequential personal resources. *Journal of Personality and Social Psychology, 95*(5), 1045–1062.

Goldstein, E. D. (2007). Sacred moments: Implications on well-being and stress. *Journal of Clinical Psychology, 63*(10), 1001–1019.

Hazard Jr., G. C. (1994). Law, morals, and ethics. *Southern Illinois University Law Journal, 19*, 447–458.

Johnson, N. (2000). *Barefoot Zen: The Shaolin roots of Kung Fu and Karate*. York Beach, ME: Samuel Weiser Books.

Jones, D. T. (2012). The five niyāmas as laws of nature: An assessment of modern Western interpretations of Theravāda Buddhist doctrine. *Journal of Buddhist Ethics, 19*, 545–582.

Kabat-Zinn, J. (1982). An outpatient program in behavioral medicine for chronic pain patients based on the practice of mindfulness meditation: Theoretical considerations and preliminary results. *General Hospital Psychiatry, 4*(1), 33–47.

Kabat-Zinn, J. (2003). Mindfulness-based interventions in context: Past, present, and future. *Clinical Psychology: Science and Practice, 10*(2), 144–156.

Kang, C. (2009). Buddhist and Tantric perspectives on causality and society. *Journal of Buddhist Ethics, 16*, 69–103.

Kaplan, K. H., Goldenberg, D. L., & Galvin-Nadeau, M. (1993). The impact of a meditation-based stress reduction program on fibromyalgia. *General Hospital Psychiatry, 15*(5), 284–289.

Keown, D. (2003). *A dictionary of Buddhism*. Oxford: Oxford University Press.

Keown, D. (2009). *Buddhism: A brief insight*. New York, NY: Sterling Publishing.

King, R. (1995). *Early Advaita Vedanta and Buddhism: The Mahayana context of the Gaudapadiya-Karika*. New York, NY: SUNY Press.

King, R. (1999). *Orientalism and religion: Post-colonial theory, India and "The Mystic East"*. London: Routledge.

Lin, W.-F., Mack, D., Enright, R. D., Krahn, D., & Baskin, T. W. (2004). Effects of forgiveness therapy on anger, mood, and vulnerability to substance use among inpatient substance-dependent clients. *Journal of Consulting and Clinical Psychology, 72*(6), 1114–1121.

Lomas, T., Cartwright, T., Edginton, T., & Ridge, D. (2013). 'I was so done in that I just recognized it very plainly, "You need to do something"': Men's narratives of struggle, distress
and turning to meditation. *Health, 17*(2), 191–208.

Lomas, T., Cartwright, T., Edginton, T., & Ridge, D. (2014a). Engagement with meditation as
a positive health trajectory: Divergent narratives of progress in male meditators. *Psychology
and Health, 29*(2), 218–236.

Lomas, T., Cartwright, T., Edginton, T., & Ridge, D. (2014b). A religion of wellbeing?: The
appeal of Buddhism to men in London, UK. *Psychology of Religion and Spirituality 6*(3),
198–207. doi:10.1037/a0036420

Maharaj, A. (2013). Yogic mindfulness: Hariharānanda Āraṇya's quasi-Buddhistic interpretation of smṛti in Patañjali's yogasūtra. *Journal of Indian Philosophy, 41*(1), 57–78.

Maslow, A. H. (1943). A theory of human motivation. *Psychological Review, 50*(4), 370–396.

McCown, D., Reibel, D., & Micozzi, M. (2010). Defining mindfulness for the moment. In
D. McCown, D. Reibel, & M. S. Micozzi (Eds.), *Teaching mindfulness* (pp. 59–87). New
York, NY: Springer.

McIntosh, E. M. (2007). *Noticing and appreciating the sunny side of life: Exploration of a novel
gratitude intervention that utilizes mindfulness techniques.* Ann Arbor, MI: ProQuest.

Meiklejohn, J., Phillips, C., Freedman, M. L., Griffin, M. L., Biegel, G., Roach, A., ... Soloway,
G. (2012). Integrating mindfulness training into K-12 education: Fostering the resilience
of teachers and students. *Mindfulness, 3*(4), 291–307.

Miller, J. J., Fletcher, K., & Kabat-Zinn, J. (1995). Three-year follow-up and clinical implications of a mindfulness meditation-based stress reduction intervention in the treatment of
anxiety disorders. *General Hospital Psychiatry, 17*(3), 192–200.

Müller, F. M. (1881). *The Dhammapada sacred books of the East* (Vol. X, F. M. Müller, Trans.).
Oxford: Clarendon Press.

Napoli, M., Krech, P. R., & Holley, L. C. (2005). Mindfulness training for elementary school
students: The attention academy. *Journal of Applied School Psychology, 21*, 99–125.

Nikaya, S. (2008). Right figures of speech. In R. Flores (Ed.), *Buddhist scriptures as literature:
Sacred rhetoric and the uses of theory* (pp. 163–178). Albany, NY: State University of New
York Press.

Peacock, J. (2014). Sati or mindfulness? Bridging the divide. In M. Mazzano (Ed.), *After
mindfulness: New perspectives on psychology and meditation* (pp. 3–22). Basingstoke: Palgrave
Macmillan.

Rao, K. R. (2007). Purposeful living. In N. K. Shastree, B. R. Dugar, J. P. N. Mishra & A. K.
Dhar (Eds.), *Value management in professions: Present scenario, future strategies* (pp. 63–71).
New Delhi: Ashok Kumar Mittal.

Recine, A. C., Werner, J. S., & Recine, L. (2009). Health promotion through forgiveness
interventions. *Journal of Holistic Nursing, 27*(2), 115–123.

Ryff, C. D. (1989). Happiness is everything, or is it? Explorations on the meaning of psychological well-being. *Journal of Personality and Social Psychology, 57*(6), 1069–1081.

Sangharakshita, U. (1997). *The rainbow road.* Glasgow: Windhorse Publications.

Sangharakshita, U. (1998). *Know your mind: The psychological dimensions of ethics in Buddhism.*
Birmingham: Windhorse Publications.

Sangharakshita, U. (2003). *Living with awareness: A guide to the Satipatthana Sutta.* Birmingham:
Windhorse Publications.

Sangharakshita, U., & Subhuti, D. (2013). *Seven papers* (2nd edition). London: Triratna Buddhist Community.

Śāntideva. (2002). *The Bodhicaryāvatāra: A guide to the Buddhist path to awakening* (K. Crosby &
A. Skilton, Trans.). Birmingham: Windhorse Publications.

Schwartz, S. H. (1999). A theory of cultural values and some implications for work. *Applied
Psychology, 48*(1), 23–47.

Seligman, M. E. P. (2002). *Authentic happiness* New York, NY: Free Press.

Shapiro, D. H. (1994). Examining the content and context of meditation: A challenge for psychology in the areas of stress management, psychotherapy, and religion/values. *Journal of Humanistic Psychology, 34*(4), 101–135.

Soeng, M. (2006). The art of not deceiving yourself. In D. K. Nauriyal, M. S. Drummond & Y. B. Lal (Eds.), *Buddhist thought and applied psychological research: Transcending the boundaries* (pp. 302–313). Oxford: Routledge.

Stanley, E. A., Schaldach, J. M., Kiyonaga, A., & Jha, A. P. (2011). Mindfulness-based Mind Fitness Training: A case study of a high-stress predeployment military cohort. *Cognitive and Behavioral Practice, 18*(4), 566–576.

Stanley, S. (2012). Intimate distances: William James' introspection, Buddhist mindfulness, and experiential inquiry. *New Ideas in Psychology, 30*(2), 201–211.

Subhuti, D. (1994). *Sangharakshita: A new voice in the Buddhist tradition.* Glasgow: Windhorse Publications.

Sundararajan, L. (2005). Happiness donut: A Confucian critique of positive psychology. *Journal of Theoretical and Philosophical Psychology, 25*(1), 35–60.

Swinburne, R. (1989). *Responsibility and atonement.* Oxford: Oxford University Press.

Taylor, C. (1989). *Sources of the self: The making of the modern identity.* Cambridge: Harvard University Press.

Teasdale, J. D., Segal, Z. V., Williams, J. M. G., Ridgeway, V. A., Soulsby, J. M., & Lau, M. A. (2000). Prevention of relapse/recurrence in major depression by mindfulness-based cognitive therapy. *Journal of Consulting and Clinical Psychology, 68*(4), 615–623.

Thera, S. (1941). *The way of mindfulness: The Satipatthana Sutta and its commentary.* Asgiriya, Kandy: Saccanubodia Samiti.

Thrangu, K. (1993). *The practice of tranquility and insight: A guide to Tibetan Buddhist meditation* (R. Roberts, Trans.). Boston, MA: Shambhala Publishing.

Wilber, K. (1995). *Sex, ecology, spirituality: The spirit of evolution.* Boston, MA: Shambhala Publications.

Wilber, K., Engler, J., Brown, D. P., & Chirban, J. (1986). *Transformations of consciousness: Conventional and contemplative perspectives on development.* Boston, MA: New Science Library.

Williams, J. M. G., & Kabat-Zinn, J. (2011). Mindfulness: Diverse perspectives on its meaning, origins, and multiple applications at the intersection of science and dharma. *Contemporary Buddhism, 12*(01), 1–18.

17

MINDFULNESS AND WELLBEING

Towards a unified operational approach

Edo Shonin, William Van Gordon,
and Mark D. Griffiths

> Upon a heap of rubbish in the road-side ditch blooms a lotus, fragrant and
> pleasing. Even so, on the rubbish heap of blinded mortals the disciple of the
> Supremely Enlightened One shines in resplendent wisdom.
>
> (Buddha, as cited in Buddharakkhita, 1986, p. 23
> [*Dhammapada*, pp. 4, 58–59])

Introduction

According to a nationally representative survey commissioned by the Mental Health
Foundation (MHF), 80% of British adults believe that contemporary pressured life-
styles cause stress and/or illness and that their health could be improved by slowing
down and learning to be more aware of the present moment (MHF, 2010). A separate
national survey commissioned by the MHF in the same report found that 72% of
general practitioners in the United Kingdom believe that their patients could derive
health benefits by practising mindfulness meditation (MHF, 2010). Such beliefs are
likely to have been influenced by findings from the increasing number of empirical
studies exploring the psychological and physical health benefits of mindfulness practice.
Indeed, clinically focussed empirical enquiry represents the primary focus of mindfulness research (Shonin, Van Gordon, & Griffiths, 2015), and a specific mindfulness-based
intervention (MBI) known as mindfulness-based cognitive therapy (Segal, Williams, &
Teasdale, 2002) is now advocated by both the UK National Institute for Health and
Care Excellence (NICE) and the American Psychiatric Association (APA) for the
treatment of recurrent depression in adults (APA, 2010; NICE, 2009).

Despite, or perhaps because of, the growing popularity of mindfulness amongst
healthcare stakeholders, an increasing number of researchers, clinicians, and Buddhist teachers/scholars have raised concerns over the rapidity at which Buddhist
principles are being integrated into clinically focussed mindfulness interventions

(e.g., Carrette & King, 2005; Howells, Tennant, Day, & Elmer, 2010; McWilliams, 2011, 2014; Rosch, 2007; Shonin, Van Gordon, & Griffiths, 2014a; Singh, Lancioni, Winton, Karazsi, & Singh, 2014; Van Gordon, Shonin, Sumich, Sundin, & Griffiths, 2014a). One of the primary concerns raised by such authors is that mindfulness was originally practised within the context of spiritual development, in which unconditional wellbeing (i.e., the complete liberation from suffering) was the ultimate goal, and where principles such as ethical awareness, compassionate outlook, and right intention underlay and supported the mindfulness practitioner's development (see Shonin et al., 2014a). This is obviously different than the use of mindfulness in most contemporary MBIs where emphasis is placed more on relieving psychological and/or somatic distress.

This chapter briefly explicates a traditional Buddhist construction of mindfulness and then goes on to (i) discuss how traditional Buddhist depictions of mindfulness differ from contemporary psychological interpretations, and (ii) propose a model and definition of mindfulness that, whilst still applicable to secular mindfulness interventional approaches, is more congruent with the traditional Buddhist understanding.

Mindfulness in Buddhism

Mindfulness is the commonly accepted English translation of the Pāli word *sati* and the Sanskrit word *smrti*. Based on their literal meaning, the terms *sati* and *smrti* have previously been defined as the process of 'remembering' or 'recollecting' past events (see, for example, Gethin's [2011] review of mindfulness definitions). However, from the Buddhist perspective, such translations are unsatisfactory and overlook the fact that both the Sanskrit root *'smr'* and the Pāli *'sati'* can also denote "intense thought" (Har, 1999), "mental activity" (Rhys Davids, 1881), or "intense cognition" (Shonin et al., 2014a). Therefore, the most widely accepted interpretations of *sati* and *smrti* (and therefore mindfulness) are that these terms imply the 'full retention of mind' or 'full awareness of mind' (and therefore mind objects) in the present moment (i.e., rather than the recollection of previous events).

In its current form, Buddhism comprises a diverse range of different practice traditions and there exist slight (and in some cases major) differences in how these traditions interpret and practise the Buddha's teachings. Consequently, there are numerous constructions and interpretations of mindfulness within the wider collection of traditional and contemporary Buddhist works. However, the authenticity of the Buddha's teachings on mindfulness as recorded in the Pāli Canon (the original collection of Buddhist scriptures comprising three categories or 'baskets' [Pāli: *pitaka*] of teachings covering (i) discipline *[Vinaya Pitaka]*, (ii) discourses on spiritual practice *[Sutta Pitaka]*, and (iii) philosophy/metaphysics *[Abhidhamma Pitaka]*) is accepted by all Buddhist traditions, and the Pāli Canon serves as an authoritative source for anybody wishing to understand the principles and characteristics of mindfulness as embodied by the Buddhist model.

Although there are numerous references to mindfulness throughout the Buddhist Pāli Canon, arguably the most important discourses include the *Ānāpānasati Sutta*

(Majjhima Nikāya [MN] 118), *Satipaṭṭhāna Sutta* (MN 10), *Mahasatipaṭṭhāna Sutta* (Dīgha Nikāya [DN] 22), and *Kāyagatāsati Sutta* (MN 119). The *Ānāpānasati Sutta* (literally the discourse on mindfulness of breathing in and out) outlines a meditative technique by which the breath is used to 'tie the mind' to the present moment whilst awareness is directed, in turn, to 16 different meditative focus points (Shonin et al., 2014a). These 16 focus points occur in groups of four (i.e., tetrads) and each tetrad corresponds to one of the following four frames of reference: (i) body, (ii) feelings, (iii) mind, and (iv) phenomena (or mind-objects).

As documented in the *Ānāpānasati Sutta,* meditatively observing the breath whilst bringing awareness to each of these frames of reference was taught by the Buddha as a means of cultivating the *Four Establishments of Mindfulness.* Understanding and cultivating the *Four Establishments of Mindfulness* (which likewise correspond to the four reference frames of body, feelings, mind, and phenomena) are the subjects of the *Satipaṭṭhāna Sutta* (literally the discourse on the establishment of mindfulness) and the *Mahasatipaṭṭhāna Sutta* (literally the great discourse on the establishment of mindfulness). Having followed the instructions recorded in the *Ānāpānasati Sutta* of how to use the breath as an attentional referent, the *Satipaṭṭhāna Sutta* and *Mahasatipaṭṭhāna Sutta* provide in-depth instructions on the intricacies of mindfulness practice and the process by which mindfulness – when correctly practised – fulfils the requirements for cultivating the *Seven Enlightenment Factors* that lead to total knowledge and release:

> And how, Bhikkhus [monks], do the Four Foundations [i.e., Establishments] of Mindfulness, developed and cultivated, fulfil the Seven Enlightenment Factors? Bhikkhus, on whatever occasion a bhikkhu abides contemplating the body as a body, ardent, fully aware, and mindful, having put away covetousness and grief for the world – on that occasion unremitting mindfulness is established in him. On whatever occasion unremitting mindfulness is established in a bhikkhu – on that occasion the mindfulness enlightenment factor [the first of the Seven Factors of Enlightenment] is aroused in him, and he develops it, and by development, it comes to fulfilment in him.
>
> *(Nanamoli & Bodhi, 2009, p. 485; MN 118)*

In terms of their context within the wider body of teachings expounded by the Buddha, the aforementioned discourses on mindfulness comprise one aspect of the *Noble Eightfold Path* to enlightenment. The *Noble Eightfold Path* is the path referred to by the Buddha in the first (and arguably the most important) teaching that he gave after attaining enlightenment. The first teaching given by the Buddha is known as the *Discourse That Sets the Wheel of Dharma in Motion* (*Dhammacakkappavattana Sutta,* Saṃyutta Nikāya, 56:11) and it was also during this teaching that the Buddha expounded the *Four Noble Truths.* In their condensed form, the *Four Noble Truths* are that (i) suffering exists, (ii) there is a cause to suffering, (iii) there is cessation of suffering (i.e., liberation), and (iv) there is a path that leads to the cessation of suffering. The *Noble Eightfold Path,* of which 'right mindfulness' constitutes the seventh aspect, is the path referred to in the last of the *Four Noble Truths* outlined above (i.e., that there is a path that leads to the cessation of suffering).

Thus, within the overall collection of the Buddhist teachings, mindfulness comprises part of the path that leads to the cessation of suffering. The cessation of suffering, which in Buddhism is basically what is implied by the term 'liberation', is the ultimate goal of the Buddhist path and is a state believed to be characterised by qualities or capabilities such as (i) omniscience, (ii) deathlessness, (iii) dwelling in emptiness, (iv) unconditional blissful abiding, (v) freedom to take rebirth in any realm according to the needs of beings, (vi) great compassion, and (vii) command over animate and inanimate phenomena (Van Gordon, Shonin, & Griffiths, 2015).

As indicated by the above description of the ultimate goal of mindfulness and Buddhist practice, the Buddhist delineation of wellbeing and happiness is one that stops nothing short of total spiritual liberation. Any other form of wellbeing, such as the wellbeing associated with material gain, favourable renown, good health, and other transitory circumstances, is considered by Buddhism to expose individuals to circumstances where it is easy to succumb to attachment – the primary cause of suffering referred to in the second of the above-mentioned *Four Noble Truths* (Van Gordon et al., 2015). Undertaking mindfulness (and other Buddhist practices) with the firm objective to attain spiritual liberation (and of helping others to do the same) is deemed in Buddhism to be a prerequisite for effective spiritual development and is referred to as *right intention* (Van Gordon et al., 2014a).

Right intention is the second aspect of the *Noble Eightfold Path* and the present authors have made a point of referring to it earlier in order to highlight a key principle of the *Noble Eightfold Path* (and of Buddhist practice more generally). As explained by the Buddha in the *Mahācattārisaka Sutta* (*The Great Forty Sutta;* MN 117), although the *Noble Eightfold Path* comprises eight individual elements (of right view, right intention, right speech, right action, right livelihood, right effort, right mindfulness, and right concentration), these elements should be practised and embodied as a single path. Indeed, just like the individual strands of a rope that have limited utility on their own but have strength and functionality when woven together, Buddhism asserts that spiritual practice is most effective when all of the individual aspects of the path are implemented in unison (Van Gordon et al., 2015). In other words, all authentic Buddhist teachings take their place as part of a cohesive whole, and isolating and/or exclusively focussing on just one minuscule facet of the Buddhist path – such as mindfulness – will inevitably yield a result that falls short of the intended goal of enduring unconditional wellbeing (i.e., wellbeing that is not reliant upon external factors and that does not abate with time).

Differences between contemporary and traditional perspectives of mindfulness

Compared to teaching mindfulness in the traditional Buddhist setting, there are obviously a range of additional factors that need to be considered when attempting to introduce and teach mindfulness to clinical populations. Of course, this is not to say that there is inherently something wrong with introducing individuals to the mindfulness teachings in a manner and context fundamentally different than that employed for over 2,500 years by Buddhist practitioners and teachers. However, it does mean that there is a risk of aspects traditionally deemed to be prerequisites for effective mindfulness practice being overlooked or underrepresented in contemporary mindfulness interventional approaches. Consequently, the remainder of this section discusses (i) what the present authors deem to be the key differences between the manner in which mindfulness is constructed, practised, and taught within Buddhist versus clinical settings, and (ii) the implications of these differences for mindfulness research and practice.

1   *Differences relating to intention for practising mindfulness:* In general, participants of MBIs choose or are referred to receive mindfulness training for the primary purposes of alleviating psychological/somatic distress, or, as is the case in certain occupation-focussed MBIs, for improving work effectiveness and professional skills more generally (Van Gordon, Shonin, Zangeneh, & Griffiths, 2014b). As already referred to above (see discussion on 'right intention'), this is fundamentally different than the Buddhist approach where mindfulness is undertaken with the intention of attaining liberation from suffering and helping others to achieve the same. The right intention required for effective mindfulness practice has been described by Buddhist teachers in the following manner:

> "It is because people don't have the right intention that their spiritual practice fails to bear fruit. Some people sit in meditation for hours each day and/or they diligently study the teachings for many decades. But right intention is something that comes from within – it can be learned but it is actually quite intuitive. You either really want to evolve spiritually or you don't. You're either willing to subdue your ego or you're not. It is quite simple. In a nutshell, right intention means that due to knowing all phenomena are impermanent and our time here is limited, we are ready to work hard in order to leave suffering behind" (Shonin & Van Gordon, 2014a).

2   *Differences relating to when to practise mindfulness:* Although certain MBIs (e.g., MBSR and MBCT) have been shown to be effective in the treatment of various different health conditions, there is a tendency for MBIs to be developed for the purposes of treating specific mental and/or somatic illnesses or complaints (e.g., stress, depression, eating disorders, addiction disorders, childbirth- and parenting-related issues, etc.). Consequently, many of the mindfulness exercises utilised in MBIs are specifically focussed on cultivating mindfulness in response to specific symptoms (e.g., somatic pain, distressing emotions, mental craving, etc.) and/or whilst engaging in specific behaviours (e.g., eating, gambling, work, etc.). This represents a departure from the Buddhist approach where far fewer divisions are made in terms of the different types of situations that warrant the spiritual practitioner to engage a mindful attention set. Indeed, as explained in the *Ānāpānasati Sutta,* Buddhism teaches that there is basically

just one type of mindfulness to be practised, which should be maintained at all times and in whatever situation a person finds themselves:

> "Again, bhikkhus, a bhikkhu is one who acts in full awareness when going forward and returning; who acts in full awareness when looking ahead and looking away; who acts in full awareness when flexing and extending his limbs; . . . who acts in full awareness when eating, drinking, consuming food, and tasting; who acts in full awareness when defecating and urinating; who acts in full awareness when walking, standing, sitting, falling asleep, waking up, talking, and keeping silent" (Nanamoli & Bodhi, 2009, p. 147; MN 10).

3 *Differences in the way importance is assigned to mindfulness practice:* Buddhism teaches that the spiritual practitioner should strive to ensure that they are continuously aware of the present moment and should regard mindfulness practice not as an optional endeavour, but as a matter of life or death (Shonin et al., 2014a). However, at the same time as educating others in the principles and importance of mindfulness, the Buddha taught that spiritual practitioners should ensure that they do not become attached to their practice:

> "He who clings to nothing of the past, present and future, who has no attachment and holds on to nothing – him do I call a holy man" (*Dhammapada,* p. 26, p. 421; Buddharakkhita, 1986, p. 165).

Remaining unattached to spiritual practice relates closely to the need to cultivate a 'right view' (the first aspect of the *Noble Eightfold Path*), which basically refers to the ability to perceive and apprehend the absolute or 'empty' nature of reality. By realising that phenomena originate in dependence upon each other and that they (therefore) lack intrinsic existence, Buddhism asserts that spiritual practitioners avoid the trap of perceiving the world in dualistic terms (Dalai Lama & Berzin, 1997). In the context of mindfulness practice, a dualistic perception means to regard mindfulness as a 'subject' that is practised by an 'object' (i.e., the self). Perceiving mindfulness practice in 'subject-object' terms creates a separation between the practitioner and the present moment that they are supposed to be observing. This is problematic from the Buddhist perspective where relating to mindfulness in a dualistic manner is understood to distance the spiritual aspirant from the realisation that they are deeply interconnected with, and inseparable from, the 'here and now' (Shonin & Van Gordon, 2014b). As a result of teaching mindfulness in isolation of core Buddhist principles such as 'right view' and 'emptiness', there is inevitably a greater tendency in MBIs for participants to become attached to the need to regard the present moment (and mindfulness practice) as something separate from themselves. This scenario has previously been referred to as the difference between 'being aware of the present moment' (i.e., the approach advocated in MBIs) and the arguably more spiritually profound position advocated by Buddhism of simply 'being in the present moment' (Shonin & Van Gordon, 2014b).

4 *Differences relating to mindfulness teacher competencies:* Some concerns have been raised by scholars in the academic literature regarding the credibility and competence of MBI program instructors (e.g., Shonin et al., 2014a, Van Gordon et al., 2014a). These concerns principally relate to the fact that – in some cases – MBI instructors can have as little as 12 months' mindfulness practice and teaching experience following completion of a single 8-week course (MHF, 2010). Although efforts are underway to disseminate best-practice and assessment guidelines for MBI teachers (see Crane et al., 2013), the relatively short training period followed by some MBI instructors constitutes a major departure from traditional Buddhist values and conventions concerning mindfulness teaching (Shonin et al., 2014a).

Within Buddhism, meditation teachers typically train for many decades before they are deemed to have acquired the necessary experience for effectively instructing and guiding others in meditation practice (Van Gordon et al., 2014a). However, it is important to emphasise that rather than years spent in training or being able to claim receipt of a recognised Buddhist practice lineage, arguably the most important factor that qualifies an individual to teach Buddhism and/or meditation is the extent to which they have accumulated authentic spiritual realisation:

> "If a person has genuine spiritual realisation, they are authorised to transmit the spiritual teachings. All titles, held-lineages, endorsements, acclamations, life accomplishments, life mistakes, and years spent in training are irrelevant. . . . If a person is without genuine spiritual realisation, they have no such authority. All titles, held-lineages, endorsements, acclamations, life accomplishments, life mistakes, and years spent in training are irrelevant. . . . Ultimately, true authorisation to transmit the spiritual teachings comes from awaking to the timeless truth of emptiness. It seems that some form of spiritual guide is required to effectuate this awakening" (Shonin & Van Gordon, 2013).

According to the *Canki Sutta* (MN 95), the Buddha explained that in order to be considered authentic, a meditation and/or Dharma teacher's actions and behaviour must not in any way be influenced by greed, hatred, or delusion (Nanamoli & Bodhi, 2009). This also appears to be the position of the 15th-century Tibetan Buddhist saint Tsong-kha-pa, who used words such as 'thoroughly pacified', 'serene', and 'disciplined' to describe the qualities of a suitable meditation instructor (Tsong-Kha-pa, 2004). Thus, in relation to contemporary interventional mindfulness approaches, it is argued that Buddhism places much greater importance on the experience and effectiveness of the meditation teacher – particularly in terms of the extent to which they can impart an embodied authentic transmission of the mindfulness teachings.

5 *Differences relating to the use of judgement and discernment:* The following definition of mindfulness, formulated and introduced by Kabat-Zinn, is arguably the most commonly employed definition of mindfulness in the scientific literature.

He defines mindfulness as "paying attention in a particular way: on purpose, in the present moment, and non-judgmentally" (1994, p. 4). The term 'non-judgemental' was probably employed in this definition in order to refer to the need for the mindfulness practitioner to accept (i.e., rather than reject or ignore) present-moment experiences. However, it has been previously argued that 'non-judgemental' could also be interpreted as meaning that mindfulness requires an attitude of indifference or even unresponsiveness to life situations and events (Shonin et al., 2014a). Consequently, from the Buddhist perspective, assigning non-judgemental awareness as a key facet of mindfulness is unsatisfactory because it appears to contradict core Buddhist principles relating to the need for the spiritual practitioner to apply discernment during all of their interactions (i.e., in order to ensure that they respond with compassion, wisdom, and ethical awareness).

6   *Differences in interpreting the meaning of concentration and insight meditation:* As referred to above, 'right mindfulness' (Pāli: *sammā-sati*), which appears as the seventh aspect of the *Noble Eightfold Path,* cannot be separated from, and is essential to the maintenance of, each of the other aspects of the *Noble Eightfold Path.* Nevertheless, the fact that in the *Noble Eightfold Path* mindfulness appears immediately prior to 'right concentration' (Pāli: *sammā-samādhi*) is significant because it implies that mindfulness is actually distinct from meditative concentration. Indeed, the Buddhist teachings explain that meditative concentration is basically the process of resting awareness on a given meditative object (e.g., the breath, a visualisation, or even the mind or present moment more generally) with the intention of effectively calming and introducing tranquillity into the mind (Shonin et al., 2014a).

However, the Buddhist teachings explain that because the tranquillity associated with meditative concentration can be so blissful and inviting, it can actually trigger a loss of meditative concentration (Dalai Lama & Berzin, 1997). Therefore, the purpose of mindfulness is essentially to watch over the concentrating mind and make attentional adjustments as required in order to ensure that meditative concentration remains at its optimum. The reason why Buddhism asserts that this is important is because meditative concentration is a prerequisite for the development of insight/wisdom and what is known as 'right view' (Pāli: *sammā-ditthi*) (Khyentse, 2007). Spiritual wisdom or right view is basically the ultimate goal of Buddhist meditation because unlike the bliss associated with meditative concentration that provides only temporary relief from *Dukkha* (the Buddhist and Pāli equivalent of the terms suffering and unsatisfactoriness), spiritual wisdom (Pāli: *paññā*) severs the causes of suffering at their roots (Shonin et al., 2014a).

Thus, mindfulness effectively regulates the breadth and intensity of meditative concentration and therefore plays a vital role in the cultivation of meditative insight. However, according to the Buddhist model and for the reasons already outlined, mindfulness itself is distinct from meditative concentration as well as the meditative insight that it yields. Consistent with the aforementioned literal meaning of the Pāli word *sati,* mindfulness is the process of 'remembering' to keep concentration placed in and on the present moment (or another meditative object) such that there is a constant arising and extraction of spiritual wisdom as the meditator attends with awareness to their daily duties and activities. This represents a fundamental departure from the way in which mindfulness is conceptualised in the contemporary scientific literature where, with differing degrees of frequency, mindfulness has been (incorrectly) described as either being a form of (i) concentrative meditation, (ii) insight meditation (also known as Vipassana mediation – vipassana translates from the Pāli as clear seeing or superior seeing), or (iii) both concentrative and insight meditation (see Shonin et al., 2014a).

7   *Differences relating to the integration of death awareness:* Each of the (previously referred to) principle Buddhist suttas on mindfulness emphasise the importance of cultivating mindfulness of death and impermanence. For example, the *Satipaṭṭhāna Sutta, Mahasatipaṭṭhāna Sutta,* and *Kāyagatāsati Sutta* each contain the *Nine Charnel Ground Contemplations* (contemplations involving seeing oneself as a decaying corpse – an inevitable outcome for the body), and the 13th exercise of the *Ānāpānasati Sutta* is specifically concerned with cultivating an awareness of impermanence. Impermanence is known in Buddhism as a 'mark of existence' and Buddhism asserts that without exception, phenomena are subject to dissolution (Khyentse, 2007). The Buddha taught that by infusing their spiritual and meditative practice with the realisation that they and everything around them are transient occurrences, individuals can begin to intuit the ultimate nature of reality and weaken their attachment to the belief in an inherently existing self (Shonin, Van Gordon, & Griffiths, 2013). It is therefore argued that the vital role that impermanence and death awareness play in supporting and optimising mindful awareness is an additional factor that has been overlooked in the majority of clinically focussed MBIs.

An alternative model and definition of mindfulness

In this section, an alternative model of mindfulness is explicated that, whilst still appropriate for use in public healthcare contexts, is intended to lessen some of the disconnect between traditional Buddhist and contemporary-secular mindfulness interpretations. However, given that mindfulness is studied and utilised by individuals from a broad range of backgrounds (e.g., Buddhist teachers, Buddhist practitioners, clinicians, health service providers and practitioners, academics, etc.), it is unlikely that there will ever be a definition and model of mindfulness that meets with universal acceptance. Therefore, readers should understand that the definition and discussion that follows is provided in the vein of attempting to advance understanding and further debate concerning mindfulness and to work alongside (i.e., rather than substitute) existent theoretical and operational models.

The present authors recently proposed that mindfulness can be defined as "the process of engaging a full, direct, and active awareness of experienced phenomena that is (i) spiritual in aspect and (ii) maintained from one moment to the next" (Shonin et al., 2014b, p.900). The principles and meaning of the key aspects of the proposed definition can be understood as follows:

1   *Full awareness* refers to the fact that mindfulness is all-embracing and requires the individual to be accepting of all physiological and psychological experiences. This is the passive aspect of mindfulness. However, implicit within the meaning of this term is that the mindfulness practitioner's awareness should extend beyond their immediate environment and keep in mind the fact that phenomena are (i) impermanent, (ii) absent of intrinsic existence, and (iii) a cause of suffering if they become the object of attachment. Thus, the term 'full awareness' also accounts for the encompassing aspect of mindfulness.

2   *Direct awareness* means that there should not be a gap or delay between the experiencing of phenomena and awareness of this experience. In other words, mindfulness is not concerned with the remembering of past events, but involves being intricately aware – in real time – of all psychological and somatic experience. Direct awareness also implies that there should not be any separation between the individual and the object or objects of one's mindful attention. This is the insight aspect of mindfulness.

3   *Active awareness* refers to the fact that mindfulness requires and facilitates the capacity to respond with skill, compassion, and discernment in any given situation. In other words, mindfulness not only involves observing the present moment, but it requires an active participation in it. Active awareness is the compassionate and ethical aspect of mindfulness.

4   *Experienced phenomena* means that mindfulness does not require excessive effort or the need to 'find' things to be mindful of. It means that 'experience now' is taken as the object of mindful awareness. This includes awareness of physiological, psychological, and environmental phenomena. This is the effortless or spontaneous aspect of mindfulness.

5   *Spiritual in aspect* refers to the traditional Buddhist meditation literature where mindfulness is contextualised as a spiritual (but not necessarily a religious) practice. It also refers to the fact that (i) mindfulness involves one aspect of consciousness observing another aspect of consciousness, and (ii) mindfulness was traditionally intended to facilitate a realisation of a person's full human potential and capacity for unconditional wellbeing. This is the transpersonal aspect of mindfulness.

6   *Maintained from one moment to the next* means that the mindfulness practitioner should try to maintain an unbroken flow of present-moment awareness throughout the day. The phrase *maintained from one moment to the next* is used in order to distinguish mindfulness from a practice that is only undertaken at certain times of day or during formal seated meditation practice. This is the enduring aspect of mindfulness.

Whilst it is unlikely that the above definition of mindfulness will meet with unanimous approval, the present authors believe that compared to existent deline-ations of mindfulness employed in the academic literature, it more accurately cap-tures and embodies the Buddhist interpretation. It is probably fair to say this newer definition also accurately captures the meaning of mindfulness as it is utilised in what have been termed 'second generation' MBIs. The introduction and early stage empirical evaluation of second-generation MBIs – such as the 8-week secular intervention Meditation Awareness Training (MAT; Van Gordon et al., 2014a) – has occurred in recent years as a remedy to the apparent deficiency of spiritual and Buddhist foundations in the first generation of MBIs. According to Singh et al. (2014), one of the primary purposes and achievements of first-generation MBIs (such as mindfulness-based stress reduction [Kabat-Zinn, 1990] and mindfulness-based cognitive therapy [Segal et al., 2002]) was to gain acceptance of the mindful-ness construct within Western clinical and scientific domains. However, given the rapidity at which mindfulness has been integrated into Western research and public healthcare settings, it was perhaps inevitable that questions would arise regarding the extent to which this pioneering work accurately embodies the Buddhist con-struction of mindfulness, and that alternative formulations and methods of practis-ing mindfulness would be proposed accordingly.

Conclusions

Scientific and public interest in the applications of mindfulness – particularly as a means of improving psychological wellbeing and mental health – has increased sig-nificantly over the last decade (Shonin et al., 2014a). However, as has been repeat-edly emphasised in this chapter, the traditional Buddhist teachings explicate that mindfulness can only remain intact where it enters into a process of cross-fertili-sation with various other meditative and spiritual practice agents (e.g., right view, right intention, right concentration, etc.). Therefore, in Westernised interventional approaches that treat mindfulness as a stand-alone spiritual or non-spiritual tech-nique, it is questionable whether such interventions are in fact still working with and teaching a method that can be accurately described as 'mindfulness' in the traditional sense.

The intention of Western science to operationalise mindfulness as a means of alleviating human suffering is admirable. However, the rapidity at which this pro-cess is unfolding and the fact that in most instances mindfulness is taught to effectu-ate what (relative to the Buddhist approach) might be seen as short-term reductions in psychological/somatic pain, mean that concerns and compatibility issues are inevitably going to arise. Indeed, from the traditional Buddhist perspective, unless an intervention targets suffering at its causes and therefore helps the individual to advance along the path towards enduring unconditional wellbeing (i.e., the com-plete and irreversible cessation of suffering), its utility becomes questionable (Van Gordon et al., 2015).

As discussed above, some academic scientists and Buddhist scholars have alleged or implied that contemporary Western psychological constructions of mindfulness reflect a superficial account of this 2,500-year-old contemplative practice. Consequently, the mindfulness research agenda appears to be undergoing a slight shift in direction, with a greater number of researchers seeking to formulate and empirically evaluate mindfulness models and interventions that more closely align with the traditional Buddhist approach. However, perhaps of greater significance, concerns over the authenticity of Western models of mindfulness may actually prompt the scientific and medical community to raise expectations in terms of the conceivable outcomes of psychological interventions. What is being referred to here is a scenario whereby empirical investigations into mindfulness focus on the extent to which it fosters wellbeing according to the intended meaning and implications of the term 'wellbeing' within Eastern contemplative systems. This is different than the current tendency to assess the utility of mindfulness according to Western parameters of wellbeing and suffering. More specifically, if a better understanding of the Buddhist model of wellbeing, suffering, and meditative/spiritual practice can make the total liberation of suffering (i.e., enlightenment) a more credible and acceptable notion within Western science, then the introduction of mindfulness to the West can undoubtedly be regarded as a success.

Bibliography

American Psychiatric Association. (2010). *American Psychiatric Association practice guideline for the treatment of patients with major depressive disorder* (3rd edition). Arlington, VA: American Psychiatric Publishing.

Buddharakkhita (Trans.) (1986). *Dhammapada: A practical guide to right living.* Bangalore: Maha Bodhi Society.

Carrette, J., & King, R. (2005). *Selling spirituality: The silent takeover of religion.* New York, NY: Routledge.

Crane, R. S., Eames, C., Kuyken, W., Hastings, R. P., Williams, J. M. G, Bartley, T., . . . Surawy, C. (2013). Development and validation of the Mindfulness-Based Interventions – Teaching Assessment Criteria (MBI: TAC). *Assessment, 20,* 681–688.

Crane, R. S., Kuyken, W., Williams, J. M., Hastings, R. P., Cooper, L., & Fennell, M. J. (2012). Competence in teaching mindfulness-based courses: Concepts, development and assessment. *Mindfulness, 3,* 76–84.

Dalai Lama, & Berzin, A. (1997). *The Gelug/Kagyu tradition of mahamudra.* New York, NY: Snow Lion Publications.

Gethin, R. (2011). On some definitions of mindfulness. *Contemporary Buddhism, 12,* 263–279.

Har, D. (1999). *The Bodhisattva doctrine in the Buddhist Sanskrit literature.* Delhi, India: Motilal Banarsidass.

Howells, K., Tennant, A., Day, A., & Elmer, R. (2010). Mindfulness in forensic mental health: Does it have a role? *Mindfulness, 1,* 4–9.

Kabat-Zinn, J. (1990). *Full catastrophe living: Using the wisdom of your body and mind to face stress, pain and illness.* New York, NY: Delacourt.

Kabat-Zinn, J. (1994). *Wherever you go, there you are: Mindfulness meditation in everyday life.* New York, NY: Hyperion.

Khyentse, D. (2007). *The heart of compassion: The thirty-seven verses on the practice of a Bodhisattva.* Boston, MA: Shambhala Publications.

McWilliams, S. A. (2011). Contemplating a contemporary constructivist Buddhist psychology. *Journal of Constructivist Psychology, 24,* 268–276.

McWilliams, S. A. (2014). Foundations of mindfulness and contemplation: Traditional and contemporary perspectives. *International Journal of Mental Health and Addiction, 12,* 116–128.

Mental Health Foundation. (2010). *Mindfulness peport.* London: Author.

Nanamoli, B. (1979). *The path of purification: Visuddhi Magga.* Kandy, Sri Lanka: Buddhist Publication Society.

Nanamoli, B., & Bodhi, B. (2009). *Majjhima Nikaya: The middle length discourses of the Buddha* (4th edition, Bhikkhu Nanamoli & Bhikkhu Bodhi, Trans.). Massachusetts: Wisdom Publications.

National Institute for Health and Clinical Excellence (NICE). (2009). *Depression: Management of depression in primary and secondary care.* London: Author.

Rhys Davids, T. W. (1881). *Buddhist suttas.* Oxford: Clarendon Press.

Rosch, E. (2007). More than mindfulness: When you have a tiger by the tail, let it eat you. *Psychological Inquiry, 18,* 258–264.

Segal, Z. V., Williams, J. M., & Teasdale, J. D. (2002). *Mindfulness-based cognitive therapy for depression: A new approach to preventing relapse.* New York, NY: Guilford Press.

Shonin, E., & Van Gordon, W. (2013). *Authentic spiritual lineage.* 11 March. http://edoshonin.com/2013/03/09/73/

Shonin, E., & Van Gordon, W. (2014a). *The scientific study of Buddhism and the Noble Eightfold Path: Dividing the whole into many.* 21 June. http://edoshonin.com/2014/06/21/the-scientific-study-of-buddhism-and-the-noble-eightfold-path-dividing-the-whole-into-many/

Shonin, E., & Van Gordon, W. (2014b). Searching for the present moment. *Mindfulness, 5,* 105–107.

Shonin, E., Van Gordon, W., & Griffiths, M. D. (2013). Buddhist philosophy for the treatment of problem gambling. *Journal of Behavioural Addictions, 2,* 63–71.

Shonin, E., Van Gordon, W., & Griffiths, M. D. (2014a). The emerging role of Buddhism in clinical psychology: Toward effective integration. *Psychology of Religion and Spirituality, 6,* 123–137.

Shonin, E., Van Gordon, W., & Griffiths, M. D. (2014b) Are there risks associated with using mindfulness for the treatment of psychopathology? *Clinical Practice, 11,* 389–392.

Shonin, E., Van Gordon, W., & Griffiths, M. D. (2015). Mindfulness in psychology: A breath of fresh air? *The Psychologist: Bulletin of the British Psychological Society, 28,* 28–31.

Singh, N. N., Lancioni, G. E., Winton, A. S. W., Karazsia, B. T., & Singh, J. (2014). Mindfulness-Based Positive Behavior Support (MBPBS) for mothers of adolescents with autism spectrum disorders: Effects on adolescents' behavior and parental stress. *Mindfulness, 5*(6), 646–657. doi:10.1007/s12671–014–0321–3

Tsong-Kha-pa. (2004). *The great treatise on the stages of the path to enlightenment* (Vol. 1, J. W. Cutler, G. Newland, Eds., & The Lamrim Chenmo Translation committee, Trans.) New York, NY: Snow Lion Publications.

Van Gordon, W., Shonin, E., & Griffiths, M. D. (2015). *Mindfulness and the four noble truths.* In E. Shonin, W. Van Gordon & N. N. Singh (Eds.), *Buddhist foundations of mindfulness* (pp. 9–27). New York, NY: Springer.

Van Gordon, W., Shonin, E., Sumich, A., Sundin, E., & Griffiths, M. D. (2014a). Meditation Awareness Training (MAT) for psychological wellbeing in a sub-clinical sample of university students: A controlled pilot study. *Mindfulness, 5,* 381–391.

Van Gordon, W., Shonin, E., Zangeneh, M., & Griffiths, M. D. (2014b). Work-related mental health and job performance: Can mindfulness help? *International Journal of Mental Health and Addiction, 12,* 129–137.

PART V

Mindful therapy

18

MINDFULNESS AND PERSON-CENTRED THERAPY

Stephen Joseph, David Murphy and Tom G. Patterson

Introduction: background to P-CT

In 1940 Rogers gave a talk at the University of Minnesota, Minneapolis, entitled 'Some Newer Concepts of Psychotherapy' and in 1942 he published his first major work entitled *Counseling and Psychotherapy: Newer Concepts in Practice,* in which he presented a revised and expanded version of his 1940 lecture. This was the beginning of what became P-CT. Initially, Rogers referred to his new approach as *non-directive therapy* to describe how it was the therapist's task to follow the client's lead. At the time this was a radical departure from the then dominant therapist-directed and advising style of the interpretive approach of psychoanalysis.

Person-centred therapy soon became known for the non-directive attitude that Rogers advocated in his approach. Raskin (1947/2005), one of Rogers's colleagues, suggested that non-directivity was not a "matter of acquiring technique, but of gradually embracing the conviction that people do not have to be guided into adjustment, but can do it for themselves when accepted" (p. 346). Non-directivity has attracted a significant amount of attention in the last 10 years within the field of P-CT. Levitt (2005) suggests that "at its most basic, non-directivity implies being responsive to the client's direction. It implies that individuals have the capacity and right to direct their own therapy and lives" (p. i).

Non-directivity is a complex concept. A distinction was proposed by Grant (1990), who distinguished two forms of non-directivity: instrumental and principled. Instrumental non-directivity is a technique that is used by the therapist in order to achieve a predetermined outcome. In contrast, principled non-directivity is when the therapist has no intention other than to create a therapeutic relationship (as defined by the six necessary and sufficient conditions described below).

Principled non-directivity but not instrumental non-directivity characterises P-CT and requires the therapist to trust in the client's self-healing capacities, their right and capacity for self-direction, and as such is directly related to the therapist's ability to offer unconditional positive regard (Bozarth, 1998; Brodley, 1997). Principled non-directivity therefore is based on the *radical ontology* that the human organism is by its nature directional, socially constructive and trustworthy. Rogers (1957a, p. 201) described his understanding of human nature as being basically trustworthy and possessing the following characteristics:

> towards development, differentiation, cooperative relationships; whose life tends to move from dependence to independence; whose impulses tend naturally to harmonize into a complex and changing pattern of self-regulation; whose total character is such as to tend to preserve himself and his species, and perhaps to move towards its further evolution.

Rogers's personality theory underpins the theory of P-CT. His theory posits that the developing infant has an inherent tendency to survive, maintain and enhance itself. This core theoretical concept is referred to as the *actualizing tendency*. As such, the infant is driven to seek new experiences and to value those experiences that enhance the organism. This is referred to as the *organismic valuing process* (OVP). The human infant is dependent on care givers for the satisfaction of their basic need for self-direction consistent with the OVP.

As development continues, parts of total experience of the organism are differentiated and the infant begins to develop a *self-concept*. With the emergence of the differentiated self-concept the infant learns the need for positive regard that becomes a potent need in its own right and is now separable from the OVP.

When the positive regard perceived by the child is consistent with their OVP, personality development is such that the child's unique potentialities are expressed. In this instance the child continues to trust in their organismic valuing. However, sometimes the OVP is at cross purposes with the introjected values of the self-concept, resulting in frustration in the need for self-direction.

Psychological maladjustment results when there is inconsistency or incongruence between the self-concept and the OVP (Rogers, 1951, 1959). Greater incongruence leads to greater psychological tension; and the greater the tension, the greater the psychological distress and dysfunction that results (Joseph & Worsley, 2005).

In P-CT Rogers (1957b) suggested that there are six necessary and sufficient conditions that when present will lead to constructive personality change. Three of these conditions are referred to as the core conditions. The core conditions that lead to change are that the therapist must experience unconditional positive regard, empathy and congruence. If the client perceives these attitudes within the therapist, it enables them to once again learn to trust their OVP. As clients grow, the values of others that have been introjected and made part of the self-concept become less influential in guiding the direction of decisions and their course for life. As the person becomes more psychologically mature, there is an increasing trust in the organismic valuing. Rather than being governed by fixed values held within the self-concept, the organism is engaged in a dynamic *process of valuing*. Rogers did not state specific or particular values that the therapist must hold. Instead the therapist engages herself in a process of valuing for her client expressed through the experience of empathy and unconditional positive regard as attitudes towards the client. It is the unconditional element of the therapist's satisfaction of the client's need for positive regard that seems to be a potent healing factor in P-CT.

The above is a brief description of Rogers's theory of personality development in that it provides an understanding of the cause of clients' difficulties. As such, P-CT practitioners do not need a taxonomy of diagnoses or psychological problems. In fact, Rogers suggests that diagnosing clients can in fact be problematic because diagnosis involves the therapist applying an external frame of reference to understanding the client, in contrast to an empathic understanding which involves understanding the client from the client's own frame of reference.

All forms of distress and dysfunction that are not biological in origin share this unitary psychological cause of incongruence between the self-concept and organismic valuing. However, distress and dysfunction find a variety of expressions according to the uniqueness of each situation and person (see Joseph & Worsley, 2005). Whilst there is no one way to communicate therapist empathy and unconditional positive regard, P-C therapists must be highly attuned to the client's expression and experience, moment-by-moment in the session. Following the development from non-directive counseling to P-CT, Rogers's (1957b) research interests turned towards empirically testing the six necessary and sufficient conditions hypothesis, which states that when certain relationship conditions are present there will be constructive personality change. The relationship conditions described by Rogers (1957b; 96) are:

1   Two persons are in psychological contact.
2   The first, whom we shall term the client, is in a state of incongruence, being vulnerable or anxious.
3   The second person, who we shall term the therapist, is congruent or integrated in the relationship.
4   The therapist experiences unconditional positive regard for the client.
5   The therapist experiences an empathic understanding of the client's internal frame of reference and endeavors to communicate this experience to the client.
6   The communication to the client of the therapist's empathic understanding and unconditional positive regard is to a minimal degree achieved.

Rogers's theory of personality development provides the rationale for the principled non-directive stance of P-CT. Rogers contended that the actualizing tendency is inherent in all people, always active and striving towards greater congruence between the self-concept and experience, directed towards development, maintenance and enhancement of the organism. P-CT is thought to provide the social environmental conditions that allow people to evaluate their experiences organismically rather than through the self-concept and thus move toward greater congruence and authenticity. This seemingly straightforward theory has been highly influential in modern psychology and psychotherapy. The impact of the theory has been significant and many of the ideas have now been integrated into mainstream psychology (Joseph & Murphy, 2013a).

Positive psychology

One of the key recent developments within mainstream psychology has been the emergence of positive psychology (Seligman & Csikszentmihalyi, 2000). It is now generally accepted that Rogers's P-CT and the person-centred approach (PCA) was one of the forerunners of the idea of positive psychology with its emphasis on fully functioning behaviour (Joseph & Linley, 2006; Joseph & Murphy, 2013a, 2013b). It has become evident that self-determination theory (SDT), developed by Ryan and Deci (2000), provides a more contemporary organismic theory largely synonymous with the PCA. Both the theories of SDT and P-CT share the basic philosophical position that human beings are intrinsically motivated towards the actualization of their potential, but that motivation can be usurped when the person does not have their basic psychological needs met, in this case for autonomy, competence and relatedness. While this is not the only reason people fail to grow, the shared theoretical ground is ripe for collaboration. A wealth of research shows that when basic needs for autonomy, competence and relatedness are satisfied in relationships, greater well-being results (Patterson & Joseph, 2007; Sheldon, 2013).

Of importance to the PCA is the observation that Deci and Ryan's conceptualisation of need satisfactions is essentially the same as Rogers's notion of unconditional positive regard, which is essentially about supporting the autonomy and relationship needs of the client (see Joseph & Linley, 2006). Other social psychological research has provided support for the notion of the OVP through the observation that over time people tend to move towards more intrinsic goals (Sheldon, Arndt, & Houser-Marko, 2003), and as people are more intrinsically rather than extrinsically motivated, increased well-being results (Joseph & Linley, 2006; Sheldon, 2013). The move towards fulfilling more intrinsically motivated aspirations supports the theory that as people psychologically mature they become more in tune with their OVP. It seems that the introjected values of others, reflected in the pursuit of extrinsically motivated aspirations, have less influence as people mature and become more psychologically adjusted. In sum, these findings from positive psychology and related social psychological fields support some important elements of the personality theory of the PCA, making them relevant for P-C therapists.

Mindfulness

Mindfulness has long been recognised as a means for improving present-moment awareness, thereby allowing one to make more informed and deliberate choices.

The concept has its roots in Buddhist philosophical and religious traditions going back about 2,500 years, and mindfulness as a discipline and practice lies at the heart of all classical systems of Buddhist meditation, where it is viewed as just one component of a web of connected factors that together make up the noble eightfold path of Buddhism, which includes "right mindfulness" (Bodhi, 2013). Mindfulness practice has been gaining increasing attention in the West over the last forty years, with a range of secular mindfulness-based interventions having been developed in the service of improving psychological and physical health. Theoretical and conceptual understanding of mindfulness in a Western context has also been a recent concern of academic disciplines and psychology in particular (Baer, 2003; Bishop et al., 2004; Brown, Ryan, & Creswell, 2007a; Malinowski, 2008). Empirical work from the positive psychology tradition has shown how mindfulness is associated with a host of well-being indicators (Brown & Ryan, 2003, 2004). It has also been shown that mindfulness-based approaches provide possible means of fostering self-determination and self-awareness, and in this way facilitate the satisfaction of basic psychological needs for autonomy, competence and relatedness (see Brown & Ryan, 2003, 2004), which are believed to underpin much of human well-being (Ryan & Deci, 2000).

Mindfulness has been defined as a receptive attention to and awareness of present events and experience (Brown & Ryan, 2003) and, elsewhere, as a multidimensional construct encompassing two elements: *self-regulation of attention* (moment-to-moment awareness) and an attitude of *curiosity, openness and acceptance towards one's experiences* including thoughts, perceptions, emotions and sensations (Bishop et al., 2004), while Kabat-Zinn defines the approach as, "paying attention in a particular way: on purpose, in the present moment, and non-judgmentally" (Kabat-Zinn, 1994, p. 4). There is ongoing debate around the conceptualisation of mindfulness in the psychological literature, suggesting that it is a difficult construct to 'pin down' and differences in operational definitions are also reflected in research and perhaps to a lesser degree in practice in this area (Brown, Ryan, & Creswell, 2007a, 2007b; Malinowski, 2008; Grossman & Van Dam, 2013). Grossman and Van Dam (2013) point out that early Buddhist texts tend to refer to mindfulness not as a mental function or trait but as a practice involving at least four distinct phases, ranging from mindfulness of bodily sensations to awareness of more expansive mental content and processes, such as emotion and an altered view of self. However, most current definitions tend to define and operationalise it as a relatively stable trait or disposition.

Typical formal mindful practices involve attention to and awareness of present-moment breathing, hearing, seeing, thoughts or bodily sensations. In formal practices there is clearly a cultivation of a *state* of mindfulness during the practice itself. For our purposes, we will consider that formal mindfulness practices are concerned with fostering state mindfulness during the actual practice but also aim to strengthen trait (dispositional) mindfulness. This latter aim is a core goal of mindfulness-based interventions, which have been shown to be efficacious in a number of meta-analyses (Baer, 2003; Grossman, Niemann, Schmidt, & Walach,

2004; Hofmann, Sawyer, Witt, & Oh, 2010). It is our view that the core skill that formal mindfulness practices target is being able to regulate attention so that the focus of awareness is on present-moment experiencing, in line with Brown and Ryan (2003) and consistent with the first part of the Bishop et al. definition. We would view the attitudinal qualities of mindfulness to be qualities that emerge as a consequence of increased ability to regulate attention to present-moment experiencing, i.e. as process outcomes that naturally emerge with the capacity to maintain awareness of present-moment experiencing.

Within therapeutic settings, mindfulness training has been allied with cognitive-behavioural therapy as a technique for therapists to use in order to try and prevent the problems of relapse following treatment for depression. According to Teasdale et al. (2000), vulnerability to relapse and recurrence of depression arises from the fact that the person makes repeated associations between their depressed mood and patterns of negative, self-devaluing, hopeless thinking during episodes of major depression. This leads to changes at both the cognitive and neuronal levels, such that people who have experienced major depression, but who have recovered, differ from people who have never experienced major depression in their patterns of thinking that are triggered by low mood or dysphoria. The important point here it seems is those at a higher risk of relapse in depression have attention regulatory systems whose focus is oriented towards the past experiences of depressed mood. The emphasis of mindfulness on present-moment awareness would then seem supportive of preventing relapse into depression.

The focus of mindfulness-based cognitive therapy is then to teach individuals to become aware of how thoughts and feelings relate to them from a wider, decentred perspective. In this way, people are encouraged to view their thoughts as "mental events" that are detached from, rather than an integral part of, the person and their psychological make-up. This detachment then provides individuals with the skills and abilities they need in order to prevent the escalation of depressive thoughts and feelings into full-blown major depression. There is growing evidence to support the effectiveness of this approach (see e.g. Ma & Teasdale, 2004; Teasdale et al., 2000) and its use with a variety of clinical as well as non-clinical conditions (Grossman et al., 2004).

The potential synergy for mindfulness-based approaches and P-CT is clearly presented through the idea of principled non-directivity. Fostering an orientation to experience with curiosity, openness and acceptance without judgement or striving towards a desired internal or external state (Bishop et al., 2004; Hayes & Feldman, 2004) seems to resonate within both. We would argue that the person-centred approach is already a mindful approach. By definition the therapist conditions of empathic understanding, congruence and unconditional positive self-regard in the service of staying present with and attentive to the client's moment-to-moment process in the therapeutic encounter is a mindful practice.

Below we will develop these ideas further to argue that (1) P-CT is a form of mindful therapy insofar as it involves the therapist being wholly responsive to the moment-by-moment experiences of the client; (2) mindful techniques can be used within P-CT; and (3) the outcomes of P-CT can be reconceptualised in the language of mindfulness.

1. P-CT as a form of mindfulness towards the client

The practice of P-CT is paradoxical in that it requires the therapist to relinquish any goal for the client to change in a particular way in order that the client may choose what and how to change. The notion of going with the client in their direction and at their pace, so central to P-CT, is often misunderstood as being little more than asking the client what they want from the sessions and then attempting to give it to them. What is actually required is the moment-by-moment attention of the therapist to the client, in every aspect of what they say and how they say it, along with their expressions and posture. In short, P-CT requires the therapist to be mindful of their client, to understand without wanting to change the client's frame of reference. This is perhaps most clearly represented in the person–centred idea of the therapist developing an unconditionally accepting empathic understanding of the client. Here we can see that the therapist is clearly required to adopt an attitude of mindful and non-judgemental curiosity about the client's experience, asking: "Can I be sensitive to every nuance of personal meaning and value, no matter how different it is from my own experience?" (Rogers, 1987, p. 38).

Bazzano (2011) suggests that mindfulness as a practice for person–centred therapists is supportive of developing the necessary therapeutic attitudes. This can perhaps be understood as meaning that as the therapist practices mindfulness; they are open to experiences that are beyond those discriminated as 'self-experiences'. The cornerstone of training as a person–centred therapist is the development of the therapist's congruence. This is usually achieved through personal therapy, personal development groups and experiential learning within training. Given the similarities between the constructs of mindfulness and congruence we would suggest that mindfulness exercises used within person–centred training are likely to be helpful. Studies of psychological therapists in training have shown that mindfulness practice/meditation is associated with developing the quality of therapeutic presence (McCollum & Gehart, 2010) as well as reduced discomfort with silence in therapy sessions, less preoccupation and self-recrimination with themselves as therapists and better tolerance of difficult emotions (Christopher & Maris, 2010). Furthermore, Grepmair et al. (2007) found that promoting mindfulness in trainee psychotherapists could positively influence therapeutic course and client outcomes.

In person–centred therapy experience can be thought of as either organismic, or as a self-experience. Some aspects of experience then are not self-experiences. Mindfulness has some overlapping qualities with the concept of congruence insofar as being congruent involves holding experience in 'accepting awareness'. That is, mindfulness requires the person-centred therapist to experience congruent acceptance for their own experience. This seems crucial for the practice of person-centred therapy. The therapist that is experiencing this congruent accepting awareness is also then free to experience greater unconditional positive regard for the client's experience. As many authors have written (e.g. Bozarth, 1998), it is the experience of unconditional positive regard for the client that is the healing and curative factor within person-centred therapy.

Consistent with the mindfulness attitudinal stance of purposefully and intentionally directing attention to what is occurring in the present moment (Kabat-Zinn, 1990), as well as with the person-centred emphasis on the importance of being sensitive to every aspect of what the client is communicating in the therapeutic encounter (Rogers 1951, 1987), is the idea of therapeutic presence. One model of therapeutic presence identifies three components: "availability and openness to all aspects of the client's experience, openness to one's own experience in being with the client and the capacity to respond to the client from this experience" (Geller & Greenberg, 2002, p. 178). Interestingly, mindfulness literature elsewhere refers to the ability to attend to the other in an open and non-judgmental manner as unconditional presence (Brown, Ryan, & Creswell, 2007a), underscoring the parallels between mindfulness and P-CT in terms of the qualities in the therapist and the relationship with the other person that the two approaches value and strive to achieve.

2. Using mindfulness techniques within P-CT

To genuinely experience and communicate empathy and unconditional positive regard in the relationship with the client is the therapist's only goal. Principled non-directivity therefore refers to the attitude of the therapist. As Raskin (1947/2005) says, non-directivity cannot be reduced to therapist technique but reflects the basic belief the therapist has in the client's resourcefulness for growth and self-direction. Non-directivity refers to the stance of the therapist in relation to the client. It does not mean that the therapy itself lacks direction but that the direction is determined by the client. As such the term non-directive gave way to the term person-centred. Furthermore, non-directivity, or client-centred, does not imply passivity on the part of the therapist. Grant (1990) suggests that from a principled position the therapist need be prepared to do whatever it takes in service to the client; this may involve offering the client techniques or interventions based on their need at that moment in therapy. Seen this way, there are exercises and techniques within the mindfulness literature that the therapist may choose to suggest to the client. To do so would not be incompatible with P-CT. Such an approach is also consistent with P-CT's recognition that the communication of unconditional positive regard to the client by the therapist is just "one way" of achieving increased unconditional positive self-regard and decreased conditions of worth (Rogers, 1959, p. 230).

Indeed, as previously described, P-CT views distress as the psychological tension that emerges from incongruence between the self-concept and the OVP (Rogers, 1951, 1959). Greater incongruence leads to greater psychological tension. Aspects of the individual's (organismic) experiencing that are inconsistent with the self-concept can be kept outside of conscious awareness because they represent a threat to the conditions of worth in which the self-concept is invested. Mindfulness techniques represent a valid attempt to encourage the individual to remain curious, open and non-judgmentally accepting of all that they experience, thus potentially facilitating conscious awareness of a range of self-experiences (Bishop et al., 2004). In addition, the decentred (less identified) observation and awareness of those self-experiences may serve to reduce defensiveness and promote openness to self-experiences that may be perceived as threatening or potentially distressing.

With a shared emphasis on a warm, open and non-judgmental approach to engaging with here-and-now experiencing, there is clearly some convergence of aims between mindfulness-based approaches and P-CT.

3. Mindfulness as an outcome of P-CT

Research into dispositional or trait mindfulness suggests that a mindful disposition may be present without formal mindfulness training or practice (Brown et al., 2007b). Nonetheless, it is recognised that there are individual differences in levels of trait mindfulness and that training in mindfulness can enhance dispositional mindfulness (Shapiro et al., 2006), a principle that underpins the various mindfulness-based approaches.

There is also a growing body of research which indicates that higher levels of dispositional mindfulness are associated with increased well-being, positive affect and lower levels of negative affect, in particular in patients with depression and anxiety (e.g. Baer, Smith, & Allen, 2004; Baer et al., 2006; Brown & Ryan, 2003). We suggest that a more mindful disposition is also a feature of growth and change within the PCA. In this regard, Rogers (1961) observed that one of the key process-changes to occur in more fully functioning individuals is a movement towards increasingly living in the here and now:

> A second characteristic of the process which for me is the good life, is that it involves an increasing tendency to live fully in each moment. Such living in the moment means absence of rigidity, of tight organization of the imposition of structure on experience. It means instead a maximum of adaptability, a discovery of structure in experience, a flowing, changing organization of self and personality. . . . It involves discovering the structure of experience in the process of living the experience. To open one's spirit to what is going on now, and to discover in that present process whatever structure it appears to have – this to me is one of the qualities of the good life, the mature life, as I see clients approach it.
>
> *(pp. 188–189)*

Mindfulness skills training focusses on developing the attitudinal aspects of curiosity, openness, acceptance, non-judgement – attitudes that converge with the process outcomes of person-centred therapy and Rogers's definition of fully functioning. As such, our opinion is that those individuals who are more fully functioning from a person-centred understanding are also likely to show higher dispositional mindfulness. While this is clearly a question that merits empirical study to determine its veracity, there is evidence to suggest that a more mindful mode of conscious processing is associated with more autonomous self-regulation and acting in ways that are congruent with chosen interests and values rather than introjected values (Brown & Ryan, 2003; Brown et al., 2007b). In addition, this more autonomously regulated behaviour has been found to be associated with a wide range of positive behavioural outcomes, particularly from research within positive psychology (e.g. Ryan & Deci, 2000).

For the mindfulness practitioner, this attitude of openness to and acceptance of present-moment experiencing is thought to represent an awareness which is more accurately informed than non-mindful awareness and which the person can consciously choose to respond to or not. Similarly for the person-centred therapist, being open and sensitive to what is occurring here and now facilitates a similar more informed, more conscious position from which to respond to the present moment, including the present-moment experience of what is present in the therapeutic encounter. There is certainly convergence between mindfulness and P-CT in their shared goal of facilitating more present-focussed living, the association with more autonomous functioning and the focus on authenticity implicit in the person-centred conceptualisation of congruence. It should probably not surprise us then, when mindfulness practitioners embrace attitudes and values that resonate with those of P-CT:

> I like to think of mindfulness simply as the art of conscious living. You don't have to be a Buddhist or a yogi to practice it. In fact, if you know anything about Buddhism, you will know that the most important point is to be yourself and not to try to become anything that you are not already. ... It (mindfulness) is simply a practical way to become more in touch with the fullness of your being through a systematic process of self-observation, self-inquiry and mindful action.
>
> *(Kabat-Zinn, 1994, pp. 6–7)*

Other research testing the correlation between psychometric scales of mindfulness and self-actualisation are consistent with the notion that there is a similarity between Rogers's views and those of the Buddhist tradition (Beitel, Bogus, Hutz, Green, Cecero, & Barry, 2014). Indeed, the very concept of congruence so central to P-CT would seem to refer to both the moment-to-moment awareness and openness and acceptance towards one's experiences including thoughts, perceptions, emotions and sensations, described by Bishop as constituting mindfulness. Recognising the similarities between the concepts of congruence and mindfulness promises to be helpful to P-CT therapists who may have overemphasised the more secondary aspect of congruence, which is the honest expression of thoughts and feelings at the expense of developing more mindful self-awareness, described by Rogers as the need for the therapist's "actual experience" to be ". . . accurately represented by his awareness of himself" within the context of the therapeutic relationship (Rogers, 1957b, p. 97). On the other hand, it may be beneficial for mindful practitioners to reflect on the wider theoretical context provided by P-CT and its non-directive stance. We would suggest that mindfulness is too easily taken out of its original theoretical context and used instrumentally when in fact it is better understood as a goal in itself.

Conclusion

Our argument is that P-CT is already a form of mindful therapy. Therapists holding the core conditions are already by definition engaged in mindful practice that is present in the moment, self-aware of inner experiencing, and acceptant of themselves. There may however be occasions when mindful practices could be incorporated by the P-C therapist if done at the pace and direction of the client, consistent with principled non-directivity. It may also be that in addition to potential benefits to clients, formal mindfulness practice may have utility as an additional means of strengthening therapists' own capacity to hold the core conditions of empathy, unconditional positive regard and congruence. In conclusion, we hope to have shown how there is common ground between mindfulness and P-CT and how these two trajectories of research and practice can inform each other in new and interesting ways.

Bibliography

Baer, R. A., Smith, G. T., & Allen, K. B. (2004). Assessment of mindfulness by self-report the Kentucky inventory of mindfulness skills. *Assessment, 11*(3), 191–206.

Baer, R. A., Smith, G. T., Hopkins, J., Krietemeyer, J., & Toney, L. (2006). Using self-report assessment methods to explore facets of mindfulness. *Assessment, 13*(1), 27–45.

Baer, R. (2003). Mindfulness training as a clinical intervention: A conceptual and empirical review. *Clinical Psychology: Science and Practice, 10,* 125–143.

Bazzano, M. (2011). The Buddha as a fully functioning person: Toward a person-centered perspective on mindfulness, *Person-Centered & Experiential Psychotherapies, 10*(2), 116–128.

Beitel, M., Bogus, S., Hutz, A., Green, D., Cecero, J. J., & Barry, D. T. (2014). Stillness and motion: An empirical investigation of mindfulness and self-actualization. *Person- Centered & Experiential Psychotherapies, 13*(3), 187–202.

Bishop, S. R., Lau, M., Shapiro, S., Carlson, L., Anderson, N. D., Carmody, J., & Devins, G. (2004). Mindfulness: A proposed operational definition. *Clinical Psychology: Science and Practice, 11,* 230–241.

Bodhi, B. (2013). What does mindfulness really mean? A canonical perspective. In J. M. G Williams & J. Kabat-Zinn (Eds.), *Mindfulness: Diverse perspectives on its meaning, origins and applications* (pp. 19–39). London: Routledge.

Bozarth, J. (1998). *Person-centred therapy: A revolutionary paradigm.* Ross-on-Wye: PCCS Books.

Brodley, B. T. (1997). The non-directive attitude in client-centered therapy. *The Person- Centered Journal, 4*(1), 67–74.

Brown, K. W., & Ryan, R. M. (2003). The benefits of being present: Mindfulness and its role in psychological well-being. *Journal of Personality and Social Psychology, 84,* 822–848.

Brown, K. W., & Ryan, R. M. (2004). Fostering healthy self-regulation from within and without: A self-determination theory perspective. In P. A. Linley & S. Joseph (Eds.), *Positive psychology in practice* (pp. 105–124). Hoboken: Wiley.

Brown, K. W., Ryan, R. M., & Creswell, J. D. (2007a). Mindfulness: Theoretical foundations and evidence for its salutary effects. *Psychological Inquiry, 18*(4), 211–237.

Brown, K. W., Ryan, R. M., & Creswell, J. D. (2007b). Addressing fundamental questions about mindfulness. *Psychological Inquiry, 18*(4), 272–281.

Campbell, J. C., & Christopher, J. C. (2012). Teaching mindfulness to create effective counsellors. *Journal of Mental Health Counseling, 34*(3), 213–226.

Christopher, J. C., & Maris, J. A. (2010). Integrating mindfulness as self-care into counselling and psychotherapy training. *Counselling & Psychotherapy Research, 10*(2), 114–125.

Geller, S. M., & Greenberg, L. S. (2002). Therapeutic Presence: Therapists' experience of presence in the psychotherapy encounter. *Person-Centered & Experiential Psychotherapies, 1*(1–2), 71–86. doi:10.1080/14779757.2002.9688279

Grant, B. (1990). Principled and instrumental nondirectiveness in person-centred and client-centered therapy. *Person-Centered Review, 5*(1), 77–88. Reprinted in D. Cain (Ed.). (2005) *Classics in the person-centered approach* (pp. 371–377). Ross-on-Wye: PCCS Books.

Grepmair, L., Mitterlehner, F., Loew, T., Bachler, E., Rother, W., & Nickel, M. (2007). Promoting mindfulness in psychotherapists in training influences the treatment results of their patients: A randomized, double-blind, controlled study. *Psychotherapy and Psychomatics, 76,* 332–338.

Grossman, P., Niemann, L., Schmidt, S., & Walach, H. (2004). Mindfulness-based stress reduction and health benefits: A meta-analysis. *Journal of Psychosomatic Research, 57*(1), 35–43.

Grossman, P., & Van Dam, N. T. (2013). Mindfulness, by any other name . . . trials and tribulations of Sati in Western psychology and science. In J. M. G Williams & J. Kabat-Zinn (Eds.), *Mindfulness: Diverse perspectives on its meaning, origins and applications* (pp. 19–39). London: Routledge.

Hayes, A. M., & Feldman, G. (2004). Clarifying the construct of mindfulness in the context of emotion regulation and the process of change in therapy. *Clinical Psychology: Science and Practice, 11*(3), 255–262.

Hofmann, S. G., Sawyer, A. T., Witt, A. A., & Oh, D. (2010). The effect of mindfulness- based therapy on anxiety and depression: A meta-analytic review. *Journal of Consulting and Clinical Psychology, 78*(2), 169–183.

Joseph, S., & Linley, P. A. (2006). *Positive therapy: A meta-theory for positive psychological practice.* London: Routledge.

Joseph, S., & Murphy, D. (2013a). Person-centered approach, positive psychology and relational helping: Building bridges. *Journal of Humanistic Psychology, 53,* 26–51.

Joseph, S., & Murphy, D. (2013b). Person-centered theory encountering mainstream psychology: Building Bridges and looking to the future. In J. H. D. Cornelius-White, R. Motschnig-Pitrik & M. Lux (Eds.), *Interdisciplinary handbook of the person- centered approach: Research and theory* (pp. 213–226). New York, NY: Springer.

Joseph, S., & Worsley, R. (Eds.) (2005). *Person-centered psychopathology: A positive psychology of mental health.* Ross-on-Wye: PCCS Books.

Kabat-Zinn, J. (1990). *Full catastrophe living: Using the wisdom of your body and mind to face stress, pain and illness.* New York: Delacorte.

Kabat-Zinn, J. (1994). *Wherever you go, there you are: Mindfulness meditation in everyday life.* New York: Hyperion.

Kirschenbaum, H. (2007). *The life and work of Carl Rogers.* Ross-on-Wye: PCCS Books.

Levitt, B. E. (2005). *Embracing non-directivity: Reassessing person-centered theory and practice in the 21st century.* Ross-on-Wye: PCCS Books.

Ma, S. H., & Teasdale, J. D. (2004). Mindfulness-based cognitive therapy for depression: Replication and exploration of differential relapse prevention effects. *Journal of Consulting and Clinical Psychology, 72,* 31–40.

Malinowski, P. (2008). Mindfulness as psychological dimension: Concepts and applications. *The Irish Journal of Psychology, 29*(1), 155–166.

McCollum, E. E., & Gehart, D. R. (2010). Using mindfulness meditation to teach beginning therapists therapeutic presence: A qualitative study. *Journal of Marital and Family Therapy, 36*(3), 347–360.

Patterson, T. G., & Joseph, S. (2007). Person-centred personality theory: Support from self- determination theory and positive psychology. *Journal of Humanistic Psychology, 47,* 117–139.

Raskin, N. J. (1947/2005). The non-directive attitude. In B. Levitt (Ed.), *Embracing non-directivity: Reassessing person-centered theory and practice in the 21st century* (pp. 329–347). Ross-on-Wye: PCCS Books.

Rogers, C. R. (1951). *Client-centered therapy: Its current practice, implication and theory.* Boston, MA: Houghton Mifflin.

Rogers, C. R. (1957a). A note on the nature of man. *Journal of Consulting Psychology, 4*(3), 199–203.

Rogers, C. R. (1957b). The necessary and sufficient conditions of therapeutic personality change. *Journal of Consulting Psychology, 21*(2), 95–103.

Rogers, C. R. (1959). A theory of therapy, personality, and interpersonal relationships as developed in the client-centered framework. In S. Koch (Ed.), *Psychology: A study of a science. Vol. 3: Formulations of the person and the social context* (pp. 184–256). New York, NY: McGraw-Hill.

Rogers, C. R. (1961). *On becoming a person.* London: Constable.

Rogers, C. R. (1963). The actualizing tendency in relation to "motives" and to consciousness. In M. R. Jones (Ed.), *Nebraska symposium on motivation* (pp. 1–24). Lincoln, NE: University of Nebraska Press.

Rogers, C. R. (1980). *A way of being.* Boston, MA: Houghton Mifflin.

Rogers, C. R. (1987). Comments on the issue of equality in psychotherapy. *Journal of Humanistic Psychology, 27*(1), 38–40.

Ryan, R. M., & Deci, E. L. (2000). Self-determination theory and the facilitation of intrinsic motivation, social development, and well-being. *American Psychologist, 55*(1), 68–78.

Segal, Z. V., Williams, J. M. G., & Teasdale, J. D. (2002). *Mindfulness-based cognitive therapy for depression: A new approach to preventing relapse.* New York, NY: Guildford Press.

Seligman, M. E. P., & Csikszentmihalyi, M. (2000). Positive psychology: An introduction. *American Psychologist, 55,* 5–14.

Shapiro, S. L., Carlson, L. E., Astin, J. A., & Freedman, B. (2006). Mechanisms of mindfulness. *Journal of Clinical Psychology, 62*(3), 373–386.

Sheldon, K. (2013). Self-determination theory, person-centered approaches, and personal goals: Exploring the links. In J. H. D. Cornelius-White, R. Motschnig-Pitrik & M. Lux (Eds.), *Interdisciplinary handbook of the person-centered approach: Research and theory* (pp. 227–244). New York, NY: Springer.

Sheldon, K., M., Arndt, J., & Houser-Marko, L. (2003). In search of the organismic valuing process: The human tendency to move towards beneficial goal choices. *Journal of Personality, 71, 835–886.*

Teasdale, J. D., Segal, Z. V., Williams, J. M. G., Ridgeway, V. A., Soulsby, J. M., & Lau, M. A. (2000). Prevention of relapse/recurrence in major depression by mindfulness-based cognitive therapy. *Journal of Consulting and Clinical Psychology, 68,* 615–623.

19

BEYOND MINDFULNESS

The power of self-compassion, purpose, play, and confidence in the clinical treatment of the depressed client

Elisha Goldstein

Introduction

Writer John Keats told of the hopelessness that depression created in his soul: "If I were under water, I would scarcely kick to come to the top." Every part of the body can feel the weight of depression and each year, in the United States alone, 25 million people experience an episode of major depression and millions more suffer with low grade chronic unhappiness. According to the Centers for Disease Control and Prevention, for people between the ages of 10 and 24, suicide is the third leading cause of death and untreated depression is the leading cause of suicide (NAMI, 2013). At the same time more people across many sectors from business, sports, entertainment, and politics are coming out of the depressive closet and speaking about their experience and the pervasive shame that stands at the heart of it.

In the past 15 years new neurobiological treatments have been gaining a lot of attention. We now have neurostimulation interventions to jumpstart the brain like magnetic coils that attach to the skull to stimulate specific brain regions or electrodes to implant to stimulate nerve cells like a pacemaker stimulates the heart. Our understanding of anti-depressants is evolving, showing how they can create slow-onset adaptive changes in brain cells, or neurons. This sends more dollars toward research for new medication-based treatment interventions.

But with all of this "progress," it's also not news that we've been pushing the medication side a bit too far. This has always troubled me and over 10 years ago I started experimenting with the integration of mindfulness as a way to work with depression. After the publication of *A Mindfulness-Based Stress Reduction Workbook* (2010), I inevitably became trained as a mindfulness-based cognitive therapy (MBCT) teacher and along with my colleague Roger Nolan, MFT, launched the first MBCT group in Los Angeles at InsightLA.

You've most likely heard of MBCT, and it has done wonders for so many people's lives in supporting them with relapse prevention, but it wasn't created for people who are actively depressed. Even so, I've learned how powerful mindfulness can be as a "natural anti-depressant" even for some who are depressed. It can still give them solace from the "rehashing" and ruminating mind and help them find some ease and peace. It can help them step into that pause between stimulus and response and begin to challenge those persistent negative thoughts. But I've also realized that for many people who were deeply depressed and unstable, this was not the first point of intervention as it's too difficult to maintain a meditation practice and this fed the depression loop, exacerbating their sense of deficiency.

I was curious; what else could create an anti-depressant effect that helped move someone out of their depressive stuckness and even promote happiness? I started looking into what we know about the depressed brain in hope for some answers. I wasn't surprised to find that a depressed brain can often look like a traumatized brain. Compared to someone who is not depressed, certain areas are overactive, while others are underactive. There are even areas of the brain that are enlarged, while others seem to have shrunken in size. This led to the next question: Are there things that I could do as a therapist to help the people I work with build up the sections of the brain that can protect them from depression and slow down the sections that foster depression?

Through some trial and error I came upon a handful of natural anti-depressant mindsets that also positively impact the brain in all the right ways. One of the key ones is the explicit training in self-compassion. I also understood how essential it is for people to get outside of their self-loathing prison by uncovering what matters to them and engaging life with greater purpose. I found how far removed from activities of play people were, and how important it was to begin discovering and engaging in life again. Finally, what pulled this all together was the understanding that in the mind of a depressed person was a performance-based mindset where any sign of failure was confirmation that they were deficient. A new mindset needed to be taught and reinforced where the process was about learning; only this would pull together the pieces to help people create an anti-depressant brain. I started to systematically work with these natural anti-depressants in my groups and with my clients. Some of the stories that came out of this work still create a quiver in my heart.

This has been a story of hope and I'm going to share my experience with you.

Understand that depression is a neurobiological trauma

This is the way I think of depression. Whether it's nature or nurture it almost doesn't matter because right now, in this moment, the person in front of me is operating with a brain on autopilot, wired in a way that reinforces a depressive loop. This isn't meant to be reductionistic; the person's family history and genetics of course matter and the person is far more than a brain. But seeing how a depressed brain can look highly similar to a traumatized brain helps both of us understand why depressed people can lack perspective at times or have difficulty with impulse control.

When you look at a depressed brain you find some interesting things. The first thing you find is that it is highly similar to the brain of someone who has been experiencing severe chronic stress or someone with post-traumatic stress disorder (PTSD). The prefrontal cortex (PFC) can be shrunken in size, making impulse control more challenging (Davidson et al., 2002). There is also greater activation toward the right side that's been associated with avoidant mindsets and negative emotions. This makes depression a recipe for avoiding life. The amygdala can be enlarged, if not just overactive, suggesting sensitivity to fearful cues. The hippocampus is also negatively impacted by repeated surges of cortisol flooding the brain in response to states of fear, which ambush people when they are stuck in a depression loop. This may be why in a depressed brain, the hippocampus is often smaller in size (Davidson et al., 2009).

Some studies show correlative findings with the vagus nerve, the nerve that appears to connect our brain to our hearts. When vagal tone is high it slows the heart rate, regulates internal systems, and is associated with a feeling of calm, rest, relaxation, and contentment. When it's low, there is flat affect, low voice tone, and difficulty regulating emotions. Low vagal tone is associated with depression and trauma (Conway et al., 2013). There are other studies that show that dopamine is low in a depressed brain, correlating with low sense of pleasure and motivation (Salamone et al., 2014).

What follows is an understanding that currently, the person in front of you is being hijacked by a traumatized brain, and explaining it to them in this way helps release the self-judgment and the sense that being depressed is somehow their fault. This loosens the shame and opens the door for hope with experience-dependent neuroplasticity. There are certainly things we can do that can be considered under the umbrella of positive psychology that create a left prefrontal shift toward more resilient emotions, cool down the amygdala, increase vagal tone, restore the hippocampus, and amp up our dopamine and oxytocin in healthy ways. Science shows us that it all resides within us and now we can begin to uncover it and even create an anti-depressant brain.

Self-compassion and its anti-depressant effects

My client Claudia loved her shoes. She loved shopping for them, dressing up in them, and talking about them with anyone. She loved shoes so much that she had a pair in a glass case that never got worn because she reveled in the sight of them. But at 38, Claudia suffered the greatest tragedy of her life – one that would change all of this. An unfortunate collision with a drunk driver left her permanently disabled, with one leg shorter than the other. After she was rushed to the hospital, the doctors were unable to perform immediate and necessary reconstructive surgery because of heavy scar tissue. This loss spiraled her into the deepest depression of her life.

When I met her she was deeply depressed. She said, "It's been years since the accident, and I can't force myself to look at my mangled ankle. Whenever I think about it, a rush of anxiety and anger washes over me, and I can't get the self-judgments out of my head. What is wrong with me?"

After hearing her story and gaining trust over some sessions I asked her to sense where anxiety and anger lived in her body (some light informal mindfulness). As she did this she said, "There's just so much sadness I could drown in it." I invited her to put her hand on her heart and asked, "Can you sense in this moment what you're needing? Is it to be free from this struggle? To feel healthy, safe or at ease?" She nodded and said, "All of those seem right." I followed: "Now silently repeat these loving intentions to yourself such as 'May I be free from this suffering,' 'May I be healthy in body and mind,' 'May I feel safe and protected,' 'May I be at peace.'"

After a few minutes, she opened her tear-filled eyes and looked down at her ankle for the first time in years. Her facial expressed had changed, it was softened, and there was more ease around it.

"What are you noticing?" I asked.

With her hand remaining on her heart, she said, "What I went through was terrible."

That was a critical moment; she was experiencing the softening effects of self-compassion, the experience where you recognize your suffering with the inclination to support or be kind toward yourself.

What happened here? She experienced self-soothing and even self-love, two things that had been residing in her all along, but were uncovered through a process of encouraging self-compassion. In all my years of working with individuals and groups with depression I've come to learn a simple truth: Self-compassion is a critical missing link. Studies show that there is an inverse relationship between self-compassion and depression. When one is high, the other is low. The experience of depression is a shadow in our culture that very few people speak about it in public. This gives a lot of fuel for people to decimate themselves in their minds to the point of feeling overwhelmed, and in that moment their mind and body don't know what else to do but shut down.

One of the main anti-depressant effects of self-compassion is the power to build an internal self-soothing system in the face of suffering; this is exactly what Claudia experienced. For some, it's easy to make the argument that just coming into therapy with the intention of supporting yourself is an act of self-compassion.

The neurobiology of self-compassion

The fact is this isn't just a feel-good psychobabble idea; there's a biological basis to how self-compassion is a natural anti-depressant as it relates to the hormone oxytocin and the vagus nerve, and to creating a left prefrontal shift in brain activity that's associated with resiliency. It's sometimes helpful to describe to clients how, like trauma, depression thrives on fear and the biology of self-compassion soothes it. I'll explain to them that when fear is aroused, the nervous system kicks into gear to keep us safe and get us ready to fight, flee, or freeze. This releases the hormone cortisol, and as it continues to surge, certain areas of our brains become impaired – including the hippocampus, which, as you may know, is responsible for learning, remembering, and putting life events in context. As the brain and body become impacted, depression often follows. Self-compassion does the opposite. Instead of stimulating cortisol, self-compassion stimulates oxytocin release in our bodies, the hormone of connection, love, and bonding.

Some studies show that compassion stimulates the vagus nerve. Stephen Porges (2011) and Dacher Keltner (2009) do a great job showing us the science behind this. Vagal tone goes up when we witness the good of another, or even just hear a score of beautiful music. It's the feeling of openness and expansion in the body where we are less reactive to depressive cues and better able to self-soothe and engage socially. This suggests that self-compassion may be a powerful cue for good vagal tone and a natural anti-depressant.

Richie Davidson's lab at the University of Wisconsin has found that the left side of the PFC is associated with an approach mindset, while the left side is associated with an avoidant mindset (Davidson et al., 2002). The left side has also been associated with positive emotions and resiliency, while the right side has been associated with negative emotions. When you look at a depressed brain you see more activity on the right side confirming this. Certain compassion studies have found that focusing on compassion is correlated with a left prefrontal shift and it wouldn't be too farfetched to guess that this can happen with self-compassion as well, balancing out the depressed brain.

Arousing the self-soothing system

There is no linear path to teaching self-compassion and of course we have to meet people where they are. Depending on their level of depression I may try and activate their self-compassion in a few different ways, through placing of hands, self-compassion breaks, or the SAFE practice.

Placing of hands

If someone is highly impaired, like with Claudia, one simple yet meaningful way to foster self-understanding and self-love is by having the patient simply putting a hand on her heart. This gesture of caring can be done anytime, anywhere and connects us with self-care. It seems so simple, but can be so powerful. The practice of placing your hand on your heart acknowledges the difficulty, but also physically makes contact with the area of the body that is most associated with love. When the brain maps the body it turns down the volume on rumination. This practice is the brain mapping the body while sprinkling in an association with caring, and this is one reason it creates that natural anti-depressant effect. People often find this simple gesture to be a powerful way to not only stop the depressive loop, but also to experience a homecoming to the heart. This is too intimate for some people to do and if so you can always have them place a hand on their abdomen, which is often considered the grounding area of the body. Just placing a hand on the center of abdomen throughout the day can be a wonderful centering practice.

Self-compassion breaks

We can help people identify small self-compassionate actions to sprinkle in their day that are on a spectrum from little effort to lots of effort. The level of effort involved in a self-compassion break will depend on the severity of their depression. If the need is ease, can they lie down on the bed and listen to some gentle music? If the need is social support, are there any friends or family to visit, or meetups in the area to begin attending? One time a client of mine really needed some humor to feel some lightness and so I sat down next to him, turned on a YouTube video of John Cleese engaging in laughing yoga and over the course of a couple minutes saw a smile break over his face. There are all kinds of examples of self-compassion breaks.

Be SAFE

Once someone has a bit of stability restored, I teach them this short self-compassion practice to give them a way to pop out of autopilot during a difficult moment, change the relationship to the feelings that are there, create insight into the need that's there, and connect to the common humanity behind the current struggle. It integrates all the essential components of self-compassion, including mindfulness, kindness, and connection to our shared humanity.

Here are the four steps for SAFE:

S – Soften into the feeling.
A – Allow it to be as it is, without resisting or clinging to it.
F – Feel into it the sensation of the emotion and uncover your need.
E – Expand awareness to all people struggling with this.

- **Soften** – When vulnerability arises, whether it's a feeling of sadness, anxiety, grief, anger, or shame, take a moment to gently soften awareness into that area of the body. At this point you are just resting your awareness into this area. If it helps you can say, "Breathing in, I am aware of this vulnerability, breathing out softening into it."
- **Allow/Accept** – We're not striving to change this feeling, or make it any different; we're just allowing and letting be. Acceptance doesn't imply that you are okay with it or want it there; it's simply acknowledging the reality of its existence. Here you are just saying to yourself, "allowing, allowing, allowing."
- **Feel into it with kindness** – Now we have the opportunity to deepen our awareness and investigate the feeling. You may choose to put your hand on your heart or wherever you feel the sensation in your body. This applies love

or kindness to the feeling, which may shift it all by itself. The brain also has to map the sensation of the touch, which is inversely correlated with mental rumination, turning the volume down on negative thinking.

> As you feel into it you might ask, "What does this feeling believe?" Does it believe you are unlovable or unworthy, or perhaps that if you allow it to be, it will consume you? Ask the question, what does this feeling need right now? Does it need to feel cared for, to feel secure, to feel a sense of belonging? Whatever the answer, see if you can wish that for yourself. For example, "May I feel loved, may I feel secure, may I feel a sense of belonging." Make this personal to whatever your needs are.

• **Expand awareness and wishes to all people** – Whatever your vulnerability, it's important you know you're not alone. Feeling vulnerable is part of the human condition and millions of people struggle with the same source of vulnerability that you experience. But when we're feeling vulnerable with anxiety, depression, or shame, it becomes all about us; we need to also impersonalize the experience and get out of ourselves.

> Now is the opportunity to make that realization real by imagining all the other people who struggle with this same feeling of vulnerability and to wish them all the same prayers that you just wished yourself. For example, "May we all feel loved, may we all feel a sense of safety and security, and may we all feel that sense of belonging."

One of the major roadblocks to self-compassion is the allegiance depression has to its self-critical nature. This can be tough for any of us to work with. I ask people, "If you were struggling with a task and on the left side you had someone shouting in your ear how screwed up you were and on the right side was someone understanding the degree of difficulty and wanting to support you, who would you want to help you get the job done?" This is who self-compassion is and it ignites the right areas of the brain to serve as a natural anti-depressant.

Purpose and compassion create needed connection

Psychiatrist and Holocaust survivor Viktor Frankl provides another clue as to what is a natural anti-depressant. When he looked around the concentration camps he realized an important truth – the people around him who were surviving the trauma had a sense of meaning and purpose in their lives. This might be something we all have a sense of, but there's also some real science behind it. Barbara Frederickson, PhD, professor at the University of North Carolina, collaborating with a team at UCLA led by Steven Cole, PhD, professor of medicine, psychiatry, and behavioral sciences, conducted research showing that people who have a high sense of purpose have stronger immune systems and experience less stress-related gene expression that is involved in cellular inflammation, two signs of health (2013). As a group, they're less likely to suffer from depression, cardiovascular disease, diabetes, and certain kinds of cancers. Also, remember the science of compassion shows it helps facilitate that left prefrontal shift and increases vagal tone. These are just a few things that make the case for being natural anti-depressants.

Depression is the mind inclined in an *antisocial* direction, meaning there is so much self-focus that people feel disconnected and hate themselves. Purpose and compassion incline the mind in a *prosocial* direction and create connection. Since science often proves things we already know from experience, it's not surprising that we're seeing anti-depressant effects from engaging more purposefully in life. But in order to actually create experience-dependent neuroplasticity, you have to have experience.

The Dalai Lama is known for having said, "It's not enough to be compassionate, you must act." Someone who is depressed might have a prosocial value for compassion, but only judges himself after "failing" to actually do anything compassionate in his life. It's important to remember that there's a level of learned helplessness in depression that disables someone to learn new strategies. Depressed clients need scaffolding. They need us to help them break down how to turn their prosocial values into doable verbs. A client of mine was an executive assistant and chronically depressed since she was a child. She also happened to have a gift for design. She had a prosocial value of bringing beauty into the world and other people's lives, but her lack of doing it only reinforced her fixed belief that she wasn't able to do anything about it. Since she was fairly depressed and arrested, we talked about a number of different options and rated them from easiest to scariest. It was easiest for her to start talking about different ideas and then eventually sketching some out. This started to give her a sense of personal control and achievement that seemed to go alongside her coming out of her depressive shell. She inevitably started some courses in design. I'm proud to say that she's now created her own line of jewelry that people are enjoying, and her sense of achievement has led to a level of confidence and resiliency.

One key to helping people uncover a sense of purpose and compassion is to help them understand what they value. Is it world peace, equality, close friendships, accomplishments, or maybe compassion? Once they do this, we want to help them understand more specifically *what* these values look like in daily life and *why* they are doing them. This is a page out of acceptance and commitment therapy (ACT). Instead of valuing world peace, a person might value volunteering or giving money to a particular organization. Instead of valuing friendship, someone might value regular visits with specific friends. This helps tether the brain to something more practical and it is far more likely to be put into practice. Next, we want to replace any negative reasons to engage these values (go to the dentist to avoid getting cavities) to a positive value (to take care of my teeth). The negative value only feeds the brain's negativity bias and we're trying to shift activity to more positive states of mind.

Play is the opposite of depression

Abraham Joshua Heschel (1955) was a philosopher and a Rabbi and he said, "Life is routine and routine is resistance to wonder" (p. 85). Brian Sutton-Smith is one of the renowned play researchers who made reference to the notion that the opposite of play is not work — it is depression. Somewhere along the way the brain makes things routine and we lose out on this vital natural anti-depressant. Psychiatrist and clinical researcher Stuart Brown (2009), who founded the nonprofit organization National Institute of Play in Carmel Valley, California, says: "Play is an ancient, voluntary, inherently pleasurable, apparently purposeless activity or process that is undertaken for its own sake, and that strengthens our muscles and our social skills, fertilizes brain activity, tempers and deepens our emotions, takes us out of time and enables a state of balance and poise" (p. 412). Play is happening when you are so engrossed in something you enjoy, that you lose all sense of time and don't want it to end. It's where that inner critic finally shuts up, self-consciousness fades away, and we can open up to new possibilities.

The table below shows exactly how play is the opposite of depression and a natural anti-depressant.

Play	Depression
Engaged (Left Prefrontal)	Disengaged (Right Prefrontal)
Absence of self-critic	Self-Judgment
Flexible Mind	Rigid Thinking
Positive Emotions	Negative Emotions
Social (High Vagal Tone)	Isolation (Low Vagal Tone)
Open to possibilities	Helplessness

Numerous studies have shown that when it comes to play, two elements are both needed to make it a natural anti-depressant: toys and playmates. In the 1960s, Marian Diamond, a professor of neuroscience and anatomy at the University of California at Berkeley and one of the world's top researchers on neuroplasticity, pioneered research to see what effects "enriched" environments had on the brains of rats. It turns out that the rodents have a similar neural development as humans do. Diamond and her colleagues (1964) took 36 rats and split them up into three different groups based on environment: (1) enriched, (2) standard, and (3) impoverished. All the cages had the basics of food, water, and lighting. The enriched environment was the play space with friends and toys. The standard environment was a cage less than half the size with friends but no toys. The impoverished environment was a single rat alone with no toys.

After the experiment ended, scientists examined the rats' brains. The rats who had toys to play with *and* other rats to socialize with had thicker *cerebral cortexes* with more neural connections than the other rats. The cortex is a critical area of the brain responsible for cognitive processing, attention, and awareness. They also found that the greatest neural change happened in the first 30 to 60 days, cluing us in to the importance of novelty in neuroplasticity. Engaging in novel things in life has also been shown to increase levels of dopamine, the motivational brain chemical, or *neurotransmitter,* that many studies suggest is low when a person is feeling depressed. Diamond's research proved a fundamental breakthrough, showing us that the environment – the toys and playmates – can actually change neural architecture for the better. What's more, the impoverished rats actually showed *decreased* cortical thickness – implying reduced cognitive processing. Still other studies found that exposing rats to cognitive, physical, and social play increased survival of nerve cells in the hippocampus, allowing this critical part of the brain to thrive. With respect to depression, when we can reduce the amount of energy the brain needs to function well and can grow parts that are responsible for learning, memory, and better discernment of optimal choices, we are nurturing a more resilient brain.

In working with our clients it's important to ask them, what does it mean to play? We have to help them discover what the toys of today are. In my experience this question can arouse a bit of confusion as the concept is foreign. One way to nurture the feeling of play is to ask the client to recall what it was like to play as a child. Have them describe it to you and see if you notice any muscles loosening or smiles breaking out. The question then is, are there things that translate from being a child to being an adult? One client of mine loved to dance as a child and then, after an initial hesitation tried out belly dancing and loved it. Another used to feel free on a ranch and went back to volunteer at the ranch (engaging play and purpose) and later went back to school to become a therapist and an equine assistant. For me, it was my love of poetry and now I have a few favorite poetry books by my bed that I engage regularly.

An enriched environment that's good for the brain doesn't only have toys, it also has playmates. It's essential to help our clients understand who is nourishing to them and who is depleting them. Is there a way to increase time for nourishing playmates and decrease time with depleting people? Are there ways to reach out and find new playmates? I often encourage clients to try out meetup.com or even online venues.

If neurons that fire together, wire together, we want to encourage the firing of these playful moments. As clients begin to bring more playful moments into their lives I ask them to consider these three questions to help savor the moments.

Three steps to savoring:

1   "This is a good moment."
2   "In life there are good moments (or joyful moments)."
3   "Can I bring gratitude to this moment?"

Practice and repeat and watch this natural anti-depressant come alive.

It's all about learning

The final mindset is what makes all the previous natural anti-depressants work. Nourishing an anti-depressant brain is not some achieved state of being but rather the *process* of growing and learning how to get continuously better at something.

This mastery mindset is what creates the most dramatic changes in the brain. Achieving self-compassion is a *performance* goal. Being able to practice self-compassion is a *learning* goal. We use both types of goals, and both can indeed lead to achievement. But only one leads to mastery and uncovers real happiness.

Carol Dweck is a psychology professor at Stanford University who has been studying the field of motivation and mastery for over 40 years. She's found that there are two different types of mindsets people hold when it comes to motivation and change. Some people believe that they have finite abilities that they cannot increase. This is called a *fixed mindset* and it's a big piece of the theory behind *learned helplessness.* Others believe that different people hold varying abilities and that ultimately with strategy and effort, we can increase these abilities. This is called a *growth mindset,* a more flexible state of mind where you believe with understanding, application, and effort that you can increase your abilities. If our clients believe that the ability to gain mastery over depression is fixed, then every encounter with the depression loop becomes a measure of how much ability they have. If they believe their ability is something you can learn to increase, like pumping iron increases muscles, then the same encounter becomes an opportunity for growth. One mindset says that your ability to cultivate an anti-depressant brain is something you exhibit, while the other is something you can nurture and develop.

In one study, Dweck (2006) enlisted college students who exhibited depression, assessed their mindset, and asked them to track their moods, activities, and coping strategies. She discovered that certain students kept rehashing their setbacks and attributed them to their fixed trait of being deficient and unworthy. One student said, "It just kept circulating in my head: 'You're a dope.'" They felt helpless, less motivated to get things done, less able to move through their difficulties. They were stuck. But other students who also felt miserable showed completely different behavior. The more depressed they were, the more actively they confronted it. They reached out for help, kept up with the responsibilities of school, and were more resilient. What was the difference between these two groups?

The members of the first group clearly had a fixed mindset, where they weren't performing well and identified themselves as failures. It became part of who they were and led to a sense of helplessness. The students in the second group had a growth mindset: They believed that they could learn to get better and better; setbacks were painful for them but didn't define them – and could even be opportunities for growth.

With a growth mindset we can help clients begin to incorporate all the previous natural anti-depressants into a strategy for daily living. They can make a list of all the things they do in a day and check off which ones seem depleting and which ones seem nourishing. We can have them extend the list with things that are helpful with depression like exercise, diet, sleep, light, small accomplishments, and connection with others. We can begin to strategize how to replace the depleting activities with some of these healthier activities or the previous natural anti-depressants that are more nourishing.

The key here is that there are no errors. Even "failing" to accomplish the schedule set out is an opportunity to learn about the obstacles that get in the way and perhaps the need to revise the schedule or create new strategies. It's all about learning and it creates hope.

Here's a sample of how we bring learning to implementing healthier changes:

Neutral Activities	Extended List Activities Accomplishment/Pleasure	Natural Anti-depressant
Wake up, check phone.	Take a few deep breaths or the "be" practice.	Mindfulness.
Make breakfast.	Healthy eating: Swap frozen waffles for healthier choices such as oatmeal or granola and yogurt. Remind myself this is taking care of me.	Self-compassion, purpose, play.
Take shower.	Bring more mindfulness to the shower experience.	Mindfulness.
Drive to and from work.	Listen to audio programs I've been wanting to hear.	Purpose, self-compassion, play.
Checking email during lunch.	Go out on a 20-minute walk.	Self-compassion, purpose.
Click through TV channels at night.	Either watch specific shows that are fun for me, take a bath, or connect with friends and family.	Play.
Check messages before bed.	Listen to relaxing old tunes, do a meditation, read a book I've been meaning to get to.	Play, self-compassion.

We each are brought into this world with a certain set of genetics, but what we're learning is that that doesn't have to determine the fate of the days to come. Science that is coming out of the fields of mindfulness and positive psychology are showing us that we have these qualities within us, and that if we tap into them and intentionally nurture them, they can balance out areas of the brain that are impacted through the trauma of depression. But ultimately none of that matters; what matters is the personal experience we and all our clients have with engaging mindfulness, self-compassion, purpose/compassion, play, and mastery. Since we are a culture based in science, that can provide an initial motivation, but ultimately our experience is our greatest teacher. May we all continue to help our clients (and ourselves) be open to discovering that all along there were tremendous capacities within us, and now we can begin to awaken to them.

Bibliography

Brown, S. L. (2009). Discovering the importance of play through personal histories and brain images: An interview with Stuart L. Brown. *American Journal of Play, 1*(4), 399–412.

Conway, C. R., Chibnall, J. T., Gebara, M. A., Price, J. L., Snyder, A. Z., Mintun, M. A., & Sheline, Y. I. (2013). Association of cerebral metabolic activity changes with vagus nerve stimulation antidepressant response in treatment-resistant depression. *Brain Stimulation, 6*(5), 788–797. doi:10.1016/j.brs.2012.11.006

Davidson, R., Pizzagalli, D., & Nitschke, J. (2009). The representation and regulation of emotion in depression: Perspectives from affective neuroscience. In I. Gotlib & C. Hammen (Eds.), *Handbook of depression* (2nd edition). New York, NY: Guilford Press.

Davidson, R. J., Pizzagalli, D., Nitschke, J. B., & Putnam, K. (2002). Depression: Perspectives from affective neuroscience. *Annual Review of Psychology, 53*, 545–574.

Diamond, M., Krech, D., & Rosenaweig, M. (1964). The effects of an enriched environment on the histology of the rat cerebral cortex. *Journal of Comparative Neurology, 123*(1), 111–119.

Dweck, C. S. (2006). *Mindset: The new psychology of success.* New York, NY: Random House.

Fredrickson, B. L., Grewen, K. M., Coffey, K. A., Algoe, S. B., Firestine, A. M., Arevalo, J. M. G., ... Cole, S. W. (2013). A functional genomic perspective on human well- being. *Proceedings of the National Academy of Sciences of the United States of America, 110*(33), 13684–13689. doi:10.1073/pnas.1305419110

Heschel, A. (1955). *God in search of man: A philosophy of Judaism.* New York, NY: Farrar Straus and Giroux.

Keltner, D. (2009). *Born to be good: The science of a meaningful life.* New York, NY: W. W. Norton.

NAMI. (2013). Major depression fact sheet. (n.d.). www.nami.org/factsheets/depression_factsheet.pdf

Porges, S. (2011). *The polyvagal theory: Neurophysiological foundations of emotions, attachment, communication, and self-regulation.* New York, NY: W. W. Norton.

Salamone, J. D., Correa, M., Farrar, A., & Mingote, S. M. (2007). Effort-related functions of nucleus accumbens dopamine and associated forebrain circuits. *Psychopharmacology (Berl.), 191*, 461–482.

Salamone, J. D., Koychev, I., Correa, M., & McGuire, P. (2014). Neurobiological basis of motivational deficits in psychopathology. *European Neuropsychopharmacology, 25*(8), 1225–1238. doi:10.1016/j.euroneuro.2014.08.014

Stahl, B., & Goldstein, E. (2010). *A mindfulness-based stress reduction workbook.* Oakland, CA: New Harbinger Publications.

20

MINDFULNESS YOGA IN PREGNANCY

A promising positive treatment augmentation for women experiencing depression or anxiety

Maria M. Muzik and Susan E. Hamilton

Introduction

Women's mental health during pregnancy has important implications not only for the well-being of the mother, but also for the development, health, and well-being of her unborn child. A growing body of empirical evidence from population-based studies suggests that psychosocial stress during pregnancy may exert a significant influence on pregnancy outcomes, fetal development, and infant birth outcomes, such as birth weight and length of gestation, even after controlling for the effects of established socio-demographic, obstetric, and behavioral risk factors (Andersson, Sundstrom-Poromaa, Wulff, Astrom, & Bixo, 2006; Stewart, 2007; Talge, Neal, & Glover, 2007). Among the most common mental illnesses occurring in pregnancy related to elevated levels of psychosocial stress are depression and anxiety.

Psychopathology during pregnancy is a serious health concern (Bonari et al., 2004; Seng et al., 2001; Steer, Scholl, Hediger, & Fischer, 1992) with perinatal major depressive disorder (MDD) impacting 1 in 5 women (O'Hara & Swain, 1996), and perinatal anxiety affecting 1 in 10 women (Andersson et al., 2006). Co-occurrence of MDD and anxiety is high and treatment is complex, with modest success rates (Andersson et al., 2006; Green et al., 2006). It is a myth that pregnancy is always a joyful time; in fact, it is one of three times in a woman's life that she is most vulnerable to depression, the other two being adolescence and menopause (National Institute of Mental Health, 2009). Hormonal changes and genetic predisposition, combined with social factors such as financial worries and lack of social support, can set up an expectant mother for a host of debilitating symptoms, including persistent depressed mood or irritability, feelings of being easily overwhelmed, excessive guilt, difficulty concentrating, decreased ability to cope with stress, and thoughts of hurting herself (American Psychiatric Association, 2013; Dayan et al., 2010). She may eat less because of a reduced appetite or eat too much, both of which put her unborn baby at risk for growth or weight problems. She may be too restless to sleep at night or be unable to stay awake during the day, affecting her ability to function at work and at home. She may find herself feeling excessively guilty about anything from forgetting her prenatal vitamin to drinking a cup of coffee to not keeping up with work because of morning sickness or fatigue. Additionally, the incidence of depression is increased when women have suffered from depression before becoming pregnant (Dayan, et al., 2010). Untreated antenatal psychopathology bears major health risks for both mother and unborn child, such as poor weight gain, preeclampsia, premature labor, and trouble bonding with the unborn baby (Bifulco et al., 2004; Bonari, et al., 2004; Kurki, Hiilesmaa, Raitasalo, Mattila, & Ylikorkala, 2000; Rondo et al., 2003; Seng et al., 2001). Thus, from a public health perspective, development of feasible treatment modalities for pregnant women suffering from psychiatric conditions is critical.

Sara, age 28, was referred to our High Risk Perinatal Team by her obstetrician around 12 weeks' gestation due to a high score on a depression screen. During her early twenties, Sara struggled with significant depression following the death of a close friend. She saw a therapist for over a year and was prescribed an antidepressant. Sara responded well to treatment, but was advised by her psychiatrist to remain on a low dose of her medication after experiencing a relapse in symptoms while tapering down. Upon discovering that she was pregnant, Sara stopped taking her medication out of concern for her unborn baby.

This pregnancy was unplanned, but desired, and she and her husband are thrilled to be starting a family. However, Sara's first trimester was physically and emotionally difficult, due to significant morning sickness, fatigue, and mood swings. She described moderate depressive symptoms, including hypersomnia, low appetite, feelings of worthlessness, and lack of interest in activities she formerly enjoyed. These symptoms impacted her job as a high school teacher, and reduced her ability to manage everyday stress.

Unfortunately, few women suffering from perinatal mental health disorders receive treatment, leaving them and their children exposed to the negative impact of psychiatric illness during this vulnerable period (Bennett, Marcus, Palmer, & Coyne, 2010; Cohen et al., 2010; Marcus, Flynn, Blow, & Barry, 2003; Muzik, Vazquez, & Marcus, 2011). The range of traditional treatments for psychopathology is limited for women during pregnancy because of potential risks to the fetus. While antidepressant medications have been proven effective to treat antenatal mood disorders (Cohen et al., 2006), many pregnant women are reluctant to take these drugs because they are concerned for their infant's safety (Battle & Salisbury, 2010; Goodman, 2009). In fact, up to 50% of women taking antidepressants prior to conception choose to discontinue medication, creating risk for relapse of symptoms during their pregnancy (Cohen, et al., 2006).

For many commonly prescribed antidepressants, concerns have been raised that their intake during pregnancy increases the risk for congenital malformations, especially when taken during the first trimester (GlaxoSmithKline, 2005). Particularly around the medicine paroxetine, there have been many concerns raised over the last decade (FDA, 2005; Myles, Newall, Ward, & Large, 2013; Painuly, Heun, Painuly, & Sharan, 2013), although a more recent study actually gives this medicine a good safety rating (CDC, 2008). Additionally, it is important to note, that the risk of congenital malformations specifically due to prenatal medication use is only 1% (Bánhidy, Lowry, & Czeizel, 2005) and, in general, every woman has a baseline teratogenicity risk of 3%. Finally, several studies have found that women's perception of risk may be heightened during pregnancy, leading many to overestimate the negative effects of medications like penicillin and antacids, both of which research has been shown to be low risk and are commonly prescribed by health care providers (Lupattelli, Picinardi, Einarson, & Nordeng, 2014; Nordeng, Ystrom, & Einarson, 2010; Widnes, Schjott, Eide, & Granas, 2013).

Given this background, many women choose not to take antidepressants even if a doctor has determined that they need them during pregnancy. Treatment of perinatal mental illness presents special challenges as many women choose not to disclose symptoms out of fear that they could be forced to take medications that may be harmful to their health or their child. Many women prefer psychosocial treatments, but face psychological and practical barriers to treatment initiation and adherence to standard longer term psychotherapy (Kopelman et al., 2008). Others may shy away from conventional psychotherapy as they may feel pregnancy is not a suitable time to unveil dormant conflicts, which would increase their stress level. There is an urgent need to improve the acceptability of and adherence to evidence-based treatments for pregnant and postpartum women suffering from depression.

Sara was reluctant to follow up on the referral for mental health treatment because she was adamant about not taking antidepressants during her pregnancy. After discussing her concerns with a nurse, she learned about a prenatal mindfulness yoga group for women with a history of depression that was being offered in the same building as her doctor's practice. The nurse explained that both yoga and mindfulness practice can help improve mood and reduce stress. Sara had no experience with yoga, but was interested in trying it out.

When traditional Western treatments are rejected or feared, evidence exists suggesting that women are more comfortable with the options offered by complementary and alternative medicine (CAM) (Harding & Foureur, 2009). A study conducted in Canada among midwives revealed that a large percentage of pregnant women were in favor of complementary and alternative medicine approaches, including relaxation, meditation, mind-body work, guided imagery, and herbal medicine, to name a few (Harding & Foureur, 2009). Lamaze and other drug-free childbirth pain management methods have been popular since the 1960s, and many of the techniques taught in these classes promote CAM concepts such as patterned breathing, hypnosis, and visualization. Although a small percentage of women decide to forgo traditional obstetric treatments entirely, resulting in the high rate of Cesarean births, episiotomies, and other labor interventions, many expectant mothers are choosing midwives over obstetricians, medication-free labor over epidurals, and Cesarean section only as a last resort (Epstein, 2008; Johnson & Daviss, 2005). For example, the number of midwives attending births has steadily risen since 1989, and increased from 3.3% in 1989 to 7.7% in 2009, reflecting a shift from viewing birth as a medical process to one that does not necessarily require intervention (Declercq, 2012). Despite limited empirical research, CAM methods are becoming more popular among pregnant women, suggesting that pregnancy may be a time when CAM is more accessible and acceptable to the average woman (Hall, Griffiths, & McKenna, 2011). This could mean that CAM may be a way to treat anxiety and depression in pregnant women who are unwilling to try antidepressants or psychotherapy, and could serve as a gateway to effective treatments for women who may have never considered CAM before becoming pregnant.

Why mindfulness yoga?

Yoga means "union" in Sanskrit, referring to the union between mind, spirit, and body. It is an ancient practice that originated in India thousands of years ago, and involves meditative practices combined with physical poses. Kabat-Zinn (2003) defines the practice of mindfulness as being fully present in the moment, without judgment or correction, starting with simple awareness of one's body and thoughts. Inherently, the human mind judges each experience we have as positive or negative, while striving for a particular outcome and becoming disappointed if that outcome is not achieved. Mindfulness practice gently pulls the mind out of this pattern by observing each experience with an attitude of curiosity, non-judgment, and patience, focusing on what is happening in the present moment, instead of worrying about the future or regretting the past (Stahl & Goldstein, 2010). Mindfulness practice cultivates stability and a sense of being grounded, with the effect of changing one's ability to adapt to all of life's ups and downs. Paying attention to the breath, sounds, bodily sensations, thoughts, and emotions with acceptance and non-attachment helps one to be fully present in the moment, and can help one manage stressful experiences with calm awareness (Kabat-Zinn, 2005).

Yoga has been shown to have many positive health effects, from reducing stress and improving chronic pain to decreasing the incidence of symptoms associated with psychiatric illnesses, such as depression, anxiety, and eating disorders (Dale et al., 2009; Javnbakht, Hejazi Kenari, & Ghasemi, 2009; Khalsa, Shorter, Cope, Wyshak, & Sklar, 2009; Uebelacker et al., 2010; Woolery, Myers, Sternlieb, & Zeltzer, 2004). In addition, mindfulness practice has been shown to successfully decrease perceived stress, fatigue, depressive symptoms, feelings of anger, and mental burnout while increasing energy, empathy, and psychological well-being (Schneider, 2009; Smith et al., 2008; Vieten & Astin, 2008). Narendran et al. (2005) and Chuntharapat, Petpichetchian, and Hatthakit (2008) have reported on the benefits of integrated prenatal yoga, such as improved adaptive autonomic response and reduced incidence of pregnancy-related hypertension and preterm labor, among healthy women in Thailand and India, both countries where yoga and mindfulness practices are widely accepted components of the greater culture. In the United States, yoga is frequently taught in gym-like settings, resulting in an epidemic of classes that omit mindfulness and concentrate on yoga as "exercise." For a beginning yoga student in the United States, "yoga and mindfulness" are not synonymous. Thus, the intentional combination of yoga and mindfulness practice can be powerful, increasing stress tolerance and sleep quality and decreasing psychological distress and chronic pain intensity (Carlson, Speca, Patel, & Goodey, 2003; Haruki, Ishikawa, Kouno, & Matsuda, 2008; Rosenzweig et al., 2010; Trotter, 2010).

Mindfulness, yoga, and positive psychology

Positive psychology accentuates strength, health, and resilience, while deemphasizing struggle, sickness, and pain. Acceptance and commitment therapy, or ACT, a mindfulness-based method of treating anxiety and depression that encourages allowing oneself to feel painful emotions in order to decrease their power, was developed only years apart from the concept of positive psychology (Kashdan & Ciarrocchi, 2013). During a major depressive episode or panic attack, it is common to try moving away from the experience or attempt to push it away. Mindfulness and yoga offer a different path. With mindful awareness, we are invited to simply be in the present moment, without judgment, gently steering our thoughts toward peace instead of striving to find more ways to avoid our emotions. Yoga can be a physical manifestation of mindfulness, bringing mind and body together, which opens up realms of possibility for healing. Mindfulness and yoga are natural partners during times of stress and physical pain, and may be particularly useful as the body progresses through the normal physical and emotional changes of pregnancy.

Mindfulness yoga during pregnancy: previous research

The impact of mindfulness yoga on pregnant women has not been studied extensively, but the research that has been done is encouraging. Mindfulness practice and yoga have been shown to decrease the perception of pain during labor, reduce physical discomfort during pregnancy, improve heart rate, and significantly reduce stress, as well as shorten the first stage of labor (Beddoe & Lee, 2008; Chuntharapat, et al., 2008; Satyapriya et al., 2009). Several studies support the acceptability of prenatal yoga among women seeking treatment for antenatal depression (Battle, Uebelacker, Howard, & Castaneda, 2010; Chuntharapat, et al., 2008; Narendran, et al., 2005; Sun, Hung, Chang, & Kuo, 2010). In addition, Vieten and Astin (2008) found that a mindfulness-based intervention alone can significantly reduce anxiety and negative emotions among pregnant women when compared to a wait-list control group who did not receive the intervention. Guardino et al. (2014) found similar results with a larger sample size, comparing a 6-week mindfulness course to a reading control group.

Very few studies examining yoga as a treatment for antenatal psychopathology have been published, and those that exist have all been published within the past 5 years. In 2009, Beddoe et al. (2009) were the first to examine the impact of a mindfulness yoga intervention on the emotional and physical distress of healthy pregnant women in the United States. Sixteen first-time mothers participated in a 7-week mindful yoga intervention that combined Iyengar yoga and mindfulness-based stress reduction (MBSR), a program developed by Kabat-Zinn (2005), incorporating yoga poses with meditation to bring mindfulness to the body during movement (Stahl & Goldstein, 2010). They found that mindful yoga significantly decreased both emotional stress and physical pain. The data suggested that the intervention may have greater impact if started earlier in pregnancy, since all participants experienced a reduction in stress, but women who started in their second trimester were more likely to have reduced physical discomfort as they progressed in their pregnancy. Three randomized control trials, two in the US and one in India, have been published supporting these results. Bershadsky et al. (2014) found that salivary cortisol levels and negative affect were reduced for women who participated in the yoga group, while Newham et al. (2014) found that pregnancy-specific anxiety, such as worry related to childbirth, significantly improved when compared to a group of women receiving treatment as usual. Finally, Satyapriya et al. (2013) reported a significant reduction in anxiety, depression, and pregnancy-related discomfort in women who completed an integrated yoga intervention when compared with a group assigned to a standard regimen of physical exercise. However, since women meeting criteria for current psychopathology were excluded in these studies, it was unclear whether the benefits of Mindfulness Yoga (M-Yoga) were limited to healthy women or can be generalized to pregnant women with psychiatric illness.

Our study (Muzik, Hamilton, Rosenblum, McGinnis, & Hadi, 2012) was the first attempt to close this gap in the literature; we explored the feasibility, acceptability, and efficacy of M-Yoga in reducing symptoms of depression among pregnant women with current and lifetime psychiatric diagnoses in an open trial format using a convenience sample. Shortly after our pilot study was made available online, Field et al. published four randomized control trials using a large sample of psychiatrically high-risk pregnant women meeting criteria for either major depression or dysthymia (Field et al., 2012; Field, Diego, Delgado, & Medina, 2013a, 2013b; Mitchell et al., 2012). In one study, both yoga and massage therapy were found to significantly decrease symptoms of depression, anxiety, and back/leg pain when compared to a third group that received standard prenatal care (Field et al., 2012). Another study found that randomization to a group receiving a combination of yoga and tai chi led to a significant decrease in depression, anxiety, and sleep disturbances when compared to a wait-list control group (Field et al., 2013a). The third study showed that a 12-week yoga intervention significantly reduced depression, anxiety, anger, and back/leg pain when compared to a 12-week social support control group, where one study staff member met with participants to provide a space for discussion without leading the group or offering comment (Field et al., 2013b). Finally, the fourth study compared women randomly assigned to either a yoga group or parenting education group, finding that yoga was significantly more likely to reduce symptoms of depression over a 12-week period (Mitchell et al., 2012). The work of Field et al. further demonstrated that prenatal yoga can be a viable alternative to traditional treatments for depression and anxiety in a high-risk sample. Our original hypothesis was that prenatal yoga will improve antenatal depression through the following mechanism: M-Yoga will enhance women's mindfulness and maternal-fetal attachment, which in turn will lead to an empowered and positive feeling towards pregnancy and motherhood and subsequently contribute to reduced symptoms of depression.

Materials and methods

Recruitment

All study procedures were approved by the institutional review board of the University of Michigan Medical School. Informed consent, including an explanation of potential risks and benefits, was obtained from all subjects prior to data collection. Participants were recruited through a university-based perinatal psychiatry clinic and flyers posted in the community. Women were invited to participate in a free 10-week prenatal "Mindfulness Yoga" class to improve well-being and decrease stress. Forty-nine were screened for eligibility within a 4-week period in the fall of 2009, and 22 were found eligible for the study. Participants were first-time mothers with the following characteristics: English speaking; at least 18 years of age; history of depression or anxiety; interested in alternative health care; not taking medications for mental health conditions; 12–26 weeks pregnant at the first yoga class; and scored 9 or higher on the Edinburgh Postpartum Depression Scale (EPDS) (Murray & Carothers, 1990) at baseline. Exclusion criteria included patients with active substance abuse, psychosis, and suicidality. Women in psychotherapy, those practicing yoga, or those with medical problems (pre-existing or pregnancy-related) were not excluded from the sample. Each eligible woman underwent a psychiatric diagnostic interview (First, Spitzer, Gibbon, & Williams, 2002) at baseline to assess both past and present DSM-IV diagnoses.

Of the initial 22 women entering the study, two dropped out after attending only one class: one because of transportation problems and the other because of back problems unrelated to yoga; thus only 20 women participated in the intervention. Lastly, for the final outcome measures, two more women did not complete surveys after the last yoga class (premature delivery; relocation), reducing the sample size to $n = 18$.

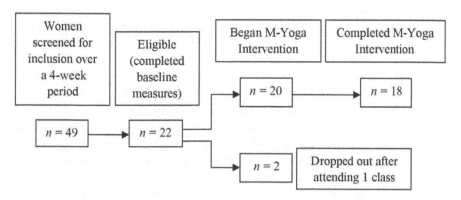

FIGURE 20.1 Recruitment

Participants

The women enrolled in this study ranged in age from 22 to 41 (mean = 32.9, SD = 4.9). Seventy-five percent were Caucasian, 10% were Latina, 10% were biracial or other, and 5% were African-American. They were highly educated, with 60% having master's degrees or higher. Eighty percent were married or living with a partner. All had significant histories of psychopathology as indicated by the Structured Clinical Interview for DSM Disorders (SCID), including current or past depression (60%), current or past anxiety disorders (55%), PTSD (55%), and a past history of substance abuse/dependence (45%). Half of the sample had an active Axis I diagnosis at baseline according to DSM-IV-TR (American Psychiatric Association, 2013), and over 85% had a lifetime psychiatric diagnosis (Table 20.1). Depression symptom severity at baseline was assessed using the Beck Depression Inventory-II (BDI-II) (Beck, Steer, & Brown, 1996). Nine participants were also engaged in outside psychotherapy while undergoing the M-Yoga class. There were no adverse events related to study participation.

Design

The M-Yoga open feasibility trial was facilitated by two instructors, both master's-level mental health professionals, certified in prenatal yoga and experienced in mindfulness techniques. Each 90-minute session focused on a variety of poses, taught specifically for the pregnant body, with awareness of the baby and modified for any level of experience or gestational age. Classes met once weekly. Two 10-session mindfulness yoga classes ran consecutively, each with 10 participants who completed the full series of sessions; one class took place during evening hours and the other during the day. Both classes received the same intervention, taught by the same instructors, and only differed by time of day delivery. Materials used during M-Yoga, such as mats, bolsters, and straps, were provided by the research study.

The M-Yoga curriculum differed from typical prenatal hatha yoga classes by highlighting mindfulness practice, with targeted instructions, reminders, and readings. Participants were taught mindfulness techniques including breathing, guided visualization, and relaxation. The instructors consciously made it a part of class to continually remind women to focus inward toward the sensations of their body, listen to the feedback of body during asana, and be aware of how their bodies are changing to support their growing baby. A significant aspect of the intervention was being "mindful" of the baby, to sense its unique persona, which in turn facilitates the attachment process. In addition, having the word "mindfulness" in the title of the class/study continually brought that awareness to the forefront.

Sessions opened with a 10–15 minute check-in, allowing each woman to share how she was feeling physically and emotionally with the group. Teachers customized the poses and instruction to address participants' current issues, cultivating a supportive atmosphere. For example, if irritability was an issue, instructions included finding compassion towards oneself as the body experiences the hormonal changes of pregnancy. If heartburn was an issue, poses were taught with an emphasis on creating more space between the chest cavity and throat. Each class

TABLE 20.1 Participant demographic and mental health baseline characteristics

Participant Characteristics (N = 22)	% Frequency (N) or M (SD)
Age	32.41 (4.98)
Gestational age at baseline (in weeks)	21.80 (5.96)
Ethnicity	
Minority	27% (6)
Caucasian	72% (15)
Education	
< Bachelor's Degree	14% (3)
Bachelor's Degree Only	32% (7)
Master's Degree or Higher	60% (12)
Marital Status	
Single	28% (5)
Living with Partner	72% (17)
Income	
Under 25,000	0% (0)
25,000–50,000	15% (3)
More than 50,000	45% (9)
Refused/Missing	40% (10)
Current Psychopathologya	
No diagnosis	50.0% (11)
Major Depression	9.1% (2)
Post-Traumatic Stress Disorder	18.2% (4)
Anxiety Disorder (GAD, Phobias, Panic)	45.5% (10)
Substance Abuse/Dependence	0%
Past Psychopathologya	
No diagnosis	13.6% (3)
Major Depression	54.5% (12)
Post-Traumatic Stress Disorder	36.4% (8)
Anxiety Disorder (GAD, Phobias, Panic)	9.1% (2)
Substance Abuse/Dependence	45.5% (10)
BDI-II Depression Severity	
Baseline BDI score (range 6–33)	15.2 (7.6)
Mild (score < 13; 45%)	9.2 (2.5)
Moderate (score > 13; 55%)	20.2 (6.8)

[a] *Axis I diagnosis assessed with SCID, 73% of participants had more than one diagnosis*

Note: Income is measured in categories 1–21 in 4K increments: 18 = 85–89k, 12 = 55–59k Minorities included: Latina (2), Multiracial (2), African-American (1), Native American (1)

included seated, kneeling, standing, and restorative poses. The instructors demonstrated each pose while including descriptions of Kabat-Zinn and colleagues' (1992) seven qualities of mindfulness: allowing presence, non-judging, patience, beginner's mind, non-striving, acceptance, and letting go, for example, "Practice the pose for your body without judgment" and "Bring your attention to your breath, always practicing with awareness of your growing baby." See Table 20.2 for more examples. Techniques supported women's comfort with their changing body, prepared the body and mind for the birthing experience, and focused awareness on the fetus. To ensure women's safety, modifications for all poses were offered and participants were reminded throughout the practice to listen to the body's cues, for example, when to move deeper in a pose and when to slow down. Classes ended with a 15–20 minute restorative pose, including a full-body relaxation exercise, along with a reading from a text such as *Everyday Blessings: The Inner Work of Mindful Parenting* (M. Kabat-Zinn & J. Kabat-Zinn, 1997) and *Bringing Yoga to Life* (Farhi, 2003) to provide more information on the benefits of a mindful practice and to increase stress reduction and connection with the body and the baby. Finally, sessions concluded with a 5–10 minute informal interaction while participants prepared to leave. Instructors and participants did not interact outside the class context, and we did not facilitate peer interactions among participants outside the M-Yoga class. Women were encouraged to also practice at home, but compliance was not assessed.

Sara came to the first class feeling nervous and tired after her day at work, but curious and ready to learn. She found the instructors to be warm, welcoming, and knowledgeable. At the beginning of each class, the instructors encouraged everyone to share how they were feeling, both physically and emotionally. At first, Sara didn't say much, but found herself feeling more comfortable every week, and was relieved to hear from other women who were struggling with depression, too. The poses helped with the tension in her neck and back, and she loved the final relaxation exercise that closed every class. When class ended, Sara often felt more energized and seemed to sleep better. Once, when her back was aching during a particularly stressful day, she tried using one of the yoga poses and it quickly became something she relied on for relief.

TABLE 20.2 Examples of M-Yoga instructor's language

Bring your awareness and focus inward to your breath
Watch your inhalation and your exhalation
Allow your inhalation to bring an extension to your spine
Allow your exhalation to bring a release of your shoulders
Observe the base of your posture equally balancing your weight on the four corners of each foot
Move into the posture without jerking or forcing
Observe your breath and body without commenting or analyzing
Observe and accept where your body is today, moving with awareness and modifying the pose as necessary
Bring your attention to your breath and to your center where your baby is, always practicing with awareness of your growing baby
Inhale the breath and lengthen the spine; on your exhalation move into the pose
Start the pose from afresh as we repeat it on the second side
Practice the pose for your body today without judgment
Observing if you need to come out of a pose, and coming out of the pose with the same awareness and attention as we had going into the pose
Release more completely into the pose with each exhalation
Relinquish your will to do, and allow yourself to be in the pose

Measures

Participating women underwent an initial psychiatric interview, and completed self-report questionnaires about depression, mindfulness, and maternal-fetal attachment, at baseline and after the final yoga class.

1   The *Structured Clinical Interview for DSM Disorders (SCID I N-P)* (First et al., 2002) is a clinician-based diagnostic interview deriving a DSM-IV Axis I diagnosis (American Psychiatric Association, 2013), administered prior to the intervention. The SCID modules assess the presence of current and past psychopathology, specifically mood disorder, psychotic symptoms, eating disorders, anxiety disorders, and substance disorders. Available data suggest good inter-rater reliability for MDD (α = .61–.80) and PTSD (α = .77–.88) and the SCID is seen as the "gold standard" among diagnostic interviews (Sanchez-Villegas et al., 2008; Zanarini et al., 2000).

2   The *Edinburgh Postnatal Depression Scale (EPDS)* (Cox, Holden, & Sagovsky, 1987) was used to determine eligibility; a cut-off score of ≥ 9 was used (Murray & Carothers, 1990). Items are scored on a 4-point scale (0–3), ranging from 0 to 30 (Cox, Chapman, Murray, & Jones, 1996). Available data suggest good reliability (α = .87) and positive predictive value (83%) (Cox et al., 1996).

3   The *Beck Depression Inventory (BDI-II)* is a 21-item survey designed to measure the severity of symptoms of depression, such as loss of interest, guilty feelings, and worthlessness (Beck, Steer, & Brown, 1996). Items are scored on a 4-point scale (0–3), ranging from 0 to 63, with higher scores indicating greater symptomatology. A score of 0–13 indicates minimal depression, 14–19 mild depression, 20–28 moderate depression, and 29–63 severe depression (Beck, Steer, Ball, & Ranieri, 1996). In this study, we sorted subjects into two groups, mild depression (range 6–13; n = 10) and moderate depression (range 14–33; n = 12). Among psychiatric samples, the internal reliability of the BDI-II has ranged from a =. 89 to a =. 92 (Beck, Steer, & Brown, 1996).

4   The *Five Facet Mindfulness Questionnaire-Revised (FFMQ-Revised)* assesses for elements of mindfulness in five areas: observing (paying attention to stimuli), describing (labeling the sensation of stimuli), acting with awareness (purposefully attending to stimuli), non-judging (not criticizing one's inner experience), and non-reactivity (allowing thoughts and emotions to come and go, without reaction) (Baer, Smith, Hopkins, Krietemeyer, & Toney, 2006). Items are scored on a 5-point scale (1–5), ranging from 39 to 195, with higher scores reflecting greater mindfulness. The FFMQ-Revised has shown good internal consistency in several samples, with Cronbach's alphas ≥ .80 (Baer et al., 2006).

5   The *Maternal Fetal Attachment Scale (MFAS)* is a 24-item scale that assesses for maternal-fetal attachment during pregnancy, made up of five factors: role taking ("I picture myself feeding the baby"); differentiation of self from fetus ("I enjoy watching my tummy jiggle as the baby kicks inside"); interaction with fetus ("I poke the baby to get him/her to poke back"); not attributing characteristics to the fetus ("It seems the baby kicks and moves just to keep

me from resting"); and giving of self ("I feel all the trouble of being pregnant is worth it") (Cranley, 1981). Available data suggests good reliability, with sub-scale Cronbach's alphas ranging from .52 to .73, and a total score alpha of .85 (Cranley, 1981).

6   Women completed a brief survey regarding acceptability of the intervention.

Results

Psychopathology and baseline characteristics

Women with and without current psychopathology did not differ on demographic characteristics. Thus, we did not control for demographics in all subsequent analyses. The 18 participants attended on average 7.83 sessions (SD = 1.62); 11 (55%) participants attended at least 8 or more groups, and 3 (16%) only attended 5 groups.

Acceptability

Overall, the women felt M-Yoga was a helpful coping strategy and benefited the child as well ("Yoga helped me to cope with a high-risk pregnancy – and my son is the most calm and gentlest of souls. The stress reduction REALLY helps the baby, too"). Social support of the group was highlighted *("Hearing from the other moms made me feel much less alone,"* and *"I really benefitted emotionally from sharing with the other participants and benefitted physically from breathing and relaxation exercises").* Teaching content and instructors were perceived positively *("The breathing and mindfulness exercises allowed me to have the delivery I wanted. It was perfect,"* or *"I loved all of it – the readings were excellent and the instructors have a true passion for helping pregnant women").*

Stability and treatment effects before and after M-Yoga intervention

We calculated the correlation coefficients from pre- to post-intervention for all measures (Table 20.3), demonstrating a negative correlation between baseline depression symptoms (BDI-II) and post-intervention mindfulness skills. In addition, we also saw negative correlations between post-intervention depression symptoms (BDI-II) and both mindfulness and maternal-fetal attachment at baseline. Furthermore, we calculated the stability coefficients from pre- to post-intervention for mindfulness ($r(18) = .85, p < .001$), maternal-fetal attachment ($r(18) = .62, p < .01$), and depression (BDI-II) ($r(18) = .64, p < .01$). Post-intervention BDI-II depression scores were significantly and inversely related with baseline mindfulness ($r(18) = -.470, p < .05$) and maternal-fetal attachment ($r(18) = -.549, p < .05$); these associations were even stronger for concurrent post-intervention mindfulness ($r(18) = -.547, p < .05$) and maternal-fetal attachment ($r(18) = -.591, p < .05$).

TABLE 20.3 Correlations between pre and post group measures

Measures	Post BDI	Post Mindfulness	Post Maternal-Fetal Attachment
Pre BDI	.642**	−.556*	−.272
Pre Mindfulness	−.470*	.853**	.234
Pre Maternal-Fetal Attachment	−.549*	.004	.623**

*$p < .05$ and **$p < .01$

Intervention effect for total group

Eighteen women provided post-intervention assessments. Using paired t-tests, we explored changes on all outcome variables from pre- to post-intervention (Table 20.4). As nine women were enrolled in outside psychotherapy, we investigated treatment effects based on psychotherapy. We found that psychotherapy enrollment did not affect M-Yoga outcomes, and thus was not controlled for in analyses. There was a significant reduction in depressive symptoms as measured by both the BDI-II and EPDS. The total score for mindfulness skills (FFMQ-Revised) improved significantly over the intervention. This result was mainly driven by significant results on the non-judgment subscale, which includes statements like "I (do not) criticize myself for having irrational or inappropriate emotions" and "When I have distressing thoughts or images, I (do not) judge myself as good or bad." Finally, maternal-fetal attachment (MFAS) significantly increased overall and on all five subscales.

After the third class, Sara started talking with two other women, Michelle and Penelope. Two weeks later, when she was having car trouble, she called Michelle and asked for a ride. They started carpooling, and Sara began to really look forward to attending each week. Another woman in the class, Jessica, invited everyone to her baby shower, including the instructors. As Sara got closer to her due date, and the end of the M-Yoga classes, she realized that she was less likely to ruminate about small mistakes she'd made at work or feel guilty about having to take maternity leave at the end of the school year. Her baby was moving a lot now, and she was pleased to notice that he would slow down if she talked softly to him and rubbed her belly. Childbirth was still stressful to think about, but she was able to talk about her fears in class and it helped to hear that she wasn't alone. The instructors demonstrated a few poses that can help with pain during contractions, and chose a reading about trusting one's body and relaxing into the present moment for the relaxation exercise at the end of class.

Discussion and conclusion

While conventional treatments for psychopathology are well researched and many are widely accepted, pregnant women may be reluctant to engage in standard treatment modalities because of possible risks to the unborn child. It is crucial to explore more acceptable treatments. Our findings suggest that the M-Yoga

TABLE 20.4 Intervention effect for total group

Time Point					
	Before M-Yoga Intervention	After M-Yoga Intervention	t	df	p
Maternal Psychopathology					
BDI score	13.95 (6.84)	9.63 (6.99)	2.40	17	.025*
EPDS score	12.45 (3.41)	7.60 (4.16)	4.41	19	.000**
Mindfulness					
Total	131.17 (14.23)	137.56 (16.79)	-3.09	17	.007**
Observe	27.78 (3.95)	29.28 (3.56)	-1.92	17	.072*
Describe	27.06 (4.00)	27.61 (3.68)	-1.13	17	ns
Awareness	27.50 (3.76)	28.11 (4.57)	-0.65	17	ns
Non-Judgment	28.89 (6.25)	28.94 (6.76)	-2.20	17	.042
Non-React	21.94 (4.76)	23.61 (5.29)	-1.71	17	ns
Maternal-Fetal Attachment					
Total	83.56 (10.12)	95.50 (10.53)	-5.65	17	.000**
Role Taking	17.39 (2.45)	18.23 (2.08)	-2.30	17	.035*
Diff. of Self from Fetus	14.17 (2.96)	17.06 (2.41)	-4.96	17	.000**
Interaction with Fetus	16.67 (3.16)	19.22 (3.42)	-4.21	17	.001**
Not Attrib. Char. to Fetus	17.72 (3.34)	22.67 (4.33)	-3.99	17	.001**
Giving of Self	19.78 (3.00)	22.22 (2.05)	-3.04	17	.007**

$'p < 10, *p < .05$ and $**p < .01$

intervention is acceptable to the target population. We found that M-Yoga reduced depressive symptoms in pregnant women. Given the small sample size, we did not have adequate representation of mildly, moderately, or severely depressed women and thus were unable to make inferences about the efficacy of M-Yoga based on depression severity. However, we speculate that M-Yoga may prove beneficial if offered as an adjunctive treatment mode in combination with traditional pharmacotherapy or psychotherapy for pregnant women struggling with symptoms of depression. Future studies should include a sufficiently large sample with a wide range of depression severity in order to make definite conclusions.

As predicted, the intervention appeared to positively impact participants' mindfulness skills, helping them to experience the present moment with an attitude of curiosity instead of judgment. This was expected as the intervention specifically targeted the capacity for mindfulness through selected readings and the guided focus on body awareness. Finally, it appeared that a potentially positive impact of M-Yoga was in the maternal-fetal attachment domain, with improvement in overall total score as well as all five subscale scores. The MFAS measured how often mothers engage in behaviors that indicate interaction and connection with their unborn child (Cranley, 1981), meaning that women who completed the intervention became more comfortable assuming the role of a mother and they enjoyed interaction with the fetus; they were also more likely to engage in healthy behaviors because of the pregnancy. This increase in fetal attachment suggests that M-Yoga provided a supportive environment in the transition to motherhood, as well as an opportunity to engage in healthy behaviors for the group as a whole (Salisbury, Law, LaGasse, & Lester, 2003). The improvements in maternal-fetal attachment were independent of depression symptom level and current psychopathology.

Limitations of this study include the small sample size, the homogeneity of the sample population, and the lack of a control group. In addition, we relied upon self-report of symptoms rather than interviewer-rated assessment of some key outcomes (BDI-II). Finally, we did not measure symptoms of anxiety, which would have been useful considering that nearly half of our sample (45.5%) met criteria for an anxiety disorder at baseline. However, given that the majority of our participants (54.5%) met criteria for past MDD and all participants scored ≥ 9 on the EPDS at baseline, indicating they were at risk for developing MDD during pregnancy, we feel that depression is an appropriate primary outcome variable. Despite a small sample size, data collected provides a solid foundation for future research in terms of documenting feasibility and acceptability of this intervention. It is notable that we were able to recruit our sample very quickly because of the tremendous response and in fact were required to turn away several women after meeting our recruitment goal. Verifying our results with a larger, more diverse sample will be important; given the interest we observed during the recruitment phase, obtaining such a sample appears realistic. Our sample consisted primarily of white, highly educated, partnered, and financially comfortable women open to alternative treatments for psychopathology. While we attempted to make the classes accessible to women of different socio-economic backgrounds and employment status by offering classes during the day and evening, enrollment in the classes was determined in part by distance traveled and was thus limited to women who had reliable transportation. More research is needed to explore the effects of M-Yoga on pregnant women who are unpartnered, under age 25, and from diverse ethnic backgrounds, and who have fewer resources (education, income, etc.). Finally, the lack of a control group does not allow us to separate the effects of M-Yoga and the social support created by meeting weekly with other pregnant women and two familiar instructors. Future research would benefit from recruiting a group who practices yoga at home using a DVD or a group that meets weekly for group exercise such as walking to use as a control in order to determine which mechanism has the greatest impact on outcomes.

This study builds on the work of Beddoe et al. (2009), Vieten and Astin (2008), and Battle et al. (2010), demonstrating the feasibility and acceptance of mindfulness yoga during pregnancy, yet for the first time targeting a high-risk population with historical and active psychiatric disorders. Our work provides promising first evidence that mindfulness yoga may improve depression symptoms, promote a mindful stance towards pregnancy, and enhance mother's attachment towards her child, which in turn, is a long-term gain promoting child well-being.

Sara left the final class with a sense of accomplishment and excitement, as well as sadness that it was ending. She kept in touch with Michelle and Penelope, continued to practice M-Yoga at home, and was excited to find a local yoga class that encourages mothers to bring their babies. When she went into labor at 38 weeks, she used many of the yoga poses learned in class to manage pain, but ultimately elected to have an epidural after 30 hours of labor. Her son, Avery, was born healthy, and she was thrilled to see that he seemed to know her voice. Sara started breastfeeding while still in the hospital and plans to continue. She is looking forward to her first postpartum yoga class.

Acknowledgments

We would like to thank all the mothers who participated in the M-Yoga groups, as well as our M-Yoga instructors, Marlene McGrath, MSW, and Barbara Brooken-Harvey, MSW, at Inward Bound Yoga in Ann Arbor, Michigan.

Bibliography

American Psychiatric Association. (2013). *Diagnostic and statistical manual of mental disorders* (5th edition). Washington, DC: American Psychiatric Association.

Andersson, L., Sundstrom-Poromaa, I., Wulff, M., Astrom, M., & Bixo, M. (2006). Depression and anxiety during pregnancy and six months postpartum: A follow-up study. *Acta Obstet Gynecol Scand, 85*(8), 937–944.

Baer, R., Smith, G., Hopkins, J., Krietemeyer, J., & Toney, L. (2006). Using self-report assessment methods to explore facets of mindfulness. *Assessment, 13*(1), 27–45.

Bánhidy, F., Lowry, R. B., & Czeizel, A. E. (2005). Risk and benefit of drug use during pregnancy *Int J Med Sci, 2*(3), 100–106.

Battle, C. L., & Salisbury, A. (2010). Treatment of antenatal depression: Letter to the editor. *J Midwifery and Women's Health, 55*(5), 479.

Battle, C. L., Uebelacker, L. A., Howard, M., & Castaneda, M. (2010). Prenatal yoga and depression during pregnancy. *Birth, 37*(4), 353–354.

Beck, A., Steer, R., Ball, R., & Ranieri, W. (1996). Comparison of beck depression inventories-IA and -II in psychiatric outpatients. *J Pers Assess, 67*(3), 588–597.

Beck, A., Steer, R. A., & Brown, G. K. (1996). *Manual for beck depression inventory-II.* San Antonio, TX: Psychological Corporation.

Beddoe, A. E., & Lee, K. A. (2008). Mind-body interventions during pregnancy. *J Obstet Gynecol Neonatal Nurs, 37*(2), 165–175.

Beddoe, A. E., Paul Yang, C. P., Kennedy, H. P., Weiss, S. J., & Lee, K. A. (2009). The effects of mindfulness-based yoga during pregnancy on maternal psychological and physical distress. *J Obstet Gynecol Neonatal Nurs, 38*(3), 310–319.

Bennett, I. M., Marcus, S. C., Palmer, S. C., & Coyne, J. C. (2010). Pregnancy-related discontinuation of antidepressants and depression care visits among medicaid recipients. [Research Support, N. I. H., Extramural]. *Psych Serv, 61*(4), 386–391.

Bershadsky, S., Trumpfheller, L., Kimble, H. B., Pipaloff, D., & Yim, I. S. (2014). The effect of prenatal Hatha yoga on affect, cortisol and depressive symptoms. *Complement Ther Clin Pract, 20*(2), 106–113.

Bifulco, A., Figueiredo, B., Guedeney, N., Gorman, L. L., Hayes, S., Muzik, M., . . . Henshaw, C. A. (2004). Maternal attachment style and depression associated with childbirth: Preliminary results from a European and US cross-cultural study. *Br J Psychiatr Suppl, 46*, s31–s37.

Bonari, L., Pinto, N., Ahn, E., Einarson, A., Steiner, M., & Koren, G. (2004). Perinatal risks of untreated depression during pregnancy. *Can J Psychiatr, 49*(11), 726–735.

Carlson, L. E., Speca, M., Patel, K. D., & Goodey, E. (2003). Mindfulness-based stress reduction in relation to quality of life, mood, symptoms of stress, and immune parameters in breast and prostate cancer outpatients. *Psychosom Med, 65*(4), 571–581.

CDC. (2008). Update on overall prevalence of major birth defects—Atlanta, Georgia, 1978–2005. *MMWR Morb Mortal Wkly Rep, 57*(1), 1–5.

Chuntharapat, S., Petpichetchian, W., & Hatthakit, U. (2008). Yoga during pregnancy: Effects on maternal comfort, labor pain and birth outcomes. *Complement Ther Clin Pract, 14*(2), 105–115.

Cohen, L. S., Altshuler, L. L., Harlow, B. L., Nonacs, R., Newport, D. J., Viguera, A. C., . . . Stowe, Z. N. (2006). Relapse of major depression during pregnancy in women who maintain or discontinue antidepressant treatment. *JAMA, 295*(5), 499–507.

Cohen, L. S., Wang, B., Nonacs, R., Viguera, A. C., Lemon, E. L., & Freeman, M. P. (2010). Treatment of mood disorders during pregnancy and postpartum. *Psychiatr Clin North Am, 33*(2), 273–293.

Cox, J. L., Chapman, G., Murray, D., & Jones, P. (1996). Validation of the Edinburgh Postnatal Depression Scale (EPDS) in non-postnatal women. *J Affect Disord, 39*(3), 185–189.

Cox, J. L., Holden, J. M., & Sagovsky, R. (1987). Detection of postnatal depression. Development of the 10-item Edinburgh Postnatal Depression Scale. *Br J Psychiatr, 150*, 782–786.

Cranley, M. S. (1981). Development of a tool for the measurement of maternal attachment during pregnancy. *Nurs Res, 30*(5), 281–284.

Dale, L. P., Mattison, A. M., Greening, K., Galen, G., Neace, W. P., & Matacin, M. L. (2009). Yoga workshop impacts psychological functioning and mood of women with self-reported history of eating disorders. *Eat Disord J Treat Prev, 17*(5), 422–434.

Dayan, J., Creveuil, C., Dreyfus, M., Herlicoviez, M., Baleyte, J. M., & O'Keane, V. (2010). Developmental model of depression applied to prenatal depression: Role of present and past life events, past emotional disorders and pregnancy stress. *PLoS ONE, 5*(9), e12942.

Declercq, E. (2012). Trends in midwife-attended births in the United States, 1989–2009. *J Midwifery and Women's Health, 57*(4), 321–326.

Epstein, A. (Writer). (2008). The business of being born [DVD]. In R. Lake (Producer): New Line.

Farhi, D. (2003). *Bringing yoga to life.* New York: Harper Collins Press.

FDA. (2005). FDA advising of risk of birth defects with Paxil. www.fda.gov/newsevents/newsroom/pressannouncements/2005/ucm108527.htm

Field, T., Diego, M., Delgado, J., & Medina, L. (2013a). Tai chi/yoga reduces prenatal depression, anxiety and sleep disturbances. *Complement Ther Clin Pract, 19*(1), 6–10.

Field, T., Diego, M., Delgado, J., & Medina, L. (2013b). Yoga and social support reduce prenatal depression, anxiety and cortisol. *J Bodyw Mov Ther, 17*(4), 397–403.

Field, T., Diego, M., Hernandez-Reif, M., Medina, L., Delgado, J., & Hernandez, A. (2012). Yoga and massage therapy reduce prenatal depression and prematurity. *J Body Mov Ther, 16*(2), 204–209.

First, M., Spitzer, R., Gibbon, M., & Williams, J. (2002). *Structured Clinical Interview for DSM-IV-TR Axis I disorders, research version, Non-patient edition (SCID-I/NP).* New York, NY: Biometrics Research, New York State Psychiatric Institute.

GlaxoSmithKline. (2005). US: December 2005 communication and recommendations to health care professionals. www.gsk.com/content/dam/gsk/globals/documents/pdf/pregnancy_hcp_letter.pdf

GlaxoSmithKline. (2013). Use of Paxil CR tablets or Paxil tablets during pregnancy. www.gsk.com/content/dam/gsk/globals/documents/pdf/pregnancy_hcp_letter.pdf

Goodman, J. H. (2009). Women's attitudes, preferences, and perceived barriers to treatment for perinatal depression. *Birth, 36*(1), 60–69.

Green, B. L., Krupnick, J. L., Chung, J., Siddique, J., Krause, E. D., Revicki, D., . . . Miranda, J. (2006). Impact of PTSD comorbidity on one-year outcomes in a depression trial. *J Clin Psychol, 62*(7), 815–835.

Guardino, C. M., Dunkel Schetter, C., Bower, J. E., Lu, M. C., & Smalley, S. L. (2014). Randomised controlled pilot trial of mindfulness training for stress reduction during pregnancy. *Psychol Health, 29*(3), 334–349.

Hall, H. G., Griffiths, D. L., & McKenna, L. G. (2011). The use of complementary and alternative medicine by pregnant women: A literature review. *Midwifery, 27*(6), 817–824.

Harding, D., & Foureur, M. (2009). New Zealand and Canadian midwives' use of complementary and alternative medicine. *New Zealand Coll of Midwives Jnl, 40*(1), 407–412.

Haruki, Y., Ishikawa, R., Kouno, R., & Matsuda, Y. (2008). Mindfulness-based stress reduction (MBSR) program and its application in health psychology. *Japanese Journal of Health Psychology, 21*(2), 57–67.

Javnbakht, M., Hejazi Kenari, R., & Ghasemi, M. (2009). Effects of yoga on depression and anxiety of women. *Complement Ther Clin Pract, 15*(2), 102–104.

Johnson, K. C., & Daviss, B. A. (2005). Outcomes of planned home births with certified professional midwives: Large prospective study in North America. *BMJ, 330*(7505), 1416–1419.

Kabat-Zinn, J. (2003). Mindfulness-based interventions in context: Past, present, and future. *Clin Psychol: Sci Pract, 10*(2), 144–156.

Kabat-Zinn, J. (2005). *Full catastrophe living: Using the wisdom of your body and mind to face stress, pain, and illness* (Delta trade pbk. reissue edition). New York, NY: Delta Trade Paperbacks.

Kabat-Zinn, J., Massion, A. O., Kristeller, J., Peterson, L. G., Fletcher, K. E., Pbert, L., . . . Santorelli, S. F. (1992). Effectiveness of a meditation-based stress reduction program in the treatment of anxiety disorders. *Am J Psychiatr, 149*(7), 936–943.

Kabat-Zinn, M., & Kabat-Zinn, J. (1997). *Everyday blessings: The inner work of mindful parenting* (1st edition). New York, NY: Hyperion.

Kashdan, T., & Ciarrocchi, J. (2013). *Mindfulness, acceptance, and positive psychology: The seven foundations of well-being.* Oakland, CA: Context Press.

Khalsa, S. B., Shorter, S. M., Cope, S., Wyshak, G., & Sklar, E. (2009). Yoga ameliorates performance anxiety and mood disturbance in young professional musicians. *Appl Psychophysiol Biofeedback, 34*(4), 279–289.

Kopelman, R. C., Moel, J., Mertens, C., Stuart, S., Arndt, S., & O'Hara, M. W. (2008). Barriers to care for antenatal depression. *Psych Serv, 59*(4), 429–432.

Kurki, T., Hiilesmaa, V., Raitasalo, R., Mattila, H., & Ylikorkala, O. (2000). Depression and anxiety in early pregnancy and risk for preeclampsia. *Obst Gynecol, 95*(4), 487–490.

Lupattelli, A., Picinardi, M., Einarson, A., & Nordeng, H. (2014). Health literacy and its association with perception of teratogenic risks and health behavior during pregnancy. *Patient Educ Couns, 96*(2), 171–178.

Marcus, S. M., Flynn, H. A., Blow, F. C., & Barry, K. L. (2003). Depressive symptoms among pregnant women screened in obstetrics settings. [Research Support, Non-U.S. Gov't]. *J Women's Health, 12*(4), 373–380.

Mitchell, J., Field, T., Diego, M., Bendell, D., Newton, R., & Pelaez, M. (2012). Yoga reduces prenatal depression symptoms. *Psychology, 3*(9A), 782–786.

Murray, L., & Carothers, A. D. (1990). The validation of the Edinburgh post-natal depression scale on a community sample. *Br J Psychiatr, 157*, 288–290.

Muzik, M., Hamilton, S. E., Rosenblum, K. L., McGinnis, E., & Hadi, Z. (2012). Mindfulness yoga during pregnancy for psychiatrically at-risk women: Preliminary results from a pilot feasibility study. *Complement Ther Clin Pract, 18*(4), 235–240.

Muzik, M., Vazquez, D., & Marcus, S. M. (2011). Treatment resistant depression in pregnant women. In J. F. Greden, M. B. Riba & M. G. McInnis (Eds.), *Treatment resistant depression:*

A roadmap for effective care (1st edition, pp. 89–114). Washington, DC: American Psychiatric Pub.

Myles, N., Newall, H., Ward, H., & Large, M. (2013). Systematic meta-analysis of individual selective serotonin reuptake inhibitor medications and congenital malformations. *Aust N Z J Psychiatr, 47*(11), 1002–1012.

Narendran, S., Nagarathna, R., Narendran, V., Gunasheela, S., & Nagendra, H. R. (2005). Efficacy of yoga on pregnancy outcome. *J Altern Complement Med, 11*(2), 237–244.

National Institute of Mental Health. (2009). Women and depression: Discovering hope. www.nimh.nih.gov/health/publications/women-and-depression-discovering-hope/women_depression_09_17_09_ln_04_final.pdf

Newham, J. J., Wittkowski, A., Hurley, J., Aplin, J. D., & Westwood, M. (2014). Effects of antenatal yoga on maternal anxiety and depression: A randomized controlled trial. *Depress Anxiety, 31*(8), 631–640.

Nordeng, H., Ystrom, E., & Einarson, A. (2010). Perception of risk regarding the use of medications and other exposures during pregnancy. *Eur J Clin Pharmacol, 66*(2), 207–214.

O'Hara, M., & Swain, A. (1996). Rates and risks of postpartum depression – A meta-analysis. *Int. Rev Psychiatr, 8*, 37–54.

Painuly, N., Heun, R., Painuly, R., & Sharan, P. (2013). Risk of cardiovascular malformations after exposure to paroxetine in pregnancy: Meta-analysis. *The Psychiatr, 37*(6), 198–203.

Rondo, P. H., Ferreira, R. F., Nogueira, F., Ribeiro, M. C., Lobert, H., & Artes, R. (2003). Maternal psychological stress and distress as predictors of low birth weight, prematurity and intrauterine growth retardation. *Eur J Clin Nutr, 57*(2), 266–272.

Rosenzweig, S., Greeson, J. M., Reibel, D. K., Green, J. S., Jasser, S. A., & Beasley, D. (2010). Mindfulness-based stress reduction for chronic pain conditions: Variation in treatment outcomes and role of home meditation practice. *J Psychosom Res, 68*(1), 29–36.

Salisbury, A., Law, K., LaGasse, L., & Lester, B. (2003). MSJAMA. Maternal-fetal attachment. *JAMA, 289*(13), 1701.

Sanchez-Villegas, A., Schlatter, J., Ortuno, F., Lahortiga, F., Pla, J., Benito, S., & Martinez-Gonzalez, M. (2008). Validity of a self-reported diagnosis of depression among participants in a cohort study using the Structured Clinical Interview for DSM-IV (SCID-I). *BMC Psychiatr, 8*. doi:10.1186/1471-244X-8-43

Satyapriya, M., Nagarathna, R., Padmalatha, V., & Nagendra, H. R. (2013). Effect of integrated yoga on anxiety, depression & well being in normal pregnancy. *Complement Ther Clin Pract, 19*(4), 230–236.

Satyapriya, M., Nagendra, H. R., Nagarathna, R., & Padmalatha V. (2009). Effects of integrated yoga on stress and heart rate variability in pregnant women. *Int J Obstet Gynecol, 104*(3), 218–222.

Schneider, C. (2009). Can mindfulness save primary care? *Altern Med Alert, 12*(12), 135–137.

Seng, J. S., Oakley, D. J., Sampselle, C. M., Killion, C., Graham-Bermann, S., & Liberzon, I. (2001). Posttraumatic stress disorder and pregnancy complications. [Research Support, Non-U.S. Gov't Research Support, U.S. Gov't, P.H.S.]. *Obstet Gynecol, 97*(1), 17–22.

Smith, B. W., Shelley, B. M., Dalen, J., Wiggins, K., Tooley, E., & Bernard, J. (2008). A pilot study comparing the effects of mindfulness-based and cognitive-behavioral stress reduction. *J Altern Complement Med, 14*(3), 251–258.

Stahl, B., & Goldstein, E. (2010). *A mindfulness-based stress reduction workbook*. Oakland, CA: New Harbinger Publications.

Steer, R. A., Scholl, T. O., Hediger, M. L., & Fischer, R. L. (1992). Self-reported depression and negative pregnancy outcomes. *J Clin Epidemiol, 45*(10), 1093–1099.

Stewart, R. C. (2007). Maternal depression and infant growth: A review of recent evidence. *Matern Child Nutr, 3*(2), 94–107.

Sun, Y. C., Hung, Y. C., Chang, Y., & Kuo, S. C. (2010). Effects of a prenatal yoga programme on the discomforts of pregnancy and maternal childbirth self-efficacy in Taiwan. *Midwifery, 26*(6), e31–e36.

Talge, N. M., Neal, C., & Glover, V. (2007). Antenatal maternal stress and long-term effects on child neurodevelopment: How and why? *J Child Psychol Psychiatr, 48*(3–4), 245–261.

Trotter, M. J. (2010). *Effects of participation in a mindfulness-based stress reduction program on college students' psychological well-being.* 70, ProQuest Information & Learning, US. http://search. ebscohost.com/login.aspx?direct=true&db=psyh&AN=2010–99070–323&site=ehost-live Available from EBSCOhost psyh database

Uebelacker, L. A., Epstein-Lubow, G., Gaudiano, B. A., Tremont, G., Battle, C. L., & Miller, I. W. (2010). Hatha yoga for depression: Critical review of the evidence for efficacy, plausible mechanisms of action, and directions for future research. *J Psychiatr Pract, 16*(1), 22–33.

Vieten, C., & Astin, J. (2008). Effects of a mindfulness-based intervention during pregnancy on prenatal stress and mood: Results of a pilot study. *Arch Women's Ment Health, 11*(1), 67–74.

Widnes, S. F., Schjott, J., Eide, G. E., & Granas, A. G. (2013). Teratogenic risk perception and confidence in use of medicines in pairs of pregnant women and general practitioners based on patient information leaflets. *Drug Saf, 36*(6), 481–489.

Woolery, A., Myers, H., Sternlieb, B., & Zeltzer, L. (2004). A yoga intervention for young adults with elevated symptoms of depression. *Altern Ther Health Med, 10*(2), 60–63.

Zanarini, M. C., Skodol, A. E., Bender, D., Dolan, R., Sanislow, C., Schaefer, E., . . . Gunderson, J. G. (2000). The collaborative longitudinal personality disorders study: Reliability of Axis I and II diagnoses. *J Pers Disord, 14*(4), 291–299.

INDEX

Note: figures and tables are denoted with italicized page numbers; end note information is denoted with an n following the page number.

acceptance: experiential, in mindful eating 84–5; as mechanism of mindfulness 158–9; Mindfulness-Based Medical Practice focus on 203, 204, 205; self-acceptance as 85–6, 164
acceptance and commitment therapy (ACT): mental health via 113, 118; mindful acceptance commitment ties to 65, 66, 70–1, 72; performance optimization interventions related to 65, 70–1; positive psychology ties to 325; values recognition in 315
agency 178–9
Ānāpānasati Sutta 282, 284–5, 288
anxiety treatment/avoidance: acceptance and commitment therapy for 113, 325; Coping with Anxiety through Living Mindfully for 52–3; mental health via mindful interventions for 111–12, 114, 116, 118, 119; mindful eating for 81, 83; mindfulness-based stress reduction for 6, 112, 114, 116, 118, 119; mindfulness yoga in pregnancy for 4–5, 321–36; performance optimization and mindfulness focus in 65–8; perinatal mindfulness training for 52–4; self-compassion for 41; see also stress treatment/avoidance
appamada 267–8, 269–73, 275
appraisal and reappraisal 165, 232–4, 235–6
The Art of Happiness (Dalai Lama) 209

Association for Contemplative Mind in Higher Education 175–6
attachment theory and security 56–60
attention: bare, with flow 144; gratitude association with 162–3; as mechanism of mindfulness 6, 109–10, 162–4, 251; mental health ties to 117; performance optimization and mindfulness enhancement of 67–8, 69; positive mindfulness program on 10; savoring association with 163–4; spirituality and positive youth development of 251, 257
attitude: autonomy association with 164–5; body awareness association with 166; flow and performance impacted by 146–7; as mechanism of mindfulness 6, 110–11, 164–6; positive mindfulness program on 10; positive reappraisal association with 165; self-acceptance association with 164
autonomy 8, 9, 164–5

body awareness 166
body image 44, 82, 83, 86
body scans 196, 197–8, 207, 208
Buddhist foundations: Ānāpānasati Sutta on 282, 284–5, 288; appamada (awareness infused with spirit of ethical care) in 267–8, 269–73, 275; bīja-niyāma in 271; character strengths in 19; citta-niyāma in 271; contemporary perspectives of

mindfulness *vs.* 283–8; *dhamma-niyāma* in 271, 274–5; *kamma-niyāma* or *karma* in 271–2; *Kāyagatāsati Sutta* on 282, 288; *Mahasatipaṭṭhāna Sutta* on 282, 288; of mindfulness-based positive behavior support 217; mortality awareness based on 129, 136–7, 288; Noble Eightfold Path in 196, 209, 249, 270–1, 274, 282–3, 285, 287, 299; overview of 4, 265–6, 275–6; Pāli as canonical language of 276n; Pāli Canon on 281–2; *paṭiccasamuppāda* (law of conditionality) in 270–1, 274; of performance optimization and mindfulness 65, 74–5; of person-centered therapy 299; of positive youth development 248, 249; *sampajañña* (awareness infused with sense of spiritual progress) in 267–8, 273–5; *sati* (awareness of present moment) in 266–9, 273, 281; *Satipatthana Sutta* on 266–7, 273, 282, 288; of self-compassion 37–8; of spirituality and mindfulness 4, 5, 19, 37–8, 65, 74–5, 129, 136–7, 156, 196, 209, 217, 248, 249, 265–76, 280–91, 299; of Triratna Buddhist Order 276n; of unified operational approach 280–91; *utu-niyāma* in 271; wellbeing and happiness in 37–8, 156

Center for Contemplative Mind in Society 175–6
character strengths *see* mindfulness-based strengths practice
Christian spirituality 19–20, 251
compassion: definition of 38; mindful eating based on 85–6; perinatal mindfulness training benefits of 59–60; positive youth development of 246, 251; self-compassion as 2, 8, *9*, 37–47, 60, 85–6, 159, 193–4, 207, 236, 251, 309, 310–15, 318–19; workplace mindfulness including 236
concentration 117, 287–8
contemplative pedagogy in nursing education: agency in 178–9; contemplative knowing as 178–9; definitions and description of 176–7, 179–80; factors to consider with 189; first-person knowing and contemplative practices in 179, 180, 181–8; free writing as 183, 184; as health practitioner-carer mindfulness 3, 175–90; integration of 181–8; learning activities for 182–8; meditation as 183–4, 187–8; overview

of 3, 175–6, 189–90; positive psychology alignment with 176–8; second-person knowing in 180, 185; student experiences and feedback with 187–8; third-person knowing in 179–80, 185; Tree of Contemplative Practices for 177
Coping with Anxiety through Living Mindfully 52–3

Dalai Lama 209
Daoist spirituality 251
death *see* mortality awareness
decentring 158–60, 165, 168
depression treatment/avoidance: acceptance and commitment therapy for 315, 325; antidepressant medication for 308, 322–3; chronic label impacting 101–2; learning or growth mindset for 317–19, *319*; meaning or purpose creating needed connections for 314–15, *319*; mental health via mindful interventions for 111–12, 114, 116–17, 118, 119; mindful eating for 81–2, 83; mindfulness-based cognitive therapy for 6, 112, 116–17, 280, 300, 308–9; mindfulness-based stress reduction for 6, 112, 114, 118, 119; mindfulness yoga in pregnancy for 4–5, 321–36; mindful therapy for 4–5, 6, 308–19, 321–36; neurobiological function and 309–10, 311–12, 316–17, 318–19; overview of 308–9; perinatal mindfulness training for 52, 54; play as means of 315–17, *319*; savoring for 317; self-compassion for 41, 309, 310–15, 318–19; self-soothing system for 312–14; spirituality and positive youth development for 247, 254
dialectical behavior therapy (DBT) 6, 113

eating issues: mindful eating for 2, 80–7, 112, 196–7, 206, 207–8; self-compassion and 44, 85–6
emotions *see* positive emotions
empathy: in person-centered therapy 296–7, 302; in positive youth development 251–2; in workplace mindfulness 232–4, *234*, 236, *239*
engagement: flow and performance impacted by 147–8; positive mindfulness program on 8, *9*; wellbeing and happiness ties to 104
ethics and morals 255, 267–8, 269–73, 275; *see also* values; virtues
exposure 158

flexibility 118, 159, 208
flow: assessment of 148–9; definition of 141;
  experience of 141–3; future research on
  148, 150–1; mechanisms of mindfulness
  in relation to 3, 141–52; mindfulness-flow
  relationship 143–5; overview of 3, 141,
  151–2; performance optimization and
  mindfulness with 73–4, 75, 143, 145–8;
  self-awareness with 145, 150–1
Frankl, Viktor 230, 231, 314

gratitude 162–3

happiness *see* wellbeing and happiness
health practitioner-carer mindfulness:
  contemplative pedagogy in nursing
  education as 3, 175–90; Mindfulness-Based
  Medical Practice as 3, 193–209;
  mindfulness-based positive behavior
  support as 3–4, 212–24; mindfulness-based
  strengths practice as 31–2; workplace
  mindfulness as 4, 31–2, 228–39
Hindu spirituality 251
hope 161

immune function 115
intellectual and development disabilities:
  behavioral interventions for 212–13,
  215–16, 217–18; mindfulness-based
  positive behavior support with 3–4,
  212–24; psychopharmacological
  interventions for 212, 213
intention: Buddhist foundations of 283, 284;
  contemporary *vs.* traditional perspectives
  on 284; hope association with 161;
  meaning association with 161–2; as
  mechanism of mindfulness 6–7, 109,
  160–2; perinatal mindfulness training
  awareness of 59; positive mindfulness
  program on 10; workplace mindfulness
  focus on 236
International Positive Psychology
  Association 176
Islamic spirituality 251

karma 271–2
Kāyagatāsati Sutta 282, 288

labels 101–2
Langerian mindfulness 74–5
laughter 97–8

Mahasatipaṭṭhāna Sutta 282, 288
Man's Search for Meaning (Frankl) 230

MB-EAT 84, 112
meaning: definition of 230; depression
  treatment/avoidance via 314–15, *319*;
  integration of mindfulness and 237–8,
  239; as mechanism of mindfulness
  161–2; motivation alignment with
  231–2; positive mindfulness program
  on 8, *9*; significance and purpose as
  229–31, 237; spirituality and positive
  youth development of 256; workplace
  mindfulness making 228–39
mechanisms of mindfulness: acceptance as
  158–9; additional 156–69; autonomy as
  164–5; body awareness as 166; changes
  in mode of mental processing as 159–60;
  changes in perceptions of self as 160;
  cognitive, emotional, and behavioral
  flexibility as 159; decentring as 158;
  established 158–60; exposure as 158;
  flow relationship to 3, 141–52; future
  research on 167–8; gratitude as 162–3;
  hope as 161; intention, attention, and
  attitude as 6–7, 109–11, 160–6, 251;
  meaning as 161–2; mental health using
  3, 108–20; mortality awareness and
  use of 3, 126–38; overview of 3, 6–7,
  156–8, 168–9; positive reappraisal as 165;
  savoring as 163–4; self-acceptance as 164;
  self-compassion as 159; self-regulation
  as 159; upward spirals of 167; values
  clarification as 159; wellbeing and
  happiness with 3, 97–105, 156–69
memory 116–17
mental health: clinical applications of
  mindfulness-based interventions for
  111–14; definition of 108; diagnostic
  disorders impacting 111–13; formal
  and informal practice of mindfulness
  for 111; future directions and research
  on 119–20; happiness and positive
  affect ties to 117; of healthy stressed
  populations 113–14; immune function
  ties to 115; life quality and satisfaction
  impacting 118–19; mechanisms of
  mindfulness for 3, 108–20; memory,
  attention, and concentration ties to
  116–17; mindfulness defined for
  108–11; neuroplasticity ties to 115–16;
  optimism ties to 117–18; overview of
  3, 108; physiological underpinnings of
  114–19; prevention to maintain 113–14;
  psychological flexibility impacting 118;
  self-esteem impacting 118; spirituality
  and positive youth development of 254

mental processing 159–60
mindful acceptance commitment (MAC)
65, 66, 70–1, 72
mindful eating: binge eating *vs.* 83, 84–5,
112; dieting or dietary restraint *vs.* 82–3;
experiential acceptance in 84–5; future
research in 86–7; MB-EAT program
for 84, 112; Mindfulness-Based Medical
Practice including 196–7, 206, 207–8;
obesity and reduced psychological
functioning necessitating 81–2; overview
of 2, 80–1, 86–7; as positive psychology
intervention 2, 80–7, 112; potential
role of, among overweight youth 83–4;
Project EAT for 83; self-acceptance,
self-care, and compassion in 85–6;
self-regulation in 85; unhealthy weight
control behaviors *vs.* 82, 83
Mindful Mother 52
mindfulness: health practitioners and carers
use of (*see* health practitioner-carer
mindfulness); mechanisms of (*see*
mechanisms of mindfulness); mindful
therapy using (*see* mindful therapy);
overview of, in positive psychology 1–10;
positive psychology interventions with
(*see* positive psychology interventions);
spirituality and (*see* spirituality and
mindfulness)
Mindfulness-Based Childbirth and
Parenting (MBCP) 53–4, 56
mindfulness-based cognitive therapy
(MBCT): advocacy for 280; character
strengths in 19; as deficit-based approach
6, 7; for depression treatment/avoidance
6, 112, 116–17, 280, 300, 308–9; mental
health via 112, 116–17; physiological
impacts of 116–17
Mindfulness-Based Medical Practice
(MBMP): beginning of 194–5; week
1 of 195; week 2 of 196–7; week
3 of 197–8; week 4 of 198–201;
week 5 of 201–2; week 6 of 203–4;
retreat day in 205; week 7 of 206–7;
week 8 of 207–9; acceptance focus
in 203, 204, 205; body scans in 196,
197–8, 207, 208; choiceless awareness
meditation in 202, 203; flexibility
in 208; as health practitioner-carer
mindfulness 3, 193–209; letting go
theme in 206; mindful eating in
196–7, 206, 207–8; overview of 3,
193–4, 209; RAIN (recognize, accept,
investigate, non-identification) in

200; relationship mindfulness in 202,
203–4; self-compassion in 193–4, 207;
soundscape meditation in 201; STOP
(slow down, take a breath, observe,
proceed) in 199, 200, 203; stress
management in 198–201; stuck position
observations in 201–2; training the mind
in 195; Triangle of Awareness in 199,
200, 201, 204
mindfulness-based positive behavior
support (MBPBS): 7-day intensive course
for 221, *222*; 8-week course for *219–20*,
219–21; behavioral interventions *vs.* or
with 212–13, 215–16, 217–18; Buddhist
foundations of 217; fidelity of training
in 223; future directions in 223–4; as
health practitioner-carer mindfulness
3–4, 212–24; measuring outcomes of
223; mindfulness defined for 214–15;
origins of 215–17; overview of 3–4, 214;
positive behavior support in 217–18;
psychopharmacological interventions
vs. 212, 213; research on 223, 224; stress
reduction via 215; trainer qualifications
for 221; training and curriculum for
218–23; wellness/wellbeing via 215
mindfulness-based relapse prevention
(MBRP) 112–13
mindfulness-based strengths practice
(MBSP): booster or maintenance sessions
for 30, 31, 32; case discussions of 28–32;
character strengths defined for 16, 18;
core topic areas of *21*, *22*; delivery
mechanisms for 30, 33; future research
on 32–3; integration of mindfulness
and character strengths in 18–20, 22,
24, 25, 33; manualized program for
20–5, *21*; mindfulness defined for 15;
overview of 2; pilot research and field
reports on 25–32; as positive psychology
intervention 2, 8, 15–33; positive
relationships benefits in 26–8; prevention
focus of 30–1; science of mindfulness
and character strengths in 15–18, *16–18*;
self-care encouragement via 31–2;
session structure and activities in 22, *22*,
23, *24*; VIA classification of character and
virtues in 16, *16–18*; workplace team
support via 28–30
mindfulness-based stress reduction
(MBSR): Buddhist foundations of
248, 249; character strengths in 19; as
deficit-based approach 6, 7; mental health
via 112, 114, 115–16, 117, 118, 119;

Mindfulness-Based Medical Practice ties to 193, 194, 195, 197, 198; mindfulness yoga in pregnancy using 325–6; performance optimization interventions related to 64, 65, 69; perinatal mindfulness training foundations in 53; physiological impacts of 115–16, 117, 119; self-awareness development in 55; self-compassion in 45

mindfulness meditation practice (MM) 68–9, *69*, 72–3

Mindfulness Meditation Training in Sport (MMTS) 72–3

mindfulness yoga in pregnancy: acceptability of 332; antidepressant medication *vs.* 322–3; benefits of/ reasons for 324–5; dangers of depression necessitating 321–2; design of program for 328–30, *330*; materials and methods used in 327; measuring outcomes of 331–3, *333*, *334*; mindfulness defined for 324; as mindful therapy for depression and anxiety 4–5, 321–36; overview of 4–5, 321–4, 333–6; participants in *327*, 327–8, *329*, 335; positive psychology ties to 325; prior research on 325–6; recruitment for 327, *327*, 335; results of 332; stability and treatment effect pre- and post- 332, *333*; total group intervention effects of 333, *334*

mindful parenting: mindfulness-based positive behavior support as 214–24; mindfulness yoga in pregnancy as 4–5, 321–36; perinatal mindfulness training for 2, 51–60

mindful self-compassion program (MSC) 2, 8, 45, 46

Mindful Sport Performance Enhancement (MSPE) 65, 69–70, 71–2

mindful therapy: depression treatment as 4–5, 6, 308–19, 321–36; dialectical behavior therapy as 6, 113; mindfulness-based cognitive therapy as 6, 7, 19, 112, 116–17, 280, 300, 308–9; mindfulness-based relapse prevention as 112–13; mindfulness-based stress reduction as 6, 7, 19, 45, 53, 55, 64, 65, 69, 112, 114, 115–16, 117, 118, 119, 193, 194, 195, 197, 198, 248, 249, 325–6; mindfulness yoga in pregnancy as 4–5, 321–36; person-centered therapy as 4, 295–305; positive mindfulness program as 2, 8–10, *9*; *see also specific topics for details*

morals *see* ethics and morals

mortality awareness: associational chatter reduction due to 134–5; Buddhist approaches to 129, 136–7, 288; contemporary *vs.* traditional perspectives on 288; facing death without danger of dying to achieve 136–8; intensified perception due to 131–2; life reevaluation due to 133–4; mechanisms of mindfulness to address 3, 126–38; near-death experiences with 127–8; overview of 3, 126–8; post-traumatic growth and 127, 131, 137; presentness due to 132, 134; relationship improvements due to 132–3; sense of connection due to 132; spontaneous mindfulness with 128–30, 133–5; terror management theory on 135–6; transformational effects of 127–8, 130–3, 136, 137–8; value of life appreciation with 133; wellbeing and happiness ties to 131; 'Year to Live' therapy for 137

neurobiological function with depression 309–10, 311–12, 316–17, 318–19

neuroplasticity 115–16, 310, 315, 316

nursing education with contemplative pedagogy *see* contemplative pedagogy in nursing education

obesity avoidance *see* mindful eating

optimism 117–18

Pāli 276n

Pāli Canon 281–2

parenting *see* mindful parenting

paṭiccasamuppāda 270–1, 274

performance optimization and mindfulness: anxiety treatment related to 65–8; audio-tapes used for 68–9; Buddhist and Langerian foundations of 65, 74–5; design and dosage of interventions for 71–2; empirical support for 68; enhanced mental efficiency for 67–8; flow with 73–4, 75, 143, 145–8; mindful acceptance commitment approach to 65, 66, 70–1, 72; mindfulness defined for 65, 74; mindfulness meditation practice for 68–9, *69*, 72–3; Mindfulness Meditation Training in Sport for 72–3; Mindful Sport Performance Enhancement for 65, 69–70, 71–2; overview of 2, 64–5, 75–6; performance dukkha impacting 70–1; as positive psychology intervention 2,

64–76, 143, 145–8; psychological skills training with 71

perinatal mindfulness training: attachment theory and security in relation to 56–60; collaborative communication via 57; Coping with Anxiety through Living Mindfully as 52–3; earned security via 58; enhancement of attachment security via 57–9; future research in 60; intergenerational transmission of attachment impacted by 58–9; mentalizing in 57–8; Mindful Mother as 52; Mindfulness-Based Childbirth and Parenting as 53–4, 56; overview of 2, 60; parental self-awareness increased via 55–6, 57–8; parent-child attunement via 56–7; parent-child relationship benefits of 55–60; partner relationship benefits of 54; positive emotions via 52, 54, 56, 59–60; as positive psychology intervention 2, 51–60; preliminary research on 51–4; psychological processes impacted by 59–60; self-compassion in 60; see also mindfulness yoga in pregnancy

person-centered therapy (P-CT): background to 295–8; Buddhist foundations of mindfulness in 299; congruence in 296–8, 301–2, 304; empathy in 296–7, 302; as form of mindfulness toward client 301–2; mindfulness as outcome of 303–5; mindfulness defined for 299; mindfulness in 298–305; mindfulness techniques used within 302–3; as mindful therapy 4, 295–305; non-directivity in 295–6, 297, 302; organismic valuing process in 296–7, 298; overview of 4, 305; personality theory underlying 296–7, 298; positive psychology ties to 298; self-determination theory in relation to 298; unconditional positive regard in 296–7, 298, 301–2

physiology/physical body: body awareness of 166; body image of 44, 82, 83, 86; body scans of 196, 197–8, 207, 208; embodiment of wellbeing and happiness 97–8, 166; immune function in 115; memory, attention, and concentration in 116–17; mental health ties to 114–19; mindfulness yoga in pregnancy impacting 325–6, 328–9, 330; neurobiological function with depression in 309–10, 311–12, 316–17, 318–19; neuroplasticity in 115–16, 316; stress markers in 235

play 315–17, *319*

positive behavior support *see* mindfulness-based positive behavior support

positive emotions: as choices 99–100; laughter creating 97; mental health ties to 117; perinatal mindfulness training benefits of 52, 54, 56, 59–60; positive mindfulness program on 8, *9*; spirituality links to 254; wellbeing and happiness ties to 97, 99–100 (*see also* wellbeing and happiness); youth emotional development of 246–7, 254

positive mindfulness program (PMP) 2, 8–10, *9*

positive psychology: interventions using (*see* positive psychology interventions); mindfulness in 1–10 (*see also* mindfulness); positive theory and mechanisms of mindfulness underlying (*see* mechanisms of mindfulness)

positive psychology interventions: mindful eating as 2, 80–7, 112; mindfulness-based strengths practice as 2, 8, 15–33; performance optimization and mindfulness as 2, 64–76, 143, 145–8; perinatal mindfulness training as 2, 51–60; positive mindfulness program as 2, 8–10, *9*; self-compassion as 2, 8, *9*, 37–47; *see also specific topics for details*

positive reappraisal 165

positive relationships: mindfulness-based strengths practice benefits to 26–8; mortality awareness creating 132–3; positive mindfulness program on 8, *9*; positive youth development of 255; self-compassion and 44

positive theory and mechanisms of mindfulness *see* mechanisms of mindfulness

positive youth development: awareness and attention in 251–2, 257; Buddhist foundations of 248, 249; clinical applications of 247–8; cognitive development in 246; emotional development in 246–7, 254; empathy and compassion in 251–2; integration of mindfulness and spirituality for 250–2, 256–9; mental health in 254; moral development in 255; origins and contexts of mindfulness for 248–9; overview of 4, 245–6; positive effects of spirituality in 253–4; positive emotions in 246–7, 254; purpose in 256; spirituality and mindfulness in 4, 245–59; spirituality and youth development overlap in 252–3; spirituality defined for 249–50; supportive relationships in 255; Tibetan monastic education system model of 257–8

post-traumatic growth (PTG) 127, 131, 137

Potter, Dennis 126

pregnancy-related mindfulness see mindfulness yoga in pregnancy; perinatal mindfulness training

Project EAT 83

psychological skills training (PST) 71

purpose see meaning

RAIN (recognize, accept, investigate, non-identification) 200

relapse prevention, mindfulness-based 112–13

relationships see positive relationships

SAFE (soften, allow, feel, expand) practice 313–14

sampajañña 267–8, 273–5

Sangharakshita (née Dennis Longwood) 276n

sati 266–9, 273, 281

Satipatthana Sutta 266–7, 273, 282, 288

savoring 163–4, 317

school-based positive youth development see positive youth development

self-acceptance 85–6, 164

self-awareness: contemplative pedagogy in nursing education including 180, 181–8; flow, mindfulness and 145, 150–1; perinatal mindfulness training benefits of 55–6, 57–8; person-centered therapy outcome of 304–5; positive mindfulness program on 8, 9; positive youth development of 247

self-compassion: breaks allotted for 313; brief interventions for 46–7; Buddhist foundations of 37–8; common humanity in 39, 41, 314; definition and description of 38–40; depression treatment/avoidance via 41, 309, 310–15, 318–19; development of 44–6; disordered eating, body image, and 44; interpersonal relationships and 44; learning or growth mindset about 318–19, 319; as mechanism of mindfulness 159; mindful eating based on 85–6; Mindfulness-Based Medical Practice including 193–4, 207; mindfulness in 39–40, 45–7, 159;

mindful self-compassion program based on 2, 8, 45, 46; motivation, health, and 42–4; neurobiological impacts of 311–12; overview of 2, 37–8, 47; perinatal mindfulness training in 60; placing of hands activating 312–13; positive mindfulness program on 8, 9; as positive psychology intervention 2, 8, 9, 37–47; positive youth development of 251; rumination as benefit of 41; SAFE (soften, allow, feel, expand) practice of 313–14; self-esteem vs. 42; self-kindness in 39; self-soothing system activating 312–14; three facets of 38–40; wellbeing and 37–8, 40–2, 159, 193–4; workplace mindfulness including 236

self-determination theory 298

self-efficacy 8, 9

self-esteem: mental health impacted by 118; mindful eating impacting 83; positive youth development of 247; self-compassion vs. 42

self-perceptions 160

self-regulation: as mechanism of mindfulness 159; mindful eating based on 85; person-centered therapy outcome of 304; positive youth development of 246–7, 255

spirituality and mindfulness: Buddhist foundations of 4, 5, 19, 37–8, 65, 74–5, 129, 136–7, 156, 196, 209, 217, 248, 249, 265–76, 280–91, 299; character strengths in 19–20; Christian practices of 19–20, 251; Daoist practices of 251; Hindu practices of 251; Islamic practices of 251; positive youth development with 4, 245–59; unified operational approach to 4, 280–91

sports performance see performance optimization and mindfulness

STOP (slow down, take a breath, observe, proceed) 199, 200, 203

strength of character see mindfulness-based strengths practice

stress treatment/avoidance: mindful eating for 81, 84; Mindfulness-Based Medical Practice for 193–209; mindfulness-based positive behavior support for 215; mindfulness-based stress reduction for 6, 7, 19, 45, 53, 55, 64, 65, 69, 112, 114, 115–16, 117, 118, 119, 193, 194, 195, 197–8, 248, 249, 325–6; perinatal mindfulness training for 51–60; positive youth development for 247; prevention for mental health of healthy stressed populations 113–14; self-compassion for 41; workplace mindfulness for 232–3, 234–7; *see also* anxiety treatment/avoidance

substance abuse treatment/avoidance: mindfulness-based relapse prevention for 112–13; mindlessness and outdated expectations impacting 100; optimism impacting 117–18; self-compassion for 43–4; spirituality and positive youth development for 254, 255, 256

terror management theory 135–6
Tree of Contemplative Practices 177
Triangle of Awareness 199, *200*, 201, 204
Triratna Buddhist Order 276n

unified operational approach: alternative model and definition of mindfulness in 288–90; Buddhist foundations examined in 280–91; concentration and insight meditation meaning considered in 287–8; contemporary *vs.* traditional perspectives of mindfulness in 283–8; death awareness integration considered in 288; importance assigned to mindfulness considered in 285; intention considered in 283, 284; judgment and discernment use considered in 286–7; mindfulness in Buddhism in 281–3; overview of 4, 280–1, 290–1; to spirituality and mindfulness 4, 280–91; teacher competencies considered in 286; timing of mindfulness practice considered in 284–5

values: depression treatment/avoidance recognition of 315; ethics relationship to 270; values clarification, as mechanism of mindfulness 159; *see also* ethics and morals; virtues
VIA classification of character and virtues 16, *16–18*
VIA Survey 16
virtues: courage as *16–17*; humanity as *17*; justice as *17*; temperance as *17*; transcendence as *17–18*; VIA classification of character and 16, *16–18*; wisdom as *16*; *see also* ethics and morals; values

wellbeing and happiness: attention promoting 162–4; attitude promoting 164–6; autonomy relationship to 164–5; body awareness relationship to 166; Buddhist foundations of 37–8, 156; as choices 97, 98–100, 102–5; control inhibiting 98–9; embodiment of 97–8, 166; engagement leading to 104; establishing via mindfulness 105; eudaimonic 5, 37–8, 40–2, 157, 162, 163, 164, 165; future research on 167–8; gratitude relationship to 162–3; hedonic 5, 37, 157, 161, 162, 163, 164; hope relationship to 161; intention promoting 160–2; labels influencing 101–2; laughter creating 97–8; meaning relationship to 161–2; mechanisms of mindfulness related to 3, 97–105, 156–69; mental health ties to 117; Mindfulness-Based Medical Practice goals of 193–209; mindfulness-based positive behavior support leading to 215; mindlessness and outdated expectations negatively impacting 100–2, 105; mortality awareness leading to 131; overview of 3; positive emotions ties to 97, 99–100; positive reappraisal relationship to 165; as product of mindfulness and choice 102–4; savoring relationship to 163–4; self-acceptance relationship to 164; self-compassion and 37–8, 40–2, 159, 193–4; unified operational approach to spirituality and mindfulness for 280–91; upward spirals of positive effects affecting 167
workplace mindfulness: appraisal in 232–4, 235–6; breath practices for 235; on compassion and self-compassion 236; empathy in 232–4, *234*, 236, *239*; as health practitioner-carer mindfulness 4, 31–2, 228–39; integration of meaning and mindfulness in 237–8, *239*; on intention 236; meaning sought via 228–39; meditation practices in 235, 236–7; mindfulness-based strengths practice for 28–33; mindfulness foundation of 234–8; on motivation and meaning in work 231–2; overview of 4, 228–9, 238–9; presentness focus in 235; on significance and purpose 229–31, 237; stress treatment via 232–3, 234–7

'Year to Live' therapy 137
yoga *see* mindfulness yoga in pregnancy
youth development *see* positive youth development
youth obesity avoidance *see* mindful eating